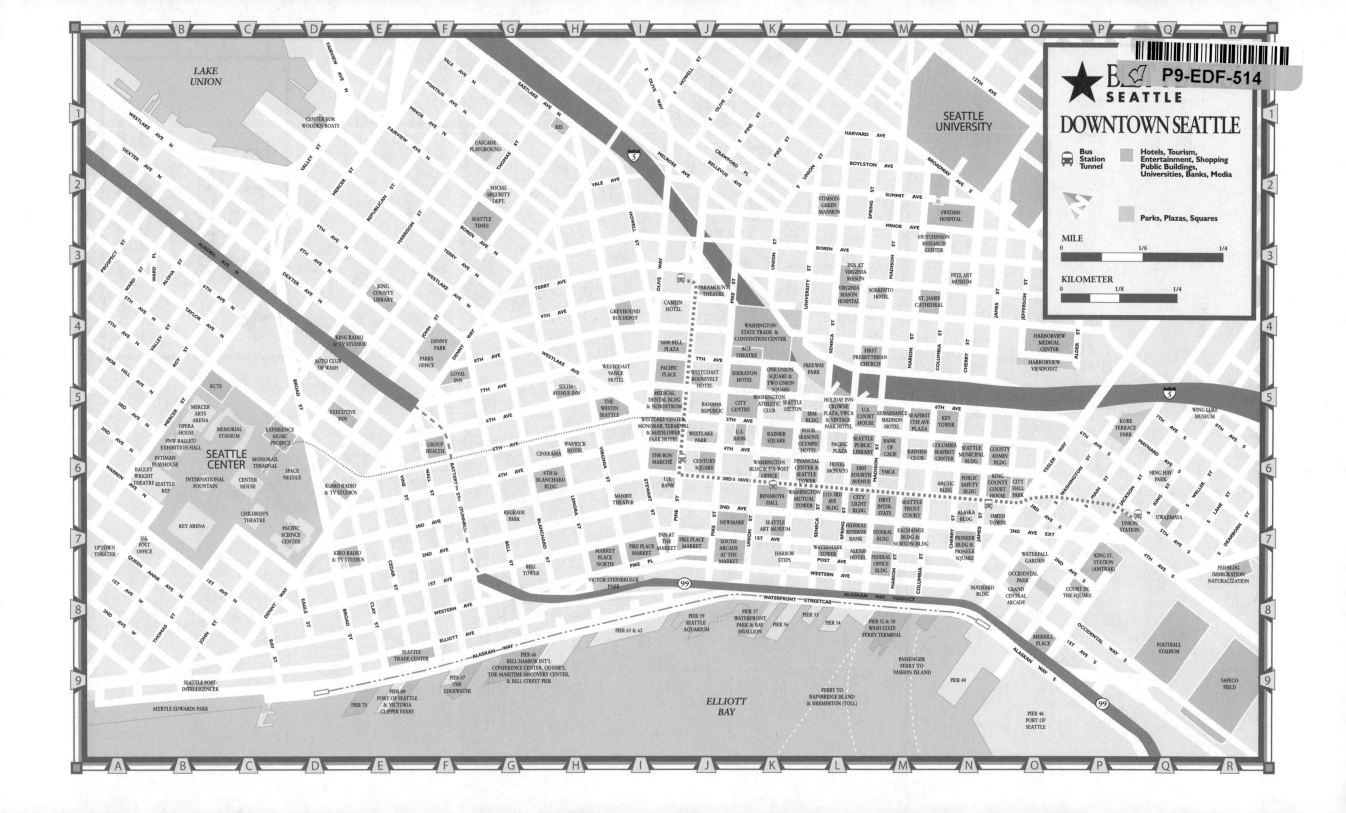

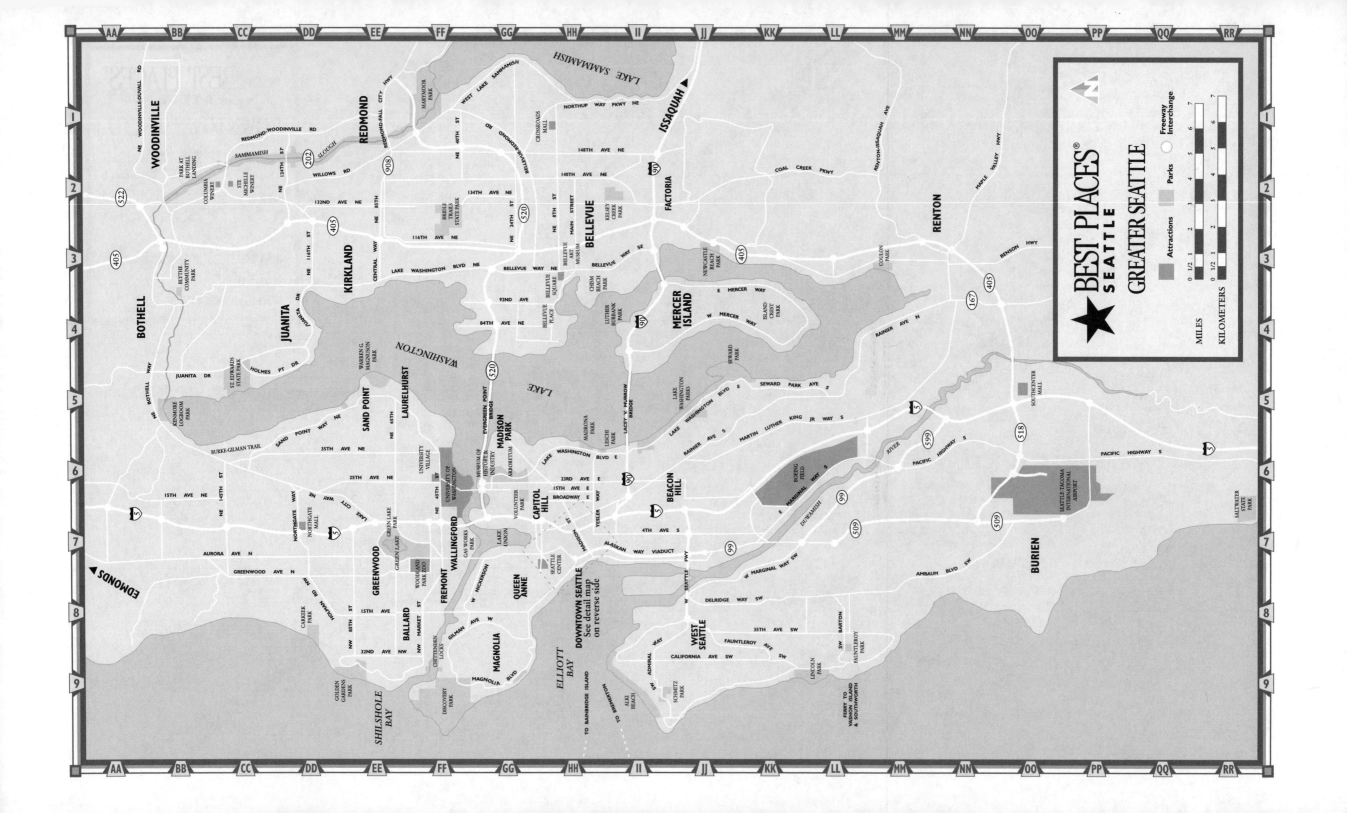

BEST PLACES®
SEATTLE
GREATER SEATTLE

Attractions   Parks   Freeway Interchange

MILES   0 1/2 1   2   3   4   5   6   7

KILOMETERS   0 1/2 1   2   3   4   5   6   7

WOODINVILLE

REDMOND

LAKE SAMMAMISH

ISSAQUAH ▶

NE WOODINVILLE-DUVALL RD

PARK AT BOTHELL LANDING

SAMMAMISH SLOUGH

REDMOND-WOODINVILLE RD

COLUMBIA WINERY

STE MICHELLE WINERY

MARYMOOR PARK

WEST LAKE SAMMAMISH PKWY NE

NORTHUP WAY NE

CROSSROADS MALL

148TH AVE NE

COAL CREEK PKWY

RENTON-ISSAQUAH RD

MAPLE VALLEY HWY

BOTHELL

NE BOTHELL WAY

522

405

BLYTHE COMMUNITY PARK

NE 124TH ST

202

908

REDMOND-FALL CITY HWY

BELLEVUE-REDMOND RD

40TH ST

NE 8TH ST

140TH AVE NE

FACTORIA

90

RENTON

BENSON HWY

405

KIRKLAND

JUANITA

CENTRAL WAY

LAKE WASHINGTON BLVD NE

132ND AVE NE

134TH AVE NE

116TH AVE NE

NE 24TH ST

520

NE 8TH ST

MAIN STREET

BELLEVUE ART MUSEUM

BELLEVUE

BELLEVUE SQUARE

BELLEVUE WAY SE

92ND AVE

84TH AVE NE

KELSEY CREEK PARK

CRESH BEACH PARK

LUTHER BURBANK PARK

NEWCASTLE BEACH PARK

167

JUANITA DR

NE 116TH ST

NE 116TH ST

BELLEVUE PLACE

MERCER ISLAND

E MERCER WAY

ISLAND CREST PARK

W MERCER WAY

405

COULON PARK

ST. EDWARDS STATE PARK

HOLMES PT DR

WARREN G. MAGNUSON PARK

SEWARD PARK

SEWARD PARK AVE S

KENMORE LOGBOOM PARK

SAND POINT

LAURELHURST

MADISON PARK

LAKE WASHINGTON

WASHINGTON

BURKE-GILMAN TRAIL

SAND POINT WAY NE

35TH AVE NE

NE 65TH ST

520

EVERGREEN POINT BRIDGE

MUSEUM OF HISTORY & INDUSTRY

ARBORETUM

LACEY V MURROW BRIDGE

LAKE WASHINGTON PARKS

LAKE WASHINGTON BLVD S

RAINIER AVE N

RAINIER AVE S

MARTIN LUTHER KING JR WAY S

RIVER

PACIFIC HIGHWAY S

PACIFIC HIGHWAY S

SOUTHCENTER MALL

518

5

599

EDMONDS ▶

15TH AVE NE

25TH AVE NE

NE 145TH ST

NORTHGATE WAY

LAKE CITY WAY NE

NORTHGATE MALL

5

5

UNIVERSITY VILLAGE

NE 45TH ST

UNIVERSITY OF WASHINGTON

LAKE WASHINGTON BLVD E

23RD AVE E

15TH AVE E

BROADWAY

90

BEACON HILL

E MARGINAL WAY S

BOEING FIELD

DUWAMISH

99

509

509

SEATTLE-TACOMA INTERNATIONAL AIRPORT

SALTWATER STATE PARK

GREENWOOD

WALLINGFORD

FREMONT

CAPITOL HILL

VOLUNTEER PARK

YESLER WAY

AURORA AVE N

GREENWOOD AVE N

GREEN LAKE

GREEN LAKE PARK

GAS WORKS PARK

WOODLAND PARK ZOO

LAKE UNION

SEATTLE CENTER

MADISON ST

4TH AVE S

ALASKAN WAY VIADUCT

W SEATTLE FWY

99

W MARGINAL WAY SW

BURIEN

AMBAUM BLVD SW

DELRIDGE WAY SW

BALLARD

MAGNOLIA

QUEEN ANNE

W NICKERSON

NW MARKET ST

15TH AVE

NW 85TH ST

NW 32ND AVE NW

ANN RD NW

HOLMAN RD NW

CARKEEK PARK

CHITTENDEN LOCKS

MAGNOLIA BLVD

DISCOVERY PARK

GOLDEN GARDENS PARK

SHILSHOLE BAY

ELLIOTT BAY

DOWNTOWN SEATTLE
See detail map
on reverse side

TO BAINBRIDGE ISLAND

TO BREMERTON

ALKI BEACH

WEST SEATTLE

ADMIRAL WAY

CALIFORNIA AVE SW

35TH AVE SW

FAUNTLEROY AVE SW

SW BARTON

SCHMITZ PARK

LINCOLN PARK

FAUNTLEROY PARK

FERRY TO VASHON ISLAND & SOUTHWORTH

ESTATES

Praise for Best Places® Guidebooks

"Best Places are the best regional restaurant and guide books in America."
—THE SEATTLE TIMES

"Best Places covers must-see portions of the West Coast . . . with style and authority. In-the-know locals offer thorough info on restaurants, lodgings, and the sights."
—NATIONAL GEOGRAPHIC TRAVELER

". . . travelers swear by the recommendations in the Best Places guidebooks . . ."
—SUNSET MAGAZINE

"Known for their frank yet chatty tone . . ."
—PUBLISHERS WEEKLY

"For travel collections covering the Northwest, the Best Places series takes precedence over all similar guides."
—BOOKLIST

"The best guide to Seattle is the locally published Best Places Seattle . . ."
—JONATHAN RABAN, MONEY MAGAZINE

"Whether you're a Seattleite facing the winter doldrums or a visitor wondering what to see next, guidance is close at hand in Best Places Seattle."
—SUNSET MAGAZINE

"Best Places Seattle remains one of the best, most straightforward urban guidebooks in the country."
—THE SEATTLE TIMES

"This tome [Best Places Seattle] is one of the best practical guides to any city in North America."
—TRAVEL BOOKS WORLDWIDE

"Visitors to Washington, Oregon, and British Columbia would do well to pick up Best Places Northwest for an exhaustive review of food and lodging in the region . . . An indispensable glove-compartment companion."
—TRAVEL AND LEISURE

TRUST THE LOCALS

The original insider's guides, written by local experts

COMPLETELY INDEPENDENT
- No advertisers
- No sponsors

EVERY PLACE STAR-RATED & RECOMMENDED

★★★★ The very best in the city

★★★ Distinguished; many outstanding features

★★ Excellent; some wonderful qualities

★ A good place

MONEY-BACK GUARANTEE
We're so sure you'll be satisfied, we guarantee it!

HELPFUL ICONS
Watch for these quick-reference symbols throughout the book:

 FAMILY FUN

 GOOD VALUE

 ROMANTIC

 EDITORS' CHOICE

BEST PLACES®

SEATTLE

The Locals' Guide to the Best Restaurants,
Lodgings, Sights, Shopping, and More!

Edited by
SHANNON O'LEARY

EDITION **10**

SASQUATCH BOOKS
SEATTLE

Printed in the United States of America
Published by Sasquatch Books
Distributed by Publishers Group West

Tenth edition
09 08 07 06 05 04   6 5 4 3 2 1

ISBN: 1-57061-408-3
ISSN: 1095-9734

Cover illustration/photograph: Paul Souders
Cover design: Nancy Gellos
Maps: GreenEye Design
Interior composition: Bill Quinby
Production editor: Cassandra Mitchell
Copyeditor: Julie Van Pelt
Proofreader: Amy Smith Bell
Indexer: Michael Ferreira

SPECIAL SALES

Best Places guidebooks are available at special discounts on bulk purchases for corporate, club, or organization sales promotions, premiums, and gifts. Special editions,
including personalized covers, excerpts of existing guides, and corporate imprints,
can be created in large quantities for specific needs. For more information, contact
your local bookseller or Special Sales, Best Places Guidebooks, 119 S Main Street,
Suite 400, Seattle, Washington 98104, 800/775-0817.

SASQUATCH BOOKS
119 South Main Street, Suite 400
Seattle, WA 98104
(206) 467-4300
www.sasquatchbooks.com
custserv@sasquatchbooks.com

CONTENTS

Introduction

In one episode of the HBO dramedy *Six Feet Under,* a Seattle tourist apparently dies of boredom. I find the circumstances highly suspicious. For one thing, the caffeine supply here alone should keep most visitors upright.

As a more or less lifelong resident, I admit to some bias, but Seattle has long since shed its cliché of being a sleep-inducing, rain-soaked city (OK, the rain part is true). Sure, in the not-so-distant past the whine of some malcontents was, "Nothing ever happens here!" (To which contented Old Timers would harrumph, "Good! Where do you think you are, New York?") Well, we're all grown up now, and just like any big city we can lay claim to a host of complications that come with maturity—traffic and business bumps (tech bust and Boeing HQ walkout), riots (WTO and Mardi Gras), political and sports scandals (city-council members caught cashing in on strip clubs; a college football coach discovered wagering on collegiate basketball), attempted civic coup d'états (we must generate more voting initiatives—from expanding the Monorail to taxing lattes—than any other constituency in the country), and so on. Not exactly marketing copy to make a chamber of commerce giddy, but surely not boring.

On the upside, while we worry over and work to solve the occasional breakouts of bad behavior, the benefits of adulthood are manifest. We have a wider circle of friends, for instance. An influx of newcomers has brought added depth to our personality and energy to our sidewalks. One need only hop a Metro bus from nearly any point in the city—whether the First-through-Fifth-Avenue downtown business district or an urban neighborhood—to be introduced to the changing face of Seattle. (Seriously, take a bus: it's the cheapest, and speediest, tour around, allowing you to mitigate the aforementioned traffic and near misses with Seattle's increasingly incomprehensible driving style—burn rubber, slow for green lights, text-message your pals). Along with more diverse populations have come distracting cultural spikes we can all exploit, namely in the triumvirate of shopping, dining, and entertainment. New life has also been injected into neighborhoods surrounding the city. In the past few years, Belltown and, more recently, Ballard and SoDo, have been transformed from neglected old farts into comely young things with their own varied attractions.

As with any city worth its ambitions (yes, Seattleites harbor aspirations to be the shiniest, smartest city on the block), Seattle is not just a one-look burg. Like one of those large families that make the most absorbing dinner theater, Seattle has the full cast of urban characters: pony-tailed rabble rousers banging convictions out on the table; teenagers catching the latest fashion, or piercing, wave; my-body-is-a-temple athletes; my-body-is-a-playground partyers; clean-cut careerists; sophisticates with gold cards; and wise, not quite out-of-it parents.

And they all find their place in the city.

There is a literary, musical, or artistic act being committed somewhere in the city nearly 24/7. Unlike the old days, when the city closed for fun around 10pm, entertaining curfews are becoming more and more passé (see the Up All Night sidebar in the Nightlife chapter for a short list): night clubs, pool halls, ethnic eateries, and cocktail lounges abound. And newer big-buck venues such as the Experience Music Project (EMP), Safeco Field and Seahawks Stadium, Marion McCaw Hall, and the soon-to-be unveiled downtown Central Library, mesh amiably with Old Seattle's icons like the Space Needle, the Pike Place Market, Pioneer Square, and mountain- and waterscapes. Just one boisterous family under ever-changing skies.

In fact, to keep up with all the comings and goings of the city, we took on even more expert guides for this 10th edition of *Best Places Seattle* (including enlisting some local notables for their "best places" tips, scattered throughout the book). My thanks goes out to all of our contributors. After all, without the heavy lifting of in-the-know reviewers (delve into their pasts on the next page), and fact checking and general eyeballing by folks such as Niki Stojnic, spying for missteps, we'd be stuck with just a real promising table of contents. In addition, the efforts of production editor Cassandra Mitchell, copy editor Julie Van Pelt, and proofreader Amy Smith Bell were essential and much appreciated.

So, whether you're a longtime local or a first-time visitor, my wish is that this book is a helpful companion in your travels around Seattle. And, of course, above all, that it keeps boredom at bay.

—Shannon O'Leary, Editor

Contributors

DOREE ARMSTRONG, who wrote our Lodging reviews, was born and raised in the Seattle suburbs. She has written about remodeled houses for *Seattle Homes & Lifestyles* and *Northwest Home + Garden* magazines, so she knows what comforts people look for in a good night's sleep. Her work has also appeared in *Seattle Magazine* and the *Seattle Post-Intelligencer.*

Her nights spent traipsing around Seattle's clubs and bars as the Club Beat columnist for the *Seattle Post-Intelligencer* made **TIZZY ASHER** an ideal reviewer for our Nightlife chapter. A long-time devotee of local and national music, her articles have appeared in *The Stranger, Seattle Weekly, Magnet, Venus,* and *Resonance.* She currently is working on a novel about four high school girls who discover the power of zines.

Seattle native **SHEILA FARR** has long been involved in the local art scene as a poet and critic. As well as reviewing the visual arts for this edition, she has authored three books on Northwest artists: *Fay Jones, James Martin: Art Rustler at the Rivoli,* and *Leo Kenney: A Retrospective* (all from University of Washington Press). Since 2000, she has been staff art critic for the *Seattle Times.*

Shopping chapter reviewer **KATE FULCHER** was raised in Edmonds, but she was close enough to fall in love with Seattle stores at a tender age. Fulcher writes for *Seattle Magazine, Seattle Bride,* and *Scopes.* When not tromping around the city with laptop in tow, she's on the other side of the North Cascades where her family has a home.

JAMES GOLDSMITH, who handled one-third of this edition's restaurant reviews, has been reviewing Seattle-area restaurants for more than a decade, currently for the *Seattle Post-Intelligencer.* A past contributor to *Best Places Seattle* and *Best Places Northwest* guides, *Seattle Cheap Eats,* and *Seattle Sidewalk Offline Restaurant Guide,* he also pens pieces on restaurants, food, and other topics for *Seattle Magazine.*

MICHAEL HOOD was a chef and restaurateur for 25 years before becoming a reporter, political analyst, and food writer. As well as reviewing one-third of the restaurants in this edition, this former restaurant critic for the *Seattle Post-Intelligencer* covers news for the French news wire service, Agence France-Presse. His writing credits include an essay anthologized in *Best Food Writing 2000* and pieces for the *New York Post* and *The Stranger.*

"Where are the palm trees?" asked seven-year-old **JAMILA ASHA JOHNSON** when she arrived in Seattle with her parents from Los Angeles. Today, the recent Seattle University journalism grad still pines over the loss of her favorite tree, but Seattle's beautiful parks keep her satisfied. As well as updating our Lay of the City chapter, she has freelanced for *Seattle Magazine* and *Northwest Home + Garden.*

JENNA LAND put her obsession with Seattle to use updating our Planning a Trip chapter. Among her favorite Seattle activities are biking the Burke-Gilman Trail, which she aims to get all the way around by the time she's 80. Executive editor for a local literary agency, Land also works for Seal Press and her freelance credits include *Seattle Magazine, Seattle Bride,* and *Northwest Home + Garden.*

JOHN LONGENBAUGH, who covered performing, film, and literary arts in our Arts chapter, is a Seattle-based writer and playwright who's still here following the boom and bust of this fair city, and looking forward to seeing it bloom all over again. His plays include *Scotch and Donuts*, *The Eternal Vaudeville*, *The Man Who Was Thursday*, and *How to be Cool*, and he's the author of the *Insight Guide to Seattle*, along with six years worth of articles and reviews while working as the theater critic for the *Seattle Weekly*.

ANNA JOE SAVAGE chased down some of the city's well-knowns for their insider tips on the "best places" in Seattle. Artists to sports figures divulged their secrets of the city—like the best place to be ignored. A Seattle native and recent University of Washington grad, Anna Joe is just beginning her freelance writing career. "I'm living the life of an aspiring writer/dedicated waitress," she admits. She has written for *Seattle Magazine* and *Northwest Home + Garden*.

When **SUZANNE SCHMALZER**, who contributed one-third of our restaurant reviews, moved to Seattle she went to a lounge where local celebutantes sipped designer martinis: "This one's too hip." Then, she went to a hotel where middle-aged men puffed on cigars: "This one's too stuffy." Suzanne picked up a copy of *Best Places Seattle* and found a bunch of places that were "just right." She wrote about her experiences for *Seattle Magazine*, *Northwest Palate*, and Gayot.com. Her readers have been dining happily ever after.

Lifelong Seattleite **GISELLE SMITH** wrote the Experience Seattle tours in the Planning a Trip chapter and updated the Recreation chapter. Besides double-digit years of editing and writing for regional magazines, she has clocked 10 years of competitive rowing and hundreds of laps around Green Lake. She is currently a database editor in Seattle's high-tech industry, a freelance writer, and is editor of the forthcoming *Best Places Northwest* 15th Edition (Sasquatch) guidebook.

Seattle freelance writer **NIKI STOJNIC** updated our Day Trips chapter, happily trekking out to points north, south, east, and west of the city. A former assistant editor at *Washington Law & Politics* magazine, she has also contributed to *Northwest Home + Garden*, *Horizon Air*, *Midwest Express*, and *Alaska Airlines*. This is her second stint with *Best Places Seattle*.

Since he moved to Seattle from New York City in 2001, exploring the area has been **MATT VILLANO**'s favorite pastime, so we tapped him to update our Exploring chapter. A long-time freelance writer, Villano's articles have appeared in *The New York Times*, *Men's Health*, and *Seattle Weekly*. When he's not writing, Villano is trail running, watching whales, or playing with his cat.

Seattle native **SHANNON O'LEARY** has been writing about the places and people of the city for more than a dozen years. She has contributed reviews and stories on local arts, architecture, restaurants, and retail to publications including *Seattle Magazine*, *Vancouver*, *Horizon Air*, *Miami Metro*, and *Best Places Northwest*. She is former editor of *Washington Law & Politics* magazine and editor of the *Buca di Beppo: Into the Sauce!* (Tiger Oak Publications) cookbook, *Northwest Home + Garden*, and this edition of *Best Places Seattle*.

About Best Places® Guidebooks

People trust us. Best Places guidebooks, which have been published continuously since 1975, represent one of the most respected regional travel series in the country. Our reviewers know their territory and seek out the very best a city or region has to offer. We are able to provide tough, candid reports about places that have rested too long on their larels, and to delight in new places that deserve recognition. We describe the true strengths, foibles, and unique characteristics of each establishment listed.

Best Places Seattle is written by and for locals, and is therefore coveted by travelers. It's written for people who live here and who enjoy exploring the city's bounty and its out-of-the-way places of high character and individualism. It is these very characteristics that make *Best Places Seattle* ideal for tourists, too. The best places in and around the city are the ones that denizens favor: independently owned establishments of good value, touched with local history, run by lively individuals, and graced with natural beauty. With this 10th edition of *Best Places Seattle,* travelers will find the information they need: where to go and when, what to order, which rooms to request (and which to avoid), where the best music, art, nightlife, shopping, and other attractions are, and how to find the city's hidden secrets.

We're so sure you'll be satisfied with our guide, we guarantee it.

NOTE: *The reviews in this edition are based on information available at press time and are subject to change. Readers are advised that places listed in previous editions may have closed or changed management, or may no longer be recommended by this series. The editors welcome information conveyed by users of this book. Feedback is welcome via email: bestplaces@SasquatchBooks.com.*

How to Use This Book

This book is divided into ten chapters covering a wide range of establishments, destinations, and activities in and around Seattle. All evaluations are based on reports from local and traveling inspectors. Final judgments are made by the editors. **EVERY PLACE FEATURED IN THIS BOOK IS RECOMMENDED.**

STAR RATINGS *(for Top 200 Restaurants and Lodgings only)* Restaurants and lodgings are rated on a scale of one to four stars (with half stars in between), based on uniqueness, loyalty of local clientele, performance measured against the establishment's goals, excellence of cooking, cleanliness, value, and professionalism of service. Reviews are listed alphabetically, and every place is recommended.

BEST PLACES® STAR RATINGS

Any travel guide that rates establishments is inherently subjective—and Best Places is no exception. We rely on our professional experience, yes, but also on a gut feeling. And, occasionally, we even give in to a soft spot for a favorite neighborhood hangout. Our star-rating system is not simply a checklist; it's judgmental, critical, sometimes fickle, and highly personal.

For each new edition, we send local food and travel experts out to review restaurants and lodgings, and then to rate them on a scale of one to four, based on uniqueness, loyalty of local clientele, performance measured against the establishment's goals, excellence of cooking, cleanliness, value, and professionalism of service. That doesn't mean a one-star establishment isn't worth dining or sleeping at—far from it. When we say that all the places listed in our books are recommended, we mean it. That one-star pizza joint may be just the ticket for the end of a whirlwind day of shopping with the kids. But if you're planning something more special, the star ratings can help you choose an eatery or hotel that will wow your new clients or be a stunning, romantic place to celebrate an anniversary or impress a first date.

We award four-star ratings sparingly, reserving them for what we consider truly the best. And once an establishment has earned our highest rating, everyone's expectations seem to rise. Readers often write us letters specifically to point out the faults in four-star establishments. With changes in chefs, management, styles, and trends, it's always easier to get knocked off the pedestal than to ascend it. Three-star establishments, on the other hand, seem to generate healthy praise. They exhibit outstanding qualities, and we get lots of love letters about them. The difference between two and three stars can sometimes be a very fine line. Two-star establishments are doing a good, solid job and gaining attention, while one-star places are often dependable spots that have been around forever.

The restaurants and lodgings described in Best Places Seattle have earned their stars from hard work and good service (and good food). They're proud to be included in this book—look for our Best Places sticker in their windows. And we're proud to honor them in this, the tenth edition of Best Places Seattle.

★★★★　The very best in the region

★★★　Distinguished; many outstanding features

★★　Excellent; some wonderful qualities

★　A good place

UNRATED　New or undergoing major changes

(For more on how we rate places, see the Best Places Star Ratings box on the previous page.)

PRICE RANGE *(for Top 200 Restaurants and Lodgings only)* Prices for restaurants are based primarily on dinner for two, including dessert, tax, and tip (no alcohol). Prices for lodgings are based on peak season rates for one night's lodging for two people (i.e., double occupancy). Peak season is typically Memorial Day to Labor Day; off-season rates vary but can sometimes be significantly less. Call ahead to verify, as all prices are subject to change.

$$$$　Very expensive (more than $125 for dinner for two; more than $250 for one night's lodging for two)

$$$　Expensive (between $85 and $125 for dinner for two; between $150 and $250 for one night's lodging for two)

$$　Moderate (between $35 and $85 for dinner for two; between $85 and $150 for one night's lodging for two)

$　Inexpensive (less than $35 for dinner for two; less than $85 for one night's lodging for two)

RESERVATIONS *(for Top 200 Restaurants only)* We used one of the following terms for our reservations policy: reservations required, reservations recommended, no reservations. "No reservations" means either reservations are not necessary or are not accepted.

PARKING We've indicated a variety of options for parking in the facts lines at the end of each review.

ADDRESSES AND PHONE NUMBERS Every attempt has been made to provide accurate information on an establishment's location and phone number, but it's always a good idea to call ahead and confirm. For establishments with two or more locations, we try to provide information on the original or most recommended branches.

CHECKS AND CREDIT CARDS Many establishments that accept checks also require a major credit card for identification. Note that some places accept only local checks. Credit cards are abbreviated in this book as follows: American Express (AE); Carte Blanche (CB); Diners Club (DC); Discover (DIS); Japanese credit card (JCB); MasterCard (MC); Visa (V).

EMAIL AND WEB SITE ADDRESSES Email and web site addresses for establishments have been included where available. Please note that the web is a fluid and evolving medium, and that web pages are often "under construction" or, as with all time-sensitive information, may no longer be valid.

MAP INDICATORS The letter-and-number codes appearing at the end of most listings refer to coordinates on the fold-out map included in the front of the book. Single letters (for example, F7) refer to the Downtown Seattle map; double letters (FF7) refer to the Greater Seattle map on the flip side. If an establishment does not have a map code listed, its location falls beyond the boundaries of these maps.

HELPFUL ICONS Watch for these quick-reference symbols throughout the book:

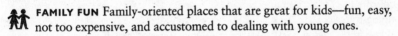 **FAMILY FUN** Family-oriented places that are great for kids—fun, easy, not too expensive, and accustomed to dealing with young ones.

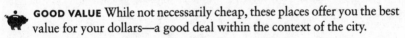 **GOOD VALUE** While not necessarily cheap, these places offer you the best value for your dollars—a good deal within the context of the city.

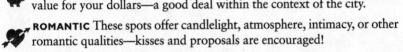 **ROMANTIC** These spots offer candlelight, atmosphere, intimacy, or other romantic qualities—kisses and proposals are encouraged!

EDITORS' CHOICE These are places that are unique and special to the city, such as a restaurant owned by a beloved local chef or a tourist attraction recognized around the globe.

Appears after listings for establishments that have wheelchair-accessible facilities.

INDEXES In addition to a general index at the back of the book, there are five specialized indexes: restaurants are indexed by star-rating, features, and location at the beginning of the Restaurants chapter, and nightspots are indexed by features and location at the beginning of the Nightlife chapter.

PLANNING A TRIP

PLANNING A TRIP

How to Get Here

BY PLANE

SEATTLE-TACOMA INTERNATIONAL AIRPORT (SeaTac, 206/431-4444; map:OO6), better known as simply Sea-Tac (not to be confused with the city of SeaTac, sans hyphen), is located 13 miles south of Seattle, barely a half-hour freeway ride from downtown. Continuing expansion, multimillion-dollar renovations to concourses in the main terminal, and an easily accessible parking facility have helped turn Sea-Tac into one of the most convenient major airports in the country, although the construction sometimes leads to delays and lines. Sea-Tac now serves between 26 million and 27 million passengers a year. A newly upgraded, high-speed, computer-controlled subway system links the main terminal to two adjoining satellite terminals; allow an extra 10 minutes to reach gates in those terminals.

Travelers who need information or directions should look for roaming airport volunteers in blue jackets or "Pathfinders" in red jackets or T-shirts carrying matching clipboards marked "Airport Information." These folks, available between 6am and 11pm daily, will point you in the right direction. Throughout the airport, families will find rest rooms with changing tables; nearly all men's and women's rest rooms, as well as the family rest rooms, have them. If you must check your e-mail, Laptop Lane, located in the north satellite terminal near the United Airlines gates, provides on-line access for computers, phones, fax machines, and photocopying. Ground transportation information booths are located on the baggage level at carousels 3 and 16. **VISITOR INFORMATION SEA-TAC AIRPORT** (206/433-5218) is located in baggage claim by carousel 8 and offers trip suggestions regarding Seattle and the state of Washington seven days a week, along with a plethora of splashy travel brochures. Foreign visitors in need of information and services should proceed to the customs area, where **OPERATION WELCOME** (206/433-5367) provides assistance in nearly 15 languages. For exhaustive information on airport services and operating conditions, call the **AIRPORT INFORMATION LINE** (206/431-4444): you can listen to recorded messages on everything from parking, paging, hotels, and customs to lost and found. Or go to the **AIRPORT WEB SITE** (portseattle.org/seatac/).

The **SEA-TAC PARKING** complex, which holds more than 11,000 vehicles, is connected to the main terminal via sky bridges on the fourth floor. The garage is slightly counterintuitive, the only way to get to it is actually via this fourth-floor sky bridge. It's self-serve when it comes to paying for parking, with automated pay stations also located on the fourth floor of the garage, so tickets should be kept with the parker, not in the car. Machines take cash and major credit cards. Short-term parkers can pick a spot anywhere in the garage and pay $2 for up to 30 minutes and $4 for 30 minutes to 1 hour. General parking, located on the top four floors of the garage, costs $6 for 1 to 2 hours and $3 each hour thereafter up to $20 maximum per day. Follow the signs in the garage for valet parking, which costs $20 for up to 4 hours and $30 for 4 to 24 hours. It's drop and go only on the ticketing/departures drive. Parties can also be dropped off on the baggage claim/arrivals drive.

For less expensive long-term parking, try the numerous **COMMERCIAL PARKING LOTS** in the vicinity of the airport. The following operate 24 hours a day and offer free shuttle service for their parking and car-rental patrons: Thrifty Airport Parking (18836 International Blvd, SeaTac; 206/242-7275), Park & Fly (17600 International Blvd, SeaTac; 206/433-6767), and Doug Fox Airport Parking (2626 S 170th St, SeaTac; 206/248-2956).

AIRPORT TRANSPORTATION

If you're traveling alone or in a very small group, one of the easiest and least spendy ways of getting to Sea-Tac Airport from downtown (or vice versa) is on the **GRAY LINE AIRPORT EXPRESS** (206/626-6088). Going to the airport, the shuttle stops every 30 minutes at downtown hotels, including the Madison Renaissance, Crowne Plaza, Fairmont Olympic, Hilton, Sheraton, Grand Hyatt, Warwick, and Westin, from about 5am until about midnight. Going from the airport to the hotels, it runs from about 5am to 11pm at the same intervals, leaving from the north and south ends of the airport baggage claim area. The ride is about 30 to 45 minutes between the Madison Renaissance and Sea-Tac. Cost is $14 round-trip ($8.50 one-way), and children under two ride free.

SHUTTLE EXPRESS (206/622-1424 or 800/487-RIDE) provides convenient door-to-door van service to and from the airport, serving the entire greater Seattle area, from Everett to Tacoma. The company also guarantees that if a rider misses a flight, Shuttle Express will pay whatever flight-changing or other fees are incurred so that the customer's travel expenses remain the same. The cost ranges from $21.50 (from within the city) to $28.50 (from outlying suburbs) one-way. Groups traveling from a single pickup point pay reduced rates. You may share the ride with other passengers, so expect to stop elsewhere enroute. To ensure availability, make reservations two to three days ahead for trips to the airport. The shuttle from Sea-Tac operates 24 hours a day and requires no advance notice; the service desk is located on the third floor of the parking garage.

Thanks to a city ordinance, **TAXIS** to the airport from downtown Seattle are a flat fee of $25 for one or two people—"downtown" limits stretch from the waterfront at Pier 70 to the intersection of Broad and Mercer Streets, east to the freeway, and south to where the freeway meets the intersection of Rainier Avenue and S Dearborn Street. A ride from the airport to downtown runs about $30. At the airport, catch a cab on the third floor of the parking garage.

METRO TRANSIT (206/553-3000; transit.metrokc.gov) offers the cheapest rides to the airport ($1.25 one-way, $2 during rush hour), via two routes: the number 174 (which can take up to an hour from downtown) and the number 194 express (a 30-minute ride via Interstate 5). Both run every half hour, seven days a week. The 194 uses the downtown transit tunnel, except on Sunday, when it travels through downtown along Third Avenue. The 174 travels through downtown along Second Avenue, with many stops through the industrial area. Both buses stop on the baggage-claim level of the airport.

BY CHARTER OR PRIVATE AIRPLANE

Most **AIRPLANE AND HELICOPTER CHARTER COMPANIES** are based at King County International Airport/Boeing Field (206/296-7380; map:KK6), south of downtown. Other airplane charters are located north of the city at Snohomish County Airport (Paine Field, Everett; 425/353-2110). Services include flying lessons and aircraft rentals. Call the Seattle Automated Flight Service Station (206/767-2726) for up-to-date weather reports and flight-related information.

BY BUS

GREYHOUND BUS LINES (811 Stewart St, Downtown; 800/231-2222; greyhound.com; map:I4) is usually the least expensive way to get to Seattle. The station is within walking distance of the downtown retail core.

BY TRAIN

The wide seats inside and beautiful vistas outside make **AMTRAK** (800/872-7245, passenger information and reservations; 206/382-4128, baggage and package express; 206/382-4713, lost and found; amtrak.com) the most comfortable and scenic mode of transportation to Seattle. Especially eye-catching is the Portland-to-Seattle route, some of which runs along the shores of Puget Sound. The Coast Starlight leaves Seattle headed south to Portland, San Francisco, and Los Angeles, and headed north to Vancouver, British Columbia; the Empire Builder heads east to Chicago via Spokane. The train pulls up to King Street Station (3rd Ave S and S Jackson St, Pioneer Square; map:P7) at the south end of downtown.

BY CAR

The primary north-south artery is **INTERSTATE 5**, which runs south from Seattle through Tacoma and the state capital of Olympia, to Portland, Oregon (185 miles south of Seattle), and on through California. To the north via I-5 lies Vancouver, British Columbia, just 143 miles away. More or less parallel to I-5 is the old north-south route, **HIGHWAY 99**, which becomes Aurora Avenue for a stretch through the city. Just south of downtown, I-5 meets **INTERSTATE 90**, Seattle's primary connection to all points east. From downtown, I-90 crosses a floating bridge over Lake Washington to the eastern suburbs, and then crosses the Cascades at Snoqualmie Pass before dropping down to the Columbia Plateau of Eastern Washington and curving its way toward Spokane, 280 miles east. The other link to the Eastside suburbs is **HIGHWAY 520**, which leaves I-5 just north of downtown, crosses a different floating bridge, and passes near the Bellevue and Kirkland town centers before ending in Redmond. Both east-west highways connect with **INTERSTATE 405**, which runs north-south through the suburbs east of Lake Washington. To go to and from the Olympic Peninsula to the west, take a scenic **FERRY RIDE** across Puget Sound (see the Ferry Rides sidebar in the Day Trips chapter).

A cautionary note: Seattle's traffic can be nerve defying. It seems at any given time, on any random street, there's a crew tearing up, digging out, or jackhammering chunks of the road. The raising of the Fremont, University, and Montlake bridges to let sailboats and barges pass through can also tack extra time onto a drive. Road warriors need to be on the defensive. Try to plan your arrival and departure times to avoid rush hours, generally 7am to 9am and 3pm to 7pm weekdays.

When to Visit

If weather is a factor in your decision of when to visit Seattle, remember that the table below shows averages; what you'll experience is unpredictable. Keep in mind that although the season from November through February may have more rain and be a little cooler, hotel rates, airfares, and admission fees are often lower at that time.

WEATHER

The toughest job in Seattle is being a weather forecaster—everyone suspects you're a liar, an idiot, or both. Between the mountains, the warm offshore currents, and the cold fronts sweeping down from the north, predicting weather here is an exercise in equivocation. Predictions are even more difficult because a torrential downpour in West Seattle might occur at the same time as blinding sunshine in Wallingford. One thing you can count on is clouds: if you don't get a glimpse of the sun for days (or weeks!) on end, you may feel as though it's rained more than it actually has. If you're trying to avoid the rain altogether, July and August are the warmest and driest months, and they usually don't reach extremes of heat and humidity. Since so few days are uncomfortably hot, air conditioners are notably absent. Things get wet in the winter, with averages of around 5 to 6 inches of rain a month from November through January, but temperatures are mild enough that snow and ice are infrequent. On those rare days when the slick stuff does appear, though, watch out: the town grinds to a halt and the streets become one big roller derby.

Average temperature and precipitation by month

Month	Daily Maximum Temp. (degrees F)	Daily Minimum Temp. (degrees F)	Monthly Precipitation (inches)
January	46	36	5.13
February	50	37	4.18
March	53	39	3.75
April	58	42	2.59
May	64	47	1.78
June	70	52	1.49
July	75	55	0.79
August	76	56	1.02
September	70	52	1.63
October	60	46	3.19
November	51	40	5.90
December	46	36	5.62

Source: weather.com

Big Events to Plan Around

FEBRUARY

Northwest Flower and Garden Show

(WASHINGTON STATE CONVENTION & TRADE CENTER; 9TH AVE AND PIKE ST, DOWNTOWN; 800/229-6311; GARDENSHOW.COM) Five days of gardens over 8 acres in the Washington State Convention Center help make this horticultural extravaganza the third largest spring show in North America. Held in early February, the nearly 300 exhibits bring an early spring to the Northwest. General admission is $18 (half day $12).

BEST PLACE TO LISTEN TO LIVE MUSIC?

"Bumbershoot—Seattle's official end-of-summer arts festival. Otherwise Pioneer Square, where one cover gets you into most of the clubs."

Greg Nickels, mayor of Seattle

APRIL

Skagit Valley Tulip Festival

(MOUNT VERNON, 60 MILES NORTH OF SEATTLE VIA I-5; 360/428-5959; TULIPFESTIVAL.ORG) Washington's temperate climate makes it a viable, if less exotic, alternative to the Netherlands when it comes to raising tulips. During early April, Mount Vernon seizes the moment and entertains visitors with a street fair and parades, and thousands of acres of tulips.

MAY

Opening Day of Boating Season

(ALONG THE MONTLAKE CUT BETWEEN LAKE WASHINGTON AND LAKE UNION; 206/325-1000; SEATTLEYACHTCLUB.ORG) Boat owners from the Northwest and beyond come to participate in this festive ceremonial regatta, which officially kicks off the nautical summer on the first Saturday in May.

International Children's Festival

(SEATTLE CENTER; 206/684-7338; SEATTLEINTERNATIONAL.ORG) Professional children's performers come from all over the world for this popular event. Crafts, storytelling, puppet shows, and musical and theater performances entertain kids and their parents for six days in early May.

Northwest Folklife Festival

 (SEATTLE CENTER; 206/684-7300; NWFOLKLIFE.ORG) Memorial Day weekend means folk fest in Seattle, with performers and artists traveling from all over the country to attend. The music is complemented by food, dance, and crafts throughout the Seattle Center.

Seattle International Film Festival

(VARIOUS THEATERS AROUND TOWN; 206/464-5830; SEATTLEFILM.COM) Film buffs schedule vacation time around this cinematic bonanza, held over a 3½-week period every May and June. Tickets can be competitive to acquire, so plan ahead. The most recent festival boasted films from 50 countries, with 226 features and documentaries and more than 80 short films. Filmgoers vote on their favorites within categories, and the winning films take home a Golden Space Needle.

JUNE

Fremont Fair

(N 34TH ST, ALONG THE FREMONT SHIP CANAL; 206/632-1500; FREMONT FAIR.COM) The artsy, eccentric Fremont neighborhood celebrates summer's beginning with a solstice parade, music, crafts booths, food, and dance. This event gets bigger and crazier every year.

Summer Nights on the Pier

(PIER 62/63 ON ALASKAN WY; 206/281-7788; SUMMERNIGHTS.ORG) Two former working piers transformed into a 3,000-seat concert ground have become a perfect place to spend a summer evening listening to such acts as Ani DiFranco or the Beach Boys. The concert series extends through the summer.

JULY

Seafair

(VARIOUS LOCATIONS THROUGHOUT TOWN; 206/728-0123; SEAFAIR.COM) Seattle's frenzied summer fete has been around since 1950 and—to the chagrin of some locals—isn't likely to go away. Highlights include the milk carton–boat races at Green Lake and the hydroplane races. Practically all Seafair events are free.

Chinatown/International District Summer Festival

(HING HAY PARK, INTERNATIONAL DISTRICT; 206/382-1197; INTERNATIONAL DISTRICT.ORG) The Chinatown/International District's mid-July extravaganza celebrates the richness and diversity of Asian culture with dancing, instrumental and martial-arts performances, food booths, and arts and crafts.

SEPTEMBER

Bumbershoot

(SEATTLE CENTER; 206/281-8111; BUMBERSHOOT.ORG) Though "bumbershoot" technically means "umbrella," the weather on Labor Day weekend, when the multiarts festival is held, usually doesn't require one. Bumbershoot has been around in various forms since the early 1970s and now hosts craftspeople, writers, comedians, poets, and select musical performers such as REM. The festival occurs in venues throughout the Seattle Center, and a $15 daily pass is all you need.

Fringe Festival

(VARIOUS PERFORMANCE VENUES ON CAPITOL HILL; 206/342-9172; SEATTLE FRINGE.ORG) Started in 1990, this festival of theatrical performances stretches over 15 days in late September. More than 90 theater companies participate, providing a wide range of entertainment.

OCTOBER

Northwest Bookfest

(SAND POINT MAGNUSON PARK; 206/378-1883; NWBOOKFEST.ORG) Seattle's first book festival debuted in 1995 and hosts a wide range of programs, including author appearances and signings, bookseller and publisher exhibits, and panel discussions. Held in late October.

DECEMBER

Christmas Ship Festival

(VISITS BEACHES CITYWIDE; 206/623-1445; ARGOSYCRUISES.COM) Since *Sleepless in Seattle*, the rest of the world has associated Christmas in Seattle with lighted boats skimming along the water. Area musical groups climb aboard to serenade folks gathered at 45 different waterfront locations. Call for a schedule.

TIME

Seattle is on Pacific Standard Time (PST), which is three hours behind New York, two hours behind Chicago, one hour behind Denver, one hour ahead of Anchorage, and two hours ahead of Honolulu. Daylight Saving Time begins in early April and ends in late October. Because Seattle is located so far north (between the 47th and 48th latitudes), residents enjoy long daylight hours in summer, with sunrises before 6am and sunsets as late as 9:45pm.

WHAT TO BRING

Given the variable nature of Seattle's weather, it's best to be ready for anything, especially if you're visiting between May and October. Bring layers that you can add or remove, with a sweater or a light jacket just in case; even summer evenings can be cool. From June through September, be sure to bring shorts and sunglasses. In the winter months, it's easy: dress for rain. If you plan to take walking tours of the city, wear water-resistant shoes and wool socks, and be sure to bring a bumbershoot— unless you want to pass for a local.

When choosing what to wear, remember that Seattle pioneered the art of dressing casual. Suits and ties are seen only on those unfortunate souls who work in the downtown business district; otherwise, jeans, khakis, T-shirts, and fleeces are ubiquitous. With a few exceptions, even the most expensive restaurants allow patrons to wear jeans, and only a select few require a jacket.

General Costs

As is the case elsewhere around the country, of late the economic outlook in Seattle has been gloomy. Deflation is a threat, and economic recovery is slow, with neither situation helped by continuing layoffs at Boeing and in government offices. But there remains a silver lining. Microsoft continues to be a titan to be reckoned with, with thousands of job openings. Starbucks is not only a thriving company but an international habit. Nordstrom continues to turn out shoppers looking their best. Biotech is now one of the area's front-runners—witness Pacific Northwest Research Institute and Fred Hutchinson's groundbreaking cancer medications. Amazon.com is a household name. REI outfits a healthy number of the country's outdoor types. And Weyerhaeuser still manufactures wood products.

Housing costs remain high, especially in comparison to other major cities. According to the National Association of Realtors, in the first quarter of 2003 Seattle ranked ninth in the nation with a median home price of $250,000, just behind Washington, D.C. and vicinity and the Los Angeles area. Fortunately, costs for quotidian items are in keeping with the region and are relative to any robust, big city.

Average costs for lodging and food

DOUBLE ROOM

Inexpensive	$55–$89
Moderate	$85–$150
Expensive	$150 and up

LUNCH FOR ONE (INCLUDING BEVERAGE AND TIP)

Inexpensive	$9–$13
Moderate	$13–$19
Expensive	$20 and up

BEVERAGES IN A RESTAURANT

Glass of wine	$5–$7
Pint of beer	$4–$5
Coca-Cola	$1.25
Double tall latte	$3

OTHER COMMON ITEMS

Movie ticket	$8–$9
Roll of film	$5
Taxi per mile	$1.80
Rain jacket from REI	$30–$549
Seattle souvenir T-shirt	$12–$15

READ ALL ABOUT IT

Seattleites are bookworms. According to a 2003 university study of the most literate cities, we ranked number two in the United States in overall literacy and were tops when it came to the ratio of booksellers to population. Our page-turning proclivities ensure that you don't have to go far in this town to find a store selling new or used titles, or both. In fact, Seattle hosts two nationally known independent bookstores, **ELLIOTT BAY BOOK COMPANY** (101 S Main St, Pioneer Square; 206/624-6600; map:O8) and the **UNIVERSITY BOOKSTORE** (4326 University Wy NE, University District; 206/634-3400; map:FF6).

And although they don't all write about the city, many well-known authors live and work in the area: Tom Robbins, Charles Johnson, David Guterson, Erik Larson, Michael Collins, Dan Savage, Rebecca Brown, Sherman Alexie, and Terry Brooks, to name just a few. True-crime masters John Saul and Ann Rule, as well as science-fiction novelists Vonda McIntyre and Greg Bear, also live here. But it's crime novelists—from J. A. Jance to G. M. Ford to K. K. Beck—and visiting writers who seem to best capture the city.

Here's a short reading list to put you in the know about Seattle and the Puget Sound region.

NONFICTION

Northwest history is recorded by those who lived it in *A Voyage of Discovery to the North Pacific Ocean and Round the World in the Years 1790–95* (Reprint Services Corp., 1992; originally published by C. G. and J. Robinson, 1798) by explorer George Vancouver and in books by early pioneers and visitors, including *Pioneer Days on Puget Sound* (Glen Adams, 1980) by Arthur A. Denny; *West Coast Journeys, 1865–1879: The Travelogue of a Remarkable Woman* (Sasquatch Books, 1995) by Caroline C. Leighton; and *Saddle and Canoe* (The Long Riders' Guild Press, 2001) by Theodore Winthrop.

Skid Road: An Informal Portrait of Seattle (University of Washington Press, 1982) by Murray Cromwell Morgan is a lively, irreverent look back at some of the events and eccentrics responsible for creating the Seattle we know today. This is the essential guide to the first 100 years of the city's history. For a more contemporary, sociological look at Seattle, don't miss *Seattle and the Demons of Ambition: A Love Story* (St. Martin's Press, 2003), by former *Seattle Weekly* editor Fred Moody. Moody's book chronicles the unsettling changes in Seattle induced by the rise of powerhouses like Microsoft and Starbucks, culminating in the 1999 World Trade Organization protests.

Walt Crowley's *National Trust Guide Seattle* (John Wiley & Sons, 1998) provides a wonderful overview of the city's architecture and history that both locals and visitors can enjoy. *Seattle City Walks* (Sasquatch Books, 1999) by Laura Karlinsey provides easy-to-use walking tours of various city neighborhoods, with historical and cultural details, directions to viewpoints, and profiles of Seattle personalities.

The Forging of a Black Community (University of Washington Press, 1994) by Quintard Taylor examines the often-troubled evolution of Seattle's Central District from the year 1870 through the civil-rights struggles of the 1960s.

Rains All the Time: A Connoisseur's History of Weather in the Pacific Northwest (Sasquatch Books, 1997) by David Laskin recounts the history of this region's relationship with its "liquid sunshine."

One of our most beloved regional books, *The Egg and I* (reprinted by Perennial, 1987; originally published in 1945) by Betty MacDonald is a delightfully whimsical memoir of life on a Western Washington chicken ranch.

Northwest poet Richard Hugo's work reflects the Seattle area he called home in *Making Certain It Goes On: Collected Poems of Richard Hugo* (W. W. Norton & Co., 1991). Tobias Wolff recollects his childhood in 1950s West Seattle in his award-winning memoir *This Boy's Life* (Grove Press, 2000). Works that offer contemporary perspectives on the region are Sallie Tisdale's *Stepping Westward: The Long Search for Home in the Pacific Northwest* (Harper-Perennial Library, 1992); *New York Times* correspondent Timothy Egan's *The Good Rain: Across Time and Terrain in the Pacific Northwest* (Vintage Books, 1991); and Bruce Barcott's *The Measure of a Mountain: Beauty and Terror on Mount Rainier* (Ballantine Books, 1998).

FICTION

In *Into the Inferno* (Ballantine Books, 2003) by Seattle Fire Department lieutenant Earl Emerson, a fire chief in nearby North Bend must discover why members of his department are succumbing to freak accidents, or within a week he'll join them.

Ten Little Indians (Grove Press, 2003) by Native American novelist and screenwriter (*Smoke Signals*) Sherman Alexie tells nine different stories, most set in Seattle, centering on love, rituals, and loss.

In *First Avenue* (Onyx Books, 2000), Seattle ex-cop Lowen Clausen writes about the beat on First Avenue in Belltown before recent gentrification.

A River out of Eden (Anchor, 2002) by John Hockenberry is a thriller set against the backdrop of the Northwest, centered on the contemporary and enmeshed issues of environmental pollution, salmon survival, and Native American ways.

In *Slant* (Tor Books, 1998) by Greg Bear, Seattle in the year 2050 is one of the principal settings for an innovative tale of nanotechnology and national madness.

Black River (Avon Books, 2003) by G. M. Ford features Seattle true-crime writer Frank Corso, hoping to get his next book from the drama surrounding an area mobster's trial.

Snow Falling on Cedars (Vintage Contemporaries, 1995) by David Guterson is a historical novel (made into a movie in 1999) about the murder trial of a Japanese American fisherman working on Puget Sound, which won considerable local and national acclaim.

Lastly, the late Oregonian Ken Kesey captures the flavor of the Northwest's timber industry in *Sometimes a Great Notion* (Penguin USA, 1998), a regional classic.

—*J. Kingston Pierce*

Tips for Special Travelers

FAMILIES WITH CHILDREN

In an emergency, call 911, 24 hours a day. For questions about your child's health, growth, or development, call the **CHILDREN'S HOSPITAL RESOURCE LINE** (206/987-2500). If you think your child has ingested a toxic substance, call the **WASHINGTON POISON CENTER** (206/526-2121 or 800/732-6985). A local publication, **PARENTMAP** (206/709-9026), serves as a resource for parents and is available free at many libraries, grocery stores, YMCAs, and other businesses catering to families.

The majority of downtown hotels cater heavily to business travelers. This means that family-oriented amenities such as swimming pools, game rooms, and inexpensive restaurants are more readily found at hotels outside the downtown area. Many hotels allow kids to stay free when traveling with their parents, so ask when you make reservations. Most major restaurants have children's menus.

Watch for this icon throughout the book; it indicates places and activities that are great for families.

SENIORS

SENIOR SERVICES OF SEATTLE/KING COUNTY (2208 2nd Ave, Ste 100, Belltown; 206/448-3110; map:H7) runs a referral service for seniors, offering information about health and welfare resources and transportation and mobility services. It also publishes a newsletter called *Passport* that lists upcoming events for seniors, including fairs, volunteer activities, opportunities for flu shots, and some happenings at neighborhood senior centers. For **PUBLIC TRANSIT**, Senior bus passes are $3 for people 65 and older. They are good for life and reduce the fare to 25 cents on all buses, or 50 cents during peak hours. Senior passes can be purchased in person either at the downtown Metro office (201 S Jackson St, Pioneer Square; 206/553-3060; map:O8) or in the transit tunnel station underneath Westlake Center (map:J6).

PEOPLE WITH DISABILITIES

For information about using public transportation, call the **METRO ACCESSIBLE SERVICES OFFICES** (206/263-3113). After registering for services, riders can then call **ACCESS** for reservations (206/205-5000 or 206/749-4286 TTY). For tour companies and other private companies offering mobility services, call the **SEATTLE/KING COUNTY CONVENTION AND VISITORS BUREAU** (206/461-5840). **THE DEAF/BLIND SERVICE CENTER** (206/323-9178) offers volunteers and helpers for hire who assist deaf or blind Washington state residents in taking walks, grocery shopping, or going to the bank. Visitors from elsewhere in Washington state can contact the center in advance of their trip for a list of volunteers to call directly for assistance. **THE WASHINGTON TALKING BOOK AND BRAILLE LIBRARY** (2021 9th Ave, Downtown; 206/615-0400; map:G4) has thousands of recorded and Braille titles available for loan.

WOMEN

Seattle is known as a relatively safe city but, as in most cities, women travelers should take extra precautions at night, especially in Downtown, Belltown, the University District, and Pioneer Square. **THE UNIVERSITY OF WASHINGTON WOMEN'S CENTER** (4014 University Wy NE, Cunningham Hall, University District; 206/685-1090; map:FF6) is open to students as well as the general public and offers an extensive library, job listings, community bulletin board, and class information. For health and reproductive services, call **PLANNED PARENTHOOD** (2001 E Madison St, Capitol Hill; 206/328-7700; map:HH6). **BAILEY/COY BOOKS** (414 Broadway Ave E, Capitol Hill; 206/323-8842; map:HH6) carries a wide range of books on women's issues and also supports a community bulletin board.

BEST PLACE TO WATCH A FOREIGN FILM?

"The Metro, because while parking isn't very good there, parking at the other foreign-film venues is horrible."

Tom Robbins, author

PET OWNERS

Travelers with pets will find themselves welcome in the most surprising places—including downtown Seattle's four-star **FAIRMONT OLYMPIC HOTEL** (formerly Four Seasons Olympic). Refer to guidebooks such as *The Dog Lover's Companion to Seattle* by Steve Giordano for other places your dog or cat is welcome to share your room.

Mid-to-high-end pet supply stores are scattered throughout town, including **RAILEY'S LEASH & TREAT** (513 N 36th St, Fremont; 206/632-5200; map:FF8) and **FETCH** (1411 34th Ave, Madrona; 206/720-1961; map:HH6). There's even an in-city doggie day care, **DOWNTOWN DOG LOUNGE** (206/282-DOGS; www.downtowndoglounge.com).

If Seattle has one militant, vocal political force, it's dog owners. As a result, Seattle boasts many spacious and well-tended off-leash areas, meaning many happy dogs. For overall information on Seattle's off-leash areas (listed below), call the **SEATTLE PARKS AND RECREATION DEPARTMENT** (206/684-4075).

GENESEE PARK (46th Ave S and Genesee St, Columbia City; map:JJ5) has an off-leash area east of the playfield.

GOLDEN GARDENS PARK (8498 Seaview Pl NW, Ballard; map:DD9) has an off-leash area in the eastern portion of the park and is the only area that provides lighting.

BLUE DOG POND PARK (Martin Luther King Jr Wy at Massachusetts St, Central District; map:II6) has a giant, blue dog sculpture at the park's entrance.

SAND POINT MAGNUSON PARK (6500 Sand Point Wy, Sand Point; map:EE5) has dog-friendly areas along the park's eastern and northern boundaries, with some water access to Lake Washington and plenty of abandoned tennis balls in case Sparky forgot his.

WESTCREST PARK (8806 8th Ave SW, West Seattle; map:KK8) has a dog area along the southern border of the reservoir.

WOODLAND PARK (N 50th St and Aurora Ave N, Wallingford; map:FF7) has a dog area in the park's northeastern portion, west of the tennis courts.

Outside Seattle, area off-leash parks include **MERCER ISLAND'S LUTHER BUR-BANK PARK** (206/236-3545; map:II4) as well as **MARYMOOR PARK** (206/296-2964; map:FF1) in Redmond.

GAYS AND LESBIANS

Seattle is a gay-friendly city. Its large gay community is mainly centered around the Capitol Hill neighborhood, with a variety of gay-focused bars, dance clubs, bookstores, and bed-and-breakfast inns. *Seattle Gay News* (1605 12th Ave, Ste 31, Capitol Hill; 206/324-4297; sgn.org; map:GG7) is a weekly community newspaper, available at many shops, bars, and bookstores around Capitol Hill. There's a helpful guide to the businesses and services of the community: the GSBA Guide & Directory, available at stores in the area or by contacting the **GREATER SEATTLE BUSINESS ASSOCIATION** (2150 N 107th, Ste 205, Northgate; 206/363-9188; map:DD7). Two community bookstores, **BEYOND THE CLOSET** (518 E Pike St, Capitol Hill; 206/322-4609; map:K2) and **BAILEY/COY BOOKS** (414 Broadway Ave E, Capitol Hill; 206/323-8842; map:HH6), offer community bulletin boards and have staffs who are knowledgeable about local resources and events. **THE LESBIAN RESOURCE CENTER** (2214 S Jackson St, Central District; 206/322-3953; map:HH6) provides business referrals, therapy and physician referrals, and housing information. For information on the city's many gay clubs and bars, see the Nightlife chapter.

FOREIGN VISITORS

Seattle hosts a number of foreign-exchange brokers and foreign banks. **THOMAS COOK** (400 Pine St, Downtown; 206/682-4525; map:I6; 10630 NE 8th St, Bellevue; 425/462-8225; map:HH3; and various Sea-Tac Airport locations) is a foreign-exchange broker. Foreign banks with branches in Seattle include the **BANK OF TOKYO** (900 4th Ave, Ste 4000, Downtown; 206/382-6000; map:L6) and the **HONG KONG BANK OF CANADA** (600 University St, Ste 2323, Downtown; 206/233-0888; map:K5).

A multitude of services are available for the foreign visitor who does not speak English as a first language. **THE AMERICAN CULTURAL EXCHANGE** (200 W Mercer St, Ste 504, Downtown; 206/217-9644; cultural.org; map:B6) offers language classes and arranges for summertime exchanges and visits by foreigners to American homes. **YOHANA INTERNATIONAL** (425/771-8465) and the **LANGUAGE CONNECTION** (425/277-9045) provide document translation as well as interpreters in dozens of languages, including those of Africa, Asia, and Europe. The **MILMANCO CORPORATION** (651 Strander Blvd, Ste 100, Tukwila; 206/575-3808; map:OO5) can help those involved in international business and in need of technical written translations (from and into foreign languages); rates vary. The **RED CROSS LANGUAGE BANK** (206/323-2345) provides on-call interpretive assistance at no charge.

Seattle's importance as a port city has brought it many foreign consulates.

BELGIUM, 2200 Alaskan Wy, Ste 470, Downtown; 206/728-5145 (call for appt).

BOLIVIA, 15215 52nd Ave S, Tukwila; 206/244-6696.

CANADA, Plaza 600, Ste 412, Downtown; 206/443-1777.

ESTONIA, 2200 Alaskan Wy, Ste 470, Downtown; 206/467-1444.

FINLAND (not open to the public), 425/451-3983 (call for appt).

FRANCE, 2200 Alaskan Wy, Ste 490, Downtown; 206/256-6184 (call for appt).

GREAT BRITAIN, 900 4th Ave, Ste 3001, Downtown; 206/622-9255.

JAPAN, 601 Union St, Ste 500, Downtown; 206/682-9107.

MEXICO, 2132 3rd Ave, Belltown; 206/448-3526.

NETHERLANDS (not open to the public), 4609 140th Ave NE, Bellevue; 425/861-4437 (call for appt).

NEW ZEALAND (not open to the public), 360/766-8002 (call for appt).

NORWAY, 1402 3rd Ave, Ste 806, Downtown; 206/623-3957.

PERU, 3717 NE 157th St, Ste 100, Lake Forest Park; 206/714-9037.

RUSSIA, 2001 6th Ave, Ste 2323, Belltown; 206/728-1910.

SOUTH KOREA, 2033 6th Ave, Ste 1125, Belltown; 206/441-1011.

SWEDEN, 1920 Dexter Ave N, Westlake; 206/622-5640.

TAIWAN, 2001 6th Ave, Ste 2410, Belltown; 206/441-4586.

BEST PLACE TO IMPRESS A DATE WITH YOUR CULTURAL SOPHISTICATION?

"Frye Museum. Architecturally elegant, out of the way, full of stunning, little-known, but dazzlingly accomplished Viennese paintings (and superior traveling collections). . .
You can cement the good impression you make with coffee at the intimate, chic cafe."

Michael Medved, film critic and host of syndicated radio talk show originating at KNWX AM 770

WEB INFORMATION

In a city as wired as Seattle, it's little wonder there's a wide range of Web sites operated by private as well as government organizations, nonprofits, and for-profit ventures. The following sites are helpful to both visitors and locals. Some point the direction to the best seafood in town and others give live-cam views of the traffic on the floating bridges. See listings within other chapters for specific site addresses, where available.

CITYOFSEATTLE.NET History, tours, city parks, employment.

HISTORYLINK.ORG Seattle and King County history.

SEATTLE.CITYSEARCH.COM In-city entertainment guide with reviews on restaurants, shopping, hotels, movie times, arts, and more.
SEATTLE.NET Community, business, information, and entertainment.
SEATTLEINSIDER.COM Classified ads, jobs, events, restaurants, and news.
SEATTLE-PI.COM *Seattle Post-Intelligencer* daily newspaper.
SEATTLETIMES.COM *Seattle Times* daily newspaper.
SEESEATTLE.ORG Seattle/King County Convention and Visitors Bureau.
WASHINGTON.EDU University of Washington.

Experience Seattle

Like most complex cities, Seattle has multiple personalities. Trying to capture every facet of the Emerald City in a week is next to impossible. So if you've got a limited amount of time, you might do well to specialize. What intrigues you most about this swelling metropolitan area on Puget Sound? Is it the water, the music, or perhaps the Asian influences?

Follow one or two of the themed guides we've assembled below and you'll realize that the true spirit of the city is a combination of many appealing elements.

Note: More information on most of the places in boldface may be found in other chapters throughout this guide.

CLASSIC SEATTLE: TOURISM'S GREATEST HITS

A young city by almost any measure, the largest city in Washington state has packed some interesting stories into its 150 years. The places and things that are classically Seattle may not be as old as the Liberty Bell or the Eiffel Tower, but they're icons just the same.

BEST PLACE TO LET THE KIDS RUN FREE?

"The Seattle Children's Museum—they've made it adult-proof."

Greg Nickels, mayor of Seattle

PIKE PLACE MARKET is part farmers market, part tourist attraction, part shopping mall. Arrive before 9am (8am May through October) to watch the market come to life: grab a latte from the original **STARBUCKS** (1912 Pike Pl; 206/448-8762), and wander among the farmers and craftspeople as they set up their wares. You'll get first pick of the abundant produce—including berries, peaches, and apples, in season—to fuel your progress. Head into the depths of the market to explore the unusual collection of shops, such as the **MARKET MAGIC SHOP** (206/624-4271), where Harry Potter wannabes can browse props or catch a prestidigitation demo, or **GOLDEN AGE COLLECTABLES** (206/622-9799), a kitschy warren of movie, comic book, and sports memorabilia. Don't miss Rachel, the giant bronze pig, or the street musicians. **THE MARKET FOUNDATION** (206/774-5249; pikeplace market.org) offers hour-long tours that cover the market's history, shopping tips, and quirky anecdotes.

Just south of the market is Seattle's historic district, **PIONEER SQUARE**, which is not so much a square as a neighborhood, centered around a triangular plaza and a two-block-long pedestrian mall, anchored by the 1909 pergola. Here you'll find the bulk of the city's **ART GALLERIES**, as well as totem poles, shops, and restaurants. Literary devotees love the independently owned **ELLIOTT BAY BOOK COMPANY** (101 S Main St; 206/624-6600); in a city full of rabid readers, it's considered by many to be the best bookstore.

Downtown, at **WESTLAKE CENTER** (5th Ave and Pine St) you can hop the **MONORAIL** (206/441-6038; seattlemonorail.com), the country's first full-scale system of its kind, originally built in 1962 for the World's Fair. Though activists are trying to get this elevated mode of transport extended citywide, so far the track is just 1.2 miles long, ending at the 74-acre **SEATTLE CENTER**, also built for the fair.

At the Center, youngsters love the rides at the **FUN FOREST**, and the smaller among them also enjoy the **CHILDREN'S MUSEUM** (Center House; 206/441-1768; thechildrensmuseum.org); kids of all ages enjoy the hands-on exhibits and two IMAX screens at the **PACIFIC SCIENCE CENTER** (200 2nd Ave N; 206/443-2001; pacsci.org) and running around the **INTERNATIONAL FOUNTAIN**, which spurts water in time with music. Another absorbing attraction is the two-stage **SEATTLE CHILDREN'S THEATRE** (2nd Ave N and Thomas St; 206/441-3322; sct.org), known for its imaginative performances of old favorites and future classics, afternoons and evenings, September through June.

The high point—literally—of the Center is the 605-foot **SPACE NEEDLE** (206/443-2145; spaceneedle.com). If it's a clear day, take a ride to the top, where you can get an unequalled 360-degree overview of the city.

WHERE TO STAY: Steps away from the bustle of Pike Place Market is the Inn at the Market (86 Pine St; 206/443-3600 or 800/446-4484), which affords excellent water views and service. For a more laid-back option (some rooms have shared baths) try Pensione Nichols (1923 1st Ave, Pike Place Market; 206/441-7125), just north of the Market.

WHERE TO EAT: The Space Needle's revolving restaurant, SkyCity (206/443-2150), is pricey but classically Seattle. The Pike Place Market's many dining options include Cafe Campagne (1600 Post Alley; 206/728-2233), Matt's in the Market (94 Pike St, 3rd floor; 206/467-7909), Shea's Lounge (94 Pike St; 206/467-9990), and the Pink Door (1919 Post Alley; 206/443-3241). Another local favorite is Ivar's Salmon House (401 NE Northlake Wy, Wallingford; 206/632-0767), where you can opt for inside menu service or order fish and chips and sit outside, watching the boat traffic on Lake Union.

ARCHITECTURALLY SPEAKING: EXPLORING THE CITY FROM BOTTOM TO TOP

Seattle is not known for its architecture. It's probably telling that locals tagged two downtown buildings with the brand names of a roll-on antiperspirant and an electric razor. Recently, however, the city's skyline has been impacted by architects such as Robert Venturi (**SEATTLE ART MUSEUM**, 1991), Frank Gehry (**EMP MUSEUM**, 2000), and Rem Koolhaas (new downtown **CENTRAL LIBRARY**, slated to open in 2004). Older buildings include the **KING STREET STATION** (1906), the **DOWN-TOWN YMCA** (1930), and the Marcus Priteca–designed **PARAMOUNT THEATRE** (1928).

If you're interested in the building of Seattle, the best place to start is under it. The **UNDERGROUND TOUR** (610 1st Ave, Pioneer Square; 206/682-4646; under groundtour.com), gives an energetic, informative, if somewhat corny, look at the city from before the Great Fire of 1889. It's a worthwhile 90 minutes, depending, of course, on the personality of your guide (and your tolerance for dank, dark spaces). For a self-guided, above-ground option, try the **MUSEUM OF HISTORY AND INDUSTRY** (2700 24th Ave E, Montlake; 206-324-1126; seattlehistory.org), near the University of Washington, for information about the Seattle Fire and more, including an impressive collection of historic photographs.

Back at street level downtown, you're surrounded by architectural history. Check out the Chicago school–style **ALASKA BUILDING** (1904) on Second and Cherry, the beaux arts–style **COBB BUILDING** (1910) on Fourth and University, and the art deco, walrus head–adorned **ARCTIC BUILDING** (1917) at Third and Cherry.

Seattle's first skyscraper was the 522-foot, white terra-cotta **SMITH TOWER** (506 2nd Ave, Downtown; 206/622-4004; smithtower.com), commissioned by L.C. Smith in 1911 and—when it opened on July 4, 1914—the tallest building west of the Mississippi and the fourth tallest in the world. The exquisite neoclassical building was renovated at the turn of the 21st century (reportedly at a cost of $28 million), retaining its attendant-operated brass-and-glass elevators and much of its early charm. Some trivia: Lyman Cornelius (L. C.) Smith was the Smith in Smith-Corona typewriters. The top few floors of the tower shelter a private penthouse apartment, but the observation deck on the 35th floor is open on a limited schedule (for a fee), and you can rent the adjacent Chinese Room for events.

Learn about the city's "built environment," both old and new, on a Saturday morning tour with the **SEATTLE ARCHITECTURAL FOUNDATION** (1333 5th Ave, Downtown; 206/667-9184; seattlearchitectural.org). The nonprofit organization offers themed walking tours (usually $10 to $20 per person), May through October. Subjects might cover a single building, an architectural style, or a particular neighborhood. The group also offers exhibits, public forums, and school programs. The (free) permanent exhibit at the foundation office features items including historic photographs, artist renderings, models, and building remains.

For another design perspective on Seattle, check out the downloadable, self-guided **PUBLIC ART WALKING TOURS** put out by the City of Seattle (city ofseattle.net/arts/publications/publicart/walkingtours/) that spotlight the use of murals, gardens, fountains, sculptures, and artist-designed functional art (benches, for example) secreted around the city. In the spring, the preservation organization **HISTORIC SEATTLE** (1117 Minor Ave, First Hill; 206/622-6952; cityofseattle.net/commnty/histsea) offers a popular lecture series focusing on local architecture.

You can look down on almost every other building in Seattle from the observation deck of the city's tallest tower, the 76-story **BANK OF AMERICA TOWER** (701 5th Ave, Downtown; 206/386-5151). Weekdays, you can take an elevator to the 73rd floor—and a panoramic view—for $5 per adult ($3 each for children and seniors).

BEST PLACE FOR SEAFOOD?

"Ponti Seafood Grill, where innovative chefs can make dead fish sing like nightingales."

Tom Robbins, author

WHERE TO EAT: You'll feel like you're in a historic men's club in the Sorrento's dark-paneled Hunt Club (900 Madison St, First Hill; 206/343-6156). For some postmodern cool, try Earth & Ocean in the W Seattle Hotel (1112 4th Ave, Downtown; 206/264-6000).

WHERE TO STAY: Some of the most historic lodgings in town include the 1908 Italian-style Sorrento Hotel (900 Madison St, First Hill; 206/622-6400) and the 1924 Renaissance Revival Fairmont Olympic Hotel (411 University St, Downtown; 206/621-1700).

SEATTLE AFLOAT: NAVIGATING THE CITY'S WATERWAYS

Seattle is a city almost surrounded by water: Puget Sound on the west, Lake Washington on the east, and Lake Union to the north of downtown. You can take in the waterways from shore or from a boat, big or small and powered by a motor, the wind, or you.

At **FISHERMEN'S TERMINAL**, wander the docks and watch the launch of a large portion of the city's fishing fleet. Just over the Ballard Bridge is the **HIRAM M. CHITTENDEN LOCKS** (3015 NW 54th St, Ballard; 206/783-7059), where you can watch boats rise and fall as they move between Puget Sound and the inland waterways. In season (generally June and July), don't miss the spectacle of thousands of salmon migrating through the fish ladder on the south side of the locks.

For hands-on water work, rent a kayak at the **NORTHWEST OUTDOOR CENTER** (2100 Westlake Ave N, Westlake; 206/281-9694 or 800/683-0637; www.nwoc.com) on the west side of Lake Union or at **AGUA VERDE CAFE & PADDLE CLUB** (1303 NE Boat St, University District; 206/545-8570; www.aguaverde.com) on Portage Bay. At either place, staff will offer basic instructions and steer you in the right direction. Paddle past houseboats or through the Montlake Cut, painted with the inspirational slogans of local crew teams. If you prefer a canoe or a rowboat, try the **UW WATERFRONT ACTIVITIES CENTER** (University District; 206/543-9433; depts.washington.edu/ima/IMA.wac.html). At the south end of Lake Union, experienced sailors can rent a sailboat at the **CENTER FOR WOODEN BOATS** (1010 Valley St, South Lake Union; 206/382-2628; cwb.org), nonsailors can rent rowboats, and landlubbers can admire a collection of boats without getting their feet wet. Not far

OUR HUMOR'S ALL WET

After a brief visit to Seattle some years back, comedian Bill Cosby worked up a skit about the rarity of good weather here. When the sun manages to claw out from behind gray clouds, he said, natives bound from their homes and run about frantically yelling, "What have we done? What have we done?"

Maybe he overstated things just a tad. Yes, the city's favorite event is a Labor Day festival called Bumbershoot, after the British term for "umbrella." Yes, a lot of visitors would take issue with the old TV theme song from *Here Come the Brides* that claimed "The bluest skies you've ever seen are in Seattle." But this place doesn't really deserve its reputation as the wetness capital of the United States. The rain that drenches Seattle every year is typically less than what falls on Miami, New York, Boston, or Atlanta. Yet Seattle's drippy rep hasn't been all bad. It has kept weather wimps away and has even inspired a wealth of dry humor.

"What comes after two straight days of rain in Seattle?" runs one popular riddle. The

away is the starting point of the quacky **RIDE THE DUCKS OF SEATTLE** amphibious tours (Seattle Center; 206/441-DUCK; ridetheducksofseattle.com).

Downtown, at the waterfront, hop an **ARGOSY CRUISE** (Piers 54, 55, and 57; 206/623-1445 or 800/642-7816; argosycruises.com) for a harbor tour of the working waterfront—or one of the company's other tours. For an unnarrated but cheaper view of Puget Sound, head for the Colman Ferry Dock (Pier 52) and a **WASHINGTON STATE FERRY** (206/464-6400, 800/84-FERRY or 888/808-7977; wsdot.wa.gov/ferries/) for the 35-minute crossing to Bainbridge Island, where you can spend an hour or so strolling its quaint downtown before the next return sailing. Or just stay aboard the ferry as the cars unload and reload, then return to Seattle. Take a seat on the south side of the boat for clear views of Mount Rainier in the distance, and to watch the seagulls race the boat.

A few piers north of the ferry dock on the waterfront is the **SEATTLE AQUARIUM** (Pier 59; 206/386-4320; seattleaquarium.org), with an impressive collection of cold- and warm-blooded creatures, including starfish, jellyfish, and cuddly looking otters. The underwater dome is a visitor favorite. Then take the **WATERFRONT STREETCAR** (206/553-3000)—a real 1927 trolley—north to the less-busy part of the waterfront and visit **ODYSSEY MARITIME DISCOVERY CENTER** (Pier 66; 206/374-4000; ody.org). The exhibits at this interactive museum bring out the kid in everyone; displays simulate kayaking, fishing, or navigating a freighter.

WHERE TO EAT: Tourists love Ray's Boathouse (6049 Seaview Ave NW, Ballard; 206/789-3770) and Palisade (2601 W Marina Pl, Magnolia; 206/285-1000), and locals agree these restaurants have two of the city's best waterside views. Also serving good, fresh seafood is Chinook's at Salmon Bay (1900 W Nickerson St, Interbay; 206/283-4665) at Fishermen's Terminal.

answer? "Monday." The most popular movie in Seattle? The Sound of Mucus. Or, "It's so wet in the Northwest you can watch people walk their fish." To the query "Whaddya do around here in the summer?" Northwesterners are said to reply cheerfully, "Well, if it falls on a weekend, we go on a picnic."

The rain joke is the local equivalent of the Chicago wind joke, the Michigan black-fly joke, and the Texas brag. It's a corny spill of overstatement that unites a diverse people because they all understand the exaggeration. Humor also helps fend off dampened spirits. Nobody wants to listen to somebody else whine about the rain—too depressing. But if they tell you they were knocked unconscious by a huge raindrop and that it took six buckets of sand in the face to bring them around, that makes it all right.

More surreptitious motives may be behind this brand of humor, of course. Residents who want to keep Seattle all to themselves use the rain—and the rain joke—as their first line of attack.

—J. Kingston Pierce

WHERE TO STAY: If you want to be lulled to sleep by the gentle sound of water, your best bet is the Edgewater Hotel (Pier 67, Waterfront; 206/728-7000 or 800/624-0670) overlooking Puget Sound.

PACIFIC RIM: DRAGONS AND DIM SUM

Seattle's geographic position on Puget Sound gives it an important role on the world's Pacific Rim. The Pacific Ocean links the city's port—and our culture—with several Asian nations. Their influences can be found throughout the city.

The best place to start is the **CHINATOWN/INTERNATIONAL DISTRICT.** Those expecting a Chinatown like that in other West Coast cities may be surprised by the mix of Japanese, Filipino, Korean, and Southeast Asian cultures. The remodeled **UWAJIMAYA VILLAGE** (600 5th Ave S; 206/624-6248) offers a wide range of Asian specialties, tanks of live fish and rare imported produce, a Japanese bookstore, and wonderful cooking accessories. In the deli and food court, you'll find hot and cold entrées plus Asian pastries (cream-filled buns, Hawaiian pineapple-coconut bread) and an espresso counter.

BEST PLACE TO SPOIL YOURSELF?

"Le Frock, temple of the fashion consignment gods. Whenever the universe knocks me around, I cruise their shoes for designer samples so I can kick it right back."

Melanie McFarland, Seattle Post-Intelligencer *TV critic*

Venture out of Uwajimaya to stroll the streets and admire the fresh produce and wares. Visit 1-acre **KOBE TERRACE PARK** (221 6th Ave S; 206/684-4075), where Mount Fuji cherry trees and a 4-ton, 200-year-old Yukimidoro stone lantern were gifts from Seattle's sister city of Kobe, Japan. For a history on Seattle's Chinese immigrants, visit the **WING LUKE ASIAN MUSEUM** (407 7th Ave S; 206/623-5124; wingluke.org), named for the city's first Chinese American city council member, to see its intriguing permanent collection of photographs and artifacts that integrates the experiences of 10 Asian Pacific American groups. Rotating exhibits also document the Northwest Asian American experience. Northeast of downtown is the **SEATTLE ASIAN ART MUSEUM** (1400 E Prospect St, Capitol Hill; 206/654-3100; seattleartmuseum.org), in Volunteer Park. Here, the original Seattle Art Museum building holds an extensive collection of Asian art; be sure to check out its Asian Art Library. Martial-arts fans might want to venture into **LAKEVIEW CEMETERY**, next to the park, to find the graves of Bruce Lee and his son, Brandon Lee.

At the **WASHINGTON PARK ARBORETUM**, visit the **JAPANESE GARDEN** (1502 Lake Washington Blvd E, Madison Valley; 206/684-4725), March through November. The authentic garden was constructed under the direction of Japanese landscape architect Juki Iida in 1960. Plan ahead if you want to attend a tea ceremony in the garden's teahouse, performed on the third Saturday of the month, April through October.

Back in the Chinatown / International District, the **NORTHWEST ASIAN AMERICAN THEATRE** (409 7th Ave S; 206/340-1445; nwaat.org) offers a variety of cross-cultural programs, which might include a festival of films by Asian Americans, a play about a historic Asian actress, or a late-night drag-queen cabaret. The 100-year-old **NIPPON KAN THEATER** (628 S Washington St; 206/467-6807) serves as the venue for many NWAAT shows.

WHERE TO EAT: For the popular nibbling festival that is a meal of dim sum, head for the spacious House of Hong (409 8th Ave S; 206/622-7997). Or treat yourself to tea at the Panama Hotel (605½ S Main St; 206/223-9242). If you're overwhelmed by the tasty selection at Uwajimaya Village (600 5th Ave S; 206/624-6248), step across the street to A Piece of Cake bakery (514 S King St; 206/623-8284) and ask for a simple slice of mango cake.

WHERE TO STAY: The historic Panama Hotel (605½ S Main St, Chinatown / International District; 206/223-9242) was designed by a Japanese architect and University of Washington graduate. It offers history in the middle of the Chinatown / International District, though befitting its early days (it was built in 1910), rooms share a bath down the hall.

LISTEN UP: SEATTLE IS FOR AUDIOPHILES

Most local musicians groan if they hear tourists talking "grunge." It's not that they have anything against bands that made Seattle world famous in the 1980s and '90s; it's just that they know that Seattle music is—and always has been—a lot more.

"Grunge was over in Seattle by the time the rest of the world ever even heard about it, but that didn't stop a thousand bands from moving to the Northwest in the '90s," explains Charles R. Cross, author of the best-selling Kurt Cobain biography *Heavier Than Heaven* (and of a forthcoming book on Seattle legend Jimi Hendrix).

"Most of those bands stayed on and the local scene continues to reflect a diverse culture that spans from hip hop to electronica."

One music lover (and sometime musician) who recognizes the diversity of the Seattle sound is local billionaire, Microsoft cofounder, and Hendrix uberfan Paul Allen, who built a shrine to Northwest music: the **EXPERIENCE MUSIC PROJECT (EMP)** (325 5th Ave N, Seattle Center; 206/EMP-LIVE or 877-EMP-LIVE; emplive.com). The Frank Gehry–designed museum building, said to resemble a gigantic smashed guitar, features a gallery on Northwest artists as well as hands-on opportunities for wannabes to play instruments. The EMP also offers concerts, a restaurant (Turntable), and bar (the Liquid Lounge).

Seattle rocks at night. Pick a genre, grab a *Seattle Weekly* or *The Stranger*, and check out club listings, or just head straight for some of the city's most reliable nightspots. For jazz, try **DIMITRIOU'S JAZZ ALLEY** (2033 6th Ave, Downtown; 206/441-9729; jazzalley.com) or **TULA'S** (2214 2nd Ave, Belltown; 206/443-4221; tulas.com). The **CROCODILE CAFE** (2200 2nd Ave, Belltown; 206/441-5611; the crocodile.com), where a lot of the aforementioned "grunge" acts once played, specializes in local and national alternative rock, folk, and blues acts. At historic Ballard's **TRACTOR TAVERN** (5213 Ballard Ave NW, Ballard; 206/782-3480), the music menu could be rock, country, Celtic, or zydeco. And in Pioneer Square, hit the **NEW ORLEANS RESTAURANT** (114 First Ave S, Pioneer Square; 206/622-2563) for Cajun or blues, or the **FENIX** (109 S Washington St, Pioneer Square; 206/405-4323) for (usually) rock 'n' roll, served loud. **THE SHOWBOX** (1426 1st Ave, Downtown; 206/628-3151; showboxonline.com), a music staple since 1939, offers live semi-established, semi-alternative bands, plus funk and dance music on alternate nights. For classical fare, try the **SEATTLE SYMPHONY** (206/215-4747; seattlesymphony. org) or the **SEATTLE OPERA** (206/389-7676; seattleopera.org).

BEST PLACE FOR A BEER?

"The Athenian Inn, because they still have regulars and petitioners. In the wintertime you can look at the rainy cold wind on Elliott Bay."

Kurt Beattie, artistic director of A Contemporary Theatre (ACT)

Love music but not quite club legal? Seattle's got that covered too. Some local musicians have been involved in the creation and perpetuation of an **ALL-AGES MUSIC** venue that's run with a strict no-drugs, no-drinking policy. **THE VERA PROJECT** (1916 4th Ave, Downtown; 206/956-8372; theveraproject.org) is largely volunteer-run by youth who adamantly enforce the rules because they know their access to live music depends on it.

While many clubs have dance space, other venues are dedicated to dancing for its own sake, sometimes even offering lessons for newbies. **SEATTLE FOLK DANCING** (seattledance.org) has information on various types of dancing styles and where to practice them in town. **BESO DEL SOL** (4468 Stone Way N, Wallingford; 206/547-8087) is a hot spot for salsa dancing, the **LAKE CITY COMMUNITY CENTER** (12531 28th Ave NE, Lake City; 206/525-0932) for contra dancing, and the **CENTURY BALLROOM** (915 E Pine St, 2nd floor, Capitol Hill; 206/324-7263; century ballroom.com) for swing dancing.

If you visit Seattle in the summer, plan ahead to get tickets for one of the area's multiple outdoor concerts. **SUMMER NIGHTS AT THE PIER** (summernights.org) regularly draws artists such as Lyle Lovett and Chris Isaak; during its 2003 inaugural season, **CONCERTS AT MARYMOOR** (concertsatmarymoor.com) brought Jackson Browne and Tracy Chapman, among others, to Redmond's Marymoor Park. Other places to enjoy music al fresco include the **CHATEAU STE. MICHELLE** winery (425/415-3300; ste-michelle.com) and the **WOODLAND PARK ZOO** (206/684-4892; zoo.org). And the summer **KPLU JAZZ AND BLUES CRUISES** (253/535-7758 or 800/npr-kplu; kplu.org) navigate Puget Sound while offering up live music and a brunch buffet.

Or time your visit around the annual festivals held at the Seattle Center that sound as good as they look (and taste): the Memorial Day weekend **FOLKLIFE FESTIVAL** (nwfolklife.org) brings a world view of music and dance; over Labor Day weekend, **BUMBERSHOOT** (bumbershoot.org) is an umbrella for arts—ranging from theater to visual arts—but has a heavy emphasis on music and consistently draws top national acts.

WHERE TO EAT: Music, not food, is the main attraction of many of these venues; however, the Crocodile Cafe (2200 2nd Ave, Belltown; 206/441-5611; the crocodile.com) and EMP's Turntable (325 5th Ave N, Seattle Center; 206/770-2777; emplive.com) also offer menus that will hit the spot.

WHERE TO STAY: Hipsters, musicians, and DJs often stay at the Ace Hotel (2423 1st Ave, Belltown; 206/448-4721), within walking distance of many venues.

LAY OF THE CITY

LAY OF THE CITY

Orientation

When it comes to natural endowments, Seattle was flat-out spoiled.

Situated on a narrow isthmus of land between **PUGET SOUND** and **LAKE WASHINGTON**, bisected north from south by **LAKE UNION** and the Lake Washington Ship Canal and east from west by the Duwamish River, the city is surrounded by watery wonders. But that's not the only lure for the droves of tourists and residents to this city of more than 550,000 people. We've also got mountains aplenty. Directly to the west of Puget Sound looms the **OLYMPIC MOUNTAINS**. East of Lake Washington, the **CASCADES** stretch in a jagged line just 50 miles away; Mount Rainier plays hide-and-seek 67 miles south of downtown, and on clear days, Glacier Peak, about 70 miles northeast, and Mount Baker, about 110 miles northeast, can be glimpsed.

Within the boundaries of these imposing geographic landmarks lies a rapidly growing urban area. Because the city's parts developed in relative isolation—cut off from one another by canals, lakes, and bridges—Seattle boasts a distinct collection of neighborhoods. At the city's heart stands the famous **PIKE PLACE MARKET** (Pike St and 1st Ave; map:J8), an authentic smorgasbord of food, flowers, entertainment, and art that has served local residents and visitors for nearly a century. Taking the steps down the steep hill just west of the market leads you to the Seattle waterfront, brimming with shops, restaurants, and the always busy ferry docks (map:M8) that link the city to Bainbridge Island and other points west. Directly east of the market is an ever-growing shopping district dominated by **WESTLAKE CENTER** (Pine St and 4th Ave; map:I6) and **PACIFIC PLACE** (600 Pine St; map:I5), and fanning out in all directions. Seattle's major office and financial district lies interspersed through the shopping area.

At the southern end of downtown lies historic **PIONEER SQUARE** (along 1st and 2nd Aves, between James St and S Jackson St; map:N8), the first area of Seattle to be rebuilt after the Great Fire of 1889. In February 2001, a 6.8 earthquake that shook this part of town caused a rain of bricks from crumbling facades and considerable damage to some of the oldest buildings. But most were left intact, including the many shops, bars, and galleries in the area. Just east of Pioneer Square is the **CHINATOWN/INTERNATIONAL DISTRICT**, and just south of Pioneer Square is the newly energized industrial area called SoDo (South of the Dome or South of Downtown), with the Seahawks' football stadium (Occidental Ave S and S King St; map:Q9) and its next-door neighbor Safeco Field, ballpark to the city's beloved Mariners.

Traveling northeast from Pike Place Market through the trendy **BELLTOWN** neighborhood (between Virginia St and Denny Wy, between Western and 5th Aves; map:G7), one comes upon the slightly grittier **DENNY TRIANGLE**, also known as the Denny Regrade (the triangle between 6th Ave, Denny Wy, and Pike St). Both neighborhoods encompass what used to be steep Denny Hill, which in the early 1900s was leveled along Denny Way from Interstate 5 to the waterfront. Across

Denny Way is the sprawling **SEATTLE CENTER** complex (between Denny Wy and Mercer St, between 1st Ave N and 5th Ave N; map:B6), home to the Pacific Science Center; the new digs of the Seattle Opera and Pacific Northwest Ballet, Marion Oliver McCaw Hall; Experience Music Project museum; and a wide variety of festivals and fairs, as well as Seattle's best-known landmark, the **SPACE NEEDLE** (Broad St and 5th Ave N). The Seattle Center is on the lower slopes of **QUEEN ANNE** hill; to the west is **MAGNOLIA**, and in between Queen Anne and Magnolia is the area called **INTERBAY** (along 15th Ave W). To the east of the Seattle Center, on the northern reaches of downtown, is the **SOUTH LAKE UNION** area (aka Cascade neighborhood); other neighborhoods surrounding the lake are **WESTLAKE** and **EASTLAKE**.

A few blocks east of downtown, the **CAPITOL HILL** neighborhood rises up from I-5 and is packed with hip people, stores, coffee shops, and nightspots. In addition to its main thoroughfares of Broadway and 15th Avenue E, Capitol Hill encompasses many residential areas mixed with small business and is the central hub of surrounding neighborhoods. Northeast, toward the ship canal, **MONTLAKE** lies at the northern foot of the hill; southeast, toward Lake Washington, are the **FIRST HILL**, **CENTRAL DISTRICT**, **MADRONA**, **MADISON VALLEY**, **MADISON PARK**, and **LESCHI** neighborhoods, a microcosm of the city's diversity.

West of downtown, across the Duwamish River, is **WEST SEATTLE**, with many residential areas, lush parks and beaches, as well as thriving commercial centers such as the West Seattle Junction. In the city's **SOUTH END** are the Rainier Valley—including Columbia City and Rainier Beach—Beacon Hill, and Georgetown, all east of the Duwamish; South Park and White Center are west of the river. **SOUTH OF SEATTLE** are the suburban cities of Burien, Tukwila, and Renton; farther south are SeaTac, Des Moines, Normandy Park, and Kent; farthest south are Federal Way and Auburn.

BEST PLACE TO LISTEN TO LIVE MUSIC?

"The Tractor Tavern remains my favorite place to see a show because of their consistent booking, the laid-back vibe, and the fact that the place feels as comfortable as an old boot (many of which hang from the ceiling)."

Charles R. Cross, author of Heavier Than Heaven: The Biography of Kurt Cobain

North of the Ship Canal, Lake Union, Portage Bay, and the Montlake Cut, you'll find **BALLARD** to the west, **FREMONT** and **WALLINGFORD** due north of downtown, and the **UNIVERSITY DISTRICT** and **LAURELHURST** to the east. Just to the north of Fremont and Wallingford is the **GREENWOOD/GREEN LAKE** area. In Seattle's

HOW TO PASS FOR A LOCAL

Every city has its own set of idiosyncrasies. Visitors who want to mesh more naturally with the locals might benefit from these insights into Seattle's native style.

UMBRELLAS: Despite the city's rep, it doesn't rain buckets here daily (Miami has more rain annually). A sure way to spot a newcomer is to see an unfurled umbrella during a light shower.

SHADES: Residents have to combat cloud glare more than unfettered sunshine; as a result, sunglasses are de rigueur nearly year-round.

ATTIRE: Varies widely by neighborhood. For example, while the Capitol Hill crowd favors black ensembles, body piercing, and Doc Martens, Green Lakers sport spandex, bare midriffs, and Nikes. The main thing is, Seattleites are flexible when it comes to degrees of formality. A night at the opera here can mean evening gowns or Gap wear.

COOLNESS: This isn't a climate reference but an attitudinal one. Frankly, natives aren't an effusive lot—just ask any touring actor waiting for a standing ovation. Rumor has it that it takes two years to make a real friend here (unless, of course, the new friend is another lonely newcomer). It's not that we're unfriendly—we're just politely reserved.

expansive residential **NORTH END**, Crown Hill and Bitter Lake are north of Ballard in the west; Northgate, a busy commercial area, and Haller Lake lie north of Greenwood/Green Lake; heading east from the Green Lake area you'll find the Roosevelt, Ravenna, and Sand Point neighborhoods, north of the University District. Maple Leaf, Wedgwood, and View Ridge are residential areas to the north of Roosevelt/Ravenna, and Lake City lies north of Wedgwood. (For an artistic but accurate look at the complexity of Seattle neighborhoods, you can order a map from Big Stick Inc. [888/507-0058; bistickinc.com] for about $25.) **NORTH OF SEATTLE** are the suburban cities of Shoreline in the west, Mountlake Terrace along I-5, and Lake Forest Park and Kenmore to the east on the north shore of Lake Washington. Farther north are Edmonds, Lynnwood, and Everett.

THE EASTSIDE is a growing part of the Seattle metropolitan area. East of Lake Washington are Mercer Island, Medina, Bellevue, and Issaquah; to the north and east lie Kirkland, Juanita, Redmond, Bothell, and Woodinville.

Visitor Information

Ever since the Klondike gold rush, Seattleites have been known to lend a helping hand to travelers. If people on the street can't point you in the right direction, try the new **CITYWIDE CONCIERGE CENTER** at the **SEATTLE CONVENTION AND VISITORS BUREAU** (710 Pike St, Ste 800, Downtown; 206/461-5800; seeseattle.org; map:J4), opened in July 2003. The first operation of its kind for the city, it is part

VOCABULARY: "Yeah" is as common a part of Seattle speech as "Oh my gawd!" is to a suburban teenager. Not to be confused with the intimidating interrogative "Oh yeah?!" favored by East Coasters, Seattle's "yeah" is simply a laid-back form of assent or agreement. (In the more heavily Scandinavian sections of the city, "Ya sure, you betcha" can be used as a synonym.)

JAYWALKING: That crowd on the corner isn't making a drug deal, they're simply waiting for the crosswalk sign to change. Natives are notorious sticklers for obeying these signs—and so are the police. Newcomers blithely crossing against lights may find themselves ticketed, at about $46 a pop.

BICYCLISTS: Some days they seem to outnumber cars. Observing the traditional politeness of the city, locals resist the urge to bump off cyclists who unconcernedly hold up traffic.

TRAVEL ESPRESSO CUPS: They're everywhere. Isn't that why car cup holders were invented? Besides, a swig of caffeine takes drivers' minds off dawdling cyclists.

—Shannon O'Leary

Ticketmaster, part tour guide, and part personal assistant, where you can get pointers on everything from where to find a spa to a babysitter.

Savvily staffed **CONCIERGE DESKS** are also available at several downtown shopping locations. The Bon-Macy's (1601 3rd Ave; 206/506-6000) and Nordstrom (500 Pine St; 206/628-2111) both have their flagship stores downtown. The concierges at these locations are exceptionally accommodating and can provide shoppers and tourists with maps and directions to attractions. In Pacific Place (600 Pine St; 206/405-2655) is another useful downtown concierge desk.

The **DOWNTOWN SEATTLE ASSOCIATION** (500 Union St, Ste 325; 206/623-0340; downtownseattle.com/GettingAround) has many helpful links to assist in the navigation of the 275 square blocks of downtown Seattle. Whether you want to know how many vendors set up shop in the Pike Place Market or how many licks it takes to get to the center of a Tootsie Pop, call the research wizards at the **SEATTLE PUBLIC LIBRARY QUICK INFORMATION LINE** (206/386-INFO). The *Newcomer's Handbook for Moving to and Living in Seattle* (First Books, Second Edition, 2003) by Monica Fischer and Amy Bellamy is a thorough, reliable resource for newcomers and longtime residents alike.

Getting Around

BY BUS

It is exceptionally easy to get around downtown Seattle without a car. **METRO TRANSIT** (201 S Jackson St, Downtown; 206/553-3000; transit.metrokc.gov;

map:O8) operates more than 300 bus routes in Seattle and surrounding King County. Many of the coaches are wheelchair accessible, and all are equipped with bike racks (mounted on the front of the bus) for bike-and-bus commuters. Bus stops have small yellow and white signs designating route numbers, and many have schedules posted. The fare is $1.25 in the city ($1.50 during peak commuter hours—6am to 9am and 3pm to 6pm) and $1.25 if you cross the city line ($2 peak). Exact fare is required. Seniors, youths, and handicapped riders are eligible for discount cards. All-day passes ($2.50) are available from drivers on the weekends and holidays only. Printed schedules and monthly passes are available at Metro headquarters and the Westlake Center bus tunnel station. You can also buy passes at many Bartell Drug Stores (cash only), at the Federal Building branch of the Northwest Federal Credit Union (915 2nd Ave, Downtown; 206/440-9000; map:M7), by phone (206/624-PASS), and online at buypass.metrokc.gov. More than 120 retail businesses in King County sell bus passes; see the Metro Web site (above) for a complete list of locations to purchase passes. Bus schedules are also available at a number of downtown office buildings, including the main U.S. Post Office (301 Union St, Downtown; 206/748-5417; map:K6) as well as the ferry terminal (Pier 52, 801 Alaskan Wy, Downtown; map:M8).

One of Metro's most valued services is the **RIDE FREE AREA** in downtown's commercial core. In the area bordered by the waterfront to the west, I-5 to the east, Jackson Street to the south, and Battery Street to the north, you can ride free on any Metro bus from 6am until 7pm. Avoid above-ground traffic snags by catching a bus in Metro's sleek, L-shaped transit tunnel within the Ride Free Area; it has five underground stations, from near the Washington State Convention & Trade Center at Ninth and Pine to the Chinatown/International District at Fifth and Jackson.

Metro also operates the **WATERFRONT STREETCAR**. The vintage late-1920s Australian green-and-yellow trolleys run from Myrtle Edwards Park along Alaskan Way on the waterfront to Main Street, then jog east through Pioneer Square to Fifth and Jackson, making nine stops. They depart at 20-minute to half-hour intervals from 7am weekdays (around 10:30am weekends) until 6pm, with extended hours in summer. The ride takes 20 minutes from one end to the other and costs $1 (exact change only), or $1.25 during Metro peak hours. The cash fare entitles riders to a transfer that allows them to disembark and sightsee for up to 90 minutes, then continue the ride. Metro monthly bus passes and discount cards are good on the streetcar. The cars can hold up to 43 passengers and have wheelchair access.

The **MONORAIL**, which connects the Seattle Center to the downtown retail district, was a space-age innovation of the 1962 World's Fair. The two-minute, 1.2-mile ride—presently the only stretch of rapid transit in town—is a great thrill for kids and passes through the Experience Music Project museum. A smart way to avoid the parking hassle at the Seattle Center is to leave your car downtown and hop on the monorail at Westlake Center (3rd floor, Pine St and 4th Ave, Downtown; seattle-monorail.com; map:I6); the station is on a platform outside, just east of the top of the escalator. Adults pay $1.50 one-way; seniors and children ages 5 to 12 pay 75 cents. Trains leave every 10 minutes Monday through Friday from 7:30am to 11pm and weekends from 9am to 11pm.

For trips from as far north as Darrington in Snohomish County, Community Transit (800/562-1375; commtrans.org) runs buses on a regular schedule. Fare is $3 per adult to Seattle from any point outside the city; fare within Snohomish County is $1.

GRAY LINE OF SEATTLE (4500 W Marginal Wy SW, West Seattle; 206/626-5209; graylineofseattle.com) has the largest fleet of charter buses and competitive prices for sightseeing tours of the city. The company also offers organized tours to destinations such as Mount Rainier, Vancouver, and the San Juan Islands. (For other bus information, see Motor Tours under Organized Tours in the Exploring chapter.)

BY CAR

Despite ongoing efforts to make mass transit accessible to more people, sometimes it takes a car to get around Seattle. Most large **RENTAL CAR COMPANIES** have offices at Sea-Tac Airport, in downtown Seattle, and in downtown Bellevue. Some larger ones, such as Enterprise (800/736-8227, out-of-town reservations) and Budget (800/527-0700), have locations in other suburbs and in various Seattle neighborhoods. Hertz (800/654-3131) is the preferred rental car company of **AAA WASHINGTON** (330 6th Ave N, Downtown; 206/448-5353; 800/AAA-HELP, emergency road service). One cautionary note: The fine for blocking an intersection is $101.

BEST PLACE TO VIEW ART?

"A screening of just about anything at the Cinerama theater. . . . It beats any moviegoing experience anywhere in the country."

Darryl Macdonald, co-founder of Seattle International Film Festival (SIFF)

Centrally located **PARKING** lots charge between $15 and $20 a day; lots on the fringes of downtown—Chinatown/International District, Belltown, and Alaskan Way on the waterfront, for instance—are usually less expensive. In downtown, most of the meters have a maximum of 30 minutes, and many are off-limits to all but delivery trucks, but if you're lucky enough to get one after 6pm or on Sundays and holidays, they're free. Most parking tickets cost $28; parking illegally in a space reserved for the disabled costs $250. Large facilities such as Safeco Field, Seattle Center, and Husky Stadium in the University District generally have their own parking areas. Meters cost 60 cents to $2 an hour throughout town.

There are more than 4,000 public parking spots downtown, including streetside metered parking and lots. In an attempt to draw shoppers to the city's retail core, the Pacific Place parking garage (6th Ave and Pine St, Downtown; map:I5) charges $2 per hour before 5pm ($3 per hour after four hours) weekdays; $3 for four hours after 5pm weeknights; and $3 for four hours or fewer on weekends and holidays.

For **LOST CARS**, begin by calling the Seattle Police Department's Auto Records Department (206/684-5444) to find out whether your car is listed as towed and

PLACES OF WORSHIP

Houses of reverence vary widely in Seattle, from classical grandeur to eclectic jumble to tumbledown storefront. Here are a few noted for their architecture, community importance, and welcoming attitudes.

In Islam, the oldest set of doctrines are those of the Sunnis. North Seattle contains a small, attractive home for local adherents in the form of the **IDRIS MOSQUE** (1420 NE Northgate Wy, Northgate; 206/363-3013; idrismosque.com; map:DD6). The compact dome and minaret-evocative tower, topped with a crescent, routinely slow down traffic.

Synagogues in Seattle serve Reform, Conservative, Orthodox, and Sephardic communities. Freestanding fluted columns lend a Hellenistic air to **TEMPLE DE HIRSCH SINAI** (1511 E Pike St, Capitol Hill; 206/323-8486; map:HH6), an airy, modern Reform complex. An extensive library includes more than 500 films with Jewish themes.

On the Jesuit Seattle University's campus is the breathtaking **ST. IGNATIUS CHAPEL** (900 Broadway, First Hill; 206/296-5588; seattleu.edu/chapel; map: N4). The brainchild of renowned architect Steven Holl (think Bellevue Art Museum meets Virgin Mary), it was conceived as "seven glass bottles of light in a stone box," each bottle a vessel of light corresponding to an aspect of Catholic worship.

The twin towers of **ST. JAMES CATHEDRAL** (804 9th Ave, First Hill; 206/382-4874; map:N4) announce an elegant and solidly impressive Roman Catholic church that boasts the city's oldest classical New Year's Eve concert and celebration, held at 11pm, featuring cathedral musicians and a chamber orchestra. The cathedral choir sings Sundays at 10am, the women's choir Sundays at 5:30pm.

ST. MARK'S EPISCOPAL CATHEDRAL (1245 10th Ave E, Capitol Hill; 206/323-0300; saintmarks.org; map:GG6), designed along traditional Gothic lines in the late 1920s, was never finished due to the Depression. After one of many renovations, the interior is now filled with pastel light streaming from a new rose window. A popular compline mass is held Sundays at 9:30pm.

impounded. If there's no record, it may have been stolen; call 206/625-5011, or in an emergency call 911.

BY TAXI

Most cabs are directed by dispatchers, but it's easy to hail one near major attractions or downtown hotels. Call ahead and one will typically meet you within 5 to 10 minutes. A cab from the airport to downtown costs about $30, but from the hotel district to the airport it's a flat rate of $25. The standard drop is $1.80, with the meter

Though it recently landed on the Washington Trust's 10 Most Endangered Properties list, as of press time the **FIRST UNITED METHODIST CHURCH** (811 5th Ave, Downtown; 206/622-7278; firstchurchseattle.org; map:M6) was still open to worshippers and those attending the popular series of concerts and readings by visiting authors such as Isabel Allende.

The white stucco curves of **PLYMOUTH CONGREGATIONAL CHURCH** (1217 6th Ave, Downtown; 206/622-4865; www.halcyon.com/plymouth; map:L5) are both intriguingly intricate and refreshingly simple. Black-and-white abstract crosses dance in starry columns down the sides of the building, inviting passersby in to lunchtime jazz services on Wednesdays at noon.

The lofty central dome of the **ST. DEMETRIOS GREEK ORTHODOX CHURCH** (2100 Boyer Ave E, Capitol Hill; 206/325-4347; map:GG6) is home to Eastern Orthodox Christianity. It stages a Greek Festival with everything from dancing to baklava in the fall.

FIRST COVENANT CHURCH (400 E Pike St, Capitol Hill; 206/322-7411; map:K1), with its gold-tipped dome surmounting a heavy classical front, is a roomy space smack in the middle of nightlife-loving Capitol Hill.

FIRST PRESBYTERIAN CHURCH (1013 8th Ave, First Hill; 206/624-0644; firstpres.org; map:L4) is a streamlined sculptural complex dating from the 1960s; the modern architecture hides the fact that, at more than 130 years old, this is one of Seattle's oldest congregations.

Look for the Buddhist festival held every July at **SEATTLE BUDDHIST CHURCH** (1427 S Main St, Central District; 206/329-0800; seattlebetsuin.com; map:R4). The long brick building with upturned roof corners sits across from a park displaying the temple bell (under a canopy) and a statue memorializing the founder of Jodo Shinsu Buddhism.

Red, white, and blue upside-down triangles along the edge of the roof make **MOUNT ZION BAPTIST CHURCH** (1634 19th Ave, Central District; 206/322-6500; map:HH6) easy to spot, and the church draws congregants from five counties.

—*Caroline Cummins*

running at $1.80 per mile. Local companies include Farwest Taxi (206/622-1717), Graytop (206/282-8222), and Yellow Cab (206/622-6500).

BY BICYCLE

Seattle is a bicycle-friendly city. Depending on the weather, between 4,000 and 8,000 bikers commute to work each day. **BIKE LANES** on arterial streets throughout the city are fairly safe routes for cyclists, and bike trails offer a reprieve from huffing and puffing up Seattle's steep slopes. For both commuting and recreation, the **BURKE-GILMAN TRAIL** is the bicycling backbone of Seattle. Extending approximately 15 miles from Kenmore at the north end of Lake Washington through the University of Washington campus to Ballard, and connecting to downtown Seattle via either the Ballard Bridge and 15th Avenue, or the Fremont Bridge and Dexter Avenue, the Burke-Gilman Trail is essentially flat because it follows a former railroad line. The trail connects in Kenmore with the **SAMMAMISH RIVER TRAIL**, which takes riders around the north end of Lake Washington and through Woodinville to Redmond's Marymoor Park on the north edge of Lake Sammamish.

The **ELLIOTT BAY TRAIL** is a scenic 2.5-mile spur running northwest from downtown along the waterfront through Myrtle Edwards and Elliott Bay Parks. The rebuilt **ALKI TRAIL** stretches along Alki Beach in West Seattle and will soon connect with the 11-mile **DUWAMISH TRAIL**, which roughly follows the west shore of the Duwamish River south to Kent (where you can pick up the Green River Trail). Recreational riders especially enjoy the bike trail in Seward Park, which circles the wooded peninsula jutting into Lake Washington. The I-90 Trail takes cyclists from just east of downtown across Lake Washington to Mercer Island. The city's *Seattle Bicycling Guide Map*, shows these trails and cyclists' street routes, including across the lower West Seattle Bridge and south to Sea-Tac Airport; call the **CITY OF SEATTLE BICYCLE AND PEDESTRIAN PROGRAM** (206/684-7583). Maps include in-depth insets on difficult-to-navigate areas, but they become scarce during summer, so call ahead if you can. For bike maps of Bellevue, call the City of Bellevue Transportation Department (425/452-2894).

BEST PLACE FOR INTELLIGENT CONVERSATION?

"In the midpriced seats at a Sonics basketball game."

Sherman Alexie, poet, novelist, and screenwriter

If in your travels you come upon a hill or body of water that looms too large, hop on a bus or ferry. All Metro buses come equipped with bike racks on the front, and using them is free, though they hold only two bikes per bus, first come, first served. The only restriction is that you can't load or unload bicycles in the downtown Ride Free Area between 6am and 7pm, except at the Convention Place and China-town/International District bus tunnel stations. For more information, call Metro's Bike and Ride program (206/553-3000). Taking a bike on most local ferry routes costs $1 on top of the regular walk-on passenger fare. For more ferry information, see the next section.

BIKE RACKS for securing your two-wheeler are conveniently located outside the Washington State Convention & Trade Center (800 Convention Pl, Downtown; map:J4), Key Tower (700 5th Ave, Downtown; map:N6) on the Cherry Street side, and in the City Centre parking garage (1420 5th Ave, Downtown; map:J5). Racks can usually be found within a block of most bus stops in commercial areas. In addition, bikes can be parked (as well as repaired and rented) 24/7 at the new **BIKESTA-TION SEATTLE** center (311 3rd Ave S; 206/332-9795; www.bikestation.org).

To **RENT A BIKE**, try Gregg's Greenlake Cycle (7007 Woodlawn Ave NE, Green Lake; 206/523-1822; map:FF7), Al Young Bike and Ski (3615 NE 45th St, University District; 206/524-2642; map:FF6), and, across the street from the busy Burke-Gilman Trail, Ti Cycles (2943 NE Blakely St, University District; 206/522-7602; map:FF6).

BY FERRY

In the Puget Sound area, ferries are commuter vehicles, tourist magnets, and shortcut alternatives to driving around large bodies of water. You can take a ferry from the downtown terminal at Pier 52 on the waterfront (801 Alaskan Wy; map:M8) across the Sound to semiresidential/semirural Bainbridge or Vashon Islands (many people who live on the islands or the Kitsap Peninsula catch daily ferries into the city), or hop one from Anacortes, 90 miles north of town via I-5, to the San Juan Islands or even Vancouver Island, British Columbia. Travelers headed for the Olympic Peninsula use them as a scenic way to cut across the Sound; some passengers just go for the ride—people have even gotten married on them. For complete schedule and route information, call **WASHINGTON STATE FERRIES** (206/464-6400 or 888/808-7977; wsdot.wa.gov/ferries). Schedules vary from summer to winter (with much longer lines in summer); cash or traveler's checks only. For more information on ferry routes, see the Ferry Rides sidebar in the Day Trips chapter.

The **ELLIOTT BAY WATER TAXI** is a cute boat run by Metro that operates every half hour between sunrise and 10:30 pm (11pm going from West Seattle, back downtown) during the summer to transport people between West Seattle's Alki beach and Pier 54 downtown off of Spring Street. Each way on the water taxi costs $2, and bikes can be brought on at no additional fee. The trip takes about eight minutes, and on Mariners game days the last boat departs from Pier 54 at 10:45pm.

Essentials

PUBLIC REST ROOMS

Public rest rooms can be found at the base of the ramp in the Main Arcade of Pike Place Market (Pike St and Western Ave, Downtown; map:J8), at Freeway Park (6th Ave and Seneca St, Downtown; map:L5), and on the Main Street side of the Pioneer Square fire station (corner of 2nd Ave S and S Main St; map:O8). Public buildings are another option (e.g., Seattle Public Library, King County Courthouse, and the Federal Building, all downtown). Downtown shopping centers, such as Westlake Center (Pine St and 4th Ave; map:I6) and Pacific Place (7th Ave and Pine St; map:I5), have a plentiful number of rest rooms. Many larger parks, such as Volunteer Park on Capitol Hill and Gas Works Park in Wallingford, also have public facilities (although most are open only until dusk).

NAMING NAMES

Most people know that Seattle was named in honor of Chief Sealth, the peace-loving leader of two local Indian tribes (the Suquamish and the Duwamish) at the time when the first white settlers landed at Alki Point in 1851. But the sources of names for other landmarks, streets, and sights are less well remembered.

DENNY WAY: This busy street near Seattle Center recalls David Denny, one of the town's pioneers, who arrived here in 1851 with 25 cents in his pocket and eventually made a fortune with his investments—before losing it all during the panic of 1893.

ELLIOTT BAY: Lieutenant Charles Wilkes, who commanded an 1841 exploration of Pacific Northwest waterways, christened today's harbor. The bay was supposedly named after one of three Elliotts in his party. But whether it was the Reverend J. L. Elliott, Midshipman Samuel Elliott, or "First Class Boy" George Elliott is open for debate.

KING COUNTY: The area containing Seattle was originally dubbed King County in honor of William Rufus DeVane King, Franklin Pierce's vice president. But it was renamed in 1986 to honor the slain civil rights leader Martin Luther King Jr.

MERCER ISLAND: There's some doubt as to which of two pioneering Mercer

MAJOR BANKS

Money-changing facilities are available at almost every major downtown bank. All of Seattle's larger banks also provide the full range of services, and you can locate neighborhood branches by contacting their downtown headquarters: Washington Mutual national headquarters (1201 3rd Ave; 206/461-6475; map:L7), located in the neoclassical Washington Mutual Tower, where a pair of peregrine falcons also reside; Wells Fargo (999 3rd Ave; 206/292-3719; map:M7); US Bank (1420 5th Ave; 206/344-2300; map:K6); and KeyBank (1329 4th Ave; 206/447-5767; map:L6).

POLICE AND SAFETY

In emergency situations, dial 911. In nonemergencies, call the Seattle Police Department (206/625-5011). Seattle is known as a relatively safe city. There are fewer violent crimes here than in many large cities, although pickpockets are a problem in crowded areas such as Capitol Hill and Pike Place Market. As in any large city, be particularly aware of your surroundings when walking around downtown at night. (A fun bit of trivia: Seattle was the first city in the nation to have bicycle cops and, along with Los Angeles, the first in the nation to employ female police officers.)

HOSPITALS AND MEDICAL/DENTAL SERVICES

Seattle has so many **HOSPITALS** located near the heart of the city that the First Hill neighborhood just east of downtown is known to locals as Pill Hill. One of the best facilities is Harborview Medical Center (325 9th Ave, First Hill; 206/731-3000; 206/731-3074, emergency; washington.edu/medicine/hmc/index.html; map:P4), managed by the University of Washington. Originally founded in 1877 as a six-bed

brothers gave his name to this lump of land in Lake Washington. The probable honoree was Thomas Mercer, who arrived here in 1852 with a team of horses to become Seattle's first teamster and later its first judge. But it could also have been Asa Mercer, first president of the Territorial University (now the University of Washington) and the man who brought the famous "Mercer Maidens," a cargo of potential brides from the East Coast, to this virgin territory in the 1860s—an entrepreneurial feat immortalized in the 1960s TV show *Here Come the Brides.*

PUGET SOUND: Our "inland sea" was named after Peter Puget, a second lieutenant under British Captain George Vancouver, who commanded an exploration of the Sound in 1792.

STARBUCKS COFFEE: Our best-known latte purveyor takes its moniker from Mr. Starbuck, a java junkie in Herman Melville's *Moby Dick.*

YESLER WAY: In the early 1850s, Henry Yesler built the town's first steam sawmill on Elliott Bay. The Pioneer Square street that bears his name was originally a path down which logs were skidded from surrounding hills for processing.

—*J. Kingston Pierce*

welfare hospital in South Seattle (its current name and locale the result of a 1931 move), Harborview is now the highest-level trauma center for a four-state region. Other hospitals in the neighborhood include Swedish Medical Center (747 Broadway Ave, First Hill; 206/386-6000, info; 206/386-2573, emergency; map:N2); Virginia Mason (1100 9th Ave, First Hill; 206/223-6600; virginiamason.org; map:N2), a hospital partnered with Group Health that boasts more than 390 physicians; a handful of neighborhood clinics; and The Bailey-Boushay House, a home for those living with AIDS. Standing apart from the Pill Hill neighborhood triumvirate is the University of Washington Medical Center (1959 NE Pacific St, University District; 206/598-3300; 206/598-4000, emergency; washington.edu/medicine /uwmc info; map:FF6).

The Seattle/King County Dental Society offers a Dentist Referral Service (206/443-7607) that refers callers to a dentist or a low-cost dental clinic. Health-South Medical Clinics (walk-in health clinics) have numerous locations around Puget Sound that can be located on the Internet at healthsouth.com.

POST OFFICE
Downtown Seattle's main U.S. Post Office (301 Union St; 206/748-5417; usps.com; map:K6) is open weekdays 7:30am to 5:30pm. Hours at neighborhood branches vary, and some are open on Saturdays, so call ahead.

GROCERY STORES
The closest major grocery stores to downtown are the Harvard Market QFC (1401 Broadway Ave, Capitol Hill; 206/860-3818; map:L1), at the corner of Broadway

and E Union, and two stores on the western edge of the Seattle Center: Larry's Market (100 Mercer St, Queen Anne; 206/213-0778; map:A7) and QFC (100 Republican St, Queen Anne; 206/285-5491; map:A7), the latter of which is open 24 hours a day. Safeway has several large locations, such as the Queen Anne Safeway (2100 Queen Anne Ave N; 206/282-8090). Stocked with beautiful produce and knowledgeable staff, Admiral Metropolitan Market (2320 42nd Ave SW, West Seattle; 206/937-0551) and the Queen Anne Metropolitan Market (1908 Queen Ave N; 206/284-2530), both formerly Thriftways, are two of the best supermarkets in the city. The Admiral location has an incredible deli with in-store sushi chefs. The newly relocated PCC Natural Markets in Fremont (600 N 34th St; 206/632-6811) has a nice selection of healthy foods and organic fruits.

BEST PLACE TO LISTEN TO LIVE MUSIC?

"The Sunset Tavern in Ballard, where you can catch barely discovered bands and get close to the stage without fear of having your rib cage crushed."

Melanie McFarland, Seattle Post-Intelligencer *TV critic*

PHARMACIES

Bartell Drug Stores is the biggest local chain in the area, and most locations have prescription departments. Downtown stores are at Third Avenue and Union St (1404 3rd Ave; 206/624-1366; map:K6) and at Fifth Avenue and Olive Way (1628 5th Ave; 206/622-0581; map:I6). The branch on Lower Queen Anne (600 1st Ave N; 206/284-1353; map:A7) is open 24 hours a day. Other 24-hour pharmacies are located in Walgreen Drug Stores in Ballard (5409 15th Ave NW; 206/781-0056; map:EE8) and Kirkland (12405 NE 85th St; 425/822-9202; map:EE3). Both Walgreen Drug Stores have convenient drive-thru pharmacies. Two local alternatives are Medicine Man (323 N 85th St, Greenwood; 206/789-0800; map:EE8) and Rainbow Remedies (409 15th Ave E, Capitol Hill; 206/329-8979; map:HH6), both of which carry homeopathic remedies, nutritional supplements, and other holistic remedies.

DRY CLEANERS AND LAUNDROMATS

Several dry cleaners operate throughout the city, and many hotels have in-house services. A couple to consider: Creases (1822 Terry Ave, Downtown; 206/382-9265; map:I3), which has an express service; and Ang's French Cleaners (2000 9th Ave, Downtown; 206/622-6727), a fixture for more than 50 years that will pick up and deliver.

Have a beer at the 5 Point Café while your clothes dry at the adjacent 5 Point Laundromat (417 Cedar St, Belltown; map:E7), patronized by an eclectic crowd 24 hours a day. An added bonus: Zeek's Pizza (419 Denny Wy, Belltown; 206/448-

6775; map:E7) is kitty-corner from the laundry just past the dry fountain and statue of Chief Sealth, Seattle's namesake.

LEGAL SERVICES

Lawyer Referral Services (206/623-2551) puts clients in touch with lawyers who are members of the King County Bar Association. The call to the service is free; lawyers charge $30 for 30 minutes for consultations, with pro bono and low-fee programs for low-income clients. Columbia Legal Services (206/464-5911; columbialegal.org) is a program that provides free legal help for clients with very low incomes. Northwest Women's Law Center (206/621-7691; nwwlc.org) provides basic legal information and attorney referrals, as well as advice on self-help methods.

BUSINESS, COPY, AND MESSENGER SERVICES

Business Service Center (1001 4th Ave, 32nd floor, Downtown; 206/624-9188; map:M6) rents office and conference space for periods of 3 to 12 months; open weekdays only. Another option is Globe Secretariat (2001 6th Ave, Ste 306, Belltown; 206/448-9441; map:H5). Services available include word processing, typing, tape transcription, résumés, 24-hour dictation, copying, and faxing. Kinko's (1833 Broadway Ave, Capitol Hill; 206/329-7445; map:GG6; and branches) is open 24 hours every day and offers copying, in-house IBM and Macintosh computer rentals, and Internet access (on rental computers).

Fleetfoot Messenger Service (206/728-7700) has quick-service, radio-dispatched bicyclists delivering packages downtown Monday though Friday (and weekends if the delivery is called in during business hours), as well as vehicle delivery of packages up to 250 pounds—or whatever fits—statewide. And there's always Federal Express (800/463-3339) and United Parcel Service (800/742-5877), better known as UPS.

BEST PLACE TO SPOIL YOURSELF?

"Ummelina's—I've never been, but it seems to work (as a gift for my sweetie) every Valentine's Day."

Greg Nickels, mayor of Seattle

PHOTOGRAPHY EQUIPMENT AND SERVICES

Seattle's professional photographers swear by Cameratechs (2034 NW Market St, Ballard; 206/782-2433; map:EE8). The shop services all makes and models, usually within 24 hours, and is open Monday through Saturday. For developing, custom printing, and digital outputting, the pros take their film to Ivey Imaging Seattle (424 8th Ave N, Downtown; 206/623-8113; map:D3).

COMPUTER REPAIRS

Uptime (2408 N 45th St, Wallingford; 206/547-1817; map:FF7), open Monday through Friday, 8:30am to 5:30pm, has been serving Seattle since the '80s repairing

STREET SMARTS

If you ask for directions in Seattle, you will likely be given an answer that omits actual street names.

Signage in Seattle can be inexplicable, so much so that locals are more apt to tell you to take a left at the auto supply store or a right just before the bridge. Northeast 45th Street in the University District, for example, starts out harmlessly enough, but then begins to vacillate between numbers and names: turning into Sand Point Way NE, then NE 125th Street, Roosevelt Way NE, and NE 130th. The key to signage smarts is proper translation—knowing, for instance, that University Way (which everyone refers to as the Ave, just to further confuse) in the University District is wholly unrelated to University Street, which is downtown. It helps to know that "Streets" run east to west and, except for downtown, have a compass direction *before* the street name or number. "Avenues" run north to south with a compass direction *after* their name. (Tip: To center yourself downtown, remember the mnemonic—"Jesus Christ Made Seattle Under Protest"—the first letter of each word in the saying reveals the south-to-north order of the main streets: Jefferson and James, Cherry and Columbia, Marion and Madison, Spring and Seneca, University and Union, and Pike and Pine.)

Part of the confusion can be traced to the city's founders. On May 23, 1853, when Arthur Denny, Carson Boren, and David Maynard gathered to file the first plats for Seattle, Maynard felt the grid should be organized according to the points of the compass, whereas Denny and Boren felt the grid should be parallel to Elliott Bay's shore. The muddled streets are a result of their compromise, and the directionally challenged have suffered ever since.

PCs and laptops. In-shop repairs are $80 an hour, or, for house calls, they'll dispatch a technician for $110 an hour. Westwind (510 NE 65th St, Greenlake; 206/522-3530; map:FF6) is a favorite of Mac users. The shop repairs laptops and desktops, has a priority service for $95, and is open Monday through Friday, 9:30am to 6pm.

PETS AND STRAY ANIMALS

If you spot a stray animal or lose your pet in Seattle, call Seattle Animal Control (206/386-7387; cityofseattle.net/animalshelter). They hold animals for three working days before putting them up for adoption, so make sure Rover has a legible license. For veterinary services, the Elliott Bay Animal Hospital (2042 15th Ave W, Interbay; 206/285-7387; map:GG8) is recommended by local vets. If your pet needs immediate attention after hours, contact the Emerald City Emergency Clinic (206/634-9000).

Seattle's hills and waterways have also contributed to the impossibility of a straight grid. And the hills become trouble for an entirely different reason: parking. Though not as extreme as San Francisco, many visitors are unpleasantly surprised at Seattle's steep hills. For those who just don't trust the emergency brake, and don't want to use the bus system, here are some stress-free parking options.

PACIFIC PLACE (6th Ave and Pine St, Downtown; map:J5) is one of the most popular places to park downtown in the evening, and for good reason. After 5pm, it's only $3 for four hours and $2 every additional hour, it's clean and well lit, and it has city names and photos to help you remember where you parked. In Pioneer Square, the **FRYE GARAGE** (117 3rd Ave S; 206/622-4367; map:O6) is a great option for weekdays, and is only $7.75 per day if you arrive by 10am. In addition, Frye offers fairly priced car washes.

A **DIAMOND PARKING SERVICE** lot between Occidental and First Avenue at the south end of Seahawks Stadium offers a bargain rate of $4 for early birds, valid from 9:30am until 5:30pm. The only catch is that the machine doesn't give change, so four crisp, one-dollar bills are a must.

Though it's only three-hour parking, free spots in Capitol Hill are usually easy to snag on Eleventh Avenue between Olive and Denny. For Pike Place Market, park one street below, at the meters on **ALASKAN WAY**, where there are more than 50 spots and a quarter buys 15 minutes. If there isn't any room, **THE MARKET PLACE GARAGE** (2001 Western Ave, Downtown; map:I7) has stalls-aplenty, and is only $5 for up to 10 hours on Sundays.

Happily, though navigating the city can be a bit confusing, the destination is always worth the trouble.

—Jenna Land

Local Resources

NEWSPAPERS AND PERIODICALS

The *Times*—and the *P-I*—might be a-changing. The biggest Seattle media story of late is an embattled joint operating agreement (JOA) that may make Seattle a one-daily-newspaper town.

For the past 20 years, the locally owned *Seattle Times* (1120 John St, Denny Triangle; 206/464-2111; seattletimes.com; map:F2)—tours of its Bothell production facilities (reservations required) are offered Thursdays (19200 120th Ave NE, Bothell; 425/489-7000)—has been joined in a JOA with the Hearst-owned *Seattle Post-Intelligencer* (101 Elliott Ave W, Belltown; 206/448-8000; seattle-pi.com; map:B9)—home to the eye-catching, rotating world globe. The JOA joined the two papers' business functions while each retained independent editorial operations. In 2003, citing financial losses, the *Times* sought to break the JOA in court and, as of our press time, the case was not resolved.

Meanwhile, the daily *King County Journal* (1705 132nd Ave NE, Bellevue; 425/455-2222; kingcountyjournal.com; map:GG2), formerly the *Eastside Journal*, provides a local voice for the Eastside. Want more local flavor? Most neighborhoods have their own weekly newspapers, usually available free at grocery stores.

Weeklies abound here. The free *Seattle Weekly* (1008 Western Ave, Ste 300, Downtown; 206/623-0500; seattleweekly.com; map:M8) and *The Stranger* (1535 11th Ave, 3rd Floor, Capitol Hill; 206/323-7101; thestranger.com; map:HH7), available Thursdays, cover politics, civic issues, and the arts. The pillar of Seattle's gay community is the 30-year-old *Seattle Gay News* (1605 12th St, Capitol Hill; 206/324-4297; sgn.org; map:HH6), which costs a quarter in bookstores (free elsewhere) and comes out on Fridays. The free upstart the *Seattle Gay Standard* (605 29th Ave E, Capitol Hill; 206/322-9027; gaystandard.com; map:GG7) arrives on newsstands on Thursdays. Claiming to be the alternative to the alternative weeklies, *Tablet* (1122 E Pike St; 206/ 374.8678; tabletnewspaper.com) is a volunteer-run biweekly covering music, art, and politics that is distributed free in orange drop boxes around Seattle as well as at Elliott Bay Books.

In the glossy publications department, the city's largest magazine is the monthly *Seattle Magazine* (423 3rd Ave W, Queen Anne; 206/284-1750; seattle magazine.com; map:A8), which is packed with insider information about the people and places of the city and can be found at newsstands and bookstores. The Pacific Northwest's only monthly, multicultural magazine, *ColorsNW* (1319 Dexter Ave N, Ste 190, Westlake, 206/444-9251; colorsnw.com), is distributed free in boxes around town. *Resonance* (resonancemag.com), which has been giving its hip take on local art, music, and literature since 1994, can be picked up at indie music stores, Borders bookstores, and Sam Goody outlets.

PUBLIC LIBRARIES

Ever since the blueprint stage, public opinion has been divided over Pritzker Prize–winning Dutch architect Rem Koolhaas's design for the Seattle Public Library's new Central Library (1000 4th Ave, Downtown; 206/386-4636; www.spl.org), scheduled for completion in 2004. Renderings of the $156-million-plus library depict a gratelike exterior of glass, copper, and steel that some have likened to a structure in a "*Blade Runner* megalopolis." Built on the same site as its 1960s predecessor, the 355,000-square-foot, 11-level library promises to be ultra-cool, with a four-story spiral constructed within to house the nonfiction collection. An underground parking garage will make trips to the castle of books far more pleasant, as will the in-library cafe. Other improvements include more computer terminals (around 130 total), where the public can reserve time to surf the Net. The main branch also hosts the Quick Information Line (206/386-INFO), for answers to almost any question you can think of. While construction goes on, an impressive temporary library is located in the convention center at 800 Pike Street. Hours at the temporary (and new) library are Monday through Wednesday 10am to 8pm, Thursday through Saturday 10am to 6pm, and Sunday 1pm to 5pm.

Besides lending books, video and audio recordings, and even artwork, the Seattle Public Library system offers readings, lectures, film screenings, and many other events in 28 branch libraries around the city. Call the individual branches for specific event information. Mobile library service is also available (206/684-4713). The **KING COUNTY PUBLIC LIBRARY** system has 43 branches countywide and an answer line (425/462-9600 or 800/462-9600).

MAJOR DOWNTOWN BOOKSTORES

Seattle's population is legendarily literary, so it's not surprising that the city is filled with bookstores. The **ELLIOTT BAY BOOK COMPANY** (101 S Main St, Pioneer Square; 206/624-6600; map:O8), which celebrated its 30th anniversary in 2003, is the best locally owned bookstore in town. The downtown branch of the **UNIVERSITY BOOK STORE** (1225 4th Ave; 206/545-9230; map:K6) features a vast selection of technical and computer titles. Large chains with downtown branches include **BORDERS BOOKS & MUSIC** (1501 4th Ave; 206/622-4599; map:J6) and **BARNES & NOBLE** at Pacific Place (7th Ave and Pine St; 206/264-0156; map:I5). For more bookstores, see the Shopping chapter.

RADIO AND TV

Amid the usual horde of stations offered by the usual nationwide radio conglomerates lie some gems. The University of Washington–owned, student-run 90.3 FM KEXP has had a cutting-edge music and no-commercials format since 1972. For a quick introduction to the issues and politics of Seattle, nothing beats the University of Washington's National Public Radio affiliate, 94.9 FM KUOW, and its daily *Weekday* program, running every morning from 9am to 11am. Here's a quick guide to the local radio dial.

Radio Stations

Talk Radio	570 AM	KVI
News/Talk	710 AM	KIRO
Sports	950 AM	KJR
24-Hour News	1000 AM	KOMO
Pacific Lutheran University, National Public Radio, Jazz	88.5 FM	KPLU
University of Washington, Alternative	90.3 FM	KEXP
Bellevue Community College, Jazz, Folk, World Music, Blues	91.3 FM	KBCS
Top 40, R&B	93.3 FM	KUBE
Country	94.1 FM	KMPS
University of Washington, National Public Radio	94.9 FM	KUOW
Oldies	97.3 FM	KBSG
Classical	98.1 FM	KING
Outrageous Talk	100.7 FM	KQBZ
Classic Rock	102.5 FM	KZOK
Adult Alternative	103.7 FM	KMTT
Alternative	107.7 FM	KNDD

TV Stations

ABC	4	KOMO
NBC	5	KING
Independent	6	KONG
CBS	7	KIRO
PBS	9	KCTS
UPN	11	KSTW
Fox	13	KCPQ
Warner/Independent	22	KTZZ

INTERNET ACCESS

Many major hotels now offer the option of Internet access for their guests, with double phone lines in rooms or sometimes even computers and business centers (see the Lodgings chapter). And though it can get crowded at times, the temporary downtown Central Library (see Public Libraries, above) has 47 **COMPUTERS** available to the public, with free Internet access and word processing, and with a 45-minute time limit. (The new library will have more than 130 computers.)

BEST PLACE TO SMOKE A CIGAR?

"Dulces Latin Bistro, because there's a varied selection of stellar cigars, fine ports and sauternes to sweeten the smoke, and Carlos is the most gracious host in Seattle: he makes you feel like you're a guest in his home, a home where nobody has a cow when you fire up a stogie."

Tom Robbins, author

Seattle is also home to several cyber cafes where, for a fee, you can log on and surf—or just check your e-mail. At the Capitol Hill Internet Café (216 Broadway Ave E; 206/860-6858; map:HH6), using the PCs will cost you $6 an hour; hours are 8am to midnight daily. Other Capitol Hill establishments include Aurafice Internet and Coffee Bar (616 E Pine St; 206/860-9977; aurafice.com; map:HH6), a hipster joint decked out in red walls and black leather chairs from the '70s. It's open 8am to 2am Tuesday, Friday, and Saturday, and 8am to midnight each other day of the week. Internet use costs 10 cents per minute, $6 per hour, or, if used for more than two hours, $5 an hour. Online Coffee Company (1720 E Olive Wy; 206/328-3731; onlinecoffeeco.com; map:HH6) is a comfy place with corner-office-style polished desks, open Monday through Friday 7am to midnight, and Saturday and Sunday 9am to midnight. Cost is 12 cents per minute, 30 minutes free with purchase of coffee or tea, and one hour free with coffee or tea before 9am.

UNIVERSITIES AND COLLEGES

The University of Washington (Visitor Information Center: 4014 University Wy NE, University District; 206/543-2100; washington.edu; map:FF6) is the largest of the Washington state public universities and has one of the biggest university bookstores in the country (4326 University Wy NE, University District; 206/634-3400; www.ubookstore.com; map:FF6). **SEATTLE PACIFIC UNIVERSITY** (3307 3rd Ave W, Queen Anne; 206/281-2000; www.spu.edu; map:FF8) is a private college associated with the Free Methodist Church. **SEATTLE UNIVERSITY** (Broadway Ave and Madison Ave, First Hill; 206/296-6000; seattleu.edu; map:N1) is a private Jesuit school. **SEATTLE COMMUNITY COLLEGES** (206/587-4100; seattlecolleges.com) operate three separate campuses in the city.

Important Telephone Numbers

AAA Washington	206/448-5353
AAA Emergency Road Service (24 hours)	800/AAA-help
AIDS Hotline	206/205-7837
Alcoholics Anonymous	206/587-2838
Ambulance	911
Amtrak	800/872-7245
Animal Control	206/386-7387
Auto Impound	206/684-5444
Better Business Bureau	206/431-2222
Birth and Death Records	206/296-4769
Blood Bank	206/292-6500
Bureau of Citizenship and Immigration Services	800/375-5283
Chamber of Commerce	206/389-7200
Children and Family Services (to report abuse/neglect)	206/721-6500
City of Seattle Information	206/386-1234
City Parks Information and Scheduling Office	206/684-4075
Coast Guard 24-Hour Emergency	800/982-8813
Community Information Line	206/461-3200
Customs (U.S.)	206/553-4676
Directory Information (first call per month from residence free, each additional call $1.25)	206/555-1212
Domestic Violence Hotline	800/562-6025
Emergency Resource Center (activated during emergencies such as earthquakes)	206/684-3355
FBI	206/622-0460
FEMA (Federal Emergency Management Agency)	800/462-9029
Fire	911
Greyhound Bus Lines Seattle Terminal	206/628-5508 OR 800/231-2222
Lost Pets	206/386-7387

Marriage Licenses	206/296-3933
Metro Transit Rider Information Line	206/553-3000
Missing Persons	206/684-5582
Passports	206/808-5700
Planned Parenthood	206/328-7700
Poison Center	206/526-2121
Post Office Information	800/275-8777
Red Cross	206/323-2345
Seattle Area Traffic Reports	206/368-4499
Seattle Convention & Visitors Bureau	206/461-5840
Seattle/King County Department of Public Health	206/296-4600
Senior Information Center	206/448-3110
Sexual Assault Resource Line	206/632-7273
State Patrol	425/455-7700
Suicide Prevention	206/461-3222
Ticketmaster	206/628-0888
Washington State Ferries	206/464-6400
Weather	206/526-6087
Zip Code Information	800/275-8777

TOP 200 RESTAURANTS

Restaurants by Star Rating

★★★★
Canlis
Campagne
Dahlia Lounge
Georgian, The
Herbfarm, The
Lampreia
Le Gourmand
Rover's

★★★½
Brasa
Cafe Juanita
Cascadia Restaurant
Flying Fish
Harvest Vine
Mistral
Nell's
Nishino
Oceanaire Seafood Room,
    The
Saito's Japanese Cafe &
    Bar
Seastar Restaurant and
    Raw Bar

★★★
Andaluca
Anthony's Pier 66
Café Campagne
Carmelita
Cassis
Chez Shea
Dulces Latin Bistro
El Gaucho
Elliott's Oyster House
Etta's Seafood
Eva Restaurant and Wine
    Bar
Fandango
Fireside Room
Geneva
Hunt Club
Il Bistro

Il Terrazzo Carmine
India Bistro
Kaspar's
Lark
Le Pichet
Marjorie
Mashiko
Matt's in the Market
Metropolitan Grill
Monsoon
Osteria La Spiga
Ovio Bistro
Ponti Seafood Grill
Restaurant Zoë
Salumi
Sans Souci
Sapphire Kitchen & Bar
727 Pine Restaurant
Shanghai Garden
Sostanza Trattoria
Stumbling Goat
Swingside Cafe
Szmania's
Tango
Thaiku
Third Floor Fish Cafe, The
1200 Bistro & Lounge
Typhoon!
Wild Ginger Asian Restau-
    rant and Satay Bar

★★½
Al Boccalino
Axis
Bandoleone
Barbacoa
Barking Frog
Bis on Main
Blue Onion Bistro
Cactus
Cafe Flora
Cafe Lago
Chiso

Daniel's Broiler Prime
    Steak & Chops
District, The
El Greco
Fish Club by Todd English,
    The
Frontier Room
Galerias
Green Papaya
Greenlake Bar & Grill
I Love Sushi
Isabella Ristorante
Kingfish Café
La Louisiana
La Rustica
Lee's Asian Restaurant
Macrina Bakery & Cafe
Madison Park Cafe
Malay Satay Hut
Marco's Supperclub
Market Street Urban Grill
Maximilien in the Market
Mona's
Palace Pigalle
Palisade
Queen City Grill
Ray's Boathouse
Ruby's on Bainbridge
St. Clouds
Sazerac
Serafina
Shallots Asian Bistro
Shea's Lounge
Shiro's
611 Supreme Crêperie
    Café
Supreme
Tempero do Brasil
Tosoni's
Union Bay Cafe
Vivanda Ristorante
Waterfront Seafood Grill
Yarrow Bay Grill

48

★★

Afrikando
Agua Verde Cafe & Paddle
    Club
Assaggio Ristorante
Bell Street Diner
Bick's Broadview Grill
Bizzarro Italian Cafe
Black Pearl
Buenos Aires Grill
Cafe Nola
Calcutta Grill
Chandler's Crabhouse
Chinoise Café
Chinook's at Salmon Bay
Doong Kong Lau
Dragonfish Asian Café
El Camino
Endolyne Joe's
Figaro Bistro
5 Spot Cafe
Four Swallows, The
Fremont Classic Pizza &
    Trattoria
Il Bacio
Imperial Garden Seafood
    Restaurant
JaK's Grill
Jitterbug Cafe
Kabul Afghan Cuisine
Luau Polynesian Lounge
Maple Leaf Grill
Matt's Rotisserie & Oyster
    Lounge

Medin's Ravioli Station
Noble Court
Orrapin Thai Food
Panos Kleftiko
Pink Door, The
Pontevecchio
Racha Noodles & Thai
    Cuisine
Ray's Cafe
Saigon Bistro
Saltoro
Sand Point Grill
Sanmi Sushi
Shamiana
Shanghai Café
Siam on Broadway
SkyCity at the Needle
Snappy Dragon
Stalk Exchange, The
Tacos Guaymas
Tia Lou's
Toi
Tup Tim Thai
21 Central
Wasabi Bistro
Wazobia West African
    Cuizine
Yanni's Greek Cuisine
Yarrow Bay Beach Cafe

★☆

Bada Lounge
Bistro Pleasant Beach
Burrito Loco Taqueria

Calypso Caribbean
    Kitchen
Coastal Kitchen
Gravity Bar
Kolbeh Persian Restaurant
Rosita's Mexican
    Restaurant
Still Life Café, The
Ten Mercer
13 Coins Restaurant
Union Square Grill

★

Anthony's Fish Bar
Bimbo's Bitchin' Burrito
    Kitchen
Chutneys
El Puerco Lloron
Garage
Hilltop Ale House
Luna Park Cafe
Mae's Phinney Ridge Café
Malena's Taco Shop
Mojito Cafe
Original Pancake House,
    The
Siam on Lake Union
Triangle Lounge

UNRATED

Earth & Ocean
La Medusa
Raga
Tulio Ristorante

Restaurants by Neighborhood

**BAINBRIDGE
ISLAND**

Bistro Pleasant Beach
Cafe Nola
Four Swallows, The
Ruby's on Bainbridge

**BALLARD/
SHILSHOLE
MARINA**

Burrito Loco Taqueria
India Bistro
Le Gourmand
Malena's Taco Shop
Market Street Urban Grill

Medin's Ravioli Station
Ray's Boathouse
Ray's Cafe
Thaiku

BELLEVUE

Bis on Main
Calcutta Grill

Daniel's Broiler Prime
 Steak & Chops
I Love Sushi
Noble Court
Sans Souci
Seastar Restaurant and
 Raw Bar
Shanghai Café
Tosoni's

BELLTOWN
Afrikando
Assaggio Ristorante
Axis
Bada Lounge
Brasa
Buenos Aires Grill
Cascadia Restaurant
El Gaucho
Etta's Seafood
Fandango
Flying Fish
Frontier Room
Lampreia
Macrina Bakery & Cafe
Marco's Supperclub
Marjorie
Mistral
Palace Kitchen
Queen City Grill
Restaurant Zoë
Saito's Japanese Cafe &
 Bar
Shallots Asian Bistro
Shiro's
Tia Lou's
Wasabi Bistro

**BROADVIEW/
 SHORELINE**
Bick's Broadview Grill
Black Pearl
Saltoro

CAPITOL HILL
Bimbo's Bitchin' Burrito
 Kitchen
Cassis
Chutneys Grille on the
 Hill
Coastal Kitchen
El Greco
Galerias
Garage
Gravity Bar
Green Papaya
Kingfish Café
Lark
Monsoon
Osteria La Spiga
Siam on Broadway
611 Supreme Crêperie
 Café
Tacos Guaymas
Tango
1200 Bistro & Lounge

**CENTRAL
DISTRICT**
La Louisiana

**CHINATOWN/
INTERNATIONAL
DISTRICT**
Chinoise Café
Malay Satay Hut
Saigon Bistro
Shanghai Garden

COLUMBIA CITY
Columbia City Alehouse
La Medusa

DENNY TRIANGLE
13 Coins Restaurant

DOWNTOWN
Andaluca
Dahlia Lounge
Dragonfish Asian Café
Earth & Ocean
Georgian, The

Isabella Ristorante
Le Pichet
Metropolitan Grill
Oceanaire Seafood Room,
 The
Sazerac
727 Pine Restaurant
Toi
Tulio Ristorante
Typhoon!
Union Square Grill
Wild Ginger Asian
 Restaurant and Satay
 Bar

EASTLAKE
Bandoleone
Serafina

FIRST HILL
Fireside Room
Geneva
Hunt Club, The

FREMONT
Chiso
El Camino
Fremont Classic Pizza &
 Trattoria
Medin's Ravioli Station
Pontevecchio
Ponti Seafood Grill
Still Life Café, The
Swingside Cafe
Tacos Guaymas
Triangle Lounge

GREEN LAKE
Eva Restaurant and Wine
 Bar
Greenlake Bar & Grill
Luau Polynesian Lounge
Mona's
Nell's
Rosita's Mexican
 Restaurant
Tacos Guaymas

GREENWOOD/ PHINNEY RIDGE
Carmelita
Mae's Phinney Ridge Café
74th Street Alehouse
Stalk Exchange, The
Stumbling Goat
Yanni's Greek Cuisine

ISSAQUAH
JaK's Grill
Shanghai Garden

KENT
Imperial Garden Seafood
    Restaurant

KIRKLAND
Cactus
Cafe Juanita
Original Pancake House,
    The
Raga
Shamiana
Szmania's
Third Floor Fish Cafe, The
21 Central
Yarrow Bay Beach Cafe
Yarrow Bay Grill

LAKE CITY
Mojito Cafe

LAKE UNION
Chandler's Crabhouse
Daniel's Broiler Prime
    Steak & Chops
I Love Sushi
Siam on Lake Union

LESCHI/MADRONA
Daniel's Broiler Prime
    Steak & Chops
Dulces Latin Bistro
St. Clouds
Supreme

MADISON PARK/ MADISON VALLEY
Cactus
Cafe Flora
Chinoise on Madison
Harvest Vine
Madison Park Cafe
Nishino
Rover's
Sostanza Trattoria

MAGNOLIA/ INTERBAY
Chinook's at Salmon Bay
Palisade
Sanmi Sushi
Szmania's

MONTLAKE
Cafe Lago

NORTHGATE
Doong Kong Lau

PIKE PLACE MARKET
Café Campagne
Campagne
Chez Shea
El Puerco Lloron
Il Bistro
Matt's in the Market
Maximilien in the Market
Pink Door, The
Place Pigalle
Shea's Lounge
Vivanda Ristorante

PIONEER SQUARE
Al Boccalino
Il Terrazzo Carmine
Kolbeh Persian Restaurant
Salumi
Wazobia West African
    Cuizine

QUEEN ANNE
Barbacoa
Canlis
Chinoise Café
Chutneys
Figaro Bistro
5 Spot Cafe
Hilltop Ale House
Kaspar's
Macrina Bakery & Cafe
Malena's Taco Shop
Mojito Cafe
Orrapin Thai Food
Panos Kleftiko
Racha Noodles & Thai
    Cuisine
Sapphire Kitchen & Bar
Ten Mercer
Tup Tim Thai

RAVENNA/ WEDGWOOD
Black Pearl
Shamiana

REDMOND
Il Bacio
Malay Satay Hut
Matt's Rotisserie & Oyster
    Lounge
Typhoon!

ROOSEVELT/ MAPLE LEAF
Calypso Caribbean
    Kitchen
Maple Leaf Grill
Snappy Dragon

SAND POINT/ LAURELHURST
JaK's Grill
Sand Point Grill
Union Bay Cafe

SEATTLE CENTER
SkyCity at the Needle

UNIVERSITY DISTRICT
Agua Verde Cafe & Paddle Club
Blue Onion Bistro
Burrito Loco Taqueria
District, The
Tempero do Brasil

WALLINGFORD
Bizzarro Italian Cafe
Chinoise on 45th

Chutney's Bistro
Jitterbug Cafe
Kabul Afghan Cuisine

WATERFRONT
Anthony's Fish Bar
Anthony's Pier 66
Bell Street Diner
Elliott's Oyster House
Fish Club by Todd English, The
Waterfront Seafood Grill

WEST SEATTLE
Endolyne Joe's
JaK's Grill
La Rustica
Lee's Asian Restaurant
Luna Park Cafe
Mashiko
Ovio Bistro
Tacos Guaymas

WOODINVILLE
Barking Frog
Herbfarm, The

Restaurants by Food and Other Features

AFGHAN
Kabul Afghan Cuisine

BAKERY
Macrina Bakery & Cafe

BARBEQUE
Frontier Room

BREAKFAST
Andaluca
Chinook's at Salmon Bay
Coastal Kitchen
Dragonfish Asian Café
Earth & Ocean
El Greco
Endolyne Joe's
Fish Club by Todd English, The
5 Spot Cafe
Georgian, The
Gravity Bar
Hunt Club
Imperial Garden Seafood Restaurant
Jitterbug Cafe
Le Pichet
Luna Park Cafe
Macrina Bakery & Cafe
Mae's Phinney Ridge Café

Mojito Cafe
Original Pancake House, The
Sazerac
727 Pine Restaurant
SkyCity at the Needle
Still Life Café, The
Tacos Guaymas
13 Coins Restaurant
Tulio Ristorante

BREAKFAST ALL DAY
Coastal Kitchen
Endolyne Joe's
5 Spot Cafe
Jitterbug Cafe
Mae's Phinney Ridge Café
Original Pancake House, The
13 Coins Restaurant

BRUNCH
Bandoleone
Barking Frog
Bistro Pleasant Beach
Café Campagne
Cafe Flora
Cafe Nola
Calcutta Grill

Chandler's Crabhouse
Dragonfish Asian Café
El Greco
Etta's Seafood
Hunt Club
Kingfish Café
Macrina Bakery & Cafe
Madison Park Cafe
Maple Leaf Grill
Maximilien in the Market
Palisade
Ponti Seafood Grill
St. Clouds
Sapphire Kitchen & Bar
Sazerac
611 Supreme Crêperie Café
SkyCity at the Needle
Stalk Exchange, The
Still Life Café, The
Supreme

BURGERS
Bell Street Diner
Cafe Campagne
Cascadia Restaurant
El Greco
Gravity Bar (vegan)
Greenlake Bar & Grill

Luau Polynesian Lounge
Luna Park Cafe
Maple Leaf Grill
Palace Kitchen
Ray's Cafe
Rosita's Mexican
    Restaurant
St. Clouds
Saltoro
Triangle Lounge
Yarrow Bay Beach Cafe

CHINESE

Black Pearl
Chinoise Café
Doong Kong Lau
Imperial Garden Seafood
    Restaurant
Lee's Asian Restaurant
Noble Court
Shallots Asian Bistro
Shanghai Café
Shanghai Garden
Snappy Dragon

CONTINENTAL

Canlis
El Gaucho
Geneva
Georgian, The
Kaspar's
Szmania's
13 Coins Restaurant
Tosoni's

CONVERSATION-
    FRIENDLY

Andaluca
Bis on Main
Burrito Loco Taqueria
Café Campagne
Calcutta Grill
Canlis
Cassis
Chez Shea
Chiso (at the sushi bar)
District, The
Dulces Latin Bistro

Figaro Bistro
Georgian, The
Herbfarm, The
Kaspar's
Lampreia
Macrina Bakery & Cafe
Market Street Urban Grill
Mona's
Pink Door, The
Pontevecchio
Ponti Seafood Grill
Sans Souci
Stalk Exchange, The
Swingside Cafe
Ten Mercer
Third Floor Fish Cafe, The
Tulio Ristorante
Yarrow Bay Grill

DELIVERY

Black Pearl
Malay Satay Hut
Snappy Dragon

DESSERTS
    (EXCEPTIONAL)

Cafe Campagne
Cafe Juanita
Dahlia Lounge
Earth & Ocean
Etta's Seafood
Eva Restaurant and Wine
    Bar
Figaro Bistro
Geneva
Georgian, The
Herbfarm, The
Hunt Club
Kaspar's
Lampreia
Le Gourmand
Nell's
Restaurant Zoë
Serafina
611 Supreme Crêperie
    Café
Szmania's

13 Coins Restaurant
Tulio Ristorante

DINER

5 Spot Cafe
Jitterbug Cafe
Luna Park Cafe
Mae's Phinney Ridge Café

DINING ALONE

Café Campagne
Carmelita
Four Swallows, The
I Love Sushi
Kaspar's Wine Bar
Marco's Supperclub
Matt's in the Market
Nishino
Place Pigalle
Saito's Japanese Cafe & Bar
Sazerac
Shiro's
Szmania's

EDITORS' CHOICE

Agua Verde Cafe & Paddle
    Club
Barking Frog
Brasa
Café Campagne
Cafe Lago
Campagne
Canlis
Cascadia Restaurant
Chez Shea
Chinook's at Salmon Bay
Dahlia Lounge
Elliott's Oyster House
Etta's Seafood
Flying Fish
Harvest Vine
Herbfarm, The
Hunt Club
Lampreia
Le Gourmand
Matt's in the Market
Nell's
Nishino

Palace Kitchen
Ponti Seafood Grill
Queen City Grill
Ray's Boathouse
Ray's Cafe
Rover's
Salumi
Seastar Restaurant and
     Raw Bar
Shea's Lounge
SkyCity at the Needle
Swingside Cafe
Third Floor Fish Cafe, The
13 Coins Restaurant
Waterfront Seafood Grill
Wild Ginger Asian
     Restaurant and Satay
     Bar

FAMILY
Anthony's Fish Bar
Anthony's Pier 66
Bell Street Diner
Bick's Broadview Grill
Black Pearl
Burrito Loco Taqueria
Calcutta Grill
Chinook's at Salmon Bay
El Puerco Lloron
Elliott's Oyster House
Endolyne Joe's
Etta's Seafood
Greenlake Bar & Grill
Lee's Asian Restaurant
Mae's Phinney Ridge Café
Malay Satay Hut
Maple Leaf Grill
Medin's Ravioli Station
Oceanaire Seafood Room
Original Pancake House,
     The
Ray's Boathouse
Ray's Cafe
Rosita's Mexican
     Restaurant
Saigon Bistro
St. Clouds

Saltoro
Snappy Dragon

FIREPLACE
Barking Frog
Cafe Juanita
Canlis
Dulces Latin Bistro
Fireside Room
Hunt Club
Ponti Seafood Grill
Raga
Saltoro
Sostanza Trattoria

FISH-AND-CHIPS
Anthony's Fish Bar
Bell Street Diner
Chinook's at Salmon Bay
Oceanaire Seafood Room,
     The
Ray's Cafe

FRENCH
Bis on Main
Café Campagne
Campagne
Cassis
Chez Shea
Figaro Bistro
Le Gourmand
Le Pichet
Madison Park Cafe
Maximilien in the Market
Mistral
Place Pigalle
Rover's
611 Supreme Crêperie
     Café
Shea's Lounge

GERMAN
Geneva
Szmania's

GOOD VALUE
Afrikando
Bimbo's Bitchin' Burrito
     Kitchen

Black Pearl
Blue Onion Bistro
Brasa
Chutneys
Doong Kong Lau
El Puerco Lloron
Galerias
Green Papaya
Hilltop Ale House
India Bistro
JaK's Grill
Kabul Afghan Cuisine
Kingfish Café
Lee's Asian Restaurant
Macrina Bakery & Cafe
Mae's Phinney Ridge Café
Malay Satay Hut
Medin's Ravioli Station
Saigon Bistro
St. Clouds
Salumi
Sand Point Grill
Shallots Asian Bistro
ShamianaTacos Guaymas
Tempero do Brasil
Thaiku
Union Bay Cafe
Wazobia West African
     Cuizine
Yanni's Greek Cuisine

GREEK
Panos Kleftiko
Yanni's Greek Cuisine

GRILL
Bick's Broadview Grill
Buenos Aires Grill
Greenlake Bar & Grill
JaK's Grill
Maple Leaf Grill
Market Street Urban Grill
Matt's Rotisserie & Oyster
     Grill
Metropolitan Grill
Ponti Seafood Grill
Queen City Grill

Triangle Lounge
Union Square Grill
Waterfront Seafood Grill
Yarrow Bay Grill

HEALTHY
Afrikando
Cafe Flora
Carmelita
Gravity Bar

INDIAN
Chutneys
India Bistro
Raga
Shamiana

INVENTIVE ETHNIC
Axis
Barbacoa
Cafe Flora
Cafe Nola
Chinoise Café
Coastal Kitchen
Dahlia Lounge
Etta's Seafood
5 Spot Cafe
Kingfish Cafe
Luau Polynesian Lounge
Maple Leaf Grill
Marco's Supperclub
Marjorie
Matt's in the Market
Mona's
Monsoon
Ovio Bistro
Sapphire Kitchen & Bar
Sazerac
Shallots Asian Bistro
Shamiana
Shea's Lounge
Szmania's
Wild Ginger Asian
   Restaurant and Satay
   Bar
Yarrow Bay Beach Cafe
Yarrow Bay Grill

ITALIAN
Al Boccalino
Assaggio Ristorante
Bizzarro Italian Cafe
Cafe Lago
Fremont Classic Pizza &
   Trattoria
Il Bacio
Il Bistro
Il Terrazzo Carmine
Isabella Ristorante
La Medusa
La Rustica
Medin's Ravioli Station
Osteria La Spiga
Pink Door, The
Pontevecchio
Salumi
Sans Souci
Serafina
Sostanza Trattoria
Swingside Cafe
Tulio Ristorante

JAPANESE
Chiso
Dragonfish Asian Café
I Love Sushi
Mashiko
Nishino
Saito's Japanese Cafe &
   Bar
Sanmi Sushi
Shiro's
Wasabi Bistro

KITSCHY
Bizzarro Italian Cafe
Blue Onion Bistro
Endolyne Joe's
5 Spot Cafe
Galerias
Pink Door, The

LATE-NIGHT
Bada Lounge
Bandoleone
Café Campagne

Campagne
El Gaucho
5 Spot Cafe
Flying Fish
Frontier Room
Garage
Luau Polynesian Lounge
Mojito Cafe
Palace Kitchen
Queen City Grill
Tango
13 Coins Restaurant
Union Square Grill
Wazobia West African
   Cuizine

LATIN
Bandoleone
Dulces Latin Bistro
Fandango
Mojito Cafe
Tango
Tempero do Brasil

MEDITERRANEAN
Andaluca
Bistro Pleasant Beach
Brasa
El Greco
Four Swallows, The
Hunt Club
Mona's
Ponti Seafood Grill
Sapphire Kitchen & Bar
Tulio Ristorante

MEXICAN
Agua Verde Cafe & Paddle
   Club
Burrito Loco Taqueria
Cactus
El Puerco Lloron
Galerias
Malena's Taco Shop
Rosita's Mexican
   Restaurant
Tacos Guaymas
Tia Lou's

NORTHWEST

Barking Frog
Brasa
Cafe Juanita
Campagne
Cascadia Restaurant
Chez Shea
Dahlia Lounge
Earth & Ocean
Eva Restaurant and Wine
  Bar
Flying Fish
Georgian, The
Kaspar's
Lampreia
Lark
Le Gourmand
Market Street Urban Grill
Nell's
Palace Kitchen
Ray's Boathouse
Ray's Cafe
Shea's Lounge
SkyCity at the Needle
Stumbling Goat
Supreme
Ten Mercer
Third Floor Fish Cafe, The
1200 Bistro & Lounge
Union Bay Cafe

OUTDOOR DINING

Anthony's Pier 66
Assaggio Ristorante
Agua Verde Cafe & Paddle
  Club
Barking Frog
Bistro Pleasant Beach
Cactus
Café Campagne
Cafe Flora
Cafe Nola
Carmelita
Cascadia Restaurant
Chandler's Crabhouse
Chinook's at Salmon Bay
El Camino

El Greco
El Puerco Lloron
Elliott's Oyster House
Hunt Club, The (Piazza
  Capri)
Il Terrazzo Carmine
Le Pichet
Luau Polynesian Lounge
Macrina Bakery & Cafe
Madison Park Cafe
Malena's Taco Shop
Maple Leaf Grill
Marco's Supperclub
Monsoon
Orrapin Thai Food
Palisade
Pink Door, The
Place Pigalle
Ponti Seafood Grill
Ray's Cafe
Rover's
Sapphire Kitchen & Bar
Serafina
Sostanza Trattoria
Tacos Guaymas (some
  branches)
Triangle Lounge
Union Bay Cafe
Waterfront Seafood Grill
Yarrow Bay Beach Cafe
Yarrow Bay Grill

OYSTER BAR

Elliott's Oyster House
Matt's Rotisserie & Oyster
  Bar

PAN-ASIAN

Chinoise Café
Dragonfish Asian Café
Lee's Asian Restaurant
Malay Satay Hut
Shallot's Asian Bistro
Wild Ginger Asian Restau-
  rant and Satay Bar

PERSIAN

Kolbeh Persian Restaurant

PIZZA

Bistro Pleasant Beach
Cafe Lago
Fremont Classic Pizza &
  Trattoria
Isabella Ristorante
La Medusa
Ruby's on Bainbridge
Triangle Lounge

PRIVATE DINING ROOMS

Brasa
Cafe Juanita
Cascadia Restaurant
Chandler's Crabhouse
Dahlia Lounge
Dragonfish Asian Café
El Gaucho
Etta's Seafood
Fandango
Flying Fish
Galerias
Georgian, The
Harvest Vine
Hunt Club
Kaspar's
Luau Polynesian Lounge
Malay Satay Hut
Matt's Rotisserie & Oyster
  Bar
Metropolitan Grill
Nishino
Palace Kitchen
Ponti Seafood Grill
Ray's Boathouse
Rover's
Seastar Restaurant and
  Raw Bar
727 Pine Restaurant
Shallots Asian Bistro
Szmania's
Tango
Third Floor Fish Cafe, The
Tulio Ristorante
Waterfront Seafood Grill

Wild Ginger Asian
Restaurant and Satay
Bar
Yarrow Bay Grill

ROMANTIC
Al Boccalino
Andaluca
Bandoleone
Bis on Main
Brasa
Café Campagne
Cafe Juanita
Cafe Nola
Campagne
Canlis
Carmelita
Cassis
Chez Shea
Dulces Latin Bistro
Eva Restaurant and Wine
Bar
Figaro Bistro
Four Swallows, The
Galerias
Geneva
Georgian, The
Hunt Club
Il Bistro
Il Terrazzo Carmine
Isabella Ristorante
La Rustica
Lark
Le Gourmand
Le Pichet
Madison Park Cafe
Marjorie
Maximilien in the Market
Mona's
Pink Door, The
Place Pigalle
Pontevecchio
Ponti Seafood Grill
Rover's
Sans Souci
Serafina
727 Pine Restaurant

Shea's Lounge
Sostanza Trattoria
Stumbling Goat
Ten Mercer
Tosoni's
Tulio Ristorante
1200 Bistro & Lounge

SEAFOOD
Anthony's Pier 66
Anthony's Fish Bar
Bell Street Diner
Chandler's Crabhouse
Chinoise Café
Chinook's at Salmon Bay
Chiso
Coastal Kitchen
Dragonfish Asian Café
Elliott's Oyster House
Etta's Seafood
Fish Club by Todd English,
The
Flying Fish
Hunt Club
I Love Sushi
Imperial Garden Seafood
Restaurant
Mashiko
Matt's in the Market
Nishino
Noble Court
Oceanaire Seafood Room,
The
Palisade
Ponti Seafood Grill
Queen City Grill
Ray's Boathouse
Ray's Cafe
Ruby's on Bainbridge
Saito's Japanese Cafe &
Bar
Sanmi Sushi
Seastar Restaurant and
Raw Bar
Shanghai Café
Shanghai Garden
Shiro's

Swingside Cafe
Third Floor Fish Cafe, The
Vivanda Ristorante
Wasabi Bistro
Waterfront Seafood Grill

SOUP/SALAD/
SANDWICH
Café Nola
Café Campagne
Columbia City Alehouse
El Greco
Gravity Bar
Hilltop Ale House
Macrina Bakery & Cafe
Maple Leaf Grill
Mojito Cafe
Saigon Bistro
74th Street Alehouse
Stalk Exchange, The
Still Life Café, The
Triangle Lounge

SOUTH AMERICAN
Buenos Aires Grill
Fandango
Tempero do Brasil

SOUTHERN
Kingfish Café
La Louisiana

SOUTHWESTERN
Cactus

SMOKE-FREE
Go online to
metrokc.gov/health/
tobacco/guide.htm

STEAKS
Buenos Aires Grill
Daniel's Broiler Prime
Steak & Chops
El Gaucho
JaK's Grill
Matt's Rotisserie & Oyster
Lounge
Metropolitan Grill

Palisade
21 Central
Union Square Grill

SUSHI
Chinoise Café
Chiso
Dragonfish Asian Café
I Love Sushi
Mashiko
Nishino
Saito's Japanese Cafe & Bar
Sanmi Sushi
Shiro's
Wasabi Bistro

TAKE-OUT
Black Pearl
Fremont Classic Pizzeria
   & Trattoria
India Bistro
Macrina Bakery & Cafe
Malay Satay Hut
Malena's Taco Shop
Salumi
Snappy Dragon
Tacos Guaymas

TAPAS
Andaluca
Bandoleone
Cactus
District, The
Harvest Vine
Tango

TAVERN
Columbia City Alehouse
Hilltop Ale House
Maple Leaf Grill
74th Street Alehouse
Triangle Lounge

THAI
Chinoise Café
Orrapin Thai Food
Racha Noodles & Thai
   Cuisine

Siam on Broadway
Siam on Lake Union
Thaiku
Toi
Tup Tim Thai
Typhoon!

VEGETARIAN
Cafe Flora
Carmelita
Cascadia Restaurant
Gravity Bar

VIETNAMESE
Chinoise Café
Green Papaya
Monsoon
Saigon Bistro

VIEW
Agua Verde Cafe & Paddle
   Club
Anthony's Pier 66
Bell Street Diner
Calcutta Grill
Canlis
Chandler's Crabhouse
Chez Shea
Chinook's at Salmon Bay
Daniel's Broiler Prime
   Steak & Chops
El Puerco Lloron
Elliott's Oyster House
Etta's Seafood
Fandango
I Love Sushi
Matt's in the Market
Maximilien in the Market
Palisade
Pink Door, The
Place Pigalle
Ponti Seafood Grill
Ray's Boathouse
Ray's Cafe
Sanmi Sushi
Shea's Lounge
SkyCity at the Needle

Sostanza Trattoria
   (Lakeside Patio)
Third Floor Fish Cafe, The
Vivanda Ristorante
Waterfront Seafood Grill
Yarrow Bay Beach Cafe
Yarrow Bay Grill

WEST AFRICAN
Afrikando
Wazobia West African
   Cuizine

WINE BAR/LIST
Assaggio Ristorante
Barking Frog
Brasa
Café Campagne
Cafe Lago
Cafe Juanita
Campagne
Canlis
Cascadia Restaurant
Earth & Ocean
El Gaucho
Eva Restaurant and Wine
   Bar
Georgian, The
Il Bistro
Kaspar's Wine Bar
Le Pichet
Metropolitan Grill
Monsoon
Palace Kitchen
Place Pigalle
Queen City Grill
Ray's Boathouse
Rover's
Sand Point Grill
Seastar Restaurant and
   Raw Bar
Serafina
Supreme
Tango
Waterfront Seafood Grill

RESTAURANT REVIEWS

Afrikando / ★★

2904 1ST AVE, BELLTOWN; 206/374-9714 If you dream of French West Africa, head for the lively Afrikando, where the menu recalls chef Jacques Sarr's native Senegal. Start with *akra*, light fritters of black-eyed peas in a spicy tomato sauce with bay shrimp. The star entrée is the *poisson frite* (French for "fried fish"), a whole fried tilapia served with rice and tomato sauce. Other favorites include *debe*, grilled lamb chops with spicy onion mustard sauce and couscous, and *thiebu djen*, the national Senegalese dish of fish in rich tomato sauce with vegetables and *jollof* rice. The beer and wine list features selections from South Africa and Kenya. For nonalcoholic alternatives, try one of the homemade Senegalese juices—hibiscus, ginger, or tamarind. Sarr's mango tart is perfect with a cup of hot ginger tea. *$; MC, V; checks OK; lunch Mon–Fri, dinner every day; beer only; reservations recommended; self parking; map:D8* ⟐

WHY GO: First-hand travel tips from chatty diners just back from their overland Safari.

Agua Verde Cafe & Paddle Club / ★★

1303 NE BOAT ST, UNIVERSITY DISTRICT; 206/545-8570 Even on the grayest Seattle days, this bayside cafe exudes the essence of sun-drenched Baja. Brightly colored walls fill the cottage with a tropical glow, while stripped floorboards resemble an oceanfront boardwalk. Around lunch, count on a crowd. The menu features Baja classics—fish tacos, salads, ceviche—and plenty of vegetarian plates. The *taco de mero*, grilled halibut and shredded cabbage enlivened with a squirt of fresh lime, is love at first bite. We also favor the *de carne*, sliced flank steak taco with onions, peppers, and crumbles of cotija cheese as well as *de carnitas*, shredded pork with cabbage and salsa. The vegetarian *de boniato* is a surprising combination of sweet potatoes sautéed with mild chiles, served with onions, cotija, and a cooling, creamy avocado sauce. Don't miss the salsa cart, which offers a smoky chipotle and a three-alarm tomato salsa. The cafeteria-style lunch, frequented by U-Dubbers, gives way to full service at dinnertime, where table service can be hit-or-miss. Partner any meal with Mexican beer, a margarita, or fresh-squeezed juice. Conclude any meal with the quivering chocolate flan, a slice of Key lime or Kahlúa pecan pie. *$; DIS, MC, V; checks OK; lunch, dinner Mon–Sat; full bar; reservations recommended; self parking; www.aguaverde.com; map:FF7* ⟐

WHY GO: Restaurant-side kayak rentals (Mar 1–Oct 31) are a great distraction while waiting for a table.

Al Boccalino / ★★★

1 YESLER WY, PIONEER SQUARE; 206/622-7688 Fragrant harbingers of delights lure hungry patrons to this pretty place just west of Pioneer Square. The triangular dining room trimmed in dark wood and stained glass has been the setting for countless marriage proposals and romantic celebrations. Sure-to-please offerings include antipasti such as the *vongole oreganate*, clams baked in the half shell with oregano and bread crumbs, or *polenta ripiena con Gorgonzola*, creamy polenta custard stuffed with sweet Gorgonzola heady with fresh sage. Northern dishes are a specialty—try the saddle of lamb with a piquant sauce of Cognac, tarragon, and Dijon mustard. There are plenty of good pastas, and seafood plays a major role here, as in the seared large scallops with pesto and white wine. Downtown denizens love the lunches in this hideaway, with its complement of pastas and reasonably priced sandwiches. Proprietor Carlos Tager (who took up the reins after the death of longtime friend and original owner Kenny Raider) sets a professional tone in the hushed dining room. *$$; AE, DC, MC, V; checks OK; lunch Tues–Fri, dinner Tues–Sun; beer and wine; reservations recommended; street parking; alboccalino.com; map:N8* &

WHY GO: Old World service and namesake wine pitchers for purchase.

Andaluca / ★★★

407 OLIVE WAY (MAYFLOWER PARK HOTEL), DOWNTOWN; 206/832-6999 Lovers who love to eat will love this romantic, informal midtown refuge that goes beyond mere ambience. In the sure hands of chef Wayne Johnson, Andaluca has become a mecca for fine food. Well-informed and lighthearted servers deftly attend to diners in this cocoon of rosewood booths, murals, and textured walls in deep reds and earthy browns. The center-stage half-moon bar is aglitter with crystal stemware, pretty bottles, and the gleaming teeth of the smart bartenders. Johnson's menus, conversant with the Mediterranean, have seasonal emphases on local seafood and produce and include well-considered wine-pairing suggestions from the extensive list. An ever-changing tapas menu of light shareables is perfect for têtes-à-têtes with a bottle of wine. Two notable signature entrées are the saffron-scented paella, loaded with shellfish, chicken, and chorizo, and the Cabrales Crusted Beef, a crusty rare tenderloin with grilled pears, and blue cheese. Johnson's Chateau Manos, a warm liquid centered chocolate cake, is a triumph of Western civilization. *$$$; AE, DC, DIS, MC, V; checks OK; breakfast every day, lunch Mon–Sat, dinner every day; full bar; reservations recommended; valet parking; andaluca.com; map:I6* &

WHY GO: Best paella this side of Barcelona.

Anthony's Pier 66 / ★★★
Bell Street Diner / ★★
Anthony's Fish Bar / ★

2201 ALASKAN WY, PIER 66, WATERFRONT; 206/448-6688 This handsome trio of restaurants at the Bell Street Pier is designed to suit any mood, appetite, or budget. Pier 66 upstairs has the most jaw-dropping view of Seattle's working waterfront, and the Asian-inflected menu of local and regional seafood is priced accordingly. Ginger Penn Cove mussels steamed with sake will get you off to a good start, as will the Potlatch, an impressive collection of Northwest steamer clams, mussels, split snow-crab legs, and half-shell oysters. Planked wild chinook salmon or Alaskan halibut are always reliable entrées.

For lunch or casual dining by Elliott Bay, the boisterous Bell Street Diner downstairs is a good choice, offering a wide selection of less formal fare: seafood, chowders, burgers, generous salads, rice bowls, and fish tacos. You'll enjoy the same view of the marina as the harbormaster, whose watchtower is right next door.

For a quick, no-frills bite, take the kids and join the sea gulls waterside at Anthony's Fish Bar and chow down on fish-and-chips, chowder, blackened-rockfish tacos, or bay-shrimp Caesar salads. *$$, $, $; AE, MC, V; checks OK; dinner every day (Anthony's Pier 66), lunch, dinner every day (Bell Street Diner, Anthony's Fish Bar); 2 full bars; reservations recommended for Pier 66; valet (at night) and validated (lunch and dinner) garage parking at Seattle Art Institute; anthonys.com; map:H9* &

WHY GO: To reconsider one's disdain for corporate restauranting.

BEST PLACE TO STAGE A PROTEST?

"Where else? The Federal Building. Or marching down Pike Street from Seattle Central Community College to Westlake, chanting, 'Hey Hey, Ho Ho.'"

Joel Connelly, Seattle Post-Intelligencer *political columnist*

Assaggio Ristorante / ★★

2010 4TH AVE (CLAREMONT HOTEL), BELLTOWN; 206/441-1399 Assaggio is one of Seattle's best Italian restaurants due in large part to the passion and presence of owner Mauro Golmarvi. The affectionate front-of-the-house man greets each guest with a hug, a kiss, or at least a handshake. When the place is in full swing, this frescoed trattoria is nothing short of a celebration. The menu features authentic cuisine from Golmarvi's hometown, Acona on Italy's Adriatic coast. At lunch and dinner luxuriate over a bowl of *brodetto*, a silken seafood soup perfumed with saffron and served with rustic Tuscan bread. Begin your feast with the piquant *carpaccio di filleti de manzo*, thinly sliced beef tenderloin with Parmesan, capers, and mustard. Primi favorites include the pappardelle with bolognese sauce and the penne with pancetta, peppercorns, and vodka. For *secondi*, order the lamb shanks braised in red wine and that longing for fall-off-the-bone lamb will be sated. The gracious staff is knowledgeable about the menu and the award-winning wine list. *$$; AE, DC, DIS, MC, V; checks OK; lunch Mon–Fri, dinner Mon–Sat; beer, wine, and service bar; reservations recommended; valet, self, and street parking; assaggioseattle.com; map:H6* &

WHY GO: Better cannoli you will not find.

Axis / ★★★

2214 1ST AVE, BELLTOWN; 206/441-9600 This sleek, soaring, multilevel space would be a drafty warehouse if it weren't for the warm lighting, neon accents, giant art, and the swarm of Belltown social bees hiving around the busy bar that specializes in exotic fresh-fruit drinks and trendy cocktails. Veteran chef Alvin Binuya's extensive dinner-house, pub-food menu provides an impressive list of global options for diners or noshers. From his kitchen that features a massive wood-burning oven, open-fire rotisseries, and grills, he turns out a planetary synthesis that includes

FAST—AND FABULOUS—FOOD

BUNS

Burgers are an important institution in American dining, and Seattle, being a town of implicit taste, has a noble history of covering the bun with relish and aplomb. **RED MILL BURGERS** (312 N 67th St, Phinney Ridge; 206/783-6362; and 1613 W Dravus St, Interbay; 206/284-6363) leads the pack with its smoky, house-made mayo, awesome onion rings, and real ice-cream shakes. The local fast-food icon is the citywide **DICK'S DRIVE-IN** (six locations, including the University District and Capitol Hill), with their instant service, legendary fries, and low prices. **PRIMO BURGERS** (6501 Roosevelt Way NE, Roosevelt/Maple Leaf; 206/525-3542) serves Hawaiian-style burgers in a busy storefront. **BING'S BODACIOUS BURGERS** (4200 E Madison St, Madison Park; 206/323-8623) and the **DELUXE BAR & GRILL** (625 Broadway Ave E, Capitol Hill; 206/324-9627) are for-sure stops for grown-up burgers and a beer. You won't find fries at **TWO BELLS TAVERN** (2313 4th Ave, Belltown; 206/441-3050), but their fat and famous burger on sourdough has a cultish following. Ballardites hang at **SCOOTER'S BURGERS** (5802 24th St NW, Ballard; 206/782-2966) for real handmade burgers and fries. Award winning is the big and messy Dock Street Burger at **BAD ALBERT'S TAP & GRILL** (5100 Ballard Ave NW, Ballard; 206/782-9623). **HERFY'S BURGERS** (5963 Corson Ave, Georgetown; 206/764-0980) is a delicious, greasy descendant of the fondly remembered Seattle burger chain and has an avid following. On the Eastside, add a fried egg to the huge patty at **FATBURGER** (17181 Redmond Wy, Redmond; 425/497-8809); pair your burger with a classic root beer at **XXX ROOT BEER DRIVE-IN** (98 NE Gilman Blvd, Issaquah; 425/392-1266), or get it charbroiled at **WIB-BLEY'S GOURMET HAMBURGERS** (2255 140th Ave NE, Bellevue; 425/747-7818).

There's a long list of delicious hotdogs served in a cute doggy-styled decor at **DIG-GITY DOG HOT DOGS & SAUSAGES** (5421 Meridian Ave N, Wallingford; 206/633-1966). **MATT'S FAMOUS CHILI DOGS** (6615 E Marginal Way S, George-town; 206/768-0418) does it Chicago-style, while there are gourmet dogs and sausages at **TAXI DOGS** (1928 Pike Pl, Pike Place Market; 206/443-1919), and for the best wurst, **ULI'S FAMOUS SAUSAGE** (1511 Pike Pl, Pike Place Market; 206/839-1000) has all manner of tube steaks in a bun or raw to take home. And for those so inclined, get your red-hot vegetarian dogs (and other styles) at **CYBER DOGS** (909 Pike St, Downtown; 206/405-3647).

PIZZA

Seattle's history doesn't include large numbers of Italian Americans. So, there's no "Seattle-style" pizza. But we've more than leaped into that breach with the help of hordes of newcomers who have brought their styles from all over the United States and, indeed, the whole world. **PAGLIACCI PIZZA**'s (550 Queen Anne Ave N, Queen Anne; and branches) Philly-style pie is an all-around favorite—but you can get 'em gourmet with sun-dried tomatoes and artichokes too. Just call the central delivery line (206/726-1717) to have it delivered hot. Hugely popular (for good reason) are two pur-veyors of thin-crust New York–style: **PIECORA'S NY PIZZA & PASTA** (1401 E Madison St, Capitol Hill; 206/322-9411) and **NEW YORK PIZZA PLACE** (8310 5th Ave NE, Maple Leaf; 206/524-1355). Get Chicago deep-dish pizza at **WALLINGFORD PIZZA HOUSE** (2109 N 45th St; 206/547-3663); or gourmet thin-crust or deep-dish at **MADAME K'S** (5327 Ballard Ave NW, Ballard; 206/783-9710), in olden days a brothel! **ATLANTIC STREET PIZZA** (5253 University Wy NE, University District; 206/524-4432) serves thin-crust, gourmet pies to rock stars and long lines of other humans. Go Brazilian at **PIZZA RIO** (5011 S Dawson St, Seward Park; 206/723-0445), with Brazilian ingredients on unique crusts. **ABBONDANZA PIZZERIA** (6503 California Ave SW, West Seattle; 206/935-8989) is winning battles in the Pizza Wars with its thin, crispy yet chewy crusts. On the Eastside, **COYOTE CREEK PIZZA** (15600 NE 8th St, Bellevue; 425/746-7460) is in Crossroads Mall, but its Southwest/Mediterranean pies have a rabid following with mall rats and discriminating Bellevue-ites.

BARBECUE

The debate never quits: hickory or applewood, alder or mesquite? Here are the best of the pits. **JONES BBQ** (3216 S Hudson St, Rainier Valley; 206/725-2728; and 15600 NE 8th St, Crossroads Mall, Bellevue; 425/746-3955) is generally rated by barbecue buffs as best in town, with its Texarkana-style ribs, chicken, and beef. But loyalists of West Seattle's **BACK PORCH BBQ** (6459 California Ave SW; 206/932-7427) may argue with that. SoDo's **PECOS PIT BBQ** (2260 1st Ave S; 206/623-0629) does weekday lunches, only with huge five-napkin Texas barbecue sandwiches. **WILLIE'S TASTE OF SOUL** (6305 Beacon Ave S, Beacon Hill; 206/722-3229) is Louisiana-style and a Seattle classic; and **THE STEEL PIG** (603 Roy St, Queen Anne; 206/213-5870) is gaining pop-ularity. On the Eastside, the popular **DIXIE'S BBQ** (11522 Northup Wy, Bellevue; 425/828-2460) serves up famous ribs and chicken and a hot sauce not for the faint of heart, while **ARMADILLO BBQ** (13109 NE 175th St, Woodinville; 425/481-1417) has a funky decor and dry, smoky meats.

—*Michael Hood*

wood-fired prime rib, fried pickles, roasted salmon, Kobe beef, pizza puttanesca, surf and turf, seafood risotto, sea bass, and ale and honey-barbecued shrimp. Filipino spring rolls, zippy jerked chicken wings, noodle salad, and blackened ahi may add to the confusion but definitely provide just about everything for everyone. *$$; AE, DC, MC V; no checks; dinner every day; full bar; reservations recommended; valet and street parking; info@axisrestaurant.com; axisrestaurant.com; map:G8* &

WHY GO: Tasty bites make good props for the fish-bowl singles scene.

Bada Lounge / ★★☆

2230 1ST AVE, BELLTOWN; 206/374-8717 They call it Bada Lounge, not Bada Restaurant, but the kitchen often surprises, usually satisfies, and sometimes delights. Call it Asian hip. One can find meats—five-spice pork tenderloin sided with satsuma yams, sweet Korean barbecue ribs, and excellent duck potstickers. But the emphasis is on raw fish: if it's not sushi or sashimi—hamachi and tuna—it's carpaccio of yellow tail. Or it's almost raw, like the de rigueur seared tuna, nicely sided with fried rice noodles and black-bean sauce. The real focus, not quite as heavy as the kidney-vibrating subwoofers, is on the bar menu—nibbles and bites and small plates. Try a hot pot, catfish with lemongrass or short rib with bok choy and cucumber. Bada seats 50 for dinner, then expands to 200 for the evening's festivities. It's as if there's a dress code: black only. This contrasts nicely with the predominant color scheme: white as good teeth, red as an open mouth. *$$; AE, MC, V; no checks; dinner every day; full bar; reservations recommended; street parking; badalounge.com; map:G7* &

WHY GO: While gnawing on sweet ribs, you just might up your coolness quotient.

Bandoleone / ★★★☆

2241 EASTLAKE AVE E, EASTLAKE; 206/329-7959 The *bandoleone*, a small accordion, sings of passion in Latin rhythm. Likewise, Danielle Philippa's Eastlake taverna. Laid-back and less trendy than its newer sibling, Tango (see review), Bandoleone roams the Carribean and beyond for flavors that provoke a loyal following. Pulled pork *carnitas* pulls them in, while sweet onion stuffed with Spanish cheese, sided with pear, apple, and flat bread holds 'em rapt. They smack lips over smoked pork ribs, habanero glazed, tender as an August night. And that's just the small plates. *Cenas* (entrées) rise to similar heights. Among the favorites entrée is Ternéra en Xeres, a veal shank soaked and braised in Spanish cream sherry and served with a rich rice spoon bread. Finish off the night with the *torta de cerezas,* a bittersweet chocolate cake with marinated cherries and vanilla whipped cream. Use of largely organic products induces feelings of health—promptly cancelled out by bar patrons, whose smoke drifts across the small dining room. *$$; MC, V; checks OK; dinner every day, brunch Sat–Sun; full bar; reservations recommended; self and street parking; bandoleone.net; map:GG7* &

WHY GO: Grazing small plates, sipping mojitos, smoking a good stogie in the bar after 10pm.

Barbacoa / ★★★☆

2209 QUEEN ANNE AVE N, QUEEN ANNE; 206/352-6213 Despite its name, this popular little place is not a Tex-Mex barbecue. Chef partners John Calderon and Bob Colegrove have created an intimate, affordable, delicious gem serving "border cuisine," which covers a large area—California, Florida, Texarkana, the Caribbean, and the Gulf of Mexico. The minimalist Iberian interior of iron chandeliers and antiqued walls is countered by a bigger-than-life wall cutout of Roy Rogers, crowds of lively diners, and intense flavors. Some of our favorites are the tangy mesquite-roasted chicken, the gigantic chile relleno stuffed with beets, roasted corn, and asadero cheese, or the crispy-moist pecan-fried catfish. Try the elegant sides like bacon-smoky *frijoles borrachos* or the cheesy, twice-baked, stacked tortilla casserole *chilaquile*. Don't say adios without lifting a fork to desserts such as the Ibarra flan and Mexican chocolate custard crusty with caramel. *$$; AE, DC, MC, V; checks OK; lunch, dinner Tues–Sun; full bar; reservations recommended for 6 or more; street parking; map:GG8* &

WHY GO: Tart Crock o' Key Lime Pie in a graham-pecan pie crust.

Barking Frog / ★★★

14580 NE 145TH ST (WILLOWS LODGE), WOODINVILLE; 425/424-2999 Located in the heart of Woodinville wine country at Willows Lodge, Barking Frog celebrates the senses Northwest-style. Under the leadership of executive chef/general manager Tom Black, the staff delivers a memorable dining experience without a whiff of the pretense one might find in the wine country of a certain state to the south. Large old-growth beams, wooden table tops, and a circular fireplace—a Knights of the Round Table meets Campfire Girls thing—create a room that is comfortably rustic. The menu changes seasonally, but some favored perennial starters are the ahi tuna poke served with ginger sorbet, pickled cucumber, and a soy-ginger sauce, as well as seared foie gras with huckleberry-vodka compote and buttery brioche. Both meat and seafood are expertly prepared. If you feel adventurous, trust Black with British Columbia elk loin and order Alaskan halibut, confident that it will be perhaps the best piece of fish you have ever had. The wine list, awarded "List of the Year" by the Washington Wine Commission in 2002, is an appropriate showcase for Washington wines, arranged by style rather than by standard varietal. Decadent desserts include the chocolate turtle tart and the ever-changing crème brûlée. *$$; AE, DC, DIS, MC, V; checks OK; lunch Mon–Fri, dinner every day, brunch Sat–Sun; full bar; reservations recommended; self parking; willowslodge.com; map:BB2* &

WHY GO: Chef's tasting menu paired with Northwest wines.

Bick's Broadview Grill / ★★

10555 GREENWOOD AVE N, BROADVIEW; 206/367-8481 Since 1977, the neighborhood has been dropping by for dinner and drinks. There's a buzz here. Partly it's because sound finds no solace in all the wood, from exposed rafters to hardwood floor. Partly it's the chiles. These show up in many menu items, from clustered bottles of hot sauce at the tables to a bookshelf crowded with souvenir hot sauces (Liquid Axe, Crying Tongue) donated by loyal locals. Spring rolls—crab, rock shrimp, or duck—jump with red curry sauce, and jalapeño-smoked duck sizzles with a chipotle dipping sauce. For dinner, try the sesame-crusted halibut on a coconut rice cake or the signature Flattop Flattened Chicken, a boneless marinated half chicken cooked on a griddle with a steak weight and garnished with basil oil and goat cheese.

Save room for the warm broken chocolate torte with vanilla ice cream. *$$; MC, V; local checks only (with ID); dinner every day; full bar; reservations accepted for 6 or more; self and street parking; map:DD8* ♿

WHY GO: Tongue afire from chiles and ears ringing from the din feels so good.

Bimbo's Bitchin' Burrito Kitchen / ★

506 E PINE ST, CAPITOL HILL; 206/329-9978 If it's reverence and decorum you want, stroll elsewhere. This tiny taco joint with great food and a sense of humor abounds with Day-Glo Hawaiian decor, loud indie rock, and black-velvet paintings. Expect to wait alongside the young Capitol Hill hipsters, who can't get enough of the humongous burritos, tacos, quesadillas, or nachos paired with sensational cumin-lime sour cream. If you have a complaint, tell it to the customer comment card safely embedded under the glass tabletop. Fuel up here, then shuffle over to the adjacent Cha Cha Lounge, where the same crowd hangs in a cigarette haze. It's got the same mood and music as Bimbo's, plus it serves great margaritas with a fresh, homemade sour blend, no bottled mixes. *$; MC, V; no checks; lunch, dinner every day; full bar; no reservations; street parking; map:J1* ♿

WHY GO: No processed ingredients, except possibly the crowd.

Bis on Main / ★★☆

10213 MAIN ST, BELLEVUE; 425/455-2033 If you say it with proper French feeling, Bis rhymes with peace, which is what you'll find in this cozy, 15-table bistro. It's the handiwork of Joe Vilardi, a warm host well known from his years at Pioneer Square's Il Terrazzo Carmine. Tasteful in muted shades and hung with good art, Bis draws a well-dressed business and social bunch. Nothing on the dinner menu is too challenging, but everything is perfectly executed and expertly served, such as a roasted tenderloin of veal in a basil–white wine sauce. Its plate companion—scallion, sweet corn, and basil risotto—can be had on its own. Mr. V's generous and crisp Dungeness crab cakes take you fondly back to the late 20th century when this dish was on every dinner menu in town. The accompanying celery root, radicchio, and savoy cabbage rémoulade is especially good. *$$; AE, DC, DIS, JCB, MC, V; checks OK; lunch Mon–Fri, dinner every day; full bar; reservations recommended; self parking; bisonmain.com; map:HH3* ♿

WHY GO: Imagine, a dining room where you can hold a quiet conversation.

Bistro Pleasant Beach / ★☆

241 WINSLOW WY W, BAINBRIDGE ISLAND; 206/842-4347 Mediterranean, Moroccan, and Northwest flavors mesh at Hussein and Laura Ramadan's classy island landmark. Flower boxes edge the brick patio outside; inside, it's postmodern Bedouin done in shades of olive, mango, and deep red. For appetizers, try Mediterranean mussels in a creamy sauce infused with lemongrass, Thai basil, cream, and Moroccan spices. Dip tender skewers of lamb in rich curried peanut sauce fragrant with coriander. Gourmet pizzas fired over applewood in the open kitchen's brick hearth come with toppings such as buffalo mozzarella, lamb sausage, pears, or sweet onions. Fresh seafood frolics in a provençal-style tomato-based stew infused with pepper, saffron, and orange zest. Shareable-size desserts, such as the tiramisu parfait-cake, are hard to pass by. *$$; AE, MC, V; checks OK; lunch, dinner Tues–Sun, brunch Sun; beer and wine; reservations recommended; self parking.* &

WHY GO: The most sought-after fair-weather tables on the island.

Bizzarro Italian Cafe / ★★

1307 N 46TH ST, WALLINGFORD; 206/545-7327 The interior looks like an Italian hangover, but the food and service have gotten better. The deliberately claptrappy decor has always separated this place from the herd of neighborhood Italian joints. The rooms are jammed with eccentric kitsch, such as the red dining table with silver- and glassware hanging upside-down from the ceiling. Even the menu slants toward the wacko, such as the Forest Floor Frenzy. Get this for its mix of shiitakes, porto-bellos, walnuts, and roasted garlic tossed with rigatoni in sherry cream, and don't be troubled by the thought of rigatoni and cream on the forest floor. True, the food can still be a bit uneven, but compared to the digs, it's Paxil, baby. We love the steamed mussels in white wine and fresh oregano, as well as the sesame-crusted seared tuna salad with citrus mint vinaigrette. The lamb shank holds a hefty cargo— until you pick it up and delightful chunks fall off the bone. *$$; AE, DIS, MC, V;*

OODLES OF NOODLES

Seattle has a long-term relationship with noodles—whether pho, yakisoba, or chow mein. That's because they're fun for everyone—even kids love them—and they fit every budget. **THAN BROTHERS** (516 Broadway Ave E, Capitol Hill; 206/568-7218; and 7714 Aurora Ave N, Green Lake; 206/527-5973) can be counted upon for great pho and free appetizer cream puffs. **PHO BAC** (1314 S Jackson St, Chinatown/International District; 206/323-4387) has some of the best pho in town. **THAIKU** (5410 Ballard Ave NW, Ballard; 206/706-7807) has soupy slurp-'em-up noodles and lots of dry phad thai–type dishes. Go to **MIKE'S NOODLE HOUSE**, (418 Maynard Ave, Chinatown/International District; 206/389-7099) for wontons and squid balls. **RACHA NOODLES** (23 Mercer St, Queen Anne; 206/281-8883) has a huge list of noodle-y things. Vegans and vegetarians are well served at **BAMBOO GARDEN VEGETARIAN CUISINE** (364 Roy St, Queen Anne; 206/282-6616). Other best noodle bets are the classy **ORRAPIN NOODLE EXPERIENCE** (2208 Queen Anne Ave N, Queen Anne; 206/352-6594), funky **NOODLE RANCH** (2228 2nd Ave, Belltown; 206/728-0463), and **SEVEN STARS PEPPER SZECHUAN RESTAURANT** (1207 S Jackson St, Chinatown/International District; 206/568-6446). Try the tortellini-like potato-cheese *pelmeni* at the **RUSSIAN CAFE YARMARKA** (1530 Post Alley, Pike Place Market; 206/521-9054).

—Michael Hood

checks OK; dinner every day; beer and wine; reservations accepted for 6 or more; street parking; map:FF7 &

WHY GO: Over-the-top decor is a built-in conversation piece.

Black Pearl / ★★

7347 35TH AVE NE, WEDGWOOD; 206/526-5115 / 14602 15TH AVE NE, SHORELINE; 206/365-8989 Many local folks don't bother waiting for tables—takeout and home delivery accounts for about 60 percent of Black Pearl's business. Marlene and Ray Chang and partners opened the Pearl as Panda's more than 13 years ago and they've been going strong ever since. The house-made, hand-rolled noodles that distinguish this place shouldn't be missed. Special Chow Mein's plump and plentiful signature noodles are tossed with shrimp, chicken, beef, and seven different vegetables. The sea bass slices are aromatically steamed with squiggles of oolong tea leaves and served in their own fragrant juices. Another house specialty is the Black Pearl hot pot. Have it with chicken and tofu, with veggies, tofu, and bean threads, with a combo of chicken/prawn/scallop, or with catfish. The diverse bunch of young servers are helpful in guiding the newcomer. *$; AE, DIS, DC, MC, V; checks OK; lunch Mon–Sat, dinner every day; beer and wine; reservations recommended for 6 or more; self and street parking; map:EE6* &

WHY GO: To watch the parade of happy campers carting off takeout.

BEST PLACE FOR BREAKFAST?

"Kingfish on Sundays, without a doubt. Bring a pal, order a plate of crab cakes eggs Benedict and another of their bread pudding. Both of you will go home gastronomically and spiritually fulfilled."

Melanie McFarland, Seattle Post-Intelligencer *TV critic*

Blue Onion Bistro / ★★★

5801 ROOSEVELT WY NE, UNIVERSITY DISTRICT; 206/729-0579 It might be lodged in a 1950s gas station. It might be filled with Depression-era knick-knacks and dooleywhacks from a time when Barnum and Bailey posters didn't even mention the Ringling Bros. It might have a deep, light, ironic sense of humor. But Blue Onion Bistro is no joke. The Blue Salad is zesty with apples, chicken, and blue cheese, and the daily soups kick butter. There is a lot of comfort food, but it's all been zapped into full flavored, imaginative new-American fare. Fat Man's Chicken—crunchy, buttermilk fried—comes with Top Secret Sweet Chili Sauce. Chef Scott Simpson turns out a mean mac-and-cheese, rendered extraordinary by a cheddar–blue cheese mix, and the Amazing Ever Changing Pasta Experiment is just that. Chef/co-owner Susan Jensen is an accomplished baker and pastry chef—her robust herbed dinner rolls are served warm in an Easter basket and her

68

desserts, posted on a blackboard, change regularly. *$$; MC, V; checks OK; lunch Tues–Fri, dinner Tues–Sun; beer and wine; reservations recommended; self and street parking; blueonionchef@aol.com; map:EE7* &

WHY GO: The kitschy location is a gas.

Brasa / ★★★☆

2107 3RD AVE, BELLTOWN; 206/728-4220 Recently, Brasa owners Tamara Murphy and Bryan Hill improved on what was already one of the most striking restaurants in the city. Awash in warm orange tones and amber light, the dual-tiered dining room is still sumptuous, while the copper-topped bar, cinched in tuck-and-roll glitter vinyl, remains one of the hippest spots in town. But gone are the white tablecloths along with any sign that might suggest Brasa was built exclusively for "them." Hill is at the door waiting to welcome everyone into his dining room, while in the kitchen Murphy cooks honest food (often over live coals) for her guests. From the bar and dinner menus, the perfume of cataplana mussels marooned in curry, coriander, and coconut milk turns heads, as does the sensual beef carpaccio with minced shallot and heady white truffle oil. Savory favorites include the Oregon hare with figs, pine nuts, and potato dumplings, as well as the grilled squab with wilted spinach, house-cured bacon, and goat cheese. Tarry over a glass of red wine from Hill's glass-pour list or shake up the routine with a frozen lemon mousse with raspberries. *$$; AE, DC, MC, V; checks OK; dinner every day; full bar; reservations recommended; self parking; brasa.com; map:G7* &

WHY GO: Best happy hour in town. Where else can you get steak frites for $7?

Buenos Aires Grill / ★★

220 VIRGINIA ST, BELLTOWN; 206/441-7076 Oh so tantalizing, tempting, arousing. And that's just the weekend-evening tango dancers, gliding among the tables and wooden booths, amid the old Argentine ranch trappings hung on walls of brick. It's the meat that matters here, far far away from your CFO's steak-house cliché. Meats are from the parrilla, a mesquite wood-fired grill that chef/co-owner Marianne Zdobysz traveled to Argentina to master after leaving a long stint at Madison Park Cafe. Buenos Aires Grill embodies the long-held dream of co-owner Argentinian Marco Casas Beaux, who has had a hand in more than a few Seattle restaurants (including Gitano in Madison Valley). Order the *parrillada mixta* and get more than a piece of the pampas. You get *vacio*, hangar steak; *asado de tira*, beef short ribs; *entraña*, skirt steak; *mollejas*, beef sweetbreads; and chorizo sausage. None is a choice cut, a filet mignon, say. You have to order that on its own, and it's a big hummer, *chimichurri* marinated. But all cuts are flavorful and compel you to order a glass or two of Malbec, to make you feel like a real *vaquero*. A glance at the leather-bound menu reveals that you can start your meatfest with yet more meat. The Picadas is a selection of chorizo, beef tongue, mortadella, salami, and pro- sciutto, along with peppers, cheese, and olives. The Argentine *empanadas*, deep-fried turnovers, can be filled with vegetables, but more to the point, with ground lamb or beef. Surprisingly, the dessert menu is void of beef. But it does list the festive *dulce de leche crepes*, filled with liquid caramel, flamed with rum. When crowded, the joint gets very, very loud. *$$; AE, DC, MC, V; checks OK; dinner every day; full bar; reservations recommended; street parking; map:H7*

WHY GO: Dr. Atkins would approve.

Burrito Loco Taqueria / ★★☆

4508 UNIVERSITY VILLAGE PLACE, UNIVERSITY DISTRICT (AND BRANCH); 206/729-2240 As with its Crown Hill cousin of the same name (9211 Holman Rd NW), this colorful outdoors-meet-indoors cafe plates up sunny Mexican *especialdades*. The huge namesake Burrito Loco is jammed with meat—*asada, al pastor,* or *pollo*—guacamole, salsa, cheese, rice, and beans. We also like the *machaca* (shredded) beef burrito. Soups are a specialty here, particularly *menudo*, the tripe-laden morning-after therapy (available Friday through Sunday), and the cure-all *albondigas* with golf ball–size meatballs, marooned in a chipotle-spiked chicken broth. It's a sign of authenticity in any taqueria to see tongue tacos—good news even if you're not adventurous enough to eat them. Order instead the spicy chorizo or barbecued pork tacos *suaves* (soft) and you will know the joys of a perfectly seasoned *parrilla* (grill). There are numerous vegetarian possibilities, including quesadillas, fat chiles rellenos, and huevos rancheros. *$; MC, V; checks OK; lunch, dinner every day; beer and wine; no reservations; self parking; map:FF6* ♿

WHY GO: *Pipian*, chicken in a sauce of crushed seeds from the owners' native Cuautla, Jalisco.

Cactus / ★★★

4220 E MADISON ST, MADISON PARK; 206/324-4140 / 121 PARK LN, KIRKLAND; 425/893-9799 Cactus owes its popularity to the consistent quality, variety, and originality of its Mexican and Southwestern food. It's been such a hit in Madison Park that they've opened another in downtown Kirkland. Bright painted tables and hanging peppers make it festive, its pioneering tapas menu makes it delicious. Among the favorites are tuna poke Mexicano, with jicama, cucumber, and prickly pear; and the $10 nachos, which are worth at least $11. The usual Mexican entrées such as fajitas, enchiladas, and tacos are worth doing, but this is the place to try the more unusual dishes, including goat-cheese pollo relleno Chimayo enchilada—blue-corn tortillas layered with chicken, chorizo, and green chile sauce; Jamaican chicken in a novel banana jerk sauce; or pork chunks roasted in banana leaves with spicy achiote, corn tortillas, and sizzling habanero *escabeche*. To put out the heat, there are plenty of fruit drinks, margaritas, and beers, but the wine list is limited. Bananas *dulce* and three-milk Cuban flan are the must-have desserts. *$$; AE, DC, DIS, MC, V; checks OK; lunch Mon–Sat, dinner every day; full bar; reservations recommended for 5 or more; street parking; cactusrestaurants.com; map:GG7* ♿

WHY GO: Tapas and top-shelf margaritas.

Cafe Flora / ★★★

2901 E MADISON ST, MADISON VALLEY; 206/325-9100 Say you're a carnivore. Say a friend asks you to vegetarian Flora. Beg off? Don't do it. You won't miss the fauna for a minute. Portobello Wellington will ensure that, with its mushroom-pecan pâté wrapped in puff pastry. Meaty. Sample the Oaxaca tacos—corn tortillas stuffed with spicy mashed potatoes, cheddar, and smoked mozzarella. Salads, like everything here, reflect the seasons—a summer offering might be chantaboon noodles and summer rolls; noodles plus ginger cilantro pistou; Asian vegetables and stone fruit stir-fried in black-bean chili oil with a caramel-ginger dipping sauce and guava berry coulis; an organic nectarine salad with toasted pecans, orange marmalade dressing, and Bleu de Basque cheese. Vegans have items to choose from too, and the kitchen will also adapt items on the menu. Flora serves beer and wine now, and the garden patio is lovely. *$$; MC, V; checks OK; lunch Tues–Fri, dinner Tues–Sun, brunch Sat–Sun; beer and wine; reservations recommended for 8 or more; self parking; www.cafeflora.com; map:HH6* &

WHY GO: Food that could convert even a carnivore to veganship.

Cafe Juanita / ★★★✫

9702 NE 12TH PL, KIRKLAND; 425/823-1505 It's still a humble little converted white-brick house, but its reputation—on both sides of the lake—is like a brick house. The theme is northern Italy. The execution by Holly Smith is precise; the presentation flawless. A professional waitstaff brings elegant cuisine changing with the seasons, created lovingly from first-rate ingredients, including herbs and such from the kitchen garden viewed through dining-room windows. Grilled octopus with fennel might start a meal, as could a pear salad with pine nuts, Parmigiano-Reggiano, and white truffle oil. Tagliatelle with sea urchin–white truffle crema could be a destination, or a stopping point before a whole roasted fish, rib-eye chop, or Muscovy duck breast, each prepared with flair. The dessert list is formidable and irresistible, with select cheeses or Valrhona-chocolate-truffle cake with vanilla gelato, espresso sauce, and crisp almond wafer. After training at Dahlia Lounge and Brasa, Smith is now the one to emulate. The carefully considered wine list has plenty of Italian bottles, with a fair Northwest representation and a range for varied pocketbooks and tastes. *$$$; AE, MC, V; no checks; dinner Tues–Sun; full bar; reservations recommended; self and street parking; cafejuanita.com; map:DD4* &

WHY GO: Navigational pride in having actually found this hidden gem.

Cafe Lago / ★★✫

2305 24TH AVE E, MONTLAKE; 206/329-8005 Locals converge nightly at this cafe near the Montlake Bridge for wonderful Italian fare from chef/owners Jordi Viladas and Carla Leonardi. Start with the antipasto plate, stacked with eggplant, bruschetta with olivata, goat cheese, roasted peppers, mozzarella, roasted garlic bulbs, prosciutto, and Asiago cheese (the plate is also available meatless), or the City of Seattle Eggplant—grilled eggplant wedges marinated in olive oil, tomato, *balsamico*, and garlic, with a wedge of Gorgonzola served with thick slices of country Italian bread from La Panzanella (see sidebar). Try one of the thin-crust wood-fired pizzas, perhaps one with *salsiccia*, roasted red peppers, marinara, and fontina. Viladas's wood-fired grill turns out a New York steak marinated in *basalmico* and herbs, covered with Gorgonzola, grilled onions, and radicchio. Finish up with a slice of Leonardi's chocolate truffle cake served in a puddle of espresso *crema inglese*. *$$; AE, DC, DIS, MC, V; checks OK; dinner Tues–Sun; full bar; reservations recommended; street parking; map:GG6* &

WHY GO: Soufflé-like lasagne that should be ordered before 8pm lest they run out.

Cafe Nola / ★★

101 WINSLOW WY E, BAINBRIDGE ISLAND; 206/842-3822 At this stylish bistro run by spouses Kevin (the former sous-chef at Seattle's Marco's Supperclub) and Whitney Warren come pleasingly eclectic dishes. Popular with lunch crowds are hearty soups—from roasted eggplant to black-bean portobello; the grilled Kodiak salmon sandwich, piled high with greens, red onion, and roasted yellow pepper aioli; and tortilla crab salad. Dinner hour brings forth Sichuan ribs basted with hoisin-pineapple sauce and sweet-potato fries; pan-seared scallops served over yellow-corn grit cakes with roasted pepper-garlic sauce; and not-to-miss desserts, such as the triple-layer chocolate hazelnut torte. The tight wine list spotlights a "wine maker of the month" along with a selection of favorite cocktails and mixed drinks. *$$; MC, V; checks OK; lunch Mon–Fri, dinner Wed–Sun, brunch Sat–Sun; beer and wine; reservations recommended; street parking; cafenola.com* &

WHY GO: Louisiana-style seafood jambalaya and sidewalk dining in summer.

BEST PLACE TO SAMPLE A MICROBREW OR THREE?

"Elliott Bay Brewery in [West Seattle's] Alaska Junction. The food is terrific, too!"

Greg Nickels, mayor of Seattle

Calcutta Grill / ★★

15500 SIX PENNY LN, NEWCASTLE; 425/793-4646 Not to be confused with the city in India, Calcutta is also the name of a golf betting game. That explains why this isn't a curry house but, rather, the Golf Club at Newcastle's clubhouse restaurant, easily the best around. Destination dining offers a stunning view from high atop a bluff southeast of Seattle—Lake Washington, the downtown skyline, and the jagged Olympic Mountains. The food in this castle-like edifice is adequate and a little pricey, but everything is well prepared. A familiar roster of salmon, halibut, steaks, and pasta cover the basic needs. Especially good is the smoky prime rib, with mashers jazzed up with Cougar Mountain cheddar. The regular wine list carries mostly domestic bottles with a Northwest emphasis, with quite a few under $30, plus a reserve list ranging up, up, and away, like a Tiger Woods eight-iron shot. Send the young 'uns to the Kids Corner at the popular Sunday brunch, while the adults enjoy a buffet complete with carved-meat, crepe, and omelet stations, and sushi, hot entrées, and desserts. The Wooly Toad Cigar Bar, a tony retreat, has a dress code, and no cheap stogies. *$$$; AE, DC, DIS, MC, V; checks OK; lunch Mon–Sat, dinner every day, brunch Sun; full bar; reservations recommended; self parking; cammyshepard@newcastle.com; newcastlegolf.com; map:JJ2* &

WHY GO: Best minigolf (Rusty Putter Putting Course, $10) of any restaurant around.

Calypso Caribbean Kitchen / ★★☆

7917 ROOSEVELT WY NE, MAPLE LEAF; 206/525-5118 On an unremarkable corner in the Maple Leaf neighborhood, the sign for Calypso is easy to miss, but the spiced aromas wafting into the street are advertisement enough. Inside chef/owner Paul Decker combines European-influenced Caribbean cuisine with classical American tastes. Decker's grandmother was from Trinidad, and though he honors her with some of the recipes she handed down, his kitchen sails around the archipelago to Jamaica, Cuba, Curaçao, Puerto Rico, and all over the West Indies. Alongside appetizers such as fried plantains and Cuban black-bean soup, Jamaican jerked meats and seafood figure prominently. Decker also offers five superior cuts of meat, ranging from pork chops to a nine-ounce beef tenderloin prepared two ways: crusted with black peppercorns and finished in a brandy-and-chutney sauce, or marinated West Indies–style in pineapple juice, molasses, and white vinegar. Conclude your island getaway with Key lime pie. *$$; DIS, MC, V; checks OK; dinner Tues–Sun; beer and wine; no reservations; self parking; map:EE7* ♿

WHY GO: Bright red conch chowder and Keshy Yena, a fondue-like appetizer.

Campagne / ★★★★
Café Campagne / ★★★

86 PINE ST (INN AT THE MARKET), PIKE PLACE MARKET; 206/728-2800 / 1600 POST ALLEY, PIKE PLACE MARKET; 206/728-2233 Tucked away in a courtyard in Pike Place Market and adjacent to the Inn at the Market, rain or shine, Campagne is a ray of light from sun-drenched southern France. As not to distract your attention from what owner Peter Lewis calls "the adventure at the table," the candlelit room and bar are warmly (and newly as of 2002) finished with cherrywood floors, farmhouse-yellow walls, and sumptuous draperies. Chef Daisley Gordon's menu is a passionate union of Northwest and French influences. Don't pass up the earthy leeks in truffle vinaigrette, served with crostini and perfect with a glass of chenin blanc from the Loire Valley. Worthy hors d'oeuvres include pan-roasted sea scallops over carrot purée; or the *tartare de boeuf aux herbes*, raw beef with herbs, capers, and parsley. (A collection of tasty "petit plats" (small plates) was added to the menu in early 2004.) For the main event, dishes range from grilled king salmon, served over chard potato gnocchi and pancetta in a sorrel cream sauce with oyster mushrooms, to grilled lamb loin and house-made lamb *crepinette* accompanied by potato galette, olives, and a red wine–fennel glaze. Pastry chef Asia Johnson haunts the Market, gathering local fruits and berries for tarts, ice creams, and granités. The crème brûlée tasting (a selection of three) is our idea of heaven. Wine director and frequent host Shawn Mead has composed a wine list that calls to mind vineyards of France. Smoking is permitted in the bar after 10pm.

Café Campagne, located just below its sibling, offers patrons a slice of French cafe life morning (on weekends), noon, and night. Prepare yourself for butter and lots of it. Weekend brunch is very popular; expect to wait for a table, perhaps at the counter with a sparkling *kir volant*. You could have a healthful bowl of house-made granola and yogurt, but then you might miss the *oeufs en Meurette*, two poached eggs resting on garlic croutons marooned in a red wine and foie gras sauce with pearl onions, bacon, and champignons. Lunch offers a lighter-than-air quiche du jour served with green salad, a line-up of *croques* (Parisian ham sandwiches), and the celebrated lamb burger. Dinners often start with a warmed asparagus topped with finely diced egg, tomato, parsley, and *beurre fondu*, and could end with pan-roasted, boneless trout with steamed potatoes and the very, very French almond, lemon, and brown butter pan sauce. Ooh-la-la! *$$$, $$; AE, DC, MC, V; no checks; dinner every day (Campagne), lunch Mon–Fri, dinner every day, brunch Sat–Sun (Café Campagne); full bar; reservations recommended; valet and street parking; campagne restaurant.com; map:I7* &

WHY GO: Cassoulet in winter and courtyard dining in summer at Campagne.

BEST CITY VIEW?

"Kerry Park, of course, on Queen Anne Hill—with exhilarating skyline, Mount Rainier as backdrop (on clear days), the Olympics to the west, and ferries chugging atmospherically across the Sound."

Michael Medved, film critic and host of syndicated radio talk show originating at KNWX AM 770

Canlis / ★★★★

2576 AURORA AVE N, QUEEN ANNE; 206/283-3313 Though star executive chef Greg Atkinson has moved on, after breathing new culinary life into Seattle's favorite special-occasion view restaurant, the beat goes on with co-chefs Jeff Taton and Aaron Wright. Those now celebrating their umpteenth whatever will still find old favorites, and the verve and zing that helped land Canlis a Top 50 rating from *Gourmet* magazine in 2001. The Northwest Seafood Extravaganza starts a meal with three tiers of fresh delights. Kobe-style Washington beef comes as impeccable steak tartare, or having done a turn in the famous copper broiler. Other broiler items—salmon, ahi, more steaks—enjoy the company of reliable sides, such as a mighty baked potato that the menu forever shall include. Dungeness crab legs come encased in a chickpea crust with ponzu and Asian vegetables. Be sure to give a half-hour notice for the knockout Grand Marnier soufflé. Sommelier Shyn Bjornholm presides over the massive and much-lauded wine list, which ranges from a $1,000 bottle to many options in the $30 range. No more kimono-wearing servers, a nice touch since some are now male. The dress code of yore has eased a bit, but men wear a jacket. Women, the restroom is indeed a haven. Expect to be treated like royalty and to pay accordingly in this beautifully delicious anachronism. *$$$$; AE, DC, DIS, MC, V; checks OK; dinner Mon–Sat; full bar; reservations required; valet parking; canlis.com; map:GG7* &

WHY GO: Sheer indulgence, telepathic valets.

Carmelita / ★★★

7314 GREENWOOD AVE N, GREENWOOD; 206/706-7703 Here is a vegetarian restaurant that the most bloodthirsty carnivore can love. With chef
Dan Braun's innovative and tasty menu, Carmelita transcends the meat-free
eating laboratories to which vegetarians are usually sentenced. And—it's gorgeous.
Owners Kathryn Newmann and Michael Hughes, visual artists in their spare time,
transformed a dilapidated retail space into a theatrically lit, art-filled haven of color
and texture. Neighbors from Greenwood and Phinney Ridge embraced Carmelita
warmly from the beginning and the sophisticated, seasonal vegetarian menu remains
enticing. Expect to find such entrées as English pea agnolotti stuffed with asparagus,
foraged mushrooms, and truffle butter sauce, or portobello mushroom roulade with
green beans, roasted-shallot mashed potatoes, and mushroom demi-glace. *$$; MC,
V; local checks only; dinner Tues–Sun; beer and wine; reservations recommended;
street parking; reserve@carmelita.net; carmelita.net; map:EE8* &
WHY GO: Inventively flesh-free fare and an intimate patio ideal for special occa-
sions.

Cascadia Restaurant / ★★★½

2328 1ST AVE, BELLTOWN; 206/448-8884 Cascadia benefits from its spare but
luxurious space and its chef/owner Kerry Sear, who uses indigenous foods and
flavors of Cascadia (the region he defines as between the Pacific Ocean and Mon-
tana) and beyond to include Northern California and New York's Hudson Valley. A
sculpted-glass wall between the dining room and kitchen has water sluicing through
it like rain against a window. The bar now offers pocketbook- and palate-friendly
noshes ranging from skillet-roasted prawns to cheeseburgers. While the dining room
features such à la carte exotica as an appetizer of foie gras torchon with brandied
cherries and black truffle jam or entrées such as pork tenderloin served with grilled
peaches, fingerling potatoes, and grilled eggplant. Or, choose from one of three
seven-course tating menues, including an ambitious all-vegetarian selection; a new
three-course menu is a deal at $25. The wine list features hand-crafted wines of char-
acter and quality, chosen for their ability to flatter Sear's cuisine. *$$$$; AE, DC, DIS,
MC, V; no checks; dinner Mon–Sat; full bar; reservations recommended; street
parking; www.cascadiarestaurant.com; map:G7* &
WHY GO: Dollar burgers during happy hour and an alpine martini with a Dou-
glas-fir snowball float.

Cassis / ★★★

2359 10TH AVE E, CAPITOL HILL; 206/329-0580 Many joints call them-
selves bistros, but this one's the real deal. Looking like it's been there since
before the French liberation, Cassis serves its neighborhood well but attracts
savvy diners from around the region. It's cozy, comfortable, and sexy, humming
along under owner Jeff Fike and serving moderately priced, finely executed French
bistro fare. Gallic classics including cassoulet, coq au vin, boeuf bourguignon, calf's
liver, pan-roasted capon, and steak with a tall haystack of perfect frites will put you
in mind of the last time you strolled the Left Bank, or at least allow you to imagine
that you once did. Desserts range from kid pleasers such as *oeufs à la niege*, floating

islands of poached hazelnut meringue in a nutty custard, to a very grown-up goat-cheese tart in a port-kissed rhubarb coulis. PS—There's a nifty little wine list and a small bar just made for sipping *pastis. $$; AE, MC, V; local checks only; dinner every day; full bar; reservations recommended; self and street parking; reservations@ cassisbistro.com; cassisbistro.com; map:GG6* &

WHY GO: Any minute, Humphrey Bogart might stroll in with Ingrid Bergman on his arm.

Chandler's Crabhouse / ★★

901 FAIRVIEW AVE N, SOUTH LAKE UNION; 206/223-2722 Along with renovation of its reception area and bar, Chandler's Crabhouse has refocused its strategy away from the Northeast to closer to home. Washington native and executive chef Dan Thiessen delivers an insightful Northwest dining experience. Try the ahi poke dressed in soy-miso vinaigrette or the decadent whisky-kissed crab soup. Although he serves a crabcentric menu, Thiessen is adept with all types of fish. The smoked Alaskan halibut served with grilled asparagus and porcini risotto regularly knocks us out. With direction and overdue media attention, waitstaff brim quietly with pride and consequently service is personal and competent. The extensive wine list is heavy on the regional labels. Even the desserts have a local angle. Warm crisps with seasonal fruit come with almond-streusel topping and vanilla ice cream. *$$; AE, DC, MC, V; local checks only; lunch Mon–Fri, dinner every day, brunch Sat–Sun; full bar; reservations recommended; valet parking; www.chandlers.com; map:D1* &

WHY GO: Guest dock for boat-commuting diners and an armada of seaplanes landing and taking off overhead.

Chez Shea / ★★★
Shea's Lounge / ★★★☆

94 PIKE ST, 3RD FLOOR, PIKE PLACE MARKET; 206/467-9990 Romance is always on the menu at this gem tucked on the top floor of the Corner Market Building, with a view through the grand arched windows of Elliott Bay and beyond. Dinner is a prix-fixe affair, with three of the four courses preset and a choice of five entrées. As they have since Sandy Shea opened the place in 1983, menus reflect the bounty of the season, employing ingredients fresh from the market stalls below. A summer meal might begin with sweet potato and lemongrass bisque with Thai peanut salsa and chive oil, then a warm Penn Cove mussel salad with caramelized onions, saffron, and sherry. Entrée selections usually include fish, meat, and game along the lines of pan-roasted wild king salmon with a Thai cucumber salad or a confit of Muscovy duck leg with herbed crepe, carrot purée, and red-wine reduction; there's also usually a vegetarian option. Service is always sure and gracious.

Shea's Lounge is a sexy bistro wed to Chez Shea by a common door. The menu offers an à la carte menu that echoes and expands upon the main room's offerings. The perfect place for a date or a friendly gathering before or after an evening on the town. *$$$, $$; AE, MC, V; no checks; dinner Tues–Sun; full bar; reservations recommended (Chez Shea); valet parking Thurs–Sat, validation for Market garage, and street parking; dinner@chezshea.com; chezshea.com; map:J8*

WHY GO: Love blossoms and/or matures above the Market.

Chinoise Café / ★★

12 BOSTON ST, QUEEN ANNE (AND BRANCHES); 206/284-6671 Eclectically but assuredly Asian, Chinoise Cafés are reliable places for Vietnamese salad rolls, Japanese sukiyaki, Thai curries, Chinese stir-fry, and noodles. The original, sunny Queen Anne location fills nightly, despite the speedy—some say rushed—service. Nevertheless, one dish, the vibrant Vietnamese lemon grass chicken salad, always drags us up the hill. For a multicourse meal, start with delicate summer salad rolls or an order of potstickers and move onto General Tsao's Chicken or a *yakisoba*. Chinoise on Madison (2801 E Madison St, Madison Valley; 206/323-0171) is calmer, reflecting that quieter neighborhood, and has a somewhat larger menu venturing farther into the "pan" of pan-Asian. Try the broiled five-spice Cornish hen or the sensational fish of the day, served with Chinese long beans in a tangy tamarind-basil oyster sauce. Opened two years ago in the Uwajimaya Village, the third Chinoise Café (610 5th Ave S, Chinatown/International District; 206/254-0413) offers some Korean dishes and a full bar in the neon-lit lounge. The newest Chinoise on 45th (1618 N 45th St, Wallingford; 206/633-1160) in Wallingford is a grown-up version of its Queen Anne sibling with a more sophisticated service style. *$; AE, DC, DIS, MC, V; no checks; lunch Mon–Fri, dinner every day; beer and wine (full bar at International District location); no reservations; street parking (validated lot parking at Uwajimaya Village); chinoisecafe.com; map:GG8* &

WHY GO: Quick quality lunches and fresh but not fussy sushi.

BEST UNKNOWN GARDEN STROLL?

"Kubota Gardens, South Seattle. Waterfalls, ponds, beautifully manicured Japanese landscaping, hillsides, vistas— an unexpected refuge in an unlikely neighborhood."

Michael Medved, film critic and host of syndicated radio talk show that originates at KNWX AM 770

Chinook's at Salmon Bay / ★★

1900 W NICKERSON ST, INTERBAY; 206/283-4665 The Anthony's folks (see review) are using the right bait here at their showplace in the heart of Fisherman's Terminal. The light-industrial decor—steel countertops, visible ventilation ducts—are secondary to the bustle of the working marina outside the big windows. The Anthony's group owns its own wholesale fish business, so count on the fish being immaculately fresh. And count on the oyster stew being creamy, with wonderful chunks of yearling Quilcene oysters throughout. The regular menu is large and can be overwhelming. Fail-safe choices are the tender halibut 'n' chips and the mahi mahi tacos. The daily special sheet is the place to be, with

GO ON, GET BAKED

Whether you hunger for a crusty Como loaf, a seeded baguette, or a chewy ciabatta, the region's best, rustic, free-formed loaves can be found in Seattle.

Some of the most widely distributed—with good reason—breads in the city come from s **GRAND CENTRAL BAKING COMPANY** (214 1st Ave S, Pioneer Square; 206/622-3644), known for loaves with a golden, nutty crust and chewy interior; **LA PANZANELLA** (1314 E Union St, Downtown; 206/325-5217), specializing in dense, Italian-style breads; and **MACRINA BAKERY** (2408 1st Ave, Belltown; 206/448-4032; and 615 W McGraw St, Queen Anne; 206/283-5900; see review). Other not-to-be-missed bakeries include the **ESSENTIAL BAKING COMPANY** (1604 N 34th St, Fremont; 206/545-0444) and the modest **TALL GRASS BAKERY** (5907 24th Ave NW, Ballard; 206-706-0991), both of which specialize in organic products.

But Seattleites do not live on bread alone. We crave sweets, too. Next door to Tall Grass Bakery waits the incomparable **CAFÉ BESALU** (5909 24th Ave NW, Ballard;

offerings such as wild king salmon charred with sun-dried tomato-basil butter or garlic-baked prawns with lemon and gremolata. There's a great all-you-can-eat tempura bar—don't miss the fat, tender *panko*-coated onion rings. For dessert, try the warm wild-blackberry cobbler. *$$; AE, MC, V; checks OK; breakfast Sat–Sun, lunch, dinner every day; full bar; no reservations; self parking; anthonysrestaurants.com; map:FF8* &

WHY GO: Great local draft beer selection and front-row viewing of commercial fishermen.

Chiso / ★★☆

3520 FREMONT AVE, FREMONT; 206/632-3430 Chiso is one of those very good Japanese neighborhood restaurants that Seattle is known for. The tasteful, Zen-like atmosphere with its khaki and sage walls and open ductwork focuses the diner on what's really important—the fish. The emphasis is on sushi: artful owner Tai Chi Kitamura is a sushi chef who, sharp knives flashing, always seems to be there, slicing the *toro* and *chutoro*, shaping the nigiri, making rolls and fishy small talk. The hot kitchen does well, too—don't miss the *panko*-breaded halibut or the geoduck sauté with shiitake mushrooms and butter. You'll be elbow-to-elbow with Japanese businessmen, chefs taking busman's holidays, Fremont hipsters, construction workers, and sushi cultists who all flock to this busy place. *$$; MC V; no checks; lunch, Mon–Fri, dinner every day; beer and wine; street parking; info@chisoseattle.com; chisoseattle.com; map:FF8* &

WHY GO: Hot Japanese comestibles.

206/789-1463). Stepping into this small, buttery patisserie you are assured to find the best pain au chocolat, orange brioche, and croissant this side of the Seine. Also nearby is **LARSEN BROTHERS DANISH PASTRY** (8000 24th Ave NW, Ballard; 206/782-8285), the home of Seattle's exceptionally flaky Danish. In the Market, let yourself be wooed by the calorific aromas spilling out of **LE PANIER VERY FRENCH BAKERY** (1902 Pike Pl, Pike Place Market; 206/441-3699). The Eastside's **HOFFMAN'S FINE PASTRIES** (226 Park Place Center, Kirkland; 425/828-0926) is a best bet.

In the midst of the mass-produced, macrodoughnut movement, a handful of hand-made doughnuts have emerged. Top among them are **TOP POT DOUGHNUTS** (609 Summit Ave E, Capitol Hill; 206/323-7841), which has a new flagship retail site, doughnut production facility, and coffee roasting plant at its Belltown location (2124 5th Ave; 206/728-1966). For an organic twist, visit **MIGHTY-O** doughnuts (2110 N 55th St, Green Lake; 206/547-0335).

—*Suzanne Schmalzer*

Chutneys / ★

519 IST AVE N, QUEEN ANNE (AND BRANCHES); 206/284-6799 Chutneys' menu suffers from being too large and trying to please too many people. Head for the hearty Indian dishes and stay away from the salads. Two solid choices are the toasted coriander-and-paprika-dusted calamari with coconut-tamarind chutney and the curried mussels with cashew curry-wine sauce. Entrées can be ordered with varying degrees of heat, to be chased with an Indian beer or a mango *lassi*, a sweet fruit smoothie. Try the lamb medallions marinated in saffron yogurt and roasted in the tandoor, the super-hot vertical clay oven, or the spinach mush-room chicken breast and the tandoori chicken in brilliant pomegranate curry. Don't forget the Indian breads, such as the *Kabuli* naan stuffed with nuts, raisins, and cherries. Chutneys Grille on the Hill (605 15th Ave E, Capitol Hill; 206/726-1000) is a more laid-back sister to the Queen Anne branch or the bustling Chutneys Bistro (Wallingford Center, 1815 N 45th St; 206/634-1000). *$; AE, DC, DIS, MC, V; local checks only; lunch Mon–Sat; dinner every day; full bar; reservations recommended; street parking; map:GG7* &

WHY GO: Milky, cardamom-infused Masala tea.

Coastal Kitchen / ★★☆

429 15TH AVE E, CAPITOL HILL; 206/322-1145 Peter Levy and Jeremy Hardy—of Queen Anne's 5 Spot Cafe, Wallingford's Jitterbug Cafe, Fauntleroy's Endolyne Joe's (see reviews), and University Village's Atlas Foods—always invent restaurants with humor and an interesting idea. Coastal Kitchen's idea is coastal foods in general, but southern American ones in particular. We're still swept away to the Louisiana Gulf with Satchmo's Red Beans and Rice or the andouille sausage sandwich, or to Baja with the fried yuca (cassava) puffs stuffed with manchego cheese. Neighbors flock in for breakfast, served all day with smoked salmon omelets, hash browns, and corn griddle cakes, as well as for the beer, pupus, and Key lime pie. *$$; MC, V; local checks only; breakfast, lunch, dinner every day; full bar; reservations recommended for 6 or more; street parking; chowfoods.com; map:HH6* &

WHY GO: Coastal culinary explorations called "Food Festivals."

BEST PLACE TO VIEW ART?

"Francine Seders Gallery in Greenwood. Not the scene of Pioneer Square and a lot better art."

Charles R. Cross, author of Heavier Than Heaven: The Biography of Kurt Cobain

---

Dahlia Lounge / ★★★★

2001 4TH AVE, DOWNTOWN; 206/682-4142 For a brief, dark moment after Dahlia moved into new digs several years ago, Tom Douglas's predictably unpredictable menus were lost, having taken a hard turn toward Asian cuisines. Today, under the direction of Tom Douglas, head chef Mark Fuller has returned the legendary restaurant to its state of grace. Matching a spirited decor of crimson, gold brocade, and papier-mâché fish lanterns is an exuberant, global approach from the kitchen. We confess to rarely ordering from the regularly updated main dishes on the right side of the menu—too many delights on the left side. That's where you'll find appetizers such as crispy veal sweetbreads masterfully presented with crayfish, fava beans, and roasted cauliflower to curried vegetable samosas with tamarind and coriander dipping sauces, and the always tempting "Little Tastes from the Sea Bar" list starring a seasonally changing Sea Bar Sampler that never fails to serve up tender chunks of smoked salmon with spicy mustard and some incarnation of fatty tuna. Select entrées based on their accompaniments because better sautéed bitter greens and toasted farro you will not find. Dessert can be such down-to-earth yet cosmic delectables as a bag of doughnuts fried to order with mascarpone and raspberry, plum, and apricot jams. *$$$; AE, DC, DIS, MC, V; local checks only; lunch Mon–Fri, dinner every day; full bar; reservations recommended; valet parking; tomdouglas.com; map:H6* &

WHY GO: Signature triple coconut cream pie and lighting that takes off 10 years.

Daniel's Broiler Prime Steak & Chops / ★★★☆

809 FAIRVIEW PLACE N, LAKE UNION (AND BRANCHES); 206/621-8262 It's all about meat at this luxurious classic steak house on the southernmost shore of Lake Union. Masculine and well-appointed in copper, wood, and windows, the yachts glide by in splendiferous lake views at this swanky Schwartz Brothers flagship. There's prime seafood too, like giant Australian lobster tails, salmon, halibut, and Dungeness crab, but the deal's definitely the meat. The beef is Midwestern, corn-fed, aged, cut huge, and cooked to order in the space-age 1,800°F-broilers. We suggest one of the mighty porterhouses, T-bones, or the herb-encrusted, cut-it-with-a-fork prime rib, but Daniel's does a great job on the veal chop and the French cut lamb chops as well. Expect slavish service, a mighty wine list, and all the usual steak-house choices—Caesar salads, garlic mashers, or a baked potato the size of your shoe. All three Daniel's Broilers—the others are in Leschi (200 Lake Washington Blvd; 206/329-4191) and Bellevue (Seafirst Building, 10500 NE 8th St; 425/462-4662)—have great water views, stellar service, and large, well-priced, and praiseworthy wine lists. *$$$; AE, DC, DIS, MC, V; checks OK; lunch Mon–Fri, dinner every day; full bar; reservations recommended; valet parking; info@schwartzbros.com; www.schwartzbros.com; map:HH6* &

WHY GO: Lake views and big meat, done well—even when well-done.

The District / ★★☆

4507 BROOKLYN AVE NE (UNIVERSITY TOWER HOTEL), UNIVERSITY DISTRICT; 206/547-4134 From this cavernous basement warren in the historic University Tower Hotel (formerly the Edward Meany Hotel) come the strains of live jazz and the smells of some of the best cooking in the neighborhood. Not known for fine dining, the University District is rich with close-to-the-ground ethnic restaurants and student eat-it and beat-it joints that are long on cheap but short on grace. However, at The District, successful downtown caterer Tony Butz has installed tasty global tapas and an all-American comfort-food menu in a hip cocktail bar. The meat-loaf sandwich is like your mother never made—on sourdough with blistered jalapeño aioli. Cool tapas, like rack of Lamb Lollipops, sesame tiger shrimp satay, fried calamari crispy with blue-corn flour, or *panko*-breaded salmon pinwheels with spinach polenta and warm sherry vinaigrette, are some of the shareables that have made this hotel bar a local an after-work hot spot. *$$; AE, MC, V; checks OK; lunch, Mon–Fri, dinner Mon–Sat; full bar; self parking; contact@universitytowerhotel.com; university towerhotel.com; map:FF6* &

WHY GO: Perfect spot for pre- or post–Husky game fodder.

Doong Kong Lau / ★★

9710 AURORA AVE N, NORTHGATE; 206/526-8828 The Hakkas are called the "gypsies of China." Though wandering the world since the third century BC, they kept their customs intact and, most importantly for us, their food traditions as well. Henry Chen has clearly marked the Hakka dishes on his menu, which are scattered among a hundred or two Sichuan, Hunan, and Cantonese offerings. The Hakka preserve vegetables and combine them with meat, as with the stir-fried sidepork with pickled cabbage and five-spice that you stuff into little buns. The sautéed long beans are cooked perfectly crisp yet are tender with pickled cabbage and garlic sauce. Chen uses no MSG or peppers, but achieves his full flavors by using the preserved vegetables, strong stocks, and special seasonings. Northern dim sum is served every day, with more choices on weekends. *$; AE, DC, DIS, MC, V; no checks; lunch, dinner, dim sum every day; beer and wine; reservations recommended for 8 or more; self parking; map:DD7* &

WHY GO: No MSG and fabulous crispy duck!

Dragonfish Asian Café / ★★

722 PINE ST (PARAMOUNT HOTEL), DOWNTOWN; 206/467-7777 Because of the proximity of the Paramount Theatre across the street, actors or rock stars, their entourages, and hot-looking wannabes inhabit the booths and tables of this easygoing pan-Asian restaurant in the Paramount Hotel. Or, patrons may just be regular Seattleites packing the place for pre-show drinks, supper, sushi, or after-theater dinners. Walls are hung whimsically with Japanese anime and baseball posters; the bar is lined with brightly colored *pachinko* (Japanese pinball) machines. Two exhibition kitchens—a wok station and a robata grill—are part of the energetic ambience. The menu specializes in such small plates of pan-Asian shareables as dim sum, sushi rolls, and satays as well as some creative entrées like red Thai curry noodles and shrimp, Sichuan (Szechwan) duck breast, or almond-crusted halibut tempura. If you are downtown for weekend shopping or a matinee, the dimsum brunch is a weekend must-stop for those in the know. *$$; AE, DC, DIS, MC, V; checks OK; breakfast, lunch, dinner every day, dim sum brunch Sat–Sun; full bar; street parking; dragon fishcafe.com; map:J4* &

WHY GO: Super sushi and *pachinko* machines.

Dulces Latin Bistro / ★★★

1430 34TH AVE, MADRONA; 206/322-5453 Dulces, which means sweets, is appropriately named—everything about this place is sweet. Chef Julie Guerrero operates this romantic nuevo Latino bistro with partner Carlos Kainz, who serves as host and sommelier. With table settings of crystal and napery and very popular in its own zip code, the place draws people from all over the city. "Latino," here is broadly defined—southern French, Spanish, Italian, and regional Mexican flavors and dishes are featured and fused. There are green chicken enchiladas (green is the color of the sauce, not the chicken); the fat chiles rellenos have both French Montrachet and Spanish manchego cheeses. Sometimes you'll even find New England clam chowder. Kainz's wine list is a wonder of width, breadth, and affordability. They didn't name this place "sweets" for nothing—try the extraordinary pecan pie, or the *cajeta* (Mexican caramel and chocolate tart). *$$; AE, DC, DIS, MC, V; no checks; dinner Tues–Sat; full bar; reservations recommended; street parking; dulces latinbistro.com; map:GG7* &

WHY GO: To watch romantic diners playing footsie.

Earth & Ocean / Unrated

1112 4TH AVE (W SEATTLE HOTEL), DOWNTOWN; 206/264-6060 Behind the glitzy W Seattle scene, award-winning chef Johnathan Sundstrom thoughtfully created some of the most dazzling food in town. That is, until recently. As this book was going to press, Sundstrom left his post to open his own place, Lark, on Capitol Hill (see review), and his opening executive sous-chef Maria Hines returned to Seattle to focus on a regional American theme. Stay tuned for Pacific halibut and Penn Cove mussels with polenta and arugula sprouts and Niman Ranch pork chop and beans with a smoky ham-hock jus. The dining room is dark and clubby with a peekaboo view of the brightly lit kitchen. Service, known to oscillate between nice and pampering and snooty and absent, has found the right balance. Sommelier Marc

Papineau is on hand to retrieve gems from this celebrated cellar. *$$$; AE, B, DC, DIS, JCB, MC, V; checks OK; breakfast every day, lunch, dinner Mon–Fri; full bar; reservations recommended; valet parking; earthocean.net; map:L6* &

WHY GO: Whimsical creations from pastry chef Sue McCown.

El Camino / ★★

607 N 35TH ST, FREMONT; 206/632-7303 The bar jumps all night because of the hip location (and, in summer, its packed deckside seating), reliably smart food from south of the border, and of course, the superb fresh-juice margaritas. The dining room has the requisite ceiling fan, ceramic tiles, wrought iron, and sequined saints to go with the retroschlock feel of this arty but rapidly changing neighborhood. Try the salmon with tamarind sauce or the fish tacos with green rice. The grilled pork with pasilla chiles is succulent and spicy, as are the mussels in a creamy ancho sauce. The ever-changing dessert menu will probably include the signature pecan tart with Kahlúa, or coconut flan. Both are great, but the traditional postprandial margarita is de rigueur. *$$; AE, MC, V; no checks; dinner every day; full bar; reservations recommended; street parking; map:FF8* &

WHY GO: Given the votives, the saints, and the statuary, the dining experience is surely blessed.

El Gaucho / ★★★

2505 1ST AVE, BELLTOWN; 206/728-1337 El Gaucho is the retroswank, Paul Mackay remake of the '70s-era uptown hangout with mink-lined booths and nearly extinct tableside service. Located in Belltown (as well as Tacoma and Portland), the current version has dark, wide-open spaces where cooks scurry at a wood-fired broiler and servers make classic Caesar salads to order, right before your eyes. Patrons seated at comfy banquettes in the senate-style dining room feast on any number of (trademarked) Custom 28-Day Dry-Aged Certified Angus Beef Prime cuts, which include New York, the Baseball cut of top sirloin, filet mignon, and filet of New York—none fewer than eight ounces. Seafood lovers don't get short shrift either, although they may be better served at Mackay's seafood palace, Waterfront Seafood Grill (see review): they can dredge garlic bread in buttery Wicked Shrimp or slurp saffron-scented broth from an artful bouillabaisse. Bananas Foster is a decadent and sublime capper to the evening. In the bar, a well-heeled crowd sips martinis as a piano player noodles jazz riffs on a baby grand. The wine card is formidable, supplemented by a premium reserve list. Serious imbibers will be heartened by the lengthy single-malt Scotch list. The Pampas Room downstairs, open for dancing and drinking on Friday and Saturday, offers the full El Gaucho menu. *$$$$; AE, DIS, MC, V; checks OK; dinner every day; full bar; reservations recommended; valet parking; elgaucho.com; map:F8* &

WHY GO: Two (count 'em) coed cigar lounges and blazing baked Alaska.

El Greco / ★★⯪

219 BROADWAY AVE E, CAPITOL HILL; 206/328-4604 With higher sensibilities and prices than most of its street-level competitors, El Greco might seem a little out of place at ground zero of the hip grit of Capitol Hill's Broadway. It always had a great reputation, but new owners Stacey Hettinger and Gary Snyder have put new paint and energy into the 10-year-old hangout. The menu is more adventurous as it meanders around the Mediterranean with Greek lamb burger, Italian risotto, Moroccan chicken, Spanish seafood paella, and occasionally sets out for the New World with dishes like South American ancho-chili pork. Lunch features satisfying sandwiches: from eggplant, pesto, and mozzarella to warm pitas wrapped around spiced lamb or grilled chicken. There's late breakfast with yummy stuff like crab Benedict and ginger pancakes every day, and lines thicken up for the mighty weekend brunch. On warm days, eat outside and witness the splendid, sordid spectacle of the Broadway foot traffic. *$–$$; AE, MC, V; no checks; breakfast, lunch, dinner Tues–Sun, brunch Sat–Sun; full bar; street parking; map:GG6* &

WHY GO: Best people-watching north of the Haight-Ashbury.

El Puerco Lloron / ★

1501 WESTERN AVE, PIKE PLACE MARKET; 206/624-0541 This delicious-smelling place is as about as authentic as you might want to get when it comes to Tex-Mex restaurants in Seattle. There are pink and aquamarine walls, cutout tin lamps, and a lady hand-forming tortillas in the dining room. Pick up your food at the serve-yourself cafeteria line—then fight for a table along with the neighboring workers who line up for the inexpensive and tasty fare (and, in nice weather, jostle for the outside tables). Eat the tamales—they're always freshly steamed; the *taquito* plate with its sliced steak and soft tortillas is the most popular dish, though the *machaca* beef comes in a close second; the chiles rellenos are fat and juicy. Most everything is served with rice and beans. Grab a Mexican beer, and it's easy to pretend for a moment you're back in San Antone. *$; AE, MC, V; business checks only; lunch, dinner every day; beer and wine; no reservations; street parking; map:J8*

WHY GO: Salsa on the jukebox as good as it is on the tables.

Elliott's Oyster House / ★★★

1201 ALASKAN WY, PIER 56, WATERFRONT; 206/623-4340 They call it Oyster House for a reason. It's the best in town, with an extensive selection. Their annual Oyster New Year is a world-class all-you-can-slurp pig out. But Elliott's is more than that. It's a classic fish house with plenty of innovative seafood alternatives served up in a sparkling redo of an old Seattle waterfront favorite. Designers envisioned a classic yacht when they spent $2 million on the remodeled setting best described as nautical but nice. Tourist boat docks next door provide appropriate visual action. Or focus on one of several excellent creamy seafood chowders, like pink-tinged Dungeness crab chowder with a touch of cayenne. The iced shellfish extravaganzas serve two, four, or six people. Whole Dungeness is offered hot and spicy, simply steamed, or chilled with dipping sauces. Alaska weathervane scallops are grilled over mesquite then drowned in crab beurre blanc. Wild, troll-caught king salmon either gets aromatically alder planked and served with smoked tomato beurre blanc, or mesquite grilled or lightly alder smoked and chargrilled. The mesquite-grilled mahi-mahi tacos at lunch are salsa mayoed and wrapped in thick tortillas. It wouldn't be Seattle without Dungeness crab cakes, and these are exceptional, with rock shrimp and a crab beurre blanc blended with the juice of blood oranges. There's a safe but seafood-friendly wine list. *$$$; AE, DC,*

DIS, MC, V; checks OK; lunch, dinner every day; full bar; reservations recommended; street parking; elliottsoysterhouse.com; map:H8 &

WHY GO: An inner-city pleasure cruise without leaving the dock.

Endolyne Joe's / ★★

9261 45TH AVE SW, WEST SEATTLE; 206/937-5637 The stable of restaurants created by Peter Levy and Jeremy Hardy take up a good chunk of this guide. That's because these guys are the undisputed champs of the lively, comfortable neighborhood restaurants Coastal Kitchen, Jitterbug, 5 Spot Cafe (see reviews), and Atlas Foods. The latest lucky neighborhood, Fauntleroy in West Seattle, got Endolyne Joe's in the summer of 2003. It's named for the '40s streetcar "lyne," the end o' which was right here. Joe's rocks with diner sass—"Adobo!" hollers the host, to whichever adept server awaits this order, now ready at the sweeping, open kitchen, visible from a precious few counter stools from which a lucky few can catch all the action. "Crab cakes!" "Cobb!" Whatever he calls, chances are it's pretty good. To keep things popping, they theme the joint differently a few times a year—Key Largo, Little Italy, Route 66—and commission local artists to create appropriate canvases, which get stapled to the walls. Key Largo produced Frank McCloud's Flank Steak, chewy but flavorful thanks partly to a dose of sherry-garlic vinaigrette. Adobo chicken has the right seasonings, a slow hand removing it from the grill, and addictive, aggressively seasoned yucca fries. The regular menu ranges among the West Coast, the East Coast, the Gulf Coast, and the Heartland. A thick-cut pork chop represents the latter, nicely marinated in hoisin and Tabasco. Roasted mushroom ravioli somehow represents our neck of the woods, stuffing rich 'shroom and spinach in locally made pasta pillows. Breakfast is the best meal—or "blunch" as it's called—with all manner of scrambles and omelets, caramel apple French toast, and fruit parfait. *$; MC, V; local checks only; breakfast, lunch, dinner every day; full bar; reservations recommended; self parking; chowfoods.com; map:LL9*

WHY GO: In the AM, Billy Bob's Biscuits & Gravy; in the PM, buttermilk-battered onion rings.

BEST PLACE FOR BREAKFAST?

"Café Campagne—you don't have to go to France
to discover great French fare."

Kathy Casey, chef and culinary diva

Etta's Seafood / ★★★

2020 WESTERN AVE, BELLTOWN; 206/443-6000 In the mid-'90s, chef/entrepreneur Tom Douglas created this hip seafood house and named it after his effervescent daughter, Loretta. Etta's is in the same freewheeling style as its notable siblings, Dahlia Lounge and Palace Kitchen (see reviews). Douglas, and chef Chris Schwarz, approach seafood with originality and a respectful light touch. For starters there are mussels or clams in broth zesty with chorizo and house-smoked salmon. In-season, this is a place to slurp local oysters on the half shell with a glass of bracing white wine. Douglas's Dungeness crab cakes spiked with green tomato relish and his spice-rubbed pit-roasted salmon are Seattle's signature versions of these dishes. Lush desserts come from dessert central in the Dahlia Bakery. Lunch can be as simple as fish-and-chips with red cabbage slaw or something more complicated, such as chilled peanut noodles with lemongrass chicken skewers. Downtowners and Market dwellers descend on Etta's for brunch on the weekends. Expect to wait for a seat in the small, conversation-friendly dining room or the other larger and much noisier noshery with bar and counter seating. *$$; AE, DC, DIS, MC, V; local checks only; lunch, dinner every day, brunch Sat–Sun; full bar; reservations recommended; street parking; tomdouglas.com; map:I8* &

WHY GO: Terrific kids' menu and Tom's Tasty Sashimi, a Salad with scallion pancakes.

Eva Restaurant and Wine Bar / ★★★

2227 N 56TH ST, GREEN LAKE; 206/633-3538 In this little subneighborhood with a handful of restaurants a few blocks east of Green Lake, James Hondros and spouse/chef Amy McCray transformed a well-windowed, warmwooded room into a first-rate bistro. The only drawback is that the wood is the only thing absorbing sound. And while an open kitchen is one thing, an open dishwashing station is a nerve-jangling something else. But dig into McCray's food and you might block out extraneous senses. McCray spent years honing her skills at the Dahlia Lounge and Chez Shea, where she was lead chef. She also lured pastry chef JoAnna Cruz away from Sandy Shea, and the resulting kitchen chemistry is captivating palates across the city with an absolute imperative: yes, enjoy dinner, but dammit, save room for dessert. Panfried oysters rolled in the crumbs of *pappadams* (Indian flatbread) and served with a raita sauce and cilantro pesto typifies the simplicity and originality of the menu. The light, smooth, Cabrales flan is a blue-cheese blast offset with a tangy-sweet pear relish and anchored to the earth with a buttery walnut cracker. There are basic bistro entrées as well: grilled and roasted fish, steaks, and poultry. Cruz's desserts are flawless, and Hondros's well-chosen wine list has plenty of bottles in the $30s—and nearly a dozen good half bottles. *$$; AE, MC, V; checks OK; dinner Tues–Sun; full bar; reservations recommended; street parking; map:FF7* &

WHY GO: Creative cuisine, artfully plated.

Fandango / ★★★

2313 1ST AVE, BELLTOWN; 206/441-1188 Fandango is a visually and culinarily capricious tour of Brazil, Colombia, Peru, Argentina, and Mexico led by chef/owner and tour-guide Christine Keff. Keff, who also owns Flying Fish (see review), has been careful to stock her huge, exhibition kitchen with talented cooks. We love passing by and watching as cooks turn tortillas that'll be brought warm to the table in the dining room lined with lipstick-red tea-cup booths big enough for an entourage. There are *antojitos* enough for tapas-style dining, with choices including a daily ceviche, swordfish *panuchos*, lamb riblets with habanero salsa, and Argentinean carpaccio with *chimichurri* sauce. Dive hands-first into the fish-taco platter sized for sharing. Expect a whole fried snapper (that you will flake for yourself) to be presented with wedges of lime, sour cream, guacamole, cilantro, a bevy of mild to hot salsas, and some of those tortillas. Other entrée options include roast suckling pig, grilled beef tenderloin, and Brazilian seafood stew that introduce authentic Latin flavors and preparations. The streetside bar has 50 tequilas, a *mojito* that'll make you think you're Hemingway in Havana, and a truly spectacular Pisco Sour. *$$; AE, DC, MC, V; checks OK; dinner every day; full bar; reservations recommended; street parking; fandangoseattle.com; map:G8* &

WHY GO: Family-style dining (for four or more) on Sunday nights and excellent selections of sherries and Madeiras.

BEST PLACE TO SPEND $5?
"The ice-cream counter at (West Seattle's) Husky Deli."

Greg Nickels, mayor of Seattle

The Fish Club by Todd English / ★★☆

2100 ALASKAN WY (SEATTLE MARRIOTT WATERFRONT HOTEL), WATERFRONT; 206/256-1040 It's on the waterfront, but there's neither deck nor view. Its claim to fame is the stellar cuisine of its namesake owner, Boston celeb-chef Todd English. With 18 restaurants, a PBS cooking show, and designation as one of *People* magazine's "50 Most Beautiful People," English has made The Fish Club his first West Coast venture. Service is warm and knowledgeable, and with the sure hand of English protégé Chris Ainsworth actually running the kitchen, it's all about top-of-the-line seafood, as you'd expect. Whole salmon twirl around the flames on the "dancing fish" rotisserie, an English invention that looks like a medieval torture device. The menu pans the continents with diverse and delicious offerings like yellowfin-tuna tartare with sushi rice; lobster paella, Louisiana seafood gumbo; or the delicious, luxury comfort food, Lobster Mac & Cheese. With all the un-Seattle celebrity glam of the opening, a slow start, and reports of unevenness in service and food, only time will tell whether The Fish Club will sign up a permanent membership in Seattle. *$$$; AE, DC, DIS, MC V; no checks; breakfast, lunch, dinner every day; full bar; reservations recommended; valet parking; toddenglish.com; map:D9* &

WHY GO: Celeb chef buzz and dancing fish.

5 Spot Cafe / ★★

1502 QUEEN ANNE AVE N, QUEEN ANNE; 206/285-7768 It always seems as if a party's going on at longtime neighborhood restaurateurs Peter Levy and Jeremy Hardy's places, which include Coastal Kitchen, Jitterbug Cafe, Endolyne Joe's (see reviews), and Atlas Foods. Indeed, food festivals celebrating cuisine of different regions of the United States change the focus every three months or so. Visit the 5 Spot during the fall to enjoy the Harvest Festival, representing such events as Bradford, Vermont's wild-game extravaganza, though here "wild" translates as hearty

COUNTER CULTURE

Dining needn't ever be a lonely affair in Seattle. Simply slide up and take a seat at one of these local counters to easily mix with other hungry strangers.

Made famous by its star turn in *Sleepless in Seattle*, the **ATHENIAN INN**'s (1517 Pike Pl, Pike Place Market; 206/624-7166) Formica counter is as much a place to eat as a tourist destination. Lunch is the best time to go to this Market eatery, when you can choose from a burger with fries or chowder, or one of the kitchen's delicious Filipino specials.

At **THE DISH** (4358 Leary Way NW, Fremont/Ballard; 206/782-9985), a plastic-countertop hideaway, sample the soup or homemade scones. For a kick, try one of the 30 hot sauces that line the back wall; you'll fit right in with the dock workers on their lunch breaks.

The counter at **HATTIE'S HAT** (5231 Ballard Ave NW, Ballard; 206/784-0175) proudly bears the scratches and gashes from years of abuse. And no wonder, night owls often make a pub-grub pit stop here before or after a show at the Tractor Tavern just down the street.

---

venison stew with roasted root vegetables, served with sweet yam dollar biscuits. Favorites include corned beef, sauerkraut, and swiss stacked high on grilled rye bread and slathered in Russian dressing—served the old-fashioned way with horseradish, cherry peppers, and a half sour pickle. Or try the pork ribs with tamarind/garlic or the marlin tacos with lime-kissed guacamole. Breakfast includes such standards as Kathryn's Grand Slam (buttermilk cakes, bacon, and two eggs). Late riser? No problem; ham and eggs are on the menu until midnight. *$; MC, V; local checks only; breakfast, lunch, dinner every day; full bar; reservations for 6 or more recommended; street parking; chowfoods.com; map:GG8*

WHY GO: Flavor, fun, and to test your tolerance of cute menu language.

Flying Fish / ★★★☆

2234 1ST AVE, BELLTOWN; 206/728-8595 Even on nights when neighboring Belltown joints are quiet, Flying Fish jumps; it leaps, it soars. And it's a foodie's dream come true. Chef/owner Christine Keff not only knows and loves seafood but has created a place where everybody seems to want to be at the same time and where ultrafriendly staffers haul platters and plates to exuberant wine-imbibing diners. Order the small starter plates, two or three of which can make a meal. Entrée choices range from lobster ravioli with yellow-foot mushrooms in a puddle of lobster velouté to a pile of crispy fried calamari with a hot-sweet honey jalapeño mayonnaise, to grilled scallops in a creamy herb polenta served with sautéed mixed greens. Everything is achingly fresh and artistically presented. Keff encourages large parties to opt for the large sharing platters that are sold by the pound, such as the whole fried rockfish or her famous Sister-in-Law Mussels with chile-lime dipping

At **LONGSHOREMAN'S DAUGHTER** (3510 Fremont Pl N, Fremont; 206/633-5169), regulars line up two and three deep on weekends to pull up a stool to the tiny marble counter, dive into some Texas eggs, and throw back a Bloody Mary or two.

Tucked into what seems like a closet on the third floor of the Corner Market Building, the tiny **MATT'S IN THE MARKET** (94 Pike St, Pike Place Market; 206/467-7909; see review) serves delicious gumbo and po' boy sandwiches on a wood-and-tile counter that spells "Counter Culture" in mosaic. The local seafood lunch specials change daily and are the favorite of the business trade.

This Lower Queen Anne mainstay is one of the oldest family-owned restaurants in the city, and rumor has it that the **MECCA CAFE**'s (526 Queen Anne Ave N; 206/285-9728) burgers and malts are as good today as when the place opened (with the same Formica counter) in 1930. The BLT is to clog arteries for, and laid-back servers will make you feel like a regular in no time.

—*Matt Villano*

sauce. The wine list is expansive and accessible, with many Northwest and California offerings as well as tons of midrange bottlings from around the world. *$$; AE, DC, MC, V; local checks only; dinner every day; full bar; reservations recommended; street parking; info@flyingfishseattle.com; flyingfishseattle.com; map:G8* &

WHY GO: So tourists can say, "Look at all the locals!"

The Four Swallows / ★★

481 MADISON AVE N, BAINBRIDGE ISLAND; 206/842-3397 The historic William Grow farmhouse, within walking distance of Bainbridge's ferry landing, houses the charming Four Swallows. Owner Mike Sharp manages the service in the dining room, while partner Gerry Ferraro does the cooking. The warren of mismatched rooms with comfy rural tchotchkes makes a pleasant place to sit, and the efforts of the chef, with their Mediterranean overtones, are stellar. The starter list is varied enough to graze as dinner with glasses of wine. Mussels with saffron, leeks, tomatoes, and cream are magical, as are the braised artichokes and the beef carpaccio. Entrées meet expectations, too. The rack of lamb with a rosemary port sauce comes with roasted figs and mashed potatoes. The crab cakes are served with a tangy lemon aioli; the clam linguine is a flavor blast with pancetta and lots of garlic. Large parties, couples, or singles are equally at home in this elegant yet easygoing island eatery. *$$; AE, DC, DIS, MC, V; local checks only; dinner Tues–Sat; full bar; reservations recommended; street parking; fourswallows.com* &

WHY GO: Clubby privacy of the black-and-ivory bar.

Fremont Classic Pizza & Trattoria / ★★

4307 FREMONT AVE N, FREMONT; 206/548-9411 This isn't just a pizza joint any more. This hugely popular neighborhood place is a righteously creative Italian trattoria. They still have thin-crusted pizzas, simple pastas, and the laid-back Fremontness that works for families as well as couples on dates. Paul and Erin Kohlenberg opened their place in 1988 and expanded a few years ago with a second dining room and an easygoing patio. Chef Paul enlarged his menu with seasonal dishes like fettuccine with fresh chanterelles, roasted pear raviolis with smoked shallots, and tortellini Gorgonzola with fresh spinach and walnuts. A new smoke house is pumping out, among many other things, smoky pork chops and chicken sausage. The service is friendly—many servers are longtime employees on a first-name basis with the neighborhood patrons. *$; AE, DC, DIS, MC, V; local checks only; dinner everyday; beer and wine; no reservations; self and street parking; fremontclassic@ fremontpizza.com; fremontpizza.com; map:FF8* &

WHY GO: Pizzas with pizzazz in a family- and couple-friendly atmosphere.

BEST PLACE TO DINE AL FRESCO?

"By the kids' wading pool at Green Lake. Get the food to go from World Wrapps and sit there and be part of Tolstoy's swarm of life."

Charles Cross, author of Heavier Than Heaven: The Biography of Kurt Cobain

Frontier Room / ★★☆

2203 1ST AVE, BELLTOWN; 206/956-7427 The original Frontier Room was a classic Seattle dive known for strong drinks and weak resolve. Gutted and re-funked in 2002, it's been transformed into a hot see-and-be-seen Belltown bar and a decent, albeit upscale, late-night barbecue. Dark corners where tanked imbibers once lurked are now lit by a faux fireplace accented by a stack of firewood placed artfully by a decorator. But don't be put off by all the Western tongue-in-chic, a Southern Pride Pit Smoker in the kitchen turns out Tennessee-style ribs, pork shoulder, Texas-style beef brisket, chicken, and sassy baked beans cooked low and slow in the smudge of applewood and hickory. The bar gets hoppin' after about 8:30pm and the noise makes speaking in a normal tone nigh impossible, so if you're into conversation over dinner, go for lunch or go early. *$$; AE, MC, V; no checks; lunch, dinner Tues–Sat; full bar; no reservations; street parking; map:G8* &

WHY GO: Down-home barbecue in a sexy city setting.

Galerias / ★★☆

611 BROADWAY AVE E, CAPITOL HILL; 206/322-5757 Since 1997, Ramiro Rubio has been wooing Seattleites over to his infinite expressions of regional Mexican cuisine. Today the papaya-colored walls at Galerias are cluttered with honors such as "Best Tamales," "Best Margarita," and "Best Mexican Restaurant" in Seattle. The large room aches for romantic trysts: high ceilings drip billowing gauze scrim, wrought-iron candelabras cast amber light on tables draped in (worn) white linen, and Diego Rivera–inspired arrangements of papier-mâché calla lilies. Start with the Galerias *taquitos papas*, half moon–shaped pockets of tender potatoes topped with smoky enchilada sauce and crumbles of cotija cheese. Entrées such as Chile en Nogada, roasted poblano chile filled with beef or pork, apples, pears, raisins, almonds, and a sweet walnut sauce; and Enchiladas Chipotle, corn tortillas filled with pork, chicken, or beef and topped with a chipotle cream sauce and crushed *cacahuetes* (peanuts), are accompanied by a tortilla cup of *refritos con arroz*. Margaritas are *muy grande* and as close to the real thing as one might find in Cabo. *$$; AE, DC, MC, V; no checks; lunch, dinner every day; full bar; reservations recommended; self parking; map:HH6* &

WHY GO: Salsa dancing on weekend nights in the dining room turned sultry disco.

Garage / ★

1130 BROADWAY AVE, CAPITOL HILL; 206/322-2296 If we were rating entertainment value, the Garage would garner four stars. What other restaurant in town with a wine list as long as a bowling lane happens to have bowling lanes—14 of them split between two levels of a one-time Plymouth car dealership? As well as 18 really good, full-size billiard tables in the equally funky old repair garage? The dining room is off the billiard room, but runners will carry the peppy tiger prawns in spicy, bacon-enhanced tequila sauce right to your table . . . or lane. Don't get any of the ever-changing, reliable risotto in the bowling ball's finger holes, and watch that you don't run a cue right through the flash-fried calamari rings and into the honey-curry aioli. Run the table then sit down to jalapeño-buttered beef medallions, a richly spiced meat loaf, or chicken picata. *$$; AE, MC, V; no checks; dinner every day; reservations recommended; self and street parking; garagebilliards.com; mapH1* &

WHY GO: Tuesdays, with purchase of a large plate, get 25 percent off already reasonably priced wines.

Geneva / ★★★

1106 8TH AVE, FIRST HILL; 206/624-2222 It's Mozart and Strauss, crystal and silver. Longtime Rainier Club executive chef Hanspeter Aebersold and his wife Margret quietly make people very happy in this intimate, elegant jewel box of a continental restaurant, with its old-world crystal chandelier and silk wall hangings. Begin with such delights as escargot broiled on mushroom caps and go on to signature entrées like *Jägerschnitzel*, lightly crusted pork medallions with wild mushroom sauce served with buttered spaetzle; or Veal Bernoise, a ragout of veal in wine and cream and loaded with mushrooms. Desserts are one of Hanspeter's specialties: try the sensational bread-and-butter pudding with vanilla brandy sauce or the bittersweet chocolate mousse and raspberry sauce in a Florentine cookie basket. The service under Margret's direction is reverent and pampering. The wine list with its wide-ranging prices is a mix of the Old World and the New, with plenty to interest serious 'bibers. *$$$; AE, MC, V; no checks; dinner Tues–Sat; full bar; reservations recommended; street parking; genevarestaurant.com; map:L4* &

WHY GO: Where else can you get spaetzle and crystal chandeliers?

The Georgian / ★★★★

411 UNIVERSITY ST (FAIRMONT OLYMPIC HOTEL), DOWNTOWN; 206/621-7889 This 1924 Italian Renaissance room with its floor-to-ceiling Palladian windows, fussy fretwork, soaring ceilings, extravagant chandeliers, and wall of art glass has been down-dressed, down-priced, and lightened up—but it'll be never anything other than drop-dead elegant. Gore-Tex and turtlenecks, black tie and ball gown are appropriate here. Chef Gavin Stephenson's notable, seasonal, regional American food is served by an informed, pampering staff. For starters try the delicata squash soup, a velvety cream garnished with truffled Brie balls; and the Quacky Duck Dumplings, poached ground breast of duck with a righteous slice of sautéed foie gras. Entrées can be well-prepared seafood—we love the apple cider–glazed weathervane scallops, with sweet white corn juice, cilantro, and lots of caviar, and a charred tender-to-the-bone Willamette lamb rack with homemade sausage and eggplant marmalade. Desserts are ever-changing and transcendent. The Chocolate Fudge Passion Cake with clotted cream would sate any chocolate fiend, and the autumn apple pie is topped with rich black walnut–caramel ice cream. This glorious food is complemented by the gigantic, well-priced, interplanetary wine list, with attendant and knowledgeable wine service. *$$$; AE, DC, MC, V; no checks; lunch, breakfast everyday, dinner Tues–Sat; full bar; reservations recommended; valet parking validated for dinner only; fairmont.com; map:EE7* &

WHY GO: Dress up or dress down for luxury treatment.

Gravity Bar / ★★☆

415 BROADWAY AVE E, CAPITOL HILL; 206/325-7186 At Seattle's coolest juice bar and vegetarian restaurant, no one tries to fool their guests into thinking about—or even missing—the "real thing." Its tables of conical, galvanized steel and glowing green glass are where Bauhaus meets *Star Trek* in Broadway Market. A tattooed, black-on-black crowd meets each other for drinks from the "pharmacy," such as the Mr. Rogers on Amino Acid (pineapple, orange, banana, yogurt, and amino acids). Plenty of the lesser chic (read: us) congregate here, drawn by healthy food that will actually challenge taste buds. Order the RV1, a bowl of nutty brown rice and steamed vegetables with lemon-tahini dressing, a garlicky concoction whose formula is impossible to coax out of the tight and pierced lips of the staff. The menu offers lots of salads, soups, and vegan dishes. There are roll-ups and sandwiches such as the Beso de Queso, with black-bean spread, sliced avocado, sun-dried tomatoes, and melted provolone cheese on rustic whole-wheat bread, or the barbecue onion and mushroom vegan burger with tomatoes, avocado, and provolone on an herb and onion bun. Service can be a bit too mellow. *$$; MC, V; local checks only; breakfast, lunch, dinner every day; no alcohol; no reservations; self parking; map:HH6* &

WHY GO: Sopa Azteca, a spirulina soup that just might cure the common cold.

Green Papaya / ★★★☆

600 E PINE ST, CAPITOL HILL; 206/323-1923 Fresh flowers, black linen, and celadon walls in the bright, airy dining room are a pleasant backdrop for the wide variety of fragrant, traditional Vietnamese dishes coming from this kitchen. It's owned and operated by a brother and sister team of corporate refugees—Van and Thuy Hong—who talked their chef/mother Suong Nguyen into relocating from California to do the cooking. There is plenty on this menu for vegetarians here—the Cho Lon rice-paper bundles with vegetables, fresh basil, mint, and bean sprouts are light little finger salads. Along with prawns, there's freshwater fish—try the Catfish Clay Pot, filets served with a brusque black-pepper sauce or a sizzling pan-fried Trout with Spicy Eggplant. Carnivores will be sated with grilled Saigon Beef Rolls, the Coconut (Chicken) Curry, or the Lemongrass Pork. The Green Papaya is upscale for the Pike-Pine corridor, but it's a well-considered melding of moderate prices and beautifully executed food. *$; AE, MC, V; no checks; lunch, dinner Tues–Sun; full bar; no reservations; street parking; papayaonpine.com; map:GG7* &

WHY GO: Authentic and wallet-friendly Vietnamese cuisine.

Greenlake Bar & Grill / ★★☆

7200 E GREEN LAKE WY N, GREEN LAKE; 206/729-6179 John Schmidt, who built the Taco del Mar burrito chain, stepped away from all that to open this laid-back little place with his brother James. It's obviously a labor of love. This comfortable Green Lake eatery serves pub food done well. The genteel atmosphere is comfortable both for neighboring families and the buff singles crowd who flock to the green midcity shores of what's known locally as Dig Me Lake. The grilled vegetable sandwich is a neighborhood lunch favorite—a tasty pile of sliced assorted peppers, summer squash, and portobellos grilled and stuffed into a bollo roll with a sun-dried tomato spread. More ambitious entrées such as halibut with strawberry-peppercorn sauce share the menu with pub faves such as bacon burgers or a New York steak with brandy-mushroom sauce and creamy mashed potatoes. A brief wine list has good choices, mostly under $30 and many of which are available by the glass. *$$; AE, MC, V; checks OK; lunch, dinner everyday; full bar; reservations accepted for large groups; street parking; map:EE7* &

WHY GO: See-and-be-seen singles scene and pub food with flair.

Harvest Vine / ★★★☆

2701 E MADISON ST, MADISON VALLEY; 206/320-9771 As in Spain, conviviality is the point of this tiny tapas emporium and Joseph Jimenez de Jimenez's infinitely shareable menu will frustrate a solo diner. Once seated, ask for a glass of fino sherry and start ordering *platitos* from the more than two dozen seasonally inspired tapas. Simply superb are the grilled sardines with lemon, the meltingly tender braised octopus with grilled potatoes, and warm salad of partridge with morels and corn. The sweet *piquillo* peppers stuffed with potato mousse and salt cod proves that good food doesn't have to be precious. A seat at the copper-top bar provides front-row-center viewing of Jimenez and his wee crew as they turn out dish after dish with precision and humor. Tables offer an intimate, although not ideal for lingering, option. The chef's wife and award-winning pastry *patrona*, Carolin Messier de Jimenez, breathes new life into classic Spanish and Basque desserts. Be advised: Harvest Vine does not take reservations, except for the "harvest table," located in the *txoko* (the small subterranean addition that doubled their seating capacity), which can be reserved for parties of eight or more. Waits can be long and

93

there is no lounge or reception area, but we think the experience is well worth any inconvenience. *$$; MC, V; checks OK; dinner Tues–Sat; beer and wine; no reservations; street parking; map:GG7* &

WHY GO: Peerless selection of Spanish cheeses and a new definition of "dinner theater."

BEST PLACE FOR A COCKTAIL?

"Cactus [Kirkland]—when Ryan Magarian, the cutest bartender, is working! He shakes up a mean one."

Kathy Casey, chef and culinary diva

The Herbfarm / ★★★★

14590 NE 145TH ST, WOODINVILLE; 425/485-5300 It is often placed in the upper echelon of American restaurants. A must-experience place for anyone who loves serious food and formal service, and can pay the freight. The nine-course prix-fixe dinner with accompanying wines costs around $175 per person. After a devastating fire followed by a short time in a temporary location, Ron Zimmerman and Carrie Van Dyke moved their foodie shrine to brand-new gorgeous digs in the Woodinville "wine country," near the Ste. Michelle and Columbia wineries, on the property of the posh Willows Lodge. Nationally renowned chef Jerry Traunfeld presides over seasonal menus of local produce and herbs—much of which is grown in the Herbfarm's own substantial gardens. The food is immaculately presented and carefully explained. A night's repast could typically encompass tempura squash blossoms stuffed with goat cheese; crab salad with fennel and chives; pea flan with caviar; sweet corn soup with smoked mussels and chanterelles; salmon smoked in basilwood; herb-crusted lamb; cheeses; desserts such as a roasted Italian plum tart and a caramelized pear soufflé with rose-geranium sauce; and a selection of small treats—miniature s'mores with cinnamon and basil, chocolates, or lemon-thyme espresso truffles—to go with your coffee. Every service detail is seen to by the army of staff, wiping your brow, pouring your wines, and clearing away the Christofle flatware and crystal as you use it. The rooms are filled with a tasteful mass of framed art and memorabilia. Arrive a half hour before dinner for Van Dyke's tour around the gardens. This is a coveted, one-of-a-kind destination—reservations usually need to be booked months in advance, especially for holidays. *$$$$; AE, MC, V; checks OK; dinner Thurs–Sun; beer and wine; reservations required; self parking; reservations@theherbfarm.com; theherbfarm.com; map:AA2* &

WHY GO: When it's this good, it is indeed possible to eat and drink for five hours straight.

Hilltop Ale House / ★

2129 QUEEN ANNE AVE N, QUEEN ANNE; 206/285-3877 This Queen Anne Hill watering hole has pub food that's a cut above the usual burgers and frozen deep-fried tidbits. There are cool little nibbly things such as the oven-roasted curried cashews. But most everything else is big enough for an entire meal: a huge cilantro pesto quesadilla, a so-called starter, is crammed with roasted peppers, Monterey Jack cheese, cilantro pesto, and grilled chicken if you so choose. The half salads (baked goat cheese or Caesar) can be dinner with a cup of soup or the spicy Hilltop Gumbo, full of shrimp, chicken andouille sausage, and veggies. The chicken-breast sandwich is a handful oozing with mozzarella and cream cheese served on toasted rye. Entrée specials change weekly, a grilled Cascioppo Bros. lamb sausage one week, lemon chicken risotto the next. This is a noisy, popular joint run by the same owners as the Columbia City Alehouse (4914 Rainier Ave S, Columbia City; 206/723-5123) and the 74th Street Alehouse (7401 Greenwood Ave N, Greenwood; 206/784-2955). The creative fare is but a worthy accompaniment to the real business at hand: the 15 beers and ales on tap. *$; MC, V; checks OK; lunch, dinner every day; beer and wine; no reservations; street parking; seattlealehouses.com; map:GG8* ♿

WHY GO: Artichoke hummus plate with grilled pita, washed down with an ice-cold brew.

Hunt Club / ★★★
Fireside Room / ★★★

900 MADISON ST (SORRENTO HOTEL), FIRST HILL; 206/343-6156 Hidden away inside Seattle's grand dame Sorrento Hotel, the Hunt Club exudes traditional elegance, impeccable service, and sumptuous meals from executive chef Brian Scheehser. The burnished mahogany and weathered-brick den got a face-lift in 2002, and although still sporting that men's club atmosphere, ladies will delight in design details such as overstuffed sofas and tasseled bolsters on banquets. Scheehser's menu is Mediterranean, a nod to the hotel's namesake city, and showcases the finest regional ingredients available. Start with any one of the luxurious appetizers: crispy Dungeness crab cakes with basil-aioli and oven-dried tomatoes or roasted beet salad (in season) topped with frizzled leeks and vinaigrette. Soup lovers will swoon over the frothy mussel bisque. Scheehser's grilled filet mignon is arguably the best in town. Look for tender, flavorful duck and lamb chops. Seafood, such as wild king salmon, served with apple-cider reduction and beurre blanc, brings the best of the Northwest to table, an ideal match for one of the region's gems (Oregon pinot noir) on the extensive wine list.

Meals at the Sorrento Hotel can be a movable feast. Take dessert, coffee, or Cognac in the octagonal Fireside Room off the hotel lobby, where piano music and board games frequently draw crowds (a light menu is available day or evening) and afternoon tea is served from 3pm to 5pm daily. *$$$, $; AE, DIS, MC, V; checks OK; breakfast, lunch, tea, dinner every day, brunch Sat–Sun; full bar; reservations recommended; valet parking (Hunt Club); hotelsorrento.com; map:L4* ♿

WHY GO: Al fresco dining and cocktailing at Piazza Capri (a pop-up cafe on the circular *porte cochere*) during warm summer months.

I Love Sushi / ★★☆

1001 FAIRVIEW AVE N, SOUTH LAKE UNION; 206/625-9604 / 11818 NE 8TH ST, BELLEVUE; 425/454-5706 This place has been serving wonderful sushi so long now (since 1986), many younger customers don't even get the word play in the name. Though it's hard to picture Lucy and Ricky, forget about Fred and Ethel, at a sushi bar, this place would be one of their better bets. At their respective bars, the cast of chefs are happy to help guide newbies and are capable of satisfying diehards. If she didn't order one of the bargain sushi specials, Lucy would have some 'splainin' to do. The à la carte dishes, such as flame-broiled mackerel or salmon, the ubiquitous tempura, or geoduck itame sautéed with spinach, are excellent. *$$; AE, MC, V; no checks; lunch Mon–Fri (Seattle), Mon–Sat (Bellevue), dinner every day; full bar; reservations recommended; self parking; ilovesushi.com; map:GG7, HH3* ⅙

WHY GO: Artful nigiri sushi—fingers of vinegared rice topped with assorted raw fish.

BEST PLACE FOR A STROLL?

"On the University of Washington campus in the spring when the cherry tree quadrangle is in bloom—could rekindle just about the deadest romantic embers."

Pepper Schwartz, PhD, sociologist/author

Il Bacio / ★★

16564 CLEVELAND ST, REDMOND; 425/869-8815 Over a decade ago, Italian-born chef Rino Baglio brought his trunkload of awards and accolades to a little Redmond strip mall and set up shop: a pasticceria and cafe. The bakery is long gone, but the restaurant expanded to three rooms painted to look like Italian verandas and such, with simple ceiling panels the color of a starry Mediterranean night sky. It was a new dawn for Eastside Italian dining. Much of the kitchen staff still works here, which accounts for the consistency. Start with Clams Casino, bivalves stuffed with herbs and bacon in a white-wine sauce. A specialty is the tenderloin of buffalo wrapped in prosciutto, with a demi-glace of Barolo wine. Try the herbed veal chop served with wild mushrooms or the Risotto di Novara, a peasant dish of Italian aborio rice, sausage, Tuscan beans, sage, and fresh tomato sauce. There are plenty of great pastas here, including Baglio's angel-hair pasta with lobster meat in a fresh tomato sauce. A small, Italian-leaning wine list, with an inadequate by-the-glass program, completes the picture. *$$; AE, DC, DIS, JCB, MC, V; no checks; lunch Mon–Fri, dinner every day; full bar; reservations recommended; self parking; ilbacioredmond@aol.com; ilbacio.com; map:EE1* ⅙

WHY GO: A *New York Times* Who's Who reviewer bestowed it five stars. Agree?

Il Bistro / ★★★

93-A PIKE ST, PIKE PLACE MARKET; 206/682-3049 One of the most enduring stars in the Seattle universe of small Italian restaurants, Il Bistro is tucked away under the eaves of the Market. The cozy warren of candlelit rooms is a perfect place to tryst again like you did last summer. For tête-à-tête suppers try any of the shareable antipasti—such as mussels or scampi, fragrant of garlic and basil, or crostini with roasted garlic and goat cheese. They're great with a bottle of wine from the daunting list topping 500 choices. The pasta must-eats are the homemade gnocchi in tomato-cream; or a tangle of linguini in spicy tomato-basil with fresh seafood from the Market. If you're in for *secondi*, the rack of lamb is heady with rosemary and sauce sweet with Sangiovese wine and there's always plenty of in-season seafood from Market vendors for a memorable *cioppino*. There's more on this menu, but save yourself for either the cheesecake with its lemon glaze and almond crust or the Marquis, a chocolate mousse cake so rich it ought to be a controlled substance. *$$$; AE, DC, MC, V; no checks; dinner every day; full bar; reservations recommended; valet parking Thurs–Sat, street parking; ilbistro.net; map:J8 &*
WHY GO: To nosh appetizers in the classically romantic Pike Place Market.

Il Terrazzo Carmine / ★★★

411 1ST AVE S, PIONEER SQUARE; 206/467-7797 More than a few consider this to be Seattle's top Italian restaurant. Those who disagree often do so without conviction. Carmine Smeraldo's handsome and romantic restaurant is nestled in an urban-renewed alley, with entrances through the historic lobby on First Avenue or through the back courtyard. The airy room and small terrace outside are a perfect environment for the kind of romantic but decisive tête-à-tête it requires to navigate the formidable and tempting menu. For a lusty starter there's calamari in *padella* (Italian frying pan), tender squid in a heady tomato-garlic sauté, or fresh spinach sautéed with lemon and garlic. The creamy soup of prawns and roast peppers is rich and unusual. Cannellonis are creamy and bubbly with ricotta and filled with veal and spinach; the fettuccine is tossed with house-smoked salmon, mushrooms, and peas. The outstanding osso buco is braised in red wine and served with buttered fettuccine. The prime-cut tenderloin is roasted and served with a wine and pancetta sauce. Tiramisu and crème brûlée are appropriately decadent and well crafted, but so are the ever-changing choices such as cheesecakes, cannolis, or house-made gelati that showcase local fruits in season. A guitarist plays classical music most nights, adding to the dreamy escapism of this exceptional restaurant. *$$$; AE, DC, DIS, MC, V; no checks; lunch Mon–Fri, dinner Mon–Sat; full bar; reservations recommended; valet parking; ilterrazzcarmine.com; map:O8 &*
WHY GO: The osso buco is oh-so-good-o.

Imperial Garden Seafood Restaurant / ★★

18230 EAST VALLEY HWY, KENT; 425/656-0999 Imperial Garden is located in the Great Wall Mall, which should tell you something. That it's Chinese? That it's a long way from Seattle? Well, not that far; just Kent. Though the high-ceilinged room is a bit stark, the food is the focus. And many consider it among the area's best. Usually kitchens need 24 hours' notice to prepare Peking duck. Not here; duckie is first carted to the table, the delectable, nearly fat-free skin cut into little patches to be eaten with little pancakes and sauces. The denuded duck is taken back to the kitchen, reappearing boneless and braised in a delicate broth of wine, more spices, and mushrooms. If duck doesn't do it for you, try the panfried black cod, whole fish steamed in clay casseroles, one of the many noodle dishes, or vegetables with roasted nuts. Dim sum is served every day at lunch: lobster dumplings, almond shrimp balls, pork buns with airy pastry as delicate as any strudel in Vienna. The pork *shiu mai* with black mushrooms are little satchel bombs of flavor, as are the panfried vegetable dumplings or shrimp-stuffed tofu. *$; DIS, MC, V; no checks; breakfast, lunch, dinner, dim sum every day; full bar; reservations recommended; self parking; imperial garden@greatwallmall.com; imperialgardenseafood.com; map:PP4* &

WHY GO: Can't-miss Peking duck!

India Bistro / ★★★

2301 NW MARKET ST, BALLARD; 206/783-5080 We cannot think of a better endorsement of any restaurant than a marked-up copy of their takeout menu magnetically secured to our refrigerator. Such is the case with India Bistro. Run by three partners—manager Mike Panjabi and chef Gian Jaswal and his assistant Gurmohan Singh—India Bistro is one of the most enduring Indian restaurants in the city. The exotic smells of the Malabar Coast or Kashmiri Province come from an unlikely corner in Seattle's old Norwegian neighborhood, Ballard, and is the destination of frequent pilgrimages by Indian nationals. The long menu has curries, vegetarian dishes, Indian breads, and meats from the tandoor—the superhot, vertical clay oven. Try the pakoras, little bundles of vegetables, chicken, or fish fried in a lentil-flour batter served with mint chutney and the mulligatawny soup. Infinitely shareable entrées include *kabli masala*, delicate garbanzo beans cooked with onions and spices, and lamb *vindaloo*, a spicy stew with potatoes, and splash of vinegar. Accompanying rice is buttery, flakey, and fragrant. Order the cooling raita on the side if these specialties are too spicy (heat is determined by the star system). From the tandoor, don't miss the delectable and inexpensive lamb rack or the fish cooked amazingly moist at 800°F. The naan is tender and the best way to soak up rich gravies and sauces. *$; AE, DC, DIS, MC, V; no checks; lunch Mon–Sat, dinner every day; beer and wine; reservations recommended; street parking; map:FF8* &

WHY GO: $5.95 lunch buffet served Monday through Saturday.

Isabella Ristorante / ★★★

1909 3RD AVE, DOWNTOWN; 206/441-8281 The walls are the color of late-August pimentos. The striking columns of Prussian blue, floral-brocaded booths, white linen, and a blue-tiled applewood-burning brick oven give Isabella a European feel. A faithful following comes for the large menu with such enduring Seattle favorites as Ravioli Bosco, fresh spinach four-cheese pasta with sautéed wild mushrooms, tomatoes, and artichoke hearts. Cannelloni di Carne stuffed with veal, pork, and spinach is a cheesy landmark in this cannelloni-deprived town. The signature lamb shanks are braised with shiitakes and fragrant with a rosemary-infused demi-glace. The thin-crusted pizzas are good for lunch or before- or after-theater suppers—with quality toppings like house-made sausage, Parma ham, or prosciutto. Finish it all off with tiramisu or the strawberry and white-chocolate torte. Service is professional, and the servers well informed. *$$; AE, CB, DC, DIS, JCB, MC, V; local checks only; lunch Mon–Fri, dinner every day; full bar; reservations recommended; street parking; isabella@isabellaristorante.com; isabella ristorante.com; map:I7* &

WHY GO: Sexy pasta, licentious decor.

JaK's Grill / ★★

4548 CALIFORNIA AVE SW, WEST SEATTLE; 206/937-7809 / 3701 NE 45TH ST, LAURELHURST; 206/985-8545 / 14 FRONT ST N, ISSAQUAH; 425/837-8834 For a no-baloney steak house that serves good corn-fed Nebraska beef that they dry-age themselves, JaK's is the place. Make that the places. The steaks are first rate, but then so are the pork chops, particularly a double-thick fella, marinated in bourbon and brown sugar, glazed with honey and peppercorn. Top of the line is the 21-ounce porterhouse, about $35. The rest check in at midtwenties down to the upper teens, grilled just right, and topped with seasoned butter. Meats come with salad and spud—fried, baked, or mashed. Wines come from California and Washington. Expect to wait for a table; concentrate on the food, not the digs; and at meal's end, expect your ears to be ringing. *$$; DC, DIS, MC, V; checks OK; dinner every day; full bar; no reservations; self and street parking; map:II8, FF6* &

WHY GO: You get your salad, you get your sides, no nickel and diming.

BEST PLACE FOR BREAKFAST?
"The Hi Spot in Madrona, outside if the weather is sunny."
Joel Connelly, Seattle Post-Intelligencer *political columnist*

Jitterbug Cafe / ★★

2114 N 45TH ST, WALLINGFORD; 206/547-6313 This little sliver of a place is another neighborhood gem from the minds of Peter Levy and Jeremy Hardy, who run a culinary empire that includes Coastal Kitchen, Endolyne Joe's, 5 Spot Cafe (see reviews), and Atlas Foods. Typically large menus are a little heavy on the schtick (Tumblewood Dan's High Desert Rumble: a scramble of Anaheim chiles, cilantro, romas, and pepperjack loaded on roasted corn cakes). Fending off boredom seems to be the intent, and it works. Breakfast is a high point: gingerbread waffles and great scrambles and omelets, such as one with chicken Italian sausage, sun-dried tomatoes, scallions, and pecorino. Dinners range from steak and frites to skewers of prawns and scallops. Eggs, spudcakes, and bacon or sausage are served up all day. *$; MC, V; checks OK; breakfast, lunch, dinner every day; full bar; reservations recommended; street parking; chowfoods.com; map:FF7* &

WHY GO: Perfect for a bite or drink before or after a flick at the Guild 45th theater across the street.

Kabul Afghan Cuisine / ★★

2301 N 45TH ST, WALLINGFORD; 206/545-9000 In Afghanistan, cooks marinate meats and infuse them with mint, coriander, cilantro, and dill. There's lots of cooling yogurt, scallions, and basmati rice. Chef Sultan Malikyar, who emigrated from Afghanistan in the late '70s, shares his family's recipes, which include his father's kebab and his mother's *chaka* (garlic-yogurt sauce). He and partner Wali Khairzada make fragrant, elegant food such as crisp *bolani* (scallion-potato turnovers with *chaka* for dipping), *ashak* (delicate scallion dumplings with either beef or vegetarian tomato sauce), and kebabs served on perfumed piles of basmati. The dining room's simple decor is as soothing as the cardamom-and-rose-water custard *firni* (sometimes known as Turkish Delight) served for dessert. *$; AE, DIS, MC,V; local checks only; dinner every day; beer and wine; reservations required; street parking; map:FF7* ♿

WHY GO: Live sitar music on Tuesdays and Thursdays.

Kaspar's / ★★★

19 W HARRISON ST, QUEEN ANNE; 206/298-0123 Just west of the Seattle Center, Kaspar Donier has been at it since 1996, coupling classic European cooking styles with fresh Northwest ingredients. His place is an easy, intimate room with bamboo accents and shoji screens in shades of brown and green, with a lattice-shaded solarium on the lower level—the favored seats. Some just stop by to duck into the cozy wine bar, with outstanding wines by the glass drawn from a broad list of mostly West Coast labels. Well-trained servers make you feel welcome and well cared for. Order the sampler tower—Donier selects three of the ever-changing appetizers. These may include broad-flavor-profiled smoked trout bruschetta with apple horseradish, salmon rice cake with black-bean aioli, juniper-cured sockeye, or his take on Vietnamese spring rolls. Though seafood gets the royal treatment, don't overlook the meats, such as the huge Chianti-braised lamb shank and a roasted duck breast with pear compote. A mushroom dusting further elevates ling cod; spicy bacon-spinach sauce raises divers scallops to the surface and beyond. Desserts, such as the fudge cake with pecans à la mode, are sublime. The pre-theater crowd loves Kaspar's, because they never miss an opening curtain. *$$$; AE, MC, V; no checks; dinner Tues–Sat; full bar; reservations recommended; valet and self parking; info@kaspars.com; kaspars.com; map:A8* ♿

WHY GO: Only place in town currently selling curried french fries with pear ketchup.

Kingfish Café / ★★☆

602 19TH AVE E, CAPITOL HILL; 206/320-8757 The Coaston sisters have their restaurant just the way they want it—busy. The cuisine is sassy Southern classics served in a stylish, casual, contemporary space with blown-up sepia-tinted photos from the family album on the walls—including one of distant cousin Langston Hughes. They take no reservations, so expect lines of chatty people, wine glasses in hand. It's worth it for the likes of Jazz It Slow Gumbo, loaded with tasso and prawns; velvety pumpkin soup; catfish cakes with green-tomato tartar sauce; and the famous buttermilk fried chicken. Lunch is even more of a bargain—try the pulled pork sandwich with peach and watermelon barbecue sauce. Save room for three-layer red velvet cake or strawberry shortcake. At Sunday brunch those crab and catfish cakes are topped with a poached egg and hollandaise. *$$; MC, V; checks OK; lunch, dinner every day but Tues, brunch Sun; beer and wine; no reservations; street parking; map:HH7* &

WHY GO: To put some South in your mouth in a hip, northern setting.

Kolbeh Persian Restaurant / ★★⯪

1956 1ST AVE S, PIONEER SQUARE; 206/224-9999 The dining room is like a living room in Tehran, but once you taste the food, you'll forgive the plastic flowers and Persian kitsch. Owner Fereydoon Aboosaidi reopened Kolbeh in spring 2003 after the damage caused by the 2001 earthquake. The King of Beef kebob is made with a pound of tenderloin; the boneless, skinless chicken kebob is marinated in lemon juice and fragrant with saffron. The meat falls off the bone of the saffron-scented roast lamb shank served with a pilau with fresh dill and lima beans. There are plenty of vegetarian dishes, such as *khoresht bademjan* (eggplant stew), hummus, and baba ghanouj. This is a baseball neighborhood, but in the spirit of cultural exchange, Kolbeh gives us the Iranian national pastime: belly dancing. On weekends after 10pm, Iranian expats unwind by winding on the dance floor to DJs spinning hot Persian hits. *$$; AE, MC, V; local checks only; lunch, dinner every day; beer and wine; reservations recommended on weekends or for groups of 10 or more; street parking; kolbehseattle.com; map:HH7* &

WHY GO: Authentic beef kebob and belly dancing.

La Louisiana / ★★★⯪

2514 E CHERRY ST, CENTRAL DISTRICT; 206/329-5007 It's Big Easy elegance and rich Creole/Cajun cooking in this busy and comfortable dining room around the corner from Garfield High School. This neighborhood is not flush with upscale restaurants, but after a rash of great reviews and lots of buzz, this one thrives both with its neighbors and as a destination for lovers of elegant N'awlins cuisine. Well-lit rooms are warm in pale yellow with dark wainscoting, soft lighting, mirrors and well-chosen tchotchkes. A good way to taste the standards is to order the Creole combo—which includes a cup of filé gumbo, jambalaya loaded with sausage, ham, and shrimp; rich red-crawfish étouffé; and red beans and rice. Chef Jemil Johnson breaks out from the standards with a delicious Northwest/Cajun take on a classic with his Blackened Salmon Rockefeller, and his bread pudding with whiskey sauce is a heart-stopping wonder. *$$; AE, MC, V; checks OK; lunch, dinner every day; liquor license pending; reservations recommended for 8 or more; street parking; map:HH6* &

WHY GO: The only upscale Creole/Cajun cooking in town.

La Medusa / Unrated

4857 RAINIER AVE S, COLUMBIA CITY; 206/723-2192 Girls rule at La Medusa and have since 1997, when Lisa Becklund and Sherri Serino opened this cozy, twinkle-lit storefront to serve what they call "Sicilian soul food" in the Rainier Valley's gently gentrifying Columbia City neighborhood. Today, new owner and chef Julie Andres (a veteran of the La Medusa kitchen who took over in 2003) leads the all-female corps de cuisine. Start with the house-smoked trout salad tossed with arugula and avocado or the seasonal Grandma's Greens braised with pine nuts, kalamatas, and golden raisins served in broth in a bowl with tiny corn muffins. The *spaghetti con le sarde* (which would be the national dish if Sicily were a nation), a rich heap of pasta, fresh sardines, fennel, raisins, pine nuts, olives, and tomatoes, will linger in your memory. Their manicotti are crespelle stuffed fat with fluffy herbed ricotta and baked with fresh mozzarella and marinara. A kids menu has Sicilian versions of spaghetti, pizza, and mac and cheese. Desserts are house-made—particularly good is the cannoli, a crispy pastry tube filled with ricotta and chocolate bits surrounded with Marsala-soaked fruits. Medium-priced wines mainly hail from southern Italy. *$$; MC, V; no checks; dinner Tues–Sat; beer and wine; reservations recommended for 6 or more; street parking; map:KK6* &

WHY GO: Irresistible hand-formed, thin-crust pizzas.

La Rustica / ★★☆

4100 BEACH DR SW, WEST SEATTLE; 206/932-3020 This cozy restaurant is on Alki Point, but it couldn't be spiritually farther from the muscle-beach scene just blocks away. Giulio and Janie Pellegrini's pretty little place, with its rough-hewn stone walls and arches, thickets of potted plants, dusty wine bottles, and summer-weather al fresco dining has more than mere physical charm. It's a destination for a crowd of not only the West Seattle neighbors, but other city folk smart and savvy enough to know about it. Giulio's signature Osso Buco Balsamico keeps them coming, as do his veal-wrapped sautéed prawns in Marsala. Fresh homemade focaccia comes with everything—such as the spaghetti with garlic and mustard greens, or the *gnocchi con salsiccia*, rich homemade dumplings in tomato sauce with Italian sausage. Janie manages the dining room but doubles as dessert chef with such memorable delectables as bittersweet-chocolate crème brûlée, chocolate decadence, and maybe the best tiramisu west of Belltown. *$$; AE, DIS, MC, V; checks OK; dinner Tues–Sun; full bar; reservations required for 6 or more; street parking; map:JJ9* &

WHY GO: Wine, love, and spaghetti in a nostalgic *Lady and the Tramp* setting.

Lampreia / ★★★★

2400 1ST AVE, BELLTOWN; 206/443-3301 From most seats in his urbane, sparely set dining room, chef/owner Scott Carsberg can be seen in the kitchen five nights a week, performing magic. How can something this simple, diners often ask themselves, be this spectacular? Maybe it's a single slice of seared tuna topped with citrus slices. Possibly it's a veal chop, drizzled with a fonduta sauce. Carsberg is often described as a minimalist, letting a few flavors speak volumes. Many in his near-cultish following consider him a genius. What keeps the sheep's milk cheese gnocchi from floating right off the plate? Others wonder why all the fuss—smallish portions, high prices, big-city attitude. He's a local boy, raised in West Seattle when it was still a blue-collar neighborhood, who made his way to the East Coast and was mentored by a master Tyrolean chef who took him to Italy. Carsberg returned to open his own show in 1992, bringing a New York sensibility and a master chef's sensitivity. Menu descriptors—appetizer, intermezzo, and main course—too are simple, such as "lentils from Verona served as a salad with guinea hen terrine," or "thin sheets of pasta filled with foie gras in beef consommé." He features prize mushrooms—matsutakes and morels, truffles and chanterelles; also, artisan cheese, served perfectly after a meal, an end unto themselves, or as prelude to a delicate lemon tart. Service, as directed by Carsberg's wife, Hyun Joo Paek, is seamless and reverential. *$$$; AE, MC, V; no checks; dinner Tues–Sat; full bar; reservations recommended; street parking; lampreiarestaurant.com; map:F8* &

WHY GO: It's a four-star experience.

Lark / ★★★

926 12TH AVE, CAPITOL HILL 206/323-5275 Bring a group of friends to this new Capitol Hill hot spot and plan to stay a while. The multi-page menu of small plates is unusual, but servers are happy to assist you in composing a meal from categories such as "cheese," "vegetable/grains," and "charcuterie." Plates--expertly prepared from perfectly fresh ingredients--are intended for sharing, but you may want to hoard every bite of dishes such as baby beets with sherry vinegar and tangerine oil; Pommes de terre "Robuchon" (baked mashed potatoes); flat iron steak with parsley salad and blue cheese; smoked prosciutto with a 12th-century chutney; and halibut cheeks with stoneground grits. Flowing white curtains can be cleverly arranged to create an aura of privacy in the softly lit, wood-floored open space. Chef Johnathan Sundstrom earned a following at Seattle's Earth & Ocean and Dahlia Lounge and the crowd here is food-savvy and sophisticated. The no-reservations policy (except for large groups) can cause a crush at the tiny bar in the back. Have patience--and a glass of wine from the small, quirky list--the meal will be worth the wait. *$$$ MC, V; checks OK; dinner, Tues–Sun; full bar; reservations recommended; street parking; map:M1* &

WHY GO: Blood Orange Pavlova, the dessert seductively combines sweet and sour flavors of blood oranges, vanilla meringue, and lemon curd.

Le Gourmand / ★★★★

425 NW MARKET ST, BALLARD; 206/784-3463 Bruce Naftaly is one of the seminal purveyors of Northwest regional cooking. He combs the region for ingredients, and in his French kitchen uses vegetables and flowers from his own garden and from producers he's cultivated for many years. With the advent of the Italian-joint-on-every-corner era, his unlikely French store-front on the edge of Ballard has endured and matured into fine-honed perfection. Service is personal and capable in this quiet, romantic room, with its ceiling painted like a clear spring day and a *trompe l'oeil* wall of trees, hollyhocks, and lupines. Naftaly's prix-fixe menu includes appetizer choices, entrées, and *salade après*. His fortes are sauces, such as the creamy one with local caviars gracing the sole, or the huskier one with shiitakes, Cognac, and fresh sage accompanying the loin of rabbit. Naftaly married Sara Lavenstein, a pastry chef, a fortunate coupling for us all. The wine list features a notable collection of French, California, and Northwest bottles, with plenty of good midrange price options. *$$$; AE, MC, V; local checks only; dinner Wed–Sat; beer and wine; reservations recommended; street parking; map:FF8* &

WHY GO: A "secret garden" dining experience and profiteroles with house-made ice cream.

Le Pichet / ★★★

1933 1ST AVE, DOWNTOWN; 206/256-1499 Stepping into this narrow *café à vin* near the Market feels like walking into a vintage black-and-white postcard taken of la Rive Gauche. Owned by chef Jim Drohman (a Campagne expat) and business partner Joanne Herron (formerly of the Ruins), this cafe features a collection of house-made charcuterie—pâtés, sausages, and confits—that lesser places would buy from France. Parisian ambience with warm overhead lighting and wood-framed mirrors put tables together so couples are seated with strangers—before long expect to be offering bites of the *tartare de boeuf* in exchange for potted pork. The petit zinc bar, manned most nights by David Butler, is just long enough to sit a handful of patrons for espresso and brioche in the morning and Alsatian beer or a glass of Bordeaux *la nuit*. Settling in with the song stylings of Edith Piaf or Maurice Chevalier, it is hard to imagine a more transporting start to a Parisian meal than the curly endive salad with lardons, fingerling potatoes, and poached egg. Your next stop on this tour de Paris should be the chicken liver terrine followed by the grilled pork and garlic sausage over red pepper and white bean stew or the sautéed hanger steak with potatoes, fava beans, and Madiera pan sauce. The how-do-they-charge-that-and-stay-in-business wine list has about 50 labels, mostly French, and most under $25 and available by the glass, *pichet* (two-thirds of a 750ml bottle), or *demi-pichet* (two glasses). *$$; MC, V; no checks; breakfast every day, lunch, dinner Thurs–Mon; full bar; reservations recommended; street parking; map:I8* &

WHY GO: *Poulet roti*, a whole chicken roasted to order (allow one hour), for two.

Lee's Asian Restaurant / ★★☆

4510 CALIFORNIA AVE SW, WEST SEATTLE; 206/932-8209 Lee's is a little place with big flavors. You'll be glad you found this unpretentious storefront gem but be warned: many already have. Owners and brothers Wei and Bill Lee have worked at Shallots Asian Bistro and Wild Ginger, respectively, and their cooking is truly pan-Asian with emphasis on their native Chinese. You can taste each flavor—lemongrass, peanuts, hoisin, chilies, basil, garlic, and ginger in the Seven Flavor Beef, a pungent dry stir-fry of thin flank steak. Crispy Pepper Tofu is fried to a crisp skin without a hint of grease and served with a jalapeño hot and sour dipping sauce. The golden Fragrant Duck is served with steamed clamshell buns to make little sandwiches with slices of duck breast with sweet sauces. The menu is huge but the two most important things to remember: order the beef and make reservations. *$; MC, V; no checks; lunch, dinner Mon–Sat; beer and wine; reservations recommended; street parking and free lot in back; map:JJ9* &

WHY GO: All the flavors of Asia, without the sticker shock of Wild Ginger.

Luau Polynesian Lounge / ★★

2253 N 56TH ST, GREEN LAKE; 206/633-5828 Contrary to what others might tell you, one can survive on a steady diet of pupus and piña coladas. The spirit of aloha greets you at the door like the sweet fragrance of plumeria in Hawai'i, thanks to owners Jessica and Thomas Price's island vibe. Chef Geoffrey Yahn's menu roams the Pacific Rim for pulled pork, pupu platters, potstickers, sticky rice, and stir-fries, and ambles down to the Caribbean with nods at Mexico and Jamaica, yet still manages to serve a darn good burger. We love the complimentary onion marmalade that comes to the table with toasted pita triangles. Served with serrano chile corn bread, you'll gnaw the Big Daddy Mack's smoked Hawai'ian-style baby back ribs to the bone. Late night, talk story at the bar sipping exotic tropical potables like the Kaha Mai Tai or the Hawai'ian Punch. Onolicious, brah. *$$; AE, MC, V; checks OK; lunch Tues–Fri, dinner every day; full bar; reservations recommended; street parking; luaupolynesianlounge.com; map:EE7* &

WHY GO: Classic Trader Vic's Zombie, made with all the rums in the house (limit two per couple).

Luna Park Cafe / ★

2918 AVALON WY SW, WEST SEATTLE; 206/935-7250 Decked out in old neon and memorabilia, this West Seattle beanery is named after the "Coney Island of the West," the amusement park that glittered on the northern tip of West Seattle from 1907 to 1913. Simpler times are celebrated with tableside jukeboxes loaded with Top 40 hits and retro foods mostly from the 1950s: burgers, real malts, grilled sandwiches, meat loaf, prime rib dip, and a popular fresh roasted turkey and Swiss. And proportions are equally old-fashioned—large. The diner will flood you with memories of those bygone days, even if you never lived them. In summer, colorful tables and shade umbrellas draw impromptu traffic. *$; MC, V; checks OK; breakfast, lunch, dinner every day; beer and wine; reservations required for 6 or more during the week, recommended on weekends; self parking; map:JJ9* &

WHY GO: When they say jumbo hot fudge sundae, they're not kidding.

Macrina Bakery & Cafe / ★★☆

2408 IST AVE, BELLTOWN; 206/448-4032 / 615 W MCGRAW ST, QUEEN ANNE; 206/283-5900 Artisanal baker Leslie Mackie cast a spell on Seattle when she opened Macrina Bakery & Cafe 10 years ago in the (then upstart) Belltown neighborhood. The enchantment renews each morning as fresh bread, pastry, and the aroma of espresso greet still-sleepy downtown residents and on-the-go commuters. Folks fortunate enough to linger over breakfast secure a table or counter stool and start their day with homemade bread pudding with fresh fruit and cream or house-made granola and yogurt. Lunch charms with simple salads, sandwiches, and a *mezze*—your choice of three Mediterranean-inspired noshes. Afternoon lulls are banished with a pick-me-up cookie and a strong cup of organic coffee. Arguably producing the best loaves in town, Marcrina's wholesale division supplies many of Seattle's best restaurants with a variety of Mackie's loaves (which are also available for purchase). Recently, Mackie came out with a new cookbook *(The Macrina Bakery & Cafe Cookbook)* and a second cafe location on the west side of Queen Anne Hill—the magic continues. *$; MC, V; local checks only; breakfast, lunch Mon–Fri, brunch Sat–Sun; beer and wine; no reservations; macrinabakery.com; street parking; map:F8,GG8* &

WHY GO: Apricot nut bread—light sourdough with dried, Turkish apricots, roasted walnuts, and pecans (Fri–Sat only).

Madison Park Cafe / ★★★

1807 42ND AVE E, MADISON PARK; 206/324-2626 In a charming converted '20s era clapboard house resides the very soul of Madison Park. Chef Adam Straatman, who took the top toque when Marianne Zdobyzs moved on to the Buenos Aires Grill, has proven to have a skilled hand with the gently French menu. There's an incredible chicken liver terrine with Dijon, cornichon, picholine olives, and warm baguette. The chèvre gnocchi elevate potatoes to the ethereal. Depend on the rich cassoulet, done right with multiple meats and white beans. If the salmon isn't wild, it's not available. Consider the lovely Lavender Honey Rack of Lamb (free-range meats here). Host/owner Karen Binder takes outdoor reservations for the weekend brunch, which offers such temptations as huevos rancheros, sourdough waffles, and ricotta pancakes. *$$; AE, MC, V; checks OK; dinner Tues–Thurs, brunch Sat–Sun; full bar; reservations recommended; street parking; madison park@aol.com; madisonparkcafe.citysearch.com; map:GG6*

WHY GO: The cobblestone courtyard is one of the city's outstanding al fresco venues.

Mae's Phinney Ridge Café / ★

6412 PHINNEY AVE N, GREENWOOD; 206/782-1222 Images of Holstein cows adorn Mae Barwick's noisy, north-end eggs-and-hashbrowns mecca, and there always seems to be a herd out front waiting for a table. Fortunately the wait is rarely very long for the four sprawling dining areas. Portions of giant omelets and scrambles, pancakes, and french toast are huge. For advanced carbo-loading there's the famous Spud Feast—a mountain of fried potatoes with onions, sweet peppers, cheese, sour cream, and salsa. Service is casually rushed, but you might have to flag down a server for a coffee refill. An espresso bar offers access from a walk-up window. *$; MC, V; checks OK; breakfast every day, lunch Mon–Fri; no alcohol; reservations recommended for 6 or more; self and street parking; maescafe.com; map:EE8* &

WHY GO: Farm-size servings of potatoes or grits with every order.

Malay Satay Hut / ★★★

212 12TH AVE S, CHINATOWN/INTERNATIONAL DISTRICT (AND BRANCH); 206/324-4091 After a fire in 2001, fans of this tasty strip-mall storefront in Seattle's Little Saigon fretted that this flavor hub where Malaysia meets China, India, and Thailand might be gone forever. But all's well. Sam and Jessy Yoo first opened a long-planned new location in Redmond, then reopened the noisy, ambience-free Seattle location. The Eastside place (15230 NE 24th St, Redmond; 425/564-0888) kitsched up with Lava Lamps and retrojunk, has the same incredible food and prices, and is every bit as busy but a little less chaotic. It's easy to get addicted to the high intensity flavors of the Huts' seafood, curries, wontons, stirfries, and satays. Order the *roti canai*, Indian flatbread served with a potato-chicken curry sauce; the *asam laksa*, Penang-style hot and sour noodle soup; or Buddha's Yam Pot, a chicken, shrimp, and vegetable stir-fry in a deep-fried basket of grated yams. The service is fast; to-go orders are recommended if you want to avoid the noisy bustle and waiting for seats. *$; MC, V; no checks; lunch, dinner every day; beer and wine; reservations accepted for 6 or more; self parking; map:HH6, EE1* &

WHY GO: Flavors of Malay Peninsula, China, India, and Thailand in one cuisine.

Malena's Taco Shop / ★

620 W MCGRAW ST, QUEEN ANNE (AND BRANCH); 206/284-0304 Sandwiched between an upholsterer and a yoga studio on the west side of Queen Anne Hill, Malena's is the little taco shop that could. Eva Coboorubias opened Malena's in 1997 and has enjoyed a line of devotees spilling out of her petite parlor ever since. A shoebox of a place with only four oilcloth-covered tables and as many counter stools, most folks order to-go from the large menu board, with sights set on a park bench. Tables turn quickly, so order, loiter, and wait for the next available seat. Combination plates come with flakey, lightly seasoned Mexican rice and a heaping spoonful of plump beans, stewed to tender perfection. Favorite combos include carne asada tacos and pork tamales. These simple, delicious meals are served on plastic plates, and counter service is gracious in this bus-your-own taqueria. A second location recently opened in Ballard (2010 NW 56th St; 206/789-8207) and offers four times the seating. *$; local checks only; lunch, dinner every day (Ballard location closed Sun); no alcohol; no reservations; street parking; map:GG8*

WHY GO: The *molcajete* of spicy salsa and salty chips.

BEST PLACE FOR A MICROBREW OR THREE?

"The thing is, I don't like guys who say the word 'microbrew.' "

Sherman Alexie, poet, novelist, and screenwriter

Maple Leaf Grill / ★★

8929 ROOSEVELT WY NE, MAPLE LEAF; 206/523-8449 In the 13 years since opening a block south from its present coordinates, the Maple Leaf Grill has seen a lot of change. There was the fortuitous move in 2000 (a year later the original site was engulfed in a fire). Rip, the legendary opening chef has come and gone and come and gone again (and with him his legendary Rocker's Iko seafood stew). Today the place is owned by music promoter Ed Beeson, who bought it in 2001, and efforts in the kitchen are led by Tony Magnelli. Order the steamers du jour or the Mars' oyster stew full of tasso ham, shallots, artichoke hearts, and spinach. Or make a meal out of roadhouse greens with herb mustard vinaigrette, a side of skin-on fries with garlicky rémoulade sauce for dipping, and a pint of Hefeweizen. It's a conversation-friendly bar filled with classic-rock tunes, where flannel- and denim-clad regulars discuss the news over bowls of Caribbean black-bean soup or the best damn grilled sandwiches in town. *$$; MC, V; checks OK; lunch Mon–Fri, dinner every day, brunch Sat–Sun; full bar; reservations recommended; self parking; www.mapleleafgrill.com; map:DD7* &

WHY GO: Addictive mozzarella and roasted red pepper sandwich.

Marco's Supperclub / ★★⯪

2510 1ST AVE, BELLTOWN; 206/441-7801 This funky place was part of the Belltown renaissance. Out front, a few covered tables afford hip, sidewalk ambience. Inside, what looks like the bookkeeping paperwork anchors one end of the bar, which runs the length of the room. Overhead hang what look like old, gold brocade sofa cushions—now absorbing sound rather than the impact of the human butt. Veteran restaurateur Marco Rulff roams the room, greeting the regulars and welcoming the uninitiated. The capable kitchen kicks out bushes and bushes of its signature fried sage leaves to get a meal started, or the shiitake mushroom spring rolls. Exotic entrées include Pork Manchamantel, a double-cut chop with pineapple–red chile sauce and poblano mashers. An eclectic collection of European and Northwest wines is available by the bottle or glass. In the fair-weather months, a deck out back doubles the seating capacity. *$$; AE, MC, V; checks OK; dinner every day; full bar; reservations recommended; street parking; map:F8* ⅃

WHY GO: Jamaican jerk chicken served with sweet potato purée and sautéed greens.

BEST PLACE TO SEE AND BE SEEN?
"Safeco Field—walking around the concourse.
You can enjoy the ballgame and the people."
Greg Nickels, mayor of Seattle

Marjorie / ★★★

2331 2ND AVE, BELLTOWN; 206/441-9842 When Donna Moodie and then-husband Marco Rulff split the linen, their two dinner restaurants stayed in the family. He got his namesake Marco's Supperclub and she the lovely Lush Life, which she transformed from dreamy Italian to romantic eclectic and renamed after her mother. In bold jewel tones, colorful raw silk, and dynamic metal work, this vaguely Moroccan room is stunning but comfortable. Chef Tyler Boring is well traveled and his menu shows it. Indian onion pakoras are thick rings fried in chickpea batter, resembling a huge cinnamon roll with layers to be pulled off and dipped in curried ketchup and green coriander chutney. There's such pan-globals as Sri Lankan curried eggplant, baked ricotta ravioli, *fleur de sel*–roasted chicken with sour-cherry sauce all served up with handmade chapatis. Moodie is the architect of simple-sounding desserts such as the huge pieces of chocolate layer or lemon chiffon cake, which are, like her restaurant, studies in richness and triumphs of presentation. *$$; AE, MC, DIS, V; checks OK; dinner Tues–Sun; full bar; reservations recommended; street parking; marjorie@trenchtownrocks.com; trenchtownrocks.com; map:G8*

WHY GO: Jewel-box interior and thick-and-tasty onion pakoras.

Market Street Urban Grill / ★★★☆

1744 NW MARKET ST, BALLARD; 206/789-6766 Ballard is rapidly transmogrifying from a neighborhood of Scandinavian fisherfolk and backyard piles of gill nets to one with Audis sporting bumper stickers that say "Visualize Ballard." It's now more than a vision, with such amenities as the Majestic Bay, a jewel-box movie theater, and a fine dining restaurant to match. Owners John and Kendell Sillers, veterans of many fine downtown restaurants, hired chef John Paul Kunselman from Rover's to make and cook the consistently imaginative, seasonally changing menus. Start with such an un-Scandinavian appetizer as smoked-prawn spring rolls with Asian slaw, then tuck away fresh crayfish linguine with a Napoleon of spring vegetables. Finish with a chocolate-chip cookie sandwich or an in-season fruit dessert like the Melon Tartare with mascarpone and raspberries. The Sillers have fought through economic thick and thin to establish this quality place on the ground floor of Ballard's gentrification. They seem to be winning. *$$$; AE, DIS, MC, V; checks OK; dinner Mon–Sat; full bar; reservations recommended; self parking; map:EE8* &

WHY GO: It's where crayfish has replaced lutefisk in Ballard.

Mashiko / ★★★

4725 CALIFORNIA AVE SW, WEST SEATTLE; 206/935-4339 It's flying pigs, strange Japanese wind-up toys, and real art on the walls. Saltwater fish tanks are filled with unlikely critters fluttering in crystalline waters. Mashiko is more than a sushi bar: it's an attitude with a sense of humor. Hajime Sato and wife Kirstin Schlecht's off-beat restaurant is where traditional flavors of Japan are served untraditionally. Sato dances behind the sushi bar to the straining strains of ABBA, juggling knives and ahi loins like a one-man chorus line. And incredibly: *there are white women making sushi!* The kitchen, under Nicaraguan native Silvio Lopez, serves delectables from the huge hot menu like teriyaki, tempura, and all that, but also offers such diversities as ceviche or Cajun tempura shrimp. *$$; AE, DC, MC, V; no checks; dinner every day; beer and wine; reservations accepted; self and street parking; sushiwhore.com; map:JJ9* &

WHY GO: Sushi outside the box.

Matt's in the Market / ★★★

94 PIKE ST, 3RD FLOOR, PIKE PLACE MARKET; 206/467-7909 Matt's is Seattle's worst kept secret. It's tucked away in a tiny space on the third floor of the Corner Market Building, with a handful of tables that look out large-paned windows over the Market to Elliott Bay and the Olympic Mountains. From the tiny kitchen space, the durable chef, Erik Canella, turns out food that's not only well crafted, but some of the freshest and most innovative downtown. It's no wonder it's fresh—cooks shop the Market twice a day. Seafood is the best bet here—like the rare-seared albacore, the smoked catfish salad, or the whopping oyster po' boys, heady filé gumbo, or clams and mussels in an ouzo-infused broth. Owner Matt Janke does everything except cook—waiting, greeting, busing, prepping, and washing dishes. Sometimes he manages to squeeze musicians in to play live jazz *$$; MC, V; no checks; lunch, dinner Mon–Sat; beer and wine; reservations recommended; street and validated parking in Market garage after 5pm; map:J8*

WHY GO: Seafood so fresh it threatens escape.

Matt's Rotisserie & Oyster Lounge / ★★

16551 NE 74 ST, REDMOND TOWN CENTER, REDMOND; 425/376-0909 Matt's adds a much-needed urbane option to shoppers and other visitors at Redmond Town Center. It's a rotisserie. It's an oyster lounge. The house specialty is paella. Is the kitchen trying to do too much? Won't say that after a simply satisfying salt-and-pepper half chicken. Nor after the fruitwood-smoked, sweetly glazed baby back ribs or the meats or fish cooked atop the wood-fired grill—especially the various steaks and the king salmon. The little oyster bar jumps, top shells of regional bivalves flying from the hands of sharp-skilled shuckers. The paella, rich with shellfish, bits of smoked meats, and tinged with saffron, arrives in traditional two-handled, hot pans. At dinner, the prime rib regularly sells out, for good reason. The setting is a big, gleaming room awash in deep golds and reds, accented with laser-tooled copper. Servers hop to, sometimes when you wish they'd relax and slow down a bit. Among appetizers, give a nod to the Manila clams, pan-roasted simply in butter and wine. Lunch and dinner menus mirror each other. So-called Argentinean street tacos are a good choice—grilled corn tortillas wrap chunks of that rotisserie-roasted salmon, along with tropical fruit chutney and chili-inflected slaw. *$$; AE, MC, V; checks OK; lunch, dinner every day; reservations recommended; self parking; map:EE1* ⅄

WHY GO: Oysters Matt, a winning combo with spinach, pancetta, and lemon butter.

Maximilien in the Market / ★★★

81A PIKE ST, PIKE PLACE MARKET; 206/682-7270 Maximilien is a charming French restaurant located in the hub of Pike Place Market, owned and operated since 1997 by chef Eric Francy and front man Axel Mace; the pair bought out their former employer, Francois Kissel, who graced the Seattle Gallic restaurant scene with various restaurants for three decades. Here, the Old World style of a Parisian hideaway is set off by panoramic views of Elliott Bay, West Seattle, and the Olympic Mountains. And French classics—tournedos Rossini, frog legs, escargot—gracefully mix with modern offerings, such as seared salmon served over fresh lentil salad dressed in a sensational purple vinaigrette, the color of which comes from the seed of a little-known French mustard. Game lovers should try the quail stuffed with wild mushrooms, foie gras, and port-wine sauce. Lunch has great entrée salads or sandwiches, such as the gooey chicken and Brie. The French-centric wine list is extensive, with a wealth of midpriced wines (wines by the glass are frequently changed) and some expensive imports. *$$; AE, DC, DIS, MC, V; no checks; lunch Mon–Sat, dinner Tues–Sat, brunch Sun; full bar; reservations recommended; valet and street parking; maximilienrestaurant.com; map:J8* ⅄

WHY GO: Superlative omelet and real French accents.

Medin's Ravioli Station / ★★

4620 LEARY WY, FREMONT/BALLARD; 206/789-6680 Make the trip to downtown Frelard, that funky warehouse-y antineighborhood that's part Ballard, part Fremont. Chef/owner Bill Medin serves a steady stream of customers from nearby neighborhoods. The bar, always occupied by a regular crowd of wine 'bibers, has a unique water-heated iron handrail and stools made from train pistons. The big, fat raviolis on the short menu are made using an iron ravioli mold, designed as is all the iron work, by Medin, a metal sculptor in his spare time. Ravioli fillings include house-smoked salmon, roasted butternut squash, three cheeses, beef, and spinach. Match your ravioli with one of the sauces—tomato-cream, marinara, Alfredo, or roasted red pepper. The low-frill dining room, tasteful with candlelight, attracts couples on dates, but the prices, casual atmosphere, and the fact that kids love raviolis make this is a good place for families. *$; MC, V; local checks only; lunch Tues–Fri, dinner Tues–Sun; beer and wine; reservations recommended; street parking; raviolistation.com; map:FF8* &

WHY GO: Sampler ravioli plate for the indecisive.

Metropolitan Grill / ★★★

820 2ND AVE, DOWNTOWN; 206/624-3287 Few Seattle restaurants appear on expense-account reports as often as the Met. Deep in the financial district, this classic but not a bit dated grill caters to local "suits" and well-heeled tourists. Lunch comes with a floorshow of financiers, power brokers, and their underlings table-hopping and networking. After work the same crowd gathers for classic cocktails and single-malt Scotch. Whether on their way to (or from) a Mariners game, the symphony, or the theater, dinner attracts folks who just want a great meal and are not afraid to pay for it. Start with the pristine Dungeness crab cocktail or artichoke hearts flash-fried in *panko* batter and served with grain-mustard aioli. To miss one of the Met's steaks is to miss the point. The cooked-to-order bone-in New York strip and prime porterhouse steaks are well seasoned and flavorful. Tournedos are meltingly tender, although hidden under too much sauce. Seafood is largely found among the specials and is executed surprisingly well, especially the king salmon. Accompaniments such as sautéed mushrooms and scalloped potatoes are offered à la carte. Expect to be well cared for by a well-trained waitstaff and impressed by the wine list, which is heavy with muscular European and domestic reds. *$$$$; AE, DC, DIS, JCB, MC, V; checks OK; lunch Mon–Fri, dinner every day; full bar; reservations recommended; valet parking; themetropolitangrill.com; map:M7* &

WHY GO: Valuable stock tips and the decadent Metropolitan chocolate sundae.

Mistral / ★★★★

113 BLANCHARD ST, BELLTOWN; 206/770-7799 At Mistral, there's no bar, no neon, no attempt to snag the hip Belltown night crawlers. Chef William Belickis, with his "French Moderne" cuisine, was controversial when his stark little luxury restaurant opened in 2000. No one ever denied the innovation, skill, and risks taken by this young chef, but he offended reviewers and diners alike with his micro-managing of the dining experience, which was seen as culinary zealotry. Belickis has mellowed; he and Seattle have gotten used to each other and Mistral is a very special place as a result. On a late-summer visit, we had a velvety sweet-corn soup with a huge Maine scallop crusted in brown phyllo. A fish course brought together a tender skate wing and a "risotto" of bean sprout "rice," tomatoes, and fresh basil. Another plate paired juicy foie gras with plums and port. Entrées are prefaced with changing *amuse bouches*. We suggest the Chef's Tasting Menu, letting Belickis choose the seven courses and match them with appropriate wines. *$$$$; AE, DIS,*

MC, V; *checks OK; lunch Fri–Sat, dinner Tues–Sat; full bar; reservations recommended; street parking; william@mistralseattle.com; mistralseattle.com; map:G8* ♿
WHY GO: First-rate treatment from flawless waitstaff.

Mojito Cafe / ★

7545 LAKE CITY WY NE, LAKE CITY; 206/525-3162 / 181 WESTERN AVE, QUEEN ANNE; 206/217-1180 Rumor has it this joint is hard to find. More likely, it's the improbable setting that throws people. The bright yellow building fairly juts out from its corner and ho-hum neighbors (where Lake City Way heads toward Roosevelt Way). Inside, tropical colors and Latin beats (staff are often moved to conga solos) perk up the eye and ear, and the kitchen takes care of the olfactory sense. If you haven't brushed up on Spanish since junior high, it can be challenging to quiz servers on mysteries of the menu that roams about Latin America. However, lingual negotiations are part of the fun. Besides, it's a good appetite accelerant for offerings such as *parrilla*, grilled slices of steak engulfed by rice, black beans, and fried plantains (made addictive by a garlicky dipping sauce) or *pollo a la parrilla*, starring a succulent, grilled half chicken. Grilled Cuban meat sandwiches—a vegetarian option combines zucchini, red pepper, and mint—are a favorite with the lunch crowd. A new Mojito's, with a fatter menu and a separate bar, opened in Lower Queen Anne in 2003 with a bonus: Friday and Saturday nights, snacks and nonalcoholic drinks are served until 4am. *$; AE, DC, DIS, MC, V; checks OK; breakfast, lunch, dinner every day (Lake City), lunch, dinner everyday (Queen Anne); wine and beer (Lake City), full bar (Queen Anne); street parking; reservations recommended; luigi@mojito.com; mojitocafe.com; map:EE7, B9* ♿
WHY GO: *Mojitos!*—crushed ice laced with lime, mint, rum, and a splash of Sprite.

Mona's / ★★★

6421 LATONA AVE NE, GREEN LAKE; 206/526-1188 It's named after the *Mona Lisa*, but smiles much broader than hers can be seen on the faces of Tito Class and Annette Serrano's satisfied customers. The charm of the candlelit dining room is due in part to Serrano's art, which is more Kahlo than da Vinci. Over the years, this enduring little restaurant has spawned some of the area's finest chefs, and no wonder, the small seasonal Mediterranean menu is reliable, sweet, and the food beautifully presented. Ensalada del Tomba is a seared, rare, black-pepper encrusted chunk of albacore, served with a toasted bread salad, light and tangy with tomatoes and basil oil. For carnivores, there are the classic Mona's pork ribs served with sautéed greens and balsamic roasted potatoes. The couple annexed the storefront next door and converted it into a conversation bar that often features live music—a great place for after-dinner drinks or dessert. *$$; AE, DC, MC, V; no checks; dinner every day; full bar; reservations recommended; street parking; map:EE7* ♿
WHY GO: The house-made tiramisu is among the best in town.

Monsoon / ★★★

615 19TH AVE E, CAPITOL HILL; 206/325-2111 Restaurant-savvy siblings Sophie, Eric, and Yen Banh took Seattle by storm when they opened Monsoon in 1999. Like the wind after which this sleek restaurant was named, the menus at Monsoon change direction with the seasons. An innovative approach to local, seasonal produce is Monsoon's calling. Dishes are prepared in a gleaming open kitchen that fills the spare dining room with exotic fragrances minutes after opening. Don't miss signature appetizers such as the crispy spring roll stuffed with Dungeness crab, shrimp or duck salad with green cabbage and vermicelli, or the traditional tamarind soup with chicken and gulf shrimp. The entrée portions are agreeably ample. Share the wokked five-spice flank steak with Chinese celery and hot-house tomatoes or the seared scallops with bok choy and black-bean sauce. Vegetable dishes, such as the oven-baked Asian eggplant with grilled lobster mushroom and spicy green beans with butternut squash, make the menu welcoming to vegetarians. Waits can be long and the dining room can be very noisy when full. *$$; MC, V; no checks; lunch Tues–Fri, dinner Tues–Sun; beer and wine; reservations recommended; street parking; monsoon seattle.com; map:HH6* &

WHY GO: Asian fare–friendly wine list brimming with rieslings, gewürztraminers, and pinot noirs.

Nell's / ★★★★

6804 E GREEN LAKE WY N, GREEN LAKE; 206/524-4044 Green Lake is a vibrant, muscular neighborhood, well-endowed with physical beauty and economic health. Spandexed hordes aerobically circle the lake as does a dynamic commercial ring that taps this energy while serving it. Since opening in 1999, Nell's has more than stayed in shape. In the hallowed space that was the iconic Saleh el Lago, chef/owner Philip Mihalski redecorated the multilevel lakeview dining room, but it's still recognizable and a comfort to old regulars. Dishes are artfully prepared and presented, and Mihalski's seasonally changing menus take full advantage of Northwest ingredients. Wonderful flavor combinations might show up in a starter of black cod with tomato salad, romano beans, and pesto or in the signature entrée of pan-seared duck breast served with baby turnips, wilted greens, and shallot vinaigrette. Or opt for the tasting menu, which might travel from lobster broth with Dungeness crab to pan-seared foie gras to Kobe hangar steak. Desserts are dreamy affairs. French toast made with brioche and accompanied by blueberry compote and apricot ice cream is as sensational as it sounds. *$$$; AE, MC, V; checks OK; dinner every day; full bar; reservations recommended; valet and self parking; info@nells restaurant.com; nellsrestaurant.com; map:EE7*

WHY GO: Indulge in sensual desserts, then work off the calories at nearby Green Lake.

Nishino / ★★★★

3130 E MADISON ST, MADISON PARK; 206/322-5800 On the fringe of moneyed Madison Park, Kyoto-born Tatsu Nishino's space is decorated with spare, Japanese elegance. Let Nishino-san, who worked five years at the famed Matsuhisa in Los Angeles, choose your dinner *omikase*-style from the voluptuous and strikingly arranged display of fresh seafood that is the centerpiece of this restaurant. Look to the fresh sheet for such richly flavored dishes as pan-seared halibut cheeks with shiitake mushrooms and spinach with bits of sea urchin, all in a luxurious butter sauce. While you can always opt for tempura or teriyaki, you would miss much of the sheer joy of dining at Nishino if you bypassed the dozens of classical sushi items listed on the menu. Don't miss the popular Banana Tempura—caramel drizzled over crispy *panko*-fried bananas and vanilla ice cream. *$$$; AE, MC, V; no checks; dinner every day; full bar; reservations recommended; self parking; map:GG6.* ♿

WHY GO: Perfection in classical sushi and seasonal Japanese cuisine.

Noble Court / ★★

1644 140TH AVE NE, BELLEVUE; 425/641-6011 Dim sum threatens to become ubiquitous. But on the Eastside, Noble Court has long been one of the top purveyors. The crowds show it, especially the lines on Sunday. In fact, it may be best to avoid the crowds and go on Saturday. Steamed shrimp dumplings, pork buns, lotus seed balls, and chicken feet with oyster and black-bean sauce are only the beginning of the movable feast carted from table to table. The regular menu is massive, too. There's a live tank with Dungeness and king crabs, lobster, prawns, tilapia, and ling cod, all plucked from the water and served with a choice of sauces. Other seafood specialties include whole flounder and rockfish, geoduck, and abalone. There are hot pots, sizzling platters, and a lot of noodles. You can also get Peking duck without a 24-hour advance order. *$$; AE, MC, V; no checks; lunch, dinner Mon–Fri, dim sum every day; full bar; reservations recommended; self parking; www.noblecourtrestaurant.com; map:GG2* ♿

WHY GO: Go for the dim sum; stay for the fresh seafood dinner.

BEST PLACE FOR EAVESDROPPING?

"The lineups at the Egyptian Theatre during SIFF. Especially during opening weekend, when filmgoers are still fresh and hungry to hear what's hot and what's not."

Darryl Macdonald, co-founder of Seattle International Film Festival (SIFF)

The Oceanaire Seafood Room / ★★★☆

1700 7TH AVE, DOWNTOWN; 206/267-2277 Seattleites were skeptical about this chain restaurant's nostalgic take on the classic fish house. But then they got a load of chef Kevin Davis's massive menu with 30 daily-changing seafoods, high standards for freshness, and huge portions. The service is seamless in this room that's a 1940s supperclub in steamship moderne, art deco, comfy booths, and walls with stuffed groupers and swordfish. There are all the fish house classics— oysters Rockefeller, fish-and-chips, but don't miss Davis's herb-crusted sturgeon or Aunt Joy's Stuffed Petrale with Dungeness crab, bay shrimp, and Brie. Everything's à la carte, which can make this an expensive outing. The good news is that half orders of the immense side dishes, such as au gratin potatoes, green beans almandine, matchstick fries, or coleslaw, will feed four. Desserts are big too—from the towering inferno of the baked Alaskas to the crème brûlée in vats. *$$$; AE, B, DC, DIS, JCB, MC, V; checks OK; lunch, Mon–Fri, dinner every day; full bar; reservations recommended; street parking; oceanaireseafoodroom.com; map:J5* &

WHY GO: Upscale doggy bag bonanza—and no distracting waterfront view!

The Original Pancake House / ★

130 PARK PL CENTER, KIRKLAND; 425/827-7575 This one's been flappin' its jacks for over a decade. The original Original Pancake House first opened in Portland in 1953. Prices have gone up a bit. In fact, for pancakes, you might think this pricey. But it's worth a drive to Kirkland just to ponder the prodigious pancake options (including buttermilk, buckwheat, sourdough, and Swedish). There's hotcakes, flapjacks, and griddle cakes, plus fruit, nut, or bacon waffles. The baked apple pancake is a single pancake the approximate size of a hubcap, smothered with apples and cinnamon sugar; Dutch babies are golden-brown, air-filled puffs served with lemon, whipped butter, and powdered sugar. There are also a lot of crepes, with fruits and conserves and syrups to roll in them, not to mention the usual breakfast works of omelets, bacon and eggs, and oatmeal. Biscuits and gravy? Sure, sausage gravy from scratch. Eggs Benedict on weekends. Kids and grandmas love this place. *$; AE, DIS, MC, V; no checks; breakfast every day, lunch Mon–Fri; no alcohol; no reservations; self parking; flapjack@seanet.com; originalpancakehouse.com; map:EE3* &

WHY GO: Free apple pancakes and coffee while waiting for a table.

Orrapin Thai Food / ★★

10 BOSTON ST, QUEEN ANNE; 206/283-7118 These understated sage-colored rooms are hung with large Thai carvings, brilliant fabrics, and antique wall hangings. It's a serene place in the bustle of the upper Queen Anne restaurant row but don't go there to meditate, go for the Yum Gai—sliced grilled-chicken salad with lemongrass, spicy lime juice, red onions, and cucumbers. We love the rice dishes here, such as the pineapple fried rice with prawns, egg, nuts, and veggies. House specials are the Shoo Shee Pla, salmon cooked in creamy coconut milk and red curry, or the Jungle Pork, a very hot sauté with lime leaves, lemongrass, green beans, and holy basil. *$; MC, V; no checks; lunch, dinner every day; full bar; reservations accepted; street parking; map:GG8* &

WHY GO: Ginger-fried rice with prawns and tofu.

Osteria La Spiga / ★★★

1401 BROADWAY AVE, CAPITOL HILL; 206/323-8881 Inspired by the cuisine and honest hospitality of sunny Emilia-Romagna, owners Pietro and Sabrina Borghesi, and Sachia Tinsley (Sabrina's sister) fashioned this rustic taverna in a street-level corner space of Capitol Hill's Harvard Market. The sincere decor is imported from Italy: long, rough-hewn picnic tables and benches, a central wrought-iron gazebo, and wood stools work together to bring in a sense of the outdoors on even the soggiest Seattle days. Start with the simple but show-stopping presentation of *prosciutto* *di parma* or the grilled *crescione* (think thinner calzone) stuffed with rapini, potato, and pecorino. Soups change every day—it could be *passatelli*, a light beef broth with egg, cheese, and little pastas. The *farrotto*, farro grain prepared in the style of risotto (preparations change seasonally), is peerless. Pastas, like that served with the wild boar ragout, are handmade. The house-made tiramisu is a dreamy puff of mascarpone with a thick layer of coarsely ground cocoa. Look for hidden gems among the mostly Italian list. *$$; MC, V; local checks only; lunch Mon–Fri, dinner Mon–Sat; beer and wine; reservations recommended; street parking; map:HH6* &

WHY GO: *Piadina*, an unleavened flatbread, ordered plain or filled with goodies, including prosciutto, black-truffle paste, and mozzarella.

Ovio Bistro / ★★★

3247 CALIFORNIA AVE SW, WEST SEATTLE; 206/935-1774 Simply one of the best neighborhood restaurants in town. This golden Ovio (means "egg") merits a drive from hither, even yon. The restaurant's subtitle, Bistro Eclectica, is a descripta exactica. Chef Eddie Montoya, a culinarily brash young chef, looses his New Mexico sensibilities on the great wide world of food. A habanero-lemon tarter sauce, for instance, as well as bold green-chili vinaigrette await dipping of blue-corn crisped calamari. Braised short ribs, cooked to the nth degree (a good thing), get kicked in the ribs with New Mexico red chiles, then plated with flour tortillas. But Montoya is not limited to the Southwest. Take the unbeatable bacon/fish mating of prosciutto-wrapped halibut cheeks. And take some home, if you can. Excellent, brined-and-applewood-smoked hangar steak hangs with goat-cheese flavored mashers. Crispy (and that's an understatement) fried chicken crowns a mound of bacon-cheddar mashers. In fact, each entrée gets its own special pairing, and these are flavorful equals to the star ingredient. This is not one of those small places that slaps five asparagus spears and a blob of garlic mashed spuds on every plate. The halibut, for instance, is matched with sweet-onion gratin. Curried braised lamb shank one week rests regally atop saffron risotto. The next visit, it pairs with toasted couscous. Though the desserts do not live up to what precedes them, the wine list covers the bases and is priced to move. *$$; MC, V; local checks only; dinner Tues–Sat; full bar; reservations recommended; street parking; map:JJ9*

WHY GO: Excellent, varietal-specific crystal stemware thrills oenophiles.

Palace Kitchen / ★★★

2030 5TH AVE, BELLTOWN; 206/448-2001 The enormous mural on the restaurant's south wall is a tip-off to what owner Tom Douglas was going for. The 17th-century period piece is a lusty scene of scullery maids and castle servants feasting on roast meats while guzzling red wine in the "palace kitchen." The palatial open kitchen staffed by talented cooks and the lively center-stage bar scene circulates a constant energy buzz. Although primarily a bar, the Palace delivers stick-to-your-ribs fare. To get in the convivial spirit, order shareable selections such as the fat and spicy grilled chicken wings, bowls of clams, or crispy-fried, semolina-coated anchovies. The goat-cheese fondue with chunks of bread and apple slices is also a crowd pleaser. For a more formal supper, order the *plin*, tender raviolis plumped with chard and sausage, or one of the night's specials from the applewood grill, including the pit-roasted lamb, chicken, or whole fish. The wine list, written by the folks at Pike & Western Wine Shop, offers well-priced accompaniments for your dinner, while a knowing crew of bartenders makes some of the best cocktails in town. If you are lucky enough to sit at one of LaDawn King's tables, you will know the joys of Seattle-style service at its best. *$$$; AE, DC, DIS, MC, V; checks OK; lunch Mon–Fri, dinner every day; full bar; reservations recommended; street parking; tomdouglas.com; map:H5* &

WHY GO: Dinner service until 1am, seven nights a week!

Palisade / ★★☆

2601 W MARINA PL, MAGNOLIA/INTERBAY; 206/285-1000 Here's one of the most incredible waterfront settings in the area with a splendid 180-degree view of Elliott Bay, Alki Point, and the Seattle skyline. The view is pretty distracting, especially during long Northwest summer sunsets, but the interior, with its huge radiating beams, Japanese garden with bonzais, and bubbling brook, is stunning. Go for an after-work drink and pupu platters of steamed butter clams and Whidbey Island mussels with sun-dried tomatoes and fresh thyme. Chefs use an applewood grill, wood oven, and wood-fired rotisserie for the extensive menu of fish and meat. Check the daily fresh sheet for local fish such as steelhead, Columbia River sturgeon, or signature wild salmon steak roasted on a red-cedar plank, which you can take home. There are steaks, chicken, and prime rib, racks of Ellensburg lamb spit-roasted over applewood. Don't miss the Granny Smith apple tart with cinnamon ice cream and warm caramel sauce. *$$; AE, DC, DIS, MC, V; checks OK; dinner every day, brunch Sun; full bar; reservations recommended; valet and self parking; palisaderestaurant.com; map:GG8* &

WHY GO: Savory wood-fired seafood and an unequalled 180-degree view.

Panos Kleftiko / ★★

815 5TH AVE N, QUEEN ANNE; 206/301-0393 Panos Marina is the chef, host, heart, and soul of this tiny traditional Greek taverna in a cozy storefront a few blocks north of the Seattle Center. Here's another place that's fun to bring along a bunch of friends and cram your table with *mezedes,* Panos's tapas-like little dishes. There are four pages to choose from; they're moderately priced and best accompanied with warm homemade pita bread, hummus, or creamy tzatziki sauce and a glass or three of retsina. Try the *melanzan salata,* an eggplant salad with good olive oil, tomatoes, and herbs; the baked kalamata olives; or the meatballs. There are entrées we liked, too—spanakopita with fresh spinach layered in crispy phyllo dough or the tender roast lamb with rich, garlicky aioli. Arrive early if you have tickets to a show; Panos encourages lingering and doesn't take reservations. *$; MC, V; local checks only; dinner Mon–Sat; beer and wine; no reservations; street parking; map:B4* &

WHY GO: Bouzouki music and real Greek food.

The Pink Door / ★★

1919 POST ALLEY, PIKE PLACE MARKET; 206/443-3241 The low-profile, Post Alley entrance (a pale pink door that can be easily missed) underscores the speakeasy style of Jackie Roberts's Italian trattoria in the Pike Place Market. In winter the funky dining room, decorated with floral oilcloth table coverings and antique mirrors, grows noisy around a burbling fountain. Come warmer weather, everyone in town vies for a spot on the trellis-covered terrace. Inside or out, despite any inconsistencies from the sometimes overwhelmed kitchen, the Pink Door is one of those rarest of places where the impromptu can be memorable. Trusting out-of-towners, who come on the recommendation of a high-staller in the Market, sup heartily on generously portioned pastas, the daily risotto, or the lusty seafood-filled cioppino. Inventive salads are composed mostly of organic local produce. Desserts, such as rich pumpkin bread pudding with warm caramel sauce, are a homey affair. The reasonably priced wine list is, understandably, mostly Italian. There's often live music in the evenings. *$$; AE, MC, V; no checks; lunch Tues–Sat, dinner Tues–Sun; full bar; reservations recommended; street parking; map:H8*

WHY GO: Elliott Bay vistas from the patio and tarot-card readers in the dining room.

Place Pigalle / ★★☆

81 PIKE ST, PIKE PLACE MARKET; 206/624-1756 For our money, Place Pigalle is Seattle's hidden jewel. At the south end of the Pike Place Market arcade this small, demure checkered-floor bistro quietly goes about its business in the shadow (and quivering glow) of the enormous neon Public Market Center clock. Despite its flashy neighbor, Place Pigalle is indeed the place for an impossibly intimate dining experience. Ask for a window table and start with the Montrachet soufflé, twice-baked goat cheese soufflé with roasted oyster mushrooms and port syrup, or the steamed mussels that are dressed with bacon, shallots, and balsamic vinaigrette. For dinner we are smitten by the sophisticated saddle of rabbit filled with apples, spinach, and blue cheese or a soup plate of saffron broth packed with seafood, shiitakes, and roast tomatoes. There's an excellent, reasonably priced artisan cheese list; and, for dessert, the signature brandied apricot–almond torte. On sunny days, a small deck is ideal for those anxious to catch every ray of sun and the comings and goings of the ferries. The little bar is perfect for dining solo—or for snuggling up to your choice of hundreds of wines, which range from Northwest to French and Australian labels. *$$; AE, DC, MC, V; no checks; lunch, dinner Mon–Sat; full bar; reservations recommended; valet and street parking; map:J8*

WHY GO: Picture-postcard views of Elliott Bay and half bottles of Northwest wine.

Pontevecchio / ★★

710 N 34TH ST, FREMONT; 206/633-3989 Pontevecchio is a place where wives are treated like mistresses and mistresses like wives. Michele Zacco's tiny bistro tucked away across the street from Fremont's famous *Waiting for the Interurban* sculpture is the most deliberately romantic place in town. Zacco, whose exuberance is reminiscent of Roberto Begnini in *Life is Beautiful*, strives to maintain this ambient love nest. A Sicilian with the heart of an impresario and the soul of an artist, Zacco can cook too. His panini are fresh, the antipasti generous; his mama's tomato sauce simmers for hours. *Dolce* is as simple as gelato or cannoli. Try shareable starters, including antipasto of roasted peppers, eggplant croquettes with porcini, and Sicilian hummus, then segue to the gnocchi al Gorgonzola and grilled lamb medallions with fresh rosemary. The menu never changes, but the music does—one night operatic tenor, the next, a flamenco guitarist enticing a couple to jump up to dance an ecstatic tango. It's always a little zany. *$$; MC, V; local checks only; lunch Mon–Fri, dinner Mon–Sat; beer and wine; reservations recommended; street parking; map:FF8*

WHY GO: Antipasti and *amore!*

Ponti Seafood Grill / ★★★

3014 3RD AVE N, FREMONT; 206/284-3000 If you squint your eyes, you can transport yourself to the Mediterranean or Venice—what with the white stucco, red-tiled roofs, and the view of the medieval-looking draw-bridge to Fremont, the Center of the Universe. Unsquint them and a tugboat, an armada of kayakers, or the funeral parlor next door will bring you back to the very Northwest reality of being on the Left Bank of the Seattle ship canal. Rich and Sharon Malia's art-filled dining rooms tucked under the Fremont Bridge get prettier and prettier; the smart cuisine gets better and better. Start with the seared weather-vane scallops with grilled Walla Walla onions or the famous Dungeness crab spring rolls with Thai red curry aioli. Entrées are ever changing (except for the perennial patron favorite: Thai Curry Penne); there are savories like grilled black cod with a lime shallot buerre blanc, salmon with Gorgonzola polenta, or a sensational pork loin with a fig balsamic glacé. *$$$; AE, DC, DIS, JCB, MC, V; local checks only; lunch Mon–Fri, dinner every day, brunch Sun; full bar; reservations recommended; valet and self parking; pontiseafoodgrill.com; map:FF8* ♿

WHY GO: Ship Canal–side balcony dining.

Queen City Grill / ★★⯪

2201 1ST AVE, BELLTOWN; 206/443-0975 Well into its second decade, Peter Lamb's venerable Belltown saloon has always been a favorite of restaurant-industry insiders. How's that for third-party credibility? The Queen City Grill exudes masculine ele-gance: exposed brick walls, dark wood accents throughout the bar and dining room, straight-backed wooden booths with views of the street, and the aura of a satisfied dining public. The tenured waitstaff are ready to make informed recommendations from the tried-and-true regular menu and award-winning wine list; and the kitchen has straightened out some of the past inconsistencies. Start with Lamb's pioneering Dungeness crab cakes with a tangy rémoulade or the pepper-encrusted tuna carpaccio with lime, ginger, and tamari dressing. Meat selections are capably exe-cuted, but seafood is king here. For one-stop Northwest seafood sampling try the mixed grill with clams, mussels, and chunks of salmon, halibut, or snapper. The trusted specials menu, determined by seasonal availability, is worth first considera-tion. Sweet tooth? Try the dense, flourless Chocolate Nemesis Cake or the mocha crème caramel. *$$; AE, DC, DIS, MC, V; no checks; dinner every day; full bar; reser-vations recommended; valet parking; map:G8* ♿

WHY GO: Vertical collections of Washington state's best, most strictly allocated wines.

Racha Noodles & Thai Cuisine / ★★

23 MERCER ST, QUEEN ANNE; 206/281-8883 In 2000 Racha took a quantum leap forward—remodeling and expanding the menu, ratcheting up from neighborhood noodle house to serious Thai cuisine. An open kitchen dominates the center of the room, creating a healthy list of *yums*, those spicy wrap salads eaten rolled up in cabbage or lettuce. The prawn rolls are golden cylinders of fried rice paper stuffed with sausage and prawns and served with plum sauce. Other delectables include the Ocean Wrap Curry, shrimps and scallops steamed in rice wontons with green curry sauce creamy with coconut milk. Desserts can be green tea or mango ice cream, or black sticky rice rich with sweet coconut milk. Saturday night's karaoke is followed by Sunday night's live Thai classical and folk tunes played on traditional instruments by local ensembles. The meditational atmosphere can too frequently be countered by inattentive service. *$; AE, MC, V; no checks; lunch, dinner every day; full bar; reservations recommended; street parking; howspicy.com; map:B4* &

   WHY GO: Sunday night's live Thai music.

Raga / Unrated

212 CENTRAL WY, KIRKLAND; 425/827-3300 The genial original owner, Kamal Mroke, moved on to Vancouver, BC, in 2003 . . . leaving behind one of the region's highly regarded Indian restaurants. But life, like curry, goes on. Lodged in downtown Kirkland, Raga is decked out with spangled Indian fabrics and exotic musical instruments. A fireplace blazes incongruously in the middle of the room. The tables are set with linen, and waiters put your napkin on your lap. Try the two dishes unique to this kitchen: The *malai* chicken kebab is a breast marinated with cashews and cream before being flash-grilled in the tandoor. And the *methi* is the pungent herb fenugreek; the dried leaves, plus garlic and curry, make a sauce for lamb, prawns, or chicken that is unforgettable. The lunch buffet brings a few Western salads, bright red chicken tikka from the tandoor, and an ever-changing selection of meat and vegetable dishes. Liquid treats include a tangy mango *lassi* (the Indian equivalent of a thinner yogurt smoothie) or a selection from the short but well-rounded wine list. *$$; AE, DC, MC, V; checks OK; lunch, dinner every day; full bar; reservations required; self parking; ragarestaurant.com: map:EE3* &

   WHY GO: Inexpensive all-you-can-eat buffet lunch.

Ray's Boathouse / ★★☆
Ray's Cafe / ★★

6049 SEAVIEW AVE NW, BALLARD; 206/789-3770 Warm wood and a greeting to match welcome locals and tourists alike to Ray's Boathouse. Regional seafood dominates the menu at this Seattle landmark restaurant. Penn Cove mussels luxuriating in a rosy, silken stew of coconut and red curry, heady with the perfume of Thai basil, chiles, garlic, lemongrass, and ginger or the Manila clams in butter and dill broth from the Skookum Inlet are both satisfying starters. Salmon is always great (Ray's was the first restaurant to acquire its own fish buyer's license) and all fish are usually wild and always fresh. The rich Chatham Straits black cod is a signature selection, which can be applewood smoked or marinated *kasu*-style in sake lees, encrusted in sesame seeds, and served with sesame-scented rice cake and wasabi-ginger emulsion. Under general manager Maureen "Mo" Shaw, the service is gracious, capable, and well trained. Expect an extensive selection of Northwest wines on the list.

Upstairs, Ray's Cafe serves up lighter fare, though guests are welcome to order from the downstairs menu. Choices include fish-and-chips, burgers, salads, or classic clam linguine. Diehard Northwesterners sit on the outside deck, toddy in hand, any time of the night or year—there are blankets for the asking if you're chilled. The cafe serves lunch, for which you should make reservations on weekdays. *$$$, $$; AE, DC, DIS, MC, V; checks OK; dinner every day (Boathouse), lunch, dinner every day (Cafe); full bar; reservations recommended; valet and self parking; www.rays.com; map:EE9* &

WHY GO: Peerless views of the Olympic Mountains and signed copies of *Ray's Boathouse: Seafood Secrets of the Pacific Northwest.*

BEST PLACE TO TAKE YOUR IN-LAWS?

"Bizzarro Café in Wallingford. The vivid artwork and decorations all around you will stir up plenty of conversation, keeping those awkward lulls in conversation at bay."

Melanie McFarland, Seattle Post-Intelligencer *TV critic*

Restaurant Zoë / ★★★

2137 2ND AVE, BELLTOWN; 206/256-2060 Windows look out on the Belltown action. Most tables have a view of the kitchen. Between street and kitchen, diners enjoy some of the most surely prepared dishes in this uptown restaurant enclave. Chef/owner Scott Staples, who made Kirkland's Third Floor Fish Cafe (see review) into a notable destination, has vision and skill. He expertly directed a large operation there; here it's small and precise. The warm Taleggio and onion tart is luscious, as is the fresh ricotta ravioli, seasonally garnished. Staples's signature grilled romaine salad is a must—whole hearts of romaine, grilled just enough to get a touch of smoke, then dressed with a bacon, apple, and Roquefort dressing. The short entrée list balances between sea and land, with equally artful treatments of pepper-crusted yellowfin, pan-seared sea scallops, and troll-caught king salmon, as well as braised veal cheeks, pan roasted pork tenderloin, and house-smoked hangar steak. Expect perfect pairings, ranging from Israeli couscous to special spaetzel to corn flan. No clichés in the dessert department: try the slice of brioche French toast with crème brûlée and maple-syrup glaze. A flakey-crusted lemon tart with in-season fruit, ice cream, and fresh berries is perfectly Northwest. The lively bar shares the small space with diners. That and the hardwood acoustics can make this place noisy. *$$$; AE, MC, V; checks OK; dinner every day; full bar; reservations recommended; street parking; restaurantzoe.com; map:G7* &

WHY GO: Feel the love, taste the love.

Rosita's Mexican Restaurant / ★★☆

7210 WOODLAWN AVE NE, GREEN LAKE; 206/523-3031 You won't find the trendy ceviche-cilantro-chipotle consciousness here, just good old-fashioned comes-with-rice-and-beans Tex-Mex. The tables and roomy banquettes are great for large parties. And Rosita's is a place kids will love, especially for the *platos pequeños*—plates with tacos, tamales, burritos, and even cheeseburgers sized and priced for smaller, younger considerations. Adults do well here too. There's super nachos, a gigantic heap of corn chips layered with chicken and cheese, guacamole and beans, and a green tomatillo sauce. Avoid the seafood, but let them get fancy with the *pollo al carbon*, chicken with creamy chipotle sauce; chile verde, long-cooked chunks of pork in a green sauce; or the sizzling fajitas (the steak is best). At night, while waiting for a table, be sure to belly up to the fresh corn-tortilla station for warm, complementary rounds so good they eclipse the forgettable salsa. There was a second Rosita's on Crown Hill, but it's been sold. *$; AE, MC, V; no checks; lunch Mon–Sat, dinner every day; full bar; reservations recommended; self and street parking; rositasrestaurant.com; map:EE8* &

WHY GO: Tortilla-making station, handing out fresh, free rounds.

Rover's / ★★★★

2808 E MADISON ST, MADISON VALLEY; 206/325-7442 Though Rover's puckish "Chef in the Hat" Thierry Rautureau has won the hearts of Seattleites, half his customers are out-of-towners making pilgrimages to get a taste of the recently expanded kitchen that has won Rautureau national renown. Guests approach through a courtyard that blossoms behind an unassuming arcade. As part of a 2002 remodel, Rover's also gained a welcoming reception area, which proffers a gentle transition from the street to the newly spruced dining room, full of sunny hues and ambient light. Choose from three prix-fixe menus (one vegetarian) that progress from delicate flavors to bolder expressions with elegant sufficiency. Rautureau is a master of sauces, using stocks, reductions, herb-infused oils, and purées to enhance slices of sturgeon, steamed Maine lobster, wild mushrooms, breasts of quail, and the requisite foie gras. Expect professional service from the loyal staff. Rautureau, a Frenchman, is serious about wine. Cellar master and sommelier, Cyril Frechier manages the 5,500-bottle collection and is on hand to bring guests the perfect partner for any meal. Dining in the courtyard, weather permitting, is an enchanting experience. *$$$$; AE, DC, MC, V; checks OK; dinner Tues–Sat; beer and wine; reservations required; street parking; rovers-seattle.com; map:GG6* &

WHY GO: Appetizer of eggs scrambled with garlic and chives, served in the topped shell and garnished with crème fraîche and white sturgeon caviar.

Ruby's on Bainbridge / ★★☆

4738 LYNNWOOD CENTER RD NE, BAINBRIDGE ISLAND; 206/780-9303 Ruby's is now housed in a handsome Tudor manor overlooking Rich Passage built a century ago by one Emmanuel Olsen. The Pleasant Beach Grill flourished here for years, and Moonfish, more recently, did not. In spring 2003, chef Aaron Crisp and wife Maura moved their popular nearby storefront bistro to this lovely manse, refurbishing it and installing a classical but eclectic fine-dining menu. Classics like baked

Brie, a hunter pâté, and a Caesar salad are balanced with fresh-made focaccia pizzas with whimsical, daily-changing toppings such as roasted fennel, sweet onions, and cheese. There's a solid choice of Angus meats—rib-eye and sirloin to tenderloin medallions—and the lamb shank in red wine is heady with herbes de Provence. Fresh seafood is featured daily and vegetarians will be thrilled with Tortino di Melanzana, eggplant layered with fresh mozzarella and marinated tomatoes. *$$$; AE, MC, V; checks OK; dinner every day; full bar; reservations recommended; self parking; rubysonbainbridge.com* &

WHY GO: Unbeatable ferry ride to fine dining combo.

Saigon Bistro / ★★

1032 S JACKSON ST, STE 202, CHINATOWN/INTERNATIONAL DISTRICT (AND BRANCH); 206/329-4939 Here is a tasty, inexpensive trip to Vietnam with a menu not too scary for the timid nor too limited for the adventurous. There's a long list of phos, those fragrant, clear-broth, fine-noodle soups with beef, chicken, duck, or tofu, served with a heap of bean sprouts, branches of basil and mint, slices of jalapeños, and lime wedges. It's soup, salad, and entrée all in one. Popular with neighborhood day workers are the huge sandwiches bursting with grilled meats, veggies, and fresh basil and mint on a baguette for only two bucks! The wonderful *goi cuon*—summer salad rice-paper rolls with vermicelli, shrimp, pork, or tofu—and the egg rolls with shredded pork and mushrooms make for a healthy lunch, as does the Vietnamese crepe, a fluffy rice-flour pancake with turmeric, mung beans, sprouts, and green onions to wrap in lettuce. Worthy entrées include roasted coconut chicken, clay-pot dishes such as spare ribs or catfish, and a delectably rich casserole of eggplant, tofu, and sea snails. Have a sweet dessert drink—navy, mung, and red beans in coconut milk over ice or a cold-brewed iced coffee with condensed milk. The branch in Uwajimaya Village (600 5th Ave S, Chinatown/International District; 206/621-2085) has only the faster, more portable items from the fuller menu of the Jackson Street location. *$; MC, V; checks OK; lunch, dinner every day; beer and wine; no reservations; self parking; map:P5* &

WHY GO: Large tables and portions make for the best family dining this side of your dining room.

St. Clouds / ★★☆

1129 34TH AVE, MADRONA; 206/726-1522 Though it's named after the orphanage in John Irving's novel *Cider House Rules*, no one feels like an orphan hanging at St. Clouds. And hang they do. This neighborly, family-friendly joint is jumping. The menu is split between "Home for Dinner" (homey, cheaper) or "Out for Dinner" (fancy, pricier). Happily, ordering from either is a good choice. Typical offerings are roasted chicken and mashers; a rice bowl with ginger-steamed vegetables or a succulent parmesan-crusted pork tenderloin. Weekend brunch is known for the Imperial Mix-up, the semilegendary jumble of rice, veggies, and Portuguese sausage that might come with white chocolate scones or a sour cream coffeecake. The kids menu has mac and cheese, spaghetti and meatballs, and burgers. But this place isn't only about kids—a grown-up crowd gathers on certain weeknights and every weekend in the cozy bar for live acoustic blues, jazz, rock, and folk music. *$$; AE, DIS, MC, V; checks OK; dinner every day, brunch Sat–Sun; full bar; reservations recommended; street parking; john@ stclouds.com; stclouds.com; map:HH5* &

WHY GO: Chocolate-chip pancakes on the kids' menu.

Saito's Japanese Cafe & Bar / ★★★☆

2120 2ND AVE, BELLTOWN; 206/728-1333 On any given night in this smart Belltown place you might see the Japanese ambassador or—more impressively—Mariners superstar Ichiro Suzuki, who are regulars. They come for Saito-san's sushi, arguably the best in town. The fish is immaculately fresh and cut thicker than you'll usually find in Seattle—one of the reasons he's so popular with Japanese visitors. The modern mirrored dining room is served well by Saito-san's vivacious wife, Anita, and a staff of knowledgeable servers. Items from the hot kitchen are innovative—stray from the teriyaki and try the butter *itame*, a geoduck sauté with sugar snaps and shiitakes. Saito's kitchen goes further than the traditional Japanese with vegetable tempura, picking what's fresh from the Market: sugar snaps, squash blossoms, and matsutake, oyster, and morel mushrooms all cut thin and fried delicately in batter. Be sure to try the house-made ice-cream sampler with flavors such as green tea, mango, or sweet plum. *$$$; AE, DIS, E, MC, V; no checks; lunch Tues–Fri, dinner Tues–Sat; full bar; reservations recommended; street parking; info@ saitos.net; saitos.net; map:F8* &

WHY GO: Superstar sushi in super sexy Belltown.

Saltoro / ★★

14051 GREENWOOD AVE, BROADVIEW; 206/365-6025 They say a maestro saltoro is a master salter of prosciutto. Not that you'll find the stuff across the menu, but it does show up fried in a spinach salad elevated by fried pockets of Brie; also in an excellent entrée-sized starter, a sweet and savory delight of big prawns sautéed with sherry-braised onions, prosciutto, and goat cheese with a Como loaf for juice dipping. The place has similarities to owner Greg Beckly's other neighborhood-style eatery, Bick's Broadview Grill (see review), also in the north end. While still technically Broadview, Saltoro nudges the Shoreline border. This 2003 opener has an attractive, open design, lots of wood, but nothing to absorb the din. The food, while no moon shot, aims higher than Bick's. The duck confit starter—leg and thigh preserved in duck fat, served with sherry jus, paired with grilled pear and braised endive—is a succulent plateful. The risotto starter brings together a trio of 'shrooms—portobello, cremini, shiitake—in rich harmony. Or you can order an entrée that pairs both duck and risotto. A sweet and chewy chunk of monkfish lolls in a broth flavored with lobster and a hint of Calvados. Saltoro's steak frites pairs flavorful hangar steak with a bleu-cheese aioli, fine for meat dippin' or addin' flavor to mediocre fries. A few sandwiches are open faced and a gruyère-topped chicken affair and a fine lamb burger round out the menu. Kids to seniors fare well here. *$$; MC, V; no checks; dinner every day; full bar; reservations for 6 or more recommended; self parking; map:CC8*

WHY GO: House-made, berry-infused vodka cocktails chase away the blues.

Salumi / ★★★

309 3RD AVE S, PIONEER SQUARE; 206/621-8772 If you're thinking of going vegetarian, eat here first. In this little wedge of Italy near the King Street train station, arias soar and the angels sing. Armandino Batali is a retired aeronautics engineer who after 31 years at Boeing dusted off his family recipes, went to culinary school in New York, worked in a salami factory in Queens, and apprenticed with butchers in Tuscany. He cures his own *coppa*, three kinds of salami, lamb or pork prosciutto, spicy finocchiona, and citrusy *sopressata*, a lamb and orange sausage. They're cut to order and all sold cheaply by the pound for takeout, or let him slice you some to lay on a crusty baguette slathered with an anchovy-rich pesto or garlic sauce. Try the braised oxtail or the amazing meatball sandwich on rosetta rolls piled high with sautéed peppers and onions. Rotating specials are indeed special—lasagne with pork cheek, fennel bulb in *vin santo*, and *hoji poji* soup (so named because it is a hodgepodge of ingredients such as greens, pancetta, and olives). If you're still considering vegetarianism, there's Swiss chard, dandelion greens, or Roman beans. Batali's weekly private dinners are booked up months in advance (reservations required for parties of 10 or more), but lunch at communal tables is for everyone right now, and we suggest you go there at once. *$; AE, MC, V; checks OK; lunch Tues–Fri, dinner Sat; beer and wine; reservations required; street parking; map:O7* &

WHY GO: Sightings of Food Network host/chef "Molto Mario" (Batali), owner Armandino's son.

Sand Point Grill / ★★

5412 SAND POINT WY NE, SAND POINT; 206/729-1303 Though circled by affluent neighborhoods, this bistro has an easygoing unpretentiousness that packs in the neighbors. It helps that the proprietors, Seattle restaurant veterans Scott MacFarlane and Andrew Walsh, keep prices in the moderate range. The spare room has a cozy feel, with warm colors and contemporary art. Expect well-crafted, though sometimes uneven, food. The seasonal menu draws from diffuse cuisines and the list of shareables is longer than that of entrées: things like saffron-braised octopus, New Zealand lamb T-bone with grilled eggplant, Penn Cove mussels with Spanish chorizo, or halibut lettuce wraps with Thai chiles are small-plated in single servings. The tapas are probably the best way to go here, but there are some tantalizing entrées as well—such as a marinated hanging tender steak with glazed red onions. The short but well-rounded wine list includes a generous offering of by-the-glass choices. *$$; AE, MC, V; local checks only; dinner every day; full bar; reservations accepted for 6 or more; self parking; SPGrill@msn.com; map:FF5* W

WHY GO: Adult-friendly bar, kid-friendly menu.

Sanmi Sushi / ★★

2601 W MARINA PL, MAGNOLIA/INTERBAY; 206/283-9978 You could come to Sanmi Sushi to enjoy the spectacular view of downtown across Elliott Bay. You could come to see Mount Rainier towering over the hundreds of yachts docked just outside the large windows. Or you could come for the sushi. Misao Sanmi, after years working around town for other people, opened his own glorious little spot next-door to Palisade. Sanmi-san is a sushi master and the seafood, of course, is as fresh as you'd expect. A good sign is the many visiting Japanese scarfing the *nigiri*. The menu also includes a lengthy list of soups, grilled meats, and fish, combination dinners, bento-box lunches, and noodles. Though it is tucked away in Elliott Bay Marina, finding it is worth the hunt. *$$; AE, MC, V; no checks; lunch Tues–Fri, dinner Tues–Sun; full bar; reservations recommended; self parking; map:GG8* ♿

WHY GO: Service that will make you feel like family.

Sans Souci / ★★★

10520 NE 8TH ST, BELLEVUE; 425/467-9490 Carefully hidden from the world in the second floor of Bellevue Place's Wintergarden, Sans Souci seems to carry on, as its name means, "without worry." No matter that few know it's there and even fewer ever penetrate this multipurpose fortress of a development kitty-corner northeast of Bellevue Square. After so many years in the restaurant business—including introducing Seattle to fine northern Italian fare at legendary Settebello (1980s)—Luciano Bardinelli can cope. More than cope; his handsome, mostly Italian/partly French restaurant usually delivers. Skilled servers deliver the Harry's Bar carpaccio appetizer, a gorgeous plate of shaved raw tenderloin as served in the famous American expat hangout in Paris. The crab cakes are just that—nothing more. The onion soup, built on a sturdy base of veal broth, can make a meal. Paniscia di Novara is a simple, meat-laden northern Italian risotto and the osso buco is a sure bet. The well-chosen wine list ranges from the upper $20s to multiple hundreds. The handsome dining room sports pumpkin-colored walls, wood accents, and white linen. Save room for super sweet tiramisu. *$$; AE, DC, DIS, MC, V; checks OK; lunch Mon–Fri, dinner every day; full bar; reservations recommended; adjacent validated garage parking; sanssoucibistro.com; map:HH3* ♿

WHY GO: Who'd a thunk it—the French and Italian Riviera right there in Bellevue.

Sapphire Kitchen & Bar / ★★★

1625 QUEEN ANNE AVE N, QUEEN ANNE; 206/281-1931 Start the evenings at Sapphire with a stop in the bar where master mixologist Patrick Caffell makes a classic, shaken-never-blended house margarita and a Sidecar that is one part sour, one part sweet, two parts strong. Sapphire's dramatic harem-tent decor transports you straight to Casablanca and the menu of chef Leonard Ruiz Rede echoes the decor while displaying his North African/Spanish roots. The sensual *mezze* plate has warm triangles of house-made pita bread for scooping the nutty hummus or the intensely deep and smoky baba ghanouj served with minty tabbouleh in a radicchio leaf. The menu changes frequently and fish dishes vary, but Rede's wild coho salmon in a traditional Moroccan *charmoula* marinade (ginger, cilantro, garlic, cumin, and olive oil) shows his mastery of fish cookery, as does the popular seafood paella with prawns, sea scallops, mussels, and chorizo in rice cooked in a saffron-scented broth. The waitstaff can be a little too chummy—nothing a chocolate-espresso torte with white-chocolate mousse and a glass of 20-year-old tawny port can't remedy. *$$; MC, V; local checks only; lunch Mon–Fri, dinner every day, brunch Sat–Sun; full bar; reservations recommended; street parking; map:GG8* ♿

WHY GO: Downtown dining without the downtown traffic.

Sazerac / ★★☆

1101 4TH AVE (HOTEL MONACO), DOWNTOWN; 206/624-7755 This downtown luxury-hotel restaurant takes to heart its motto: "Serious fun—damn good food." The room is disarming in dizzy chandeliers and Mardi Gras colors. "Chef and Big Dawg" Jan Birnbaum splits his time between this and his new Napa Valley restaurant, Catahoula. In a witty, deep menu, his Louisiana roots show. Executive chef Jason McClure makes it happen, over and over. Appetizers truly tease: crab cakes with harissa mayo with a shaved fennel salad, or andouille sausage (the stuff's all over the menu) pizza pie. The kitchen does well with broiler and smokehouse preparations such as "The Best Fish We Can Catch Today," or the applewood-smoked pork back ribs with molasses barbecue sauce, or the hickory-smoked porterhouse. If you think that's tempting, you'll be bowled over by the warm and gooey chocolate-pudding cake served with its own pitcher of cream. Equally grand is the Sazerac, a New Orleans–invented cocktail that's a wicked blend of rye, Peychaud bitters, and Herbsaint, an anise-y faux absinthe liqueur. More down-to-earth is the wine list with its concentration of midpriced California and Northwest offerings. Servers are funny and capable. *$$$; AE, DC, DIS, MC, V; no checks; breakfast, lunch Mon–Fri, dinner every day, brunch Sat–Sun; full bar; reservations recommended; valet parking; brian.reed@sazerac.com; www.kimptongroup.com/sazerac.html; map:L6* ♿
WHY GO: Because Bourbon Street is too damn far.

BEST PLACE FOR A SLUMBER PARTY?
"The new James Turrell SkySpace at the Henry Art Gallery, because it's a skylight open to the stars and without the city lights shining in your eyes."

Greg Kucera, owner of Greg Kucera Gallery

Seastar Restaurant and Raw Bar / ★★★☆

205 108TH AVE NE, BELLEVUE; 425/456-0010 It seemed a bold move when John Howie, who had served as executive chef at Palisade for nearly a decade, left to open an upscale seafood restaurant smack dab in the middle of a recession. How bold you discover when you step into his sparkling seafood emporium. The horseshoe-shaped restaurant wraps sensually around Howie's state-of-the-art kitchen: nary a corner is to be found in the shimmering, curvy ocean-inspired rooms. Don't let a glossy clique of hostesses at the door throw you. The waitstaff has fun with playful guests and converses easily about the food. Best of Show cold appetizer is the multilevel raw bar sampler: Hawaiian ahi poke, California roll, and scallop ceviche. On the hot side, we like the flash-seared divers sea scallops with tropical fruit chutney and ginger-soy reduction and the Kauai shrimp, wrapped in *saifun* noodles, deep fried and drizzled with Sriracha (an Asian chili-garlic concoction) butter and scallions. At dinner or lunch request the sesame-peppercorn crusted ahi with creamy wasabi and ginger-soy reduction. And while it's clear the lure of Seastar is seafood, carnivores will never go hungry, not with a 9-ounce Snake River Farms American Kobe beef rib-eye on the grill. Seastar's nationally celebrated wine list is written by the ever-affable Erik Liedholm, who is on the floor most nights to lull winer-diners into a true sense of security with knowing recommendations and tailored service. $$$; AE, DC, DIS, MC, V; local checks OK; lunch, dinner every day; full bar; reservations recommended; valet and street parking; seastarrestaurant.com; map:HH3 &

WHY GO: Chef's communal table and the Thai hot and sour soup.

BEST PLACE TO FIND INSPIRATION?
"The industrial sheds in South Seattle. It's an evocative area to walk around in. It's old Seattle—what's left of the blue-collar industrial city. It's very moving."
Kurt Beattie, artistic director of A Contemporary Theatre (ACT)

Serafina / ★★☆

2043 EASTLAKE AVE E, EASTLAKE; 206/323-0807 One cannot help but be seduced by Serafina. In fact, this unapologetically romantic neighborhood restaurant is so darn sexy, don't be surprised if you make a "love connection" with someone you don't even like. Longtime devotees of Susan Kaufman's Eastlake supperclub recently detected a marked change. Three years ago Kaufman hired the ever-capable executive chef John Neumark to take charge of her Italian kitchen and take charge he did. Today the menu is focused and tucked neatly in a jacket reproduced from commissioned artwork. Tapping Kaufman and Neumark's deep knowledge of food and wine, the kitchen shoots for "Italian food with room to play" and is hitting the target dead on. *Tacchino tonnato*, thin slices of delicately poached turkey breast served with a caper-tuna sauce, is a premier example of Neumark's golden touch with Piedmontese classics, and grilled pork tenderloin with sour cherry chutney and grilled radicchio reflects his joy of cooking outside the box. Desserts are all amazing, but the biscotti and Vigna del Papa Vin Santo makes for an indulgent dipping experience. $$; MC, V; checks OK; lunch Mon–Fri, dinner every day; full bar; reservations recommended; street parking; serafinaseattle.com; map:GG7 &

WHY GO: Live make-out music and a secret garden patio during summer months.

727 Pine Restaurant / ★★★

727 PINE ST (ELLIOTT GRAND HYATT), DOWNTOWN; 206/774-6400 727 Pine Restaurant scratches that hard-to-reach itch that plagues local and visiting diners: striking the perfect balance between tragically hip and old-school sophistication. Street and lobby entrances invite you into the gleaming, split-level restaurant, while above red velvet banquettes, gigantic mirrors are angled to afford views of the dining room and the exhibition kitchen where chef Shannon

Galusha produces dishes inspired by seasonal ingredients. Knowing bartenders pour well-made cocktails at the grown-up, not grown-old, bar. Start your evening with such delights as a fig and fennel salad kissed by aged balsamic vinegar; olive oil–poached lobster on toasted brioche with frisée and tarragon; or chilled white gazpacho with divers scallops, Marcona almonds, and smoked duck. Favorite entrées include the Alaskan halibut with corn chowder and chanterelles and the 12-ounce veal chop with horseradish whipped potatoes and garlicky rapini with lemon. Expect meals to be paired with thoughtful (but too frequently Californian) wine selections. *$$$; MC, V; breakfast, lunch, dinner every day; full bar; reservations recommended; valet parking; 727pine.com; map:J4* &

WHY GO: To sip house-infused spirits in the lounge.

Shallots Asian Bistro / ★★☆

2525 4TH AVE, BELLTOWN; 206/728-1888 Shallots Asian Bistro is not just a quick fusion of kim chee, roll sushi, and chow mein, like too many other so-called pan-Asian restaurants around town. This hip little Belltown gem has a lot of Chinese but also an intriguing mix of Thai, Vietnamese, Cambodian, Japanese, and Korean. Dark wood booths, elaborately folded napkins, tasteful Asian art, and a sweet patio make for an agreeable ambience just steps away from the bustle of Fourth Avenue. Portions are generous and well priced. Satays and satay-roll appetizers, for example, can come as full meals with a bowl of fragrant rice and a mini salad. Lunch choices include kung pao chicken or black-bean salmon or a wok fry of the wide rice noodles, chow fun, and seafood. Some specialties make Shallots worth coming downtown for: like the subtly flavored steamed sea bass, the French Cambodian New York steak salad; or the amazing Nine Flavor Beef. *$$; AE, DC, DIS, MC, V; checks OK; lunch Mon–Fri, dinner every day; full bar; reservations recommended; street parking; map:E7* &

WHY GO: Belltown hipness with real pan-Asian food.

Shamiana / ★★

10724 NE 68TH ST, KIRKLAND; 425/827-4902 / 2255 NE 65TH ST, RAVENNA; 206/524-3664 Shamiana is a rare thing: an Indian restaurant not run by Indians. It's also more than an "Indian" restaurant in that it's often interpretive, with influences from Bangladesh, Kenya, and Pakistan. Those are a few of the places Eric and Tracy Larson spent their youth as Foreign Service kids. Vegetarians do well with curries and such Indian veggie dishes as eggplant *bartha* or peas and cumin. Curries and chutneys are made in-house. Vegan dishes are plentiful. There are good rice and grain dishes such as dhal with red lentils or pulao with fragrant basmati rice. Meat lovers do well too—try the chicken, lamb, and prawns in traditional spicy Pakistani barbecue. Consistent winners are Velvet Butter Chicken and the Chile Fry Lamb, chunks of lamb slow-cooked in coconut milk, chiles, and tomatoes. One of the big draws at the Kirkland original is its good-value luncheon buffet. A second location in Ravenna opened in 2002. *$; AE, DC, DIS, MC, V; checks OK; lunch Mon–Fri (Kirkland), dinner every day; beer and wine; reservations accepted for 6 or more; self parking (Kirkland), street parking (Ravenna); map:EE3* &

WHY GO: Three kinds of naan—the delicious, clay-oven-cooked, unleavened bread.

Shanghai Garden / ★★★
Shanghai Café / ★★

524 6TH AVE S, CHINATOWN/INTERNATIONAL DISTRICT; 206/625-1689 / 80 FRONT ST N, ISSAQUAH; 425/313-3188 / 12708 SE 38TH ST, BELLEVUE; 425/603-1689 Shanghai Garden chef/owner Hua Te Su and family cater to a largely Chinese clientele in this luscious pink restaurant in the Chinatown/International District. Su attracts diners from every Chinese province with Shanghai dishes that change seasonally. Try the Shanghai favorite—soupy buns, the flowery little packets of delicate dough twisted at the top containing combinations of minced pork, shrimp, or crab in a spoonful of hot broth. The flavors explode in the mouth and, even when nibbled expertly, it's hard to eat a soup dumpling without leaving some on your shirt. Prepare to be wowed by anything made with snap-pea vines or with the chef's special hand-shaved noodles. The vivid green tendrils of the sugar-snap plant are amazingly tender and clean tasting, especially when paired with plump shrimp. The noodles, shaved off a block of dough (rice, corn, or barley green), make the best chow mein you'll ever eat. The Shanghai emphasis is on seafood. Especially memorable are the pepper-salted scallops or pepper-salted shrimp with a thin, crunchy shell that when chomped gives a mouthburst of the sea along with the sedate heat of white pepper. Someone in the group should order the crispy shrimp with sweet chili sauce. Su's Issaquah branch has attracted its own lines-out-the-door following. A brother owns Shanghai Café in Bellevue, similar but not to scale. *$; MC, V; no checks; lunch, dinner every day; beer and wine (Seattle), full bar (Issaquah); reservations recommended; self parking; map:Q7, II2* &

WHY GO: To order anything with hand-shaved noodles.

Shiro's / ★★☆

2401 2ND AVE, BELLTOWN; 206/443-9844 Shiro Kashiba introduced the concept of sushi to several generations of Seattleites at his venerable Nikko and they've loved him and his seafoody perfectness for nearly 30 years. In the simple dining room, a small menu offers full-course dinner entrées such as tempura, sukiyaki, and teriyaki. The *kasu*-style black cod, that elegantly rich fish marinated and broiled, is not to be missed. But the hundreds of sushi variations are the main event, with the blond hardwood sushi bar always jammed with Shiro's regulars, an amazing mix of people: Japanese tourists, Belltown hipsters, business types—sushi fanatics all. There's a great selection of premium sakes, a bar stocked with Japanese scotches, and desserts such as red-bean ice cream and peeled persimmons. *$$$; AE, MC, V; no checks; dinner every day; full bar; reservations recommended; valet, self, and street parking; map:F8* &

WHY GO: Sushi that meets the taste test of Japanese tourists.

Siam on Broadway ★★
Siam on Lake Union / ★

616 BROADWAY E, CAPITOL HILL; 206/324-0892 / 1880 FAIRVIEW AVE E, LAKE UNION; 206/323-8101 Thai restaurants have surpassed in number even Italian ones in Seattle these days, and that's saying a lot. But no matter how many phad thai slingers there may be out there, Siam, on the busy Harvard Exit end of Broadway, always has lines out front. The seats at the front counter are a great place to watch the ballet performed by women chefs who work the woks and burners in the tiny open kitchen. They produce, among other flavorful dishes, one of the best *tom kah gai* soups—the chicken soup spicy with chiles, pungent lemongrass, and coconut milk. While the menu doesn't stray far from Bangkok standards, the dishes created by the skilled hands in the kitchen are distinctive and consistent. Sit at the counter and enjoy the show or wait for one of only 15 tables in the back.

At the Lake Union location, a larger outpost built into the railcar structure on a long-forgotten Victoria Station, you probably won't have to wait. And the huge, private parking lot offers ample space for the car you couldn't park on Broadway. The food here is now equal to its Broadway sibling's. *$, $; AE, DC, MC, V; checks OK; lunch Mon–Fri, dinner every day; beer and wine (Broadway); full bar (Eastlake); reservations recommended (Broadway); reservations recommended for 6 or more (Lake Union); street parking (Broadway); self parking (Lake Union); map:HH6, GG7* &

WHY GO: To slurp noodles at the counter while watching the Broadway crowds go by.

611 Supreme Crêperie Café / ★★⯪

611 E PINE ST, CAPITOL HILL; 206/328-0292 This cafe is like a crumbling, romantic Parisian dive, though the decor and food are quite intentionally fashioned by owner Margaret Edwins and her staff. There are bare brick walls, stressed wooden floors, unobtrusive art, and high ceilings. From the open kitchen with hanging pans and utensils comes an impressive list of entrée crepes such as cheese, almond, ham, roasted eggplant, and smoked salmon, all with choices of sauces; or create your own from a long list of sexy ingredients. There are tempting salads, like the Cambazola—Bibb lettuce tossed with a creamy dressing made from that wonderful hybrid of Camembert and Gorgonzola—and an onion soup full of Gruyère and croutons. A full bar serves *pastis*, Calvados, Armagnac, and Pernod; the inexpensive wine list is all European bottlings, but even these are mostly French. *$; MC, V; no checks; dinner Tues–Sun, brunch Sat–Sun; full bar; reservations recommended; street parking; map:J1* &

WHY GO: Dessert crepes with garnishes such as orange butter and shaved chocolate.

SkyCity at the Needle / ★★

219 4TH AVE N, SEATTLE CENTER; 206/905-2100 Chances are you've already made a reservation at SkyCity and, having heard mixed reviews about the food from cynical locals, you're vacillating. It's a reasonable reaction. Revolving landmarks are not typically known for their cuisine, no matter how good it is. No fear at the Needle, however. In the hands of chef Girard Bengle, the tried-and-true Northwest menu—line-caught salmon, peppercorn New York steak, crab cakes, seared ahi —is well considered and well executed. From the dinner menu, you'll be pleased with the smoked-salmon crisp and Nebraska prime rib. The fixed-price weekend brunch offers a selection of breakfast foods, poultry, or seafood courses and sweets. Desserts trend toward standard offerings—cheesecakes, mousses, and a delightful lemon tart—with one exception known as Mount Rainier, an ice-cream sundae nestled in fog-producing dry ice. Service is friendly and solicitous, but can be hurried. If you feel rushed, let your server know you would prefer dining at a more leisurely pace. Time your reservation to catch the sun going to bed behind the Olympics for the night. *$$$; AE, DIS, MC, V; local checks only; lunch Mon–Fri, dinner every day, brunch Sat–Sun; full bar; reservations recommended; valet parking; space needle.com; map:D6* ♿

WHY GO: Jetsonian '60s flashback and stunning 360-degree rotating views of Seattle.

Snappy Dragon / ★★

8917 ROOSEVELT WY NE, MAPLE LEAF; 206/528-5575 Judy Fu's Maple Leaf house-turned-restaurant serves up some of the snappiest Chinese food around. House-made noodles head the bill here, in various guises. Don't miss the soft-noodle chow meins or the *jaio-zi*, boiled dumplings. Maple Leafers and others flock to the joint, often for takeout. Be sure to order the crispy tea-smoked duck, aromatic foul served with hoisin and steamed buns. Other big sellers are the spicy-sweet Sichuan favorite, General Tsao's Chicken; the clay-pot stews (especially with shrimp); chicken meatballs; prawns; scallops; and veggies. Almond Cranberry Chicken is an unusual sweet-sour-savory mélange that makes something lush, complex, and very Chinese out of the simple puritanical New England sour fruit we usually equate with Thanksgiving. *$; AE, DC, MC, V; local checks only; lunch, dinner Mon–Sat; full bar; reservations accepted for 5 or more; street parking; snappy dragon.com; map:DD7* ♿

WHY GO: Yum-yum stir-fried glass noodles and a minced pork dish called Ants Climb Up a Tree.

Sostanza Trattoria / ★★★

1927 43RD AVE E, MADISON PARK; 206/324-9701 The charm here is all in the ingredients and the centuries-old traditions of northern Italy. Add a romantic sky-lighted dining room, opening onto a balcony with a peekaboo view of Lake Washington, and you have chef/owner Lorenzo Cianciusi's charming bilevel trattoria. Cianciusi's food is straightforward, fresh, and true to his northern Italian roots. Try the beef carpaccio, served with mustard dressing; or the signature veal pappardelle, tossed tableside with mushrooms, goat cheese, tomatoes, fresh basil, and Barolo. Distinctive Italian bottlings join a few domestic favorites on the limited but well-chosen wine list. At the lake end of Madison Park's tony commercial strip, Sostanza is a popular hangspot for a well-dressed neighborhood crowd who stop by to schmooze in the bar upstairs or for dinner in the warmly lit terra cotta dining room. *$$; AE, DC, MC, V; no checks; dinner Mon–Sat; full bar; reservations recommended; street parking; map:GG6* ♿

WHY GO: Fireplace in winter and lakeside patio in summer.

The Stalk Exchange / ★★

611 GREENWOOD N, GREENWOOD; 206/782-3911 Converted from a Greenwood junk store, The Stalk Exchange serves only lunch and weekend brunch in funky art-filled rooms of aubergine, yellow, and cornflower blue. But Laurie Dent's kitchen distinguishes itself from the usual over-easy and hash-brown mills—with the weekend lines out front to prove it. Emphasis is on creative, organic, and seasonal; though there's plenty of meat for carnivores. At brunch, the cloud-like lemon soufflé pancakes with berries and crème fraîche are best-selling as are a variety of pastries from the brick oven, like raspberry coffee cake. The scramble with andouille sausage or with organic bacon and Castello blue cheese comes with a light and creamy potato cake, crispy with *panko*. At lunch, there are homemade soups, entrée salads—we love the spinach mango with honey-mustard dressing. The honkin' sandwiches like the Irish Cheddar Melt are on home-baked breads. *$; MC, V; checks OK; lunch Wed–Fri, brunch Sat–Sun; beer and wine; no reservations; street parking; map:EE7* &

WHY GO: Weekend brunches worth standing in line for.

BEST PLACE FOR LIVE MUSIC?
"It's a toss up between Benaroya Hall and the Seattle Opera House because of the acoustics."
Kurt Beattie, artistic director of A Contemporary Theatre (ACT)

The Still Life Café / ★★☆

709 N 35 ST, FREMONT; 206/547-9850 Earning its rep as a haunt for coffee-swilling students and others with seemingly endless time on their hands, The Still Life has grown up. While some may be saddened by the change, viewing it as yet another sign of Fremont going mainstream, many will be impressed by the maturation. A new owner is on the scene, which has been spruced up (though, happily, mismatched wooden tables remain) with attractive art for sale on the walls and a brand-new dinner service. Slated to change seasonally, dinner runs from appetizers such as chanterelle mushrooms sautéed in sherry, garlic, and scallions and paired with crostini, to entrées of pan-seared halibut, fresh raviolis (perhaps stuffed with roasted beets), or a garlicky, roasted boneless half chicken, comfortingly sided with roasted Yukon potato wedges, corn cobs, and green beans—a dish bound to be a regular. Fitting for even new Fremont, there are several well-considered vegetarian offerings. The espresso chocolate torte is so rich it demands sharing. Lunches, previously hearty though uninspiring, got a make-over too—delivering plates such as braised venison goulash with fresh herbed spaetzle and sour cream. Though it's anything but "still," the cafe is far less noisy during dinner service because, unlike breakfast and lunch, you don't have to bus your own dishes. In warm weather, outdoor tables beckon you to bring a book. *$; AE, DC, DIS, MC, V; checks OK; breakfast, lunch, dinner every day, brunch Sat–Sun; wine and beer; reservations accepted; street parking; info@stilllife.com; stilllifefremont.com; map:FF8*

WHY GO: Half-price coffee between 10am and 11am.

Stumbling Goat / ★★★

6722 GREENWOOD N, GREENWOOD; 206/784-3535 If you don't live in this popular little bistro's Greenwood neighborhood, you'll wish it lived in yours. Erin Fetridge's cozy rooms are painted scarlet and forest green with red velvet draperies and cheap 1950s lamps, achieving an idiosyncratic hominess. In summer, expect squash-blossom fritters or pomegranate barbecued pork tenderloin with rapini and grilled peaches. The boneless pan-roasted chicken, a bistro standard, is always on the menu and not to be missed—it's on an island of rich mashed potatoes in a pond of pan juices and roasted garlic cloves. The short, well-considered wine list has many attractive wines by the glass. Desserts range from a crème brûlée trio (typical flavors: raspberry, espresso, and coconut) to a warm apple tart with ginger caramel. The service can be laid back in a neighborly sort of way, but forgivable since all the neighbors seem to be here and loving it. *$$; MC, V; checks OK; dinner Tues–Sun; full bar; reservations recommended for weekends or groups of 4 or more; street parking; map:EE7* ♿

WHY GO: Bistro charm and upscale food at midscale prices.

Supreme ★★☆

1404 34TH AVE, MADRONA; 206/322-1974 The stark postmodern decor with stressed, paint-spattered cement floor, and exposed ductwork has a mural on the south wall of a farmscape on the Great Plains. The tables and pew-like benches are as unadorned as Kansas. The brave visuals are from owner and designer Tova Cubert. The food is mostly great, with some reports of inconsistencies and revolving chefs. We were happy with the succulent house-brined pork loin with minted mashed potatoes, the sautéed chard, and grilled plums; the vegetarian contingent in our party was excited by squash blossoms filled with herbed chèvre and served with baby beets and snap peas. And oh the desserts!—such as profiteroles filled with honey-orange ice cream and homemade caramel sauce or poached fresh peaches with balsamic glaze on vanilla semifreddo. The award-winning wine list is well written, helpful, and free of winespeak. It's a thoughtful collection of European, California, and Northwest wines, including some from the neighboring Wilridge Winery. *$$; AE, MC, V; local checks only; dinner Tues–Sat; full bar; reservations recommended; street parking; map:HH3* ♿

WHY GO: Madrona's claim to Belltown chic.

Swingside Cafe / ★★★

4212 FREMONT AVE N, FREMONT; 206/633-4057 This cramped, funky, homey living room hung with Pittsburgh Pirates memorabilia and pictures of saints is off-beat and charming. Chef/owner Brad Inserra runs this unassuming place in an innovative, gregarious, Sicilianiac way that's made his place a beloved neighborhood classic. The dining room and kitchen are the only puny things here—flavors, portions, and hospitality are huge. You'll find all manner of seafood in pan-Mediterranean styles and aromatherapeutic sauces. Pastas are hard to pass up—especially the *aglio e olio*, ordinarily simple fare with garlic and olive oil but here an elaborate plateful of linguini lavished with capers, sun-dried tomatoes, anchovies, Marsala, and ground hazelnuts. Be sure to grab some when it's offered with Dungeness crab.

There's a muscular wine list and a good selection of beers. Reservations are only for parties of six or more, so plan a visit strategically—this place has never not been hot. *$$; MC, V; checks OK; dinner Tues–Sat; beer and wine; reservations accepted for 6 or more; street parking; map:FF8* &

WHY GO: For the dish that made the Swingside famous: *aglio e olio* pasta.

Szmania's / ★★★

3321 W MCGRAW ST, MAGNOLIA; 206/284-7305 / 148 LAKE ST S, KIRKLAND; 425/803-3310 The Magnolia original, which Ludger and Julie Szmania (pronounced "SMAHN-ya") opened in 1990, became a Seattle culinary landmark. Ludger, a German-born chef trained in Europe, created a stylish respite with a modern feel, warm lighting and artwork, expert service, and fireside tables. His seasonally changing menus offer a mix of European, Northwest, and pan-Asian cuisines with artful presentation. Homage to Ludger's Düsseldorfian roots is paid with the *Jäger-schnitzel*, three thick slices of lightly crusted, crispy pork tenderloin served with red cabbage and cheese spaetzle. The Kirkland restaurant opened in 2001 in a bright, much larger, wide-open space and has proven to be very popular with Eastsiders. The menu is more extensive, the decor more contemporary. Each iteration features an entertaining exhibition kitchen. *$$$; AE, MC, V; local checks only; lunch Tues–Fri (Kirkland), dinner Tues–Sun (Magnolia and Kirkland); full bar; reservations recommended; self parking; szmanias.com; map:FF8, EE3* &

WHY GO: Best spaetzle in town.

Tacos Guaymas / ★★

6808 E GREEN LAKE WY N, GREEN LAKE (AND BRANCHES); 206/729-6563 With expansion plans and locations popping up all over town, Tacos Guaymas is giving Starbucks's real-estate group a run for its money. Happily, here's a family-owned restaurant chain that serves genuine Mexican food that doesn't vary in quality or consistency no matter the location—including Capitol Hill's two taquerias (1415 Broadway Ave 206/860-3871; and 213 Broadway E 206/860-7345), West Seattle (4719 California Ave SW; 206/935-8970), White Center (1622 Roxbury St SW; 206/767-4026), and most recently, Fremont (100 N 36th St; 206/547-5110). Excellent soft tacos and burritos can come with the usual suspects (beef, chicken, or pork) or more authentic features (tripe, tongue, or beef cheeks). These are more than cafeteria-style taquerias—the enchiladas are some of the best in the area, as is the chile verde. On weekends try the menudo, a therapeutic soup for hangovers. White Center keeps a cooler full of ice-cold beer while Green Lake has a full, premium-service bar that keeps the whistles of frat boys and sports fans wet. *$; MC, V; checks OK; breakfast, lunch, dinner every day; beer only (Capitol Hill, Fremont, West Seattle, White Center), full bar (Green Lake); no reservations; street parking; tacos-guaymas.com; map:LL8* &

WHY GO: Thirst-quenchers, such as *horchata* (a cinnamon-spiced, rice-based drink), ladled from big glass jars.

Tango / ★★★

1100 PIKE ST, CAPITOL HILL; 206/583-0382 Looking like an airy Spanish hacienda, Tango stands as a sexy sentry over downtown, with windows reaching from tiled floor to high ceiling. It's something of a fitting reputation: Danielle Philippa's sibling to Bandoleone (see review) was formerly Apple Theater, a 1970s porn house. While chef Michael D. Bruno offers more formal entrées, this is a place to dine in the Spanish tapas tradition. Bruno works freestyle with local ingredients and influences, so the tapas, though not strictly Spanish, are innovative and fabulous. Dine from light to more formidable plates, starting with ceviche al mercado (which changes daily per market offerings) to *kefta de bistec*, Moroccan-spiced beef served with tapenade and roasted-garlic aioli, with a break in the middle for the knockout *queso azul*, a fallen Valdeon blue cheese soufflé served with fruit compote and port-wine syrup. Servers are fun and, better yet, knowledgeable about the menu, the aptly Spanish wine list, and the all-too-rare selection of dry sherries. Desserts assiduously avoid the mundane and are listed with beverage pairings. The animated bar scene is a good spot for a nightcap. *$$; MC, V; local checks only; dinner every day; full bar; reservations recommended; self parking; bandoleone.net; map:J3* &

WHY GO: El Diablo—a dark chocolate cube (with a devilish hint of cayenne) perched on burnt meringue, spiced almond, and cocoa nibs, with a tequila caramel sauce.

BEST PLACE TO BE IGNORED?
"'Stalag Steinbrueck,' the admission checkpoint for Seattle City Council offices at our new gold-plated city hall."

Joel Connelly Seattle Post-Intelligencer *political columnist*

Tempero do Brasil / ★★☆

5628 UNIVERSITY WY NE, UNIVERSITY DISTRICT; 206/523-6229 Despite our gray skies, the number of transplanted Brazilians in Seattle increases. Assorted expats, graduate students, and samba fanatics have been heartened by this hangout. From Bahia come Antonio and Graca Ribeira, in other lives dancers and artists (their art hangs in the dining room). Their partner, sax player Bryant Urban, helps Graca do the cooking, while Antonio tends bar. Bahia's bar/beach/street food is exemplified by *tira-gustos* (appetizers). The salt cod cakes, the ubiquitous Bahian bar food, are served with fresh limes and are great with a beer. The national dish, *feijoada* (pronounced fay-ZWHA-duh), traditionally available on weekends, is a stew of black beans, long-cooked with ham, garlic, sausage, and beef and served with *couve* (julienned collard greens with orange wedges). Weekend evenings there's live music—chef Urban has been known to burst from the kitchen playing his soprano sax. Otherwise, the well-lit ambience throbs with the Brazilian pop-jazz sounds of Caetano, Djavan—or Jobim, for the older folks. *$; DC, MC, V; no checks; dinner Tues–Sat; full bar; reservations recommended; street parking; map:EE7* &

WHY GO: Caipirinha, made authentically with *cachacha*, liquor distilled from the juice of fresh sugar cane.

Ten Mercer / ★★☆

10 MERCER ST, QUEEN ANNE; 206/691-3723 This tall, skinny, bilevel space, once an aging parking garage, is now a gorgeous place for gorgeous people drinking Skyy Vodka out of frosty vats shaped like martini glasses. Downstairs is a lovely seat-yourself bistro with a bar filled with the hip, well-dressed Queen Anne drinking class or theatergoers on the way to or from Seattle Center venues. On a rolling bookstore ladder, nimble bartenders climb up and swing limb to limb fetching premium bottles of Armagnac and Glenfiddich from the upper branches of a handsome centerpiece oak booze bin. After an ambitious run at fine dining, menus have been slimmed down to a short and sweet list that serves this elegant conversation-friendly bar well. Recommendables include the yellowfin tuna carpaccio or the flat-iron steak salad. Upstairs is romantic with napery, candlelight, and a view of the street. Appetize or nosh with the sensational oven-roasted curried mussels, the salmon with crushed seed crust, or the fresh artichoke risotto. *$$; AE, DC, DIS, MC, V; no checks; dinner every day; full bar; valet parking; dinneranddrinks@tenmercer.com; tenmercer.com; map:B4* &

WHY GO: Fuel up for Seattle Center events or converse intimately, glass in hand.

Thaiku / ★★★

5410 BALLARD AVE NW, BALLARD; 206/706-7807 Owner Jon Alberts calls it "culinary Zen." But unlike that austere practice, this Old Ballard reincarnation of the beloved Fremont Noodle House has the atmospherics of an opium den decorated from a Bangkok PTA garage sale. Dark red walls are graced by bright Thai fabric, Indonesian antiques, and the head of a Javanese carnivorous wooden deer. A rubber-tired Djakarta pony cart hangs from the ceiling alongside balloon-tired bicycles. Votives flicker on every surface. The authentic food from an expanded menu is as good as ever, with soupy slurp-'em-up noodles such as Guay Tiow Talay, prawns, scallops, squid, and vegetables; or dry stir-fries like that popular classic phad thai or a list of rice dishes. Nang Kwak, the ubiquitous goddess serving Thai businesses, beckons you and prosperity in the door. Her juju seems to be working, though she can't take all the credit—the food and service matches the incredible decor. *$; AE, DIS, MC, V; no checks; lunch, dinner every day; full bar; reservations accepted for 6 or more; self parking; map:EE8* &

WHY GO: Great noodles and authentic Thai in a room full of pan-Asian funkerata.

The Third Floor Fish Cafe / ★★★

205 LAKE ST S, KIRKLAND; 425/822-3553 Start with a no-expectations, office-building elevator ride to dinner, but when you get to your third-floor destination, you'll be delighted. A set of well-windowed rooms look out on Lake Washington with views that invite lingering, especially when the sun starts to set. Chef Greg Campbell took the top toque position seamlessly when his predecessor, Scott Staples, opened his Belltown Restaurant Zoë. Staples's signature grilled heart of romaine with apples, crispy bacon, and Roquefort is still here and a must-sample. A Yukon-gold potato soup with Cougar Gold cheddar is a hearty choice when available. But, as the restaurant's name suggests, the best option is to order fish, such as the pan-seared salmon with fennel and red-onion salad; or at least the seafood, such as sea scallops with stewed organic vegetable ragout in a tarragon broth. Campbell makes five- and seven-course tasting menus with accompanying wines that are quite good, showing off his skills beyond fish. Desserts range from an oven-roasted plum cake with plum caramel and whipped cream to a triple chocolate semifreddo. Service is unwaveringly polished and professional. The wine list of mostly domestics is carefully selected, but short at the low end. *$$$; AE, DC, DIS, MC, V; local checks only; dinner every day; full bar; reservations recommended; valet parking; www.fish cafe.com; map:EE3* &

WHY GO: The coolest piano bar (the glass-topped instrument includes neon) in the area.

13 Coins Restaurant / ★★☆

125 BOREN AVE N, DENNY TRIANGLE; 206/682-2513 / 18000 PACIFIC HWY S, SEATAC; 206/243-9500 Founded in 1967 by Jim and Elaine Ward—the force behind the original El Gaucho steak house (opened in 1953 at the corner of 7th and Olive)—13 Coins remains a resolute reminder of Seattle's gracious dining past. Seattle restaurateurs owe the Wards, and others, a debt of gratitude for their pioneering efforts that established Seattle as a fine-dining town decades ago. This is why cheap shots about 13 Coins's "out of date" style irritate us. Granted, not one tile or high-back leatherette booth has changed in 30 years, but that is the charm of 13 Coins. The menu is dated, but perfectly so—offering daily specials such as Sunday's Chicken Cordon Bleu. The regular menu, overseen by chef Tony Zamora, is peppered with old-school favorites such as veal picata and the zesty pepper steak Dijon, both served with perfectly cooked spaghettini tossed with butter and parsley. The wine list has kept up with the times, offering plenty from Washington and California, but given the surroundings we gravitate to cocktails and can vouch for the Sidecar and the Old Fashioned. Desserts, by pastry chef J. D. Calhoun, are a nostalgic triumph. When was the last time you had pineapple upside-down cake? Buttery cake and chewy pecans update this Betty Crocker classic. Open 24/7, if a cocktailing spin has you craving hazelnut cappelletti at 3am, this is the place. And if the city ever bans smoking in restaurants, even nonsmokers will lobby hard for one exception. *$$$; AE, DC, MC, V; checks OK; breakfast, lunch, dinner every day; full bar; reservations recommended; self parking; map:F3* &

WHY GO: Bucket seats at the counter for up-close viewing of the city's best short-order action.

Tia Lou's / ★★

2218 1ST AVE, BELLTOWN; 206/733-8226 Greg Contreras named it after his cookin' grandmother and put her traditional Mexican family recipes into a sleek Belltown eatery that's evolved into a cookin' Belltown disco. It's Mexican high concept, with pillared adobe-style facades, a gorgeous tiled fountain, iron chandeliers, red Spanish roof tiles, and old hardwoods. The food is done well and fairly authentically, albeit upscale. The carne asada is made with flank steak and served with good guacamole, pico de gallo, and real tortillas to roll it all up in. Homemade tamales, posole, enchiladas, and green chile stew are homey and delicious. The Lico

Lounge—the dark ultracool upstairs cantina with its top-shelf tequila cocktails, gigantic fair-weather rooftop deck, and DJs spinning a wide-ranging mix of music—is the real center of this faux Mexican universe. *$$; AE, DIS, MC, V; dinner Tues–Sat; full bar; reservations required for large parties; self parking; map:G7* &

WHY GO: Disco, DJs, and dining.

Toi / ★★

1904 4TH AVE, DOWNTOWN; 206/267-1017 In ruby reds and with huge light projections of the Buddha in bigendered forms on the high walls, Toi (pronounced TOY) has the feel of a temple shrine. But there's no meditation going on here—Toi throbs nightly with techno music and young, gorgeous, casually clad bodies and matching waitstaff grounded in the glandular aspects of the temporal world. This is another bar that's incidentally a restaurant. But the short menu of Bangkok street food and Thai home cooking is good and well priced. There are great bar snackables, like the Crackling Prawn rolls, fresh salad rolls, or satay sticks strung with prawns, pork, or beef. Try the Mam's Heavenly Beef Salad, a mélange of chargrilled beef, veggies, and young herbs, or one of the classic noodle bowls like phad thai or *phad see iew*. The single menu runs day and night and is very reasonably priced—virtually a dinner menu with lunch prices. *$; AE, MC, V; lunch Mon–Fri, dinner every day; no checks; full bar; reservations recommended for groups of 5 or more; street parking; toiseattle.com; map:I7* &

WHY GO: Thai home cooking in a techno club.

BEST PLACE TO SEE AND BE SEEN?
"Frontier Room—if you can get in!"
Kathy Casey, chef and culinary diva

Tosoni's / ★★★½

14320 NE 20TH ST, BELLEVUE; 425/644-1668 One of the Eastside's enduring treasures, Tosoni's is known to its many regulars simply as "Walter's place." Look hard, or you could miss it, hidden in an Overlake strip mall. But this humble exterior belies the Old World delights awaiting inside, where chef Walter Walcher and a sous-chef work the open kitchen, presiding over a small dining room filled with antique-looking cabinets and armoires. The menu, written out on a blackboard hung over the kitchen, tends toward the continental (Walcher hails from Austria, but feels more kinship with northern Italy). Meats are a sure bet, and diners are as likely to encounter ostrich or venison as they are rack of lamb. There's also a nice Wiener schnitzel. Look for fresh fish and poultry dishes such as duck or chicken. Choices depend on the season, the night, and Walter's fancy. *$$$; AE, MC, V; local checks only; dinner Tues–Sat; beer and wine; reservations recommended; self parking; map:GG2*

WHY GO: Watching the open kitchen turn bare plates into culinary art.

Triangle Lounge / ★

3507 FREMONT PL N, FREMONT; 206/632-0880 This neighborhood icon is like a wedge pointed at the heart of the Center of the Universe, aka Fremont. At the point, sidewalk tables bounded by whimsical wrought-iron fencing afford the same great people-watching as the tables inside. In this windowed dining room, servers might call you honey, then do their job efficiently, bringing upscale pub food and beyond. New owners reinvigorated the kitchen, but it's still mostly a salad/sandwich/ pizza/pasta scene. Among the many good choices is a salad with greens, apples, toasted almonds, and breaded, seasoned goat cheese. The portobello sandwich is a big, meaty affair, as are the half-pound hamburgers, available with Gorgonzola and fresh tarragon leaves. Raviolis are made in-house, like the sweetly stuffed roasted pumpkin pillows. The bar, backed by a big, neon sign—Prescriptions—is lively and smoky. *$; AE, MC, V; no checks; lunch, dinner every day; full bar; no reservations; street parking; thetrianglelounge.com; map:FF8* ♿

WHY GO: To hold drink in one hand, a slice of vegan pizza in the other, and know the universe is expanding, all around little ol' you.

Tulio Ristorante / Unrated

1100 5TH AVE (HOTEL VINTAGE PARK), DOWNTOWN; 206/624-5500 This bustling Italian trattoria belies its busy downtown hotel location. Roasted garlic hangs in the air, a wood-burning oven and an open kitchen create an atmosphere reminiscent of a graceful Tuscan villa with dark woods and soft lighting. Service is swift, knowledgeable, and attentive. Menus change every day or two, reflecting the seasons. We were delighted with fresh mozzarella with baby tomatoes, pine nuts, and white-balsamic syrup; and a risotto of Dungeness crab and tomato mascarpone. At Tulio, baked focaccia, gelatos, granitas, and desserts are all made fresh on the premises daily. Chef Walter Pisano has been a major part of what has made this place so special. As we go to press, he had just departed to venture out on his own. He leaves a staff that's been with him for his long duration—management says nothing will change. Stay tuned. *$$; AE, DC, DIS, JCB, MC, V; no checks; breakfast, lunch, dinner every day; full bar; reservations recommended; valet parking; www.hotelvintagepark.com; map:L6* ♿

WHY GO: Budino chocolate cake!

Tup Tim Thai / ★★

118 W MERCER ST, QUEEN ANNE; 206/281-8833 Tup Tim Thai is all about serving inexpensive, well-prepared Thai food to as many people as possible. Some say it's the best Thai food in town (a good way to start an argument in Seattle); there's certainly no shortage of clientele. Spring rolls or chicken satay are classic starters, and reliable entrée choices include the slightly sweet chicken phad thai, the fragrant red and yellow curries, or sweet-and-sour pork. Try the intensely flavored garlic prawns, without a doubt some of the best in town. Extinguish any entrée-induced fires with mango or coconut ice cream, or savor the black-rice pudding. Be sure to make a reservation and give yourself time to park. *$; DC, MC, V; checks OK; lunch*

Mon–Fri, dinner Mon–Sat; beer and wine; reservations recommended; street parking; map:GG7 &

WHY GO: Good old number 69—Tup Tim Noodles, panfried rice noodles with ground beef, onions, and tomatoes.

1200 Bistro & Lounge / ★★★

1200 E PIKE ST, CAPITOL HILL; 206/320-1200 It's small, sexy, and sophisticated— an adult experience in ways not often associated with Capitol Hill. Big, abstract art hangs on red and brown walls, lit by gorgeous, intensely colored, hand-crafted lamps. Since opening in fall 2001, 1200 has steadily improved, with a short, well-chosen menu. The mushrooms and scallops appetizer provides a wealth of fried shiitakes and a trio of perfectly grilled sea scallops kissed with sherry vinaigrette. A salad of grilled asparagus and baby beets finds apt company with avocado and sautéed onions in balsamic syrup. A perfect filet mignon derives from high-quality Vashon Island Misty Isle beef. Ling cod meets pearls of Israeli couscous, flavored pomegranate and orange, melon, and cucumber. The lounge is a bit more playful, as personified by the portrait of a naked man adorned with fruit. It has its own menu: mussels, cheese plate, and braised beef short ribs included. The wine-by-the-glass program fits most needs. A short dessert menu stars an orange caramel custard with anise cookie. *$$$; AE, MC, V; no checks; dinner every day; full bar; reservations recommended; street parking; 1200bistro.com; map:L1* &

WHY GO: Food as sexy as the staff.

BEST PLACE FOR SEAFOOD?
"The simplicity of Chinook's."
Sherman Alexie, poet, novelist, and screenwriter

---

21 Central / ★★

21 CENTRAL WY, KIRKLAND; 425/822-1515 Mike Brown fired up an 1,800°F broiler in this opulent little steak house with the clubby feel of a Gilded Age saloon. In the tradition of the other Seattle glam steak houses, Daniel's Broiler and the Metropolitan Grill (see reviews), 21 Central has a commitment to the trappings of luxury, pretentious service, and, of course, large pieces of meat cooked the way you want it. There's a menu glossary of how 21 Central defines doneness, making sure you know how you want it. The offerings are much the same as in other steak houses of this price range: oysters Rockefeller, Caesar salads, premium shellfish, all manner of potatoes. Steaks come in all the usual cuts but only one size: big. Dining is all à la carte, which adds up—salad, sauce, veggie. The wine list favors the well heeled, which comprises 21's crowd. *$$$$; AE, DC, DIS, MC, V; checks OK; dinner Mon–Sat; full bar; reservations recommended; valet parking Wed–Sat, street parking; 21central.com; map:EE3* &

WHY GO: The brandy-chanterelle sauce would be good on corn flakes; on a porterhouse, it's heavenly.

Typhoon! / ★★★

1400 WESTERN AVE, DOWNTOWN; 206/262-9797 / 8936 161ST AVE NE, REDMOND; 425/558-7666 Typhoon occupies a hallowed place in Seattle dining history. It's in the space of the original Wild Ginger, since moved uptown to bigger digs (see review). That is a big root to fill, but the new kid is far from bashful. From out of Portland, owner/executive chef Bo Lohasawat Kline has built a small empire, cooking up a storm in four Oregon locations, and two in our area. It's nouvelle Thai here, with no sense of obligation to the done-and-done-and-done-again traditional. Monster Prawns, served whole, look like they've just finished a communal shower in red garlic sauce. Pine Cone Fish resembles one—little chunks of halibut crispy fried and uniquely clumped together. Grilled Beef with Grapes is a stunner. The *lahd nah* features eggs, mushrooms, vegetables, and the lightest of gingery gravies. Those coconut-milk curries, the mainstay of Thai restaurant cuisine, are velvety and rich but not too heavy handed. The Redmond location in Bella Bottega Center has much the same menu but better parking. *$$; AE, DC, DIS, MC, V; checks OK; lunch Mon–Sat, dinner every day; full bar; reservations recommended; street parking (Downtown), self parking (Redmond); typhoonrestaurants.com; map:I7, DD2* &

WHY GO: To get out of the red-curry rut.

Union Bay Cafe / ★★★

3515 NE 45TH ST, LAURELHURST; 206/527-8364 Chef/owner Mark Manley consistently offers excellent Northwest/Mediterranean fare from an ever-changing menu in his gently lit, respiteful restaurant on the University of Washington side of Laurelhurst. He uses plenty of seasonal and regional ingredients, as in an offering on one of our visits of coastal troll salmon with chanterelles, blackberries, and Madeira with a citrus risotto. Look for game and exotics, including rabbit, venison, ostrich, or breast of Muscovy duck sauced with tamarind, orange, and cilantro. A reasonably priced wine list boasts a wide variety of premium selections by the glass. Manley often wanders out of the kitchen to mingle with guests; and every night tables are filled with folks doing anniversary and birthday celebrations, romantic evenings, after-work relaxations, or Husky game socializing. A courtyard offers outdoor seating in good weather. *$$$; AE, DC, DIS, MC, V; checks OK; dinner Tues–Sun; beer and wine; reservations recommended; self parking; ubc cafe@aol.com; map:FF6* &

WHY GO: Reliable Northwest/Mediterranean cuisine in a remember-your-name ambience.

Union Square Grill / ★★

621 UNION ST, DOWNTOWN; 206/224-4321 The Union Square Grill is a dependable downtown steak house for the beef and martini set. There's a hearty, masculine yet glitzy feel to the dining room, with its dark wood and oversize antique posters. Lunch is busy with power lunchers doing business while enjoying the chowder, entrée-sized Caesars, sandwiches, and a good London broil. Dinner features prime ribs and the usual cuts of steak broiled on the mesquite grill and accompanied by garlic mashers or baked potatoes. À la carte sides of fresh asparagus, sautéed button mushrooms, sauce béarnaise, or wild mushroom demi-glace should satisfy just about anyone in the mood for this clubby, meaty cuisine. There's some seafood, too, such as grilled salmon or halibut, weathervane scallops in lobster cream, or a pricey bouillabaisse. The bar is a favorite downtown business watering hole, with a flashy selection of martinis, single-malt Scotches, and a full bar menu. *$$$; AE, DC, DIS, MC, V; no checks; lunch Mon–Fri dinner every day; full bar; reservations recommended; valet parking, validated parking in 7th Ave and Union garage; union squaregrill.com; map:K5* &

WHY GO: Martini-and-meat power lunching.

BEST PLACE FOR A COCKTAIL?

"The Sorrento Hotel. They mix a good drink and it's an environment that's relaxing."

Kurt Beattie, artistic director of A Contemporary Theatre (ACT)

Vivanda Ristorante / ★★☆

95 PINE ST, PIKE PLACE MARKET; 206/442-1121 Vivanda is a low-key, upscale seafood fisher plying the abundant waters of the Pike Place Market. Though pleasant, the rooms are unnoteworthy except for partial views of the Market and Elliott Bay. Opened in 2002, this restaurant has grown into a darned good fish house. The service, though a little impersonal, is attentive and competent; the kitchen, despite early reports of inconsistencies, seems to have found its stride. We had a perfectly broiled chunk of swordfish served on a ragout of kalamatas, roasted peppers, and capers. A pistachio-crusted halibut filet with a delicate orange-basil beurre blanc was gloriously undercooked and moist; and the fat, hand-made raviolis stuffed with smoked-salmon mousse and mascarpone was a comforting plate of quintessential Seattle dining. Pray the chocolate-banana bread pudding will be on the day's menu, but, if it isn't, a fall-back with a very soft landing is the excellent tiramisu. *$$$; AE, DIS, MC, V; no checks; lunch, dinner every day; full bar; reservations recommended; street parking; vivanda.com; map:I7* &

WHY GO: Standout seafood and a partial but pleasant Market view.

Wasabi Bistro / ★★

2311 2ND AVE, BELLTOWN; 206/441-6044 Black-clad servers as hip as the ultra-modern digs—and the clientele for that matter—deliver generous martinis, lotsa sake, and chichi sushi. Aptly named in this seafood-rich environment, chef Billy Beach creates such makimono as the BLTA (avocado, that is) Roll and the Godzilla Roll, featuring tempura shrimp. Get into the appetizers and encounter tempura portobello and wasabi aioli for the snow-crab cakes. Among a short list of entrées, the salmon and the rib-eye steak are both Japanese inflected, to good effect. At lunch, rice bowls and noodles, salads and bento boxes complement the sushi selections. It's a hot little hangout, and the bar is the place to be. *$$; AE, DC, DIS, MC, V; no checks; lunch Mon–Fri, dinner every day; full bar; reservations recommended; street parking; wasabibistro.net; map:F8* &

WHY GO: Isn't traditional Japanese just so yesterday?

Waterfront Seafood Grill / ★★★

2815 ALASKAN WY, PIER 70, WATERFRONT; 206/956-9171 The glassed-in Waterfront Seafood Grill is a visual antithesis to Paul Mackay's steak-and-cigars place, El Gaucho (see review), where the only view is from the dish pit. Perched at the end of Pier 70, Waterfront sports sweeping harbor views from the 80-foot serpentine bar, the 175-seat dining room with elegant, whimsical touches in bold colors, and from the two private dining rooms. In fact, the only spaces without views are the restrooms. Diners will find El Gaucho steaks and a Dijon-herb crusted rack of lamb on the menu, but astonishing seafood is what this place is about. Get started on the right foot, rather claw, and order a classic, cascading *fruit de mer* presentation of lobster, prawns, oysters, cured salmon, and smoked sturgeon over cracked ice. Entrées under the straightforward heading "a beautiful piece of fish simply grilled" let you design your meal. Select a fish and pair it with either herb butter, sundried tomato beurre blanc, mango-pepper salsa, or pineapple chutney and one of the "shareable sides." You could make a meal of lobster mashed potatoes. For dessert we love that they suggest a glass of ice-cold milk to accompany the chocolate-cookie sundae. The wine list features well-priced bottlings with an emphasis on the Northwest and California. *$$$; AE, B, DC, JCB, MC, V; checks OK; dinner every day; full bar; reservations recommended; valet and self parking; waterfrontpier70.com; map:D9* &

WHY GO: Flights of dessert wine after dinner and a free shuttle service to El Gaucho.

Wazobia West African Cuizine / ★★

170 S WASHINGTON ST, PIONEER SQUARE 206/624-9154 Wazobia's dark orange walls are hung with batiks, Malian mud-cloth tapestries, and Yoruba belts with trade beads and cowries. Chef/owner Jerry Emmatrice is from Lagos, Nigeria, and his restaurant serves large portions of down-home food that is the mother of American Creole cooking. This is a magnet for local West Africans, and weekends thump with Afro-pop DJs, Congolese Soukou, or Nigerian Fuji bands. A good bet here is the Wazobia Combo Plate; you'll get *jollof* rice (a classic West African pilaf with vegetables), a huge plate of black-eyed peas, fried plantains, greens, and chicken or fish. There's a half page of vegetarian dishes, such as the vegetarian combo with rice, greens, black-eyed peas, and *fufu*, which are starchy pounded yams mixed with palm oil. Lunch is a good-valued, all-you-can-eat buffet. *$; MC, V; checks OK; lunch Tues–Fri, dinner every day; full bar; reservations recommended; street parking; map:O7* &

WHY GO: West African hospitality and a kitchen open till 4am on weekends.

Wild Ginger Asian Restaurant and Satay Bar / ★★★

1401 3RD AVE, DOWNTOWN; 206/623-4450 After a move to massively larger digs (some say too large) in 2000 that made locals whine about the prospect of Wild Ginger losing its soul, this landmark is still remarkable and wildly popular with Seattleites and visitors as well—especially those going to and fro from a Seattle Symphony performance at Benaroya Hall down the street. The dining room is a huge, bilevel space with streetside views and an elegant spiral stairway leading up to private banquet rooms. Owners Rick and Ann Yoder's culinary vision, inspired by time spent in Southeast Asia, changed the Seattle restaurant scene and pan-Asian cuisine everywhere. Wild Ginger offers a wide range of multiethnic dishes from Bangkok, Singapore, Saigon, and Djakarta. At the mahogany satay bar, order from a wide array of sizzling skewered selections like the mountain lamb and Saigon scallop satay. Indulge in the succulent Singapore-style stir-fried crab, fresh from live tanks and redolent of ginger and garlic; the celebrated fragrant duck served with steamed buns and plum sauce; or *laksa*, a spicy Malaysian seafood soup whose soft, crunchy, and slippery textures and hot and salty flavors encompass everything good about Southeast Asian cookery. *$$; AE, DC, DIS, MC, V; no checks; lunch Mon–Sat, dinner every day; full bar; reservations recommended; valet parking; map:L8* &

WHY GO: Fragrant duck and a singles satay bar like nothing in town.

BEST PLACE TO GET A LATTE?

"The name suits Diva Espresso in West Seattle, where you can sip espresso in high-backed, brocade-upholstered chairs under chandeliers, ministered to by friendly, beautiful baristas."

Melanie McFarland, Seattle Post-Intelligencer *TV critic*

Yanni's Greek Cuisine / ★★

7419 GREENWOOD AVE N, GREENWOOD; 206/783-6945 Yanni's is a comfortable joint with the simple comforts of a Greek taverna. Any night will find the place packed with locals. The deep-fried calamari, with perfectly fried, tender squid rings and *skordali* dipping sauce, is an appetizer big enough for an entrée. Add a *horiatiki* salad—a huge pile of tomatoes, cucumbers, feta, kalamata olives, and a little pita—and you have a meal for two. The huge, seven-page menu lists all the classic Greek dishes including spanakopita and moussaka. Yanni's also offers an extensive selection of Greek wines and beers to accompany your meal. *$; MC, V; checks OK; dinner Mon–Sat; beer and wine; reservations recommended; street parking; map:EE8* &

WHY GO: Spit-roasted chicken, which you can eat in or take home.

Yarrow Bay Grill / ★★☆
Yarrow Bay Beach Cafe / ★★

1270 CARILLON POINT, KIRKLAND; 425/889-9052 (GRILL); 425/889-0303 (CAFE)
Yes, you can go home again. Chef Vicky McCaffree did, back to the Yarrow Bay
Grill in summer 2002 after a two-year term opening the Waterfront Seafood Grill
(see review) in Seattle. Her purview here, the upstairs Grill, still has the great views
and the understated, elegant décor. The service has slipped at times, beyond what
one would expect at a fine venue. Now McCaffree, who made a name for herself
with pan-Asian cuisine, has downplayed that part of her repertoire. You still can get
the Seven-Spice Seared Ahi, thank goodness, and Thai Seafood Stew, with its
coconut milk/lemongrass broth. But a grilled nectarine chutney graces the seared
pork tenderloin, and Gorgonzola-Madeira demi-glace accompanies the beef tenderloin. New Mexico corn ravioli further stretch the geographical perspective.

Downstairs in the more casual Beach Cafe, Cameon Orel has been quietly turning
out great plates from menus themed from around the globe, including eye openers
like shark quiche, tuna muffaletta, and Vietnamese spring rolls with chorizo. When
she "stays at home," the cafe burger or the portobello sandwich hit the right notes—
chords of them. Delectable desserts range from the Black Bottom Banana Cream Pie
in the Cafe to, if you're lucky, the Mexican Caramel Apple Flauta on the ever-
changing upstairs Grill menu. *$$$, $$; AE, DC, DIS, JCB, MC, V; no checks; dinner
every day (Grill), lunch, dinner every day (Cafe); full bar; reservations recommended;
valet and validated lot parking; ybgrill.com, ybbeachcafe.com; map:FF3* &

WHY GO: Adjacent marina perfect parking spot for hungry boaters; plus captivating westward-facing Lake Washington views.

LODGINGS

LODGINGS

Downtown/Belltown

Ace Hotel / ★★

2423 IST AVE, BELLTOWN; 206/448-4721 The 30-room Ace is *A Clockwork Orange* without the bright colors. This futuristic, hostel-like hotel is so hip it hurts. White wood floors, white walls (some rooms have black-and-white Andy Warhol–like murals), mostly white bedding, and white robes give the Ace a stylishly clean, spare look. Fourteen standard rooms have a stainless sink and counter and baths down the hall. Sixteen deluxe rooms have their own bath and king- or queen-size beds. No down comforters here; low beds have simple wool French Army blankets. With its ultracool location above the Cyclops Cafe and within walking distance of Pike Place Market and Belltown galleries and shops, this is the place to be to experience the urban hipness of Seattle. Amenities include small wall TVs, phones with data ports, minibars, CD players. There's no room service, but with all of Belltown's eateries at your command, you can eat around the world during your stay. Rooms on First Avenue can be noisy. Pets OK. *$$–$$$; AE, DC, DIS, JCB, MC, V; checks, travelers checks OK; self parking; acehotel.com; map:F8*

Alexis Hotel / ★★★

1007 IST AVE, DOWNTOWN; 206/624-4844 OR 888/850-1155 The luxurious Alexis takes its motto "A Work of Art" seriously, placing original artwork throughout the guest rooms and common areas. This whimsical yet elegant boutique-style hotel inside a turn-of-the-19th-century building has 109 rooms, including spacious executive suites, fireplace suites, spa suites, and one- and two-bedroom suites with kitchens. Theme suites include the John Lennon Suite, with reproductions of his artwork and CDs of his music; the Author's Suite, with autographed copies of books by authors who have stayed there, such as Chuck Palahniuk (*Fight Club*) and Donna Tartt (*The Little Friend*); and the Honeymoon Suite, with in-the-mood music by Marvin Gaye and Barry White. In the romantic spa suites on the top floor, step up to a giant, two-person tub surrounded by mirrors. North-facing rooms have a view of Elliott Bay; First Avenue rooms might be a little noisy. Amenities range from voice mail, data ports, and complimentary morning tea and coffee and newspaper of your choice, to shoeshines, fitness room, on-call masseuse, and the Aveda Day Spa. Live jazz every Wednesday provides nice background for evening wine tasting. The Library Bistro, which replaced the Painted Table in 2003, serves breakfast and lunch only, but it also will provide guests with picnics to go and tours of Pike Place Market. Pets OK. *$$$–$$$$; AE, DC, DIS, JCB, MC, V; checks OK; valet parking; seattleres@kimptongroup.com; alexishotel.com; map:L7* &

Best Western Executive Inn / ★

200 TAYLOR AVE N, DENNY TRIANGLE; 206/448-9444 OR 800/351-9444 It's not much to look at, but this 123-room motor inn provides all the basics and a great location to boot. Walking into the comfy lobby with gas fireplace, you might think you're getting the warmth and charm of a rustic lodge

148

experience, but the rooms are pretty basic. No matter, all rooms have views of the city or of the Space Needle and Experience Music Project, just a block away. Hop on the Monorail at the Seattle Center and ride 1 mile to the heart of downtown. The inn has a Jacuzzi and workout room, as well as an informal restaurant and lounge. There's no charge for children under 17, and parking is free. Pets OK. *$$; AE, DC, DIS, JCB, MC, V; no checks; self parking; bestwestern.com/prop_48068/; map:E5* &

Best Western Pioneer Square Hotel / ★★

77 YESLER WY, PIONEER SQUARE; 206/340-1234 OR 800/800-5514 Situated in an elegant, turn-of-the-19th-century brick building in Seattle's historic neighborhood, it's hard to remember this is now part of the mammoth Best Western chain. Warm, comfortable, and oozing with history, the 75 guest rooms are tastefully appointed but quite small; some have sitting alcoves. The rooms are surprisingly quiet considering the hotel is just one block from the busy Alaskan Way Viaduct, ferry dock, and waterfront. South-side rooms get you a view of the back of another building; other rooms have territorial views. Pioneer Square can be edgy at night, so timid travelers might opt for a more gentrified neighborhood. But those looking for great restaurants and bars with a variety of live music will find almost anything they want here. Waterfront streetcar and walking/jogging path one block away. Kids under 12 stay free. *$$; AE, DC, DIS, JCB, MC, V; checks OK with 2-week advance deposit; self parking; info@pioneersquare.com; pioneersquare.com; map:N8* &

BEST PLACE TO LET THE DOG OFF THE LEASH?

"The dog park above Golden Gardens—it's great to be able to have a BBQ and a place for your dog to run around in such close proximity."

Kathy Casey, chef and culinary diva

Hotel Ändra / Unrated

2000 4TH AVE, BELLTOWN 206/448-8600 OR 877/448-8600 Travelers looking for prime location and posh accommodations will find both in this handsome 1926 building: located three blocks from the Pike Place Market and Pacific Place mall and a block and a half from the Monorail. Formerly the Claremont, the hotel recently underwent a massive renovation that ranged from a name change (fittingly Ändra means "change" in Swedish) to the revamping of 119 rooms, now sporting a contemporary Scandinavian style and stocked with fluffy spa robes, two-line cordless phones, high-speed Internet access, and flat-screen TVs (suites feature plasma TVs). Reopened in April 2004 as a boutique-style hotel, the Ändra still boasts upper floors views of downtown, Puget Sound, the Space Needle, Lake Union, and the Olympic Mountains. As well as an excellent northern eatery, Assaggio Ristorante (see review in the Restaurants chapter), as of press time, the hotel was working on a deal with celeb chef Tom Douglas (owner of Etta's Seafood, Dahlia Lounge, and Palace Kitchen) to open a second restaurant in the hotel. *$$$, AE, DC, DIS, JCB, MC, V; checks OK; self parking; hotelandra.com; map:I6* &

Crowne Plaza Seattle / ★★☆

1113 6TH AVE, DOWNTOWN; 206/464-1980 OR 800/227-6963 The lobby of this 34-story gleaming tower constantly bustles with activity. Its convenient downtown location (right off the freeway and about four blocks from the convention center) and nine meeting rooms for groups small or large (up to 400, with high-speed Internet and video conferencing) means this hotel is booked with repeat and corporate visitors. All 415 rooms come with one king or two double beds, and the top Executive Floors are corporate, comfortable, and clean, with amenities such as bottled water and robes. Business travelers taking advantage of "club-level" services receive a lot of individual attention in addition to free papers, a lounge, complimentary breakfast, and evening hors d'oeuvres. Lower-floor guest rooms are spacious and were undergoing renovation in mid-2003. Some pets OK with deposit. *$$–$$$; AE, DC, DIS, JCB, MC, V; no checks; valet parking; basshotels.com/crowne-plaza; map:L5* &

The Edgewater / ★★★

2411 ALASKAN WY, PIER 67, WATERFRONT; 206/728-7000 OR 800/624-0670 A longtime waterfront landmark, the Edgewater is home to some of the Emerald City's most unusual claims to fame. It's the only Seattle hotel literally over the water (you've probably seen the famous 1964 photo of the Beatles fishing out their hotel window—which isn't allowed anymore, unfortunately). Just throw open your window to breathe the fresh, salty air, listen to the ferry horns, and watch parasailers float by. The 234-room hotel has a metal log-cabin exterior, with aluminum shingles meant to evoke silvery fish scales, and a Northwest lodge theme inside. All rooms have fireplaces and log bed frames. The sleek Six Seven Restaurant & Lounge (named for the pier) serves Northwest cuisine with pan-Asian influences. The eatery's uninterrupted views of Elliott Bay, Puget Sound, and the Olympics extend to a balcony over the water. It's a short walk to Bell Street Pier (Pier 66), with restaurants, the Odyssey Maritime Discovery Center, and an overpass to nearby Pike Place Market. Pets OK. *$$$; AE, DC, DIS, MC, V; checks OK; valet parking; edgewater hotel.com; map:F9* &

Elliott Grand Hyatt Seattle / ★★★

721 PINE ST, DOWNTOWN; 206/774-1234 OR 800/233-1234 It's big, yes, but this three-year-old Hyatt tries to make you feel like you're more than a number. The 425 guest rooms (including 113 suites) could feel cold, but warm woods and glass art throughout the building make you feel at home in the Northwest. In the heart of high-tech land, you can flip a bedside switch to raise and lower drapes, or change your room's doorbell to a mute "do not disturb" mode. Adjacent to the convention center, the Elliott provides a host of large meeting rooms and an amphitheater. Rooms begin on the 10th floor, so nearly every view in the house reveals at least a sliver of lake or mountain; floors 20 and higher have great views of Elliott Bay or Lake Union. All rooms have refrigerators, free high-speed Internet access, separate glassed-in marble showers, and deep bathtubs with cascading faucets. Huge 800-square-foot suites with separate living and sleeping areas also have wet bars; the Governor Suites have dual-head showers; the Presidential Suite has a flat-screen TV. Guests receive guaranteed reservations at 727 Pine (see review in the Restaurant chapter), which serves "eclectic Northwest cuisine," with an emphasis on seafood and steak, and an extensive wine list. *$$$; AE, DC, DIS, JCB, MC, V; checks OK; valet and self parking; sales@seaghpo.hyatt.com; grandseattle.hyatt.com; map:J5* &

Executive Pacific Plaza Hotel / ★

400 SPRING ST, DOWNTOWN; 206/623-3900 OR 800/426-1165 Catering to business travelers and foreign tourists, this 1928-built European-style boutique hotel offers easy access to downtown businesses, entertainment, and stadiums. A magnet for Japanese business people and tourists, the hotel's staff includes several Japanese speakers; signs, brochures, and maps are in English and Japanese. The 160 guest rooms and suites are simple but comfortable and have small, clean bathrooms. All rooms have 25-inch TVs, in-room movies, and two-line phones. There's no air-conditioning, but all rooms are equipped with fans. You probably won't want to open the window because of noisy downtown streets. Seattle's Best Coffee is just off the lobby, so you can grab your java on the way to a business meeting or the ballgame. *$$; AE, DC, DIS, JCB, MC, V; checks OK; self parking; pacificplazahotel.com; map:L6*

Fairmont Olympic Hotel / ★★★★

411 UNIVERSITY ST, DOWNTOWN; 206/621-1700 OR 800/441-1414 It may be a cliché, but "Old World luxury" is the perfect description for the 80-year-old Fairmont Olympic. On the site of the original University of Washington, and formerly named the Four Seasons Olympic, the only four-star hotel in our guidebook was bought by Fairmont Hotels in August 2003. The changeover didn't significantly change this historic landmark: impeccable service and exceptional pampering are hallmarks of this 1924 Italian Renaissance icon. Creamy white walls, warm wood accents, huge chandeliers, and rich fabrics make you feel as if you've stepped back in time to an era when travelers expected opulent accommodations. That opulence extends from the 450 guest rooms (219 of them suites), including baths with showers, soaking tubs, and terry robes; to the venerable restaurant, The Georgian (see review in the Restaurants chapter). Executive suites feature king-size beds separated from elegant sitting rooms by French doors. Amenities include 24-hour room service, 24-hour concierge staff, twice-daily housekeeping service, complimentary shoeshine, three-line telephones (so you can e-mail, fax, and talk at the same time), phone in bathroom, CD player, town-car service, high-speed Internet access, Schuckers Oyster Bar, and two lounges. Several swank meeting rooms and 12 chichi shops flank the lobby. Enjoy afternoon tea in The Georgian (or in The Garden restaurant during the holidays), work out in the health club, or relax in the hot tub and pool (a massage therapist is on call). The Fairmont's prices are steep, but this is Seattle's one world-class contender. And it's not just for grown-ups. The hotel goes out of its way for children and infants, including providing them with their own welcome bag with toy and edible goodie, loaner Sony PlayStation, video tapes, cribs, kid-size bathrobes, and even bottle warmers and babysitting service. Pets OK. *$$$$; AE, DC, DIS, JCB, MC, V; checks OK; valet parking; fairmont.com; map:K6* &

Hotel Monaco / ★★★

1101 4TH AVE, DOWNTOWN; 206/621-1770 OR 800/945-2240 The Monaco's bold style is a welcome respite from a gray Seattle day. All 189 rooms are sumptuously appointed in a blend of eye-popping stripes and florals in reds and yellows, which may strike some as insanely busy, others as utterly charming. All rooms have queen- or king-size beds; 10 Mediterranean Suites feature deluxe bathrooms with two-person Fujijet tubs. As with many downtown hotels, views take a backseat to service and design (business travelers appreciate 6,000 square feet of meeting space). Amenities include complimentary high-speed Internet, 24-hour business services, evening wine tasting, 24-hour room service, a CD player, two-line phones, leopard-print bathrobes, a fitness center, and privileges at a local health club. Monaco's campy principality extends to the Southern-inspired Sazerac restaurant, named for the bar's signature drink (see review in the Restaurants chapter). Pets OK; they'll even provide monogrammed dog rain coats, or ask for a loaner goldfish in its own bowl. *$$$–$$$$; AE, DC, DIS, JCB, MC, V; checks OK; valet parking; monaco-seattle.com; map:L6* &

BEST PLACE TO TAKE YOUR IN-LAWS?

"Teatro Zinzanni, because the show will make them laugh and the food is excellent."

Phil Borges, photographer

Hotel Vintage Park / ★★★

1100 5TH AVE, DOWNTOWN; 206/624-8000 OR 800/624-4433 From the lobby's plush velvet settees and leather armchairs to the Grand Suite's double-sided fireplace, the Vintage Park looks like the ideal spot to break out a smoking jacket and a nice chianti. The 126 rooms are named after Washington wineries and vineyards, with Tuscany-inspired decor and cherry furniture, and a fireside Northwest wine tasting is complimentary every evening. Part of the San Francisco–based Kimpton Group, the personable Park offers rooms facing inward or outward (exterior rooms have a bit more space but not much of a view, but corner rooms on the west side have views of the courthouse's row of maple trees). Rooms come with fax machines, double phone lines with data ports, and phones in the bathrooms. Nice touches include "left arm" chairs (the left arm is high, the right arm is low, providing a very comfortable sort of slouch), in-room fitness equipment, privileges at a local health club, and 24-hour room service (including lunch or dinner from the hotel's excellent Italian restaurant Tulio; see review in the Restaurants chapter). A nearby Interstate 5 on-ramp makes lower floors a bit noisy; upper floors are more removed from traffic noise. Pets OK. *$$$; AE, DC, DIS, JCB, MC, V; checks OK; valet parking; www.hotelvintagepark.com; map:L6* &

Inn at Harbor Steps / ★★

1221 1ST AVE, DOWNTOWN; 206/748-0973 OR 888/728-8910 Tucked inside a swanky high-rise retail-and-residential complex across from the Seattle Art Museum, rooms at the Inn are shielded from the surrounding urban hubbub. It's hard to remember you're in the middle of downtown with views of the Inn's quiet interior courtyard with its lush greenery and arch from the old Victoria Hotel, which occupied this site decades ago. Part of the California-based Four Sisters Inns (another Northwest property is Whidbey Island's Saratoga Inn), Harbor Steps offers 28 rooms with sleek furnishings, garden views, fireplaces (excepting five of the rooms), air-conditioning, king- or queen-size beds, sitting areas, wet bars, fridges, data ports, and voice mail. Deluxe rooms include spa tubs. Double-queen rooms have an angled wall that extends partway into the room, separating the beds for a bit of privacy. Among the amenities are 24-hour concierge/innkeeper services, room service from Wolfgang Puck Cafe (4–10pm), complimentary evening hors d'oeuvres and wine, and a full gourmet breakfast. Guests have access to an indoor pool, resistance pool, sauna, Jacuzzi, exercise room, and meeting rooms. Complimentary fresh cookies and computers with Web access in the lobby. *$$$; AE, DC, MC, V; no checks; self parking; foursisters.com; map:K7* &

Inn at the Market / ★★★★

86 PINE ST, PIKE PLACE MARKET; 206/443-3600 OR 800/446-4484 Everything about the Inn at the Market oozes quintessential Seattle atmosphere: views of Elliott Bay and the Olympics from most rooms, the proximity to bustling Pike Place Market, and room service from country-French Campagne (see review in the Restaurants chapter). An ivy-draped courtyard wraps around its entrance amid high-end retailers and restaurants. The 70 rooms are handsomely dressed in soft taupe, copper, and green, and have oversized bathrooms, robes, two-line phones with data ports, Nintendo, and floor-to-ceiling bay windows that open. West-facing windows have incredible views of the Sound. (Don't fret if the weather turns gloomy; some of the most memorable views come through rain-streaked windows.) Rise early to sample the Market's fresh pastries (try Le Panier Bakery) and fruit. Or sleep late and indulge in room service from Bacco in the courtyard. In-room dinners come courtesy of Campagne (5–10pm). Campagne's bar is a snug, if smoky, spot for a nightcap. *$$$–$$$$; AE, DC, DIS, JCB, MC, V; checks OK; valet parking; info@innatthemarket.com; innatthemarket.com; map:I7* &

Inn at Virginia Mason / ★

1006 SPRING ST, FIRST HILL; 206/583-6453 OR 800/283-6453 The Inn at Virginia Mason is right next to the emergency entrance to Virginia Mason Medical Center, but the 75 rooms are not just for people visiting patients or out-of-town specialists. Nestled on a mostly residential street of First Hill, across Interstate 5 from downtown, the location is convenient to the convention center, but you will have to listen to the occasional ambulance siren. The standard rooms are on the small side, but they're comfortable and feature European-style decor. It's probably worth it to splurge for a larger suite with a king-size bed—a few suites also have jetted tubs. The suite on the top floor sports a fireplace, bar, and view of Puget Sound. There's also a rooftop patio open to all guests. Enjoy a meal at the pleasant Rhododendron Restaurant or, in warm weather, its patio tucked into a quiet courtyard, or take a short walk downhill for a good selection of downtown restaurants. *$$–$$$; AE, DC, DIS, MC, V; checks OK; street parking; vmmc.org/dbAccommodations/sec1315.htm; map:L3* &

Lake Union Courtyard by Marriott Seattle / ★★

925 WESTLAKE AVE N, SOUTH LAKE UNION; 206/213-0100 OR 800/321-2211 Catering mostly to the business crowd, but with a location near downtown attractions such as the Seattle Center, this is a good option for tourists, too. You can even watch the float planes landing on Lake Union. Rooms are furnished with the usual business-hotel amenities such as data ports and free wireless Internet. The hotel has 250 rooms with either city or lake views, a small business center, a pool, a hot tub, a restaurant with standard American fare, room service, and free passes to a nearby fitness center. The denlike cocktail lounge offers a place to curl up with a book. A free shuttle is available to popular downtown destinations. *$$–$$$; AE, DC, DIS, MC, V; checks OK; self parking; courtyardlakeunion.com; map:C2* &

Marriott Residence Inn Lake Union / ★★

800 FAIRVIEW AVE N, SOUTH LAKE UNION; 206/624-6000 OR 800/331-3131 Situated on busy Fairview Avenue, this Marriott hotel emphasizes longer stays. About half of the 234 rooms are one-bedroom suites, some boasting lake views (request one on the highest floor possible). Rooms are spacious with fully outfitted kitchenettes. Continental breakfast and evening dessert are presented in the lobby—a light- and plant-filled courtyard with a seven-story atrium and a waterfall. The hotel has no restaurant, but several great lakeside eateries across the street provide room service. Amenities include meeting rooms, a lap pool, an exercise room, a sauna, a business center, two-line phones with data ports, and high-speed Internet (daily, weekly, or monthly charge). Pets OK. *$$$; AE, DC, DIS, MC, V; checks OK; self parking; www.residenceinn.com/sealu; map:D1* &

Mayflower Park Hotel / ★★

405 OLIVE WY, DOWNTOWN; 206/623-8700 OR 800/426-5100 Past and present come together at this handsome 1927 hotel set in the heart of the city's retail district (it's connected to popular Westlake Center mall). A member of the National Trust Historic Hotels of America™, the Mayflower's lobby is decorated with lovely antique Chinese artwork and furniture. The 171 rooms are fairly small but preserve reminders of the hotel's past: oriental brass and antique appointments, elegant dark-wood furniture, deep tubs, thick walls, and double-glazed windows that keep out noise. Twenty suites offer comfortable sitting areas, and most have wet bars. The slightly bigger corner suites have better views; ask for one on a higher floor, or you may find yourself facing a brick wall. Amenities include free high-speed wireless Internet, robes, Nintendo, telephones with data ports, 24-hour room service, and same-day laundry service. For refreshments, you can't beat Andaluca, an upscale restaurant combining Northwest and Mediterranean themes (see review in the Restaurants chapter), or you can sip one of Seattle's best martinis at the popular bar, Oliver's. Kids 10 and under get a free, full breakfast. *$$–$$$; AE, DC, DIS, MC, V; checks OK; valet parking; mayflowerpark@mayflowerpark.com; mayflowerpark.com; map:I6* &

Panama Hotel / ★★☆

605½ S MAIN ST, CHINATOWN/INTERNATIONAL DISTRICT; 206/223-9242 This historic European-style hotel with shared bathrooms down the hall was built in 1910 in old Japantown as a workingman's hotel for Japanese immigrants, Alaskan fisherman, and international travelers. Remodeled into a regular hotel in the late 1980s (although a few old-timers still have apartments there), 100 rooms have hardwood floors, antique furnishings, unique bedding collected from around the world, down comforters, lace curtains, and single sinks. Men's and women's baths are small but clean. Streetside rooms can be a little noisy at times. Ask for a tour of the basement to see the only remaining Japanese bathhouse left intact in the United States. There's no room service, but the adjacent Panama Hotel Tea & Coffee House has yummy snacks and teas and also displays artifacts left behind by Japanese families going to WWII internment camps. Pets OK, but let them know beforehand. Weekly rates available. *$–$$; AE, MC, V; no checks, travelers checks OK; self parking; reservations@panamahotelseattle.com; panama hotelseattle.com; map:P6*

Paramount Hotel / ★★

724 PINE ST, DOWNTOWN; 206/292-9500 OR 800/325-4000 Ideally located for all sorts of diversions, whether it's business, culture, or shopping, the Paramount is kitty-corner from the historic Paramount Theatre, in the lap of posh midtown retailers, and near the convention center. The Paramount's modest size—146 guest rooms and two small meeting rooms—appeals to those who eschew nearby megahotels. Standard guest rooms are prettily appointed, though small, as are bathrooms. Each room includes a phone with data port and voice mail, and movie and game systems. Consider splurging for an "executive king," which is always on the corner, quite a bit roomier, and outfitted with fireplaces and a whirlpool jet tub. The tasty pan-Asian-inspired Dragonfish Asian Café is adjacent (see review in the Restaurants chapter). Part of the Coast Hotels & Resorts chain, the Paramount has a 24-hour fitness center and high-speed wireless Internet. *$$$; AE, DC, DIS, MC, V; checks OK; valet parking; coasthotels.com/home/sites/seattleparamount/; map:J4* &

Pensione Nichols / ★★☆

1923 1ST AVE, PIKE PLACE MARKET; 206/441-7125 OR 800/440-7125 If you're turned off by megahotels but want the ambience of downtown, Pensione Nichols (the only bed-and-breakfast in Seattle's downtown core) is the place to be. Perched above Pike Place Market and furnished with antiques from the 1920s and '30s, 10 guest rooms share four bathrooms. Some rooms face noisy First Avenue; others have bright skylights instead of windows and are quieter. Two spacious suites have private baths, full kitchens, and living rooms with jaw-dropping water views. A large, appealing common room on the third floor has a similarly spectacular view of Elliott Bay; it's here the bountiful continental breakfast—including fresh treats from the Market—is served. Couch potatoes be warned—the stair climb from street level is super steep. There's a two-night minimum stay on summer weekends; discounts for long-term stays. Kids OK, as well as pets. *$$; AE, DC, DIS, MC, V; checks OK; street parking; seattle-bed-breakfast.com; map:H8*

Red Lion Hotel on Fifth Avenue / ★★

1415 5TH AVE, DOWNTOWN; 206/971-8000 OR 800/733-5466 Formerly the West-Coast Grand Hotel (and prior to that, Cavanaugh's on Fifth), this midsize hotel changed its name in February 2003. But since Red Lion and WestCoast have the same owners, very little else was changed in this 297-room former office building. All rooms provide feather beds, robes, game players, and wireless Internet access. Most of the standard rooms also provide honor bars and vanity counters outside the bathrooms. If you move up to one of the suites, you'll have a separate parlor and better views of downtown or the Sound. Rooms higher up are best for people who want to shut out noise from busy Fourth and Fifth Avenues. Amenities include room service (7am–10pm), fitness center, and 14,000 square feet of meeting space. The fifth-floor Terrace Garden Restaurant & Lounge serves Northwest cuisine; when the weather is warmer, diners can be served on the large outdoor terrace. The British-style pub and restaurant, Elephant & Castle, is below the lobby, serving up fish-and-chips and bangers and mash, in addition to American burgers. *$$$; AE, DC, DIS, JCB, MC, V; checks OK; valet and self parking; redlion.com/5thave/; map:K6* &

Renaissance Madison Hotel / ★★

515 MADISON ST, DOWNTOWN; 206/583-0300 OR 800/278-4159 This 553-room hotel is aimed mostly at the business and convention crowd, but it doesn't have the carnival atmosphere of some of the busier downtown hotels. Many professional sports teams also stay there because of its convenient location to stadiums and arenas. Most rooms have great city and mountain views, but avoid rooms on the freeway side—windows are soundproofed but noise still seeps in. Some rooms have window seats, and all rooms were scheduled to be remodeled starting in summer 2003. Guests enjoy complimentary coffee, morning newspapers, shoeshine service, a rooftop pool, a Jacuzzi, and a fitness center. Amenities on the pricey Club Floors include free in-town transportation, hors d'oeuvres and a continental breakfast at the Club Lounge, and the best views. Pellini, the recently renamed restaurant on the 28th floor, offers a fine selection of Italian food and gorgeous views. *$$$; AE, DC, DIS, JCB, MC, V; checks OK in advance; valet and self parking; themadison.com; map:M5* &

Seattle Marriott Waterfront / ★★

2100 ALASKAN WY, WATERFRONT; 206/443-5000 OR 800/455-8254 Cruise-ship passengers ready to hop the next Alaskan-bound ship at Bell Street Terminal/Pier 66 now have a convenient choice of where to stay the night before or after their trip. Marriott opened its new hotel right across the street in April 2003. This 358-room hotel has standard rooms and suites, with views toward Elliott Bay, Mount Rainier, or downtown; about half the rooms have a tiny balcony. Amenities include 24-hour room service, two-line phones with data ports, high-speed Internet access, 24-hour fitness center, indoor pool with a portion that extends outside (with plastic flaps hanging from the ceiling that you can move aside as you swim), view of the bay from the pool, and 11,000 square feet of meeting space. Some suites have sofa beds and room for a roll-away cot. The massive lobby is divided into several parts, each with comfortable chairs and tables for visiting or working: the main reception lobby with a large glass-art fixture and twinkling ceiling lights, bar, library/piano bar, and Trolley Café. *$$$; AE, DC, DIS, JCB, MC, V; checks OK; valet or self parking; marriott.com; map:G9* ♿

Sheraton Seattle Hotel and Towers / ★★☆

1400 6TH AVE, DOWNTOWN; 206/621-9000 OR 800/325-3535 A giant megalith looming over the downtown convention center, the Sheraton bustles with business folks morning, noon, and night. While its 840 guest rooms are smallish and standard, emphasis is given to meeting rooms and restaurants. On the first floor are the lobby lounge and an oyster bar, as well as the casual Pike Street Café (home to a famous 27-foot-long dessert bar). A private dining facility is available for bookings by individuals or companies. Convention facilities at the Sheraton are second to none in the city. Head for the upper four Club Rooms (31–34), where you'll find your own lobby, concierge, private lounge, and complimentary continental breakfast and hors d'oeuvres. The 35th-floor health club features a heated pool and knockout city panorama (unfortunately, if you're not staying in the Club Rooms, you'll have to pay $5 per day). *$$$–$$$$; AE, DC, DIS, JCB, MC, V; no checks; valet and self parking; sheraton.com/seattle; map:K5* ♿

BEST PLACE TO STAGE A PROTEST?

"In front of the Westin Hotel behind sawhorses and
police on horses. At least that's the place to be
when a visiting head of state comes by."

Charles R. Cross, author of Heavier Than Heaven: The Biography of
Kurt Cobain

Sixth Avenue Inn / ★

2000 6TH AVE, BELLTOWN; 888/865-2748 Catering to tourists and conventioneers, this personable motor inn has 167 guest rooms, including 1 suite and 1 junior suite. It's much cuter on the inside than on the plain outside. Rooms were remodeled in 2002, including new carpets, furniture, and wall treatments. The clean, simple, but spacious rooms feature TVs with pay-per-view movies and game players. There's less street noise on the east side. Service is professional and friendly, and you'll also find room service (limited hours), a bar and restaurant with fireplace lounge, a selection of books for check-out at the front desk, same-day laundry and dry cleaning, and a good location, both central to downtown shopping and not too far from the Seattle Center. *$$; AE, DC, DIS, JCB, MC, V; checks OK; self parking; sixthavenueinn.com; map:H5*

Sorrento Hotel / ★★★⯪

900 MADISON ST, FIRST HILL; 206/622-6400 OR 800/426-1265 When it opened in the first decade of the 1900s, the Sorrento was a grand Italianate masterpiece holding court on a corner of the First Hill neighborhood, just east of downtown. And it's every bit as grand today. Evoking a classic European hostelry, the beauty of the Sorrento is in the details: elegant furnishings, Italian marble bathrooms, an assortment of pillows in four different firmness levels, and the plush Fireside Room just off the lobby for taking afternoon tea or a cocktail while listening to evening jazz. If you splurge for one of their special packages, such as the Sorrento Romance or Breakfast-in-Bed, you'll get rose petals on your pillow or a hot water bottle in the winter months. They even change the carpet in the single elevator every day—proclaiming the day of the week. The 76 rooms and suites are comfortably luxurious in an old-fashioned way, but still bow to technology with DIRECTV, CD players, free high-speed Internet access, and a fax/printer/scanner. There's also a small exercise room. Top-floor suites make posh quarters for meetings or parties—the showstopper being the 1,000-square-foot, $2,500-a-night penthouse, with a grand piano, fireplace, patio, Jacuzzi, view of Elliott Bay, and luxurious rooms. The Hunt Club serves Northwest and Mediterranean cuisine (see review in the Restaurants chapter). Complimentary town-car service takes guests downtown. The Sorrento is a short, though hilly, five-minute walk to the heart of the city—perfect for getting away from it all, without being too far away. Small pets OK. *$$$$; AE, DC, DIS, JCB, MC, V; checks OK; valet parking; reservations@hotelsorrento.com; hotelsorrento.com; map:M4* &

Summerfield Suites by Wyndham / ★★

1011 PIKE ST, DOWNTOWN; 206/682-8282 OR 800/996-3426 Just steps away from the convention center, this 193-room hotel offers homey comfort in standard, junior, or one-bedroom suites. Junior and one-bedroom suites have a living room and full kitchen, including dishwasher, coffeemaker, microwave, and stovetop (four units have full ranges with ovens). Earthtone rooms have CD alarm clocks, cordless phones, high-speed Internet, and desks with ergonomic Herman Miller chairs. Some rooms have fireplaces, others have jetted tubs. Expect all the amenities of a full-service hotel: conference rooms and catering staff, exercise rooms, sauna, Jacuzzi, laundry service, extensive continental breakfast buffet, free shuttle service downtown. There's even a 24-hour convenience store in the lobby that stocks frozen dinners to pop in your microwave. Summerfield Suites is ideal for corporate clients on long-term stays or families on vacation who want a little room to spread out (one-bedroom suites have two TVs and there's a heated outdoor pool). *$$$; AE, DC, DIS, JCB, MC, V; checks OK, credit card required for check-in; valet parking; wyndham.com; map:K3* &

Vance Hotel / Unrated

620 STEWART ST, DOWNTOWN; 206/441-4200 OR 800/325-4000 This old building has been renovated before, and it's happening again. But this time, in a refreshing change of pace, it's changing from a WestCoast chain to an independent hotel owned by the Northwest-based Aspen Group, owners of Portland's Hotel

Lucia. Remodeling of the 165 rooms is set to be finished by summer of 2004, turning the once stodgy Vance (which may also get a name change) into an upscale boutique hotel. Amenities will include phones with data ports and high-speed Internet. North-facing rooms above the fifth floor are best, with a view toward the Space Needle. Room service will still come from the Latin restaurant downstairs, Yakima Grill. *$$–$$$; AE, DC, DIS, MC, V; checks OK; valet parking; vancehotel.com; map:H5*

W Seattle Hotel / ★★★☆

1112 4TH AVE, DOWNTOWN; 206/264-6000 OR 877/W-HOTELS The W is in a class all its own: dressed in postmodern art, velvet drapes, plush modern furniture, and oversize chess sets—and that's just the lobby. The two-story lobby is one of those see-and-be-seen kind of places—especially once a month when a DJ gives the place a nightclub feel. Though the all-black clad staff is hard to see in the much-too-dark hallways (it's supposed to set a mood, but instead makes it hard to find your room key), they're friendly and helpful. Rooms are stylishly simple: taupe and black, with stainless-and-glass bathrooms, coffeemakers, desks, and Zen-inspired water sculptures. Many rooms (particularly higher corner rooms) have impressive downtown views. Goose-down duvets and pillows, and honor bar with wax lips and "intimacy kits," make for a sexy stay. Room service is available 24 hours, as is the fitness room; and meeting space totals 10,000 square feet. The W is also totally wired: each room comes equipped with a 27-inch TV with Internet access, CD and video player, two-line desk phone with high-speed Internet connection, conference calling, and cordless handset. A Pet Amenity Program provides pet beds and treats for your pooch. You don't have to go far for great food, just cross the lobby to Earth & Ocean (see review in the Restaurants chapter). And if you want a little privacy, unequivocal do-not-disturb signs tell visitors to "Go Away." *$$$$; AE, DC, DIS, JCB, MC, V; checks OK; valet parking; whotels.com; map:L6* &

Warwick Hotel / ★★☆

401 LENORA ST, BELLTOWN; 206/443-4300 OR 800/426-9280 The Warwick makes up for its dated '70s-era exterior on the inside, which is warm and inviting. The 225 rooms and four suites are large and comfortable, with elegant furnishings, floor-to-ceiling windows, small balconies (ask for a room above the sixth floor for a great view), and marble bathrooms. TVs, movies, phones with data ports, robes, and minibars complete the business-friendly rooms. The 24-hour health club includes a short pool, spa, and sauna. The hotel's restaurant, Brasserie Margaux, features Northwest and French-inspired seafood and local produce. Room service is available 24 hours, as is the courtesy van service for downtown appointments. *$$$; AE, DC, DIS, MC, V; checks OK; valet and self parking; res.seattle@warwickhotels.com; warwickhotels.com; map:H6* &

WestCoast Roosevelt Hotel / ★

1531 7TH AVE, DOWNTOWN; 206/621-1200 OR 800/852-0157 Built in 1929 but updated for the contemporary traveler, the Roosevelt is a lovely bit of architecture, even if some locals still bemoan the loss of the original grand skylit lobby. Much of that space is now Von's Grand City Café, famous for martinis and Manhattans. The hotel's current lobby is still fairly large, with cozy couches and chairs for listening to the piano man playing his nightly jazz. The hotel's 151 guest rooms include Jacuzzi Rooms with jetted tubs, and Roosevelt Rooms with separate seating areas. Those are good choices, because the standard rooms are so small you practically have to squeeze around the bed. The hotel has a fitness center, and all rooms have a coffeemaker, movie and game systems, two phones, and a separate work area. The Roosevelt is in the heart of the shopping and theater district and close to the convention center. *$$–$$$; AE, DC, DIS, JCB, MC, V; checks OK, credit card required for check-in; valet parking; roosevelthotel.com; map:J5* &

The Westin Seattle / ★★☆

1900 5TH AVE, DOWNTOWN; 206/728-1000 OR 800/WESTIN-1 The Westin's twin cylindrical towers evoke all sorts of comparisons by local wits: corncobs, trash cans, mountain-bike handlebars. It's a '60s-era kind of look (and not in the good way). However, the spacious rooms provide some of the best views in the city, especially above the 20th floor. The gargantuan size of the hotel (891 rooms and 34 suites) contributes to some lapses in service: the check-in counter can resemble a busy day at Sea-Tac Airport, and the harried concierge staff may have little time for your requests. But rooms are comfortable, and beds have cozy pillow-top mattresses. Hotel amenities are corporate minded: a business center, convention facilities, and a multilingual staff. You'll also find a large pool and Jacuzzi with city view, an exercise room, and a large lobby suitable for cocktails or business meetings. On the top floors are some ritzy suites suitable for all manner of CEOs, finance ministers, and sultans. The Westin's location, near Westlake Center and the Monorail station, is excellent, as are meals at Nikko, a Japanese restaurant, and Roy's (where gooey-in-the-center chocolate soufflés are reason enough to pay a visit). There's also the casual 5th Avenue Corner Café. *$$$$; AE, DC, DIS, JCB, MC, V; checks OK; valet and self parking; westin.com/seattle; map:H5* &

Capitol Hill

Bacon Mansion / ★★

959 BROADWAY AVE E, CAPITOL HILL; 206/329-1864 OR 800/240-1864 Built by Cecil Bacon in 1909, this Edwardian Tudor-style mansion is home to a classy bed-and-breakfast, with lovingly restored woodwork and common areas featuring antique rugs, a grand piano, and a library. Sixty percent of the interior burned in 1984, leading to a massive renovation, but the beautiful wood and glass pocket doors in the day rooms survived. Nine rooms in the main guest house (seven with private baths) are appointed with antiques and brass fixtures. The top of the line is the Capitol Suite, a huge room on the second floor with a sunroom, a fireplace, a pine empress bed, sofa sleeper in the sunroom, and a view of the Space Needle (though surrounding trees are somewhat eclipsing the view). The lovely Emerald Suite sports a sleigh bed, fireplace, and claw-footed bathtub with shower. The Carriage House, a separate two-story building with adjoining rooms, is appropriate for a small family or two couples. All rooms have TVs and phones with data ports. There's a peaceful flower garden in the courtyard, and the inn is a brief walk to Broadway's numerous restaurants and shops. Proprietor Daryl King is an enthusiastic, friendly host. *$$–$$$; AE, DIS, MC, V; no checks; self and street parking;* info@baconmansion.com; baconmansion.com; map:GG6

Bed and Breakfast on Broadway / ★

722 BROADWAY AVE E, CAPITOL HILL; 206/329-8933 Conveniently located just one block north of the popular (and hiply alternative) Broadway strip of shops, restaurants, and movie theaters, this distinctive turn-of-the-century house features beautiful stained-glass windows, grand piano, fireplace, hardwood floors, and Oriental rugs. Hosts and proprietors Russel Lyons—whose original paintings are on display throughout, along with original work by other Northwest artists—and Don Fabian preside over four spacious guest rooms, all with private baths. The Penthouse has a private deck lined with flower pots. A generous continental breakfast, which often features homemade coffee cake, is included. No children; check in after 5pm unless by prior arrangement. *$$; AE, MC, V; checks OK; self parking; reservation@* bbonbroadway.com; bbonbroadway.com; map:GG6

BEST PLACE TO VIEW ART?
"Benham Gallery on First Ave, next to SAM [Seattle Art Museum]. Besides being the only all-photography gallery, Marita Holdaway, the owner of the gallery, often displays the work of new artists."

Phil Borges, photographer

Capitol Hill Inn / ★★

1713 BELMONT AVE, CAPITOL HILL; 206/323-1955 This lovingly restored 1903 Queen Anne–style home is conveniently located within walking distance of the convention center and Broadway shops and restaurants. It's not in the prettiest neighborhood, but the house is lovely, and you'll get a good workout on Seattle's hills. Mother-daughter team Katie and Joanne Godmintz, who live on the premises, have beautifully restored the former boarding house and bordello down to its custom-designed wall coverings, period chandeliers, carved wooden moldings, and sleigh and brass beds. There are four guest rooms upstairs (two with full baths, two with toilets and sinks and a shower down the hall) and three lower-level guest rooms in the daylight basement (all with private bath, fireplace, and two of them have a romantic Jacuzzi for two). The Sherlock Holmes Room is filled with books and Holmes memorabilia and has a fireplace that faces both the bedroom and bath (right next to the tub—oh, so romantic). Full breakfast is included. Three-night minimum during summer and holidays. No children under 10. *$$; AE, MC, V; checks OK; street parking;* caphillinn@aol.com; capitolhillinn.com; map:HH6

SPA TREATMENT

Everyone needs respite from the stresses and strains of daily life—even if you're on a vacation. Fortunately, you don't have to travel far in Seattle to get away from it all. Here are some in-and-out-of-city pampering best bets:

The energetic staff at **SPA BELLISSIMA** (2620 2nd Ave, Belltown; 206/956-4156; spabellissima.com; map:E7) is almost as refreshing as the organic ingredients they harvest from Pike Place Market to use in their treatments. Owner Kristi Eyre Frambach creates everything by hand, using natural ingredients such as honey, sesame seeds, yogurt, lavender, and ginger. An organic healing facial ($75 for one hour) uses many of these edibles.

Slipped into historic Ballard is local favorite **HABITUDE AT THE LOCKS** (2801 NW Market St; 206/782-2898; habitude.com; map:FF8). When its former location burned down in 2001, it created a gorgeous new light-filled space just down the street. Opt for the Under a Northern Rainforest spa package ($200), which includes a sampling of pampering for the whole body. Between services, spa-goers are treated to herbal teas, fresh fruits, and nuts. A complimentary cosmetic touch-up is part of the experience; just ask.

Inside the tranquil, Asian-inspired environs, **ROBERT LEONARD DAY SPA AND SALON** (2033 6th Ave, Belltown; 206/441-9900; robertleonard.net; map:H5) offers everything from a $30 classic manicure, to an eight-hour day of beauty (underwater and table massage, body scrub, manicure, pedicure, facial, hair styling, makeup, and lunch) for $455.

Owner Nina Ummel conjures a global environment at **UMMELINA INTERNATIONAL** (1525 4th Ave, Downtown; 206/624-1370; www.ummelina.com; map:K6) with themed "journeys." One such journey, the Equator, makes for a romantic spa interlude where you can spend the day au naturel with your significant other underneath a real waterfall, a gentle rain from the "rain forest," and mud-caked baking in the "desert." Scrub clean with a return visit to the waterfall, all for $180 each. For less adventurous (and less expensive) treatments, choose from the "rituals" (facials, massages, or manicures starting at $50). Book early—appointments are at a premium.

One of three Juarez spas in the Seattle area, **GENE JUAREZ SALON AND SPA** (607 Pine St, Downtown; 206/326-6000; genejuarez.com; map:F9) contains fountains and fireplaces that provide an opulent but cozy atmosphere. You'll move from room to room for services (there are many) for massages, facials, and pedicures. In the "envelopment" room, clients lie on a floating bed while wrapped like a burrito in a body mask (order the Signature Envelopment Therapy, which includes foot soak, steam and Swiss shower, and massage for $150). Don't miss the waterworks—the European jet spa, an underwater massage with no less than 77 jets, and the Vichy shower with overhead rain bars will wash stress right down the drain.

It's convenient—shop, drop, and get a hot-rock massage at **SPA NORDSTROM** (500 Pine St, 5th Floor, Downtown; 206/628-1670; nordstrom.com/spanordstrom; map:J5). Within Nordstrom's flagship store lies an escape from all those pesky shopping decisions. There are services aplenty, such as body cocoons (aka wraps, $80), mustard baths ($60), and signature facials ($85–$178). But, as one fellow spa-goer put it, "I couldn't forget I was naked in a department store."

Topnotch treatments for the digits are the forte at the very fem **FRENCHY'S** (3131 E Madison St, Ste 103, Madison Park; 206/325-9582; frenchys.qwestdex.com/frenchys; map:GG6). There are no wham-bam-thank-you-ma'am pedicures here. Sink into a cream-colored leather chair to soak your tootsies in style while staff offers coffee and tea. Manicures range from $18 to $31, and a pedicure runs $35 to $51; both use aromatherapy exfoliating scrubs. Get a massage or one of their phenomenal facials while your nails dry.

Aestheticians dressed in no-nonsense whites take their skin seriously at **JAROSLAVA** (1413 4th Ave, Downtown; 206/623-3336; jaroslavaspa.com; map:K6). Trained at Carlsbad in the Czech Republic, the veritable birthplace of spas, Jaroslava Stovickova and her staff deliver deft treatments to the face and body, slathering on lots of product to soften and rejuvenate in this intimate, very European spa. Facials start at $75.

Right behind the Wild Rose, the singular nightspot for lesbians, is a clothing-optional bathhouse for (surprise!) girls only. The modern, minimalist decor at **HOTHOUSE** (1019 E Pike St, Capitol Hill; 206/568-3240; hothousespa.com; map:K3) makes for a soothing, relaxing, inexpensive indulgence where for only $12 gals can enjoy a deep, blue-tiled jetted tub, steam room, and sauna. Massage therapists are available by appointment. Towels and lockers are $1 more; cash or check only, please.

Just 45 minutes east of Seattle, **SALISH LODGE SPA** (6501 Railroad Ave, Snoqualmie; 425/888-2556; salishlodge.com), with its plummeting waterfall and lavishly appointed lodge, is the quintessential Northwest retreat. Try a heated river-rock massage ($99), but arrive 30 minutes before to soak or sweat in the pools, sauna, and steam room for free. One design flaw: the waiting room of the spa is adjacent to the workout room, so a hotel guest may traipse by as you sit in nothing but your robe.

—*Kathy Schultz*

Gaslight Inn / ★★☆

1727 15TH AVE, CAPITOL HILL; 206/325-3654 Not your traditional lace-and-antique kind of bed-and-breakfast, the Gaslight mixes modern elements like vibrant glass art with period pieces such as a stuffed gazelle head mounted over the living room fireplace—befitting its turn-of-the-last-century pedigree. Of the eight guest rooms, five have private baths (shared baths are accessed by a staircase), one has a fireplace, and all are gorgeously decorated in a distinct style—some contemporary, some antique, and some Mission. The outdoor heated swimming pool is open Memorial Day through Labor Day. Seven suites in the annex next door (one is a studio) are targeted at businesspeople and come with private baths, wet bars, coffeemakers, microwaves, refrigerators, and phones with data ports. One suite takes up the entire top floor and has a spectacular view of downtown and the Olympic Mountains. The 1906 main house features a living room with fireplace and a library. Though the Gaslight's aesthetics are impeccable, the same cannot always be said for the people skills of its proprietors, who can be a bit gruff. Three-night minimum on summer weekends. No kids or pets (except the inn's dog and cat). *$$–$$$; AE, MC, V; checks OK; self parking; innkeepr@gaslight-inn.com; gaslight-inn.com; map:HH6*

BEST PLACE TO SPEND $5?

"The Pike Street Market—great organic food by local growers."

Ann Lovejoy, gardening author

Hill House Bed and Breakfast / ★★★
Amaranth Inn / ★★

1113 E JOHN ST, CAPITOL HILL; 206/720-7161 OR 800/720-716 / 1451 S MAIN ST, CENTRAL DISTRICT; 206/720-7161 OR 800/720-7161 The special touches and personal service from innkeepers Herman and Alea Foster are what make the Hill House memorable. With fresh flowers in all guest rooms, down comforters, and handmade soaps, some guests find it hard to even leave the room. But be sure you do, because you won't want to miss Herman's exceptional two-course gourmet breakfasts, with entrées such as smoked-salmon omelets and walnut-bread French toast, cooked to order and served on china and crystal. This elegantly restored 1903 Victorian, located in the heart of historic Capitol Hill and filled with antiques and original artwork, offers guests a choice of seven beautifully decorated rooms, five with private baths. Off-street parking is provided (a great boon in this crowded neighborhood), but you won't need your car if you're not afraid to do a little walking or to hop the frequent buses. The Fosters also own and operate Amaranth Inn, a similarly appointed eight-room bed-and-breakfast housed in a 1906 Craftsman about a mile south in the Central District. The location is more convenient to the Chinatown/International District and Pioneer Square, and it contains eight spacious rooms (all named after flowers) with boatlike antique beds, some with private baths, seven with gas fireplaces, and a few with jetted tubs. Two-night midweek minimum; three-night weekend minimum during the summer. Children 12 and over are OK at both places. A third property by the same owners, 11th Avenue Inn, opened in May 2003, with eight rooms in a 1906 home near Capitol Hill Inn (see review). *$$–$$$; AE, DC, DIS, MC, V; no checks; self parking; hillhouse@seattlebnb.com; seattlebnb.com, amaranthinn.com; map:GG6, HH6*

Salisbury House / ★★★

750 16TH AVE E, CAPITOL HILL; 206/328-8682 This bed-and-breakfast in an elegant turn-of-the-19th-century Capitol Hill home is an exquisite hostelry on a tree-lined residential street near Volunteer Park, one of Seattle's biggest and lushest parks. Glossy maple floors and lofty beamed ceilings lend a sophisticated air to the guest library (with a chess table and a fireplace) and the living room. Up the wide staircase and past the second-level sun porch are four guest rooms, each with full baths. One room has a romantic canopied bed, popular with honeymooners. For longer stays, try the lower-level suite with its private entrance, fireplace, refrigerator, and whirlpool tub (also available for weekly "lodge only" rates). Each room has a phone with data port. Friendly innkeepers Mary and Cathryn Wiese serve a sumptuous breakfast—for a sunny treat, eat on the terrace. Classy and dignified, devoid of televisions (except the suite), the Salisbury is a sure bet in one of Seattle's finest neighborhoods. Two-night minimum during summer, although they can be flexible. No children under 12. *$$; AE, MC, V; checks OK; street parking; sleep@salisbury house.com; salisburyhouse.com; map:HH6*

University District/North End

Best Western University Tower Hotel / ★★

4507 BROOKLYN AVE NE, UNIVERSITY DISTRICT; 206/634-2000 OR 800/899-0251 It's a Best Western, yes, but this U District landmark has an appealingly boutique feel. (Long-time Seattle travelers will lament the loss of its original name, the Edmond Meany Hotel, named in honor of the famed University of Washington professor and mountaineer.) The 16-story art deco tower encases 155 rooms beautifully styled in yellows, reds, and blues around comfortably appointed rooms with plush feather beds, coffeemakers, phones with data ports, and WebTV. The octagonal-tower design allows every one of the rooms a bay window with an incredible view of water and/or mountains. South-facing rooms are sunnier. Some rooms have refrigerators and microwaves—all were scheduled to have them as part of a late-2003 remodel (three new suites were scheduled to open in fall 2003, two honeymoon suites and a presidential suite). The rates include free parking and a continental breakfast buffet in the swanky lounge. The hotel is 100 percent nonsmoking. Six meeting rooms have high-speed Internet. The District lounge (see review in Restaurants chapter) on the lower level is a restaurant and bar with occasional live music, and there's a Tully's in the lobby. The hotel is just one block away from the bus line, shopping on the Ave, and two blocks from the UW campus. *$$; AE, DC, DIS, MC, V; no checks; self parking; www.bestwestern.com/universitytowerhotel; map:FF7* &

Canal Cottages / ★

 3443 NW 54TH, BALLARD; NO PHONE, CELL NUMBER PROVIDED TO GUESTS EN ROUTE; RESERVATIONS ONLINE ONLY If you're looking for a true Seattle experience of water and boats, stay at the Canal Cottages in the historically Scandinavian neighborhood of Ballard. Two bright and cozy renovated cottages on the Ship Canal, near the mouth of Puget Sound, provide privacy, views of the commercial ships and pleasure boats using the Hiram M. Chittenden Locks, the occasional loud rumble of trains on the trestle overhead, and charter fishing boats on the adjacent dock. The Boathouse Cottage offers one bedroom, a fully stocked gleaming white kitchen, living room, good-size bathroom, bay window, and private deck. The spacious Caretaker's Cottage has two bedrooms with checked bedspreads and quilt tapestries, a den, kitchen, living room, large bathroom, woodstove, and wraparound deck with outdoor dining table. For an additional fee, get a breakfast picnic. Take a short stroll to the Locks and watch the boats; cross the bridge and visit Discovery Park, with miles of walking trails, beaches, and breathtaking views of the Sound and the Olympic Mountains. Two-night minimum stay on weekends and holidays; special rates available for extended stays. Closely supervised children 10 and older are welcome; no smoking; no pets. *$$; no credit cards; checks, travelers checks OK (half due in advance to hold reservation); self parking; stay@canal cottages.com; canalcottages.com; map:FF8*

Chambered Nautilus / ★★★

5005 22ND AVE NE, UNIVERSITY DISTRICT; 206/522-2536 OR 800/545-8459 This lovely guest house is set on a steep, woodsy hillside just one block below the University of Washington's Greek Row. But unless it's pledge week, you won't know it. Six charming and very comfortable guest rooms share the main house. Formerly the residence of UW professor Edmond Meany, this 1915 Georgian colonial has wood floors, antiques, and private baths (one bath is a few steps outside the bedroom door). Four rooms open onto porches with views of the Cascades; the Rose and Garden rooms share a porch. The Crows Nest has a cozy window seat and fireplace. An annex next-door houses four University Suites; one has two bedrooms, the remaining three have one bedroom—and all suites are appointed with full kitchens, antique iron queen beds, and sofa couches. Suites are available for long-term stays between October and May and are popular with visiting professors. All of the rooms have robes, antique writing desks, flowers, reading material, bottled water, gourmet chocolates, and resident teddy bears (in case you forget your own). A full breakfast is included, and complimentary coffee, tea, and cookies are always available in the living room. Make prior arrangements for kids under 8. *$$; AE, MC, V; checks OK; street parking; stay@chambered nautilus.com; chamberednautilus.com; map:FF6*

Chelsea Station on the Park / ★★

4915 LINDEN AVE N, FREMONT; 206/547-6077 OR 800/400-6077 Across the street from the Woodland Park Zoo and a 20-minute bus ride to downtown—and a downhill walk to Seattle's gemlike Green Lake with 3 miles of walking paths and boat rentals—Chelsea Station is a great getaway from the hustle and bustle of the city. Situated in two 1929 brick homes in the federal colonial revival style, the inn is thoughtfully dressed in Craftsman-style furniture. Each of the nine guest rooms comes with antique bed, private bath (two rooms come with shower only), and phone. The Margaret suite on the top floor offers three rooms and a view out to the Cascades, the Sunlight suite features a small kitchen, and the Morning Glory suite boasts its own in-room piano. Traffic is a little noisy on the north side, but in general this is a quiet neighborhood. Generous gourmet breakfasts of stuffed French toast, Mexican scrambles, smoked-salmon hash, or banana-nut pancakes are served in the sunny common area downstairs. Three-night minimum April through October and some holidays; sometimes bookings allow for shorter-than-minimum stays. Kids age 6 and over OK. Pets can be boarded nearby. *$$–$$$; AE, DC, DIS, MC, V; checks OK; self parking; info@bandbseattle.com; bandbseattle.com; map:FF7*

College Inn Guest House / ★

4000 UNIVERSITY WY NE, UNIVERSITY DISTRICT; 206/633-4441 This is Seattle's best version of a European hostel—27 private rooms in a 1909 Tudor building with Historic Register status. Just steps from the University of Washington, the hotel is appealingly collegial, with locker-room-type facilities for men and women on each floor, an atticlike communal sitting area (where they serve a generous continental breakfast), and a young and knowledgeable staff. No TVs or radios, but all rooms have phones. It can get a little noisy from the street and a cafe and pub downstairs. For peace and quiet, stay on the third floor. Each room has a sink, desk, and a single or double bed, and the best of the lot have window seats. Kids of any age are OK. Take advantage of the wild and wacky world that is the University District, or hop on the bus for a short ride to downtown. *$; MC, V; no checks; street parking; collegeinnseattle.com; map:FF6*

University Inn / ★★

4140 ROOSEVELT WY NE, UNIVERSITY DISTRICT; 206/632-5055 OR 800/733-3855 This is a bright, clean, well-managed establishment. Rooms in the newer south wing are more spacious; some have king-size beds. North-wing rooms are more standard, with shower stalls in the bathrooms (no tubs). Some have small balconies overlooking the heated outdoor pool and hot tub (pool is open seasonally, usually closing in late September). All 102 rooms have a really cool triangular, floor-to-ceiling bay-window nook, just big enough for a small chair so you can enjoy the territorial views. All rooms offer voice mail, small safes, data ports, and free wireless Internet access. Other amenities include a complimentary continental breakfast, free morning paper, a tiny exercise room, free off-street parking, laundry facilities, business center with free DSL Internet access, and two conference rooms. Extended-stay rooms are available. The hotel's Portage Bay Café serves up breakfast, lunch, and weekend brunches. The entire hotel is nonsmoking. *$$; AE, DC, DIS, JCB, MC, V; checks OK; self parking; reservations@universityinnseattle.com; university innseattle.com; map:FF7* &

Watertown / ★★

4242 ROOSEVELT WY NE, UNIVERSITY DISTRICT; 206/826-4242 OR 866/944-4242 This is the upscale sister hotel of the University Inn just two blocks south (see review). Built in 2002, Watertown is more luxurious, with postmodern furniture, bamboo floors in the lobby, and TVs that swivel to face the bathroom if you need your news fix while shaving. One hundred studios and suites in this totally non-smoking hotel come with free high-speed Internet access, microwave, refrigerator, and coffeemaker. Closets open from both the bedroom and bathroom side. Suites have a pull-out sofa bed and wet bar. Two-person Jacuzzi suites have two-person tubs. The hotel has a fitness center, general store, free underground parking, free local shuttle, and three meeting rooms, and offers free newspapers and continental breakfast, and access to the seasonal pool and spa at University Inn. Thoughtful amenities include loaner bicycles and "Ala Carts" (push carts filled with board games or spa amenities delivered to your room). The hotel is secure—guests must use room cards to access guest floors. *$$; AE, DC, DIS, MC, V; checks OK, credit card required for check-in; self parking; reservations@watertownseattle.com; water townseattle.com; map:FF7* &

Queen Anne/Seattle Center

Hampton Inn & Suites / ★★☆

700 5TH AVE N, SEATTLE CENTER; 206/282-7700 OR 800/426-7866 Located within strolling distance from the Seattle Center and Lower Queen Anne eateries, this efficient and friendly facility houses 124 rooms and 74 suites. A practical, though not luxurious, place to lay your head, guests here are mostly business travelers and families with full tourist schedules that keep them away most of the day. All rooms are comfortable and include high-speed Internet access, coffeemakers, and irons. One-bedroom and two-bedroom suites feature multiple televisions and a gas fireplace, small kitchen, and balcony. The hotel has free parking in a gated, underground garage, an exercise room, laundry facilities, a business center with Internet access, and complimentary continental breakfast. *$$; AE, DC, DIS, JCB, MC, V; no checks; self parking; hamptoninn.com; map:A4* &

Inn of Twin Gables / ★

3258 14TH AVE W, INTERBAY; 206/284-3979 OR 866/466-3979 For a quieter vacation away from the hubbub of the city, take a 10-minute drive from downtown to the west slope of Queen Anne Hill, where you'll find the serene Inn of Twin Gables. Set high on the corner of a quiet residential neighborhood, mother and daughter innkeepers Fran and Katie Frame turned this Craftsman home into a comfy inn in 1999. The three guest rooms are all decorated with period antiques, distinctive quilts, and fresh flowers from the garden. Each room has a fan and private bath, but one room's bath is a few steps down the hall. Two rooms have an adjoining door for families of four. Hearty breakfasts include scones and egg dishes seasoned with home-grown herbs from the backyard. The downstairs living room has a fireplace and is filled with overstuffed chairs and knickknacks. But the best seat in the house is in the glassed-in sun porch, a great spot to curl up with a novel, sip your coffee, and watch the sun set behind the Olympics. The inn is just a few blocks from bus lines to down-town and the Ballard/Fremont neighborhoods. Kids 12 and over OK. No pets, but two adorable resident dogs will greet you at the door. *$$; AE, MC, V; checks OK; street parking; info@innoftwingables.com; innoftwingables.com; map:GG8*

MarQueen Hotel / ★★☆

600 QUEEN ANNE AVE N, QUEEN ANNE; 206/282-7407 OR 888/445-3076
Entering the MarQueen Hotel, it seems you've stepped into an Edith Wharton novel. The opulent lobby of this 1918 building is lined in dark mahogany wainscoting and stocked with graceful fin de siècle furnishings. You almost expect a lady in corsets, long dress, and feathered hat to come floating down the hotel's grand staircase. Remodeled from apartments in 1998, the original wood floors remain. Modern amenities in the spacious 54 rooms include TVs, minikitchens with a built-in table and benches, coffeemakers, microwaves, refriger-ators, robes, a free newspaper, complimentary overnight shoeshine, and phones with data ports. Some rooms have full ranges with ovens, and a few rooms have glassed-in parlors. Rooms on the east side are darker than the sunlit rooms facing west. Lunch and dinner room service is available from the nearby Ten Mercer (see review in the Restaurants chapter) and T.S. McHugh's restaurants; breakfast room service is provided by the hotel's bakery and espresso bar Caffe Ladro. Intermezzo salon and La Pelle day spa are located in the lobby. *$$$; AE, DC, DIS, JCB, MC, V; no checks; valet parking; info@marqueen.com; www.marqueen.com; map:A7*

BEST PLACE TO FIND INSPIRATION?
"St. Ignatius Chapel on the Seattle University campus,
and the Suzzallo Library undergrad reading room
on the University of Washington campus."
Walt Crowley, president of HistoryLink

Bainbridge Island

The Buchanan Inn / ★☆

8494 NE ODDFELLOWS RD, SOUTH BAINBRIDGE; 206/780-9258 OR 800/598-3926 Close enough to Seattle for easy access but far enough to leave the city sounds behind, this beautifully renovated 1912 bed-and-breakfast (formerly an Odd Fellows Hall) is set in one of the island's most picturesque and sunny neighborhoods. Run by a friendly team of innkeepers, Judy and Ron Gibbs, the Buchanan features four suites with large private baths, separate sitting areas, CD players, coffeemakers, and minifridges stocked with complimentary beverages. Two rooms have gas fireplaces. A short stroll away are Fort Ward State Park and Pleasant Beach (ask Judy for the lowdown on other sights), and it's just steps to the Victorian greenhouse and the rustic cottage with its bubbling hot tub. Wine and hors d'oeuvres are served in the evening. Children over 16 OK. No pets (though dogs are on-site). *$$; AE, DC, DIS, JCB, MC, V; checks OK; self parking; jgibbs@buchananinn.com; buchananinn.com* &

Eastside

Bellevue Club Hotel / ★★★

11200 SE 6TH ST, BELLEVUE; 425/454-4424 OR 800/579-1110 One of the most elegant hotels in the Seattle area, the Bellevue Club is part hotel, part upscale athletic club. It's hidden inside lush plantings in an office park just blocks from Interstate 405. The 67 rooms feature sunken tubs and original pieces by Northwest artists, as well as cherrywood furniture custom-made on Whidbey Island. Many of the Asian-inspired rooms overlook the tennis courts; Club Guest rooms' French doors open onto private terra-cotta patios. The greatest benefit is the attached athletic facilities, including an Olympic-size swimming pool, indoor tennis, racquetball, squash courts, and aerobics classes. Oversize limestone-and-marble bathrooms—with spalike tubs—are perfect for postworkout soaks. The club offers fine dining at Polaris restaurant and casual fare at the Sport Cafe. *$$$–$$$$; AE, DC, DIS, MC V; checks OK; valet and self parking; bellevueclub.com; map:HH3* &

Hilton Bellevue / ★★

100 112TH AVE NE, BELLEVUE; 425/455-3330 OR 800/BEL-HILT The Hilton Bellevue's 179 rooms are fairly plain, done up in muted tans and burgundy—although a remodel is planned for 2004. All rooms are essentially the same size, although sixth- and seventh-floor executive-level rooms have more work space. However, its close proximity to the Meydenbauer Center for conferences, amenities such as use of a nearby health-and-racquet-ball club, free transportation around Bellevue (generally within a 5-mile radius, although they'll take you a spec further to Microsoft and Kirkland), complimentary room service (until midnight), a Jacuzzi, a sauna, a pool and exercise area, cable TV, and two restaurants, make the Hilton a solid lodging bet. Working stiffs will appreciate the high-speed Internet access and desks in every room; computer, fax machine, and copy machine are also available. *$$$; AE, DC, DIS, MC, V; checks OK; self parking; hilton.com; map:HH3* &

Hyatt Regency at Bellevue Place / ★★

900 BELLEVUE WY NE, BELLEVUE; 425/462-1234 OR 800/233-1234 A platinum card's throw from Bellevue Square, this Hyatt is part of the splashy, sprawling retail-office-restaurant-hotel-health-club complex called Bellevue Place. You can't miss the 24-story-tall, 382-room hotel with its two-toned brick exterior. But it's not just big—you get many extras: some great territorial views (particularly southside rooms above the seventh floor), two big ballrooms, several satellite conference rooms, use of the neighboring Bellevue Place Club, and a restaurant, Eques, serving Pacific Rim cuisine for breakfast and lunch. Chadfield's Sports Pub serves casual dinner fare. *$$$–$$$$; AE, DC, DIS, JCB, MC, V; checks OK; valet and self parking; hyatt.com; map:HH3* &

Residence Inn by Marriott–Bellevue/Redmond / ★★★☆

14455 NE 29TH PL, BELLEVUE; 425/882-1222 OR 800/331-3131 These 120 condolike suites just off Highway 520 in east Bellevue are a comfortable home away from home for business travelers or families on extended stays. Each unit has separate bedrooms, a living room with fireplace, a full kitchen (they'll even do your grocery shopping), a two-line phone with data port, high-speed Internet, and a free evening snack with beer and wine. A complimentary breakfast buffet is provided in the main building. Less than 1 mile from Microsoft, the complex has an outdoor pool, three spas, a workout room, and a sports court; passes to a nearby health club are also provided. Other amenities include laundry facilities and a complimentary van shuttle within a 5-mile radius of the hotel. Pets OK. Travelers with smaller budgets might try the moderately priced basic hotel rooms next door at the Courtyard by Marriott (425/869-5300), which was being renovated in 2003. *$$$; AE, DC, DIS, MC, V; checks OK; self parking; marriott.com; map:GG2* &

BEST PLACE FOR A COCKTAIL?

"A tie between the West 5 (in West Seattle), the only place I've been where none of the signature cocktails taste like iced Robitussin—believe me, that's achievement in this town—and happy hour at Dragonfish. Two hungry, cash-strapped people can gorge themselves on $2 sushi plates and wash 'em down with refreshing lime rickeys and sake drops, all for under $30. Delovely."

Melanie McFarland, Seattle Post-Intelligencer *TV critic*

Shumway Mansion / ★★

11410 99TH PL NE, KIRKLAND; 425/823-2303 In addition to hosting retreats for the likes of Bill Gates and other Eastside tech-glitterati, this gracious 1909 estate has welcomed regular folks to its eight guest rooms since owners Richard and Salli Harris rescued the Shumway from the wrecking ball in 1985. The couple had the whole building moved to its current location, a quiet residential street just blocks from the main road. The animal-themed guest rooms are furnished with antiques (some might find the stuffed animals a bit cloying), and all have private baths. Public rooms overlook Juanita Bay and the lower parking lots. Common areas are decorated with period furnishings and frilly details, but also feature business-practical data ports. The ballroom downstairs, often used for weddings or meetings, opens onto a flowering patio in summer. A full breakfast buffet is served in the dining room, and the Harrises also provide an evening snack. The beach as well as the nature trails at Juanita Bay Park are just blocks away. Children over 12 welcome;

no pets. *$$; AE, MC, V; checks OK; self parking; info@shumwaymansion.com; shumwaymansion.com; map:DD3* &

Willows Lodge / ★★★⯪

14580 NE 145TH ST, WOODINVILLE; 425/424-3900 OR 877/424-3930
Willows Lodge is the quintessential Northwest hotel, combining casual grace with a recycling aesthetic unique to the region. It's only two stories tall, so it blends in with its wooded surroundings instead of shouting "look at me!" While the burned-out shell of a 1,500-year-old cedar—trucked over from the Olympic Peninsula—stands sentinel near the entry, one-hundred-year-old reclaimed Douglas fir forms the beams and stairs in the two-level lobby. World-class wineries and lush gardens surround this 88-room luxe lodge. Rooms are classified as "nice," "nicer," and "nicest." Even the "nice" rooms are fabulous. Slate bath tile, recycled slate desk, balcony or patio, reclaimed timber shelves, rock-lined fireplaces, stereo-DVD-CD systems (borrow CDs and DVDs at the front desk), free high-speed Internet connections, lush bathrooms ("nicest" rooms have jetted tubs and heated towel racks), safes large enough for your laptop, and complimentary breakfast are just a few of the reasons to stay here. Add to that enticing views of the gardens, Chateau Ste. Michelle and Columbia wineries next door and across the street (a dozen more are a short drive away), Sammamish River (and its popular bike trail), or Mount Rainier (on a clear day). Service is Northwest casual but quick and professional. The "nicest" of the six suites ($750 per night) boasts a whirlpool bath and flat-screen TV. Other lodge amenities include a spa, 24-hour fitness room, Japanese garden, and evening wine tastings. The Barking Frog restaurant (see review in the Restaurants chapter) serves Mediterranean-influenced dinners and weekend brunch. Guests also have access to nine-course meals at the renowned Herbfarm Restaurant (see review in the Restaurants chapter), which, along with its famed herb gardens, occupies its own site on the grounds. *$$$$; AE, DC, DIS, JCB, MC, V; checks OK; self parking; mail@willowslodge.com; willowslodge.com; map:BB2* &

The Woodmark Hotel on Lake Washington / ★★★

1200 CARILLON POINT, KIRKLAND; 425/822-3700 OR 800/822-3700
The only hotel nestled right on the shoreline of Lake Washington, the Woodmark is tucked inside the elite enclave of Carillon Point on the east side of the lake. The four-story brick hotel blends seamlessly with surrounding shops and restaurants and is just steps from the marina and shoreline walking path. Away from busy streets, you're more likely to hear the rustling of boat sails than a car. One hundred guest rooms, about half with stunning lake views, offer a relaxing retreat of cream-color furnishings and extras such as minibars and refrigerators, the comfiest robes (terry on the inside, silky on the outside), and prompt, friendly service. Some rooms have balconies with table and chairs; the others at least have doors that open to let in the sound of lapping water. Suites include the palatial Woodmark, with a lake and mountain view, dining space for six, a lavish bathroom with Jacuzzi, 950 square feet of parlor space, an entertainment center, and a wet bar. Smaller suites feature varying parlor sizes. All guests get a complimentary newspaper, free Internet access, and a chance to "raid the pantry" when the restaurant lays out a complimentary

late-night buffet. Down the grand staircase is the comfortable Library Bar, with grand piano and overstuffed chairs in front of the fireplace. The hotel's restaurant, Waters, features Northwest cuisine focusing on local and organic farmers; other restaurants and specialty shops (including The Spa at Woodmark) are nearby. *$$$–$$$$; AE, DC, JCB, MC, V; checks OK; valet and self parking; mail@thewoodmark.com; the woodmark.com; map:EE3* &

Airport Area

Doubletree Hotel Seattle Airport / ★★

18740 INTERNATIONAL BLVD, SEATAC; 206/246-8600 OR 800/222-TREE Guests at this enormous 14-story hotel enjoy the spoils of a well-calibrated operation and, in the east-facing rooms, a view of the Cascades. With 850 rooms and 12 suites, services here are primed to handle scores of conventioneers and business travelers with 24-hour airport shuttle and room service. Diners can choose from two full restaurants, and two lounges provide weekend entertainment such as dancing, televised sports, and interactive video. On-site amenities include a workout room and pool. Despite the hotel's gargantuan size, guests feel a little more at home when they're greeted with freshly baked chocolate-chip cookies—a Doubletree tradition. Small pets OK. *$$; AE, DC, DIS, JCB, MC, V; checks OK; self parking; doubletree hotels.com; map:PP6* &

Hilton Seattle Airport Hotel / ★★★

17620 INTERNATIONAL BLVD, SEATAC; 206/244-4800 OR 800/HILTONS A huge renovation a few years back doubled the size of this well-run hotel to a total of 396 rooms, including seven suites. Rooms are set around two landscaped courtyards with a pool and indoor/outdoor Jacuzzi. The hotel also has a fitness room and a 40,000-square-foot, state-of-the-art conference center. Rooms include comfortable desks, computer hookups, high-speed Internet access, coffeemakers, and WebTV. A 24-hour business center caters to worker bees. The hotel's restaurant, Spencer's for Steaks and Chops, serves all meals. Room service is 5am to midnight, but the complimentary airport shuttle is 24 hours. *$$–$$$; AE, DC, DIS, JCB, MC, V; checks OK; self parking; hilton.com; map:OO5* &

Radisson Hotel Seattle Airport / ★★

17001 INTERNATIONAL BLVD, SEATAC; 206/244-6000 OR 800/333-3333 On sunny summer days, the large outdoor pool at this spic-and-span 308-room airport hotel gets plenty of traffic from its littlest guests. Family-friendly accommodations are coupled with 12 meeting rooms, workout room, sauna, and amenities such as in-room voice mail, data ports, cable TV, coffeemakers, and sleeper sofas for additional guests. The rooms are clean, and those in the newer wing on the hotel's south side sport a more updated decor. The restaurant was being remodeled in 2003; the lounge is open until 11pm. Room service is available 6am to 11pm. Complimentary 24-hour airport shuttle. No pets. *$$$; AE, DC, DIS, JCB, MC, V; no checks; self parking; www.radisson.com/seattlewa; map:OO5* &

Red Lion Hotel Seattle Airport / ★

18220 INTERNATIONAL BLVD, SEATAC; 206/246-5535 OR 800/RED-LION Formerly the WestCoast Sea-Tac Hotel, this no-nonsense hotel has easy airport access. Meeting facilities can handle up to 200 people; an outdoor pool, Jacuzzi, exercise room, and sauna are open to everyone who stays in the bright rooms here. King rooms include bathrobes and newspaper. All 146 rooms contain hair dryers and coffeemakers. Pets OK. Free valet parking and a 24-hour airport shuttle. *$$; AE, DC, DIS, MC, V; checks OK; valet parking; redlion.com; map:PP6* &

Seattle Marriott at Sea-Tac / ★★

3201 S 176TH ST, SEATAC; 206/241-2000 OR 800/228-9290 It's no surprise that this hotel one block from the airport attracts travelers who want to get in and out of town with a minimum of stress. The swift service at this 459-room megamotel makes transfer to and from Sea-Tac Airport virtually painless. Convenience doesn't come at the expense of enjoyment, though. The lobby, with its warm Northwest motif, opens into an enormous atrium complete with indoor pool and two Jacuzzis. For slightly higher rates than the standard rooms, five more-spacious, handsomely appointed suites are available, and rooms on the concierge floor include turndown service and a lounge that serves continental breakfasts and nightly nibbles. All rooms have high-speed Internet and a phone with data port. All guests have access to a sauna and well-equipped exercise room. A casual dining room and the lounge offer the usual hotel fare. Pets OK. *$$$; AE, DC, DIS, JCB, MC, V; checks OK; self parking; marriott.com; map:PP6* &

EXPLORING

EXPLORING

Top 25 Attractions

1) PIKE PLACE MARKET

PIKE ST TO VIRGINIA ST, BETWEEN 1ST AND WESTERN AVES, CENTERED ON PIKE PL, DOWNTOWN; 206/682-7453 If cities have souls, then Pike Place Market is Seattle's. Opened on August 17, 1907, in response to the demands of housewives who were angry at having to pay exorbitant food prices padded by middlemen, this oldest continuously operating farmers market in the United States remains a boisterous bazaar, aggressively eschewing chain stores or franchise operations (except, of course, for Starbucks, which opened its first store in 1971—at the Market).

Visit before 9am to watch the Market come alive as the farmers set up, then spend the day meandering its crannies, nibbling from its astonishing variety of ethnic and regional foods, browsing the shops, and watching the street-corner musicians, puppeteers, and mimes. The official entrance is at the corner of First Avenue and Pike Street, at the **INFORMATION BOOTH** (206/682-7453), where you can pick up a map and some advice on sights, or just a self-guided-tour pamphlet. (The booth doubles as a day-of-show, half-price ticket outlet, called Ticket/Ticket, noon–6pm Tues–Sun.) **FIRST AND PIKE NEWS** (206/624-0140), an extensive newsstand carrying national and international newspapers and magazines, anchors this busy corner. So does the recently remodeled **DELAURENTI SPECIALTY FOOD MARKET** (206/622-0141), a beloved Italian deli/cafe. Just to the south is the **SOUTH ARCADE**, home to modern-looking shops and condos that have spread forth from the 7-acre Market Historic District (created by voters in 1971).

Walking west from here, down the covered corridor, you'll come to the elbow of the L-shaped market, home to the big bronze piggy bank named **RACHEL** and weekend crowds that delight in the salmon-throwing antics of salespeople at **PIKE PLACE FISH** (206/682-7181). This is the start of the **MAIN ARCADE**—the famous neon Pike Place Market sign and clock are just above you—where produce vendors called "high-stallers" display beautifully arranged (don't touch!) international produce and "low-stallers" sell seasonal, regional produce. In the midst of this is a Market institution: the **ATHENIAN INN** (206/624-7166), a smoky, working-class cafe that's been the favorite haunt of Market old-timers ever since 1909 (and was one of the settings for 1993's *Sleepless in Seattle*). Engraved floor tiles were part of a 1986 fund-raising project. The Main Arcade also has two labyrinthine levels below the street, where you can find the **MARKET MAGIC SHOP** (206/624-4271) and maybe catch owners Darryl Beckman and Sheila Lyon demonstrating their slights of hand. An outdoor staircase on the Main Arcade's west side leads to the Pike Market **HILLCLIMB**, a steep cascade of steps that connects the Market (at Western Ave) with the waterfront below.

TOP 25 ATTRACTIONS

1) Pike Place Market
2) Pioneer Square
3) Space Needle and the Seattle Center
4) Safeco Field
5) Experience Music Project (EMP)
6) Ballard Locks
7) Washington State Ferries
8) Monorail
9) Seattle Asian Art Museum
10) Odyssey Maritime Discovery Center
11) Seattle Art Museum
12) Underground Tour
13) Seattle Aquarium
14) Museum of Flight
15) Woodland Park Zoo
16) Pacific Science Center
17) Washington Park Arboretum
18) Fisherman's Terminal
19) Burke-Gilman Trail
20) Smith Tower
21) Nordstrom and REI
22) Alki Beach Park
23) Henry Art Gallery
24) Gas Works Park
25) Discovery Park

In summer, the artists' and craftspeople's tables stretch along the Main and North Arcades all the way along Pike Place to Virginia Street and **VICTOR STEINBRUECK PARK** (see Parks and Beaches in this chapter), a splash of green that marks the Market's northern border. Across Pike Place from the Main and North Arcades, you'll discover shops, ethnic eateries, and the original **STARBUCKS** (206/448-8762) in low buildings that lead to a shady courtyard in the back, where covered tables are set out for **EMMETT WATSON'S OYSTER BAR** (206/448-7721), a folksy seafood joint named in honor of the late, lamented Seattle newspaper columnist and raconteur.

If you take a short detour here, up the wooden stairs to **POST ALLEY**, you'll find **THE PINK DOOR** (206/443-3241; see review in the Restaurants chapter), a funky trattoria with terrific summertime porch seating, and **KELLS** (206/728-1916), a lively, rough-hewn Irish pub and restaurant. Follow Post Alley south, back toward Pike Place; you'll pass the stylish, 70°-room **INN AT THE MARKET** (206/443-3600; see review in the Lodgings chapter), the Market's only sizable hotel. In the next block you'll go by the see-and-be-seen sipping bar at **SEATTLE'S BEST COFFEE** (206/467-7700) and the entrance to a wide variety of shops and eating places in the **POST ALLEY MARKET BUILDING.**

Back on Pike Place heading south, across the street from the high-stallers you'll encounter **TOTEM SMOKEHOUSE** (206/443-1710), where you can pick up smoked salmon (or arrange to have it shipped). Stop by **MEE SUM PASTRIES** (206/682-6780) for savory Chinese potstickers, or score balcony seating and a dish of flavorful paella at the **COPACABANA CAFE** (206/622-6359), the city's only Bolivian restaurant. **SUR LA TABLE** (206/448-2244) is a nationally acclaimed cook's emporium.

Inside the **SANITARY MARKET** (so named because horses were not allowed inside) is a chaotic jumble of produce stands and eating places, including the **PIKE**

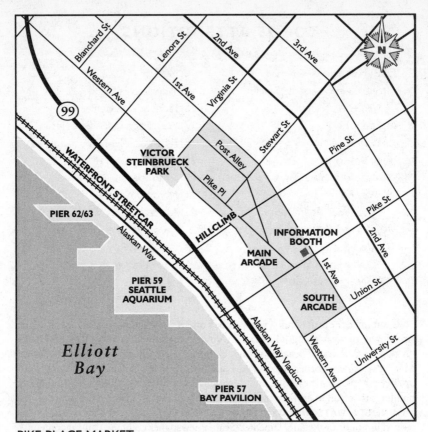

PIKE PLACE MARKET

PLACE MARKET CREAMERY (206/622-5029), which sells delicious dairy goods; **JACK'S FISH SPOT** (206/467-0514), purveyor of steaming cups of cioppino from an outdoor bar; and **THREE GIRLS BAKERY** (206/622-1045), an excellent sandwich counter that's easily identified by its long line of regulars. Just to the south is the last building in this historic stretch: the picturesque **CORNER MARKET** houses produce and flower stalls. A couple of restaurants are hidden in its upper reaches: the tiny **MATT'S IN THE MARKET** (206/467-7909), a cozy perch from which to enjoy an oyster po'boy; and **CHEZ SHEA** (206/467-9990), perhaps the most romantic nook in town, with an adjoining bistro/bar called **SHEA'S LOUNGE** (see reviews of all three in the Restaurants chapter). Post Alley continues on the south side of Pike Street, as it dips below street level and passes the dimly lit Italian restaurant **IL BISTRO** (206/682-3049; see review in the Restaurants chapter) and the **MARKET THEATER** (206/781-9273), home to Unexpected Productions, an improvisational comedy-theater troupe.

It's almost impossible to get a parking space on congested Pike Place, so either come by bus or splurge for a space in the 550-slot parking garage on Western Avenue, with its elevator that opens directly into the Market (some merchants help defray the cost by giving out parking stamps, free with purchase, so be sure to ask). Alternatively, try one of the lots a little farther south on Western or along First Avenue to the north. *Every day; information@pikeplacemarket.org; pikeplace market.org; map:J8–I8*

2) PIONEER SQUARE

S KING ST TO YESLER WY, ALONG 1ST AND 2ND AVES, DOWNTOWN At the risk of using an adjective diminished by a certain TV show, this neighborhood located just south of the modern business district is a survivor. Originally the site of a Native American village, it was settled by white pioneers in 1852, but the Great Fire of 1889 reduced the city's original downtown to cinders. Although rebuilt according to more architecturally coherent—and less flammable—standards, by the 1960s Pioneer Square had become so run-down that city officials proposed leveling it. Fortunately, wiser heads fought to save Pioneer Square to turn it into Seattle's first historic district. Accidents and disasters continue to threaten, however; in 2001 a semitruck accident collapsed the square's graceful **PERGOLA**, followed by the deadly Mardi Gras riots and the Ash Wednesday earthquake, which brought building bricks crashing down into the streets. (Both the pergola and buildings damaged in the quake have been rebuilt and reinforced.)

Encompassing almost 90 acres, Pioneer Square is one of the largest historic districts in the nation. It's a busy place filled with bookstores, art galleries, restaurants, antique shops, and nightclubs. Lawyers, architects, and media folk dominate the workforce. Panhandlers and transients are also drawn here by a preponderance of social services (and park benches).

Seattle's earliest intersection, at First Avenue and Yesler Way, is home to triangular **PIONEER PLACE PARK**. The park's most prominent fixtures—national historic landmarks both—are its 1909 iron-and-glass pergola (a waiting area during the days of cable cars) and a Tlingit totem pole (a replacement for one originally stolen from Alaska in 1899 by a group of Seattle businessmen). Facing the park is the **PIONEER BUILDING**, designed by Elmer Fisher, a prolific Scotsman who established the architectural vernacular of post–Great Fire Seattle, synthesizing his Victorian philosophies about facades with the weighty Romanesque revival look. The building houses a maze of antique shops on its lower level and the headquarters of the **UNDERGROUND TOUR**, a fun subterranean prowl through the original streets of downtown (see listing #12 below).

In the mid-19th century, greased logs and trees cut in the Seattle hills were dragged down diagonal **YESLER WAY** to feed pioneer Henry Yesler's waterfront sawmill. The avenue quickly became familiar as "skid road" (often mangled into "skid row"), an early-20th-century insult used to describe inner-city neighborhoods that—like Pioneer Square—had fallen on hard times. Just across Yesler from Pioneer Place is **MERCHANTS CAFE** (109 Yesler Wy; 206/624-1515), Seattle's oldest restaurant. To the west, you'll find a tasty breakfast or late-night dinner at **TRATTORIA MITCHELLI** (84 Yesler Wy; 206/623-3883). **AL BOCCALINO** (1 Yesler Wy;

FARMERS MARKETS

For perfect postcard imagery, or if you want to get a fish hurled at you, you can't beat Seattle's Pike Place Market. But if you want to eat your way through truly local goods *and* avoid tourist bustle, head to some of the city's smaller neighborhood farmers markets, where you'll be lured by an array of edibles—organically grown produce, jams, honey, and much more—harvested from small farms across Washington.

The Neighborhood Farmer's Market Alliance organizes five of the following markets. For more information, go online to seattlefarmersmarkets.org. For a listing of all the farmers markets in Washington, go to www.wafarmersmarkets.com.

Operating since 1993, the **UNIVERSITY DISTRICT FARMERS MARKET**'s (University Ave and NE 50th St; Sat 9am–2pm, May–Nov; map:FF6), located at the University Heights Center Playfield, is the oldest and largest (with more than 50 vendors) farmers-only market. As you walk in, check the chalkboard for the day's freshest buys—depending on the month, tomatoes, peppers, or baskets of berries. All the fixings for a same-night feast are here—yellow and red cherry tomatoes, red, green, and purple peppers, fragrant rosemary, Samish Bay cheeses, smoked salmon, and hazelnuts in every form (oil, chopped, sliced, or candied) from Lynden. There's even fresh pasta, courtesy of Queen Anne restaurant Nonna Maria. Grab a slice of strudel and some fresh cider (apple, raspberry, cherry, and apricot).

WEST SEATTLE FARMERS MARKET (Alaska Junction, corner of California Ave and SW Alaska St; Sun 10am–2pm, May–Nov; map:JJ9) is a newer market; you'll see many of the same vendors here as in the U District selling Walla Walla sweet onions, bunches of fresh basil, and artisan bread from the Great Harvest Bread Company. A crafty gift fair across the street is an extra perk.

COLUMBIA CITY FARMERS MARKET (Rainier Ave S at S Edmunds St; Wed 3–7pm, May–Oct; map:JJ6), located south of Mount Baker and neighbor to the Chinatown/International District, attracts diverse and chatty crowds—from Muslim women in traditional garb to yuppies in traditional Lexuses. Along with organic seasonal crops, Cousin's Gourmet Dip Mixes hawks homemade natural spices—just add sour cream or mayo to create delicious dips—and Skagit River Ranch stocks coolers with certified organic meats, from grass-fed-only Angus beef and burger patties to whole chicken.

Like Columbia City, **MAGNOLIA FARMERS MARKET** (2550 34th Ave W; Sat 10 am–2pm, June–Oct; mapGG9) truly reflects it neighborhood: in this case, affluent. Pleasantly nestled in the below-street level Magnolia Community Center parking lot (across from a high school), it was founded in 2003 and is the youngest of the markets. But it does tempt with bunches of flowers, honey, fruit and veggie vendors, and slices of pie. Try a few flaky rugelach, a rolled flaky pastry made with cream cheese and filled with nuts and fruit (the currant or chocolate are divine), to fuel your stall cruising. After you've collected your goodies, a prime spot for a picnic is right on Magnolia Bluff overlooking the Sound.

FREMONT SUNDAY MARKET (N 34th St, between Phinney Ave and Evanston Ave N; fremontmarket.com; Sun 10am–5pm, April–Nov; 10am–4pm, Dec–Mar; map:FF8) bills itself as a European-style street market, and you can find anything from old and new furniture to cowboy boots. Goods of the more than 150 vendors range from handcrafted jewelry and hats galore to choice antique and vintage items. Fremont originally encompassed produce and local crafts as well, but with flea market booths straining for space, in 2000 food (raw and prepared) and strictly original and locally made craft vendors moved to Ballard, creating a complementary sister market to Fremont's flea market.

The year-round **BALLARD SUNDAY MARKET** (Ballard Avenue NW, between 22nd Ave NW and 20th Ave NW; 206/781-6776; ballardsundaymarket.com; Sun 10am–4pm in summer, 11am–3pm in winter; map:EE8) is part street fair, part farmers market. This is also the only neighborhood market licensed to sell wines—made only with organic grapes in Washington, please. Along with seasonal produce (and, in winter, a smaller selection of hothouse grown greens) and organic meats and cheeses, find pleasing aromatherapy oils and balms (even get a back massage) or browse handmade jewelry and art (the Chinese silk art is a steal) while serenaded by Spanish music from a live band. The market's locale makes it doubly fun, situated as it is between the trendy rows of Ballard shops, so you can meander between shops and vendor stalls.

—Niki Stojnic

206/622-7688; see review in the Restaurants chapter) is a wonderful nook for a romantic (and pricier) Italian meal.

First Avenue is the main, tree-lined artery through the historic district, intersected by streets that terminate at the waterfront a block west (the best chance for parking in this area is under the Alaskan Way Viaduct; bring quarters for the meters). Heading south you'll see the **NEW ORLEANS RESTAURANT** (114 1st Ave S; 206/622-2563), a Creole/Cajun eatery known as well for its mint juleps as its Dixieland acts. On the next block is the **GRAND CENTRAL ARCADE.** Opened in 1879 by entrepreneur (and later Washington governor) Watson C. Squire, the structure housed Seattle's first real theater. It now contains two levels of eclectic retail, including the excellent **GRAND CENTRAL BAKING COMPANY** (214 1st Ave S; 206/622-3644). Immediately across from the Grand Central on S Main Street is the unusual **KLONDIKE GOLD RUSH NATIONAL HISTORICAL PARK** (117 S Main St, 206/553-7220), which pays homage to those who headed north during the 1890s in search of gold in Canada's Yukon. Really a storefront museum, the free "park" is

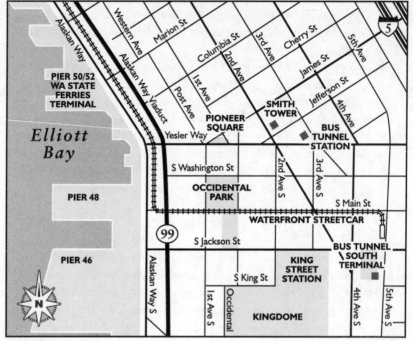

PIONEER SQUARE

the southernmost unit for the National Park Service's Klondike gold rush historical sites. (Other units are the town of Skagway and the famous Chilkoot Trail, both in southeast Alaska.) Exhibits highlight the use of placer-mining equipment and the decisive role newspapers played in spreading word of that subarctic mother lode.

At First Avenue S and S Main Street is the renowned **ELLIOTT BAY BOOK COMPANY** (101 S Main St; 206/624-6600). Since opening in 1973 the shop has become Seattle's premier independent bookstore, boasting more than 150,000 new and used titles and readings and signings that draw the nation's most distinguished authors almost nightly.

OCCIDENTAL AVENUE S, a sun-dappled, brick-lined pedestrian walkway between First and Second Avenues S, is studded with galleries. On the **FIRST THURSDAY GALLERY WALK** of every month, all of Pioneer Square fills up with art appreciators (see the Arts chapter); one gallery/store on this walk is **NORTHWEST FINE WOODWORKING** (1st Ave S and S Jackson St; 206/625-0542), with its exquisite handcrafted furniture and sculptures. Occidental Avenue S segues into **OCCIDENTAL PARK**, a Northwest attempt at a Parisian park setting with cobblestones, trees, and totem poles. The international feeling is enhanced by the occasional horse-drawn buggy or rickshaw-like pedicab. A more novel park, the **WATERFALL GARDEN**, is tucked into a corner at Second Avenue S and S Main Street (see Parks and Beaches in this chapter).

King Street is Pioneer Square's southern boundary. Look farther south and you can't miss **SAFECO FIELD** (see listing below), as well as the Seahawks' football stadium (Occidental Wy S and S King St). **F. X. MCRORY'S STEAK, CHOP AND OYSTER HOUSE** (419 Occidental Ave S; 206/623-4800) is the restaurant and watering hole of choice for game-goers. Just north of the stadiums is **KING STREET STATION** (2nd Ave S and S Main St; 206/382-4125). With its striking clock tower, the station opened for business in 1906 and still receives Amtrak trains as well as a commuter train, the Sounder. A pricey restoration scheduled for completion in 2004 promises to give the station new life and new retail. West on King is **MERRILL PLACE**, once Schwabacher's Hardware, a revitalized building that conceals an enclave of apartments and **IL TERRAZZO CARMINE** (411 1st Ave S; 206/467-7797; see review in the Restaurants chapter), an esteemed Italian restaurant with a romantic bar and a terrace overlooking a fountain—the ideal place to wind up a Pioneer Square tour. *Map:O9–M8*

BEST PLACE TO SPEND MONEY?

"Mario's or Nordstrom's, to buy that special pair of shoes or a special sport coat. For that matter, you can also buy tails and tuxedos, my work clothes."

Gerard Schwarz, music director of the Seattle Symphony

---

3) SPACE NEEDLE AND THE SEATTLE CENTER

DENNY WY TO MERCER ST, 1ST AVE N TO 5TH AVE N, QUEEN ANNE; 206/684-8582 More than 10 million visitors walk through the Seattle Center every year. This 74-acre park north of downtown, at the base of Queen Anne Hill on the edge of the Denny Regrade, is the prized legacy of the 1962 Century 21 Exposition—Seattle's second world's fair (after the 1909 Alaska-Yukon-Pacific Exposition). The center is the entertainment hub of this city—one of its biggest draws being the **EXPERIENCE MUSIC PROJECT** museum (see listing #5 below)—playing host to such popular annual events as the Northwest Folklife Festival (Memorial Day weekend), the Bite of Seattle (mid-July), and Bumbershoot (Labor Day weekend).

Legend has it that the city's most recognized symbol, the 605-foot **SPACE NEEDLE** (206/905-2100), originally called the Space Cage, began as a doodle sketched on a cocktail napkin by world's fair chairman Eddie Carlson. Architects John Graham Sr., Victor Steinbrueck, and John Ridley translated that into a futuristic concept in metal and glass. When King County commissioners refused to fund the project, a private corporation stepped in and completed the work in an astonishing eight months at a cost of $4.5 million. (The Needle is still privately owned.) Anchored to terra firma by almost 6,000 tons of concrete, the tower was built to withstand winds of up to 200 miles per hour and has already survived two major earthquakes (in 1965 and 2001) unscathed. **SKYCITY AT THE NEEDLE** (206/443-2150), formerly the Space Needle Restaurant, is located at the 500-foot level and revolves 360 degrees every hour (thanks to two gearboxes equipped with one-horse-power motors), giving diners and slow sippers in the bar panoramic views of Puget Sound, the Olympic Mountains, and the city center. The 43-second ride up (restaurant patrons ride free) provides panoramic views on clear days for only $11 ($9 seniors, $5 kids 5–12, free for younger children). *Every day; marketing@space needle.com; spaceneedle.com; map:B6* &

The Seattle Center's visitors who arrive with children head for the dinosaurs and dynamos at the **PACIFIC SCIENCE CENTER** (see listing #16 below). Chances are, they'll also visit the **FUN FOREST** (206/728-1585), a small-scale amusement park near the Space Needle that contains a Ferris wheel, a wild river ride, a roller coaster, and an indoor pavilion offering laser tag and video games. Ride tickets—purchased individually or in discounted packs—are available at booths within the Fun Forest. Just past the Fun Forest is **MEMORIAL STADIUM**, where high-school football games and outdoor concerts are frequently held. The **SEATTLE CHILDREN'S THEATRE**'s two stages—the 485-seat Charlotte Martin Theatre and the smaller Eve Alvord Theatre—provide surprisingly sophisticated youth entertainment.

Adults enjoy the performing arts at a string of other stages arranged along Mercer Street at the center's northern edge. The neon-adorned **BAGLEY WRIGHT THEATRE** is home to the Seattle Repertory Theatre (206/443-2210 for free tour of the theater, September–May). The **INTIMAN PLAYHOUSE** currently houses the Intiman Theatre. The spectacular $127 million **MARION OLIVER MCCAW HALL** opened in June 2003 and now houses the **SEATTLE OPERA** and the **PACIFIC NORTHWEST BALLET**. (For more on all of these, see the Arts chapter.)

A good place to get refreshed (especially on a summer day) is the **INTERNATIONAL FOUNTAIN**, near the center of the Seattle Center's grounds, which shoots enormous jets of water from a metal dome into the sky, sometimes synchronized with music and lights. Just to the north is the **NORTHWEST CRAFT CENTER** (206/728-1555), displaying a variety of pottery, crafts, paintings, and jewelry for sale. Beyond them are the Northwest Rooms, where traveling exhibitions such as Bumbershoot's Bookfair are shown; to the east is the exhibition hall for larger shows. Should you grow hungry, stop in at the nearby **CENTER HOUSE** (206/684-8582), a cavernous structure filled with ethnic fast food, conventioneers, pre-adolescents looking to be seen, and senior citizens. On the lower level of the Center House is the world-class **CHILDREN'S MUSEUM** (see the Arts chapter).

There is no admission charge to get onto the Seattle Center grounds (except during a few major festivals such as Bumbershoot), but parking can be a problem. The cheapest lots are on the east side. For events at McCaw Hall, Mercer Arts Arena, and the Intiman Playhouse, the covered parking garage directly north across Mercer Street from McCaw Hall affords easy access, but the egress can be maddeningly slow on busy nights. One way to avoid the problem is to take the **MONORAIL** from downtown (see listing below) that drops you off at the Center House. (The Monorail stops running at 11pm, however, so you may have to hail a cab back downtown after a late show.) *Every day; seattlecenter.com; map:B6*

4) SAFECO FIELD

1ST AVENUE S AND S ATLANTIC ST, **SODO; 206/346-4287** The mania to build new baseball-only stadiums has yielded some beautiful ballparks, but few are as impressive as Seattle's $517-million Safeco Field. With a retractable roof, comfortable sight lines from just about every seat, public art installments throughout, and more food options than a Vegas-style buffet, the new home of the Seattle Mariners is one of the best in the Majors. Even visiting teams agree: in a 2003 survey by *Sports Illustrated,* players tagged "The Safe" as their favorite ballpark.

The gates open two hours before each game, and autograph seekers should be among the first inside, since space near the dugouts is limited. If you're looking for a Mariners souvenir, try the **MARINERS' TEAM STORE** (1250 1st Ave S; 206/346-4287). Some of the best merchandise sales are when the team is on the road or down in Peoria, Arizona, for spring training. The store even sells a VIP look at Safeco itself; a **ONE-HOUR TOUR** of the ballpark is available for $7 during the off-season and on days when the Mariners are away. At the **BULLPENS** located by centerfield, fans get up-close looks at what a 90-mile-per-hour fastball looks and sounds like whizzing plateward. The celebrated retractable roof, designed by engineers to cover but not enclose the ballpark, an option unavailable in the now-defunct (or "now-a-parking-lot") Kingdome, is entertaining in its own right. If you don't get a chance to see it in action during the game, stick around—groundskeepers show off the technology at the end of every game, provided it's not raining too hard.

No visit to Safeco is complete without a Mariner Dog and a serving of the park's famously fragrant garlic fries. If you're craving sushi, a stand sells $7 Ichirolls, named after Mariners star Ichiro Suzuki. For those who prefer their fish cooked, try Ivar's Original Acres of Clams. Other options include the **BULLPEN BBQ**, serving pulled barbecue pork sandwiches that could tempt a vegetarian. Or show up early for countertop dining at the **HIT IT HERE CAFÉ** in the rightfield corner, which has unobstructed views and where all seats become reserved about 30 minutes before game time (season ticket holders have first dibs). Ticket prices range from $6 for bleacher seats to $45 for lower box seats. *Every day; mariners.com; map:R9* &

5) EXPERIENCE MUSIC PROJECT (EMP)

325 5TH AVE N, **SEATTLE CENTER; 206/367-5483** Love it or hate it (and many locals do), you can't miss the giant polychromatic metal blob (said to resemble fused electric guitars) that is the EMP. The $240-million museum conceived by Microsoft co-founder Paul Allen (originally to be devoted to his boyhood idol, Seattle's own Jimi Hendrix) and designed by Southern California architect Frank Gehry, contains 140,000 square feet celebrating modern music—mostly rock but also blues, funk, and the culture that surrounds them all. Memorabilia scattered about the place includes Elvis Presley's motorcycle jacket, Janis Joplin's bell-bottoms, and guitars once played by Hendrix and Nirvana's Kurt Cobain. Visitors tour at their own pace, clutching shoulder-slung digital devices that allow them to access snippets of display interpretation and musical clips. While the glitziest draw here may be **ARTIST'S JOURNEY**, a roller coaster–like experience that immerses you in the realm of rock 'n' roll, other don't-miss attractions include the **GUITAR GALLERY**, featuring versions of the instrument that date back to 1770; the **HENDRIX**

GALLERY, which recounts that cult guitarist's rise from his days playing teen dances in Seattle to holding forth at the original Woodstock; **ON STAGE**, where—with the help of screaming-crowd effects—you can satisfy your childhood dream to be a rock star; and Sky Church, with its giant LED screen on which concert videos are shown at the top of every hour. EMP also hosts rotating exhibits (such as one on disco) and concerts by big-name musicians, from Dave Matthews to Emmylou Harris.

And Allen isn't done with his Experience experiment . . . he recently announced plans to add on a multimillion-dollar wing dedicated to science fiction. Admission is $19.95 for adults, $15.95 for seniors and students, and $14.95 for children ages 7–10. *Every day; emplive.com; map:D6* &

6) BALLARD LOCKS

3015 NW 54TH ST, BALLARD; 206/783-7059 You don't have to go to Panama to see working ship locks; just head out to the Hiram M. Chittenden Locks in Ballard, where Seattle's busy locks are always abuzz. Talk of digging a navigable canal between the fresh water of Lakes Washington and Union and the salt water of Puget Sound began shortly after Seattle's pioneers arrived in the 1850s. Numerous engineering challenges ensued: the biggest was the design and construction of locks near the canal's western end that could control the difference in water levels between the Sound and the much higher Lake Washington. (In the end, the latter was lowered by 9 feet, exposing new lakefront property and interfering with salmon migrations.) Not until 1917 was the 8-mile-long **LAKE WASHINGTON SHIP CANAL** dedicated, and another 17 years would pass before it was officially declared complete. In 1936, the U.S. Army Corps of Engineers named the locks in honor of Major Hiram M. Chittenden, who had supervised the canal project.

Today around 100,000 pleasure and commercial boats per year go through the canal and what are colloquially known as the Ballard Locks. Couples and families trot down to watch this informal regatta as it works its way through the "water elevator." The descent (or ascent) takes 10 to 25 minutes, depending on which of the two locks is being used. A particularly good people-watching time is during Seafair in July, when boats filled with carousing men and women crowd the locks, impatient to get through.

Across the waterway in **COMMODORE PARK**, the **FISH LADDER** that bypasses the locks entices struggling salmon bound for spawning grounds in Lake Washington and Cascade mountain streams. You can watch the fishes' progress from a viewing area with windows onto the ladder: sockeye salmon in summer (peak viewing is in early July) and steelhead or coho in winter.

Call the **VISITORS CENTER** for tour times (206/783-7059; free daily in summer, weekends only the rest of the year); there's also an interesting exhibit that explains the use and building of the locks. The green lawns and tree-lined waterside promenade of the park, along with the impressive rose display at the **CARL S. ENGLISH JR. BOTANICAL GARDENS** (see Gardens in this chapter), make grand backdrops for summer picnics. *Every day; cityofseattle.net/tour/locks.htm; map:FF9*

7) WASHINGTON STATE FERRIES

COLMAN DOCK, DOWNTOWN (AND VARIOUS LOCATIONS); 206/464-6400 The Washington State Ferry system, which stretches from as far south as Tacoma to as far north as British Columbia, carries some 27 million passengers every year, making it the busiest such system in the country. The system as it exists today came into existence with the state's buyout of Puget Sound Navigation in 1951. Before that, Puget Sound ferry service was initially provided by a number of companies using small steamers known as the Mosquito Fleet. By 1929, the ferry industry had consolidated into two companies: Puget Sound Navigation Company and Kitsap County Transportation Company. A strike in 1935 forced Kitsap County Transportation Company out of business and left the Puget Sound Navigation Company, commonly known as the Black Ball line, with primary control of ferry service on Puget Sound until the state came in 16 years later.

On most of the ferries, you can take your car, driving on in one location and driving off at the next. Rates range from $3.50 one-way for foot passengers traveling from West Seattle to Vashon Island to $44.25 for a car and driver going from Anacortes to Sidney, British Columbia (rates are higher in the summer than in the winter). The bike surcharge is $1, and passenger fares are collected only on westbound routes (vehicle and driver pay both ways on most routes), so if you're island hopping, head to the westernmost destination first and work your way back. (For more information on routes, see the Day Trips chapter.) *Every day; wsdot.wa.gov/ferries/; map:M8* &

8) MONORAIL

400 PINE ST OR THE SEATTLE CENTER; 206/905-2620 Not since the fight over the building of two sports stadiums has as much citizen passion been evoked as over plans to expand the city's beloved, though short-flung, elevated transport. Way back in 1910, a local inventor named W. H. Shephard suggested that the city construct an elevated monorail network to reduce traffic on its streets, but not until Seattle hosted the 1962 world's fair was a monorail erected here. Although it cost $3.5 million at the time, it was basically just a space-age gimmick (built by Sweden's Alweg Rapid Transit Systems) that shuttled tourists between downtown and the fairgrounds at what's now the Seattle Center. Yet it was so popular that even after the fair closed down, the city continued to operate the Monorail. The elevated trains presently carry about 40,000 riders each year, making this one of the world's few profitable rapid-transit operations. The Monorail travels 1.3 miles (a 90-second ride) between Westlake Center (400 Pine St) and the Seattle Center. Tourists are the principal users—except during Bumbershoot and the Folklife Festival (both guaranteed to fill parking lots around the Seattle Center), when many city residents prefer to park downtown and hop the Monorail to the festivities.

In a hotly contested 2002 vote, Seattleites approved use of state and city funds to expand the Monorail to encompass a 14-mile route from Ballard to West Seattle at a cost of $1.29 billion tax dollars; there's also been talk of laying tracks to the Eastside and elsewhere. Keep track of the latest developments via the Seattle Monorail Project Web site (www.elevated.org). Until this system is built, which is years away, trains depart Westlake and Seattle Center stations every 15 minutes. Fare is $1.50

one-way for adults, 75 cents one-way for kids and seniors (double the price for a round-trip ticket). *Every day; map:I6* &

9) SEATTLE ASIAN ART MUSEUM

1400 E PROSPECT ST, CAPITOL HILL; 206/654-3100 Sitting atop the serene Volunteer Park, the Seattle Asian Art Museum commands perhaps the best vista in town. With the opening of the downtown Seattle Art Museum in 1991, this original building (designed in moderne style by local architect Carl F. Gould) was renovated to house the museum's extensive Asian art collections. Built in 1931 by Richard Fuller and his mother, Margaret E. MacTavish Fuller, the museum contained their 1,700-piece collection of Asian art before growing into a more eclectic institution. Now the carefully lit galleries once again hold the kind of art (the Hindu deities Siva and Parvati rapt in divine love) that draws you away from daily obsessions and expands the soul. In addition to old favorites from the collection—such as the Fullers' array of elaborate netsuke—don't miss the ancient Chinese funerary art and the collection of 14th- to 16th-century ceramics from Thailand. An Educational Outreach Gallery offers hands-on displays. Admission for adults is $3, free for children 12 and under, and free to all the first Thursday and Saturday of each month. (Admission tickets also may be used for entry to SAM downtown—see listing below—within a week of purchase.) *Tues–Sun; seattleartmuseum.org; map:GG6* &

10) ODYSSEY MARITIME DISCOVERY CENTER

2205 ALASKAN WY, PIER 66, WATERFRONT; 206/374-4000 Seven piers north of the Seattle Aquarium sits a complementary museum that shifts the focus from water life to shore life. Odyssey is an interactive museum celebrating the natural and commercial uses of Seattle's marine environment, with exhibits that allow visitors to experience simulated kayaking, fishing, and freighter navigation. Geared toward children but entertaining for adults too, the educational center emphasizes technology, human interactions with the maritime environment, and an overall "you-are-there" exhibit feel. Enter a full-size crane cab and race against a clock to load containers onto a virtual ship. Use the power of your legs to spin a propeller that's 10 feet in diameter, bringing home the fact that it takes a lot of power to move ships. Learn just how significantly ocean trade routes have expanded over the last 3,000 years. In a city still known for its 1999 anti–World Trade Organization (WTO) riots, this center's promotion of international trade may seem anachronistic, but don't mention that to the kids who are dreaming of working heavy machinery on the water. Admission is $7 for adults, $5 for children ages 5–8, $2 for children ages 2–4, and children under 2 are free. *Every day (mid-May–mid-Sept), Tues–Sat (mid-Sept–mid-May); education@ody.org; ody.org; map:G9*

11) SEATTLE ART MUSEUM

100 UNIVERSITY ST, DOWNTOWN; 206/654-3100 The Robert Venturi–designed Seattle Art Museum has a worldwide focus, with particular emphasis on Asian, African, and Northwest Coast Native American art. Each gallery is tailored to the collections—for example, dark, dramatically lit rooms for the ceremonial works of Africa and the Northwest Coast; tall ceilings with ornate moldings for European decorative arts; and white loftlike spaces for New York School paintings. All told, the museum contains 145,000 square feet of space, though only a third of it is actually gallery space.

The **JAPANESE GALLERY** features an authentic bamboo-and-cedar teahouse, where a Japanese master performs the tea ceremony for small groups of visitors two or three times a month (reservations required). A big **SPECIAL EXHIBITIONS GALLERY** houses periodic traveling shows, an occasional in-house exhibit, and events geared to mass audiences, such as the 2003 show of works by Mexican painters that highlighted Frida Kahlo and Diego Rivera.

A lecture room and a 300-seat auditorium lend themselves to talks, films, music, and dramatic performances; there's a fully equipped art studio for children's and adult classes; and a good cafe faces the immense hallway connecting the First and Second Avenue lobbies. The **MUSEUM STORE** is first-rate. And you can't miss sculptor Jonathan Borofsky's 48-foot mechanical Hammering Man at SAM's First Avenue entrance. On the first Thursday evenings of the month, SAM stays open late, with refreshments, live music, and performances scheduled each week; and admission is free to all. General admission is a suggested $7 donation for adults, $5 donation for students, and is free for children 12 and under. Special exhibit rates are $10 for adults, $7 for students and seniors. (Admission tickets also may be used for entry to the Seattle Asian Art Museum in Volunteer Park—see listing #9 above—within a week of purchase.) *Tues–Sun; seattleartmuseum.org; map:K7* &

12) UNDERGROUND TOUR

610 1ST AVE, DOWNTOWN; 206/682-4646 You wouldn't know it from walking the sidewalks of Pioneer Square, but beneath those cubes of oxidized glass embedded in the sidewalk rests a whole other Seattle. Once home to sailors, shysters, prostitutes, and city bigwigs, these remnants of Seattle are the subject of Bill Speidel's Underground Tour—an institution since 1965 when an item in the *Seattle Times* spurred late-journalist Bill Speidel to organize public tours of the subterranean world. Although the 2001 earthquake caused damage to the exterior of some Pioneer Square buildings, it didn't lead—as feared—to the closure of this popular attraction. These tours are mostly one story down—the level of the city before it was rebuilt after the Great Fire of 1889. It's all pretty cornball, but you'll get a salty taste of the pioneers' eccentricities and some historical insights, with plenty of puns from the guides. The 90-minute tours begin at **DOC MAYNARD'S PUBLIC HOUSE** in Pioneer Square. The tour operates year-round but varies seasonally. Cost is $10 for adults, $8 for seniors and students, $5 for children 7–12, and free for kids under 6. The tour is first come, first served, so try to arrive half an hour prior to tour start time. *Every day; undergroundtour.com; map:N8*

13) SEATTLE AQUARIUM

1483 ALASKAN WY, PIER 59, WATERFRONT; 206/386-4320 While plans are under consideration for a new, much larger Seattle Aquarium, the original facility continues to rake in crowds of students and travelers with its **UNDERWATER DOME**. The 400,000-gallon fish tank causes heads to swivel as they try to take in the myriad king salmon, reef sharks, snappers, and other colorful Puget Sound and Pacific Ocean inhabitants whisking by. Topside tanks are home to seals and sea otters acting clownish at feeding times.

Entrancing exhibits include **LIFE ON THE EDGE**, which debuted in 2002 and allows visitors to experience the tidepool life of Washington's outer coast and Seattle's inland sea while meeting such creatures as aggregating anemones and sunflower sea stars. There are two large exhibit pools, which include touch zones staffed by naturalists, and video screens demonstrating the lifestyles of these amazing creatures who thrive in the harsh conditions of Washington's tidal zones. New in 2003, the **LIFE OF A DRIFTER** exhibit stars a giant "Jelly Donut," a luminous, 12-foot-high crystal ring filled with dozens of mystical moon jellyfish, as well as a multi-species tank with the giant pacific octopus and wolf eels. There's also a hands-on area featuring a 13-foot wet table for an interactive experience with juvenile rockfish, sea stars, the life stages of moon jellies, and plankton. Admission is $9 for adults, $6.25 for youths, $4.25 for children 3–5, and free for children 2 and under. *Every day during summer, call about Mon during winter; www.seattleaquarium.org; map:J9* &

The adjacent **SEATTLE IMAX DOME** theater (206/622-1868) is a dramatic cinema-in-the-round, featuring *The Eruption of Mount St. Helens* and other spectacles in more than a dozen showings daily. Admission is $11 for adults, $7 for children ages 6–12, $5 for children ages 3–5, and free for children under 3. Combination IMAX Dome/Seattle Aquarium tickets are available. *Every day; info@seattleimax dome.com; seattleimaxdome.com* &

14) MUSEUM OF FLIGHT

9404 E MARGINAL WY S, GEORGETOWN; 206/764-5720 Corporate Boeing may have abandoned Seattle as its home base, but the **RED BARN**, where Boeing started in 1910, proudly sits next to the Museum of Flight. Other than its location at Boeing Field, located 10 miles south of Seattle, the museum doesn't actually have a formal affiliation with the aircraft manufacturer. It does have more than enough flying machines, including a 40,000-pound B-17, to keep even the most passive aviation buffs interested.

The museum takes you from the early legends of flying (including a replica of the Wright brothers' original glider) through the history of aviation, with special emphasis on Pacific Northwest flight—military, commercial, and amateur. Highlights include a 707 version of Air Force One; Apollo and Mercury space capsules; and the 98-foot Lockheed A-12 Blackbird, the fastest plane ever built (it has flown coast to coast in 67 minutes). Another attraction is the first-ever Air Force One, on display for visitors to walk through at their leisure. The newest exhibit, The Birth of Aviation, reveals the lives and times of Orville and Wilbur Wright, celebrates their first powered flight on December 17, 1903, and spotlights their unheralded sister, Katharine, after whom the Wrights named their plane, *Kitty Hawk*.

The Museum of Flight also offers a variety of workshops, films, tours, and special programs. Children especially enjoy the hangar with three explorable planes, and hands-on learning areas with paper airplanes, boomerangs, and other toys that fly. Admission is $11 for adults, $6.50 for children, and free for kids under 4; free on the first Thursday evening of each month, 5–9pm. *Every day; museumof flight.org; map:NN6* &

15) WOODLAND PARK ZOO

5500 PHINNEY AVE N, GREENWOOD; 206/684-4800 Get deceptively up-close to the animals at this superbly designed zoo. Occupying what was once the "country estate" of an eccentric 19th-century Canadian real-estate baron named Guy Phinney, Woodland Park Zoo has been hailed as one of the nation's 10 best zoological gardens. It's shed its roots as an animals-behind-bars facility in favor of lifelike re-creations of natural habitats ("bioclimatic zones," in zoo lingo). Among these habitats are a grassy **AFRICAN SAVANNA** populated with giraffes, zebras, and hippos that wallow merrily in their own simulated mud-bottomed river drainage (the lions, though nearby, enjoy their own grassland); **TROPICAL ASIA**, with its Elephant Forest—4.6 acres that include an elephant-size pool, a replica of a Thai logging camp and Thai temple (this last serving as the elephants' nighttime abode), and Hansa, the most recent baby pachyderm born at this zoo; and the **TRAIL OF VINES**, an adjoining 2.7-acre exhibit that takes visitors on an imaginary voyage through India, Malaysia, and Borneo with its display of orangutans, siamang apes, Malayan tapirs, and lion-tailed macaques. The heavily planted **LOWLAND GORILLA ENCLOSURES** conceal a brooding troop of adults and their precocious offspring. An exotic new exhibit is the long-awaited **JAGUAR COVE**. Opened in 2003, it quadrupled the size of the old jaguar space and, with thousands of tropical plants and a freshwater pool, realistically captures the natural habitat of the biggest cat in the Western Hemisphere.

On the tamer side, the **FAMILY FARM** (inside the Temperate Forest) is a wonderful place for human youngsters to meet the offspring of other species. At the indoor-outdoor **RAIN FOREST CAFE** (a great place to throw a birthday party), you might not love the food, but the kids, no doubt, will. The zoo also offers a rich schedule of family programming, including orientation walks, classes, sleepovers, and lectures. Its popular ZooTunes concert series, held outdoors on summer evenings, draws a panoply of top musicians (206/615-0076). Zoo admission is $9 for adult residents of King County, $10 for adult nonresidents; $8.25 for senior residents, $9.25 for senior nonresidents; $6.75 for residents ages 6–17, $7.50 for nonresidents in the same age group; and $4.75 for residents ages 3–5, $5.25 for nonresidents of the same age. *Every day; zoo.org; map:FF7* &

16) PACIFIC SCIENCE CENTER

200 2ND AVE N, SEATTLE CENTER; 206/443-2001 The Science Center was originally designed as part of the 1962 world's fair by Minoru Yamasaki, the architect responsible for the inverted-pencil Rainier Square tower downtown (as well as New York City's iconic twin-towered World Trade Center brought down in the September 11th, 2001 terrorist attacks). Since then, more than 30 million people have trooped through the 6 acres of this complex to see hands-on science and math exhibits for school-age children as well as traveling shows aimed at all age groups.

One of several permanent exhibits, **DINOSAURS: A JOURNEY THROUGH TIME**, introduces five roaring robotic creatures from Earth's Mesozoic period, including a flesh-eating Tyrannosaurus rex and a three-horned, herbivorous Triceratops. In the **TECH ZONE**, children can play virtual basketball, hang-glide through a virtual city, and match wits with a robot. The **SCIENCE PLAYGROUND** offers a kid-friendly introduction to physics. There are also insect and tropical butterfly exhibits. Outside the center, kids can take aim with a water cannon or explore their center of gravity on the **HIGH RAIL BIKE**. Admission is $6.75 for adults; $5.75 for kids; and free for children under 3, members, and disabled persons.

Also in this complex, an **IMAX THEATER** (206/443-IMAX) boasts a six-channel surround-sound system and a 35-by-60-foot screen on which viewers can thrill to experiences such as a trip to Alaska or a climb up Mount Everest. Admission is $9.50 for adults, $7.00 for kids, and free for children under 3. Combination IMAX–Science Center tickets are available. *Tues–Sun; pacsci.org; map:C7* &

17) WASHINGTON PARK ARBORETUM

2300 ARBORETUM DR E, MADISON VALLEY; 206/543-8800 Seattle's answer to Central Park, the Arboretum was set aside as urban wilderness in 1904 and developed beginning in the 1930s. Today, all year-round, naturalists and botanists rub elbows with serious runners and casual walkers, for this 200-acre public park doubles as a botanical research facility for the nearby University of Washington. The arboretum stretches from Foster Island, just off the shore of Lake Washington, through the Montlake and Madison Park neighborhoods, its rambling trails screened from the houses by thick greenbelts. More than 5,000 varieties of woody plants are arranged here by family. (Pick up maps or an illustrated guide at the visitors center if you want to find specific trees.)

From spring through autumn, the arboretum's **JAPANESE GARDEN** (1502 Lake Washington Blvd E; 206/684-4725) is well worth a visit. Just off Lake Washington Boulevard E, which winds north-south through the park, this authentic garden of pruned living sculptures was constructed in 1960 under the direction of Japanese landscape architect Juki Iida. Several hundred tons of rock hauled from the Cascades were incorporated into the design, as were stone lanterns donated by the city of Kobe and a teahouse sent by the governor of Tokyo. The graceful carp pond, spanned by traditional bridges of wood and stone and lined with water plants, is home to countless ducks, herons, and muskrats. Though the original teahouse was destroyed by vandals years ago, it has since been replaced, and the tea ceremony is still performed on the third Saturday of the month, April through October, at 1:30pm by members of the Seattle branch of the Urasenke Foundation. Guided tours are available by arrangement for a fee. Call for admission prices, event schedules, and operating hours; closing time varies seasonally. *Every day; map:GG6*

Just across the road to the north runs **AZALEA WAY**, a wide, grassy thoroughfare that winds through the heart of the Arboretum. (No recreational running is permitted on this popular route.) Azalea Way is magnificent in April and May, when its blossoming shrubs are joined by scores of companion dogwoods and ornamental cherries. Drop in on the **JOSEPH A. WITT WINTER GARDEN**, especially from November through March, which focuses on plants that show distinctive seasonal bark, winter flowers, or cold-season fruit to attract birds. Side trails lead through the Arboretum's extensive **CAMELLIA AND RHODODENDRON GROVES** (the latter collection is world famous).

Follow Azalea Way to the copper-roofed **DONALD A. GRAHAM VISITORS CENTER** (2300 Arboretum Dr E; 206/543-8800), where you can find maps and arboretum guides as well as horticulture-related books, gifts, and informational displays. The arboretum also hosts an annual spring plant sale each April, a fall bulb sale each October, and guided weekend tours. *Every day, 7am–dusk; wpa@u.washington.edu; depts.washington.edu/wpa; map:GG6*

18) FISHERMAN'S TERMINAL

3919 18TH AVE W, INTERBAY; 206/728-3395 This working terminal is the busiest of its kind in the North Pacific. Built in Ballard in 1913, it was one of the Port of Seattle's first facilities and is now home base to some 700 commercial fishing vessels (ranging in length from 30 to 300 feet), most of which head north into Alaskan waters. The terminal sits on the south shore of protected Salmon Bay, the last stretch of the Lake Washington Ship Canal before it reaches the **BALLARD LOCKS** (see listing #6 above) and meets the waters of Puget Sound.

Head out to the crowded piers to inspect hundreds of gillnetters and crab boats that make up the Northwest's most active fleet. Look also for trawlers (they're the ones with two tall poles stuck straight up in the air) and the big factory processors, on which fish are cleaned at sea. This freshwater terminal is an optimal choice for fishers, since their boats are protected from the corrosion and other problems associated with saltwater storage.

The terminal includes docks, a large public plaza (with interpretive panels detailing the development of the local fishing industry), and the **SEATTLE FISHERMEN'S MEMORIAL**, a bronze-and-concrete pillar created by Seattle sculptor Ron Petty to honor local fishers lost at sea. **CHINOOK'S** (206/283-4665) offers tasty seafood dishes and a splendid view of the waterway; or try its annex next door for quick fish-and-chips. At the **WILD SALMON SEAFOOD MARKET** (1900 W Nickerson St; 206/283-3366), mere feet from the boats, you can purchase fresh fish for your dinner table. Time your visit with an incoming fishing boat, and you might get an even fresher catch. *Every day; map:FF8*

19) BURKE-GILMAN TRAIL

BETWEEN LAKE WASHINGTON SHIP CANAL (IN BALLARD) AND BOTHELL Few cities have a trail system as extensive as Seattle's, and the Burke-Gilman is the undisputed centerpiece of it all. Originally part of a railroad right-of-way, today it runs from Ballard's busy ship canal, past Lake Union, through the University of Washington, along the west shore of Lake Washington, to Kenmore's Logboom Park. From here cyclists can continue to Bothell and links to Sammamish River Trail. The rules of the highway apply—stay to the right—and keep an eye out for crossing rabbits and, at night, feisty raccoons.

If you're planning a trip on the trail, bring rain gear, because although the Burke-Gilman enables you to escape automobile traffic, the trail is not immune to Seattle's unpredictable weather. Once you're out there, you'll find ample opportunities to turn off and buy snacks or relax and read a book. If you bring a satchel, you can even use the trail to do major shopping. Just past the University District, the trail runs by University Village, an upscale, open-air shopping mall. *Map:FF7–AA5*

20) SMITH TOWER

506 2ND AVE, DOWNTOWN; 206/622-4004 Against the picket fence of skyscrapers that currently make up Seattle's skyline, the Smith Tower looks almost puny. Yet when it was first opened in the summer of 1914, this 42-story (522-foot) terra-cotta-and-steel spire was the tallest building west of the Mississippi. It remained the highest in Seattle until 1969, when the old Seattle First National Bank Tower (now the 1001 Fourth Avenue Building) rose to 50 stories, or 609 feet. (The 605-foot Space Needle, finished in 1962, is also taller than the Smith Tower but doesn't usually count in the record books since it isn't a "building" per se.) Even now, though, the Smith Tower is considered the most beloved of this city's cloud-kissing edifices.

The building is the legacy of New Yorker Lyman C. Smith, an armaments manufacturer turned typewriter magnate, who commissioned the Syracuse, New York, architectural firm of Gaggin & Gaggin to design an office structure both distinctive and tall enough that it wouldn't be exceeded in Seattle during his lifetime. He got what he'd ordered, if not what he'd intended; Smith died in November 1910, before his skyscraper was finished.

Despite now being an address of choice for high-tech firms, the Smith Tower retains what are reportedly the West Coast's only manually operated elevators—eight brass-caged beauties. Its 35th-floor Chinese Room, an elaborate space that's popular for weddings, is surrounded by an observation deck from which visitors can take in magnificent views of downtown for $6 (cash or check only). Hours vary by season and private bookings, so call ahead, or check the online schedule, to be sure you can access the deck. *Every day (mid-Apr–Oct 31), weekends only (Nov 1–mid-Apr);chuckr@smithtower.com; smithtower.com; map:O7* &

21) NORDSTROM AND REI
500 PINE ST, DOWNTOWN; 206/628-2111 / 222 YALE AVE N, CASCADE; 206/223-1944 Retail therapy beckons, whether you're a fashion maven or an incurable gearhead, at this city's two premier shopping destinations. In 1998 locally grown retail giant **NORDSTROM** opened its flagship store across the street from its old location (the new building was once the flagship for the defunct Frederick & Nelson chain). It boasts a whopping five spacious floors of clothes, shoes, accessories, cosmetics, fine jewelry, and fabled customer service. Special attractions of this Nordy's include a full-service day spa and a complimentary wardrobe consulting service; besides the customary cafe, there's the Nordstrom Grill, featuring fresh market seafood. And the shoes: 150,000 pairs (including hard-to-find sizes, 3AAAAA to 14EE for women) are spread among five departments. Befitting a store that first made its mark in shoe leather, Nordstrom has installed glass cases around the store displaying examples of footwear, ranging from turn-of-the-19th-century ankle boots to 1970s ankle-challenging platform shoes. Nordstrom's two-week anniversary sale in late July is a bona fide Northwest event. *Every day; nordstrom.com; map:J5* &

At **REI** (Recreational Equipment Inc.), the nation's largest consumer co-op (60 stores in 24 states), you'll find basically everything you need for mountaineering, backpacking, camping, cross-country skiing, biking, and other energetic outdoor pursuits. Seattle's high-visibility, two-level location just off Interstate 5 features a 65-foot indoor climbing pinnacle (show up early as there's usually a line), mountain-bike and hiking test paths, a rain simulator in which to try out the latest Gore-Tex gear, a children's play area, a deli/cafe, and a wide assortment of fleece items, as well as maps, trail food, and outdoor books. For trip planning, the U.S. Forest Service's Outdoor Recreation Information Center is also located here (206/470-4060).

Anyone can shop here, but members (who pay only $15 once to join for a lifetime) receive at least a 10 percent yearly dividend on their purchases. Founded in 1938 by Lloyd Anderson and a group of Seattle mountaineers who wanted to import European equipment, the co-op was presided over for years by Everest conqueror Jim Whittaker, and it is still staffed by knowledgeable outdoorspeople. Many lectures, events, and courses take place here; call for a current schedule. Rentals at good prices, too. Smaller branches are in Bellevue, Federal Way, and Lynnwood. *Every day; www.rei.com; map:H1* &

22) ALKI BEACH PARK

BETWEEN DUWAMISH HEAD AND ALKI POINT IN WEST SEATTLE, ALONG HARBOR AVE SW AND ALKI AVE SW While Pioneer Square likes to be thought of as the cradle of Seattle, the city's real birthplace is in what's now West Seattle. It was there, on November 13, 1851, that a party of midwesterners led by Arthur Denny stepped off the schooner *Exact*. They dreamed of building a western version of New York City at Alki Point, but it took only a year—including one wind-whipped winter—to convinced them to retreat eastward across Elliott Bay in search of more sheltered ground.

Today, however, this migration is often reversed—especially on sunny summer days, as winter-pale Seattleites head to Alki Beach (along Alki Ave SW). With its numerous in-line skaters, volleyball games, picnicking families, and body-conscious teens, this 2-mile-long stretch of sand is the closest thing we have to California's Venice Beach. The paved path that parallels the beach starts at the **TERMINAL 5 PUBLIC SHORELINE ACCESS SITE** and runs around the rocky shoreline all the way to the **ALKI POINT LIGHTHOUSE**. Heading north and west along the path is **SEACREST PARK**, where the **ELLIOTT BAY WATER TAXI** runs shuttles across the bay to Pier 57 every hour on the hour from Memorial Day weekend through the end of the year. Nearby is the former site of Luna Park, the "Coney Island of the West" amusement park that burned down in 1930.

To fuel your fun-in-the-sun, there's **SALTY'S ON ALKI** (1936 Harbor Ave SW; 206/937-1600), **DUKE'S CHOWDERHOUSE** (2516 Alki Ave SW; 206/937-6100), **SPUDS FISH & CHIPS** (2666 Alki Ave SW; 206/938-0606), and the brand-new **BAMBOO BAR & GRILL** (2806 Alki Ave SW; 206/937.3023). If you're looking for a coffee and a snack, try the **ALKI MAIL & DISPATCH** (2536 Alki Ave SW; 206/932-2556), where you also can mail a postcard home.

The highlight of Alki Beach comes at day's end, when the sun edges toward the Olympic Mountains to the west and sunbeams shoot across the Sound to reflect off of the downtown skyscrapers. On clear nights, you can spot the alpenglow bouncing off the snowy peaks of the Cascade Mountains to the northeast. Most Alki Beach residents plan their entire evenings around these few brief moments. *Map:II9*

23) HENRY ART GALLERY

15TH AVE NE AND NE 41ST ST, UNIVERSITY DISTRICT; 206/453-2280 Founded in 1927, the Henry was the first public art museum in the state of Washington. After a 1997 expansion project that quadrupled its size, the Henry continues to forge a challenging identity that builds on its exemplary past, which, in the early '90s, brought works by such artists as Gary Hill, Ann Hamilton, and James Turrell. The new permanent James Turrell Skyspace—*Light Reign* (which features embedded LED lights)—is drawing crowds (especially at twilight), and the Henry retains its national reputation for mounting shows with an eye toward experimental installations, video, and unusual media such as digital art. Located on the University of Washington campus, the museum has permanent stand-out collections in photography and textiles. Recent additions to the museum include an outdoor sculpture court, a 150-seat auditorium, a cafe, and an education center for children. Admission is $8 for adults, $6 for seniors, and free for children under 13, UW students, and faculty. *Tues–Sun; henryart.org; map:FF6* &

24) GAS WORKS PARK

N NORTHLAKE WY AND MERIDIAN AVE N, WALLINGFORD; 206/684-4075
What do you do when the piece of property with the grandest skyline and lakeside view in the city is dominated by a greasy old coal-gasification plant? In Seattle, you turn it into a park. Wallingford's Gas Works Park represents urban reclamation at its finest. A quarter century after the Seattle Gas Company plant shut down here in 1956, landscape architect Richard Haag re-created the industrial eyesore as one of Seattle's most delightful greenswards, with a high grassy knoll for kite flying, a large picnic shelter with reservable space (206/684-4081), a wonderful play barn, and a multitude of front-row spots from which to watch sailboats bounce around on Lake Union. Climb the grassy knoll to enjoy a huge mosaic sundial (created by artist Charles Greening) and a view of the downtown towers just 2 miles south. The threat of lurking pollutants has led to periodic soil cleansings, but risks are few, provided you don't eat the dirt. (Parents with toddlers, beware.) The park has become so popular that in 2003, parks officials announced plans to expand it right up to the side of Northlake Way and incorporate an off-leash dog area. Cutting east from Gas Works is the Burke-Gilman Trail (see listing #19 above). *Map:FF7*

25) DISCOVERY PARK

3801 W GOVERNMENT WY, MAGNOLIA; 206/684-4075 Formerly the site of Seattle's Fort Lawton Army base, this densely foliated Magnolia wilderness has been allowed to revert to its premetropolitan natural order. Self-guided interpretive nature loops and short trails wind through 513 acres of thick forests, along dramatic sea cliffs (where powerful updrafts make for excellent kite flying), and across meadows of waving grasses. The old barracks, houses, and training field are the few vestiges of the Army's presence. Discover the park's flora and fauna yourself, or take advantage of the scheduled walks and nature workshops conducted by park naturalists. On weekends, the park offers free guided walks and, in spring and fall, bird tours—call ahead to check the schedule, or stop by the visitors center in the east parking lot, near the Government Way entrance (206/386-4236). Groups can also arrange their own guided walks. Check the tall trees frequently; there's often a bald eagle in residence.

Two well-equipped kids' playgrounds are here, along with picnic areas, playfields, tennis and basketball courts, and a rigorous fitness trail. The network of trails is a favorite among runners; the 2.8-mile Loop Trail circles the park, passing through forests, meadows, and sand dunes. Daybreak Star Cultural Arts Center (206/285-4425; unitedindians.com/daybreakrates.html) sponsors Native American activities and gallery exhibits of contemporary Indian art in the **SACRED CIRCLE GALLERY**. West Point Lighthouse, built in 1881, is the oldest lighthouse in the Seattle area. *Map:FF9*

Neighborhoods

DOWNTOWN/BELLTOWN

BETWEEN WESTERN AVE AND BOREN AVE, YESLER WY AND DENNY WY
Seattle's commercial district has shifted over time. Before 1900, most government and business offices huddled in Pioneer Square (see Top 25 Attractions in this chapter), at the south end of today's downtown. After the Great Fire of 1889, crowding in that historic district drove the city's expansion northward.

Today's **RETAIL CORE** lies basically between Third and Sixth Avenues from Stewart to University Streets (for details, see the Shopping chapter). It's anchored by

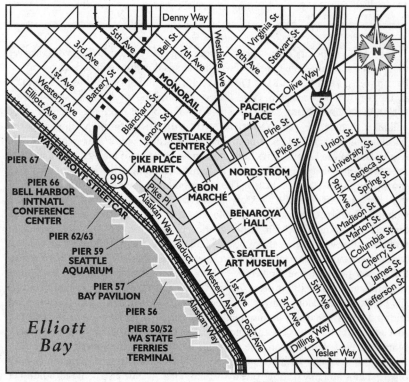

DOWNTOWN/BELLTOWN

two big department stores—**BON-MACY'S** (3rd Ave and Pine St) and **NORDSTROM** (5th Ave and Pine St)—as well as two high-end malls. **WESTLAKE CENTER** resides at Fourth and Pine and airy **PACIFIC PLACE**, which opened in 1998, sits two blocks east, at Sixth Avenue and Pine Street. Colorful smaller shops line Fourth and Fifth Avenues south to **RAINIER SQUARE** (4th Ave and Union St), an elegant three-story atrium at the base of **RAINIER TOWER**, a modernist box of a building that's balanced atop a tapered 12-story pedestal. Across University Street to the south is the **FAIRMONT OLYMPIC HOTEL** (4th Ave and University St; see the Lodgings chapter), the grand dame of Seattle hostelries, formerly the Four Seasons Olympic Hotel, opened in 1924.

BEST ACOUSTICS FOR MUSIC?

"Benaroya Hall. Sound so lively and detailed, with such jaw-dropping dynamic range, that it ranks not only as the best in town, but arguably the best in the country."

Michael Medved, film critic and host of syndicated radio talk show
originating at KNWX AM 770

It seems as if the city's construction boom, begun in earnest in the 1980s, has yet to hit a speed bump. Some of the newest buildings downtown include the soon-to-be completed **SEATTLE PUBLIC LIBRARY** (4th Ave and Spring St), as well as **CITY HALL** (5th Ave between James and Cherry Sts) and the **WILLIAM K. NAKAMURA FEDERAL COURTHOUSE** (750 Stewart St). Some of the more eye-catching older buildings include the **1201 THIRD AVENUE BUILDING** (formerly known as the Washington Mutual Tower), a postmodern confection with a stair-stepped profile reminiscent of the Empire State Building's and a covering of pink granite; and **CITY CENTRE** (5th Ave and Pike St), with its light-filled lobby, three floors of exclusive shops, and the **PALOMINO** bistro. The tallest building downtown—but also one of the least attractive—is the 76-story **BANK OF AMERICA TOWER** (formerly the Columbia Seafirst Center), about six blocks south at Fourth Avenue and Columbia Street. For a grand view, visit its observation platform on the 73rd floor; check in with the security desk in the lobby ($3.50 adults, $1.75 children and seniors; Monday–Friday). More interesting are the older towers, such as the **1910 COBB BUILDING** (4th Ave and University St), an elegant 11-story brick-and-terra-cotta structure, and the 1929 art deco, 26-story **SEATTLE TOWER** (3rd Ave and University St). Walk west along University Street to reach **BENAROYA HALL** (between 3rd and 2nd Aves), the classy young home of the Seattle Symphony, and the **SEATTLE ART MUSEUM** (between 1st and 2nd Aves; see Top 25 Attractions in this chapter). North on First Avenue from the museum is **PIKE PLACE MARKET** (see Top 25 Attractions), popular with both shoppers and people watchers. Leaving its history of strip clubs and pawn shops mostly behind, First Avenue also contains a number of upscale restaurants and shops.

Shopping and entertainment opportunities now stretch well north of Virginia Street into the hip enclave of **BELLTOWN** (Virginia St to Battery St, Western Ave to 5th Ave). Known for its music clubs, such as the famed **CROCODILE CAFE** (2200 2nd Ave; 206/441-5611), Belltown also attracts with an abundance of stylish shops, such as the sleek modern furnishings of **URBAN EASE** (2512 2nd Ave; 206/443-9546), and restaurants, including the Latin American–flavored **FANDANGO** (2313 1st Ave; 206/447-1188); **MARCO'S SUPPERCLUB** (2510 1st Ave; 206/441-7801), with a 'round-the-world menu served on a pleasant back patio during the summer; and **DAHLIA LOUNGE** (2001 4th Ave; 206/682-4142), celebrity chef Tom Douglas's first place. (For reviews of all three, see the Restaurants chapter.)

The **DENNY REGRADE** (aka Denny Triangle), home to nightspots such as sister clubs **TINI BIGS** (100 Denny Wy; 206/284-0931) and **WATERTOWN** (106 1st Ave N; 206/284-5003), extends a block or two on either side of Denny Way from Interstate 5 to Western Avenue; beyond is the waterfront. North of the Regrade, between the Seattle Center and I-5, is the booming South Lake Union area and the residential/industrial Cascade neighborhood. The eastern foot of Queen Anne Hill along the west shore of Lake Union is the Westlake area, and the western foot of Capitol Hill along Lake Union's east shore is the Eastlake neighborhood.

East of the retail core, the **WASHINGTON STATE CONVENTION & TRADE CENTER** (8th Ave and Pike St), a mammoth, glass-enclosed building, sprawls atop 12 lanes of freeway and adjoins **FREEWAY PARK** (6th Ave and Seneca St), an extraordinary park that forms a grassy lid over thundering I-5. On the east side of I-5 is the First Hill neighborhood. Five bus stations of the underground **METRO TRANSIT TUNNEL** opened in late 1990 to ease Seattle's downtown traffic woes (it hasn't really worked). From the convention center to the Chinatown/International District, each station is lined with different kinds of public art (from sculpture to poetry), the fruits of Metro's $1.5-million arts program. *Map:F5–N5, F9–N9*

BALLARD

FROM LAKE WASHINGTON SHIP CANAL TO 85TH ST NW, FROM 15TH AVE NW TO SHILSHOLE BAY, CENTERED ALONG NW MARKET ST AND BALLARD AVE NW Ballard began as an industrial burg, full of sawmills, shingle mills, and shipyards, and it has retained its distinctive character ever since (despite its annexation by the City of Seattle in 1907). Much of its current flavor derives from the hordes of Scandinavians who flocked to the shores of Salmon Bay looking for work in the late 19th and early 20th centuries. Traces of the Nordic life show up in the *Velkommen to Ballard* mural at Leary Avenue NW and NW Market Street and in the neighborhood's unofficial slogan of affirmation: "Ya sure, you betcha." In no other corner of town are you likely to find lutefisk for sale.

Its ethnic history is also apparent along NW Market Street, Ballard's main commercial hub. **NORSE IMPORTS SCANDINAVIAN GIFT SHOP** (2016 NW Market St; 206/784-9420) has more trolls than you would know what to do with, and **OLSEN'S SCANDINAVIAN FOODS** (2248 NW Market St; 206/783-8288) sells homemade specialties and imported foods with tastes (and names) that celebrate their foreign roots. The **NORDIC HERITAGE MUSEUM** (3014 NW 67th St; 206/789-5707)

NORDIC HERITAGE MUSEUM

NW 67th St

NW 65th St

Earl Ave NW
27th Ave NW
32nd Ave NW
30th Ave NW
28th Ave NW
26th Ave NW
24th Ave NW

NW 64th St

NW 63rd St

NW 62nd St

NW 61st St

NW 60th St

NW 59th St

NW 58th St

22nd Ave NW
20th Ave NW
17th Ave NW
15th Ave NW
14th Ave NW

NW 57th St

NW 56th St

Market St NW

NW 54th St

BOTANICAL GARDENS

◄ TO SHILSHOLE BAY AND GOLDEN GARDENS PARK

HIRAM M. CHITTENDEN LOCKS

Leary Ave NW

Ione Pl

NW Vernon

Ballard Ave NW

Dock Pl

Shilshole Ave NW

Salmon Bay

NW 54th St

NW 53rd St

NW 52nd St

NW 51st St

NW 50th St

NW 49th St

NW Leary Way

NW Ballard Way

N

TO FISHERMEN'S TERMINAL ◄

BALLARD BRIDGE

BALLARD

displays textiles, tools, and photos from the Old Country and the Ballard of long ago (see the Arts chapter).

BALLARD AVENUE NW, a Historic Landmark District since 1976, gives you an idea of how this area looked a century ago—and how much it is changing now. Small retailers, scared off by climbing rents in Fremont, have moved in here instead, making the street both a good strolling and shopping locale. **CAMELION DESIGN** (5335 Ballard Ave NW; 206/783-7125) sells furniture and artists' wares, **OLIVINE** (5344 Ballard Ave NW; 206/706-4188) deals in very French women's clothing, and **SOUVENIR** (5325 Ballard Ave NW; 206/297-7116) specializes in ultrahip handmade greeting cards.

The most prominent landmark along here is the **BALLARD CENTENNIAL BELL TOWER** (Ballard Ave NW and 22nd Ave NW), a cylindrical, copper-topped monument holding a 1,000-pound brass bell that was saved from Ballard's 1899 city hall, which stood on this corner until it was torn down after a severe earthquake in 1965. Farther down the street, **HATTIE'S HAT** (5231 Ballard Ave NW; 206/784-0175), with its imposing back bar and patrons fresh off the fishing boat, retains a welcome seedy tone. While the **BALLARD FIREHOUSE** (5429 Russell Ave NW; 206/784-3516), a converted 1908 fire station, burns it up with everything from blues to rock to reggae, the best place to see a live show is the **TRACTOR TAVERN** (5213 Ballard Ave NW; 206/789-3599), which frequently schedules a form of country/bluegrass known as twang.

To the west, Ballard encompasses Salmon Bay and the **BALLARD LOCKS** (see Top 25 Attractions in this chapter), Shilshole Bay Marina, and Golden Gardens Park, a perennial favorite for beach fires at sunset. One good way to get a feel for this area is to take a tour with the **BALLARD HISTORICAL SOCIETY** (206/782-6844). Call for reservations and information, or pick up a copy of the self-guided walking tour at the **BALLARD CHAMBER OF COMMERCE** (2208 NW Market St, Ste 100; 206/784-9705) or area merchants. *Map:FF8*

CAPITOL HILL

FROM MADISON ST TO MONTLAKE CUT, FROM I-5 TO 23RD AVE, CENTERED ALONG BROADWAY FROM E PINE ST TO E ROY ST, AND ALONG 15TH AVE E FROM E DENNY WY TO E MERCER ST Along the spine of Capitol Hill lies Broadway Avenue, Seattle's answer to the effervescent spirit of San Francisco's Castro Street. **BROADWAY** has established itself as a haven for black clothes and pierced body parts, as Seattle's unofficial gay district, and as one of the few areas of town where sidewalks are still busy after 10pm.

The northern end of the district is at Harvard Avenue E and E Roy Street, home to the **HARVARD EXIT** (807 E Roy St; 206/323-8986), one of Seattle's foremost art-film theaters; and the **DELUXE BAR & GRILL** (625 Broadway Ave E; 206/324-9697), crowded with folks who want their burgers and microbrews served without chichi decor on the side. Just across the boulevard, Thai fanciers will find sufficiently tongue-searing dishes at **SIAM ON BROADWAY** (616 Broadway Ave E; 206/324-0892; see review in the Restaurants chapter). Capitol Hill's free-stepping spirit is expressed in Jack Mackie's inlaid bronze *Dancers' Series: Steps*, offbeat public art that appears at intervals as you walk south along Broadway, inviting strollers to get in step with the tango or the foxtrot.

Vintage and imported fashion, books, and home accessories are the focus of Broadway's best stores. **BROADWAY MARKET** (between Republican and Harrison Sts; 206/322-1610), featuring a florist, an oxygen bar, clothing and card shops, a movie complex, and the futuristic, vegetarian **GRAVITY BAR** (206/325-7186; see review in the Restaurants chapter), is an imposing symbol of the continuing million-dollar enfranchisement of this once-funky street. On the other side of Broadway are a well-stocked newsstand, **BROADWAY NEWS** (204 Broadway Ave E; 206/324-7323), and a warmly eclectic bookstore, **BAILEY/COY BOOKS** (414 Broadway Ave E; 206/323-8842).

The southern end of the strip is permeated with Seattle Central Community College's diverse students; across Pine Street from the campus is a second excellent movie house, the **EGYPTIAN** (801 E Pine St; 206/323-4978), perched on the edge of

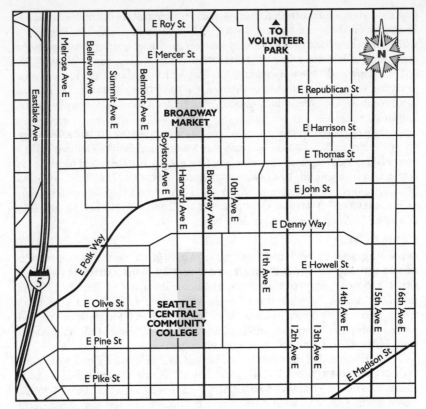

CAPITOL HILL

the so-called **PIKE-PINE CORRIDOR**. Just east of Broadway, continuing a few blocks between Pike and Pine Streets, this neighborhood is getting known for its rising housing costs, trendy little shops, and its nightclubs. Two to look out for are the graceful **CENTURY BALLROOM** (915 E Pine St; 206/324-7263) and Goth-rock club, **THE VOGUE** (1516 11th Ave; 206/324-5778). Distinctly less chic—and proud of it— is the **COMET TAVERN** (922 E Pike St; 206/323-9853), a smoky pool joint. The less flamboyant **15TH AVENUE E** is lined with shops and eateries, including **COASTAL KITCHEN** (429 15th Ave E; 206/322-1145; see review in the Restaurants chapter), a loud, fun diner-cum-grill-house with kickin' flavors from coastal regions worldwide. Several blocks farther north on 15th Avenue E, **VOLUNTEER PARK** drapes its grassy lawns among the stately mansions of north Capitol Hill. *Map:HH6–GG6*

CENTRAL DISTRICT

FROM E MADISON ST TO JACKSON ST, FROM 12TH AVE S TO MARTIN LUTHER KING JR. WY Historically Seattle's predominant African American neighborhood, the Central District is known for its churches and cultural institutions. The neighborhood is one of Seattle's oldest and largest, founded by some of the city's original settlers in the late 1870s. Once a hotbed of the civil rights movement, today the Central District is predominantly a residential neighborhood with a mix of family-owned businesses and historic houses designated as city landmarks. It also still is a neighborhood in transition; like Pioneer Square, there are pockets to avoid. The major thoroughfare is Martin Luther King Jr. Way, a street that eventually feeds into the Chinatown/International District and straight into downtown. Along this stretch, are the residential pockets of First Hill, Squire Park, and Jackson Square. In the south part of the Central District is the **LANGSTON HUGHES PERFORMING ARTS CENTER** (104 17th Ave S; 206/684-4757; cityofseattle.net/langstonhughes/) where, on any given day, you might catch a local boys choir or a performance of a play written by its namesake. Another point of pride is **GARFIELD HIGH SCHOOL**, which has produced the majority of Seattle's National Merit Scholars as well as an internationally known jazz band. The historic **DOUGLASS-TRUTH PUBLIC LIBRARY** (2300 E Yesler Way; 206/684-4704) houses the largest African American collection in the Seattle Public Library system.

The Central District also claims a burgeoning share of good restaurants. For an authentic soul food, there's **NELLIE'S PLACE CAFE** (1319 E Jefferson St; 206/322-1902), where the cornbread is plentiful and the collard greens are fresh; **EZELL'S FRIED CHICKEN** (501 23 Ave; 206/324-4141), a Seattle institution, is famous for its fried bird; or **LA LOUISIANA** (2514 E Cherry St; 206/329-5007; see review in the Restaurants chapter) and **CATFISH CORNER** (2726 E Cherry St; 206/323-4330) serve up tasty Creole/Cajun food. For good eats in the south part of the neighborhood, hop in the line forming outside the **SEATTLE DELI** (225 12th Ave S, No. 101; 206/328-0106), where $2 will buy perhaps the best Vietnamese sandwich around. Toward the eastern part of the Central District, **SAM SMITH PARK** is where you can watch pick-up basketball, soccer, or cricket. *Map: HH7-JJ5*

CHINATOWN/INTERNATIONAL DISTRICT
S DEARBORN ST TO S WASHINGTON ST, BETWEEN 4TH AVE S AND 14TH AVE S
The history of white treatment of Asians in Seattle is not a pleasant one, but you wouldn't know that to look at this peaceful and unpretentious neighborhood southeast of Pioneer Square. Seattle's Chinatown/International District is a collection of distinct ethnic communities (the Chinese have their own newspapers and opera society, the Japanese have a theater) and a cohesive melting pot (a community garden, museum, and neighborhood playground are shared by all). The influx of Southeast Asian immigrants and refugees in recent decades has only served to enrich this neighborhood's longstanding mix of Chinese, Japanese, Filipinos, Koreans, and African Americans and has given the "ID" a new vibrancy.

The southern edge of this district is marked by the handsome, barrel-vaulted **UNION STATION** (4th Ave S and S Jackson St; 206/622-3214), opened in 1911 for the Union Pacific Railroad and refurbished not long ago as the headquarters for Sound Transit. A centerpiece of the neighborhood is the emporium **UWAJIMAYA** (600 5th Ave S; 206/624-6248), the closest thing this city has to a real Japanese supermarket/department store—its cooking school is well regarded throughout the region, and it also houses **KINOKUNIYA** (206/587-2477), a branch of the largest Japanese bookstore chain in the United States. To get an idea of the engaging

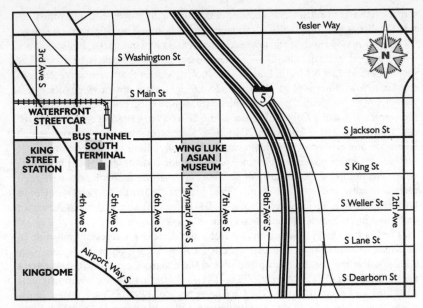

CHINATOWN/INTERNATIONAL DISTRICT

contrasts of the ID, drop in at tiny **HOVEN FOODS** (508 S King St; 206/623-6764), which sells excellent fresh tofu and soybean milk as well as take-home bags of plump, frozen potstickers.

A honey of a lunch can be had at the **HONEY COURT SEAFOOD RESTAURANT** (516 Maynard Ave S; 206/292-8828). Try **TOP GUN** (668 S King St; 206/623-6606) or **HOUSE OF HONG** (409 8th Ave S; 206/622-7997) for dim sum. **SHANGHAI GARDEN** (524 6th Ave S; 206/625-1689; see review in the Restaurants chapter) offers the cuisines of varying regions of China and what many consider to be the best Chinese food this Pacific Rim city has to offer. The oldest continuously operated Chinese restaurant in town—which is saying something—is **TAI TUNG** (659 S King St; 206/622-7372).

On Seventh Avenue is the **WING LUKE ASIAN MUSEUM** (7th Ave S and S Jackson St; see Museums in this chapter), which sensitively chronicles the experience of early Asian immigrants to the West Coast. Across Jackson Street to the north is the main Japanese district, where you'll find a real Japanese pre–World War II five-and-dime, the **HIGO VARIETY STORE** (604 S Jackson St; 206/622-7572). This is also where many of the ID's Japanese restaurants are clustered, including **BUSH GARDEN** (614 Maynard Ave S; 206/682-6830) and the tiny, inexpensive **KORAKU** (419 6th Ave S; 206/624-1389). North on Sixth Avenue and then east on Washington a short way are the **NIPPON KAN THEATRE** (628 S Washington St; 206/467-6807), known for its annual Japanese Performing Arts Series, and **KOBE TERRACE PARK**, with a noble stone lantern from Seattle's Japanese sister city of Kobe. Here, too, you'll get a splendid view of the district, including the **DANNY WOO INTERNATIONAL**

DISTRICT COMMUNITY GARDENS (206/624-1802). Built in the late 1970s, these gardens were parceled out to low-income elderly inhabitants of the neighborhood, who tend their tiny hillside plots with great pride.

East of here on Jackson, the Chinatown/International District takes on a Vietnamese air; the area surrounding 12th Avenue S and S Jackson Street is known as Little Saigon. **VIET WAH** (1032 S Jackson St; 206/328-3557) provides an excellent selection of fresh and packaged foods at very low prices and the most comprehensive selection of Chinese and Southeast Asian ingredients in town. Seattle has a well-deserved reputation for fine Vietnamese restaurants, and this is where you'll find many of them: **HUONG BINH** (1207 S Jackson St; 206/720-4907), **THANH VI** (1046 S Jackson St; 206/329-0208), and **A LITTLE BIT OF SAIGON** (1036-A S Jackson St; 206/325-3663). Or stop by **THE SAIGON DELI** (1200 S Jackson St; 206/322-3700) for spring rolls and grilled beef sandwiches. *Map:O6–R6, O2–R2*

QUEEN ANNE

FROM DENNY WY TO LAKE WASHINGTON SHIP CANAL, FROM 15TH AVE W TO AURORA AVE, CENTERED ALONG QUEEN ANNE AVE N Seattle's Queen Anne is divided into two districts—Upper and Lower—joined by "the Counterbalance," the part of Queen Anne Avenue that climbs up the steep south slope and owes its nickname to the days when weights and pulleys helped haul streetcars up that incline.

LOWER QUEEN ANNE is anchored by the Seattle Center (see Top 25 Attractions in this chapter). The area also claims some fine restaurants: within a few blocks' radius you can eat Mediterranean, Chinese, Thai, fondue, or Mexican food. Seattle Center and KeyArena events, along with the neon-deco triplex **UPTOWN CINEMAS** (511 Queen Anne Ave N; 206/285-1022), disgorge patrons to fill up late-night espresso and dessert spots. Alternatively, folks may take in the congenial bar scene at **T. S. MCHUGH'S RESTAURANT & PUB** (21 Mercer St; 206/282-1910) or the more stylin' **TEN MERCER** (10 Mercer St; 206/691-3723; see review in the Restaurants chapter).

Move north up the hill and the area becomes more residential. **UPPER QUEEN ANNE**'s big attractions include grand old-money mansions, many of them spread along **HIGHLAND DRIVE**—once considered the finest address in all of Seattle—and **KERRY PARK** (3rd Ave W and W Highland Dr), affording a smashing outlook (especially at sunrise) over downtown, Elliott Bay, the Space Needle, and even hide-and-seek Mount Rainier. Farther west is **BETTY BOWEN VIEWPOINT** (named in memory of one of the local art scene's great patrons), providing another perspective on Seattle's beauty: Puget Sound, West Seattle, the ferries, and the islands.

Queen Anne Avenue N is dominated by restaurants. The **5 SPOT CAFE** (1502 Queen Anne Ave N; 206/285-7768) is rich in attitude and American regional cuisines; **SAPPHIRE KITCHEN & BAR** (1625 Queen Anne Ave N; 206/281-1931) deals in Mediterranean meals and tapas; the often-noisy **HILLTOP ALEHOUSE** (2129 Queen Anne Ave N; 206/285-3877) concentrates on pub grub and beers (for reviews of all three, see the Restaurant chapter); **PARAGON BAR & GRILL** (2125 Queen Anne Ave N; 206/283-4548) serves traditional American dishes with elegant twists. Deserving attention, too, is **QUEEN ANNE AVENUE BOOKS** (1629 Queen Anne Ave N; 206/283-5624), strong on fiction and children's lit; **A & J MEATS AND**

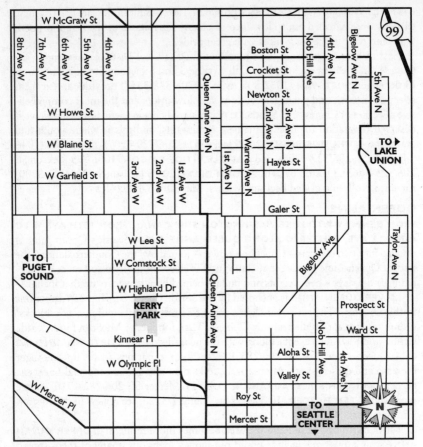

QUEEN ANNE

SEAFOODS (2401 Queen Anne Ave N; 206/284-3885), offering a diverse selection of basic cuts and prepared meals; and the tempting **MACRINA BAKERY** (615 W McGraw St; 206/283-5900; see review in the Restaurants chapter). *Map:GG7*

FREMONT/WALLINGFORD
NORTH OF LAKE WASHINGTON SHIP CANAL AND LAKE UNION, FROM 15TH AVE W TO I-5, CENTERED ALONG FREMONT AVE N AND N/NE 45TH ST Like so many of the hippies who once gave the neighborhood its funky charm, Fremont seems to have gone mainstream. Yes, it still boldly proclaims itself the "Center of the Universe" and delights in the occasional shock of nude bicyclists in its summer **SOLSTICE PARADE** every June. But the development of new commercial and office buildings on and nearby Fremont's waterfront—including those that house **ADOBE** software company's Seattle outpost—is starting to clog surrounding streets and is causing observers to worry over the district's eroding soul.

Still, streets are filled with highly browsable antique, secondhand, and retrokitsch stores that have names such as **FREMONT ANTIQUE MALL** (3419 Fremont Pl N; 206/548-9140), **THE DAILY PLANET** (3416 Fremont Ave N; 206/633-0895), and **DELUXE JUNK** (3518 Fremont Pl N; 206/634-2733). Drop into one of the slew of stylish eateries/bars, such as **TRIANGLE LOUNGE** (3507 Fremont Pl N; 206/632-0880; see review in the Restaurants chapter) and **TOST** (513 N 36th St; 206/547-0240). If you're screaming for ice cream, get in line at the new **COLD STONE CREAMERY** (624 N 34th St; 206/547-3200) near the new **PCC** (Puget Consumers Cooperative) market in the Block 40 building. Walk off those calories by strolling the park strip along the **LAKE WASHINGTON SHIP CANAL** or take in Fremont's popular—and populist—sculpture art, such as *Waiting for the Interurban* (Fremont Ave N and N 34th St), which locals revel in decorating year-round; the huge—and controversial—statue of Vladimir Lenin (Fremont Pl N and N 36th St); and the **FREMONT TROLL** (under the north end of the Aurora Bridge).

To the east lies "the James Garner among Seattle neighborhoods," as one local magazine dubbed Wallingford, and its population of mostly young marrieds. Most of the businesses hug N 45th Street. A warren of restaurants and jewelry, clothing, and book shops are inside **WALLINGFORD CENTER** (N 45th St and Wallingford Ave N; 206/547-7246). Just across Wallingford Avenue is **WIDE WORLD BOOKS** (4411 Wallingford Ave N; 206/634-3453), a great resource for both real adventurers and armchair travelers. Heading east on 45th Street, you can't miss the very Irish

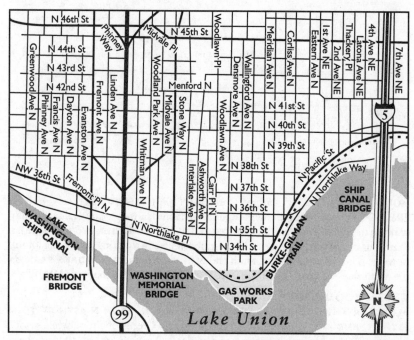

FREMONT/WALLINGFORD

WINERY TOURS

It used to be when Washington vintners traveled abroad, or even to the East Coast, the usual question was which side of the Potomac was better for growing their grapes? Now Washington state is regularly included in any survey of the world's best wine-producing regions. With more than 200 wineries across the state, Washington is second only to California in U.S. wine production.

Although the first European grape varieties were planted here in the late 1800s, fledgling winemaking efforts were hurt by icy winters and limited demand, and Washington vintners resigned themselves to producing safe, sweet dessert wines from winter-hardy vines instead. It wasn't until the late 1960s that the potential of Washington's soil and climate was fully appreciated and the first real premium wines were made. Washington's initial fame came from its full-flavored whites; only in recent years have reds equaled and surpassed the whites in reputation. Though most of the grapes are grown in the sun-soaked Yakima River and Columbia River valleys east of the Cascades, the Seattle-area oenophile can find plenty of tastings close to home. Most of the wineries in the greater Seattle area are located on the Eastside.

CHATEAU STE. MICHELLE (14111 NE 145th St; 425/488-3300; ste-michelle.com; map:CC2), 2 miles south of Woodinville off Highway 202, is the state's largest winery, occupying showplace headquarters on the 87-acre former estate of industrialist Henry Stimson. This is a popular destination for locals and visitors alike, since it offers the region's most comprehensive tour and, in summer, a lively outdoor concert series on its beautifully manicured grounds, which also provide lovely picnicking opportunities (you can buy picnic food to go with your wine in the gourmet shop on the premises). The single-vineyard wines are the winery's most exciting, but its winemakers also produce consistently well-made whites and reds with the Columbia Valley appellation. The winery has also collaborated with top Italian and German wineries to make great Washington wines, including Eroica and Col Solare.

MURPHY'S PUB (1928 N 45th St; 206/634-2110); **JITTERBUG** (2114 N 45th St; 206/547-6313; see review in the Restaurants chapter), a wonderfully relaxed eatery with a pan-ethnic menu; and **DICK'S DRIVE-IN** (111 NE 45th St; 206/632-5125), a Seattle classic serving up some of the best french fries in town and a parking lot full of teens in lust. Anchoring the south end of Wallingford is **GAS WORKS PARK** on the north shore of Lake Union (see Top 25 Attractions in this chapter). *Map:FF7*

GREENWOOD/GREEN LAKE
ALONG GREENWOOD AVE N AND PHINNEY AVE N, FROM N 45TH ST TO N 85TH ST, AND EAST TO I-5 People who've lived in Greenwood for a while say it's "like Wallingford before it became so popular." Once considered a far-northern

You'll get a different perspective across the street at **COLUMBIA WINERY** (14030 NE 145th St, Woodinville; 425/488-2776; columbiawinery.com; map:BB2). Originally located in Bellevue, this is one of the region's pioneer wineries. Its varied picnic facilities, where you can sprawl out after a wine tasting, are open daily and offer a pretty view of Ste. Michelle's grounds. The winery has an annual calendar of concerts and events. To reach both wineries, from Interstate 5 take the NE 124th Street exit, proceed east across the valley, then turn left at Highway 202/Redmond-Woodinville Road NE and left again on NE 145th Street.

Smaller wineries provide an interesting counterpoint to the giants. To taste the wines made by Chateau Ste. Michelle alum Cheryl Barber Jones, stop by **SILVER LAKE WINERY** (15029 Redmond-Woodinville Rd NE, Ste A, Woodinville; 425/486-1900; silverlakewinery.com; map:CC2). The state's only customer-owned winery, you can taste daily, noon to 5pm. This growing winery now has additional tasting rooms in Yakima Valley, as well as producing Spire Mountain hard cider. **FACELLI WINERY** (16120 Redmond-Woodinville Rd NE, Ste 1, Woodinville; 425/488-1020; facelli winery.com; map:BB2), inconspicuously tucked into an industrial office park, is worth a visit if only to meet one of the area's most exuberant (and entertaining) winemakers, Lou Facelli. Open Saturday and Sunday, noon to 4pm.

Other worthwhile winery stops in the area include **BAINBRIDGE ISLAND VINE-YARD AND WINERY** (682 Hwy 305, Bainbridge Island; 206/842-WINE) for estate-grown wines in the European style, with a picnic area (open Wednesday through Sunday). To see a wine-glass museum and wine-related antiques for sale, or to buy wines or sample them in the tasting room, visit **HEDGES CELLARS** (195 NE Gilman Blvd, Issaquah; 425/391-6056; www.hedgescellars.com).

suburb of Seattle, barely connected to downtown by a rattling municipal streetcar line, Greenwood remains more family-oriented than commercial, with a preponderance of secondhand stores, such as **PELAYO ANTIQUES** (7601 Greenwood Ave N; 206/789-1999). But since about the mid-1980s it has been attracting many younger residents and the diversity of restaurants they crave.

The neighborhood's most interesting stretch runs south from N 85th Street along Greenwood Avenue N. The **PIG 'N WHISTLE** (8412 Greenwood Ave N; 206/782-6044) is a cozy pub and eatery offering fine ribs and ample sandwiches (try the savory meat-loaf variety). For a dollop of attitude with your latte, there's **DIVA ESPRESSO** (7916 Greenwood Ave N; 206/781-1213). The comfort-food craze rules at **PETE'S EGGNEST** (7717 Greenwood Ave N; 206/784-5348); **YANNI'S** (7419 Greenwood Ave N; 206/783-6945; see review in the Restaurants chapter) is one of the top Greek restaurants in the city; **CARMELITA** (7314 Greenwood Ave N; 206/706-7703; see review in the Restaurants chapter) dispenses inventive vegetarian meals; and the **74TH STREET ALE HOUSE** (7401 Greenwood Ave N; 206/784-2955)

GREENWOOD/GREEN LAKE

is known for its chicken sandwiches and spicy soups. **TERRA MAR** (7200 Greenwood Ave N; 206/784-5350) offers handmade clothing, masks, and folk art from national and international makers.

Greenwood Avenue N becomes Phinney Avenue N at N 67th Street, which is also where you'll find **RED MILL BURGERS** (312 N 67th St; 206/783-6362), addicting crowds with its wide selection of juicy burgers. And weekends rarely fail to cause a lineup of breakfast aficionados outside **MAE'S PHINNEY RIDGE CAFE** (6412 Phinney Ave N; 206/782-1222; see review in the Restaurants chapter). Continue south on Phinney, and you'll hear the trumpeting of elephants and cackling of wild birds that signals your approach to the **WOODLAND PARK ZOO** (see Top 25 Attractions in this chapter).

East of Greenwood, the **GREEN LAKE PARK** area is busy with runners as well as patrons of the many businesses that ring the water. On the lake's east side, **NELL'S** (6804 E Green Lake Wy N; 206/524-4044; see review in the Restaurants chapter) gives a Mediterranean accent to regional foods such as Columbia River sturgeon and Dungeness crab. **SPUD FISH 'N' CHIPS** (6860 E Green Lake Wy N; 206/524-0565) wraps up orders of flaky fish and greasy fries. **GREGG'S GREENLAKE CYCLE** (7007 Woodlawn Ave NE; 206/523-1822) stocks a wide variety of bicycles and in-line skates for sale, but also rents wheels to fair-weather athletes. *Map:EE7*

MADISON PARK/MADRONA/LESCHI

FROM 23RD AVE TO LAKE WASHINGTON, FROM LAKE WASHINGTON BLVD TO I-90, CENTERED ON MADISON ST Quaint shops, restaurants, cafes—and some of Seattle's wealthiest blue bloods—fill **MADISON PARK** on the shores of Lake Washington. Though the neighborhood technically spans a good stretch of Madison Street, its main "downtown" consists of four lively blocks near the lake itself. If you're driving here, leave extra time for parking—weeknights after 5pm, squeezing between the Mercedes and Jaguars can be tricky.

Madison Park eateries attract upscale patrons day and night. Up near the Arboretum, in **MADISON VALLEY**, are the incomparable Japanese and French restaurants **NISHINO** (3130 E Madison St; 206/322-5800) and **ROVER'S** (2808 E Madison St; 206/325-7442), respectively. **MADISON PARK CAFE** (1807 42nd Ave, E; 206/324-2626), hidden away in a small house, serves bistro-style food at bistro-style prices. While down in the heart of Madison Park, you'll find young urbanites chowing on tapas and sipping $10 margaritas at **CACTUS** (4220 E Madison St; 206/324-4140), widely regarded as the best Mexican joint in the city. (For the preceding foursome, see reviews in the Restaurants chapter.) If a pint and a burger is more your style, head next door to the authentic pub **ATTIC** (4226 E Madison St; 206/323-3131).

BEST PLACE FOR EAVESDROPPING?
"Copacabana at the Market."

Joel Connelly, Seattle Post-Intelligencer *political columnist*

An outcropping of appealing shops includes **MADISON PARK BOOKS** (4105 E Madison St; 206/328-7323), which carries an extensive section of work by local authors, and **PEARSON & GRAY** (4110 E Madison St; 206/322-2765) and **MAISON MICHAEL** (4118 E Madison St; 206/325-4600), which both stock a good selection of quality antiques.

The neighborhood of **MADRONA**, whose center runs along 34th Street E, is both ethnically and commercially diverse. It is home to an eclectic collection of businesses, from the well-regarded **SPECTRUM DANCE THEATRE** (800 Lake Washington Blvd; 206/325-4161) to **WILRIDGE WINERY** (run in the cellar of Madrona Bistro). The best breakfast and brunch action is at the **HI SPOT CAFE** (1410 34th Ave E; 206/325-7905); try the Bengal Benedict, a curry-infused variation on the traditional breakfast treat. **ST. CLOUDS** (1131 34th Ave; 206/726-1522; see review in the Restaurants chapter) is popular for dinner and drinks. Other notable establishments include the charming flower shop **FLEURISH** (1411 34th Ave E; 206/322-1602) and the **CONLEY HAT MANUFACTURING COMPANY** (1112 34th Ave E; 206/322-1868), where Alexander Conley III still makes the same hats his grandfather did. If you've got time, check out the **MADRONA AUTO** building (1435 34th Ave E), a vintage auto repair shop that is now the site of various art classes and an ever-changing display of local artwork.

By far the smallest of the three neighborhoods, **LESCHI** is not without its share of attractions. For delicious steaks and a delightful view of Lake Washington, try **DANIEL'S BROILER** (200 Lake Washington Blvd; 206/329-4191; see review in the Restaurants chapter); for a more pub-like experience, try **LESCHI LAKECAFE** (102 Lakeside Ave; 206/328-2233), the lakefront iteration of Pioneer Square's F. X. McRory's. If you ride your bike to this neighborhood and you get a flat, fear not— the fellas at **IL VECCHIO BICYCLES** (140 Lakeside Ave; 206/324-8148) will get you on your way.

Parks are plentiful in this trio of neighborhoods. At the end of Madison Street sits **MADISON PARK BEACH**, one of the city's most popular sunbathing (and singles) spots. In Madrona, right along the lake, is **MADRONA PARK**, where on any given afternoon you'll count more nannies with babies than seagulls. If you continue south toward the I-90 floating bridge, you'll hit **FRINK PARK**, the centerpiece of the tiny, white-collar neighborhood of Leschi.

UNIVERSITY DISTRICT

FROM PORTAGE BAY/MONTLAKE CUT TO NE 65TH ST, FROM I-5 TO 35TH AVE NE, CENTERED ALONG UNIVERSITY WY NE Just 15 minutes north from downtown on the freeway, the 694-acre **UNIVERSITY OF WASHINGTON** campus is the center of a vital and diverse community as well as the Northwest's top institute of higher learning. The university was founded in 1861 on a plot of land downtown (on University St) and moved to its present site in 1895. In 1909, the campus played host to Seattle's first world's fair—the Alaska-Yukon-Pacific Exposition—and inherited from that not only some grand buildings, but infrastructure improvements to support the neighborhood's growth. The "U District" is the city's most youth-dominated area, with street life running the gamut from fresh-scrubbed college students to panhandling teens. The **UW VISITOR INFORMATION CENTER** (4014 University Wy NE; 206/543-9198) has maps and information regarding the large, well-landscaped campus.

The university's **MAIN ENTRANCE** is on NE 45th Street at 17th Avenue NE opposite **GREEK ROW**, a collection of stately older mansions inhabited mostly by fraternities and sororities. Just inside that entrance, to the right, is the **BURKE MUSEUM OF NATURAL HISTORY AND CULTURE** (17th Ave at 45th St; 206/543-5590; www.burkemuseum.org), displaying Native American artifacts and natural-history exhibits. Wander south past the Burke on Memorial Way to see **DENNY HALL**, the oldest building on campus (circa 1895) and the source of the hourly chimes that can be heard ringing throughout the district. Continuing south, you'll find **CENTRAL PLAZA**—aka Red Square—a striking marriage of brutalist architecture with Siena's town square. Adjacent are **MEANY HALL** and the **HENRY ART GALLERY** (see Top 25 Attractions in this chapter), but most noteworthy there is **SUZZALLO LIBRARY** (206/543-9158), the UW's main research library, with a Gothic exterior and stained-glass windows, as well as its modern **ALLEN LIBRARY** addition (donated by Microsoft co-wizard Paul Allen). Walk south between Suzzallo and the adjacent administration building and you'll reach **DRUMHELLER FOUNTAIN** ("Frosh Pond"), a pleasant stopping point among rose gardens, from which (on a clear day, anyway) you can see Mount Rainier.

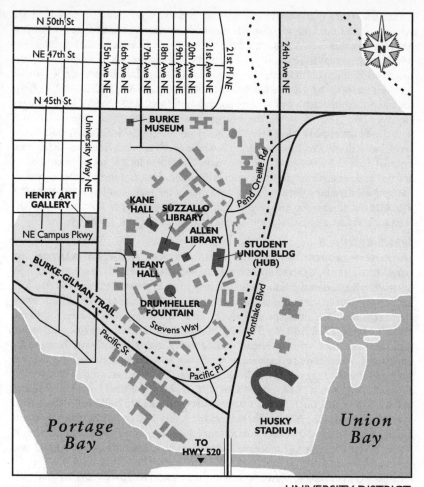

UNIVERSITY DISTRICT

If the university is the brains of this district, **UNIVERSITY WAY NE**, known to all as "the Ave," is its nerve center. The Ave is undergoing revitalization efforts to try and reverse the damage done by drug dealers and homeless teens who drove out some retailers. Already the neighborhood looks more spruced up and feels safer. Though chain stores are prominent here, there are still some distinctly local and often eccentric spots. **FOLK ART GALLERY/LA TIENDA** (4138 University Wy NE; 206/632-1796) carries select art objects and exotic crafts from several continents. Across the street is the **BIG TIME BREWERY AND ALEHOUSE** (4133 University Wy NE; 206/545-4509), offering good sandwiches and beers made on the premises. Just off the street in an alley you'll find **CAFE ALLEGRO** (4214½ University Wy NE; 206/633-3030), serving excellent espresso in a counterculturish atmosphere.

BULLDOG NEWS (4208 University Wy NE; 206/632-6397) is a browser's paradise where you can flip leisurely through hundreds of periodicals. But the real bibliophile's dream is the **UNIVERSITY BOOK STORE** (4326 University Wy NE; 206/634-3400), in perpetual rivalry with the Harvard Coop for the title of biggest, best, and most varied university bookshop in the country. Other must-visits in the U District include **FLOWERS BAR & RESTAURANT** (4247 University Way NE; 206/633-1903), for interesting (though smoky) surroundings and food; **RED LIGHT** (4560 University Way NE; 206/545-4044), the most popular vintage clothing shop on the Ave; and the **BLUE MOON TAVERN** (712 NE 45th St; 206/675-9116). A half-dozen blocks west of the Ave, the Blue Moon is where poet Theodore Roethke—and, later, novelist Tom Robbins—held court for years, and where Jack Kerouac (according to legend) and other Beats did their inimitable thing. Heading in the other direction (geographically and spiritually), just northeast of the main campus is **UNIVERSITY VILLAGE**, an upscale shopping center that keeps shoppers happy with big-name vendors such as Crate & Barrel, Ann Taylor, Sephora, and more. *Map:FF6*

WEST SEATTLE

FROM W MARGINAL WY SW TO ALKI AVE SW, FROM SW BARTON TO DUWAMISH HEAD, CENTERED ALONG CALIFORNIA AVE SW The surprisingly-for-Seattle bronze bodies that line the sandy strip of **ALKI BEACH** (along Alki Ave SW; see Top 25 Attractions in this chapter) make West Seattle a gawker's paradise during summer. But it's not all biceps and bikinis. Step right across Alki Avenue SW to the **LIBERTY DELI** (2722 Alki Ave SW; 206/935-8420), which serves terrific sandwiches and clam chowder, and on Friday and Saturday nights offers some better-than-expected dinner-theater performances. Given the New York attitude in this deli, it's only appropriate that the place should be located right across from a 3-foot-high replica of Manhattan's **STATUE OF LIBERTY**. If you prefer your landmarks full-size and tourable, check out the **ALKI POINT LIGHTHOUSE** (3201 Alki Ave SW), located at the southern end of Alki Beach. Built in 1913, this 37-foot functioning U.S. Coast Guard facility offers 30-minute guided tours. Continue farther south, along Marine View Drive all the way to Fauntleroy Way SW, and you'll reach **LINCOLN PARK** (see Parks and Beaches in this chapter) and the ferry dock to Vashon Island.

Also worth visiting in West Seattle is an area called **THE JUNCTION** (around California Ave SW and SW Alaska St), known for its historical murals as well as the **WEST SEATTLE FARMERS MARKET** (see the Farmers Markets sidebar in this chapter). While in the neighborhood, swing by **EASY STREET RECORDS** (4559 California Ave SW; 206/938-EASY), which boasts a savvy staff and expansive listening stations; the **ARTSWEST** theater and gallery (4711 California Ave SW; 206/938-0339 box office); and **CAPERS** restaurant (4521 California Ave SW; 206/932-0371), known for its scones, quiches, and gift shop. Also stop by the **HUSKY DELI** (4721 California Ave SW; 206/937-2810), famous for its homemade ice creams, and when you're ready for a nightcap, try the new **WEST 5** (4539 California Ave SW; 206/WE5-1966).

On the east side of the West Seattle ridge is the Delridge neighborhood and, to the south, South Park and White Center, home to a growing Hispanic community and South Seattle Community College. To get the best perspective on West Seattle, reach the neighborhood via **WATER TAXI** (206/205-3866). This 8-minute boat ride travels from Pier 54 on the downtown Seattle waterfront to West Seattle's Seacrest Park. The taxi runs seven days a week, from Memorial Day weekend through the end of the year. Adults pay $2 (one-way), and children under 5 ride free. *Map:JJ8*

BELLEVUE

FROM LAKE WASHINGTON TO LAKE SAMMAMISH, FROM I-90 TO HWY 520, CENTERED ON NE 12TH ST AND MAIN ST This largest city on the east side of Lake Washington now rivals Seattle for its downtown skyline of hotels and office towers. And though Bellevue does seem to be mostly about shopping (one of the city's most recognizable landmarks is **BELLEVUE PLACE**, a hotel, restaurant, and chichi shopping complex downtown), past the parking lots full of BMWs are parks, streets lined with small shops, and a surprising variety of ethnic foods.

This is not to say the shopping should be missed. With hundreds of fashion outlets, fast-fooderies, and stores, the constantly metamorphosing **BELLEVUE SQUARE** (NE 8th St between Bellevue Wy NE and 110th Ave NE; 425/454-8096) is the proverbial one-stop-shopping center and a focus for the community. Some people even show up there on weekday mornings just to walk for exercise. Across the street is the **BELLEVUE ART MUSEUM** (see Museums in the Arts chapter). On nice days, wander through the 19-acre **DOWNTOWN PARK**, also adjacent to the Square, where you'll find a 240-foot-wide, 10-foot-high waterfall, a canal enclosing a 5-acre meadow, and a 28-foot-wide promenade.

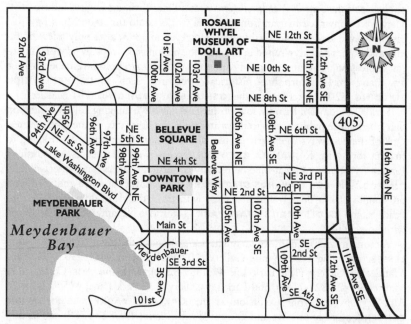

BELLEVUE

Art-fair lovers shouldn't miss the **PACIFIC NORTHWEST ARTS AND CRAFTS FAIR** (held the last weekend in July), which attracts hundreds of artists from throughout the West. It is said to be the largest crafts fair in the Northwest, and local legend holds that it never rains on the weekend of the fair (Eastsiders plan weddings and barbecues accordingly). Before leaving this area, you might want to make two last stops: at **UNIVERSITY BOOK STORE** (990 102nd Ave NE; 425/462-4500 or 206/632-9500), the Eastside outlet of Seattle's famed store (minus the textbook and buy-back options), and the **ROSALIE WHYEL MUSEUM OF DOLL ART** (1116 108th Ave NE; 425/455-1116; see review in the Arts chapter), with its diverse selection of dolls, teddy bears, and miniatures.

East of town, out SE Eighth Street, is **KELSEY CREEK PARK**, a good place for sub-urban kids to get a taste (albeit a tame one) of the country. A demonstration farm offers up-close contact with pigs, horses, chickens, and rabbits. Farther east lies **CROSSROADS SHOPPING CENTER** (NE 8th St and 156th Ave NE; 425/644-1111), a midsize mall where the emphasis shifts from shopping to community events and ethnic foods. Crossroads sponsors free live musical entertainment—featuring some of the area's most talented musicians playing anything from jazz to polka (Thursday night is open mike, for those who dare). *Map:HH3–HH1*

KIRKLAND

EAST OF LAKE WASHINGTON TO 132ND AVE NE, FROM CARILLON POINT/HWY 520 TO NE 116TH ST This town was supposed to be "the Pittsburgh of the West"— or at least that was the dream shared in the late 19th century by Leigh S. J. Hunt, publisher of the *Seattle Post-Intelligencer*, and Peter Kirk, an English industrialist. They were convinced that an iron-and-steel works could thrive on Moss Bay, just east of Seattle across Lake Washington. However, in 1893, after only a few build-ings and homes had been raised in the area, the nation was struck by its worst finan-cial depression. All that remains of Kirkland's campaign to become Pittsburgh are a few handsomely refurbished historical structures, such as the **PETER KIRK BUILDING** (620 Market St) and the **JOSHUA SEARS BUILDING** (701 Market St).

Kirkland today is a friendly, low-profile Eastside town hugging Lake Washington that offers more public access to the water than any other city on the lake's shores. One of the best ways to experience the lake is to head a bit north of Kirkland to Juanita for a visit to **JUANITA BAY PARK** (access is off Market St just south of Juanita Dr), home to great blue herons, owls, turtles, beavers, and other wildlife. Also strollable is **ST. EDWARDS STATE PARK** (take Market St north and head west on Juanita Dr), a densely forested park with trails that lead down to lakefront beaches, and **BRIDLE TRAILS STATE PARK** (116th Ave NE and NE 53rd St), laced with horse trails.

A more urban tour of the town might begin at one of the town's many **ART GAL-LERIES**, including Foster/White Gallery (107 Park Ln; 425/822-2305), Howard Mandeville Gallery (120 Park Ln; 425/889-8212), Kirkland Arts Center (620 Market St; 425/822-7161), and Park Ln Gallery (130 Park Lane; 425/827-1462). And perhaps end your excursion at the **KIRKLAND PARKPLACE SHOPPING CENTER** (corner of 6th Ave and Central Wy, Kirkland; 425/827-7789) and its mix of shops and a cinema.

When you need to nourish your body instead of your soul, try the northern Italian **RISTORANTE PARADISO** (120-A Park Ln; 425/889-8601). Or, for smashing lake views, there's **ANTHONY'S HOMEPORT** (135 Lake St; 425/822-0225) or **THE THIRD FLOOR FISH CAFE** (205 Lake St; 425/822-3553; see review in the Restaurants chapter). If all you really want is a cup of coffee, head to the **TRIPLE J CAFÉ** (101 Central Wy; 425/822-7319).

CARILLON POINT, south of downtown proper, is a luxury waterfront complex that includes the **WOODMARK HOTEL** (1200 Carillon Point; 425/822-3700 or 800/822-3700; see review in the Lodgings chapter), specialty shops, waterfront walkways, paths, and benches. **YARROW BAY GRILL** (1270 Carillon Point; 425/889-9052) features fancy food at fancier prices, while downstairs the **YARROW BAY BEACH CAFE** (425/889-9052) offers simpler fare (see reviews of both in the Restaurants chapter). Fortunately, the best thing about Carillon Point is free: the view west over the lake toward Seattle. *Map:EE3*

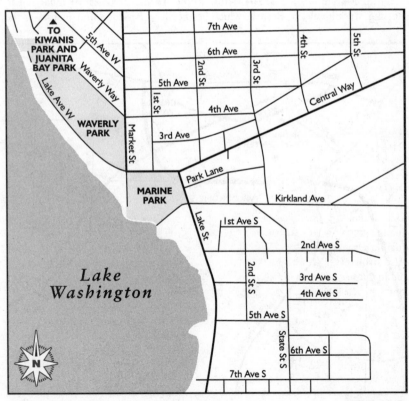

KIRKLAND

REDMOND

EAST OF LAKE WASHINGTON, FROM HWY 520 TO NE 124TH ST, FROM 132ND AVE NE TO 164TH AVE NE Even many people who have lived in Seattle for years know Redmond as nothing more than the headquarters for two corporate giants: **MICROSOFT** and **NINTENDO**. But like neighboring Bellevue, Redmond has a bustling downtown shopping mall: **REDMOND TOWN CENTER** (near NE 74th St and 164th Ave NE; 425/867-0808), with more than 50 stores and the **REDMOND TOWN CENTER CINEMAS** arranged around plazas and a large open space used for musical performances. This city also offers some more distinctive delights, including **MARYMOOR PARK** (6046 W Lake Sammamish Pkwy NE; 206/205-8751). Located south of downtown, Marymoor comprises 522 acres of playfields, running and horseback-riding trails, tennis courts, an interpretive nature trail, and even a 45-foot climbing wall. The park also hosts an annual concert series. This is also where you'll find the **MARYMOOR VELODROME** (2400 Lake Sammamish Pkwy; 206/205-3661), a 400-meter oval bicycle-racing track that attracts championship riders from around the country and picnickers who come to watch them go round and round. (Spectators pay $3 to attend Friday-night races.)

From Marymoor, the **SAMMAMISH RIVER TRAIL** stretches 10 miles north, skirting Woodinville, to Bothell, which lies north of Kirkland and Juanita at the

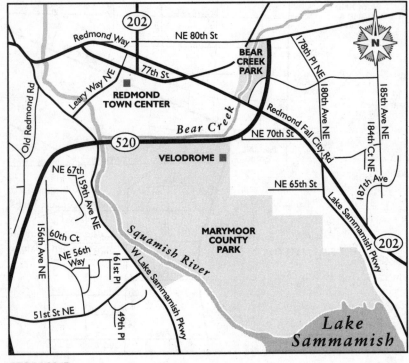

REDMOND

north end of Lake Washington. The trail is a flat but circuitous route ideal for fair-weather bicyclists, runners, and skaters who enjoy views of the surrounding mountains, slow-moving livestock, and even a few wire sculptures of cows. In Bothell the trail can be linked to the Burke-Gilman Trail (see Top 25 Attractions in this chapter) along the west shore of Lake Washington into Seattle. *Map:EE1–FF1*

Gardens

Here's the upside to all of that rain that falls on the Pacific Northwest: the region ranks among the world's best places for gardening. The **SEATTLE P-PATCH PROGRAM** (206/684-0264), a community gardening program begun in 1973, is one of the largest in the country, with 38 sites throughout Seattle. All P-Patch sites are organic and provide gardening space for families and individuals throughout the city. And downtown rooftops and terraces are green with gardens. **FREEWAY PARK** (6th Ave and Seneca St) drapes the midcity interchanges with verdant curtains of ivy, the incessant roar of the traffic obscured by whispering stands of bamboo. The University of Washington campus is rich with trees; pick up the **BROCKMAN MEMORIAL TREE TOUR** pamphlet for a small fee at the bus shelter across from Anderson Hall (Stevens Wy). **VOLUNTEER PARK** (1400 E Prospect St) on Capitol Hill boasts magnificent specimen trees and a splendid Victorian conservatory overflowing with flowers. The **WASHINGTON PARK ARBORETUM** (2300 Arboretum Dr E; see Top 25 Attractions in this chapter) offers more than 200 acres of wandering trails.

Bellevue Botanical Garden

 12001 MAIN ST, BELLEVUE; 425/452-2750 The botanical garden, which sits on 36 acres within Wilburton Hill Park, contains several smaller display gardens. The Waterwise Garden features descriptive signage detailing techniques to conserve water; specially selected plants are well labeled to provide ideas for the home gardener. The Alpine Garden boasts a generous display of flora found in rocky alpine settings (visitors are asked not to sit or climb on the rocks). The half-mile trail that rings the botanical garden winds past several other gardens, including the Yao Japanese Garden, a well-executed garden incorporating modern and traditional Japanese features. The trail continues on to the Perennial Border—a 20,000-square-foot mixed planting of perennials, bulbs, trees, shrubs, and grasses.

Its largest event, Garden d'Lights, is a holiday light festival that extends from late November through early January nightly. The Shorts Visitor Center, open 10am to 4pm daily, houses a gift shop and provides maps. Docents are available Saturday and Sunday, March through October, and group tours can be arranged by calling ahead. No pets, bicycles, or skateboards are allowed in the garden. Admission is free. *Every day; bellevuebotanical.org; map:HH3*

Bloedel Reserve

 7571 NE DOLPHIN DR, BAINBRIDGE ISLAND; 206/842-7631 Since the late 1980s, this 150-acre Bainbridge Island estate has been open to the public on a limited basis. The manse, which overlooks Puget Sound, is now a visitors center where interpretive material is available to guide your walk through the property. The parklike grounds contain a number of theme gardens, including a Japanese garden, and nature trails lead through native woods and wetlands. A small pond attracts birds in increasing numbers. This is not a place for a family picnic or a romp with the dog, and reservations for entrance are required (call well in advance during the busy spring months). Guided tours can be arranged for groups, and many of the trails are wheelchair accessible (the reserve has two sturdy wheelchairs available for public use; call ahead). Admission is $6 for adults; $4 for seniors, students, and children 5–12; and free for children under 5. *Wed–Sun; bloedelreserve.org.*

BEST PLACE TO DINE AL FRESCO?

"Ray's Boathouse, right on the water. A deck, a cocktail, some appetizers, and good friends. Few things can beat that on a clear, warm summer night."

Melanie McFarland, Seattle Post-Intelligencer *TV critic*

Carl S. English Jr. Botanical Gardens

3015 NW 54TH ST, BALLARD; 206/789-2622 One of the region's great horticulturists, Carl English made Seattle a horticultural hotspot in the last century through his plant- and seed-collecting efforts. Here at the Ballard Locks, you can explore 7 acres of gardens containing more than 500 species of plants, including those that made up English's personal arboretum. The English gardens are worth a visit even in winter, when the tapestry of bark and berry and the perfume of winter-flowering plants brighten the grayest day. In summer, the Seattle Fuchsia Society's display garden enlivens the spacious lawns, where one can picnic and watch the boats make their way through the lock systems that connect Lake Washington to Puget Sound. A summer band concert series and special theme family events, such as Scandinavian Day, provide further entertainment on the weekends. Guided tours of the locks, fish ladder, and garden are held daily in summer (June 1–September 30) and on weekends during the rest of the year; special in-depth tours can be arranged. (See also Ballard Locks under Top 25 Attractions in this chapter.) Admission is free. *Every day; nps.usace.army.mil/opdiv/lwsc/garden.htm; map:FF9*

Kubota Gardens

55TH AVE S AT RENTON AVE S, RAINIER BEACH; 206/725-5060 This Japanese garden tucked away in the Rainier Beach neighborhood at the south end of the Rainier Valley is a surprising oasis, home to such exotics as dragon trees. The large area encompasses many styles, from traditional Japanese garden to expansive lawns perfect for picnicking. The grounds are laced with winding paths that open onto ethereal views framing the many artfully trained pines and pruned plantings. A number of benches provide places for quiet contemplation. The north-central area of the garden is the site of the Necklace of Ponds, a network of waterfalls and ponds with a recirculating water system. Admission is free, and free tours are available on the last Saturday and Sunday of each month at 10am, starting in the parking lot; tours can also be arranged at any time for groups of eight or more. The Kubota Gardens Foundation holds plant sales in May and September, which are open to the public. *Every day; map:MM4*

Pacific Rim Bonsai Collection

WEYERHAEUSER WY S, FEDERAL WAY; 253/924-5206 The corporate head-quarters of the Weyerhaeuser Company, America's biggest timber business, also houses a pair of significant plant collections, both open to the public (see also next listing). Frequently changing exhibits showcase the diminutive gems of the bonsai collection, including a 1,000-year-old dwarf Sierra juniper. On alternate Sundays at 1pm, mid-April to mid-October, professional bonsai artists demonstrate pruning, propagation, and caretaking techniques. Basic bonsai care lectures are offered the second Saturday of the month, June through September. Tours are Sunday at noon or by appointment. Admission is free. *Sat–Wed (June–Feb), Fri–Wed (Mar–May); weyerhaeuser.com/bonsai.*

Rhododendron Species Botanical Garden

WEYERHAEUSER WY S, FEDERAL WAY; 253/661-9377 The Rhododendron Species Foundation's plantings encompass the largest, most comprehensive collection of rhododendron species and hybrids in the world. This is as much a preserve as a garden—more than 60 of the 500-plus species growing here on 22 acres at the Weyerhaeuser Company's corporate headquarters are endangered in the wild. A pair of study gardens are open throughout the year, so visitors can observe the rho-dodendron family's changing beauties through the seasons; though most are spring bloomers, others peak in winter or in summer, and many deciduous species take on magnificent fall foliage color. The garden has a gift shop and a plant sale pavilion. This is not a garden for picnicking or pets. Admission March through October is $3.50 for adults; $2.50 per person for students, seniors, and tour groups; and free to children under 12 and school groups. Free to all November through February. *Sat–Wed (June–Feb), Fri–Wed (Mar–May);rsf@rhodygarden.org; www.rhodygarden.org/index.html*

Seattle Tilth Demonstration Gardens

4649 SUNNYSIDE AVE N, WALLINGFORD; 206/633-0451 Urban gar-deners find a world of practical assistance at the Tilth gardens on the grounds of Wallingford's Good Shepherd Center. Self-guided instructional walks lead visitors through the gardens and an impressive array of composting units. The thriving gardens are tended organically and are kept healthy through natural pest controls and environmentally sound horticultural practices. Edible landscaping is a specialty here, but many of the 1,200 plants grown are also ornamental (including edible flowers). This midcity greenery serves everyone from raw beginners interested in learning how to prepare soil and sow carrots to advanced gardeners who trade her-itage vegetable seeds or rare border plants. The Children's Garden, east of the demon-stration gardens, lets young green thumbs practice organic and sustainable gardening too. The west end of the garden houses the Good Shepherd P-Patch. Numerous workshops and classes are offered. Tilth activities also include a spring plant sale at the end of April. Admission is free. *Every day; seattletilth.org; map:FF7*

University of Washington Medicinal Herb Garden

STEVENS WY AT GARFIELD LN, UNIVERSITY DISTRICT; 206/543-1126 First established in 1911 by the UW School of Pharmacy on a single acre, the Medicinal Herb Garden currently occupies a little more than 2 acres on the University of Washington campus and is reportedly the largest such garden in the Western Hemisphere. It serves as an accurate specimen garden for botanists, herbalists, medics, and gardeners. (It is not meant to provide medical information, however, and none is posted.) The garden displays more than 600 species and is divided into seven areas running west to east. A centrally located office displays a map of the garden and gives descriptions of each "room." Admission is free, and free tours are available the second Sunday of every month at noon, May through October. In-depth tours can be arranged by appointment for groups of 10 or more for a fee of $5 per person. The garden is located across from the Botany Building and extends east to Rainier Vista. *Every day; map:FF6*

Woodland Park Rose Garden

5500 PHINNEY AVE N, GREEN LAKE; 206/684-4863 Seattle's premier rose garden offers gardeners a chance to evaluate the regional performance of several hundred kinds of roses. Two acres of permanent plantings hold some 5,000 shrubs, both old-fashioned varieties and modern hybrids. Newest of all are the unnamed roses grown each year in the Seattle Rose Society's trial beds. Here likely candidates are tested for two years; the best of the bunch will become All-America Rose Selections. The Seattle Rose Society offers rose care and pruning demonstrations in the appropriate seasons (call the garden for information). Admission is free. *Every day; zoo.org/zoo_info/special/rose.htm; map:EE7*

Parks and Beaches

At last count there were 397 parks and playgrounds in the city of Seattle alone; the following are some of the best. The Seattle Parks and Recreation Department, which manages many city parks, maintains a comprehensive park list on its website at www.cityofseattle.net/parks. See also Top 25 Attractions and neighborhood write-ups in this chapter for more information.

Alki Beach Park

BETWEEN DUWAMISH HEAD AND ALKI POINT IN WEST SEATTLE, ALONG HARBOR AVENUE SW AND ALKI AVE SW See Top 25 Attractions in this chapter.

Bridle Trails State Park

116TH AVE NE AND NE 53RD ST, KIRKLAND; 425/455-7010, 425/828-1218, OR 800/233-0321 GENERAL INFORMATION, 360/902-8500 STATE PARKS DEPARTMENT HEADQUARTERS IN OLYMPIA As its name suggests, this 480-acre park is a densely wooded equestrian paradise laced with horse trails (one links up with Marymoor Park) and even an exercise ring. Though you may feel like an alien if you come to do anything but ride (even the private homes in the area all seem to have stables), the park also features picnic sites. Warning: The overgrowth is so dense that it's easy to get lost on the trails; also, for obvious reasons, watch where you step. *Map:FF2*

Camp Long

5200 35TH AVE SW, WEST SEATTLE; 206/684-7434 West Seattle's Camp Long, run by the Seattle Parks and Recreation Department, has a variety of broader functions: a meeting/conference facility (a lodge holds 75 people in its upper room and 35 in the basement), an in-city outdoor experience for family or group use (10 rustic bunk-bed-equipped cabins sleep up to 12 people at $35 a cabin—make reservations at least two weeks in advance), and simply a 56-acre nature preserve. The park also offers interpretive programs, perfect for school or Scout groups, and family-oriented nature programs on weekends. The lodge and cabins feature 1930s-style log architecture. Climbers can sharpen their skills on a climbing rock and a simulated glacier face. *Map:JJ8*

Carkeek Park

NW CARKEEK RD AND 9TH AVE NW, CROWN HILL; 206/684-4075 Carkeek Park is 186 acres of wilderness in the city's northwest corner. Forest paths wind from the parking lots and two reservable picnic areas (206/684-4081) to a footbridge spanning the railroad tracks, and then down a staircase to the broad beach north of Shilshole Bay. (Use caution around the tracks; trains run frequently through the park, and you may not hear them clearly.) Grassy meadows (great for kite flying), picnic shelters, and pretty, meandering Pipers Creek are other good reasons to relax here. *Map:DD8*

Chism Beach Park

1175 96TH AVE SE, BELLEVUE; 425/452-6885 One of Bellevue's largest and oldest waterfront parks, Chism sits along the handsome residential stretch south of Meydenbauer Bay. There are docks and diving boards for swimmers, picnic areas, a playground, and a large parking area above the beach. *Map:HH4*

Discovery Park

3801 W GOVERNMENT WY, MAGNOLIA; 206/684-4075 See Top 25 Attractions in this chapter.

Fay-Bainbridge State Park

15446 SUNRISE DR NE, BAINBRIDGE ISLAND; 206/842-3931 OR 800/233-0321 GENERAL INFORMATION, 360/902-8500 STATE PARKS DEPARTMENT HEADQUARTERS IN OLYMPIA, 800/452-5687 CAMPING RESERVATIONS About a 15-minute drive from the downtown ferry dock on Bainbridge Island, Fay-Bainbridge is a smallish (17-acre) park known for its camping areas and views of Mount Rainier and Seattle. The log-strewn beach has pits for fires; other features include a boat launch, horseshoe pits, and two kitchen shelters. It's a popular stop for cyclists on their way around the hilly isle.

Gas Works Park

N NORTHLAKE WY AND MERIDIAN AVE N, WALLINGFORD; 206/684-4075
 See Top 25 Attractions in this chapter.

Golden Gardens Park

 NORTH END OF SEAVIEW AVE NW, BALLARD; 206/684-4075 A breezy, sandy beach, nearby boat ramp, beach fire pits, and the pretty—but cold—waters of Shilshole Bay are Golden Gardens's biggest lures, although fully half of the park's 88 acres lie to the east of the railroad tracks along the wooded, trail-laced hillside. The marina here is home to a small village of sailboats. *Map:EE9*

Hing Hay Park

S KING ST AND MAYNARD AVE S, CHINATOWN/INTERNATIONAL DISTRICT; 206/684-4075 Hing Hay Park (the Chinese words translate as "pleasurable gathering") is a meeting and congregating place for the International District's large Asian community. From the adjacent Bush Hotel, an enormous multicolored mural of a dragon presides over the park and the ornate grand pavilion from Taipei. A great place to get a feel for the rhythms of ID life. *Map:Q6*

Kirkland Waterfront

ALONG LAKE WASHINGTON BLVD, KIRKLAND; 425/828-1218 A string of parks, from Houghton Beach to Marina Park at Moss Bay, line the shore of Kirkland's beautiful Lake Washington Boulevard. Kids feed the ducks and wade (only Houghton Beach and Waverly Beach have lifeguards); their parents sunbathe and watch the runners lope by. This is as close to Santa Cruz as the Northwest gets. *Map:DD4*

Lake Sammamish State Park

20606 SE 56TH ST, ISSAQUAH; 425/455-7010, 425/837-3300, OR 800/233-0321 GENERAL INFORMATION, 360/902-8500 STATE PARKS DEPARTMENT HEADQUARTERS IN OLYMPIA, 800/452-5687 CAMPING RESERVATIONS The sprawling beach is the main attraction of this state park at the south end of Lake Sammamish just off Interstate 90. Shady picnic areas, grassy playfields, and volleyball courts are excellent secondary draws. Large groups must reserve day-use areas—the place can be overrun in summer. Issaquah Creek, fine for fishing, runs through the park's wooded area.

Lake Washington Parks

FROM E MADISON ST AND 43RD AVE E, MADISON PARK, TO 5800 LAKE WASHINGTON BLVD S, RAINIER VALLEY; 206/684-4075 This string of grassy beachfronts acts as a collective backyard for several of the neighborhoods that slope toward Lake Washington's western shore. Bicycle Saturdays and Sundays take place in the summer, when the route from Colman Park to Seward Park is closed to cars from 10am to 6pm. **MADISON PARK** (E Madison St and 43rd Ave E) is a genteel neighborhood park, with a roped-in swimming area and tennis courts. If you head east on E Madison Street and turn left onto Lake Washington Boulevard, you'll wind down to meet the beach again, this time at **MADRONA PARK** (Lake Washington Blvd and Madrona Dr), a grassy strip with a swimming beach, picnic tables, a (summer-only) food concession, and a dance studio. Farther south is **LESCHI PARK** (Lakeside Ave S and Leschi Pl), a handsomely manicured retreat that occupies the hillside across the street from the lake. The park offers great views of the Leschi Marina and the dazzling spinnakers of sailboats, as well as a play area for kids. Another greenbelt, **COLMAN PARK** (36th Ave S and Lakeside Ave S), also with a play area, marks the start of the seamless lakefront strip that includes **MOUNT BAKER PARK** (Lake Park Dr S and Lake Washington Blvd S), a gently sloping, tree-lined ravine; the hydroplane racing Mecca—once a marshy slough, now a manicured park and spectator beach with boat launches—called **STAN SAYRES MEMORIAL PARK** (3800 Lake Washington Blvd S); and the lonely wilderness peninsula of **SEWARD PARK** (5800 Lake Washington Blvd S; see listing below). *Map:GG5–JJ5*

Lincoln Park

FAUNTLEROY AVE SW AND SW WEBSTER ST, WEST SEATTLE; 206/684-4075 Lincoln Park, a 130-acre jewel perched on a pointed bluff in West Seattle, offers a network of walking and biking paths amid grassy forests, reservable picnic shelters (206/684-4081), recreational activities from horseshoes to football to tennis, and expansive views of the Olympic Mountains from seawalls and rocky beaches. There are tide pools to be inspected and beaches to roam, and kids delight in the playground equipment. Don't miss the (heated) outdoor saltwater **COLMAN POOL** (summer only), which began as a tide-fed swimming hole. *Map:LL9*

Luther Burbank Park

2040 84TH AVE SE, MERCER ISLAND; 206/236-3545 Occupying a good chunk of the northern tip of Mercer Island, Luther Burbank Park is the Eastside's favorite family park. There are picnic areas, barbecue grills, a swimming area, nicely maintained tennis courts, an outdoor amphitheater for summer concerts, a first-rate playground, several playing fields, docks for boat tie-ups (the haunt of sun-worshiping teens in summer), and green meadows that tumble down to the shore. *Map:II4*

Sand Point Magnuson Park

SAND POINT WY NE AND NE 65TH ST, SAND POINT; 206/684-4075 This 194-acre park fronts Lake Washington just southeast of now-closed Sand Point Naval Station, with a mile of shoreline, a boat launch, a playing field, and six tennis courts. The Burke-Gilman Trail winds past Magnuson Park, linking it to Ballard and Bothell. Just north of the park is the National Oceanic and Atmospheric Administration (NOAA), where you'll find a series of unique artworks along the beach. One sculpture, the Sound Garden, is fitted with flutelike aluminum tubes that create eerie music when the wind blows. The site is open every day from dawn to dusk and is a hauntingly wonderful spot to sit on a blue whale bench, listening to the wailing wind chimes and watching the sun come up over Lake Washington. *Map:EE5*

Myrtle Edwards Park

ALASKAN WY BETWEEN BAY ST AND W THOMAS ST, WATERFRONT;
206/684-4075 Myrtle Edwards and adjacent **ELLIOTT BAY PARK** provide a front
lawn to the northern section of downtown. This breezy and refreshing strip is a
great noontime getaway for jogging (the two parks combined form a 1.25-mile trail),
picnicking on benches that face Puget Sound, or just strolling. Parking at the Pier 70
lot just south of Myrtle Edwards is at a premium, but the Waterfront Streetcar stops
nearby. *Map:B9*

Newcastle Beach Park

4400 LAKE WASHINGTON BLVD S, BELLEVUE; 425/452-6885 This Bellevue
park takes full advantage of its waterfront location with a fishing dock, swimming area, and bathhouse facility (complete with outdoor showers). Walking
paths—including a three-quarter-mile loop—weave throughout the 28 acres, and a
wildlife area offers the chance to see animals and birds in their natural habitat.
Map:JJ3

Ravenna Park

**20TH AVE NE AND NE 58TH ST, RAVENNA/UNIVERSITY DISTRICT; 206/684-
4075** This steep woodland ravine strung between residential districts north of the
University District is a lush sylvan antidote to the surrounding city. At the west end
is **COWEN PARK** (University Wy NE and NE Ravenna Blvd), with tennis courts and
play and picnic areas. Trails along burbling Ravenna Creek lead to the eastern end
of the park in the Ravenna neighborhood and more picnic areas, tennis courts, and
playing fields, plus a wading pool. The whole expanse is a favorite haunt of runners,
as is Ravenna Boulevard, a tree-lined thoroughfare that defines the park's southern
flank and leads west to Green Lake. *Map:EE6*

Schmitz Park

SW STEVENS ST AND ADMIRAL WY SW, WEST SEATTLE; 206/684-4075 Just
south of West Seattle's Alki Beach is this 53-acre nature preserve, full of raw trails
through thickly wooded terrain. The largest western red cedars and hemlocks here
are likely to be about 800 years old—seedlings back when Richard the Lionhearted
was leading his troops on the Third Crusade. No playgrounds, picnic areas, or other
park amenities. *Map:II9*

Seward Park

LAKE WASHINGTON BLVD S AND S JUNEAU ST, RAINIER VALLEY;
206/684-4075 This majestic wilderness, occupying a 277-acre knob of land
in southeast Seattle, gives modern city dwellers an idea of what this area
must have looked like centuries ago. At times the park is imbued with a primal sense
of permanence, especially on misty winter days when the quiet of a solitary walk
through old-growth Douglas fir forest is broken only by the cries of a few birds. But
at other times—hot summer Sundays, for instance—Seward turns into a frenzy of
music and barbecues. You can drive the short loop road to get acquainted with the
park, past the bathhouse and beach facilities; **SEWARD PARK ART STUDIO**
(206/722-6342), which offers classes in the arts; some of the six reservable picnic

shelters (206/684-4081); and some of the trailheads, which lead to the fish hatchery and the outdoor amphitheater, and into the forest preserve. Cyclists and runners can make an even better loop on the scenic 2.5-mile lakeside trail encircling the peninsula. *Map:JJ5*

BEST PLACE TO WATCH
A FOREIGN FILM?

"The Grand Illusion, the only place that's cozy
yet has a classic grandeur to it, owing to its pressed-tin
ceiling and red velvet chairs. You'll catch foreign films here few
other people will have heard of. Do this enough times and you'll
evolve into a man or woman of cultural wisdom and mystery.
That, or a snob people secretly want to coldcock."

Melanie McFarland, Seattle Post-Intelligencer *TV critic*

Victor Steinbrueck Park

WESTERN AVE AND VIRGINIA ST, PIKE PLACE MARKET; 206/684-4075 Pike Place Market's greatest supporter and friend is the namesake of this slice of green at the north end of the market. With the Alaskan Way Viaduct right below, the park can be quite noisy during peak traffic hours. It also tends to be a favorite hangout for street people. Despite those caveats, the park's grassy slopes and tables make a fine place for a market picnic, and the view of blue Elliott Bay and ferry traffic is refreshing. *Map:H8*

Waterfall Garden

2ND AVE S AND S MAIN ST, PIONEER SQUARE; 206/624-6096 The waterfall in this tiny Pioneer Square park was built to honor the United Parcel Service, which started at this location in 1907. It does crash (this is no place for quiet conversation), and the benches fill up by noon on weekdays, but the park (on the northwest corner of this intersection) makes for a marvelous little nature fix in the middle of a busy urban day. *Map:O8*

Waterfront Park

PIER 57 TO PIER 61 ON ALASKAN WY, WATERFRONT; 206/684-4075 A park that spans three piers between the Seattle Aquarium and Pier 57 provides a break from the bustling activity of the rest of the waterfront. The park contains a tree-encircled courtyard, raised platforms with telescopes for a view of Elliott Bay and islands, plenty of benches, and—strange for a park in this town—nary a blade of grass. *Map:J9*

Woodland Park

✝ **5200 GREEN LAKE WY N, GREEN LAKE; 206/684-4075** This 188-acre park abuts Green Lake on one side and has busy Aurora Avenue running through the middle. On the west side are the rose garden (see listing above in the Gardens section of this chapter) and Woodland Park Zoo (see Top 25 Attractions in this chapter). On the east are playfields, picnic areas, lawn bowling, and tennis courts. *Map:EE7*

Organized Tours

To get beneath the city's surface, nothing beats a tour. Clearly fun for visitors, a tour is also a great chance for locals to learn something new about their hometown. Tours can be as informational as one of the **SEATTLE ARCHITECTURAL FOUNDATION'S VIEWPOINTS WALKING TOURS** (206/667-9184; seattlearchitectural.org), which examine the mix of art and architecture throughout the city; to as colorful as Jeri Callahan's specially tailored **DISCOVER HOUSEBOATING** (206/322-9157; discover houseboating.com) tours-by-water of Lake Union's quirky houseboat neighborhoods. And for $7, volunteers with the **MARKET HERITAGE TOURS** (206/774-5262; pikeplacemarket.org/about/visiting_market/tours.asp) reveal the nooks and crannies of the Pike Place Market that you might otherwise miss.

AIR TOURS

Kenmore Air

950 WESTLAKE AVE N, SOUTH LAKE UNION / 6321 NE 175TH ST, KENMORE; 425/486-1257 OR 800/543-9595 The largest seaplane operator in the area, Kenmore Air has a fleet of 20 planes that make scheduled and charter flights around Puget Sound and to Victoria, British Columbia, from seaports on Lake Union and north Lake Washington. A one-way passage to the San Juan Islands is $98 or $108 per person on a scheduled flight ($98 May 1–June 30; $108 July 1–Sept 2), or $436 for a 1-hour charter for one to three people. A two-hour round-trip scenic flyover of the San Juans is $75 per person; or sign up for a spring or summer day-trip package (including lunch and ground transportation on San Juan Island) for $163. Round-trip all-day excursions to Victoria are $184 per person. The company also offers a 20-minute city tour (which originates from the Lake Union location only) for $218 for three passengers, $249 for up to six. Be sure to call ahead; several tours are available on a day-of-flight basis only, and advance reservations are required for other trips. *kenmoreair.com; map:GG7, BB5*

Seattle Seaplanes

1325 FAIRVIEW AVE E, EASTLAKE; 206/329-9638 OR 800/637-5553 Seattle Seaplanes does its main business in charters to Canadian fishing camps, but also offers a 20-minute exhaustive airborne tour of Seattle (University of Washington, Lake Washington, the waterfront, Magnolia, the Locks, Shilshole, Green Lake, and back to Lake Union) for $67.50 per person. Consider taking a flight to and from majestic Mount Rainier ($395 for one to four passengers, $410 for five), Mount St. Helens

($790 for one to four passengers), the San Juan Islands ($550 for one to four passengers), or Victoria ($580 for one to four passengers). Call for reservations. *info@seattleseaplanes.com; seattleseaplanes.com; map:E1*

BOAT TOURS

Given Seattle's watery surroundings, it's only natural that waterborne travel is one of the best ways to get a look around the Puget Sound area. Besides customizing your own tour via one of 29 **WASHINGTON STATE FERRIES** (206/464-6400; wsdot.wa.gov/ferries)—a handful of which leave from downtown's Colman Dock throughout the day en route to Bainbridge Island or Bremerton—there are a boatload of boat tours available. (See also the Top 25 Attractions in this chapter and "Experience Seattle" section in the Planning a Trip chapter.)

Argosy Cruises

PIERS 54, 55, AND 57, WATERFRONT/1200 WESTLAKE AVE N, SOUTH LAKE UNION; 206/623-1445 OR 800/642-7816 Scheduled tours departing from Lake Union include daily, year-round, 1-hour narrated cruises along the Seattle waterfront and Elliott Bay ($17.50); 2½-hour tours through the Ballard Locks and Lake Washington Ship Canal ($31.50); and a 2-hour Lake Washington excursion ($27.25), featuring peeks at the pricey palaces surrounding the lake—including the 40,000-square-foot Xanadu that Microsoft CEO Bill Gates has erected. Charters for private parties or special events are available for groups of 10 to 400. *sales@argosycruises.org; argosycruises.com; map:L9–K9, A1*

Emerald City Charters (Let's Go Sailing)

PIER 54, WATERFRONT; 206/624-3931 A 70-foot custom-built former racing sloop, the *Obsession* cuts through Elliott Bay waters May 1 to October 15. Star of the movie *Masquerade* (along with Rob Lowe), the yacht can comfortably carry up to 49 passengers, who should count on packing their own meals for the scheduled 1½-hour trips that leave from the north side of the pier at 11am, 1:30pm, and 4pm daily. Costs for day cruises are $23 for adults, $20 for seniors, $18 for children 12 and under. A 2½-hour sunset sail leaves between 6pm and 7pm daily and costs $38 for adults, $35 for seniors, and $30 for children 12 and under. Private charters are also available year-round. Call to check on sailing times and availability. *plamarche@qwest.net; sailingseattle.com; map:K9*

Mosquito Fleet San Juan Orca Cruises

1724 W MARINE VIEW DR, EVERETT / CAP SANTE MARINA, FLOAT D, SPACE 0, ANACORTES; 425/252-6800 OR 800/325-ORCA Whale-watching cruises leave daily from Everett and Anacortes June through September, and on a limited basis during April, May, September, and October. The 9½-hour cruises are narrated by a naturalist, who lectures on orcas (and identifies their pods) as well as on other marine life and San Juan maritime history. Depending on the time of year, tickets range from $34.50 to $79. Call for reservations. *info@whalewatching.com; whalewatching.com*

Ride the Ducks of Seattle

5TH AVE N AND BROAD ST, SEATTLE CENTER; 206/441-DUCK OR 800/817-1116 RESERVATIONS See the city's sights by land and sea aboard amphibious vehicles (aka "ducks"). The refurbished World War II landing craft are piloted by Coast Guard–certified sea captains who motor visitors about the streets of downtown, Pioneer Square, and Fremont before launching into the waters of Lake Union for tours past Seattle's houseboats and glass artist Dale Chihuly's studio. The 90-minute rides are $22 for adults and $12 for kids 12 and under. The ducks take off hourly throughout the year from the northeast corner of Fifth and Broad (across from the Space Needle). Drop by that same location for tickets, or call for reservations; private duck tours are also available. *info@seattleducktours.net; ridetheducks ofseattle.com; map:C6*

BEST PLACE FOR A COCKTAIL?
"Vito's on First Hill—like a scene from Hitchcock's *Vertigo*."
Greg Nickels, mayor of Seattle

Tillicum Village Tour

PIER 55, WATERFRONT; 206/443-1244 A Northwest tourist staple, this four-hour narrated voyage from downtown Seattle to nearby Blake Island (reputedly the birthplace of Seattle's namesake, Chief Sealth) has been operating for more than 35 years. The highlight of the hyped-up look at Northwest Indian culture is a salmon bake and a Native American dance. $65 adult, $59 seniors, $25 for kids 12 and under, and free for children 4 and under. (Also accessible from Bremerton.) *tillicumvillage.com; map:L9*

MOTOR TOURS

GRAY LINE OF SEATTLE

4500 W MARGINAL WY SW, WEST SEATTLE; 206/624-5813 This popular bus-touring service offers several choice trips: Mount Rainier (May–Sept, $54 per person); the Boeing plant in Everett ($39 per person); the popular Seattle city tours ($49 per person for seven hours or $29 per person for three hours); overnighters to Victoria, British Columbia, and more. Free pickup at several downtown hotels. *Info@graylineofseattle.com; graylineofseattle.com; map:JJ8*

Private Eye on Seattle

206/365-3739 Take your seat in a blood-red van as it weaves in and out of some of Seattle's most notorious crime scenes. A Haunted Happenings ghost tour (including a scene-of-the-crime stop at the 1983 Wah Mee Massacre) and crime tours of Queen Anne and Capitol Hill are both available (famous and infamous locals visited along the way include Kurt Cobain and Ted Bundy). Be advised, these are not excursions for children or squeamish adults. Cost for the two-hour macabre adventure is $22–$25 per person; group discounts are available. Minimal walking required; van picks up guests from downtown hotels or restaurants. *jake13@fox internet.com; privateeyetours.com*

Seattle Tours

206/768-1234 Ballard's Locks and downtown shops as well as Fremont, Alki Beach, the floating bridges, and more are on the itineraries for these three-hour minicoach tours. Custom-designed coaches hold up to 20 people and cost is $39 per person. Another tour features a day-long trip to Mount Rainier for $73 per person. Closed December 15 through January. *info@seattlecitytours.com; seattlecitytours.com*

Show Me Seattle

206/633-CITY Colorfully decaled vans holding a maximum of 14 lookie-loos per ride hit downtown Seattle hot spots—the waterfront, Pike Place Market, Chinatown/International District—and do drive-bys of the city's more remarkable neighborhoods, including Fremont (and its lurking Aurora Bridge Troll), Green Lake, and Queen Anne. The *Sleepless in Seattle* houseboat on Lake Union is an oft-requested stop. Cost is $36 adults, $24 kids 12 and under; reservations required. *geoffand jacqueline@showmeseattle.com; showmeseattle.com*

Spirit of Washington Dinner Train

425/227-RAIL It's not exactly the Orient Express, but the Spirit of Washington Dinner Train attracts diners who crave a bit of nostalgia and adventure with their meals. At downtown Renton's **SPIRIT DEPOT**, passengers board a train composed of Depression-era rail cars and engines, all immaculately restored. The highpoint of the 45-mile, 3¼-hour round-trip around the eastern shore of Lake Washington is when the train passes over Bellevue's **WILBURTON TRESTLE**, the longest wooden trestle still in use in the Northwest. For the best views, pay a $15 premium to secure seats in one of the three dome cars. Fare is $59.99 for dinner; $49.99 for lunch or brunch. *Every day (June–Sept), Tues–Sun (Oct–May); spirit ofwashingtondinnertrain.com; map:NN3–CC2*

WALKING TOURS

Chinatown Discovery

425/885-3085 Humorous Seattle native Vi Mar conducts four walking tours of the Chinatown/International District, providing a historical and cultural perspective that, in some cases, comes with a meal. For instance, the Chinatown by Day tour features a six-course dim sum lunch; the nighttime tour is an eight-course affair. Reservations required. Rates for adults range from $14.95 to $39.95, and for children from $9.95 to $22.95. Group rates for 10 or more adults are available. *heking@juno.com; seattlechinatowntour.com*

Seattle Walking Tour

425/885-3173 This two-hour tour led by Duse McLean (author of tourist-friendly books such as *The Pocket Guide to Seattle*) concentrate on the architecture and history of downtown. The $15 tours begin outside Westlake Center (400 Pine St) on

Wednesday and Thursday at 5:30pm and Saturday at 10:30am, June through September. *dusem@aol.com; thistlepress.com/thistle_press_tours.htm; map:I6*

See Seattle Walking Tours

425/226-7641 Catering to those with no time to waste finding Seattle's favorite sights on their own, these tours take in Pike Place Market, the waterfront, Pioneer Square, Chinatown/International District, and other downtown points of interest. Custom tours are available for groups, including mystery and scavenger hunts (perfect for parties or corporate groups). Typical cost is $20 per person (excluding lunch and trolley-car fee); free for children under 12. *Daily; walking@see-seattle.com;see-seattle.com*

Underground Tour

 610 1ST AVE, DOWNTOWN; 206/682-4646 See Top 25 Attractions in this chapter.

SHOPPING

SHOPPING

Neighborhoods, Shopping Districts, Malls

DOWNTOWN

Amid first-rate restaurants, cafes, and theaters, nearly every downtown corner sports a megaretailer. **BANANA REPUBLIC**, located in the historic Coliseum movie theater building, dresses up the northeast corner of Fifth Avenue and Pike Street; **KENNETH COLE** is on the southeast corner of Sixth and Pike; **NIKETOWN**, a three-story tabernacle of sneakers and sportswear, dominates the northeast corner of Sixth and Pike; arch rival **ADIDAS** is just down the street on the corner of Fifth and Pike; the **ORIGINAL LEVI'S STORE** fits into the Meridian shopping/entertainment complex on Sixth between Pike and Pine; just down the street is flagship **NORDSTROM**, while clothing store **OLD NAVY** weighs anchor on the corner of Sixth and Pine.

Bon-Macy's

3RD AVE AND PINE ST, DOWNTOWN; 206/506-6000 The staple of Seattle department stores for more than 100 years, the old Bon Marché got a new name in 2003. However, we expect Bon-Macy's to continue its role of fulfilling clothing, household, and wedding registry needs, and to mark the start of the holiday season with its annual hoisting of the 3,600-bulb Holiday Star. *Every day; bonmacys.com; map:I6*

City Centre

1420 5TH AVE, DOWNTOWN; 206/624-8800 Upscale clothier Barneys New York flaunts its wares on one side of this urban mall, while Design Concern's sleek innovation rules on the other. Ritzy retailers prevail here, from Italian handbag purveyor Furla to always appropriate Ann Taylor. To sweeten the appeal there's the posh Palomino Euro-bistro and 1,100 underground parking spots. *Every day; info@shopcitycentre.com; shopcitycentre.com; map:J5*

Nordstrom

500 PINE ST, DOWNTOWN; 206/628-2111 See Top 25 Attractions in the Exploring chapter.

Pacific Place

600 PINE ST, DOWNTOWN; 206/405-2655 Inside a 12,000-square-foot skylit atrium, Pacific Place shelters a wealth of retailers: Tiffany & Co., Cartier, J. Crew, Ann Taylor, Restoration Hardware, Pottery Barn, and Williams-Sonoma Grande Cuisine. To ease shopper headaches, the center has 1,200 surprisingly cheap underground parking spaces, several strength-sustaining restaurants, and a state-of-the-art 11-screen cinema, fashioned after a Northwest lodge that caps the complex. *Every day; pacificplaceseattle.com; map:J5*

Rainier Square

1335 5TH AVE, DOWNTOWN One of downtown's smaller malls, (and getting smaller as its tenant shuffling continues), Rainier Square still has a few notable retailers, including Barcelino and David Lawrence. *Every day; rainier-square.com; map:K6*

Westlake Center

400 PINE ST, DOWNTOWN; 206/467-1600 Westlake offers the full range of top-of-the-line retailers, from the arty (Fireworks) to the aromatic (Aveda) and some that you won't find elsewhere in Seattle, like Jessica McClintock, Talbot's, and April Cornell. An upper-level food court has more than 18 eateries. Boasting the city's largest lighted Christmas tree, complete with Santa pictures, Westlake draws crowds during the holidays. *Every day; info@westlakecenter.com; west lakecenter.com; map:I6*

HISTORIC DISTRICTS

PIONEER SQUARE (between 1st and 2nd Aves, from Yesler Wy to S King St, Downtown; map:N8) is where Seattle shopping really got its start in 1852 and today it's chock full of a appealing shops, art galleries, cafes, and bars. **PIKE PLACE MARKET** (between Western and 1st Aves and Pike and Virginia Sts, Downtown; open every day; map:J8–I8), founded in 1907, is a local favorite for its quality produce and flowers. The most unusual spot for shopping in town, because they won't allow stores that aren't one-of-a-kind, its arcades are packed with vintage apparel, antiques, arts, and crafts. An upscale overspill of shops stretches from the South Arcade (1st Ave between Pike and Union Sts, Downtown; map:J8) southward down First Avenue. Another egress from the market is via retail wedged along the **PIKE MARKET HILLCLIMB** (Pike St to Pier 59, Downtown; map:J8) toward the waterfront, where during the summer tourists swarm the colorful collection of emporiums. (Also see Top 25 Attractions in the Exploring chapter.)

NEIGHBORHOODS

ALONG THE AVE (University Wy NE from NE 41st St to NE 50th St, University District; map:FF6), a stretch of road in the **UNIVERSITY DISTRICT** neighborhood a block from the University of Washington campus, you'll find a typical university mix of stores, including chain and independent coffee, tea, book, and music shops, alternative boutiques, and ethnic restaurants. The distinctive student/bohemian flavor was being eclipsed by panhandlers and chain stores, but recent revitalization efforts are attempting to reclaim the lively neighborhood as it slowly spreads north. East down the 45th Street viaduct from the UW campus is the casually upscale **UNIVERSITY VILLAGE** (NE 45th St and 25th Ave NE).

Just west from the Ave, the family-friendly **ROOSEVELT** area (Roosevelt Wy NE from NE 55th St to NE 70th St; map:EE6) has a mix of kids' specialty foods, video, and book stores. **WALLINGFORD** (45th St from Stone Wy N to Latona Ave NE; map:FF7) combines funky gift and retail shops (like an erotic bakery) with **WALLINGFORD CENTER** (1815 N 45th St)—an old school building converted to house about a dozen shops focusing on home decor, children's books, toys, and fashion for moms and babes.

CAPITOL HILL is the city's apex of the alternative, with lots of piercings, tattoos, and a large gay community, making for a memorable shopping experience. The three most concentrated areas for eclectic clothing (especially vintage), eateries, and home stores are **BROADWAY AVENUE** (E Pine St to E Roy St; map:GG6), **E PIKE AND PINE STREETS** (between Melrose Ave to Broadway Ave E; map:J2), and **15TH AVENUE E** (Madison St to Yesler Wy; map:HH6). South of here, E Madison Street intersects 15th Avenue E on its way from downtown to **MADISON PARK** (along E Madison St from McGilvra Blvd E to 43rd Ave E; map:GG6). If you wander off its main drag, you'll see homes typically picked to star in movies shot in Seattle; the shopping in this lakeside neighborhood, with stores dedicated to home design, gift items, and high-end fashion, reflects that mix of Americana domesticity and Hollywood glam. Closer to downtown is the browsable retail of **MADISON VALLEY** (along E Madison St from 23rd Ave to 32nd Ave E; map:GG6).

BEST PLACE FOR SEAFOOD?

"Oceanaire—the food, the service—it doesn't
get better than this."

Kathy Casey, chef and culinary diva

Challenging the Hill for the cool title is **BELLTOWN** (Western to 5th Ave, between Virginia St and Denny Wy, Downtown; map:G8–D8), full of blocks of trendy shops and see-and-be-seen dance clubs, billiard halls, restaurants, and bars—and, as with Pioneer Square and Capitol Hill, its share of panhandlers.

To the north is **QUEEN ANNE** (map:GG8), where up at the top of Queen Anne Hill you can see some of the best views of the city as you wander through a village-like community of good restaurants, shops, and grocery stores. Down the northern slope of Queen Anne Hill and over the ship canal lies **FREMONT** (Fremont Ave N and N 34th St; map:FF7), or the "Republic of Fremont" or the "Center of the Universe" as residents affectionately labeled it for its funky boutiques, kitsch stores, and some of the city's better pubs. To the dismay of many, it has also attracted a lot of growth, most recently on the corner of N 34th Street and Fremont Ave N, where new condos, retail, and restaurants are creating a stir. West of Fremont is **BALLARD** (map:EE8), famous for its Scandinavian and senior community, whose Ballard Avenue, south of Market Street, has morphed into quite the fashionable shopping row. Home to popular pubs and restaurants that rock with local bands, old Ballard is not completely a thing of the past. Stores like Scandinavian Specialties and Larsen's bakery are still around—ya sure, you betcha.

SUBURBAN STOPS

Alderwood Mall

OFF I-5 AT ALDERWOOD MALL EXIT, LYNNWOOD; 425/771-1211 A recent renovation has turned this once substandard suburban mall into competition for newer malls outside the city. Improvements include a parking garage with a sky bridge leading to a new Nordstrom, a collection of new restaurants, and an open-air courtyard. *Every day; alderwoodadmin@generalgrowth.com; alderwoodmall.com; map:7AA*

Bellevue Place

10500 NE 8TH ST, BELLEVUE; 425/453-5634 Just down the street from its fellow Kemper Freeman–designed mall, Bellevue Square, Bellevue Place boasts 20 high-end shops and a number of excellent restaurants, some of which occupy the dramatic glass-walled Wintergarden atrium. *Mon–Sat; map:HH3*

Bellevue Square

NE 8TH ST AND BELLEVUE WY NE, BELLEVUE; 425/454-2431 Still Eastside's brightest shopping beacon, Bellevue Square is constantly adding new attractions for all ages to keep the cars streaming into its mammoth parking garage. Beyond the Big Three department stores (Nordstrom, Bon-Macy's, and J. C. Penney), is an ever-expanding coterie of high-quality shops ranging from Crate & Barrel to Pottery Barn (and Pottery Barn Kids). *Every day; information@ bellevuesquare.com; bellevuesquare.com; map:HH3*

Crossroads Shopping Center

NE 8TH ST AND 156TH AVE NE, BELLEVUE; 425/644-1111 With its concentration of such stores as Party City, Circuit City, and Old Navy, 23 restaurants, a 12-screen cinema, a communal giant chessboard, and live music, Crossroads Shopping Center is aptly known as "the Eastside's living room." *Every day; cross roadsbellevue.com; map:HH1*

Factoria Mall

4055 FACTORIA MALL SE, BELLEVUE; 425/641-8282 Just off exit 10 of Interstate 405 is this suburban mall with all of the stores you'd expect—Gottschalks, Mervyns California, Target, plus the Eastside's only Nordstrom Rack. No surprises here, but with the remodel of Alderwood Mall, this old-stand-by sort of mall may soon be a rarity among the trend of high-end "villages." *Every day; factoriamall.com; map:II3*

IKEA

600 SW 43RD ST, RENTON; 425/656-2980 The arrival of this Swedish-owned warehouse-style store a decade ago gave Seattleites reason to venture south. IKEA's room-by-room showrooms are filled with furniture, art, and accessories that you can purchase in pieces, which allows for the lowest prices around. Perfect for the college-bound, newly married, or budget-conscious shopper. *Every day; ikea.com; map:II3*

Kirkland Parkplace

EXIT 18 OFF I-405, CORNER OF 6TH AVE AND CENTRAL WY, KIRKLAND; 425/827-7789 Parkplace fills a community village function with its convenient services and shops including Parkplace Book Company, Ceramic Gallery, a florist, shoe repair shop, and pharmacy. It is home to Kirkland Cinema 6— where Monday mornings are for first-run films for parents with babes and small children—as well as a tasty range of dining options, including the new Purple Cafe and Wine Bar. *Every day; www.kirklandparkplace.com; map:EE3*

Northgate Mall

N NORTHGATE WY AND 1ST AVE NE, NORTHGATE; 206/362-4777 This is a no-frills shopping experience, but it had the distinction (or shame, depending on your opinion of malls) of being the first mall in the nation when it opened in 1950. Northgate (off I-5 at the Northgate exit) has the full complement of stores, including Nordstrom and Bon-Macy's, as well as an excellent food court and newsstand. Right across the street is a Target and a Best Buy. *Every day; simon.com; map:DD7*

Redmond Town Center

16495 NE 74TH ST, REDMOND; 425/867-0808 The newest mall in the area, Redmond Town Center (off Hwy 520 at W Lake Sammamish Pkwy) caters to Eastsiders who don't want to stray far from Microsoft. The open-air mixed-use mall has an array of retail—Abercrombie & Fitch, The Gap, Victoria's Secret—and now an REI and Bon-Macy's. The mall becomes an entertaining nighttime destination as well, flanked by restaurants such as Smoke Jumpers and an eight-screen movie complex. *Every day; www.shopredmondtowncenter.com; map:FF1*

SeaTac Mall

1928 S 320TH ST, FEDERAL WAY; 253/839-6150 Known mostly for its convenience from Interstate 5 and the airport and for staple stores such as Sears and Bon-Macy's, the sale of the mall in 2003, and the naming of a "redevelopment team," promises a face- and attitude-lift soon. *Every day; seatacmall.com; map:II3*

SuperMall of the Great Northwest

1101 SUPERMALL WY, AUBURN; 253/833-9500 This supersize mall encompasses discount outlet stores you won't find anywhere else in the state—Banana Republic and Ann Taylor to name a couple biggies—and anchor stores such as Marshall's and Bed, Bath and Beyond. Seventeen eateries will fuel your trek. Mall walker's start your engines. *Every day; seea@glimcher.com; supermall.com; map:PP2*

University Village

♦ **NE 45TH ST AND 25TH AVE NE, UNIVERSITY DISTRICT; 206/523-0622** This open-air mall has become one of the hottest shopping spots in Seattle. A new north-end quadrant includes a parking garage to alleviate the maddening weekend circling, and a two-level Crate & Barrel, along with a Storables and the baby clothing chain The Land of Nod. Perennial faves such as Restoration Hardware, Pottery Barn, and Ravenna Gardens have been joined by a new Smith & Hawken gardening store, which moved into the old Molbak's space in 2003. There are also more than 17 restaurants—from Atlas Foods to Zao Noodle Bar. *Every day; uvillage.com; map:FF6*

Shops from A to Z

ANTIQUES/VINTAGE/RETRO

Antique Liquidators

503 WESTLAKE AVE N, SOUTH LAKE UNION; 206/623-2740 What Antique Liquidators lacks in ambience, it makes up for in sheer volume. The largest antique store in town, its 22,000 square feet of sales and storage space house a slew of practical furnishings (mostly Danish and English; lots of chairs and drop-leaf tables). Endless variety and good prices, but don't expect perfect quality. *Every day; antiqueliquidators.com; map:D2*

Antiques at Pike Place

92 STEWART ST; DOWNTOWN; 206/441-9643 The beauty of an antique store like this one (which is somewhat rare) is that it's not musty or cluttered with junk, but is actually an enjoyable shopping experience. Sure, there are knickknacks, but they are kept clean and behind a case for the most part. The store is large and fun to roam while hunting vintage linens, jewelry, lamps, rare accent furniture, and a whole room filled with aprons. *Every day; map:I7*

Area 51

401 E PINE ST, CAPITOL HILL; 206/568-4782 Area 51 sells functional, modern pieces, perfect for a city apartment with a trendy but not overdone look. The shop's futuristic five-piece bar sets, retro '50s dining sets, and wheeled low-to-the-ground beds and minipod speakers have a futuristic *Jetsons* flair. The polka-dot bed linens and '70s prints are a relatively new addition to the store's eclectic mix. *Every day; map:J2*

City Chic Antiques

709 BROADWAY AVE E, CAPITOL HILL; 206/323-9911 Shabby-chic pieces at not-too-shabby prices make this shop a real gem. You'll find a mix of small gifts, from soaps to frames, Bella Notté baby blankets, a kitchen section with retro cloths and quilts, dishes, and dish racks. The antique end tables and bed frames may trigger nostalgia. *Tues–Sat; map:HH6*

The Crane Gallery

104 W ROY ST, QUEEN ANNE; 206/298-9425 Spare and uncluttered, the Crane's selection speaks to its reputation as a purveyor of fine Asian antiques and artifacts. Paintings, ceramics, bronzes, ivory, jade, prints, netsuke, and furniture from the Orient are museum quality—and priced accordingly. *Tues–Sat; map:GG7*

David Weatherford Antiques & Interiors

133 14TH AVE E, CAPITOL HILL; 206/329-6533 / 1200 2ND AVE, DOWNTOWN; 206/624-3514 This antiques seller doesn't muck about with reproductions. Housed in a Capitol Hill mansion, David Weatherford sells exquisite 18th-century English and French furniture, as well as Oriental rugs, porcelain, screens, and art glass. A resident design team advises clients on integrating antiques with their present furnishings. The downtown location specializes in commercial collections. *Mon–Sat; drw@davidweatherford.com; davidweatherford.com; map:HH6, L7*

Deluxe Junk

3518 FREMONT PL N, FREMONT; 206/634-2733 Fifties music from the speakers sets the mood for browsing vintage men's and women's clothes, shoes, accessories, furniture, and a clutter of appealing knickknacks—hence the name. *Wed, Fri–Sun; deluxejunk@comcast.net; map:FF7*

Fritzi Ritz

750 N 34TH ST, FREMONT; 206/633-0929 Under the Aurora bridge sits a new locale for this veteran of the vintage clothing scene. Price ranges and specials are smartly advertised in clear sight, such as "neck ties five for $1." Be warned, they don't keep early hours. *Fri–Tues; map:FF7*

Greg Davidson Antique Lighting

1020 1ST AVE, DOWNTOWN; 206/625-0406 Greg Davidson's shop glows with excellently restored relics from the days when Thomas Edison lit his first bulb. The cavernous shop stocks mostly American vintage lighting elements and a few pieces of period furniture. *Tues–Sat; map:L8*

Honeychurch Antiques

1008 JAMES ST, FIRST HILL; 206/622-1225 When out-of-towners go looking for superior Asian antiques, the Seattle Art Museum has been known to send them to Laurie and John Fairman's renowned shop—and not simply because Honeychurch stocks a few museum-quality pieces. The Fairmans' scholarly knowledge of their high-quality wares is paralleled only by their approachability. John's parents opened the original Honeychurch in Hong Kong more than 40 years ago, and he's been doing business in Seattle for more than 25 years. The store's attraction lies in its tasteful blend of Asian fine art, folk art, and furniture, which spans the Neolithic period to the Han Dynasty (206 BC) to early-20th-century basketry. The shop puts on occasional wares shows. *Tues–Sat; info@honeychurch.com; honeychurch.com; map:O3*

Isadora's Antique Clothing

1915 1ST AVE, DOWNTOWN; 206/441-7711 Impeccable antique clothing is the rule here. Custom-made in-house wedding gowns, as well as designs by Vera Wang and others, hang in the back among antique Battenburg lace tops, white mink coats, and vintage tuxedos. An estate jewelry case displays collections from Georgian to retro and art nouveau to moderne. *Every day; isadoras@earthlink.net; isadoras.com; map:I7*

Jean Williams Antiques

115 S JACKSON ST, PIONEER SQUARE; 206/622-1110 Family-owned and run for 32 years, Jean Williams is one of the more established places in Seattle to find, restore, or sell serious antiques. They even produce a handmade-to-order drop-leaf walnut dining set that seats 12 to 14. Most furniture is in heavy wood in superb condition—

a smart place to look for French-country farmhouse tables and armchairs. *Mon–Sat; jwantique@msn.com; jeanwilliamsantiques.com; map:O9*

Le Frock

317 E PINE ST, CAPITOL HILL; 206/623-5339 Even nonvintage shoppers love this store. The designer brands and popular styles of T-shirts, shoes, dresses, pants, and purses are worth the search through the racks. We're talking pre-owned Ann Taylor, Prada, Betsey Johnson, Coach, Laura Ashley, and Anne Klein. *Every day; lefrockonline.com; map:K2*

Les Piafs

600 PINE ST, PACIFIC PLACE, DOWNTOWN; 206/956-8366 Formerly in Belltown, this Frenchified shop carries antique furniture from the 1800s, including an array of American farmhouse pieces as well as some new pieces. Be sure to check out their custom-designed lampshades and pillows. Their vintage and couture bulk fabric, linens, and soft cotton loungewear line are also hard to resist. *Every day; map:J5*

Pelayo Antiques

7601 GREENWOOD AVE N, GREENWOOD; 206/789-1999 Pedro Pelayo has been stocking his expansive Greenwood store with imports of fine quality and unrivaled beauty since 1973. You'll find aisles of Euro antique furniture and decorating pieces as well as country-pine furniture. The shop also has a large selection of paintings, sculptures, and Russian religious icons. *Every day; inquiries@pelayoantiques.com; pelayoantiques.com; map:EE8*

Private Screening

3504 FREMONT PL N, FREMONT; 206/548-0751 / 1530 MELROSE AVE, CAPITOL HILL; 206/839.0759 If you can't drive past a garage or estate sale, this is the place for you. Besides a diverting classic games section—dominos to dice games—they have apparel from every decade. *Every day; map:FF7, K2*

Rhinestone Rosie

606 W CROCKETT ST, QUEEN ANNE; 206/283-4605 Those who know their faux jewels turn to Rhinestone Rosie (Rosie Sayyah). Rosie rents, buys, sells, and repairs an inventory of thousands of estate and costume jewelry treasures, and hers is the only store on the West Coast with a rhinestone repair service; she will search her rhinestone vaults to find replacement stones, convert clip earrings to pierced, or lengthen necklaces and bracelets. She's also an *Antiques Roadshow* appraiser. *Tues–Sat; rhinestonerosie@yahoo.com; map:GG8*

The Spunky Punker

1211 PINE ST, CAPITOL HILL; 206/652-0444 Spunky Punker's racks of mainly women's fashion are a mix of vintage (by various designers) and new designs, the majority of which were started from scratch by the owner, Kristin Lee. A disco ball turning on the ceiling conjures up visions of middle-school dances, if the bangle bracelets and little cotton sundresses didn't already. And the best part is, the prices are low. *Every day; map:HH6*

Stuteville Antiques

1518 E OLIVE WY, CAPITOL HILL; 206/329-5666 There is nothing chintzy in this two-level collection of antique furniture and accessories. Stuteville Antiques handle mostly things from before the 1850s, with the exception of their lamps for obvious reasons. The restoration studio in the basement is a major part of their business and they do appraisals and estate sales as well. *Tues–Sat and by appointment; map:HH6*

Two Angels Antiques and Interiors

1527 WESTERN AVE, DOWNTOWN; 206/340-6005 The store is so tiny, you may wonder where all the antiques are, but there is a 4,000-square-foot warehouse just five minutes away that stores the majority of Two Angels's continental-, French-, and Italian-bought pieces—releasing items for showcasing in the shop one tantalizing piece at a time. Two Angels has been in this spot since 1998, but the home-design business is only two years old. *Mon–Fri; twoangels@nwlink.com; map:J8*

Unique Finds

1950 1ST AVE S; SODO; 206/923-0160 In this recently transported West Seattle shop offerings can range from classy pounded-silver serving pieces and 1950s vintage kitchen pieces to an old *Little House on the Prairie*-style iron bed and ornate wooden furniture. *Every day; map:II7*

Very Cherry

1314 N 45TH ST, WALLINGFORD; 206/632-8100 Most of the blast-from-the-past pieces here—cotton apron dresses and terry-cloth bathing suit covers from the '50s and '60s—are true vintage. Also fun to check out are the purses, plastic dishes, and sunglasses. *Every day; map:FF7*

Vintage Chick

303 E PINE ST, CAPITOL HILL; 206/625-9800 Unlike many stores on the Hill, which mix vintage with new, this store phased out its selection of new apparel to carry only reproductions. Here you will find fashion trends from the '20s to the '70s. Be sure to browse the under $10 rack. *Tues–Sat; chickie@vintagechick.com; vintagechick.com; map:HH6*

Window on the Past

322 OCCIDENTAL AVE S, DOWNTOWN; 206/622-1846 Around the corner from sister store Jean Williams Antiques is this shop of inspiring custom-order antique reproductions—choose your own wood, style, and dimensions to fit your needs. *Every day; windowonthepast.com; map:O8*

APPAREL

Alhambra

101 PINE ST, DOWNTOWN; 206/621-9571 Alhambra's urban style ranges from out-there mesh pants and skirts to slinky leather high-wedge shoes and sexy evening dresses. Their clothes and jewelry come from all over the world. There's also a warehouse open to the public in the University District (4600 NE Union Bay

Pl #C; 206/522-4570). *Every day; alhambra@alhambranet.com; alhambranet.com; map:I6*

Baby & Co.

1936 1ST AVE, DOWNTOWN; 206/448-4077 Don't let the name fool you, this store has nothing to do with babies, except that it's the owner's first name. When this French couture clothing store opened on First Avenue 27 years ago, it was on the edge of town, but it's been here long enough that now it's in the middle. It is known by its loyal clientele (that grows with each new referral from downtown concierges in-the-know) for having European designs for the well-traveled, fashion-conscious consumer. *Every day; map:H8*

Barneys New York

1420 5TH AVE, CITY CENTRE, DOWNTOWN; 206/622-6300 Seattle is fortunate to have had one of the few West Coast Barneys locations for years. This two-level City Centre attraction is known for some of the best men's and women's suits you can find by Prada, Dries Van Noten, Armani, Paul Smith, Jil Sander, and Martin Magella, to name a few. Barneys also has designer casual lines, including a huge selection of denims and an impressive shoe and cosmetic section. *Every day; seattle@ barneys.com; barneys.com; map:J5*

BCBG Max Azria

600 PINE ST, DOWNTOWN; 206/447-3400 / BELLEVUE SQUARE, BELLEVUE; 425/454-7691 Parisian designer Max Azria fills his stores with what looks like stock from a couture house, but which retails at less stratospheric prices. Women who can't swing haute couture price tags, but don't bat an expertly coiffed eyelash at $128 pants, are in their element among the suits, semiformal dresses, and backless sequin tops. Shoe fetishists find ample distraction among the 4-inch heels and funky flats. *Every day; map:J5, HH3*

Betsey Johnson

1429 5TH AVE, DOWNTOWN; 206/624-2887 Betsey Johnson evidently revels in being a girl. Many of her shoes feature funky straps in floral, crochet, and glitter. The trademark baby-doll dresses are uberfeminine, though her newest line, Betseyville, is less dressy, with a focus on separates, heavier fabrics, and a lower price point. *Every day; betseyjohnson.com; map:J5*

Brooks Brothers

1335 5TH AVE, DOWNTOWN; 206/624-4400 / BELLEVUE SQUARE, BELLEVUE; 425/646-9688 Established in 1818, this elegant men's suit and casual clothing store (the Bellevue Square also has a women's department) is the longest standing of its kind. Their celebrity fan base has included Ralph Lauren, JFK, and Abraham Lincoln. Now that's longevity. Their trademark depth of inventory, fine special-order system, and gracious service is welcome, as are their two yearly sales (in June and after Christmas). *Every day; www.brooksbrothers.com; map:K6, HH3*

Butch Blum

1408 5TH AVE, DOWNTOWN; 206/622-5760 / UNIVERSITY VILLAGE, UNIVERSITY DISTRICT; 206/524-5860 Butch Blum sees wardrobes as investments and shies away from trendy fads in favor of classic men's and women's wear lines from venerated labels such as Giorgio Armani and Versace. The University Village store carries similar quality clothes sans the suits. *Mon–Sat (Downtown), every day (University Village); info@butchblum.com; butchblum.com; map:FF6, K6*

Damsel

2222 2ND AVE, DOWNTOWN; 206/374-8669 Selected as the best new store by *Seattle Magazine* readers in 2003, Damsel is the only retailer in town to sell exclusively independent handmade and designed creations. Techie owners Cathy Edens and Cristina Meyer stock an eclectic collection of everything from bathing suits, bags, soaps, and pillows to artwork (see the Sewn in Seattle sidebar). *Every day; damselcollective.com; map:HH7, I7*

David Lawrence

1318 4TH AVE, DOWNTOWN; 206/622-2544 / BELLEVUE SQUARE, BELLEVUE; 425/688-1699 Both stores of David Lawrence stock brands with heavy runway presence, such as Dolce & Gabbana, Hugo Boss, and Donna Karan. The *GQ* set will find togs, from Versace tuxes to tattered D&G jeans, for looking smashing at any occasion. Smaller dimensions and approachable staff make shopping here a less intimidating experience than at some comparable retailers. *Every day; davidlawrence.com; map:K6, HH3*

Enexile

611 N 35TH ST, FREMONT; 206/633-5771 It took a few years for the word to spread about this funky-yet-chic Fremont clothing shop, but now it's on most savvy shoppers' radar. Enexile's more "bad girl" than "girly girl" women's garments and accessories are studded, patched, laced, and ribboned. The shop carries some vintage garb and some duds for guys; its in-house label, "dogma," is feminine but racy with a hint of '80s punk. Enexile also will update customers' favorite old denim and army gear. *Every day; map:FF8*

Fini

86 PINE ST, DOWNTOWN; 206/443-0563 Fini is definitely "the end" when it comes to accessories. You'll find such goodies as miniclock cuff links that actually tell time, lightweight woven hats, mesh handbags, embroidered lingerie bags, calf-skin sunglass cases, and handmade greeting cards. The hottest item (thanks to celeb owners pictured with them in magazines) are the special-order monogrammed JAM leather-and-woven handbags. *Every day; map:I7*

Ian

1907 2ND AVE, DOWNTOWN; 206/441-4055 / 401 E PINE ST, CAPITOL HILL; 206/322-7380 Twentysomethings (and ageless funky types) who dig the retro-urban look will love this store populated with such labels as Ella Moss, paper denim & cloth, Stüssy, Fred Perry, and Blue Cult. The store, opened in 2003, also has fresh

SEWN IN SEATTLE

Seattle may not be first on the high-fashion-city list (or even second), but we definitely beat the competition when it comes to resourceful and recycled fashion statements.

The versatile Glam Garb from Swedish-born designer Gunlis Alainentalo, available at **DAMSEL** (2222 2nd Ave, Ste 100, Downtown; 206/374.8669), include hand-dyed vintage slips and lingerie in styles from the '30s to the '50s that can be worn as under- or outerwear. Designer Suzanne Jaberg, otherwise known as "Suzabelle," tweaks worn dresses into one-of-a-kind vintage revamps that occupy racks at **HELLO GORGEOUS** (411 E Pine St, Capitol Hill; 206/621-0702) and **LE FROCK** (317 E Pine St, Capitol Hill; 206/623-5339). "Indie" community artist Jamie Stratton has developed Agent X (agent Xclothing.com), a line focusing on refurbished vintage accessories—leather cuffs, makeup bags, and belts. Her pieces, along with April Goettle's vintage creations called **SATANGIRL** (satangirl.com), can be picked through at Damsel. In his new Capitol Hill store **VU** (313 E Pine St; 206/621-0388), owner Huan Vu reincarnates designs from past eras with inventive detailing that can turn a basic shirt or dress into an entirely modern creation.

Beyond our passion for recycling, Seattleites know how to bring a sense of style to the daily grind. Bike-messenger-turned-designer Victoria Howe (victoria@houseof bunnytron.com) has come out with vibrantly colored vinyl messenger bags inspired by her work on wheels. She uses a seat-belt material for the straps for her bags labeled Deer Whistle (read more about them at houseofbunnytron.com). Find them in Damsel, along with work by other local bag-making talents, such as Sarah Jane (sjaney77@yahoo.com) and Bags by Libby.

—*Kate Fulcher*

takes on classics such as men's button-down shirts. Look for the newly opened men's-only shop on Capitol Hill. *Every day; ianshop.com; map:J7*

Jeri Rice

421 UNIVERSITY ST, DOWNTOWN; 206/624-4000 Jeri Rice exudes exclusivity . . . but in a good way. It's a Seattle original, located off the lobby of the chic Fairmont Olympic Hotel, and carries clothes and accessories in the finest fabrics and leathers and by the best designers (with prices to match). In addition to European cashmere and suiting, American designer jeans and casuals, accessories, and shoes, its signature is an amazing collection of evening gowns. *Every day; jeririce.com; map:K6*

La Femme

1622 QUEEN ANNE AVE N, QUEEN ANNE; 206/285-2443 La Femme's young designer fashions, which range from relaxed office-worker wear to weekend sophisticate, are tantalizingly dispersed throughout the openly spaced store. An extensive selection of lacy, pretty-colored lingerie has its own section in back; accessories are delicately revealed on white French tables. Ooh-la-la. *Tues–Sun; map:GG8*

Les Amis

3420 EVANSTON AVE N, FREMONT; 206/632-2877 Les Amis is the boutique for those with celebrity fashion sense—and a celeb budget. The clothing lines you'll find here are not represented elsewhere in the Seattle area—hand-spun and hand-woven dresses, cute little lacey numbers, and lingerie. *Every day; lesamis-inc.com; map:FF8*

Lipstick Traces

500 E PINE ST, CAPITOL HILL; 206/329-2813 A remodel of this fun little shop for girls left it more with a focus on clothes and accessories than its previous "lifestyle" theme that included knickknacks and magazines. This Capitol Hill shop not only supports small indie designers by selling their goods, but also holds a show for visual artists once a month. *Every day; jenn@lipsticktraces.net; lipsticktraces.net; map:J2*

Mario's of Seattle

1513 6TH AVE, DOWNTOWN; 206/223-1461 When you walk into Mario's, you know you are among the height of men's and women's fashion—and prices. The European interior, with white pillars and iron staircase, is fitting for the labels it hangs—Boss, Zegnas, Loro Piana, Jil Sander, Prada, and Yves Saint Laurent, not to mention Mario's own label. The store carries luggage, suiting, and shoes, as well as casual, evening, and outer wear. *Every day; jeffray@marios.com; www.marios.com; map:J5*

The Powder Room

101 STEWART ST, STE 101, DOWNTOWN; 206/374-0060 For styles so current you're not likely to ever find them in a mall store, prices are shockingly low. Living up to the shop's name, femininity is paramount in the cuts of the late teen to twentysomething numbers. *Every day; map:I7*

Reputation

1622-B N 45TH, WALLINGFORD; 206/632-4999 This welcome addition to the Wallingford boutique scene is sure to be a favorite among young women (or young at heart) and budget-conscious trendsetters. Featuring mostly new clothing and accessory designs from all over, Reputation also brings in local designers to create on consignment. Once a month, the owner hosts a "deconstruction" party, where a designer updates old T-shirts by any means necessary. *Every day; shop-reputation.com; map:FF7*

Sway & Cake

1631 6TH AVE, DOWNTOWN; 206/624-2699 The pinkness of this store is somewhat overwhelming, but at least you can tell the marketing niche from a block away: girls! Styles range from little cotton tees to spaghetti-strapped silk dresses and funky, urbanite shoes. *Every day; map:I5*

Totally Michael's

521 UNION ST, DOWNTOWN; 206/622-4920 The look of the clothes at Totally Michael's is not totally modern, but their classic lines are timeless. It's not surprising that a good portion of the store's loyal client base of professional women is comprised of attorneys and judges looking for clothes with conviction. The shop also carries a number of rotating casual lines, as well as Cambio, Babette, and Peter Nygard. *Mon–Sat; map:K5*

Urban Outfitters

1507 5TH AVE, DOWNTOWN; 206/381-3777 / 401 BROADWAY AVE E, BROADWAY MARKET, CAPITOL HILL; 206/322-1800 So-called Generation X has in Urban Outfitters a store that it can relate to and that most parents will never understand. Intentionally dirtied, slashed, and frayed clothes often find their way to the racks here; home accessories and gifts are equally antiestablishment. For scandalously low prices, check out the upstairs racks at the Broadway store, which consolidates clearance items across the West Coast. *Every day; urbanoutfitters.com; map:J5, GG6*

BEST PLACE TO BUY A CD?
"Easy Street Records."
Sue Bird, Seattle Storm

Yazdi
Yazdi II

1815 N 45TH ST, #203 AND #204, WALLINGFORD; 206/547-6008 (AND BRANCHES) Bold batik dresses and pants and shirts that let you move are a staple here. The wide range of sizes helped to create a devoted female customer base that made new branches boom. Additional locations are in the Broadway Market (401 Broadway Ave E, Capitol Hill; 206/860-7109; map:HH7) and downstairs at the Pike Place Market (206/682-0657; map:J8). *Every day; map:FF7*

Zebraclub

1901 1ST AVE, DOWNTOWN; 206/448-7452 / 423 BROADWAY AVE E, BROADWAY MARKET, CAPITOL HILL; 206/325-2452 This urban-wear store is most popular among city men and women in their 20s, although some middle-aged shoppers are hip enough to pull the look off. The clothes are comfortable and sturdy enough for teenagers, with brands such as Paul Frank, Adidas, Puma, Mecca, and Alpha Numeric. Zebraclub also carries Italian brands, including cotton/elastane T-shirts by Fornarina. *Every day; zebraclub.com; map:I7, HH6*

BODY CARE

Dandelion Botanical Company

708 N 34TH ST, FREMONT; 206/545-8892 OR 877/778-4869 The low lighting and soothing music in this natural health shop might make you feel healed just by walking through the door. For seven years, Dandelion's has been offering classes and books on everything from herbalism to the healing power of animals. Aromatic handmade soaps come in scents such as chocomint. *Every day; marykachi@ dandelionbotanical.com; dandelionbotanical.com; map:FF7*

Essenza

615 N 35TH ST, FREMONT; 206/547-4895 For beauty lovers with means, this is heaven. The makeup, lotion, and perfume laid out like paint on a palette are impossible to resist. T. LeClere—a popular lotion in France—is Essenza'a pride, as is the line of all-natural body and hair products called Fresh. *Every day (summer), Tues–Sun (winter); essenzainc.com; map:FF7*

The Herbalist

♱ **2106 NE 65TH ST, RAVENNA; 206/523-2600** Even in Seattle, the depth of this natural remedy and health store is one difficult to match. You can research an ailment or methodology by browsing their books, which cover topics from destiny cards to natural pregnancy, or find most any kind of organic or wildcrafted herb, homeopathic flower essence, or custom herbal tincture. The "herbal tonic bar" supplies good-for-you beverages. *Every day; theherbalist@theherbalist.com; theherbalist.com; map:FF6*

L'Occitane

600 PINE ST, PACIFIC PLACE, DOWNTOWN; 206/903-6693 / UNIVERSITY VILLAGE, UNIVERSITY DISTRICT; 206/529-0801 The Provence-made Shea-Butter lotions, candles, soaps, room sprays, and iron water, also found in the rooms of the Fairmont Hotels worldwide, are the stars of this shop—as are the occasional bunches of lavender imported from France. *Every day; www.loccitane.com; map:I5, HH7*

Olivine Atelier

5344 BALLARD AVE NW, BALLARD; 206/706-4188 Most brands of Provençal lotions, soaps, and sprays that you can imagine, as well as fine French linens for the bathroom, are tastefully displayed on shabby-chic tables. *Every day; map:EE8*

Parfumerie Elizabeth George

1424 4TH AVE, DOWNTOWN; 206/622-7212 It can be hard to find this exclusive store inside a downtown office building (between the Red Lion Hotel and a walking-shoes store), but considering it's open by appointment only, foot traffic isn't really an issue. Instead, clients are drawn to the shop's reputation for specializing in custom and hard-to-find fragrances, as well as to its line of designer-matched scents (less expensive than the originals) and its appealing atomizers and bath products. *By appointment; map:J6*

Parfumerie Nasreen

1005 1ST AVE, DOWNTOWN; 206/682-3459 OR 888/286-1825 If you haven't been fortunate enough to stay at the Alexis Hotel, then most likely you haven't seen this tiny parfumerie just inside. Small in size, it's large enough to hold 780 fragrances, including imports from all over Europe. The crowded stacks of small boxes make maneuvering difficult, but the staff are happy to assist. *Mon–Sat; contact@ parfumerienasreen.com; parfumerienasreen.com; map:L8*

Tenzing Momo

93 PIKE ST, PIKE PLACE MARKET; 206/623-9837 This herbal apothecary and parfumerie has been on the same block for the past 30 years. In fact, it's the oldest medicinal herbal apothecary on the West Coast. There is a lot of energy flowing in this small shop filled with exotic Tibetan incense, tinctures, massage oils, books, and above all herbs. Ingredients and products are resourced locally if possible, but otherwise hail from Nepal, India, or Tibet. *Every day; map:J8*

BOOKS AND PERIODICALS

All for Kids Books and Music

2900 NE BLAKELEY ST, STE C, RAVENNA; 206/526-2768 From the *Green Eggs and Ham* years through young-adult novels, there's enough literature here to keep a growing mind occupied. The store stocks plenty of kits, tapes, and activities as well. There's a weekly story hour on Tuesdays during the school year and plenty of author events. *Every day; allforkidsbooks.com; map:FF6*

Bailey/Coy Books

414 BROADWAY AVE E, CAPITOL HILL; 206/323-8842 This friendly book shop is geared to the diverse expectations of its neighborhood. There are profound greeting cards, journals, and paper gifts up front, and the rest of the store is devoted to a reading rainbow of books, from lesbian and gay studies to poetry and philosophy. *Every day; map:GG7*

Barnes & Noble

UNIVERSITY VILLAGE, UNIVERSITY DISTRICT; 206/517-4107 (AND BRANCHES) It's been the scourge of independent booksellers around town, and the staff is generally not a fount of literary acumen, but Barnes & Noble's reliably huge selection garners plenty of customers. The colossal University Village store has the area's best selection. Eight branches in the Seattle area include one in Pacific Place. *Every day; bn.com; map:FF6*

Beyond the Closet Bookstore

518 E PIKE ST, CAPITOL HILL; 206/322-4609 This gay-and-lesbian-focused bookstore abounds with selections on the homosexual experience and political struggle that general bookstores simply can't touch. But it's not all serious—there are also coming-of-age and romance novels with gay protagonists, magazines, comic books, magnets, and a huge collection of postcards. The store also carries travel guides, children's books, and Gay Pride banners and flags. *Every day; admin@beyondthe closet.com; beyondthecloset.com; map:K1*

Borders Books & Music

1501 4TH AVE, DOWNTOWN (AND BRANCHES); 206/622-4599 The general collection here is respectable, but it's the broad selection of CDs that sets Borders apart from the competition. Regular events and signings, a varied Northwest section, and a small cafe give it local credibility. Branches are in Redmond, Bellevue, and Tukwila. *Every day; borders.com; map:J6*

Broadway News
Fremont News

204 BROADWAY AVE E, CAPITOL HILL; 206/324-7323 / 3416 FREMONT AVE N, FREMONT; 206/633-0731 There are no frills to these indoor magazine stands, but they are well organized and well stocked with magazines and newspapers from around the globe. In addition, there are turning racks of eclectic greeting cards and small gifts. *Every day; map:GG7, FF7*

Bulldog News

4208 UNIVERSITY WY NE, UNIVERSITY DISTRICT; 206/632-6397 / 401 BROADWAY AVE E, BROADWAY MARKET, CAPITOL HILL; 206/322-6397 With one of the fiercest foreign-press selections in town, this venerable newsstand on the Ave has prevailed in the face of big-name bookstore encroachment. There's a magazine (or newspaper) for everyone here. Customers can sip espresso from the counter and surf the Web at Internet kiosks. *Every day; info@bulldognews.com; www.bulldognews.com; map:FF6, GG6*

Cinema Books

4753 ROOSEVELT WY NE, UNIVERSITY DISTRICT; 206/547-7667 Packed with new and used, rare, out-of-print and collectible books relating to movies, television, and theater, this movie-lover's paradise is aptly located downstairs from the cozy Seven Gables theater. You'll also find magazines, screenplays, posters, stills, and technical books for filmmakers. *Mon–Sat; cinemabooks.net; map:FF6*

David Ishii, Bookseller

212 1ST AVE S, PIONEER SQUARE; 206/622-4719 Peering through the window at David Ishii, Bookseller, you might think it was the studio apartment of a scholar, except for the many titles having to do with fly-fishing or baseball. Inside, tables have stacks up to 20 books high of used, out-of-print, and hard-to-find books on these and other subjects. *Every day; map:O8*

East West Bookshop of Seattle

6500 ROOSEVELT WY NE, ROOSEVELT; 206/523-3726 OR 800/587-6002 This store is a comprehensive blend of Eastern and Western religions, philosophies, and lifestyles. Where other bookstores may have one shelf dedicated to Eastern philosophy, this one breaks the subject area down into an amazing variety of categories. With flute music playing and wind chimes and other ornamental pieces for sale, it is a peaceful place to contemplate. *Every day; eastwestbookshop@qwest.net; eastwest bookshop.com; map:EE7*

Elliott Bay Book Company

101 S MAIN ST, PIONEER SQUARE; 206/624-6600 Don't be fooled by the size of this multistoried bookstore that's been on the same corner since 1973—inside is the heart of a charming small-town oasis. Old, rickety flooring, high ceilings, and wall-to-wall wood (not to mention the quiet atmosphere) make Elliott Bay a hazard for any book lover with a time constraint. The children's section has expanded to fill a large area of the store. Travel has its own room, filled with guidebooks, maps, atlases, volumes of travel essays, and foreign-language references, and the crime-fiction department offers one of the best selections in the city. Friendly and learned employees will field any question (be sure to check out staff recommendation postings) and will wrap and ship all your gift purchases. Readings and signings take place here on most evenings (also see the Literary section in the Arts chapter). A cafe downstairs invites nibbling while thumbing through new purchases. *Every day; queries@elliottbaybook.com; elliottbaybook.com; map:O8*

Fillipi Book & Record Shop

1351 E OLIVE WY, CAPITOL HILL; 206/682-4266 Fillipi's collection of rare general books, records of all sizes, and sheet music ranges from hard-to-find 78s and 45s (especially jazz records) to single sheets of music. The all-used inventory's prices tend to be higher than elsewhere in the city, but many an idle hour has been happily passed perusing the shelves here. *Tues–Sat; map:HH7*

First and Pike News

93 PIKE ST, PIKE PLACE MARKET; 206/624-0140 What better locale for a newsstand than on the corner of milling humanity that is Pike Street and First Avenue? And this one seems to have a magazine, newspaper, or book for each of those people. Like the sign says, just ask for a title if you don't see it. With some 1,600 publications—from *People* to *African Business*—it rivals the best stands of its kind in the world. *Every day; map:J8*

Flora & Fauna Books

121 1ST AVE S, PIONEER SQUARE; 206/623-4727 In this modest basement bookshop, you'll find more titles on nature than you can shake a stick at. Whether a gorgeously illustrated volume on gardening or birding or a practical field guide, you're bound to find a new, used, or rare book that will satisfy. *Mon–Sat; ffbooks@blarg.net; ffbooks.net; map:N8*

Fremont Place Book Company

621 N 35TH ST, FREMONT; 206/547-5970 The sign in the front window says it all: "Where is human nature so weak as in a bookstore?" This small but well-stocked shop doesn't hide its devotion to the written word (look for the classic poetry posted on beams), and the store benefits from its charming setting in an old building. *Every day; fremontbks@aol.com; map:FF8*

The Globe Books

5220 UNIVERSITY WY NE, UNIVERSITY DISTRICT; 206/527-2480 / 999 3RD AVE, DOWNTOWN; 206/682-6882 This unstuffy purveyor of new and used books specializes in the humanities (especially literature and reference books) and carries a growing section of natural-science books. Don't be intimidated by the specialized inventory; this is a wonderfully down-to-earth shop. Browse through the antique maps and replicas, too. Trades are welcome. The downtown store has an impressive selection of automotive books. *Thurs–Tues (closed every other Fri); globe@ zipcon.net; map:FF6, L7*

Half Price Books, Records, Magazines

4709 ROOSEVELT WY NE, UNIVERSITY DISTRICT (AND BRANCHES); 206/547-7859 Those who happen on Half Price rarely go back to regular retail. The store sells used and new books at, well, half price. The large selection of classical literature and huge line of discounted new and used software and coffee-table books galore make it a literary lover's nirvana. The store also buys used books daily. Branches are in Bellevue, Capitol Hill, Redmond, Tukwila, and Edmonds. *Every day; halfpricebooks.com; map:FF7*

Horizon Books

425 15TH AVE E, CAPITOL HILL (AND BRANCHES); 206/329-3586 Readers looking to wax philosophical should swing by Horizon Books, where Don Glover buys and sells used general books with an emphasis on literature, criticism, history, mystery, and philosophy. His second store (6512 Roosevelt Wy NE, Roosevelt/Ravenna; 206/523-4217; map:EE7) is well stocked and eminently browsable, and a third location is now open in Greenwood (8570 Greenwood Ave N; 206/781-4680; map:EE7). *Every day; map:GG6*

Island Books

3014 78TH AVE SE, MERCER ISLAND; 206/232-6920 OR 800/432-1640 Mercer Islanders rely on Island Books for a good general selection. Besides a fine assortment of children's books, nice touches for kids include a playhouse and story hours on Saturday throughout the year. Owner Roger Page has added a small but growing section of carefully chosen used books. Gift wrapping and domestic shipping are additional free services. *Mon–Sat; islandbooks@seanet.com; map:II4*

BEST PLACE TO SPEND $5?

"Emerald Downs, where five bucks on a long shot can buy a hundred bucks worth of thrills."

Tom Robbins, author

Kinokuniya Bookstore

525 S WELLER ST, CHINATOWN/INTERNATIONAL DISTRICT; 206/587-2477 In addition to a selection of Japanese books and magazines large enough to keep a Tokyo native endlessly occupied, this bookstore inside megagrocery Uwajimaya carries books in Chinese, English-language books relating to Asia, and a sizable selection of general books in English. Children's books, cookbooks, stationery, and Eastern medicine volumes also line the shelves. *Every day; map:Q7*

M Coy Books

117 PINE ST, DOWNTOWN; 206/623-5354 Ahh . . . the smell of books. This friendly, uncluttered, independent bookstore features most categories you might find at one of the book-selling giants, but it will only take you 10 minutes to browse the perimeter. Just try to make it to the back of the store for a cappuccino and Top Pot donut without being stopped by a title on such topics as nature and pets, travel, health, philosophy, women studies, and architecture. *Every day; mcoybooks@att.net; map:J8*

Madison Park Books

4105 E MADISON ST, MADISON PARK; 206/328-7323 Right at home in its upscale neighborhood, this brightly-colored bookstore has a wood-fire stove in the quaint organized-by-grade-level children's corner. Books cover every genre from fiction to women's studies and staff recommendations throughout are always helpful when browsing the fairly standard sections. *Every day; mpbooks@hotmail.com; map:GG6*

Magus Bookstore

1408 NE 42ND ST, UNIVERSITY DISTRICT; 206/633-1800 Magus has rescued many a starving student from full-price sticker shock with its 60,000-strong used-book inventory. A staple in this student-dominated neighborhood, the store carries everything from classical literature to engineering; it has a large science-fiction selection and tons of Cliff Notes, as well as a poetry section that would do any new-book store proud. *Every day; magusbks@halcyon.com; magusbks.com; map:FF6*

Marco Polo

713 BROADWAY AVE E, CAPITOL HILL; 206/860-3736 Those with wanderlust will find a welcome home at this shop stocked with travel guides and literature covering the globe. There's also a small back room with travel clothes and gifts and a bookcase housing hour glasses, watercolor kits, clocks, calendars, and globes. *Every day; travel@marcopoloseattle.com; marcopoloseattle.com; map:HH7*

Open Books: A Poem Emporium

2414 N 45TH ST, WALLINGFORD; 206/633-0811 A book store devoted to poetry—what a novel idea. Shelves with books ranging from out-of-print volumes of poetry to new and used titles, neatly line each wall. Open Books regularly hosts poetry readings and signings. *Tues–Sat; openpoetrybooks.com; map:FF7*

Parkplace Book Company

348 PARKPLACE CENTER, KIRKLAND; 425/828-6546 Children's books, mystery, and fiction are all culled with expertise by book rep and co-owner Ted Lucia. He and his wife, Kathi, own this impeccably organized general bookstore, which has a friendly staff. *Every day; map:EE3*

Peter Miller Architectural and Design Books and Supplies

1930 1ST AVE, DOWNTOWN; 206/441-4114 The clientele of this bookstore/architect supply store are devoted. Even when filled with people, you can hear a pin drop. The walls are covered with glossy architecture magazines and books on topics such as single-family houses, earth buildings, stainless steel, and landscape design. *Every day; petermiller@petermiller.com; petermillerbooks.com; map:I7*

Queen Anne Books

1811 QUEEN ANNE AVE N, QUEEN ANNE; 206/283-5624 Tight quarters prompted a short-distance move for this popular neighborhood shop in January 2004 to a space with twice the browsing and book room. Thankfully, the well-versed, genial staff is still on hand to make thoughtful title recommendations (look for special orders to be handled quickly and efficiently). Beyond square footage, the bookstore also gained a connecting door to El Diablo Coffee (see review in the Nightlife chapter), where you'll no doubt be lured to linger with your new purchase over a cup of Cuban coffee. *Every day; queenannebooks.com; qaabooks@qwest.net; map:GG8*

Seattle Mystery Bookshop

117 CHERRY ST, DOWNTOWN; 206/587-5737 For those who simply must know whodunnit, this is the place. Or at least it's where to find mystery books of all types: from the well-known (Martha Grimes, Janet Evanovich, Michael Connelly) to the up-and-comers. *Every day; staff@seattlemystery.com; seattlemystery.com; map:N8*

Second Story Bookstore

1815 N 45TH ST, WALLINGFORD; 206/547-4605 Trolling the second level of Wallingford Center, unsuspecting shoppers are snagged by the new releases displayed outside of Second Story. Once inside, a well-crafted selection of fiction and nonfiction, self-help, gardening, and kids' books keep them hooked. The reading-friendly ambience is supported by a few comfy chairs and a dedicated staff. *Every day; map:FF7*

Secret Garden Bookshop

2214 NW MARKET ST, BALLARD; 206/789-5006 Seattle's oldest exclusively children's bookstore now includes books for grown-ups, too. In addition to comprehensive parenting and children's nonfiction sections, there is a solid general selection. Special events (musical performances, classes, signings, and occasional readings) are entertaining, and the Secret Garden does programs for teachers and parents and book fairs for local schools. There are also story times twice every Thursday. *Every day; staff@secretgardenbooks.com; secretgardenbooks.com; map:FF7*

Twice Sold Tales

905 E JOHN ST, CAPITOL HILL (AND BRANCHES); 206/324-2421 If someone wanted to create the evil twin of a Barnes & Noble, this would be it. The first tip-off is a sign on the *garbage* can by the counter, labeled "complaints." Twice Sold Tales on Capitol Hill is an institution of eccentricity in a neighborhood known for its love of the different. But, aside from entertaining people- and cat-watching opportunities (overhead planks are for the benefit of roaming felines), it is the extensive title offerings that have kept this store thriving . . . that and its being open 24 hours on Fridays. Branches are in the University District and Fremont. *Every day; tst@twicesoldtales.com; twicesoldtales.com; map:GG7*

University Book Store

4326 UNIVERSITY WY NE, UNIVERSITY DISTRICT (AND BRANCHES); 206/634-3400 Now in its second century of operation, the University of Washington's bookstore is arguably the best spot in town to find whatever you seek on the printed page: from science fiction and travel books to weighty academic tomes. One of the largest bookstores in Washington State and the largest independent college bookstore in the United States (unless you ask the Harvard Coop), the UW's primary bookstore has a vast selection (especially the gardening, arts, and design departments). Customer service goes far beyond the usual, with free book shipping, gift wrapping, and parking validation; and in the rare event that your title is not in stock, staff will promptly special-order it. The store often sponsors large events and readings (see the Literary section in the Arts chapter) in conjunction with the university, and if you want a computer, a camera, or a stuffed Husky dog, you'll find them here. The smaller branch in Bellevue (990 102nd Ave NE; 425/462-4500; map:HH3) does not carry textbooks or offer the buy-back service; it does carry an extensive general literature and children's selection. In 1995 a branch opened downtown (1225 4th Ave; 206/545-9230; Mon–Sat; map:K6) with a solid selection of business and computer titles. *Every day; ubsbooks@u.washington.edu; www.book store.washington.edu; map:FF6*

Wessel and Lieberman Booksellers

208 IST AVE S, PIONEER SQUARE; 206/682-3545 Wessel and Lieberman may hold just as many people as it does books. To add to its already well-rounded selection, there is an annex on the lower level that houses books categorized as fiction, U.S. and world history, natural history, performing arts, children's books, artist books, broadsides, literary criticism, travel, gardening, true crime, illustrated books, arts and crafts, and sets. *Mon–Sat; www.wlbooks.com; map:N8*

Wide World Books & Maps

4411 WALLINGFORD AVE N, WALLINGFORD; 206/634-3453 OR 888/534-3453 In this store, you'll find what you need to take with you (like a toiletry kit) on your next adventure, to plan your next destination (through a vast selection of literature), or at least what you need to fuel dreams of going to an exotic place (such as a clear "globe" piggy bank to help you save for the next trip). Books are categorized by region: USA, Pacific Northwest and Canada, AustralAsia, Latin America, Africa, and Europe. The shelf in the back can help you find tour groups and companies. *Every day; travel@speakeasy.net; travelbooksandmaps.com; map:FF7*

CHILDREN'S CLOTHING AND ACCESSORIES

Boston Street

1815 N 45TH ST, WALLINGFORD; 206/634-0580 / 16515 NE 74TH ST, REDMOND; 425/895-0848 They call it the children's everything store, but, more specifically, it's everything you need or want to dress the kiddies in—from active and durable to frilly and delicate. The fashion outfits are not run-of-the-mall, but truly "in," as well as sweet, reasonably priced (check out their cotton line), and a safe gift bet. *Every day; map:FF7, FF1*

Flora and Henri

717 PINE ST (ELLIOTT GRAND HYATT), DOWNTOWN; 206/749-0004 OR 888 /749-9698 / 705 BROADWAY AVE E, CAPITOL HILL; 206/323-2928 Five years ago, a local designer began selling her you-won't-believe-your-eyes cute baby apparel on First Avenue. Since then, she has moved to a more spacious space on Pine Street and opened another shop on New York's Madison Avenue. Her designs, in soft, high-quality European fabrics, are stylish enough that Mom might be tempted to ask if they come in her size. (Select styles do.) The shoes are Italian-made and the retro-striped two-piece bathing suits are more than you ever thought you'd pay for so little material. *Every day; info@florahenri.com; florahenri.com; map:J4, GG7*

The Kids Club

UNIVERSITY VILLAGE, UNIVERSITY DISTRCIT; 206/524-2553 / CROSSROADS SHOPPING CENTER, BELLEVUE; 425/643-5437 The Kids Club has an abundance of baby paraphernalia, from car seats to bottle warmers to baby carriers. The store also has a kiddie hair salon (the Hair Chair) and TVs with videos running to divert kids while their fashion fates are determined by Mom or Dad. *Every day; map:FF6, HH1*

Rising Stars

7404 GREENWOOD AVE N, GREENWOOD; 206/781-0138 No cookie-cutter kids walk out of this Greenwood shop, where local designers (some of whom live mere blocks away) create some of the clothing. You'll find an eclectic selection of pajamas and cotton casuals for boys and girls, plus lots of handmade dolls, art supplies, books, and a large playroom with a tree house. *Every day; map:EE8*

Sweet Baby Jess

1535 1ST AVE, DOWNTOWN; 206/340-0900 The dreamlike decor of this new-to-First-Avenue baby boutique makes shoppers want to take a piece of it home. The store makes all its own product line (from sizes infant to toddler, except for some specialty dresses up to size 8) in a factory a couple miles down the road and have sold nationwide for 14 years. *Every day; map:I7*

The Tin Horse

1815 N 45TH ST, WALLINGFORD; 206/547-9966 A retro white baby crib, rolling pink bassinette, and carousel horse on display turn the heads of passing Wallingford Center shoppers. In sizes and styles for tiny baby to toddler, the Tin Horse has shabby-chic nursery pieces with themed accent pillows and lamps, rockers in various sizes, bedding, petunia pickle-bottom diaper bags, and hutches filled with inspiring fabrics. Interior design services are also available. *Every day; info@thetin horse.com; thetinhorse.com; map:FF7*

ETHNIC AND SPECIALTY FOODS

DeLaurenti Specialty Food Market

1435 1ST AVE, PIKE PLACE MARKET; 206/622-0141 All ingredients for a Mediterranean diet can be found at this Market cornerstone. For more than 50 years, DeLaurenti has served as a failsafe source for international foodstuffs and is nearly as well known for its surpass-your-expectations service. The narrow aisles are dense with canned goods, olives, olive oils, imported pasta, and truffles. The deli is noted for its excellent meats and carries more than 160 kinds of cheese. The wine department upstairs is known for its Italian labels and good selection, and the baked-goods department features breads from some of the area's best bakers. A recent remodel has brought the sandwich counter out from hiding, so now you can taste what's on the shelves while watching people along First Avenue. *Every day; delaurenti.com; map:J8*

Dish D'Lish

1505 PIKE PL, PIKE PLACE MARKET; 206/784-7840 Local chef and cookbook diva Kathy Casey opened this fine-food takeout shop just inside the main entrance to the Pike Place Market in 2002. Pick up one of her tasty ready-to-eat creations—such as smoked wild salmon with wasabi—to dine like a gourmand without putting in kitchen time. Or pick up a tasty picnic basket lunch or dinner. There is also a tempting variety of salads, dressings, and dips (even cocktail mixes!) to choose among. Gift "bundles" are a sure bet for your favorite foodie. *Every day; map:J7*

El Mercado Latino

1514 PIKE PL, PIKE PLACE MARKET; 206/623-3240 This little store has the essence of a country mercantile in Mexico, with colorful *ristras* (wreaths of chili peppers and garlic) hanging under the arbor out front and plantains in boxes by the door. Inside, there are piñatas, dried fruit, candies, a huge selection of hot sauces, and shelves of canned foods. Caribbean, South America, Spanish, and Creole foods are all represented here. *Every day; map:J8*

Market Spice

85-A PIKE PL, PIKE PLACE MARKET; 206/622-6340 One of the longest residents of the Pike Place Market, Market Spice has been selling teas, coffees, cooking spices, and other goodies here since 1911. As well as boasting Indian and other spices from around the world (big jars of spices hold everything from chamomile to catnip), there are jellies, cooking utensils, and a plethora of china cup and pot patterns and tin and pottery tea sets. *Every day; marketspice.com; map:J8*

The Mexican Grocery

1914 PIKE PL, PIKE PLACE MARKET; 206/441-1147 Come in around lunchtime and you'll see the name the grocery has made for itself with local merchants who gather for takeout of nachos, sandwiches, burritos, and maybe some fresh flan for dessert. The grocery shelves hold bagged Mexican cooking spices, peppers, chili pods and beans, and the refrigerated case keeps cheeses and salsas fresh. *Mon–Sat; map:J8*

Oliviers & Co.

600 PINE ST, PACIFIC PLACE, DOWNTOWN; 206/381-1418 Many seasoned cooks preach that a good olive oil is the foundation of a well-prepared meal, and this store with a European mercantile ambience proves that many are listening. Co-branded with family farms and cooperatives from the Mediterranean, everything in the store carries the Oliviers & Co. label—jars of tapenade, straw shopping bags, and every kind of olive-related accessory, tool, or dish you can dream up. *Every day; oliviers-co.com; map:I5*

Uwajimaya

600 5TH AVE S, CHINATOWN/INTERNATIONAL DISTRICT; 206/624-6248 / 15555 NE 24TH ST, BELLEVUE; 425/747-9012 Asian megagrocery Uwajimaya cemented its reputation as the center of the Chinatown/International District with its move to the sprawling retail-residence complex Uwajimaya Village. The store still carries a vast selection of Asian foods, small electrical appliances (rice cookers, woks), housewares, gifts, and makeup. But now it also boasts a bank, condos above the store, and pan-Asian restaurant Chinoise Café (see review in the Restaurants chapter), located on the village's southwest corner. As always, the real distinctions here are the variety of canned goods, depth of choice (one aisle is wholly devoted to rice), fresh shellfish tanks, and produce department. You'll find fresh geoduck, live prawns and crabs, bitter melons, water chestnuts, and all the makings for sushi. Check out the yummy pastries at the Yummy House in the food court; the Bellevue store has a fine Asian bakery case. Both branches have in-store cafes with Asian food for eating in or carrying out. *Every day; uwajimaya.com; map:Q7, GG1*

FLORISTS, GARDENING SHOPS, AND NURSERIES

Bainbridge Gardens

9415 MILLER RD NE, BAINBRIDGE ISLAND; 206/842-5888 This destination nursery sprawls over 7 acres with a fine selection of woody plants, theme gardens for herbs, perennials, grasses, water plants, and shade plants. There's also a well-stocked garden gift shop. The nursery's partnership with renowned garden writer Ann Lovejoy includes education programs on sustainable gardening. The restored Harui Memorial Garden showcases bonsai trees, and a nature trail loops through native woods. A small outdoor cafe offers beverages, snacks, and light lunches. *Every day; info@bainbridgegardens.com; bainbridgegardens.com*

Ballard Blossom

1766 NW MARKET ST, BALLARD; 206/782-4213 Traditional arrangements at this Ballard shop are FTD in nature, and the business has been family run since 1927—its blazing neon sign is a neighborhood landmark. The friendly staff presides over a cheerful profusion of fresh, silk, and dried flowers, potted plants, and gift items. Customers can have many selections sent anywhere in the world, while personally chosen arrangements can be delivered areawide. *Mon–Sat (every day in Dec); ftd.com/ballardblossom; map:FF8*

Bay Hay and Feed

10355 VALLEY RD, BAINBRIDGE ISLAND; 206/842-2813 An authentically useful rural outfitter and delightfully shoppable gift spot, this shop housed in a 1912 general storefront has served the Rolling Bay neighborhood of Bainbridge Island for more than 20 years. There's an abundant selection of farm- and garden-related toys, gifts, books, and clothing. The garden center is ably staffed, specializes in organic gardening, and offers a full range of edible and ornamental plants, including some collectors' treasures. Rustic lawn furniture, hand tools, and unusual clay pots are specialties. The new espresso bar in the nursery features goodies from Bainbridge Bakers. *Every day.*

Blooms on Broadway

433 BROADWAY AVE E, CAPITOL HILL; 206/324-8845 This tight-quartered flower stand on the corner of the Broadway Market is impressive for its unusual selections and freshness. They specialize in a mix of English garden varieties and modern Japanese flowers—all arriving from around the world daily. *Every day; map:GG6*

City People's Garden Store & Mercantile

2939 E MADISON ST, MADISON VALLEY; 206/324-0737 / 5440 SAND POINT WY NE, SAND POINT; 206/524-1200 The mix of things you'll find in City People's is a reminder that there aren't very many true neighborhood mercantiles anymore, and what a shame. It's such a convenience to be able to go to one store for gardening, household, and hardware needs, as well as perfect last-minute gifts (unlike what you'd find in a pharmacy or "everything" store). They have furniture and accessories for the kitchen and bath and everything for a well-planned patio, including the plants. *Every day; map:GG6, EE5*

Crissey Flowers and Gifts

617 E PIKE ST, CAPITOL HILL; 206/448-1100 Traditionalists appreciate Crissey's arrangements, which run to English garden and tropical hi-style (a synthesis of Dutch and Japanese traditions). And with more than 110 years in the business, Seattle's oldest established florist has plenty of experience with blooms of all varieties. From private dinner parties to weddings or wakes, Crissey is a full-service florist that does everything with excellence, delivering throughout the area and worldwide. *Mon–Sat; crisseyflowers.com; map:H6*

Martha E. Harris Flowers and Gifts

4218 E MADISON ST, MADISON PARK; 206/568-0347 Martha E. Harris often fills out her English garden–style arrangements with native evergreenery and local flowers. The florist shop here is way at the back, past fine accessories, jewelry, and accent pieces for the home. Expect extravagant, dramatic, bountiful arrangements. Parties and weddings are Harris's specialties, and she maintains a bridal registry. (Recently she also opened Frog Hollow, a whimsical paper and party goods store, just up the street at 4111 E Madison St; 206/568-7707). Deliveries within greater Seattle and worldwide daily except Sunday. *Every day; map:GG6*

Megan Mary Olander Florist

222 1ST AVE S, PIONEER SQUARE; 206/623-6660 In the heart of hip Pioneer Square is this tiny, sweet-smelling flower and gift shop that feels like it could just as easily sit in a quaint English village. Displayed on an old-fashioned flower-cart are potted plants and delicate floral finishing touches for the home. Treasures of baby clothes on baby hangers and various French soaps are neatly presented on vintage furnishings. For custom orders, there is an arranging room in the back of the store. *Mon–Sat; map:O8*

Molbak's Greenhouse and Nursery

13625 NE 175TH ST, WOODINVILLE; 425/483-5000 Since 1956, Molbak's has catered to Northwest gardeners with plants that thrive in the Emerald City and environs. The novice and the expert gardener will find plenty to explore among the hundreds of houseplants and the full range of outdoor plants (everything from trees to ground covers). Molbak's also offers gifts, a Christmas shop (lavish holiday displays bring visitors here in droves), a garden store, and distinctive floral designs. *Every day; molbaks.com; map:BB2, I8*

Pike Place Flowers

1ST AVE AND PIKE ST, PIKE PLACE MARKET; 206/682-9797 There's nothing like passing bunches of vibrant flowers or plants on a city street corner, except stopping to buy some. Take something home to plant in the garden, such as impatiens, salvia, or Gerber Daisies, create a fresh-cut bouquet for the kitchen table, or bring a single pale pink rose to someone who loves roses. At an average price of $19.99 for bouquets, Pike Place Flowers can help with all of these things and more. They can also make special-order arrangements with your wedding or party theme in mind. *Every day; pikeplaceflowers.com; map:J7*

Swanson's Nursery and Greenhouse

9701 15TH AVE NW, CROWN HILL; 206/782-2543 Five acres of annuals, perennials, trees, shrubs, and display gardens make this a fun and worthwhile stop for serious gardeners and a decent diversion for those with undeveloped green thumbs. This full-service nursery includes uncommon plants of all kinds and emphasizes choice offerings over sheer quantity. A cafe in the gift shop offers light meals and espresso amid European garden tools, books, knickknacks, and handsome planting containers. *Every day; garden@swansonsnursery.com; swansonsnursery.com; map:DD8*

Wells Medina Nursery

8300 NE 24TH ST, BELLEVUE; 425/454-1853 Many a swanky Medina home has a landscape graced with flora from this 5-acre nursery. A favorite among perennial lovers, and regionally famed for its variety, this is also the place to buy choice shrubs—the selection of rhododendrons and Japanese maples is unmatched in the area. Look here for unusual vines, bulbs, and ground covers as well, and check out the long demonstration border. The excellent plant range and prices are complemented by a helpful staff. *Every day; map:GG4*

Young Flowers

1111 3RD AVE, DOWNTOWN; 206/628-3077 If you pass a young man on Fifth Avenue with his arms hugging a brilliant bouquet of flowers, chances are he got them here. A perfect distance from the tall office buildings, Young Flowers makes its way to the desks of many an unsuspecting birthday girl or newly promoted associate. It's not just proximity that keeps customers coming back, but the shop's exceptional quality, special orders, and deliveries to all over the area. *Every day; map:L7*

GIFTS AND HOME ACCESSORIES

The Best of All Worlds

523 UNION ST, DOWNTOWN; 206/623-2525 The concept here is stuff you won't find other places: the largest selection in Seattle of German nutcrackers, Parisian marionettes, original Kemper ware, and, the most popular item, poster calendars from local artist, Linnea. *Every day; map:J5*

Bitters Co.

513 N 36TH ST, FREMONT; 206/632-0886 This charming old building in Fremont is the perfect spot for an eclectic general store, which is what sisters Amy and Katie Carson had in mind. Rustic walls and flooring and low lighting enhance the mystique of modern rustic furniture such as tables, chairs, and daybeds, as well as folk art, Filson clothing, Norwegian sweaters, jewelry, and gift-worthy items. *Tues–Sun; info@bittersco.com; bittersco.com; map:FF8*

Burke Museum Store

17TH AVE NE AND NE 45TH ST, UNIVERSITY DISTRICT; 206/685-0909 The ideal venue to find gifts for nature and museum lovers, this shop (also a branch of the University Book Store) is located in the Burke Museum on the University of Washington campus. Browse the selection of Northwest Coast Native American art, silkscreen prints, basketry, and wooden boxes, and don't miss the geological specimens, books, and dinosaur replicas. *Every day; map:FF6*

Burnt Sugar

601 N 35TH ST, FREMONT; 206/545-0699 The pink ceiling and Martha-green walls in here should be a husband or boyfriend's first clue that she'll probably be in here a while, so best find a chair. Every corner is a cute display of fine knickknacks for herself or the home—fun cotton lingerie, makeup, designer walking (or shopping) shoes, French cheese and dessert plates, bright purses, stylin' little lamps, and a baby section that is just cause for oohs and aahs. *Every day; map:FF8*

Casa Compagna

462 N 34TH ST, FREMONT; 206/634-3109 After first occupying the land where the new PCC grocery sits, Casa Compagna now calls busy N 34th Street and Fremont Avenue home. The gifts and home accessories in this shop cover a broad range of origins from French shabby chic to country American. *Every day; casacompagna.com; map:FF8*

Egbert's

2231 1ST AVE, BELLTOWN; 206/728-5682 With some traditional pieces thrown in, many of the high-end home furnishings in this gallery showroom are an industrial-design student's dream. Even the children's corner has toys for budding designers. Also on offer are collections of Scandinavian- and Asian-influenced furniture, books, housewares, and jewelry. *Tues–Sat; map:G8*

Fireworks Gallery

210 1ST AVE S, PIONEER SQUARE (AND BRANCHES); 206/682-8707 A favorite with visitors, Fireworks displays a fiery array of ceramics, glass, and other hand-crafted wares—from the wild and whimsical to the elegantly functional—plus art jewelry, fiber art, and woodwork pieces. Holidays usher in a selection of surprising tree-trimming options. Other branches are at Westlake Center, Bellevue Square, and University Village. *Every day; fireworksgallery@mindspring.com; fireworks gallery.net; map:O8*

Flourish

1705 45TH ST. N, WALLINGFORD; 206/675-0777 Wallingfordians suffered from a sad lack of greeting card options before Minneapolis ex-pats Christine and Bob Lynch brought their charming stationery, fine papers, and small gifts shop to the neighborhood in 2001. With backgrounds in graphic design, the owners are skilled at choosing cards (some by local artists) that have definite flourish. Locally made bath and body products also demand perusing. *Mon–Sat; flourishgreetings.com; map:FF7*

Frank and Dunya

3418 FREMONT AVE N, FREMONT; 206/547-6760 Vibrant local art of various mediums has been passing through this funky shop (on its way to people's abodes) for more than 15 years. Somewhat reminiscent of an art gallery gift shop, it features fused-glass ceiling fixtures by local artist Susanna Prince, Native jewelry, wine glasses with beaded stems, and a room full of modern clock designs and child's art. Don't be too shocked, though, if you see the work of non-Seat-tleites—they do slip in, says an employee. *Every day; map:FF7*

Glenn Richards

964 DENNY WY, DOWNTOWN; 206/287-1877 Imagine 30,000 square feet of Asian antiques and a floor beneath for retrofitting old pieces (for instance, making Chinese chests into entertainment centers). This is how big Laurie and John Fairman's second store, Glenn Richards, is. (Their original store is Honeychurch Antiques, see review in Antiques/Vintage/Retro in this chapter.) The couple shops in Asia for both stores and has a crew of woodworkers who customize pieces with architectural elements. The staff also custom designs carpets and tables (constructed of rare woods and arti-facts) that are then made in Nepal by Tibetan refugees. *Every day; info@glenn richards.com; glennrichards.com; map:F4*

Great Jones Home

1921 2ND AVE, DOWNTOWN; 206/448-9405 If you're into shabby chic, you'll love this store. Offerings might include gift wrap and cards, a display of all orange-and-black furniture and accent pieces (like a feather-shaded lamp), and monogrammed lavender sachets made in the south of France. There's also a lovely linen section in the back where you can choose custom bedding. *Every day; map:I7*

Herban Patio and Herban Pottery

3200 1ST AVE S, SODO; 206/749-5112 Seattle's old factories are brought back to life in a sophisticated way at these two family-owned sister stores in SoDo. Herban Patio, the larger of the stores, is a well-designed showroom of all things for the patio, including furniture sets in metal, iron, and teak. Herban Pottery has immense pots for plants or garden water features, both in antique looks and new designs at surprisingly affordable prices, as well as an array of vases. If the need strikes, be sure to drop by the bathroom by the cottage area that's like a cute little finished outhouse. *Every day; map:JJ7*

Kasala

1505 WESTERN AVE, DOWNTOWN; 206/623-7795 OR 800/KASALA1 / 1014 116TH AVE NE, BELLEVUE; 425/453-2823 OR 800/418-2521 One-stop shopping for urban decor: Kasala's contemporary, design-conscious furniture includes trendy European furniture and home accessories—with an emphasis on lighting systems—plus glassware and gift items. *Every day; seastore@kasala.com; kasala.com; map:J8, HH3*

Lucca Great Finds

5332 BALLARD AVE NW, BALLARD; 206/782-7337 The owners of Lucca Great Finds, Francine Katz and Peter Riches, opened up this small shop in 2001 and have kept it filled ever since with authentic Euro gifts such as fine stationeries, French ribbon, Mariage Frères teas, and a line of bath and body products made in Florence, as well as quirkier gifts from Chinese lanterns to tin toys. They also carry some of their own statuaries in the garden courtyard that range from European fountains to birdbaths to bookends. You can find more statuaries at the couple's other ventures: Lucca Statuary (7716 15th Ave NW, Ballard; 206/789-0623) and nearby Lucca Manufacturing (8022 15th Ave NW, Ballard; 206/297-7474), which produces one-of-a-kind pieces finished by hand for wholesale and retail in all of the stores. *Every day; francine@luccastatuary.com; luccastatuary.com; map:EE8*

Made in Washington

1530 POST ALLEY, PIKE PLACE MARKET (AND BRANCHES); 206/467-0788 There are a plethora of take-home-a-piece-of-Seattle shops downtown, but for more quality with less cheese, Made in Washington highlights include a variety of Native artwork as well as prepackaged gift baskets of Red Hook beer, smoked salmon, and Biringer Farms jams. *Every day; madeinwashington.com; map:J8*

ROCK 'N' ROLL CITY

It's a running joke that Seattleites don't know how to drive in the snow, given how infrequently the white stuff falls here. But it's even more true that we haven't a clue about dealing with earthquakes. Residents of San Francisco and Los Angeles are so accustomed to periodic shakings that they barely notice them anymore, and they're prepared when a quake of any consequence hits. Seattleites, however, will sit before their televisions for every bit of breaking news if a tremor barely strong enough to register on the Richter scale unsettles the area's equilibrium. And then, when a truly violent quake does strike, as it did in 2001, they run out into the streets (a no-no when bricks are falling all around), bewildered and waiting for somebody to tell them what to do next.

Whether you knew it or not, the Emerald City has always been on shaky ground. More than a thousand earthquakes with magnitude 1.0 or greater rumble through Washington and Oregon every year, most of them in the Puget Sound region. (Each unit of increase in magnitude represents about a 30-fold increase in energy release; so a magnitude 6.0 quake, considered a damaging intensity, has approximately a thousand times as much energy as a magnitude 4.0 quake.) Few of these shivers of the earth—maybe two dozen—are strong enough to be felt.

However, the area has withstood three substantial temblors over the past half century. Most destructive was the 7.1 magnitude quake on April 13, 1949, centered between Tacoma and Olympia, which damaged 30 Seattle schools, caused local power outages, and killed 8 people. Less intense, with a 6.5 magnitude and centered between Seattle and Tacoma, was the quake of April 29, 1965. It damaged almost all waterfront facilities in Seattle, cast building rubble down on parked cars, made the Space Needle sway enough that the water in its toilet bowls spilled out, and was blamed for seven deaths. More recent was the February 28, 2001, shaker—measuring 6.8 on the Richter scale and centered 11 miles north of Olympia—which substantially harmed several of Pioneer Square's historic masonry buildings, shattered windows in the control tower at Sea-Tac Airport, and forced the closure of the Alaskan Way Viaduct, a potentially early casualty of any truly serious quake.

So when is "the big one" due? Seismologists wisely avoid making such predictions. But they are more than willing to say why the Seattle area is in for more bumpy rides on the earth's crust. There are three different sources of local earthquakes.

First is the **CASCADIA SUBDUCTION ZONE**, a 750-mile-long stretch located in the Pacific Ocean about 50 miles off the West Coast, where an eastward-moving structural plate of the ocean floor—the Juan de Fuca Plate—is being forced very slowly beneath the North American Plate, on top of which sits the land we see around us. These plates tend to shove against one another, then suddenly break apart again with a violence that can produce quakes of magnitudes 8.0 or greater anywhere along the zone.

The second source of drastic local shakings is the **BENIOFF ZONE**, an area of faulting that radiates out from the Cascadia Subduction Zone and may cause deep quakes with magnitudes of up to 7.5.

Finally, there are shallow earthquakes—maybe the worst-case scenario for Seattle. These upheavals occur within the North American Plate, close to the ground's surface, and (especially with aftershocks) can do considerable damage to whatever rests upon that surface, be it skyscrapers or highways or people. This area's best-known weakness in the earth's crust is the **SEATTLE FAULT**, which runs east-west through the city from Issaquah to Bremerton. Geological evidence indicates that the Seattle Fault has been quiet for something like 1,100 years. But its last convulsion was a real humdinger, provoking landslides into Lake Washington and a tsunami (or tremendous wave) on Puget Sound. Seattle's 1949, 1965, and 2001 quakes were all deep quakes, and most buildings here are designed to withstand those. However, seismologists are becoming increasingly concerned about the Seattle Fault, as small quakes occur with greater frequency along its length.

In the event of a significant quake, stay inside if you're already there and squeeze yourself under something that can protect you from falling debris, such as a sturdy desk or table. If you're outside, duck into a doorway or move into an open area, staying clear of telephone poles and overhead wires. And for heaven's sake, tell those dumbfounded Seattleites milling in the streets to take cover too.

—*J. Kingston Pierce*

Milagros Mexican Folk Art

1530 POST ALLEY, PIKE PLACE MARKET; 206/464-0490 Tucked into the Pike Place Market is this fine collection of the best Mexico's artisans have to offer. Milagros is named for the small religious trinkets that many Latin Americans use to petition saints for help (*milagros* is Spanish for "miracles"). The owners travel to Mexico every five months to bring back Oaxacan wood carvings, authentic dance masks, original Huichol Indian yarn paintings and beadwork, clay figures by the Aguilar sisters, and hand-pounded tinwork and Talavera, many of which are shipped to clients all across the country. *Every day; milagrosseattle.com; map:J7*

Northwest Discovery

ELEMENTS GALLERY, BELLEVUE SQUARE, BELLEVUE; 425/454-1676 / 10500 NE 8TH ST, BELLEVUE; 425/454-8242 Locally-made and Northwest-inspired art—such as bead and semiprecious stone jewelry; furniture, frames, and boxes of smooth, shiny wood; laser-engraved crystal images; cut-glass plates; Native American prints;

and mixed-media greeting cards—are displayed in the museumlike settings of both stores. *Every day; nwdiscovery.com; map:HH3*

Phoenix Rising Gallery

2030 WESTERN AVE, BELLTOWN; 206/728-2332 Since 1989, Steven M. Dickinson has been drawing praise for his shop filled with beautifully hand-crafted, and beautifully displayed, contemporary art (blown glass, ceramics, jewelry, and furnishings) culled from America's best designers and craftspeople. *Every day; info@prgallery.com; prgallery.com; map:H8*

Portage Bay Goods

706 N 34TH ST, FREMONT; 206/547-5221 Stocked with earth-friendly, healthy gifts, much of them made by local artisans, this shop demands loitering. Check out such creations as the frames and boxes made from recycled rulers. *Every day; portage baygoods.com; map:FF8*

Price Asher

970 DENNY WY, DOWNTOWN; 206/254-9226 / 635 SPRING ST, FRIDAY HARBOR; 206/370-5880 Dramatic sofas and chairs, hutches, mirrors, decorative pieces such as picture frames and silk arrangements, and small gift items abound. The selection of patio furniture is somewhat lacking, but ordering Brown Jordan by catalog is an option. *Every day; priceasher.com; map:F4*

Watson Kennedy Fine Home
Watson Kennedy Fine Living

1022 1ST AVE, DOWNTOWN; 206/652-8350 / 86 PINE ST, PIKE PLACE MARKET; 206/443-6281 There is no mistaking these two stores were created by the same selective hands. The bed-and-bath-focused Fine Living, in the courtyard of the Inn at the Market, also offers a broad range of tasteful gifts. The newer Fine Home is a delightful mix of old and new furniture, French linens, table wares, and everything that makes a house a home. *Every day; fineliving@watsonkennedy.com; fine home@watsonkennedy.com; watsonkennedy.com; map:I7, M7*

Zanadia

1815 N 45TH ST, WALLINGFORD; 206/547-0884 The home furnishings at this Wallingford Center store—from large furniture reproductions to small velvet tasseled pillows—are reliably classy. A kitchen corner is fully stocked with a mix of beautiful and practical cooking, baking, and dinnerware. Downstairs holds even more spill-over furniture, lamps, and mirrors. *Every day; zanadia.com; map:FF7*

JEWELRY AND ACCESSORIES

Alvin Goldfarb Jeweler

305 BELLEVUE WY NE, BELLEVUE; 425/454-9393 A small colonial-style house holds one-of-a-kind sapphires, crystal gift items, sterling watches, jewelry cases, and diamonds, diamonds, diamonds—and this family-owned business is known for its customer service. *Mon–Sat; alvingoldfarbjeweler.com; map:HH3*

Ben Bridge

1432 4TH AVE, DOWNTOWN (AND BRANCHES); 206/628-6800 Ben Bridge began in Seattle in 1912. While the shop has expanded to malls nationwide, its original downtown location is still a landmark and a decent diamond-shopping destination. Mountings are fairly traditional, but custom design work is also offered. *Every day; benbridge.com; map:K6*

Carroll's Fine Jewelry

1427 4TH AVE, DOWNTOWN; 206/622-9191 This eye-catching green marble–fronted store has been in the same spot since 1895. Specializing in modern and antique settings, Carroll's also offers custom designs and has a quality selection of watches, silver flatware, and baby gifts. The experienced staff still serves home-made cookies and tea on a silver platter to browsing customers. *Mon–Sat; carrolls finejewelry.com; map:K6*

Facèré Jewelry Art Gallery

1420 5TH AVE, CITY CENTRE, DOWNTOWN; 206/624-6768 It may be in the middle of a mall (City Centre), but this is not your average mall inventory. Here you'll find antique and modern pieces from all over; large, metal, dramatic pieces made by U.K. artists, brushed metal broaches, and bright, colorful, beaded link necklaces are examples. *Mon–Sat; facereart@aol.com; facerejewelryart.com; map:J5*

Fancy

1932 2ND AVE, DOWNTOWN; 206/443-4621 Even from the outside, you won't be able to miss Fancy's popping pink, striped interior—and you won't want to miss what's on the inside. Most of the jewelry, bags, watches, and arm bands are locally made creations. The store also stocks fun vinyl traveling cases and wool patchwork pillows. *Every day; fancyjewels.com; map:H7*

Fox's Gem Shop

1341 5TH AVE, DOWNTOWN; 206/623-2528 This is the kind of place people dress up to shop at. The specialties are glittering gemstones and dazzling diamonds. The gift section has some silver and a large selection of clocks. Fox's carries gems from Cartier as well as Mikimoto pearls and jewelry. *Mon–Sat; www.foxsgemshop.com; map:K6*

GSS Jewelers

BELLEVUE SQUARE, BELLEVUE; 425/462-8202 The one-of-a-kind sparkles at GSS are designed and made in Seattle but can only be found in this corner of Bellevue Square mall. The purchase of custom wedding rings make up about half of the store's total sales and the diamonds for these come from the owner's native Israel. GSS also has unique settings of freshwater pearls, as well as other precious stones, watches, chains, and cuff-links for "less engaged" customers. *Every day; map:A7, HH3*

Philip Monroe Jeweler

519 PINE ST, DOWNTOWN; 206/624-1531 This veteran Seattle jewelry store imparts a touch of Northwest class with its grand chandelier, marble countertops, and pre-Columbian artwork. Selling mostly custom pieces, Philip Monroe's diamonds come from New York and Chicago and are used both in their new designs and to remake rings and other pieces. Friendly staff is happy to help. *Mon–Sat; map:J5*

Turgeon-Raine Jewellers

1407 5TH AVE, DOWNTOWN; 206/447-9488 When you see the unique settings and sparkles coming from these cases, it may be love at first sight. Estate, antique, contemporary, and high-fashion jewelry and only one kind of watch—Patek Philippe—offer choices for the most simple to the most grand occasion. *Every day; jewellers@turgeon-raine.com; turgeon-raine.com; map:J5*

MUSIC (CDS, RECORDS, AND TAPES)

Bop Street Records

5219 BALLARD AVE NW, BALLARD; 206/297-2232 This Ballard record shop has a huge selection of jazz, blues, rock, and funk. Plenty of used CDs, 78s, and cassettes are hanging around, but the main draw is its inventory consisting of some 500,000 albums and 45s. If you're overwhelmed, owner Dave Voorhees is more than willing to help you navigate, just as he has for the British megaband Radiohead, the drummer from the Roots, and Miles Davis's drummer John Schofield. *Mon–Sat; bopstreet@foxinternet.com; map:EE8*

Bud's Jazz Records

102 S JACKSON ST, PIONEER SQUARE; 206/628-0445 When the new owner took over several years ago, he carried on Bud's name but began incorporating visual art into the repertoire of traditional/Dixieland jazz, blues, Latin, big band, and local jazz by featuring emerging Seattle artists on the walls and hosting a gallery opening on the first Thursday of every month. The event offers refreshments in a cool setting and the opportunity to take in great art and great jazz in one mouthful—yeah, baby. *Every day; map:O9*

Django's Cellophane Square

4538 UNIVERSITY WY NE, UNIVERSITY DISTRICT (AND BRANCHES); 206/634-2280 Of Cellophane Square's three branches, the U District location maintains the best stock (likely fed by the area's population of penniless students, since the store pays top dollar for good-condition used CDs). As a group, the stores carry one of Seattle's most extensive selections of used rock CDs. Good news for reclusive types: Cellophane Square's Web site (now run by Portland-based Djangos.com) lets you download the entire inventory so you can do all your shopping online. Branches are in Bellevue and on Capitol Hill. *Every day; djangos.com/stores_seattle.asp; map:FF6*

Easy Street Records

4559 CALIFORNIA AVE SW, STE 200, WEST SEATTLE; 206/938-3279 / 20 E MERCER ST, QUEEN ANNE; 206/691-3279 Downtown dwellers with a hankering for new and used vinyl and rare imports can easily find the huge Queen Anne location or make the trek to the West Seattle Junction institution. The store's sales list is an indie-rock barometer for the Northwest, and the coffee bar and cafe on-site provide yet another reason to loiter (at the West Seattle location). Seattle-music luminaries shop here, as do visiting bands. Easy Street carries new and used CDs and features plenty of in-store performances. *Every day; easystreetonline.com; map:JJ8, A6*

Golden Oldies

201 NE 45TH ST, WALLINGFORD (AND BRANCHES); 206/547-2260 Pick any decade, genre, or place—and Golden Oldies can have you there with the spin of a record. Their vast compilation of records (lots of 45s) and tapes (and fewer compact discs) are bought and sold, new or used. Categories and artists are labeled with cardboard and permanent-marker signs separating them, and a music expert is always on hand to assist you. *Every day; oldies@ix.netcom.com; goldenoldies-records.com; map:FF7*

Singles Going Steady

2219 2ND AVE, BELLTOWN; 206/441-7396 This is a sure-find for punk rock and independent records, with a strong local collection. The store is organized into new and used vinyl, CDs, reggae, hip-hop, hardcore XXX, jazz, garage, and psychedelic/rockabilly. If you don't know what some of those categories are, the staff will enlighten. *Every day; orders@singlesgoingsteady.com; singlesgoingsteady.com; map:G7*

Sonic Boom Records

3414 FREMONT AVE N, FREMONT; 206/547-BOOM What makes this thriving independent music store so special is that it caters not only to a specific type of music (rock mostly), but most of its customers even listen to the same radio station. They say that if something is played on 90.3FM KEXP, this store has it. Sonic Boom also has most things other music stores do—popular titles, a listening station, used albums—but, sorry, no classical music. *Every day; sonicboom@sonicboom records.com; sonicboomrecords.com; map:FF7*

Wall of Sound

315 E PINE ST, CAPITOL HILL; 206/441-9880 If you're in search of off-the-beaten-path CDs and records, you're in luck. The key word here is "eclectic" (in fact, it's the most common filing category in the store). From French hip-hop to Peruvian percussion, the inventory offers a round-the-world tour. The other side of the shop belongs to Confounded Books & Hypno Video and its cache of zines, comics, and indie-press books. *Every day; map:J2*

Zion's Gates Records

1100 E PIKE ST, CAPITOL HILL; 206/568-5446 You may have seen the Zion's Gate name on posters plastered in the area, for hosting dance parties of underground dance music and reggae. You'll find vinyls and mostly new CDs, but some used. The four-year-old store has a "chill" atmosphere, with record-player listening stations in the window and a T-shirt rack. *Every day; zionsgate.com; map:L2*

OUTDOOR GEAR

Alpine Hut

2215 15TH AVE W, INTERBAY (AND BRANCHES); 206/284-3575 This no-frills shop outfits patrons for fun on the water, the slopes, or the trail. Look here for good deals on all kinds of ski gear in winter or in-line skates, mountain bikes, and bike wear in summer. The owner is friendly and the store aims to please. *Every day; map:EE8*

C. C. Filson Co.

1555 4TH AVE S, SODO; 206/622-3147 Some of the virtually indestructible wear—heavy wool jackets, canvas hunting coats, oil-finish hats, and wool pants—at this centenarian Seattle outfitter hasn't altered in design since 1914. The original C. C. Filson sold clothes to the men headed north to Alaska during the gold rush, and today's clothes are still attractive and tough. There's also a complete line of handsome luggage (including gun bags). *Every day; ccfilson.com; map:R9*

Crossings

901 FAIRVIEW AVE N, STE C120, SOUTH LAKE UNION; 206/287-9979 / CARILLON POINT, KIRKLAND; 425/889-2628 Nautical fashions for landlubbers and water fiends alike. Though Crossings emphasizes its sailing wear (it's the official outfitter for the Windermere Cup), the classic clothing here is suited for any boating adventure. The outer wear keeps you dry on deck, and the natural-fiber fabrics keep you looking the sailor. *Every day; crossings-crew.com; map:D1, EE3*

Eddie Bauer

600 PINE ST, DOWNTOWN (PACIFIC PLACE); 206/622-2766 Eddie Bauer isn't the sporting apparel giant that it was five years ago (though it raised its profile a bit when it moved from Rainier Square to Pacific Place mall in March 2004). But they still have the same styles and dependable fabrics for the most part. Their Polar-Tec line of fleece-lined jackets is a wintertime staple, often with more feminine cuts for women. *Every day; eddiebauer.com; map:J5*

Elliott Bay Bicycles

2116 WESTERN AVE, BELLTOWN; 206/441-8144 Titanium frames and shop talk rule in this Bentley of bike stores. Elliott Bay is regarded as something of a pro shop: it sells bikes to cyclists who know what they're doing and do enough of it to justify paying high prices. Among its other attributes, the shop is home base for Bill Davidson, a nationally known frame builder, whose designs include aforementioned custom titanium frames. *Every day; feedback@elliottbaybicycles.com; elliottbay bicycles.com; davidsonbicycles.com; map:H9*

Feathered Friends

119 YALE AVE N, DOWNTOWN; 206/292-2210 Feathered Friends carries a number of quality outdoor labels in addition to their own line of bulky down jackets and vests. Much of the gear in here is somewhat hard-core, for real protection from the elements and for those requiring the necessary tools for rock-climbing, camping, backcountry skiing, and such. But you can also find stylish and durable pieces from

Watergirl, Patagonia, Jade, and Arc'teryx. *Every day; featheredfriends.com; map:H1*

Gregg's Greenlake Cycle

7007 WOODLAWN AVE NE, GREEN LAKE (AND BRANCHES); 206/523-1822 Gregg's is a high-volume, high-pressure Seattle institution. Gregg's stocks kids' bikes, all-terrain bikes, and Japanese-, Italian-, and American-made racing bicycles, along with Seattle's largest collection of touring bikes. If you do buy from Gregg's, you'll get good follow-up service. The Green Lake location, just yards from the lake's busy bike path, has a large clothing and accessories department and rents bikes, roller skates, in-line skates, and snowboards. Branches are in Bellevue (121 106th Ave NE; 425/462-1900; map:HH3) and at Aurora Cycle (7401 Aurora Ave N, Green Lake; 206/783-1000; map:EE7). *Every day; seattle@greggscycles.com; greggscycles.com; map:EE7*

Il Vecchio

140 LAKESIDE AVE, LESCHI; 206/324-8148 George Gibb's Leschi shop is the bicycle equivalent of a Gucci boutique. The award-winning Weinstein-designed store is minimalist in appeal—there are very few bikes here—and maximalist in quality (and price): Italian racers De Rosa and Pinarello, and American-made Landshark. Proper frame fit is a certainty. In addition to the road and racing bicycles, the shop sells top components and cycling apparel. *Tues–Sat and by appointment; ilvecchio@mind spring.com; ilvecchio.com; map:HH6*

Mariner Kayaks

2134 WESTLAKE AVE N, WESTLAKE; 206/284-8404 Owners and brothers Cam and Matt Broze bring years of paddling experience and sea-kayak expertise to their operation—and they're always available to debate the finer points of hull shape and function. Mariner kayaks are considered by many sea kayakers as some of the best in the world. Matt developed the modern paddle float used for rescues and has written numerous articles on sea-kayaking skill and safety. In addition to the Mariner line, which includes kayaks for sea touring and the outer coast surf, Mariner Kayaks sells the Seda, Nimbus, and Feathercraft lines, Lightning and Epic paddles, and everything else you need to get out on the water. *Tues–Sat; marinerkayaks.com; map:GG7*

Marley's Snowboards and Skateboards

5424 BALLARD AVE NW, BALLARD; 206/782-6081 When co-owner Ian Fels took up snowboarding more than a decade ago, he never looked back at skiing. He's a friendly, talkative guy who can tell you anything you need to know about getting extreme or getting started. Marley's carries top brands that range in price from reasonable to jaw dropping. There's a wide selection of snowboarding wear, too. In summer the emphasis switches to skateboards. *Every day; map:FF8*

Marmot Mountain Works

827 BELLEVUE WY NE, BELLEVUE; 425/453-1515 This store opened in the REI-starved city of Bellevue more than a decade ago and they have quickly made a name for themselves. For one, it's not just an all-around sporting store like an REI—Marmot specializes in backcountry skiing and alpine climbing. The store is known for having hard-to-find odds and ends as well, evidenced by loyal, out-of-the-area customer calls. *Every day; www.marmotmountain.com; map:HH3*

The North Face

1023 1ST AVE, DOWNTOWN; 206/622-4111 This outdoor performance store is surprisingly small for the size of the label it carries. It's certainly not the only store in Seattle to sell North Face, but it is the only one that carries the popular brand exclusively. Even if the store selection can't match REI, the expert salespeople and huge catalog selection make it worth the trip for gear that will last. *Every day; thenorth face.com; map:L8*

Northwest Outdoor Center

2100 WESTLAKE AVE N, WESTLAKE; 206/281-9694 OR 800/683-0637 Located on the somewhat inconspicuous Julie's Landing, the water-sport-focused Northwest Outdoor Center can prepare you for an off-land journey with wet suits, helmets, life jackets, casual attire, and tools, as well as the boats themselves. The store's kayak rental business stays busy during summer months—you can leave right from the shop's Lake Union dock. *Every day; nwoc.com; map:GG7*

Patagonia

2100 1ST AVE, BELLTOWN; 206/622-9700 This inspired-by-nature store has the greatest selection of purely Patagonia. From breathable short-sleeve shirts to heavy snow parkas, this outfitter helps Seattleites weather the weather. Not only can you load up for an excursion in the fly-fishing or backcountry sections, but you can decide where to go next by looking through the store's many guide books to the Northwest region. *Every day; patagonia.com; map:H8*

Patrick's Fly Shop

2237 EASTLAKE AVE E, EASTLAKE; 206/325-8988 While Patrick's does have a large variety of flies, the shop isn't just about flies. The 50-year-old-plus store can also satisfy any other fly-fishing needs you may have, from apparel to technique classes. Gift certificates are available (a great option for the hard-to-shop-for dad) as are all of the supplies and tackle, instructional videos and books, fishing rods, sunglasses, and information on local boat shows and fish updates. *Every day; patricksflyshop.com; map:GG7*

R & E Cycles

5627 UNIVERSITY WY NE, UNIVERSITY DISTRICT; 206/527-4822 A stronghold of custom frame-building expertise (the shop has crafted bikes for one-armed customers), R & E specializes in hand-built Rodriguez frames. And owners Dan Towle and Estelle Gray include tandems, racing bikes, and wheel building in their repertoire. They also operate Seattle Bike Repair (5601 University Wy NE; 206/527-0360; map:EE7). The shop opens at noon, but is open mornings and after hours by appointment. *Tues–Sun and by appointment; sales@rodcycle.com; rodcycle.com; map:FF6*

REI (Recreational Equipment Inc.)

222 YALE AVE N, DOWNTOWN (AND BRANCHES); 206/223-1944 See Top 25 Attractions in the Exploring chapter.

Recycled Cycles

1007 NE BOAT ST, UNIVERSITY DISTRICT; 206/547-4491 OR 877/298-4683 One side of this store sells the bicycles, with a couple hundred on the sales floor at a time, while the other side covers parts and repair. The mix of new and used, both bikes and parts, has no rhyme or reason, they say, so you may have to ask which is which. Recycled Cycles makes a perfect pit stop along the Burke-Gilman Trail and consequently stays pretty busy. *Every day; steve@recycled cycles.com; recycledcycles.com; map:FF6*

Second Ascent

5209 BALLARD AVE NW, BALLARD; 206/545-8810 Frugal adventurers turn here for a wide range of new and used quality gear for climbing, mountaineering, cycling, paddling, and general camping. The store is folksy, with excellent help, and owners know their business, carrying the right products at bargain prices. Buy, sell, trade, and consign. *Every day; secondascent.com; map:EE8*

Snowboard Connection

604 ALASKAN WY, WATERFRONT; 206/467-8545 Not to say that women and middle-aged extreme athletes won't love this converted warehouse devoted to boarding on snow, street, or water, but dorm-dwelling college boys are going to feel right at home. Not only is the laid-back staff extremely helpful, but there is a big-screen TV if you just want to hang out. With the selection of clothes and gear for all seasons, sometimes you do have to take a break from decisions like what to wear on the slopes. *Every day; snowboardconnection.com; map:N8*

Super Jock 'n Jill

7210 E GREEN LAKE DR N, GREEN LAKE; 206/522-7711 OR 800/343-4111 Pinpoint your footfalls' downfalls with analysis from the staff at Super Jock 'n Jill. These salespeople know their metatarsals and their merchandise and understand the mechanics of running and power walking. A podiatrist is in the store once a week to answer questions and help with problems. The selection of other merchandise (running gear, bathing suits) is smaller than the footwear choices, but carefully chosen. This is also a good source for race registration and info, fun runs, routes, and training. *Every day; sjnjill@uswest.net; superjocknjill.com; map:EE7*

Swiftwater

4235 FREMONT AVE N, FREMONT; 206/547-3377 Get rolling on a river with a craft from this little Fremont storefront, which specializes in rafts and inflatable kayaks. Swiftwater will rent you one, sell you one, or help you organize a trip on one (for fly-fishing). These guys know their waterways. *Mon–Tues, Thurs–Sat; map:FF7*

Urban Surf

2100 N NORTHLAKE WY, WALLINGFORD; 206/545-9463 You wouldn't think there would be much of a market for surf shops in Seattle, but this store makes it possible by diversifying into sports like in-line skating, windsurfing, and snowboarding. Urban Surf has a wide selection of apparel that isn't really sport-specific, such as brands like Billabong, Rip Curl, and Roxy. Upstairs, you'll find the larger items like kayaks and different types of boards, along with an expert staff to make sure you get the right one. *Every day; usurf@urbansurf.com; urbansurf.com; map:FF7*

Wright Brothers Cycle Works

219 N 36TH ST, FREMONT; 206/633-5132 The front door of this specialty bike repair shop has a sign that reads, "A bad day cycling is better than a good day at work." Only bicyclists can fully appreciate this sentiment, but the message is universal. These people have been replacing and servicing quality Italian bike parts for many years and it is their passion. *Tues–Sun (summer), Tues–Sat (winter); map:FF7*

SEAFOOD

City Fish Company

1535 PIKE PL, PIKE PLACE MARKET; 206/682-9329 OR 800/334-2669 The first fish stand when entering the Market from the north, City Fish has been in business since 1917. While not the famous fish throwers, they do put on a show for the mob of tourists that eat it up. With seven helpful guys working the busy days, they all have a job to do. They work hard to make it possible for there to be "no line, no wait, no limits"—just like the sign says. They offer overnight shipping to anywhere in the world. *Every day; cityfish.com; map:J8*

Jack's Fish Spot

1514 PIKE PL, PIKE PLACE MARKET; 206/467-0514 For 23 years, Jack has been selling fresh seafood in the front of his "Spot" and serving fish and chips at his bar in the back. Jack's is known by locals for friendly service, huge selection, and the best prices in town. On busy days, there are as many as eight workers on hand to help you find what you need. *Every day; jfishspot@aol.com; jacksfishspot.com; map:J8*

Metropolitan Market
West Seattle Admiral Metropolitan Market

1908 QUEEN ANNE AVE N, QUEEN ANNE; 206/284-2530 (AND BRANCHES) These grocery stores (formerly known as Thriftways) recently adopted a more upscale name to match their quality. At the Queen Anne store, fish guru Rick Cavanaugh runs one of the best seafood departments in the United States: pristine stock and 20 to 30 kinds of fish and shellfish, from here and all over. He's also usually the first local to score the sought-after Copper River salmon, available only for a limited time each spring. Savvy cooks call ahead to tailor their menus to what's in that day. Special orders welcome; free packing for travel. There's a new location in Sand Point (420 40th Ave NE; 206/938-6600; map: EE6), and the West Seattle store (2320 42nd Ave SW; 206/937-0551; map: II9) carries on the same fine tradition with a stunning service counter. *Every day; metropolitan-market.com; map:GG8, EE6*

Mutual Fish Company

2335 RAINIER AVE S, RAINIER VALLEY; 206/322-4368 Mutual Fish fillets and steaks turn up on plates in many of Seattle's fanciest restaurants—and in the kitchens of the city's more discerning gourmets. This is the best in town: top quality and a dazzling selection are the result of the undivided attention of the Yoshimura family. Fresh tanks are full of several types of local oysters and crabs, and the seafood cases present the best from the West and East Coasts. Seattleites are pleased to find mahi mahi, tilefish, Maryland soft-shell crabs (in season), and other exotics. Prices are good, and staff will pack for air freight or carry-home. Located just south of Interstate 90, where Rainier Valley squeezes between Beacon Hill and the Mount Baker neighborhood. *Every day; www.mutualfish.com; map:II6*

Pike Place Fish

86 PIKE PL, PIKE PLACE MARKET; 206/682-7181 OR 800/542-7732 If you've ever been a tourist in Seattle or shown one around, you've been to see the notorious fish throwers. Aside from offering fresh seafood from salmon to scallops, on any given day guys in overalls shout out a ceremonial chant, echoed by about 10 other guys in overalls, all watched by a crowd that holds up foot traffic. A fish is thrown overhead, someone pays for it, and the ritual repeats itself over and over again. It's like our changing of the guard. *Every day; pikeplacefish@pikeplace fish.com; pikeplacefish.com; map:J8*

Seattle Caviar Company

2833 EASTLAKE AVE E, EASTLAKE; 206/323-3005 The offerings at the pick-up window of Seattle's only caviar importer put other drive-throughs to shame—as does the shop's regal interior. Owners Dale and Betsy Sherrow sell the finest beluga, osetra, and sevruga caviar from the Caspian Sea, in addition to Northwest fresh American malossol caviar and all the froufrou accoutrements of serious roe eating (such as pretty mother-of-pearl spoons and caviar *présentoirs*). They'll gladly arrange beautiful gift packages and even handle shipping. Stop in for a Saturday caviar tasting, too. *Tues–Sat and by appointment; dale@caviar.com; caviar.com; map:GG7*

University Seafood & Poultry Company

1317 NE 47TH ST, UNIVERSITY DISTRICT; 206/632-3900 Although students, who make up the bulk of this neighborhood's population, aren't known for their culinary prowess, Dale Erickson's shop continues to thrive in the heart of the University District. The selection includes salmon, halibut, lingcod, seasonal treats such as local sturgeon, and an amazing array of caviars—from flying fish to Columbia River sturgeon to beluga. Hard-to-find game birds, free-run chickens, and the freshest eggs, too. Prices are not posted but, surprisingly enough, are in line with supermarket prices. The fishmongers at the counter are friendly, and are all good cooks with recipes to share. *Mon–Sat; map:FF6*

Wild Salmon Seafood Market

1900 W NICKERSON ST, INTERBAY; 206/283-3366 OR 888/222-FISH This neighborhood fishmonger boasts personal service and fresh seafood in a dockside setting.

In addition to tanks filled with live lobsters, oysters, clams, and mussels, this small seafood specialist sells good-looking fish fillets, steaks, and whole fish and shellfish from its large service counter. Crab cakes and salmon cakes are usually available for impressive yet low-maintenance meals. *Every day; ask@wildsalmonseafood.com; wildsalmonseafood.com; map:FF8*

SHOES

Duncan & Sons Boots and Saddles

1946 1ST AVE S, SODO; 206/622-1310 If you are an equine lover, you know that it's not easy to find a good Western store in these parts. Fortunately, Duncan & Sons, established 1898, can take care of all your needs from tackle to boots. They are known for their quality leather goods, including handcrafted saddlery, and good old-fashioned service. Prices run from $90 to $350 on their boots for men and women that are mostly handmade in Texas. (Children's boots are only $60). *Mon–Sat; map:P9*

Edie's

319 E PINE ST, CAPITOL HILL; 206/839-1111 Edie's isn't your every day, cram-a-bunch-in shoe store with barely enough room to sit and try on a pair. On the contrary, its interior takes "minimalist" to new heights. Inside its high-ceilinged space are displays of brightly-colored tennis shoes, such as the popular brand Camper, more classic men's and women's dress shoes, beaded jewelry, and city bags by Nanna and gravis. *Every day; map:K1*

Enzo Angiolini

BELLEVUE SQUARE, BELLEVUE; 425/450-5582 Bellevue Square houses the only location in the state that exclusively sells designs by Enzo Angiolini—a maker of sleek-styled, mostly leather shoes and accessories. The prices are reasonable for shoes made in Brazil, China, Italy, and Spain. The same high-quality leather is used in jackets and there are only some synthetic fabrics in the boots and purses. *Every day; map:HH3*

J. Gilbert Footwear

2025 1ST AVE, BELLTOWN; 206/441-1182 The big selling point at this European boutique–fashioned shoe store is it has the largest selection anywhere of Taryn Rose—an orthopedic surgeon/designer who gains a lifetime customer every time a pair is purchased. These shoes' comfort is unbeatable, and the best part is they don't look like orthopedics but are stylish dress and walking shoes—even strappy sandals. The store's handloomed cotton sweaters are also big draws, as are the Cambio jeans in almost 40 different styles. *Every day; info@jgilbertfootwear.com; jgilbertfoot wear.com; map:H8*

John Fluevog Shoes

205 PINE ST, DOWNTOWN; 206/441-1065 OR 800/568-DDFT The John Fluevog label satisfies a niche in this town of people who make statements on their feet. Handmade originals like red-and-white extra-tall cowboy boots and purple-and-red double-strapped Mary Jane's, keep company with. stylish men's shoes and a range of women's shoes, from sexy pointed-toe to school-girl fashions from the past. Keep an eye out for the twice-yearly sales that attract swarms of shoe fanatics. *Mon–Sat; seattle@fluevog.com; fluevog.com; map:I7*

Maggie's Shoes

1927 1ST AVE, DOWNTOWN; 206/728-5837 You'll need to know your Italian shoe size in here because it's mostly Italian leather, with the exception of European travel brands like Berkemann and Hartjes. The men's and women's shoes are special, from classic pumps with tiny bow straps to double Velcro pink loafers. Maggie's also carries handbags and a few racks of designer dresses and suiting. *Every day; map:I7*

M. J. Feet

4334 UNIVERSITY WY NE, UNIVERSITY DISTRICT; 206/632-5353 / 15 103RD AVE NE, BELLEVUE; 425/646-0416 While the Pike Place Market location closed, comfortably shod college kids keep this U District location going strong. The sturdy sandals that are a staple of the Northwest high-tech uniform can be found in many hues and styles here. The cheerful shop carries creative socks and tights, plus a small selection of clothing. It's also a good place to get hard-to-find Ellington school bags and quality repair service. *Every day; mjfeet@aol.com; mjfeet.com; map:FF6, HH4*

Ped

1115 1ST AVE, DOWNTOWN; 206/292-1767 Because many of Ped's largely leather shoes and bags are made by small designers, if you buy a pair (like their exclusive brand CYDWOQ), you stand a good chance of not passing your shoes on the street. The store also sells some handmade European shoes and leathers from Italy, Spain, London, and the United States. *Every day; pedshoes.com; map:L*

BEST PLACE TO SPOIL YOURSELF?

"A night in one of the upper-floor suites at the W Hotel; it's getting away from it all without really getting away at all."

Darryl Macdonald, co-founder of Seattle International Film Festival (SIFF)

Seattle Retro Shoe Store

1524 E OLIVE WY, CAPITOL HILL; 206/322-2305 The shoes sold here are retro in the sense that they stopped being made back in the '80s and early '90s. Some are limited edition, Euro-exclusive, or Asia-exclusive—it truly is hard to find these shoes anywhere else in the Northwest. Shoe collectors (yes, shoe collectors) visit every month or so to see what is in stock: names like Nike Air Jordan's, Air Max, and PF Flyers. If only we'd kept them the first time around. *Every day; seattle retroshoestore.com; map:I1*

Shoefly

7900 E GREEN LAKE DR N, STE 109, GREEN LAKE; 206/729-7463 Set in the walking capital of Seattle, Shoefly has shoes for most any occasion. There are designer brands such as Kenneth Cole, as well as the more unusual such as Cordani. Locally-made jewelry and handbags are also perched in the brightly colored window, testing the will of passing walkers who have a fetish for other-than-walking shoes. *Every day; shoefly.com; map:EE*

The Woolly Mammoth
5 Doors Up

4303 UNIVERSITY WY NE, UNIVERSITY DISTRICT; 206/632-3254 / 4302½ UNIVERSITY WY NE, UNIVERSITY DISTRICT; 206/547-3192 Most shoes in the original store are as rugged and weatherproof as their name. The Woolly Mammoth mostly carries sensible European comfort brands such as Josef Seibel, Ecco, and Naot. A second store up the street, 5 Doors Up, carries trendier stuff—Steve Madden, John Fluevog, and the like. *Every day; map:FF6*

SPECIALTY SHOPS

Arcade Smoke Shop

1522 5TH AVE, DOWNTOWN; 206/587-0159 Tobacco, pipes, cigars, and accessories are all that you will find in here, setting it apart from other smoke stores in Seattle. Call them purists. The crystal ashtrays are popular, as are the hand-carved and ivory lighters. There is a humidor in the back containing premium cigars for the ever-growing number of stogie enthusiasts. *Mon–Sat; map:J6*

Archie McPhee

2428 NW MARKET ST, BALLARD; 206/297-0240 Pop-culture icons such as the boxing nun puppet and the wiggling hula girl dash ornament get center stage—instead of just a junk-near-the-checkstand nod—at this longtime purveyor of kitsch. Archie McPhee's is a great place to stock up on cheap toys and party favors or just to browse the memorable catalog. Plenty of grown-ups confess shameful inclinations to lose themselves among the windup toys and bendable plastic creatures. *Every day; mcphee.com; map:FF8*

Dusty Strings

3406 FREMONT AVE N, FREMONT; 206/634-1662 Come here for all your stringed instrument needs. Not only will Dusty Strings take in your violin or guitar for repair, but the store is the only manufacturer of harps in Seattle. No where else can you find this selection of bagpipes, accordions, banjos, mandolins, and hammered dulcimers, as well as their specific sheet music. Planning an event with live music or want to learn an instrument yourself? Come look through the musician directory or take a workshop. *Every day; musicshop@dustystrings.com; www.dustystrings.com; map:FF7*

Metsker Maps

1511 1ST AVE, PIKE PLACE MARKET; 206/623-8747 OR 800/727-4430 After calling an edge of Pioneer Square home longer than even the owner knows, Seattle's fabled map shop moved in 2003 to a slightly larger, busier spot in the Sanitary Market Building. However, it's still the perfect place to create dreams or plans of really getting out in the world. There are fold-up maps for road trips to wherever your heart desires, maps lining the walls like artwork, world travel books, atlases, and a friendly person behind the counter to lead you in the right direction. *Every day; sales@metskers.com; metskers.com; map:N8*

Michael Maslan Historic Photographs Postcards & Ephemera

214 1ST AVE S, PIONEER SQUARE; 206/587-0187 Though Michael Maslan's hours vary according to whim (call before stopping in), once inside you'll find such treasures as vintage lithographs of jungle scenes, faded portraits of stiff-lipped Victorian-era families, and endless postcards from every location and era from the turn-of-the-19th century: vintage maps, photographs, and posters, mostly elegant samples from the era of shipboard travel or kitschy ads from the post–World War II airline boom. Prices range from extremely reasonable to heirloom level. *Mon–Fri; map:O8*

Paperhaus

2008 1ST AVE, BELLTOWN; 206/374-8566 The shelves of sleek albums, portfolios, and (of course) paper at Paperhaus are made by award-winning manufacturers like NAVA, MH Way, Prat, and Rexite. The shop also has a wide assortment of sleek pens and vinyl briefcases made in Milan. And the wares here are eco-conscious: paper products are made from recycled materials, leather items from by-products. *Every day; info@paperhaus.com; paperhaus.com; map:H7*

Scarecrow Video

5030 ROOSEVELT WY NE, UNIVERSITY DISTRICT; 206/524-8554 This packed two-floor store carries almost everything ever committed to celluloid anywhere in the world. Scarecrow's immense collection of new and used videocassettes, DVDs, and laserdiscs is cataloged not just by new releases and top rentals but by director (alphabetically), place of origin ("Balkan States"), and unusual category (animé, blaxploitation, hip-hop, experimental, and so on). VCR (both American and PAL, a European VHS format) players and DVD players are available for nightly rental for under $10. *Every day; scarecrow@scarecrow.com; www.scarecrow.com; map:FF7*

Silberman
Brown Fine Stationers

1322 5TH AVE, DOWNTOWN; 206/292-9404 / 10220 NE 8TH ST, BELLEVUE; 425/455-3665 This shop does the lost art of letter-writing proud. It has been selling richly colored pens by Cartier, Waterman, and Mont Blanc, leather frames, hand-crafted silver pen sheaths, floral painted stamp dispensers, clocks, inkwells, and dipping pens—in addition to their shelves of fine stationery and invitations—since 1977. *Mon–Sat; map:K6, GG3*

Ye Olde Curiosity Shop

✝ **1001 ALASKAN WY, PIER 54, WATERFRONT; 206/682-5844** There are few words that adequately describe this Seattle waterfront landmark—around since 1899—but hilarious, dusty, and yuck come to mind. You'll find something here for those with an appreciation for the stranger things in life. Some of the most notable treasures are Sylvester, the famous desert dummy, and a fortune-telling gypsy machine like the one in the movie *Big*. And, of course, it's always stocked with "of the moment" tacky, such as Britney Spears dollar bills. Aptly, the novelty shop has now been immortalized with its own book (*1001 Curious Things*, University of Washington Press, 2001). *Every day; yeoldecuriosityshop.com; map:L9*

TOYS

The Great Wind-Up

93 PIKE PL, PIKE PLACE MARKET; 206/621-9370 Devoted entirely to wind-up toys for 18 years, this store continues on with more than 350 toys in stock, one wind at a time. The try-before-you-buy table is alive with mechanical animals, Santas, nuns, among other things, such as battery-operated wind-ups and tin lunch boxes. Classic toys, such as Mickey riding Pluto and the clapping monkey, are fun to peruse, and then there's the section of tin collectibles that are too fragile for children to handle. Who knew? *Every day; greatwindup.com; map:J8*

Imagination Toys

1815 N 45TH ST, WALLINGFORD; 206/547-2356 / 2236 NW MARKET ST, BAL-LARD; 206/784-1310 Here you'll find diversions for all ages and types of children— from the educational arts and crafts or board games to bouncy balls and princess costumes, a large Playmobil section, big plastic infant toys and puzzles of all complexity levels. And, if you're stumped, just look for staff recommendations taped to the shelves. *Every day; map:FF7, FF8*

Magic Mouse Toys

603 1ST AVE, PIONEER SQUARE; 206/682-8097 The magic starts at the entrance with the bubbling Lava lamps and swimming fish frames, but it's the interactive toys that keep shoppers enthralled. A monkey rides the length of the ceiling on a trapeze bike while "squiggle balls" roll about in every direction on the floor. There are also toys that stand still—flight attendant Barbie, tub toys, and the like. *Every day; map:N8*

Pinocchio's Toys

4540 UNION BAY PL NE, UNIVERSITY VILLAGE, UNIVERSITY DISTRICT; 206/528-1100 This U Village store sells toys with a purpose: puzzles, interactive play media (such as Playmobil and Brio), nature-exploring aides (binoculars and science workbooks), and a wide variety of paints (nontoxic watercolors and tie-dyeing kits). Books are geared more toward adults reading bedtime stories to the little 'uns than toward older children who read on their own. *Every day; map:FF6*

WINE AND BEER

Bottleworks

1710 N 45TH, WALLINGFORD; 206/633-2437 This store proves that the term "connoisseur" isn't just reserved for wine enthusiasts. More than 700 different kinds of beer are properly chilled here, and you can buy beer from the bottle or the case, individualized gift packs, as well as find the perfect glassware and cigars to complement your frothy selection. *Tues–Sun; bottleworks.com; map:FF7*

City Cellars Fine Wines

1710 N 45TH ST, WALLINGFORD; 206/632-7238 An unpretentious neighborhood wine shop, City Cellars's customers keep coming back for another glass of warm service and well-informed advice. And a huge selection doesn't hurt. There are close to 800 labels in stock, but the specialties are Old World Wines. There is a $10 wall for those not looking to make an investment, and at regularly scheduled events the staff crack open a bottle or two for customers. *Tues–Sat; map:FF7*

Esquin Wine Merchants

2700 4TH AVE S, SODO; 206/682-7374 OR 888/682-WINE Close to 500 labels at Esquin boast many choices in the $5 to $15 range, and the store stocks close to 3,200 in all. Monthly specials reflect the best wines from all regions at some of the best prices in town. The owner seeks out the special or unique, occasionally acquiring wines no one else has. The French, Italian, Australian, and American selections are all good. You'll find case discounts, free twice-weekly tastings, and outstanding sales. *Every day; wine@esquin.com; esquin.com; map:II7*

La Cantina Wine Merchants

5346 SAND POINT WY NE, SAND POINT; 206/525-4340 / 10218 NE 8TH ST, BELLEVUE; 425/455-4363 These two small specialty shops are separately owned but equally well stocked. Owners are knowledgeable and, by getting to know their regular customers, are able to make suggestions based upon the customers' tastes. With an emphasis on French bottlings, this is the shop for fine Burgundies and Bordeaux. The Bellevue store offers discounts through its buying club. *Mon–Sat (Sand Point); Tues–Sat (Bellevue); map:FF6, HH3*

Market Cellar Winery and Home Brew Supplies

1432 WESTERN AVE, PIKE PLACE MARKET; 206/622-1880 The only winery in the downtown area, this tiny shop sells its own vintages exclusively and also stocks an extensive array of supplies for home wine and beer brewing. *Mon–Sat; market cellarwinery.com; map:J7*

McCarthy & Schiering Wine Merchants

6500 RAVENNA AVE NE, RAVENNA; 206/524-9500 / 2401B QUEEN ANNE AVE N, QUEEN ANNE; 206/282-8500 Dan McCarthy (at Queen Anne) and Jay Schiering (at Ravenna) are authorities on the nose, bouquet, and body of the wine world's rising stars. The pair seek out the newest and most promising producers from Europe and the United States. Regular Saturday-afternoon in-store tastings and a special rate for Vintage Select club members make it a good place to find a rare bottle. California and the Northwest are as well represented as France. *Tues–Sat (Ravenna), Tues–Sun (Queen Anne); map:FF6, GG8*

Pete's Wines
Pete's Wines Eastside

58 E LYNN ST, EASTLAKE; 206/322-2660 / 134 105TH AVE NE, BELLEVUE; 425/454-1100 There may be some confusion over the official name of the roughly 40-year-old store—the business cards say Pete's Wine Shop and the sign out front says Pete's Market. But regardless of what you call it, it is well known for carrying more than 1,000 wines from every region domestically and internationally. Popular attractions: low prices for sparkling wine and champagne, and the deli sandwiches. *Every day; map:GG7, HH3*

Pike & Western Wine Shop

1934 PIKE PL, PIKE PLACE MARKET; 206/441-1307 This Seattle wine shop has a couple claims to fame that keep the connoisseurs (and wine rookies) coming back for more. One is their location. Being just at the north end of Pike Place Market means shoppers happen right by with their fresh dinner ingredients, in need only of a perfect libation for their meal. The other is, though the shop carries wines from all over the world, it specializes in Washington and Oregon labels. And the owner is such a wealth of knowledge he has assisted local restaurants in designing winning wine lists. *Every day; map:J8*

ARTS

ARTS

Museums

During the boom years of the 1990s, Seattle-area museums pumped money into expansion and renovation, with every major museum improving its facility or building a new one. The **SEATTLE ART MUSEUM** opened a downtown branch; the **HENRY ART GALLERY** quadrupled in size; and the **BURKE MUSEUM OF NATURAL HISTORY AND CULTURE**, also on the University of Washington campus, extensively remodeled. Catching the tail of the economic high times, the **BELLEVUE ART MUSEUM** moved out of its suburban shopping mall space in 2000 and into its own shiny Steven Holl–designed building across the way. (Whether the museum will survive remains to be seen; see listing below.) Surprisingly, with the economy down and many of the city's cultural institutions struggling to make ends meet, there's another flurry of artistic growth. Seattle Art Museum has continued plans for a two-pronged expansion: its **OLYMPIC SCULPTURE PARK**, slated to open in 2006 on the downtown waterfront, will feature rotating exhibits and outdoor sculpture from the permanent collection. And plans are developing for an expansion of the museum's main facility in an unusual building-share arrangement with Washington Mutual Bank in a new office tower adjacent to the Seattle Art Museum. Details of the complex agreement—a multiarchitect conundrum—are still being ironed out, but SAM has hired Portland architect Brad Cloepfil of Allied Works to design its part of the proposed office tower, which will connect to the Robert Venturi–designed museum. In a more straightforward move, in the next few years, the **WING LUKE ASIAN MUSEUM** will move from its converted garage in the heart of the Chinatown/International District to roomier digs nearby, and the **MUSEUM OF HISTORY AND INDUSTRY (MOHAI)** will relocate from the U-District to downtown.

Bellevue Art Museum

510 BELLEVUE WY NE, BELLEVUE; 425/637-1799 Since moving out of its third-floor perch in the Bellevue Square mall into its piece-of-art architecture, BAM has struggled to establish a new identity geared more to design, fashion, and community activities than to traditional shows of painting and sculpture. Following the exodus of the director, lead curator, and several board members in late 2003, the museum dramatically closed its doors and announced the plan to reopen in 2004 under a new business plan. One consistent crowd pleaser expected to be unaffected by the shakeup is the museum's popular annual Bellevue Art Museum Fair held for three days in July across the street at Bellevue Square. Call for admission prices. *Call for hours; bam@bellevueart.org; bellevueart.org; map:HH3* &

Burke Museum of Natural History and Culture

17TH AVE NE AND NE 45TH ST, UNIVERSITY DISTRICT; 206/543-5590 Once an eccentric treasure trove of dusty relics, the Burke—named in honor of Judge Thomas Burke, an early Seattle mover and chief justice of the Washington State Supreme Court—is an attention-grabbing place. From its collections of more than 3 million artifacts and specimens, the museum has created three permanent exhibits. Life and Times of Washington State looks back over 500 million years of regional history, examining how nature shaped the land and the life upon it. Telling that story has meant assembling prehistoric plant and animal fossils; a selection of cast dinosaur skeletons as well as the Northwest's only real dinosaur skeleton, a 140-million-year-old, flesh-eating allosaurus; a walk-through volcano; and even a glass case of 600 native (and sometimes bizarre) Washington insects, with an accompanying interactive information center. Another permanent fixture, Treasures of the Burke, can be seen lining the museum walls, highlighting its most unique collections. Probably better appreciated by adults, though, is Pacific Voices, which delves into the richness of 19 cultures all over the Pacific Rim. A main-floor gift shop sells curiosities from around the Pacific Rim; the downstairs cafe is an especially comfy espresso-and-pastries spot. Admission for permanent exhibits is a suggested $6.50 donation for adults and $3 for students; free for children 5 and under, museum members, and UW students/staff. Charges for special exhibits vary. *Every day; recept@u.washington.edu; www.burkemuseum.org; map:FF6* &

Center for Wooden Boats

1010 VALLEY ST, **SOUTH LAKE UNION**; **206/382-2628** This maritime museum, which has its own little harbor at the southern tip of Lake Union and is kept afloat financially by private donations and a contingent of volunteers, celebrates the heritage of small craft before the advent of fiberglass. Of the 75 vintage and replica wooden rowing and sailing boats in the collection, more than half are available for public use. Admission is always free. Rentals range from $10 to $46 an hour. Lessons in sailing, traditional woodworking, and boatbuilding are offered for all ages. *Every day May 5–Sept 7, otherwise Wed–Mon; cwb.org; map:D1*

The Children's Museum

CENTER HOUSE, **SEATTLE CENTER**; **206/441-1768** Located on the fountain level of the Seattle Center's busy Center House, the Children's Museum has tripled in size since its opening. It's an imaginative learning center that stresses hands-on activities and exploration of other cultural traditions, and it houses a number of permanent features, including a play center, a mountain, and a global village with child-size houses from Japan, Ghana, and the Philippines. The variety of special programs—Mexican folk dancing, Native American games, Chinese storytelling, Japanese kite making—is impressive. The Imagination Station features a different artist every month guiding activities with various materials. The Discovery Bay exhibit is geared to infants and toddlers. The Children's Museum now has an Eastside branch at the Crossroads Shopping Center called Imagination Studio (15600 NE 8th St, Ste G-1, Bellevue; 425/644-5689; admission $4; every day), which is geared to art projects and activities. At the main branch admission is $6 per person; $5.50 over 55; and annual family memberships are $60–$120. *Every day; tcm@thechildrensmuseum.org; thechildrensmuseum.org; map:C6* &

Experience Music Project

325 5TH AVE N, SEATTLE CENTER; 206/367-5483 See Top 25 Attractions in the Exploring chapter.

Frye Art Museum

704 TERRY AVE, FIRST HILL; 206/622-9250 This once-stodgy museum, known for sentimental 19th-century German salon paintings from the collection of late Seattleites Charles and Emma Frye (who made their fortune in meat processing), underwent a dramatic expansion and remodel in 1997. Since reopening, it's become a lively hub of activities, with a pleasant cafe, poetry readings, chamber music, and other performances in addition to frequently changing exhibits. (Though lately it has been undergoing a catharsis as the museum searches for new leadership.) Shows in recent years have been as diverse as the metaphorical paintings of Norwegian artist Odd Nerdrum; the art of Russian ballet dancer Vaslav Nijinsky; a tribute—in words and imagery—to National Poetry Month; and an exhibit of women painters from the collection of Russia's Hermitage museum. Free admission and parking. *Tues–Sun; fryeart.org; map:N3* &

Henry Art Gallery

15TH AVE NE AND NE 41ST ST, UNIVERSITY DISTRICT; 206/453-2280 See Top 25 Attractions in the Exploring chapter.

Museum of Flight

9404 E MARGINAL WY S, GEORGETOWN; 206/764-5720 See Top 25 Attractions in the Exploring chapter.

Museum of History and Industry

2700 24TH AVE E, UNIVERSITY DISTRICT; 206/324-1126 The rambling, amiable MOHAI is a huge repository of Americana, with artifacts pertaining to the early history of the Pacific Northwest. There's an exhibit about Seattle's Great Fire of 1889 (which started in a glue pot on the waterfront), a hands-on history of the fishing and canning industry in the Northwest, and a half-dozen immense wooden female beauties—and one male counterpart—who once rode the prows of ships in Puget Sound. Locally oriented exhibits change throughout the year. At some point, the museum is slated to move downtown into a space at the Washington State Convention & Trade Center. Admission is $7 for adults, $5 for seniors and children 5–12, and free for kids under 5. *Every day; seattlehistory.org; map:FF6* &

Nordic Heritage Museum

3014 NW 67TH ST, BALLARD; 206/789-5707 Established in a stately restored schoolhouse, the Nordic Heritage Museum focuses on the history of Nordic settlers in the United States, with exhibits of maritime equipment, costumes, and photographs, including an Ellis Island installation. Periodic traveling exhibits

have included a show of 18th-century Alaskan and Northwest Coast Native artifacts from the National Museum of Finland, as well as artworks by contemporary
Scandinavian artists. Holidays bring ethnic festivals. Admission is $6 for adults, $5
for seniors and students, $4 for children 5–17, and free for kids under 5. *Tues–Sun;
nordic@intelistep.com; nordicmuseum.com; map:EE9* &

BEST PLACE TO FIND INSPIRATION?
"The ferry. The water is peaceful, it's quiet.
You find perspective."

Ann Lovejoy, gardening author

Rosalie Whyel Museum of Doll Art

1116 108TH AVE NE, BELLEVUE; 425/455-1116 Occupying a pink confection
of a building near Bellevue Square, this privately owned museum opened in
1992 and was an instant hit in the insular world of doll collecting. Don't be
put off by that. You'll find more than 3,000 dolls, including everything from effigies
and ancient Egyptian burial charms to extravagantly outfitted porcelain princesses—
not to mention a few of their modern, mass-produced counterparts. A gift shop with
a pricey selection of new and antique toys caters to collectors. Admission is $6 for
adults, $5 for seniors, $4 for children 5–17, and free for kids under 5. *Every day;
dollart.com; map:HH3* &

Seattle Art Museum

100 UNIVERSITY ST, DOWNTOWN; 206/654-3100 See Top 25 Attractions in the
Exploring chapter.

Seattle Asian Art Museum

1400 E PROSPECT ST, CAPITOL HILL; 206/654-3100 See Top 25 Attractions in the
Exploring chapter.

Wing Luke Asian Museum

407 7TH AVE S, CHINATOWN/INTERNATIONAL DISTRICT; 206/623-5124 Named
after Seattle's first Chinese-American city councilman, this lively little museum in the
Chinatown/International District is devoted to the Asian American experience in the
Northwest. Particularly moving is the small exhibit of photographs and artifacts
relating to the internment of Japanese Americans during World War II. Changing
exhibits are devoted to Chinese, Korean, Filipino, Vietnamese, and Laotian peoples
and their often difficult meetings with the West. Soon Wing Luke will move to a
larger building in the district. Admission is $4 for adults, $3 for students and seniors, $2 for children 5–12, and free for kids under 5. Free for everyone on the first
Thursday of every month. *Tues–Sun; folks@wingluke.org; wingluke.org; map:R5* &

ART APPEAL

When the Seattle Art Museum opens its new **OLYMPIC SCULPTURE PARK** in 2006, the waterfront near the Seattle Center will be a major art destination. Until then, discriminating art lovers can find public art worth pondering in nearly every corner of the city.

In Myrtle Edwards Park the massive Michael Heizer stone sculpture *Adjacent, Against, Upon* is one the city's subtle treasures. In the downtown business district, standout artworks include the four-story Joseph Borofsky *Hammering Man*, outside the Seattle Art Museum, whose motorized arm and hammer are set to pound out four beats per minute; Henry Moore's beloved bronze *Vertebrae* (1001 4th Ave Plaza, Downtown); and a contemplative Isamu Noguchi stone installation *Landscape of Time*, outside the Henry M. Jackson Federal Building (915 2nd Ave, Downtown). Symbolic **TOTEM POLES** in Pioneer Square and at the Pike Place Market recall the city's cultural origins. Fountains by the late Seattle artist George Tsutakawa crop up in many locations around the city, including *Fountain of Wisdom*, which graced the courtyard of the former downtown public library and will find a new home outside the new Rem Koolhaus–designed Central Library (1000 4th Ave, Downtown). Duck into any of the **METRO BUS TUNNEL STATIONS** for a quick immersion in Northwest art. A highlight is Robert Teeple's deliciously witty electronic LED light sculpture *Electric Lascaux*, at the Third and University station, where you exit for the Seattle Art Museum.

Scattered around the Seattle Center grounds you'll encounter a number of imposing sculptures, including the towering persimmon-colored cylinders of *Olympic Iliad* by Alexander Lieberman, and inside KeyArena, the expansive *Rain Wall* by sound artists Trimpin and Clark Wiegman. Outside the newly remodeled opera house, McCaw Hall, you can see a **NIGHTTIME LIGHTSHOW** projected on hanging scrims designed by

Galleries

Since the 1970s, when a few entrepreneurs and architects elbowed in to save Pioneer Square from urban renewal, Seattle's main gallery scene has been situated there, with additional galleries sprinkled to the north along First Avenue, especially in the vicinity of the downtown Seattle Art Museum. One good way to sample the fare is to roam with the crowds around Pioneer Square on the **FIRST THURSDAY GALLERY WALK** each month (6pm–8pm), when new shows are previewed. A lot of other galleries and alternative art spaces have popped up in other parts of town as well, with a particularly energetic art scene on Capitol Hill.

Leni Schwendinger and an understated waterscape by internationally acclaimed Seattle landscape designer Kathryn Gustafson. (Gustafson made headlines recently when she was chosen to design the London memorial for Princess Diana.)

The University District has a new night-time treat: a shifting light installation on the exterior walls of the new **JAMES TURRELL SKYSPACE**, an architectural addition to the Henry Art Gallery that stops passersby at the edge of the University of Washington campus. Not far from there, on campus, visit the powerful Barnett Newman *Broken Obelisk*. For a look at Seattle's quirkiest public art, visit Fremont, the self-proclaimed "Center of the Universe." Here art is by the people, for the people, and includes Richard Beyer's delightful—and regularly embellished by locals—assemblage of life-sized figures, *Waiting for the Interurban*. More controversially, a huge recycled Communist-era bronze statue of **LENIN** serves as an ironic reminder of how the mighty fall.

Another lively arts hub has sprung up at Sand Point Magnuson Park, on the Northwestern shore of Lake Washington. The park hosts sculpture exhibits each summer in and around the converted buildings of the former naval base. One imposing permanent display is John T. Young's *The Fin Project: From Swords into Plowshares*, which uses partially buried fins of decommissioned nuclear submarines to mimic a surfacing pod of whales.

Seattle's most beloved public artwork may be Isamu Noguchi's riveting *Black Sun*, perfectly sited outside the Seattle Asian Art Museum in Capitol Hill's Volunteer Park. Framing a gorgeous view of the Olympic Mountains, the Space Needle, and the setting sun, Noguchi's elegant stone form is pleasingly accessible to all. In the nearby Broadway district, another loveable artwork is Jack Mackie's lighthearted series of Arthur Murray–inspired **BRONZE DANCE STEPS**, set into the sidewalk to cha-cha-cha people through the busy shopping district.

—Sheila Farr

Benham Studio Gallery

1216 1ST AVE, DOWNTOWN; 206/622-2480 From its roots as a photographic exhibition in a passport studio entryway, the Benham has grown into one of Seattle's finest photo galleries. The gallery represents primarily Northwest photographers, from the well-known to up-and-comers, whose work is mounted here in a popular group show in December or January. *Tues–Sat; benham@benhamgallery.com; benhamgallery.com; map:L7* &

Bryan Ohno Gallery

155 S MAIN ST, PIONEER SQUARE; 206-667-9572 With connections in Japan, Ohno presents an intriguing mix of artists from the United States and abroad, with an emphasis on sculpture. Expect to find anything from abstract paintings to classical Japanese prints. His biggest draws have been two exhibits of sculpture by the late, great Isamu Noguchi (Noguchi's *Black Sun* outside the Seattle Asian Art Museum is a Seattle favorite). *Tues–Sat; bryanohnogallery.com; map:O8*

Carolyn Staley Fine Prints

314 OCCIDENTAL AVE S, PIONEER SQUARE; 206/621-1888 The specialty here is fine old prints, including Japanese *ukiyo-e* woodblock prints, antique maps, and botanical prints. Staley also hosts occasional book-art shows. *Tues–Sat; carolyn staleyprints.com; staleyprints@earthlink.net; map:O8* &

Center on Contemporary Art

1420 11TH AVE, CAPITOL HILL; 206-728-1980 CoCA is a long way from its stellar beginnings in the early 1980s as the city's top venue for outside-the-mainstream art. After many incarnations and directors and with scanty funding, it hangs on in a tiny, out-of-the-way space, hosting hit-and-miss shows by outside curators as its board tries to reignite. The best recent exhibit was selected by Microsoft curator Michael Klein to showcase Northwest artists. Call for event info. *Call for hours; cocaseattle.org map:GG6*

Consolidated Works

500 BOREN AVE N, SOUTH LAKE UNION; 206-381-3218 Visual-art exhibits are sporadic and theme driven at this venue—tending toward new media and conceptual works—with high ambitions and a huge space that also produces theater and shows. The recent hiring of a new visual-art director may change the look of things. Call for event info. *Call for hours; conworks.org; map:E2* &

Davidson Galleries

313 OCCIDENTAL AVE S, PIONEER SQUARE; 206/624-7684 Formerly geared to traditional tastes, Davidson has recently branched out from its usual shows of landscapes and figurative works by contemporary artists. Now you might also find the barest abstractions, multimedia sculptures, and gutsy surveys that include work by internationally known artists. The back gallery features contemporary printmakers from around the world. Upstairs, check out the antique print department with loads of work on file, as well as rotating shows of everything from William Blake illustrations to Indian miniature paintings. *Tues–Sat; davidson galleries.com; map:O8* &

Foster/White Gallery

123 S JACKSON ST, PIONEER SQUARE (AND BRANCHES); 206/622-2833 Under new Canadian ownership, Foster/White showcases paintings, sculpture, and ceramics—usually abstract and decorative—by Northwest artists living and dead. The gallery is also one of the major local dealers in contemporary glass by Pilchuck School stars, most notably Dale Chihuly. An Eastside outpost is located in downtown Kirkland (107 Park Lane, 425/822-2305; map:EE3) and a downtown branch at Rainier Square (1331 5th Ave; 206/583-0100; map: K5) caters to tourists and shoppers. *Every day; ask@fosterwhite.com; fosterwhite.com; map:O8* &

Francine Seders Gallery

6701 GREENWOOD AVE N, GREENWOOD; 206/782-0355 In judicious operation since 1966, Seders represents some venerable members of Seattle's art community, including the late Jacob Lawrence, Gwen Knight, Robert Jones, and Michael Spafford. New additions to the stable include generous numbers of minority artists, among them painters, sculptors, and assemblagists. *Tues–Sun; sedersgallery.com; map:EE7* &

G. Gibson Gallery

514 E PIKE ST, CAPITOL HILL; 206/587-4033 Gibson, one of the city's top photography dealers, recently moved from Pioneer Square to a Capitol Hill storefront. This is the place to find work by stellar 20th-century photographers such as Imogen Cunningham, Ansel Adams, Jacques-Henri Lartigue, Ruth Bernhard, and Marion Post Wolcott as well as by adventurous contemporary Northwesterners. *Wed–Sat; ggibson@halcyon.com; ggibsongallery.com; map:K2*

Greg Kucera Gallery

212 3RD AVE S, PIONEER SQUARE; 206/624-0770 Smart and outspoken, Kucera maintains a carefully chosen stable of artists, many with national reputations. He has a great eye for emerging talent but also shows editioned works by established blue-chip artists such as Frank Stella, Robert Motherwell, and Helen Frankenthaler. One thematic exhibit each year addresses a touchy topic: sex, religion, and politics. *Tues–Sat; staff@gregkucera.com; gregkucera.com; map:O7*

Grover/Thurston Gallery

309 OCCIDENTAL AVE S, PIONEER SQUARE; 206/223-0816 In the heart of the gallery district, Grover/Thurston gained considerable status when it picked up one of the region's most popular painters, Fay Jones, just before her 1997 retrospective at the Seattle Art Museum. The gallery also represents esteemed ceramic sculptor Akio Takamori and Oregon painter James Lavadour. *Tues–Sat; rcthurson@world net.att.net; groverthurston.com; map:O8* &

Howard House

2017 2ND AVE, BELLTOWN; 206/ 256-6399 An ambitious younger dealer with an eye toward the international scene, Billy Howard showcases up-and-coming talent. His stable also includes one of the Northwest's premier ceramic sculptors and former University of Washington professor, Patti Warashina. *Tues–Sat; info@howard house.net; howardhouse.net; map:H7*

James Harris Gallery

309A 3RD AVE S, PIONEER SQUARE; 206/903-2339 The space is small and the shows often include just four or five paintings or sculptures, but the offerings at James Harris are always fresh and distinctive. With roots in the San Francisco Bay Area art scene, Harris shows established California artists and emerging talent from the Northwest. *Wed–Sat; ottoharris@aol.com; jamesharrisgallery.com; map:O7*

Kirkland Arts Center

620 MARKET ST, KIRKLAND; 425/822-7161 In a historic brick building near the waterfront, this publicly funded center puts on several shows each year by Puget Sound–area artists. A variety of art classes are open to children and adults. *Mon–Sat; kirklandartscenter.org; map:EE3*

Linda Hodges Gallery

316 1ST AVE S, PIONEER SQUARE; 206/624-3034 Hodges shows contemporary paintings, and occasionally photography and sculpture, by artists from Seattle, Portland, and other Northwest burgs. The art ranges from fantasy to realism, with the biggest draw being the zany, countrified mythology of adored Eastern Washington painter Gaylen Hansen. *Tues–Sun; ldhgallery@aol.com; lindahodgesgallery.com; map:O8* &

Lisa Harris Gallery

1922 PIKE PL, PIKE PLACE MARKET; 206/443-3315 Amid the jostling crowds of the Market, this small upstairs gallery can be an oasis of calm. Harris favors expressionistic landscape and figurative works, with several Bellingham artists forming the core of her stable. *Every day; staff@lisaharrisgallery.com; lisaharrisgallery.com; map:I7*

Martin-Zambito Fine Art

721 E PIKE ST, CAPITOL HILL; 206/726-9509 These two guys from the East Coast know more about the obscure corners of Northwest regionalism than almost anybody. And they're on a mission: to bring recognition to overlooked early artists of the area, especially women—such as photographer Myra Wiggins, whose work attracted international attention in the early 1900s and then disappeared in the shifting tides of art history. *Tues–Sat; info@martin-zambito.com; martin-zambito.com; map:K1* &

Northwest Fine Woodworking

101 S JACKSON ST, PIONEER SQUARE; 206/625-0542 This cooperatively owned gallery offers one-of-a-kind tables, desks, chairs, cabinets, sideboards, screens, boxes, and turned bowls, all by local craftspeople. An Eastside gallery is in Bellevue (601 108th Ave NE, Plaza 100; 425/462-5382; map:GG3). *Every day; sales@nwfinewoodworking.com; map:O8*

Soil

1317 E PINE ST, CAPITOL HILL; 206-264-8061 The space is small and unassuming and some of the shows forgettable, but this artists' collective gallery has a history of launching topnotch new artists, many fresh from the University of Washington MFA program. The hours are iffy, so always call ahead. *Thurs–Sun; soilart.org; map:GG6*

Snow Goose Associates

8806 ROOSEVELT WY NE, MAPLE LEAF; 206/523-6223 Gallery space here is filled with art and artifacts of Alaskan and Canadian Eskimos and Northwest Coast Indians. Annual shows include the fall exhibit of prints by Inuit artists from Cape

Dorset on Baffin Island. Snow Goose has been in operation for more than 30 years. *Tues–Sat; sgassociates@qwest.net; snowgooseart.com; map:DD7* ♿

William Traver Gallery

110 UNION ST, DOWNTOWN; 206/587-6501 Glass is the focus at Traver and there's always an array of work by local and internationally known talent to choose from. The window-wrapped second-story space at First Avenue and Union Street, near the Seattle Art Museum, also showcases paintings, sculptures, photographs, ceramics, and assemblages, mostly by Northwest artists. *Every day; www.travergallery.com; map:K7* ♿

Woodside/Braseth Gallery

1533 9TH AVE, DOWNTOWN; 206/622-7243 You'll find strictly Northwest fare in the city's oldest gallery (founded in 1962): paintings by Mark Tobey, William Ivey, Morris Graves, Paul Horiuchi, and a varying selection of midcareer artists. *Tues–Sat; info@woodsidebrasethgallery.com; woodsidebrasethgallery.com; map:J4*

Wright Exhibition Space

407 DEXTER AVE N, DOWNTOWN; 206/264-8200 Built to showcase the world-class contemporary art collection of Virginia and Bagley Wright, this private gallery also hosts solo shows, most recently by Los Angeles artist Ed Ruscha and the late Northwest abstract painter William Ivey. *Limited hours and by appointment; map:D4* ♿

Theater

Seattle's theater scene had the luck to be part of the city's cultural explosion of the early '90s, when grunge and a national media designation as "the most livable city" brought busloads of young artists to the Northwest. These newcomers bypassed mainstream houses like Intiman, the Seattle Repertory Theatre, and A Contemporary Theatre (ACT)—which cast primarily out-of-town talent—in favor of starting their own companies. This led to an astonishing number of smaller fringe companies in a wide variety of venues: over shops, under shopping centers, in leaky basements, and even, memorably, in a converted funeral home. Many of these original artists have moved on, or found that their day job designing Web sites has become a career. But, by most estimates, outside of New York, LA, and Chicago, there are more productions here per year than any place in the United States.

Seattle's biggest celebration of theater is the annual **SEATTLE FRINGE THEATRE FESTIVAL** (various venues; 206/342-9172; seattlefringe.org). Running in late September to catch performers from the North American fringe theater circuit, the Fringe Festival offers some 500 hundred shows over two weeks at every available theater space on Capitol Hill, along with some spaces set up just for the event. Since the festival is open to all, the quality varies considerably, but a thorough check of the program guide (available at coffee shops, bookstores, and other places in the month prior to the festival, as well as at the Fringe Web site) will help you navigate your way.

EXERCISE FOR ART

Leave it to health-conscious Seattleites to favor an athletic form of arts appreciation.

The granddaddy of all the ambulatory art walks that have mushroomed around town is the monthly **FIRST THURSDAY GALLERY WALK**. Centered in downtown Seattle's historic Pioneer Square, it is draws milling crowds of sophisticates, posers, and art-loving singles who cruise the area's dozens of galleries, which stay open for extended hours, 6pm to 8pm, and the Seattle Art Museum, which waives its entry fee for the evening tour.

Other Seattle art rambles include the **BALLARD ART WALK** (second Saturday of each month, 6–9pm; call the Ballard Chamber of Commerce for more info, 206/784 9705) and the **GREENWOOD/PHINNEY ART WALK** (in early May). In Kirkland, the **SECOND THURSDAY ART WALK** takes in several closely packed galleries and some quirky public art on the second Thursday of each month, 6–9pm. Free 4-hour parking is available at the Kirkland Library (808 Kirkland Ave, Kirkland).

To check up on what's being shown in local art galleries and museums, pick up a free copy of *Art Guide Northwest* (artguidenw.com; available in many Pioneer Square galleries and bookstores), or *Seattle Weekly* or *The Stranger*, found in sidewalk newsboxes all over town.

—Shannon O'Leary

Nonmainstream theaters tend to come and go, but the following groups have established track records. Check the city's two free weeklies, *Seattle Weekly* and *The Stranger*, for event listings and opinionated reviews. **ANNEX THEATRE** (various venues; 206/728-0933; annextheatre.org) was once the flagship alternative theater in Seattle, but since losing their Belltown home they've become a nomadic company that produces infrequently. Some of the magic still remains at their regular cabaret *Spin the Bottle*, offered on the first Friday of every month at various Capitol Hill venues. Keep an eye out for place and time. **THEATER SCHMEATER** (1500 Summit Ave, Capitol Hill; 206/324-5801; schmeater.org; map:K2) is currently the most regularly producing company in town. This is in large part due to two long-running late-night cash cows: *Twilight Zone: Live on Stage*, which recreates episodes from the classic black-and-white series (some of the scripts hold up remarkably well, some can't be salvaged even with liberal doses of camp), and *Money and Run*, an inspired and original send-up of bad '80s television of the *Dukes of Hazard* variety. Tickets for those under 18 are free.

A company that is growing steadily in terms of professionalism and risk taking is **THEATRE BABYLON** (theatrebabylon.org), a scrappy collection of local artists who have a passion for original work. They share a Capitol Hill theater, the Union Garage (1418 10th Ave; 206/720-1942; map:HH6), with another worthy company, **A THEATRE UNDER THE INFLUENCE** (www.theatreinfluence.org), which includes a healthy range of older and younger theater artists and focuses on revivals of for-gotten American classics.

Also on Capitol Hill are two drama schools that rent out their spaces to home-less theater companies, as well as occasionally producing shows themselves. **FREE-HOLD THEATRE** (1529 10th Ave, Capitol Hill; 206/323-7499; freeholdtheatre.org; map:HH6) offers courses for actors, directors, and other artists, and also runs the Freehold Theatre Lab, which develops and supports the work of local artists. The **NORTHWEST ACTORS STUDIO** (1100 E Pike St, Capitol Hill; 206/324-6328; nwactorsstudio.org; map:HH6) also offers regular classes and features two theaters that get a lot of rentals from smaller companies, as well as featuring students from the Studio Conservatory. Another group, **THEATER SIMPLE** (various venues; 206/784-8647; theatersimple.org), is cheerfully vagabond and defiantly lower case and do as many shows out of town at various festivals as they do locally. They've got a strong track record of smart, big, cheap theater that engages the brain as well as the heart, including adaptations of Bulgakov's *The Master and Margarita* and Dostoevsky's *Notes from the Underground*. The multiethnic **REPERTORY ACTORS WORKSHOP** (various venues; 206/364-3283; reacttheatre.org), under the direction of David Hsieh, produces plays that heighten awareness of issues faced by minori-ties. The group can tackle everything from a musical about the Japanese American internment (*Miss Minidoka 1943*) to the work of Romanian surrealist Eugene Ionesco.

A Contemporary Theatre (ACT)

700 UNION ST, DOWNTOWN; 206/292-7676 Large productions and larger admin-istrative staffs were fine in the '90s, but after the boom went bust and arts funding diminished, what had been the luxurious new three-stage theater complex of ACT suddenly looked like a vast white elephant. One of the big three theaters in Seattle, along with Intiman and the Seattle Rep (see reviews), ACT was on the verge of bank-ruptcy in early 2003, but an 11th-hour fundraising campaign and massive reorgan-ization pulled them back from the brink. Now newly committed to local artists and under the leadership of local artistic director Kurt Beattie, the company is tentatively on its feet again, with a mix of new work and the occasional American classic tossed in for good measure. During the Christmas season, ACT presents its extremely pop-ular adaptation of Dickens's *A Christmas Carol. acttheatre.org; map:K4* &

ArtsWest

4711 CALIFORNIA AVE SW, WEST SEATTLE; 206/938-0339 Home to West Seattle's beautiful midsize theater, ArtsWest is steadily evolving from its community-theater roots toward a full-on professional company, with programming choices that have been increasingly daring. *artswest.org; map:JJ8*

Book-It Repertory Theatre and Seattle Shakespeare Company

CENTER HOUSE THEATRE, LOWER LEVEL OF CENTER HOUSE, SEATTLE CENTER; 206/216-0833 (BOOK-IT); 206/325-6500 (SHAKESPEARE) Sharing the-ater and literary ambitions, Book-It produces dramatic adaptations of literary works in an idiosyncratic fashion that's a bit hit-or-miss (some books are best left as books) but are generally inventive, while Seattle Shakespeare takes on the Bard with results that vary from uninspired to very good indeed. *www.book-it.org; seattleshakes.org; map:C6*

Crêpe de Paris Cabaret

RAINIER SQUARE, 1333 5TH AVE, ATRIUM LEVEL, DOWNTOWN; 206/623-4111 For wacky musical dinner theater laden with awful Seattle jokes, check out the action taking place on this modest stage in a downtown French restaurant. *Map:K6*

The Empty Space Theatre

3509 FREMONT AVE N, FREMONT; 206/547-7500 If there's a company in town that deserves cultural support it's the Empty Space. For more than 30 years it's been the standard bearer for the alternative and the avant-garde in Seattle. Helmed by mercurially minded artistic director Allison Narver, the company is in the awkward position of seeking to challenge and disturb its audiences with world premieres and daring theatrical experiments during a time of economic uncertainty. They manage in part by tossing in the occasional goofball comedy with a racy subtext, along with inspired crowd-pleasers such as *Wuthering! Heights! The! Musical!* and an original stage version of *Valley of the Dolls. www.emptyspace.org; map:FF8* &

5th Avenue Theatre

1308 5TH AVE, DOWNTOWN; 206/625-1900, TICKETS 206/292-ARTS Opened in 1926 as a venue for vaudeville, the fabulously ornate 5th Avenue (designed in its opulence to resemble the interior of China's Forbidden City) is home to its own resident musical theater company that specializes in revivals of mainstream Broadway musicals and an occasional world-premiere musical that the management hopes will make it big (such as 2003's *Hairspray*, which went on to Broadway raves). One or two Broadway touring shows are thrown into the schedule to sweeten the mix for subscribers. Not the most adventurous house in town, but the 25,000 or so subscribers don't seem to mind. *5thavenuetheatre.org; map:L6* &

Intiman Theatre

INTIMAN PLAYHOUSE, 201 MERCER ST, SEATTLE CENTER; 206/269-1900 Artistic director Bartlett Sher's visually adventurous productions of Shakespeare got him his position a few years ago, and he has focused on putting together smart seasons that mix up off-Broadway scripts, unusual takes on classic texts, and the occasional world premiere (such as the Lucas/Guettel musical *The Light in the Piazza*). Intiman has had to trim its budget and may well have to do more soon, but Sher seems intent on trying new things to get audiences in the seats. *intiman.org; map:A6* &

Northwest Puppet Center

9123 15TH AVE NE, MAPLE LEAF; 206/523-2579 Kids are the target audience for the Northwest Puppet Center, but adults being dragged along may be in for a pleasant surprise. The resident company, the Carter Family Marionettes, produces some truly charming work (including an oft-revived series adapted from the *Babar the Elephant* books) and also hosts guest artists from around the world. *nwpuppet.org; map:6EE*

On the Boards

BEHNKE CENTER FOR CONTEMPORARY PERFORMANCE, 100 W ROY ST, QUEEN ANNE; 206/217-9888 On the Boards occupies an intermediate place between fringe and mainstream theater and has been offering an eclectic blend of dance, theater, and multimedia performance for more than a quarter century (see also Dance in this chapter). It's here you'll see both cutting-edge performance art from around the world (Japan, Croatia, Belgium, England, you name it) and new creations by Pacific Northwest artists (UMO Ensemble, Typing Explosion, and many other groups). Every spring the Northwest New Works Festival offers a kind of juried fringe festival for locally brewed experimental performance. *onthe boards.org; map:GG8*

Paramount Theatre

911 PINE ST, DOWNTOWN; TICKETS 206/292-ARTS For the latest touring Broadway musical, your best bet is the Paramount Theatre. Jointly managed with the Moore Theatre by the nonprofit Seattle Theatre Group, it plays host to Broadway tours and pop headliners of all descriptions. You can buy tickets through Ticketmaster or in person at the Paramount box office. *soldout@the paramount.com; theparamount.com; map:J3*

Seattle Children's Theatre

CHARLOTTE MARTIN THEATRE, SEATTLE CENTER; 206/441-3322 Challenging Minneapolis's Children's Theater Company in size and prestige, SCT presents six beautifully mounted productions a year for young and family audiences. More than half the performances on the theater's two stages (the mainstage Charlotte Martin and more intimate Eve Alvord) are world premieres commissioned from leading playwrights and based on both classic and contemporary children's literature. The theater stages three evening and two matinee shows per week (with other daytime performances available to school groups), so sometimes tickets can be hard to come by. But they're worth the effort—for children and adults alike. SCT also sponsors a year-round youth drama school for ages 3½ through high-school age, with performances staged in the summer. *sct.org; map:C7* &

Seattle Repertory Theatre

BAGLEY WRIGHT THEATRE, 155 MERCER ST, SEATTLE CENTER; 206/443-2222 Established in 1963, the Rep is the oldest and best-known theater in town. Under artistic director Sharon Ott, it's also pretty staid. A typical season may not look too different from what Intiman or ACT have to offer, but the theater tends to put on lavish physical productions in place of inspired ones. They still manage to pull off a couple of noteworthy shows each season (such as a recent sterling production of Frayn's *Copenhagen*), and their own budget woes may steer more attention to audience satisfaction and less to expensive sets. *seattlerep.org; map:A6* &

Taproot Theatre

204 N 85TH ST, GREENWOOD; 206/781-9707 Taproot has become a major player in Seattle's professional theater scene in the last few years. A "Theatre of Faith," the company has transcended its church-theater roots to become a critically respected venue for mainstream audiences, featuring a smart mix of contemporary scripts and classic revivals, with an occasional world premiere tossed in. Artistic director Scott Nolte has a great rapport with his audiences, knowing when to play it safe and when to push the envelope. Particularly worth seeing are the small-cast musicals and the work of associate director Karen Lund, who's adept at mining classical texts for contemporary laughs and drama. *www.taproot.org; map:7EE*

Teatro Zinzanni

2301 6TH AVE, BELLTOWN; 206/802-0015 Teatro Zinzanni is one of Seattle's greatest theatrical successes (the dinner theater/cabaret has a successful spin-off in San Francisco). An unlikely cross between Northwest cuisine, cabaret, and European-style circus acts, it's one of the priciest tickets in town but if the waiting list is to be believed, also one of the most popular. It's a pretty remarkable evening, one that combines comedy, good food, and some truly spectacular moments of theater. If you've got the cash you can't arrange a better date, give it a try. *dreams.zinzanni.org; map:F6* &

University of Washington School of Drama

UW ARTS TICKET OFFICE, 4001 UNIVERSITY WY NE, UNIVERSITY DISTRICT; 206/543-4880 The nationally recognized UW School of Drama sometimes presents first-rate productions directed by jobbed-in big-name professionals and featuring students from the school's Professional Actor Training Program. Other productions are all-student work—some outstanding, others less so; inform yourself before you go. Performances are at four theaters on campus. *depts.washington.edu/uwdrama/; map:FF6*

Village Theatre

FRANCIS J. GAUDETTE THEATRE, 303 FRONT ST N, ISSAQUAH; 425/392-2202 The Village is all about entertaining their audiences, and they do a remarkably good job of it with a surefire season of classic American comedies and, above all, musicals. Not just the standard musical fare either; the theater has a strong development department dedicated to new musicals, which are workshopped and often make their world premiere at the Village. For lovers of this particular sort of theater, it's worth the trip out to Issaquah. *villagetheatre.org* &

Classical Music and Opera

Classical music has a relatively large and devoted following here in the Emerald City. The symphony and opera are firmly on the national map, and chamber music is a local passion. Excellent early music and choral music groups abound. Several musicians of national and international reputation make their homes here and share their musical expertise generously. And Seattle is also a regular stop for major performers on tour.

The biggest recent change to Seattle's classical music landscape was the 2003 opening of the **MARION OLIVER MCCAW HALL**, now the new home of both the Opera and the Pacific Northwest Ballet. The Opera inaugurated McCaw Hall with

Wagner's *Parsifal*, which allowed them to show off the stage's new features that include such technical marvels as a 79-foot-tall digital screen. Best of all is the sound: "extraordinary" and "spectacular" were just two of the critics' comments at the opening night of this state-of-the-art facility.

Belle Arte

KIRKLAND PERFORMANCE CENTER, 350 KIRKLAND AVE, KIRKLAND; 425/893-9900 The Belle Arte concert series on the Eastside presents five superlative chamber music concerts per season. Director Felix Skowronek has attracted national and international groups of the highest caliber, along with the best that the Northwest has to offer. Recent performers have included the Florestan String Trio and the Miami Wind Quintet. *info@bellearte.org; bellearte.org; map:EE3*

Early Music Guild

VARIOUS VENUES; 206/325-7066 For more than 25 years, the Early Music Guild has helped make Seattle a center of historically informed early-music performance. EMG's popular International Series comprises five concerts of medieval, Renaissance, baroque, or other classical music, and features top international ensembles. The fine Recital Series, with three concerts, highlights performers whose art is best presented in an intimate venue. EMG also gives concert assistance to many early-music performers in the area. *emg@earlymusicguild.org; earlymusicguild.org*

Gallery Concerts

VARIOUS VENUES; 206/726-6088 For more than 15 years, this plucky group has been performing baroque and other classical music on period instruments in a variety of intimate spaces. They typically feature heavy-hitters such as Vivaldi, Bach, and Mozart, but check in with them for some lesser-known surprises as well. *info@galleryconcerts.org; galleryconcerts.org*

Mostly Nordic Chamber Music Series and Smörgåsbord

NORDIC HERITAGE MUSEUM, 3014 NW 67TH ST, BALLARD; 206/789-5707 Sibelius and Meatballs! Begun in 1996 under the auspices of the Nordic Heritage Museum Foundation, Mostly Nordic presents five concerts per season, one for each of the Scandinavian countries. Contemporary and classical chamber music from Denmark, Finland, Iceland, Norway, and Sweden is performed by local (and occasionally Scandinavian) musicians, and is followed by an authentic smorgasbord. The museum also offers various other classical programming; call for details. *nordic@intelistep.com; www.nordicmuseum.com; map:EE9* &

Northwest Chamber Orchestra

BENAROYA RECITAL HALL, 200 UNIVERSITY ST, DOWNTOWN; 206/343-0445 Offering up small-scale classical works for more than 25 years, the Northwest Chamber Orchestra is one of the region's few professional chamber orchestras, and the group has masterfully adapted to the bright acoustics of Benaroya's small recital hall. Finnish pianist Ralf Gothoni was appointed music director in 2001 and has retained the orchestra's commitment to bold interpretations of works spanning the 17th to 20th centuries. Each season, NWCO performs seven mainstage concerts, five showcase events, and also puts on five Music in the Park concerts at the Seattle Asian Art Museum (1400 E Prospect St, Capitol Hill; 206/654-3100; map:GG7). *nwco@nwco.org; www.nwco.org; map:K7* &

Northwest Mahler Festival

MEANY THEATER, UNIVERSITY OF WASHINGTON, UNIVERSITY DISTRICT; 206/667-6567 It takes a lot of bodies to perform the symphonies of Gustav Mahler. So during the summer, when amateur orchestra players around Seattle are looking for something to do outside of the regular performance season, they band together to play several symphonies by Mahler and other Late Romantic compositions requiring big, noisy orchestras. *horndude1@yahoo.com; nwmahlerfestival.org; map:FF6* &

Seattle Baroque

VARIOUS VENUES; 206/322-3118 Seattle Baroque was founded in 1994 and, under the leadership of baroque violinist Ingrid Matthews and harpsichordist Byron Schenkman, the group has been winning critical praise all around, scoring broadcasts on public radio and recording several acclaimed CDs. Seven concert pairs are presented between fall and spring at several venues both in Seattle and on the Eastside. The orchestra also sponsors the new Seattle Baroque Summer Festival, encompassing three days of 18th-century music performed at Town Hall (1119 8th Ave, Downtown; map:L4). *info@seattlebaroque.org; seattlebaroque.org*

Seattle Chamber Music Society

LAKESIDE SCHOOL, 14050 1ST AVE NE, HALLER LAKE; 206/283-8808 Founded by University of Washington cello professor Toby Saks some 20 years ago, the Seattle Chamber Music Society presents a popular monthlong series in July showcasing local and international talent as well as a brief Winter Interlude in January at Benaroya Hall (200 University St, Downtown; map:K7). The performances are spirited, oftentimes exceptional, and almost always sold out. The recitals feature the performers' own choices (and often rarely heard pieces). *scmfmail@scmf.org; scmf.org; map:CC7* &

Seattle Chamber Players

BENAROYA RECITAL HALL, 200 UNIVERSITY ST, DOWNTOWN; 206/367-1138 An unusual grouping of flute, clarinet, violin, and cello, Seattle Chamber Players adds guests and high-quality out-of-town soloists, as needed, to perform chamber music of the 20th and 21st centuries (the latter being newly commissioned works). The players approach the series of six to eight concerts with style, imagination, and occasional humor (a piece entitled *Dead Elvis* featured a hip-swiveling bassoonist). *paultaub@dbug.org; map:K7* &

Seattle Men's Chorus

BENAROYA HALL, 200 UNIVERSITY ST, DOWNTOWN / MEANY THEATER, UNIVERSITY OF WASHINGTON, UNIVERSITY DISTRICT; 206/323-2992 The Seattle Men's Chorus is the world's largest and most successful gay men's chorus. It's also one of the country's busiest, with about 30 appearances a year at various events and a local subscription series of four concerts: an always-sold-out, family-fun

TICKET ALERT

Tickets to many local performing-arts events are available from **TICKETMASTER** (various locations around town; 206/292-ARTS; ticketmaster.com), and some are also online at **TICKETWINDOW** (ticketwindowonline.com) and **TICKETS.COM**. To avoid the mark-ups of these services, many theaters and other live performance venues have phone or walk-up box offices; take a look at listings for details. A pretty good alternative is **TICKET/TICKET** (206/324-2744; ticketwindowonline.com), with three outlets that sell half-price, day-of-show tickets to theater, music, comedy, and dance performances: Broadway Market (401 Broadway Ave E, Capitol Hill; map:GG6), Pike Place Market Information Kiosk (1st Ave and Pike St, Pike Place Market; map:J7), and Meydenbauer Center (11100 NE 6th St, Bellevue; map:HH3). Ticket/Ticket is closed on Monday and accepts cash only.

—Andrew Engelson

holiday concert in December, a popular-music spectacular during Gay and Lesbian Pride Week in the summer, and two spring shows that vary in content. *info@seattle menschorus.org; seattlemenschorus.org; map:K7, FF6*

Seattle Opera

MARION OLIVER MCCAW HALL, SEATTLE CENTER; 206/389-7676 Seattle Opera made its name with the Wagner *Ring Cycle*, so it makes sense that they'd open at McCaw Hall with his lesser-known *Parsifal*. But Executive Director Speight Jenkins, who celebrated 20 years on the job in 2003, doesn't confine himself to Wagner or any other single composer when choosing a season. He's shown himself particularly adept in programming seasons that mix up the classical canon with more obscure works, as well as providing a home for original work (such as Marvin Levy's operatic adaptation of O'Neill's *Mourning Becomes Electra*). When the *Ring* comes around every six years though, it's still a major event; tickets generally sell out a year in advance. *seattleopera.org; map:B5* &

Seattle Symphony

BENAROYA HALL, 200 UNIVERSITY ST, DOWNTOWN; 206/215-4747 The Seattle Symphony celebrates its 100th season in 2004 as one of the most vital and stimulating orchestras in the nation, now well situated in the palatial surroundings of Benaroya Hall. The Symphony has an impressive track record of supporting classical works by contemporary composers with the help of its composer-in-residence program. As well as its 18 sets of season subscription concerts under longtime maestro Gerard Schwarz, the orchestra performs shorter series packaged for every kind of music lover: from pops to light classics to baroque, from performances for children to adult concerts with insightful commentary by the conductor, plus a distinguished artist series featuring international stars such as Jessye Norman. The Symphony sponsors a host of community outreach and educational programs, including a new, popular interactive music center at Benaroya Hall. *info@seattlesymphony.org; seattlesymphony.org; map:K7* &

Seattle Youth Symphony

BENAROYA HALL, 200 UNIVERSITY ST, DOWNTOWN; 206/362-2300 The largest youth symphony organization in the country, these talented young musicians give three usually dazzling concerts, plus a benefit performance, during the winter season. Five feeder orchestras train a large number of younger musicians and perform during the summer. *info@syso.org; syso.org; map:K7* &

UW International Chamber Music Series
UW President's Piano Series
UW World Music and Theatre

MEANY THEATER, UNIVERSITY OF WASHINGTON, UNIVERSITY DISTRICT; 206/543-4880 OR 800/859-5342 The University of Washington's 1,210-seat Meany Theater is home to three excellent music series. The popular six-concert International Chamber Music Series brings to Seattle the best of the nation's chamber music ensembles (and an occasional group from abroad), with an emphasis on string quartets and trios. The President's Piano series attracts pianists of international stature, including Garrick Ohlsson, Murray Perahia, András Schiff, and the winner of the prestigious Van Cliburn Gold Medal. The fascinating World Music and Theatre Series features seven famous ethnic performing-arts groups from around the world—you'll see an eclectic mix ranging from the Throat Singers of Tuva to the Guinean dance/music troupe WOFA and Turkish finger-drum master Burhan Öçal. *meany.org; map:FF6* &

Dance

Seattle is no longer home to Merce Cunningham, Trisha Brown, and wonderboy Mark Morris, but a new crowd of choreographers such as Pat Graney, Amii LeGendre, 33 Fainting Spells, Crispin Spaeth, K.T. Niehoff, and the Maureen Whiting Company are themselves now local stars. One of the best opportunities to see these choreographers' work is to catch several performances during On the Boards's popular Northwest New Works Festival. Check out local listings for recitals staged around town, particularly in two popular venues, **VELOCITY DANCE CENTER** (915 E Pine St, Ste 200, Capitol Hill; 206/325-8773; velocitydancecenter.org; map:HH7) and **BROADWAY PERFORMANCE HALL** (1625 Broadway Ave E, Capitol Hill; 206/325-3113; broadwayperfhall.com; map:HH7). Velocity offers regular classes and is the center of the younger dance community, while the Performance Hall is favored by self-producing companies for its professional facilities.

On the Boards

BEHNKE CENTER FOR CONTEMPORARY PERFORMANCE, 100 W ROY ST, QUEEN ANNE; 206/217-9888 Long *the* source of cutting-edge works that merge dance, music, theater, and visual media, On the Boards is still the single most important showcase for local choreographers, even as the theater has shifted away from dance-centric programming. The sellout New Performance Series (October to May) brings in internationally known contemporary artists such as Anne Teresa De Keersmaeker, Meredith Monk, and Ronald K. Brown, as well as established local artists. Every six weeks throughout the year, a series known as 12 Minutes Max showcases five to seven short performances of new and experimental work by regional artists. The Northwest New Works Festival, which runs for several weekends in late spring, presents longer, more polished versions of similar work. *otb@ontheboards.org; ontheboards.org; map:GG8*

Pacific Northwest Ballet

MARION OLIVER MCCAW HALL, **SEATTLE CENTER; 206/441-2424** Under the guidance of artistic directors Kent Stowell and Francia Russell, former dancers with New York City Ballet, PNB has earned recognition as one of the top-five regional companies in America. The company seems to have little connection to local artists and is often criticized for emphasizing work that is conventional. Facing some economic hardships from fall-offs in corporate and individual giving, PNB still mounts a five-show season that features large-scale classical works and story ballets by director Stowell, and contemporary offerings by the likes of Val Caniparoli, William Forsythe, Nacho Duato, and Mark Dendy. PNB's annual *Nutcracker* has become something of a cliché, but the Maurice Sendak sets and quality performances still make it an enjoyable spectacle. *pnb.org; map:B5*

Spectrum Dance Theater

MADRONA DANCE STUDIO, **800 LAKE WASHINGTON BLVD, MADRONA (AND VARIOUS VENUES); 206/325-4161** Donald Bird, the new artistic director of Spectrum, is from New York and a choreographer of some renown. His presence has certainly reenergized the company (which was founded in 1982), although being a modern jazz choreographer working with a classical jazz company makes for some interesting artistic friction. The company offers two mainstage concert series at Meany Theater at the University of Washington every fall and spring, as well as informal Dance in the Making studio performances that include audience question-and-answer sessions with the dancers and a lecture on American jazz dance traditions. The company is very family friendly and features instructional classes for kids and adults. *spectrumdance.org; map:HH6*

33 Fainting Spells

VARIOUS VENUES; 206/568-8640 Founded in 1994 by Dayna Hanson and Gaelan Hanson (who both happen to share the same last name), 33 Fainting Spells is gaining national attention as one of the region's most original up-and-coming dance troupes. Their dance-theater quality annoys some fellow dancers (who find it precious) but there's no denying that their work, which features sly humor and weirdly frivolous themes, is a crowd-pleaser. The group stages one or two performances per year in various venues. *33fs@33faintingspells.org; 33faintingspells.org*

UW World Dance Series

✝ **MEANY THEATER, UNIVERSITY OF WASHINGTON, UNIVERSITY DISTRICT; 206/543-4880 OR 800/859-5342** Six world-renowned dance groups come to town every year as part of Meany Theater's World Dance Series. The October-through-May series almost always includes such tried-and-true top draws as the Merce Cunningham Dance Company, the Alvin Ailey American Dance Theater, and Seattle-boy-done-good, choreographer Mark Morris. The series doesn't always find the ideal mix between the exotic and the popular, but there's an attempt to keep the "world" in World Dance Series, with several non-Western dance groups usually added to the mix to keep things lively. *uwworldseries.org; map:FF6*

Film

Though we don't attract many big-budget film crews anymore (hefty tax credits and good exchange rates send most film production companies north to Vancouver, BC), Seattle is still a movie-lovers town. In fact, due to our rep as sophisticated *cinéastes*, many Hollywood films preview here first. And you can still find dedicated young filmmakers and video artists shooting all sorts of experimental work in the city, some of which shows up on the screens of microcinemas and at local and national film festivals.

One microfilm venue is the well-established **911 MEDIA ARTS CENTER** (117 Yale Ave N, South Lake Union; 206/682-6552; 911media.org; map:F2), an independent film and video school that maintains a busy schedule of documentaries and experimental work, as well as open screenings where anyone can show work in progress to an opinionated audience. Two others are run by **NORTHWEST FILM FORUM** (nwfilmforum.org), a nonprofit center that offers classes and equipment rentals to local filmmakers, as well as operating the **GRAND ILLUSION** (1403 NE 50th St, University District; 206/523-3935; map:FF7) and the **LITTLE THEATRE** (608 19th Ave E, Capitol Hill; 206/675-2055; map:GG6). These venues feature not only local artists, but regular programs of little-shown underground, avant-garde, foreign, and just plain unclassifiable films. (What else can you call the Little Theatre's architectural film series, By Design?)

Seattle also hosts at least one seriously macro festival. In mid-May through mid-June, the crowds go wild for the **SEATTLE INTERNATIONAL FILM FESTIVAL** (Broadway Performance Hall, 1625 Broadway, Capitol Hill; 206/324-9996; mail@seattlefilm.com; seattlefilm.com; map:HH7). Thirty years old and one of the biggest fests in the country, SIFF is a juggernaut that seems overwhelming at first glance. But a seasoned staff at Cinema Seattle—SIFF's nonprofit umbrella organization—has made the event (staged at a handful of movie houses throughout the city) easy to navigate. Cinema Seattle also sponsors activities year-round that include the outstanding Women in Cinema Film Festival, which usually takes place in January; Talking Pictures, a series of movies screened with an après-film discussion hosted by critics and directors; and the Screenwriters Salon series, held July through April, which presents live readings of new scripts at Capitol Hill's **RICHARD HUGO HOUSE**

(1634 11th Ave; 206/322-7030; hugohouse.org; map:HH6), with the participation of noted local actors.

Coming somewhere between the local microfestivals of places like Northwest Film Forum and SIFF is the **SATELLITES FESTIVAL OF FILM AND VIDEO** (for dates and details, check www.emeraldreels.com), which features films for the sort of people who make, or really want to make, films.

Curated for more than 30 years by the Seattle Art Museum film department's founder, Greg Olson, the quarterly **SEATTLE ART MUSEUM FILM SERIES** (100 University St, Downtown; 206/654-3100; seattleartmuseum.org/calendar/calendar.asp; map:K7) usually focuses on the work of a renowned actor or director (Cary Grant, Billy Wilder) or on a theme such as French comedy or American film noir. Frequent short programs are featured as well: a few weekends of Yasujiro Ozu, an evening of David Lynch, an afternoon with Marcel Pagnol. For less polished surroundings, the **FREMONT OUTDOOR FILM FESTIVAL** (3400 Phinney Ave N; 206/781-4230; www.outdoorcinema.com; map:FF8) screens a purposefully odd mix of flicks, from *Fight Club* to *Casablanca*. Surviving Fremont's rapid gentrification by moving to the parking lot across from the old Trolleyman Pub, the festival requires that you bring your own seating—movie-themed costume optional. At last tally, Seattle was also home to a Polish film festival, a Jewish film festival, a lesbian and gay film festival, a couple more outdoor film festivals, an Asian American film festival, a Scandinavian film festival, a human rights film festival, an Arab film festival, an Irish film festival, a couple of different children's film festivals, a short-film film festival . . . well, you get the idea. Check the arts listings in local publications to find out which one is playing this week.

In between festivals, film nuts have plenty of other year-round viewing options. The city boasts a venue—from old movie houses with creaky character and smaller independent theaters to, yes, a good number of multiplexes—sure to fit nearly every genre of film fancier. Splashy first-run multiplexes include the roomy, three-screen **UPTOWN CINEMA** (551 Queen Anne Ave N, Queen Anne; 206/285-1022; map:A8), Lowes Cineplex Odeon's downtown **MERIDIAN 16** (1502 7th Ave; 206/223-9600; map:J5), and the upscale **PACIFIC PLACE 11** (600 Pine St; 206/652-2404; map:J5)—decorated in a faux ski-lodge style—in downtown's chic Pacific Place shopping center.

The minichain **LANDMARK THEATRES** (www.landmark-theaters.com), which makes its living serving up a mix of select Hollywood films and foreign releases, currently operates an eclectic collection of theaters throughout the city. The **METRO CINEMAS** (NE 45th St and Roosevelt Wy NE, University District; 206/633-0055; map:FF7) offer films on several screens. Capitol Hill's **HARVARD EXIT** (807 E Roy St; 206/323-8986; map:GG6), with its huge lobby and stately air, was founded ages ago by a pair of eccentric film fans. Also on Capitol Hill is the **EGYPTIAN** (801 E Pine St; 206/323-4978; map:HH6), once a Masonic temple. The **GUILD 45TH** (2115 N 45th St, Wallingford; 206/633-3353; map:FF7) is actually two neighboring theaters, where you can usually find the latest Henry James adaptation. The small, dreamy **SEVEN GABLES** (911 NE 50th St, University District; 206/632-8820; map:EE7), the anchor of the theater chain, makes for a very pleasant experience—even more so

FESTIVAL FUN

Summertime in Seattle. It's no longer a secret to outsiders that summer in this city means balmy and mostly rain-free days. To take advantage of the fine weather, locals have developed a passion for outdoor events. Back in the old days, about the only big al fresco attraction was **SEAFAIR** (206/728-0123; seafair.com), a bizarre amalgam of roaring hydroplanes, jets, and drunken bands of clowns and pirates that seems more anachronistic every year. You can still do Seafair every August, but it's just one of many festivals filling up our calendar.

During Memorial Day weekend, the unofficial start of the summer season, **NORTH-WEST FOLKLIFE FESTIVAL** (206/684-7300; nwfolklife.org) rolls into action at the Seattle Center. The free event, which has been around for more than three decades, gets crowded, but where else can you see local hip-hop, Polynesian drumming, Balkan dancing, and alternative country music all in one weekend?

Two neighborhood street fairs on the cusp of summer offer an amusing mix of food, music, crafts, and assorted antics by local eccentrics. The **UNIVERSITY DISTRICT STREET FAIR** (206/547-4417; udistrictchamber.org) invades the Ave every May, while the **FREMONT FAIR** (206/632-1500; fremontfair.com) defiantly reasserts Fremont's fading eccentricities with parades, booths, and the banned-but-still-inevitable nude bicyclists as it has each June for more than 30 years.

The excellent **SUMMER NIGHTS AT THE PIER** (Pier 62/63, Waterfront; 206/281-8111; summernights.org) series of pop-rock outdoor concerts stages shows next to the

when the scent of delicious sauces from the Italian restaurant downstairs comes wafting up. Also in the U District, you'll find the single-screen **NEPTUNE** (1303 NE 45th St; 206/633-5545; map:FF6) and the three-screen **VARSITY** (4329 University Wy NE; 206/632-3131; map:FF6), where one of the screens offers a repertory of one-night double features of classic and cult movies. In the far north, head to Shoreline for the **CREST** (16505 5th Ave NE, Shoreline; 206/363-6338; map:BB7), where second-run movies are screened at bargain prices ($3 for all shows).

The best place to see first-run movies, as well as occasional revivals of special-effects classics, is on the giant screen of **CINERAMA** (2100 4th Ave, Belltown; 206/441-3080; seattlecinerama.com; map:H6). Seattle mogul Paul Allen bought the landmark movie house in 1998 to screen both 35- and 70-millimeter films and stocked it with state-of-the-art digital sound equipment, a digital projection system (ready for Hollywood's first digital movie), and innovative assistance tools for both blind and deaf moviegoers.

And speaking of Allen, his *other* Seattle playpen, the **EXPERIENCE MUSIC PROJECT** (325 5th Ave N, Seattle Center; 206/770-2702 box office; emplive.com;

waters of Puget Sound. The **SUMMER FESTIVAL ON THE GREEN** series of concerts at Chateau Ste. Michelle (14111 NE 145th St, Woodinville; 425/488-3300; ste-michelle. com) serves up a mix of pop and acoustic sounds aimed at the NPR crowd. The **CONCERTS AT MARYMOOR** series (6046 W Lake Sammamish Pkwy NE, Redmond; 206/628-0888; concertsatmarymoor.com) hosts a popular summer program at Marymoor Park that runs the smooth listening gambit from Hall and Oates to Irish folk music. The **ZOOTUNES** concert series (206/615-0076; zoo.org) at the Woodland Park Zoo presents reasonably priced folk and pop performances on summer evenings; children under 12 are free. Also free is the **OUT TO LUNCH** series of jazz, classical, and R&B concerts at various locations downtown (206/623-0340; downtownseattle.com).

BUMBERSHOOT (various locations, Seattle Center; 206/281-8111; bumber shoot.com) is the biggest and best of Seattle's arts festivals, and its music programming has been called some of the best in the nation. About the only festival that rivals it in number and quality of musical acts is the New Orleans Jazz and Heritage Festival. Bumbershoot is held Labor Day weekend at the Seattle Center, and lineups are usually announced a month in advance. While music is the dominant Bumber-phenomenon, the festival's literary events, dance, theater, and visual-art displays are all worth noting (particularly because it gets you away from the omnipresent music and crowds for a bit!). Ticket prices have been inching up over the past several years, and the crowds can sometimes leave you feeling like cattle in a feedlot, but it's still the region's best entertainment bargain.

—*Andrew Engelson*

map:C6; see Top 25 Attractions in the Exploring chapter) offers irregular film series usually tied to special exhibits; phone for times and details.

Retro charm is the selling point of Ballard's new **MAJESTIC BAY THEATRE** (2044 NW Market St, Ballard; 206/781-2229; www.majesticbay.com; map:FF8), a three-screen gem filled with character—nautical themes in the lobby evoke Ballard's fishy history—and buoyed by digital sound and comfy chairs. And want to see the latest output of Bollywood (as Bombay's cinema is affectionately known)? Cruise down to Kirkland's **TOTEM LAKE CINEMA** (12232 Totem Lake Wy, Kirkland; 425/820-5929; roxycinema.com; map:NN3), which screens first-run Indian movies Friday through Monday. The movies are in Hindi, without subtitles; you'll do fine if you just stick to the madcap musical comedies, where the plots are rather obvious and the song-and-dance numbers quite a spectacle.

Literary

It says something about the reading passion of a city when it has a celebrity *librarian* with her own action figure and a trail of national press clippings. In fact, in Seattle literary types are apt to have more groupies than our local rock residents. Besides the aforementioned Nancy Pearl (shushing librarian action figure available at local fun shop Archie McPhee), the Puget Sound area is home to a diverse universe of writers, including Ivan Doig, Sherman Alexie, Neal Stephenson, Rebecca Brown, mystery maven J. A. Jance, and Englishman-turned-Seattleite Jonathan Raban. Touring writers have made Seattle a mandatory stop on the book circuit, and local institution Elliott Bay Book Company practically invented the notion of the author tour. For better or for worse, Seattle-based Amazon.com introduced the world to online bookselling. Naturally, this city of book lovers has page upon page of literary events on offer throughout the year.

ELLIOTT BAY BOOK COMPANY has probably the city's best reading series (see listing below). However, a multitude of other Seattle and Eastside bookstores (see Books and Periodicals in the Shopping chapter) also vie for visiting authors. Among the heavyweights are the **UNIVERSITY BOOK STORE** (4326 University Wy NE, University District; 206/634-3400; ubsbooks@u.washington.edu; www.bookstore. washington.edu; map:FF6) and **THIRD PLACE BOOKS** (Lake Forest Park Towne Centre, 17171 Bothell Wy NE, Lake Forest Park; 206/366-3333; www.thirdplace books.com; map:BB5). On the smaller side, **BAILEY/COY BOOKS** (414 Broadway Ave E, Capitol Hill; 206/323-8842; map:HH6) caters to the alternative Capitol Hill crowd and holds several readings per month; **OPEN BOOKS: A POEM EMPORIUM** (2414 N 45th St, Wallingford; 206/633-0811; www.openpoetrybooks.com; map:FF7) also offers a first-rate reading series.

Scores of coffeehouses, cafes, and bars are host to open mikes, poetry slams, and oddball literary happenings. Open-mike poetry generally ranges from rotten to mildly interesting, while the slam scene is either a kick in the pants or a desperate, alcohol-fueled battle of bellowing between audience and performer. **THE GLOBE CAFÉ** (1531 14th Ave, Capitol Hill; 206/324-8815; map:HH6) is home to the grand-daddy of the recited poetry scene: **RED SKY POETRY THEATER**, which has been around for more than a decade and features a group of older poets who gather to perform on Sunday night. The Globe's Salon Poetry Series on Tuesday night appeals to the Hill's younger set. Local hipsters head for the open mike on Monday and Wednesday nights at **COFFEE MESSIAH** (1554 E Olive Wy, Capitol Hill; 206/861-8233; map:I1) and then give thanks by downing cup after cup of communal caffeine. More sedate is the Poets West open-mike series at **WIT'S END BOOKSTORE & TEA SHOP** (4262 Fremont Ave N, Fremont; 206/547-2330; map:FF7). At the University District branch of the Seattle Public Library (5009 Roosevelt Wy NE; map:FF7) the long-running **IT'S ABOUT TIME WRITERS' READING SERIES** (206/527-8875; itsaboutimewriters.homestead.com/) allows poets and writers of all experience levels to read from their work every second Thursday evening of the month. The peripatetic **SEATTLE POETRY SLAM** has settled, for a bit anyway, at the Bad Juju Lounge on Capitol Hill (1518 11th Ave, 206/709-9951; map:HH7), but it's not a good fit (dark and noisy) so you might find it elsewhere via the entertainment listings or the Slam's Web site (poetryfestival.org/slam).

Bumbershoot Literary Arts

NORTHWEST ROOMS, SEATTLE CENTER; 206/281-8111 The Bumbershoot arts festival held during Labor Day weekend offers an impressive literary arts program packed with readings, performances, poetry slams, and panel discussions involving world-class authors. The festival's long-running Bookfair boasts the largest West Coast concentration of small presses, which come from around the country to promote and sell their collections of fiction, poetry, nonfiction, hand-set letterpress books, and zines. *bumbershoot.org; map:C6*

Elliott Bay Book Company Reading Series

101 S MAIN ST, PIONEER SQUARE; 206/624-6600 Elliott Bay Books is a local literary landmark with a well-deserved national reputation for spotting talent: Amy Tan gave one of her first public readings here, as did Sherman Alexie. Elliott Bay's daily reading series, organized by bookseller extraordinaire Rick Simonson, annually brings more than 600 authors of national caliber—ranging from Chuck Palahniuk to Terry McMillan—into the cozy brick-walled cavern of the store's basement reading room each year. The bulk of the offerings are free; on rare occasions, typically for special benefit events, tickets cost $5–$10. *elliott baybook.com; map:O8*

Northwest Bookfest

SAND POINT MAGNUSON PARK, 7400 SAND POINT WY NE, SAND POINT; 206/378-1883 The city's premier literary happening, now housed in a rehabilitated naval base at Sand Point, has hit some hard economic times. The recent implementation of an admission fee brought disappointing results, and, as of press time, the debate continued on whether the Fest would revert to a free event. Still, this gigantic book love-in is a fall draw for readers and writers alike—past guests have included Pam Houston, T. C. Boyle, Amos Oz, Ha Jin, and local guy David Guterson. There's plenty to do for the little ones as well: hands-on activities such as book making, a storyteller's stage, and those oh-so-cute costumed fictional characters. Hundreds of mainstream and small-press titles are for sale at 180-plus booths. *info@nwbook fest.org; nwbookfest.org; map:Q9*

Richard Hugo House Events

1634 11TH AVE, CAPITOL HILL; 206/322-7030 Named in honor of the late Seattle poet Richard Hugo, this writers' resource center on Capitol Hill hosts writing classes, readings, book groups, screenwriters' salons, and other literary programs. Hugo House maintains a busy schedule of its own events, as well as hosting other organizations, including the Subtext Reading Series (a showcase of local avant-garde poetry readings throughout the year) and the Stage Fright open-mike series for teenagers, held every other Wednesday night. Hugo House's biggest event, the Annual Inquiry symposium, takes place over three days in October and features a full schedule of readings and writers' panels centered around a common theme (past events have had such captivating titles as Maps, Disappearances, Shelter, and The Power of Place). Most events are free or low cost. *hugohouse.org; map:HH6* &

Seattle Arts & Lectures

BENAROYA HALL, 200 UNIVERSITY ST, DOWNTOWN; 206/621-2230 At the top of the local literary food chain is this evening lecture series, founded in 1987, which runs from fall through spring. Whether it be an evening of witty exchanges between a panel of top-drawer writers or strictly a solo affair, the lecturers always manage to surprise (resident writer Sherman Alexie caused a minor sensation with his assertion that writers peak at 25). The list of guests reads like a veritable who's who of great modern writers: Gary Wills, Salman Rushdie, Michael Ondaatje, Margaret Atwood, Philip Roth, Susan Sontag. Oftentimes the source of the best moments is the post-lecture audience question-and-answer period. Tickets for the seven-event series range from $40 to $245; individual tickets cost $18–$23 and are half price for students, though be warned—for popular lecturers, they can be as hard to come by as Mariners playoff tickets. *sal@lectures.org; lectures.org; map:K7* &

Seattle Poetry Festival

VARIOUS VENUES; 206/725-1650 At press time, the Seattle Poetry Festival was still in planning for its next season. It's not clear, given the economics of the city, whether it'll be on hiatus in 2004 or a scaled-down event, but when the festival happens it's normally worthy of notice. The focus of the poetry tends to be social-political material and the form usually free verse. *poetryfestival.org*

Seattle Public Library/Washington Center for the Book

TEMPORARY CENTRAL LIBRARY, 800 PIKE ST, DOWNTOWN; 206/386-4650 OR 206/386-4184 When the Seattle Public Library selected Dutch architect Rem Koolhaas to design its new downtown library, they knew they'd be in for a wild ride. His dream was of an oblong glass bookpile of a library, stocked with all sorts of interactive and user-friendly goodies. While waiting for its new home (New Central Library, 1000 4th Ave, Downtown; map:L6) to open in 2004, SPL finds itself in temporary digs across from the Washington State Convention & Trade Center but still offers a full plate of absolutely free events that include lectures, readings, storytelling, and workshops. Much of this programming happens thanks to the efforts of Nancy Pearl, the director of the Washington Center for the Book. Each year, the library and the Center for the Book undertake the ambitious If All of Seattle Read the Same Book program, in which one lucky author becomes the subject of numerous book groups, lectures, and radio discussions. *www.spl.org; map:J4* &

NIGHTLIFE

Nightlife by Feature

ALTERNATIVE
Baltic Room
Cafe Venus and the marsBar
Catwalk
Cha-Cha Lounge
Chop Suey
Comet Tavern
Crocodile Cafe
Elysian Brewing Company
Experience Music Project
Graceland
Noc Noc
Old Firehouse, The
Rainbow, The
Re-bar
Rendezvous (Jewel Box
    Theater)
Showbox
Studio Seven
Sunset Tavern
ToST
Tractor Tavern
Vera Project, The
Vogue, The

BLUES
About the Music
Ballard Firehouse
Conor Byrne's Public
    House
Dimitriou's Jazz Alley
Experience Music Project
    (Liquid Lounge)
Fiddler's Inn
Scarlet Tree, The

COCKTAIL
LOUNGES
Alibi Room
Axis
Bada Lounge
Ballroom in Fremont
Baltic Room
Barça

BLU Video Bar
Brooklyn Seafood, Steak
    and Oyster House
Cafe Venus and the marsBar
Catwalk
Capitol Club
Cha-Cha Lounge
Club Contour
DeLuxe Bar and Grill
Experience Music Project
    (Liquid Lounge)
Fireside Room
Five Point Café
Fu Kun Wu
Hattie's Hat
Last Supper Club
Linda's Tavern
Luau Polynesian Lounge
Manray
Marcus' Martini Heaven
Mecca Cafe
Nitelite, The
Noc Noc
Paragon Bar and Grill
Queen City Grill
Rainbow, The
Rendezvous (Jewel Box
    Theater)
Scarlet Tree, The
Showbox
Shea's Lounge
Tini Bigs Lounge
ToST
Twilight Exit, The
Virginia Inn
Vito's Madison Grill

COFFEE, TEA,
DESSERT
B&O Espresso
Bauhaus Books and
    Coffee
Cafe Allegro
Caffe Ladro

Caffé Vita
Chocolati
Coffee Messiah
Dilettante Chocolates
    Cafe and Patisserie
Diva Espresso
El Diablo Coffee
Espresso Express
Joe Bar
Mr. Spot's Chai House
Panama Hotel Tea and
    Coffee House
Simply Desserts
611 Supreme Crêperie
    Café
Star Life on the Oasis
Teahouse Kuan Yin
Top Pot Donuts
Uptown Espresso and
    Bakery
The Urban Bakery
Victrola Coffee and Art
Zeitgeist Coffee
Zoka Coffee Roaster and
    Tea Company

COMEDY
Comedy Underground
Giggles

COUNTRY
Little Red Hen
Sunset Tavern
Tractor Tavern

DANCING/
DANCE FLOORS
About the Music
Alibi Room
Aristocrat's Nightclub
Ballard Firehouse
Ballroom in Fremont
Baltic Room
Belltown Billiards
BLU Video Bar

Catwalk
Century Ballroom
Chop Suey
Club Contour
Fenix Underground
Last Supper Club
Little Red Hen
Manray
Neighbours
Noc Noc
Re-bar
Showbox
Vogue, The

DRINKS WITH A VIEW

Leschi Lakecafe and
  G.B.B. Bar
Shea's Lounge
SkyCity at the Needle

EDITORS' CHOICE

Bada Lounge
Blue Moon Tavern
Cha-Cha Lounge
Chop Suey
Comet Tavern
Crocodile Cafe
Dilettante Chocolates
  Cafe and Patisserie
Dimitriou's Jazz Alley
Fenix Underground
Fu Kun Wu
Garage
Panama Hotel Tea and
  Coffee House
Pioneer Square Saloon
Showbox
SkyCity at the Needle
Sunset Tavern
Teahouse Kuan Yin
Virginia Inn

FAMILY

Experience Music Project
  (JBL Theater, Sky
  Church)

F. X. McRory's Steak,
  Chop, and Oyster
  House
Old Firehouse, The
Studio Seven
Vera Project, The

FOLK/ACOUSTIC

Conor Byrne's Public
  House
Experience Music Project
  (JBL Theater, Liquid
  Lounge)
Fiddler's Inn
Hopvine Pub
Irish Emigrant
Kells
Latona by Green Lake
Murphy's Pub
Old Pequliar, The
Owl 'n' Thistle Irish Pub
  and Restaurant
Paragon Bar and Grill
Rainbow, The
Showbox (Green Room)
Sunset Tavern
ToST
Tractor Tavern
Zoka Coffee Roaster and
  Tea Company

GAY/LESBIAN

BLU Video Bar
Manray
Neighbours
Re-bar
Wildrose, The

GOOD VALUE

Attic Alehouse & Eatery
Buckaroo Tavern
Cafe Venus and the
  marsBar
Eastlake Zoo
Hattie's Hat
Mecca Cafe
Nitelight, The

Owl 'n' Thistle Irish Pub
  and Restaurant
Rainbow, The
Stella Pizza and Ale

HIP-HOP

About the Music
Baltic Room
Chop Suey
Club Contour
Last Supper Club
Noc Noc
Re-bar

JAZZ

About the Music
Ballard Firehouse
Century Ballroom
Dimitriou's Jazz Alley
Latona by Green Lake
Old Town Alehouse
Paragon Bar and Grill
Rainbow, The
Scarlet Tree
Tula's
Vito's Madison Grill

KARAOKE/OPEN MIKE

BLU Video Bar
Little Red Hen
Manray
Neighbours
Ozzie's Roadhouse
Rainbow, The
Sunset Tavern
Tula's
Twilight Exit, The
Wildrose, The

OUTDOOR SEATING

Axis
Ballroom in Fremont
BLU Video Bar
Capitol Club
DeLuxe Bar and Grill
Fiddler's Inn

Kells
Kirkland Roaster & Ale-
house
Leschi Lakecafe and
G.B.B. Bar
Linda's Tavern
Luau Polynesian Lounge
Manray
Pacific Inn Pub
Pioneer Square Saloon
Red Door Alehouse
Roanoke Inn
Sitting Room, The
Twilight Exit, The

PIANO BARS

Fireside Room
Fu Kun Wu
Sunset Tavern

POOL TABLES/
BILLIARDS

Attic Alehouse & Eatery,
The
Bada Lounge
Ballroom in Fremont
Belltown Billiards
Big Time Brewery and
Alehouse
Blue Moon Tavern
Buckaroo Tavern, The
Cafe Venus and the marsBar
College Inn Pub
Comet Tavern
Duchess Tavern, The
Eastlake Zoo
Garage
Grady's Grillhouse
Linda's Tavern
Old Pequliar
Owl 'n' Thistle Irish Pub
and Restaurant
Pioneer Square Saloon
Roanoke Inn
Temple Billiards
Twilight Exit, The
Wildrose, The

PUBS/ALEHOUSES

Attic Alehouse & Eatery,
The
Big Time Brewery and
Alehouse
College Inn Pub
Conor Byrne's Public
House
Cooper's Alehouse
Duchess Tavern, The
Elysian Brewing Company
Grady's Grillhouse
Hale's Brewery and Pub
Hopvine Pub
Irish Emigrant
Kells
Kirkland Roaster
& Alehouse
Latona by Green Lake
Lava Lounge
Leschi Lakecafe and
G.B.B. Bar
McMenamins Queen
Anne Pub & Brewery
Murphy's Pub
Old Pequliar, The
Old Town Alehouse
Owl 'n' Thistle Irish Pub
and Restaurant
Pacific Inn Pub
Pioneer Square Saloon
Prost!
Red Door Alehouse
Roanoke Inn
Roanoke Park Place
Tavern
74th Street Ale House
Six Arms Brewery and
Pub
Stella Pizza and Ale
Two Bells Tavern

ROCK

Ballard Firehouse
Cafe Venus and the marsBar
Chop Suey

Comet Tavern
Crocodile Cafe
Experience Music Project
(Liquid Lounge, Sky
Church)
Graceland
Old Firehouse, The
Paragon Bar and Grill
Rainbow, The
Re-bar
Showbox
Studio Seven
Sunset Tavern
Tractor Tavern
Vera Project, The

ROMANTIC

Baltic Room
Capitol Club
Century Ballroom
Dimitriou's Jazz Alley
Fireside Room
Fu Kun Wu
Shea's Lounge
Sitting Room, The

SMOKE-FREE

Big Time Brewery and
Alehouse
Dimitriou's Jazz Alley
Experience Music Project
Fiddler's Inn
Fu Kun Wu
Hale's Brewery and Pub
Latona by Green Lake
McMenamins Queen
Anne Pub & Brewery
Old Firehouse, The
Old Town Alehouse
Uptown Espresso and
Bakery
Vera Project, The
Virginia Inn

SPORTS BARS

Big Time Brewery and
Alehouse

Cooper's Alehouse
Duchess Tavern
F. X. McRory's Steak, Chop, and Oyster House
Rocksport

SWING
Century Ballroom
Dimitriou's Jazz Alley
Paragon Bar and Grill
Showbox

UNDERAGE/NO ALCOHOL
Aristocrat's Nightclub (some 18-and-over shows)
Dimitriou's Jazz Alley
Experience Music Project (JBL Theater, Sky Church)
Graceland (some all-ages shows)

Mr. Spot's Chai House (some all-ages shows)
Old Firehouse, The
Showbox (some all-ages shows)
Studio Seven
Vera Project, The

Nightlife by Neighborhood

BALLARD
Ballard Firehouse
Conor Byrne's Public House
Fu Kun Wu
Hale's Brewery and Pub
Hattie's Hat
Mr. Spot's Chai House
Old Pequliar, The
Old Town Alehouse
Sunset Tavern
Tractor Tavern

BELLTOWN
Axis
Bada Lounge
Belltown Billiards
Crocodile Cafe
Lava Lounge
Queen City Grill
Rendezvous (Jewel Box Theater)
Tula's
Two Bells Tavern
Uptown Espresso and Bakery

CAPITOL HILL
Baltic Room
Barça

B&O Espresso
Bauhaus Books and Coffee
BLU Video Bar
Caffe Ladro
Caffé Vita
Capitol Club
Century Ballroom
Cha-Cha Lounge
Chop Suey
Coffee Messiah
Comet Tavern
DeLuxe Bar and Grill
Dilettante Chocolates Cafe and Patisserie
Elysian Brewing Company
Garage
Hopvine Pub
Joe Bar
Linda's Tavern
Manray
Neighbours
Roanoke Park Place Tavern
Six Arms Brewery and Pub
611 Supreme Crêperie Café
Top Pot Donuts

Victrola Coffee and Art
Vogue, The
Wildrose, The

CENTRAL DISTRICT
Twilight Exit, The

CHINATOWN/ INTERNATIONAL DISTRICT
Aristocrat's Nightclub
Panama Hotel Tea and Coffee House

DENNY TRIANGLE
Five Point Café
Graceland
Re-bar
Tini Bigs Lounge

DOWNTOWN
Brooklyn Seafood, Steak, and Oyster House
Caffe Ladro
Dilettante Chocolates Cafe and Patisserie
Dimitriou's Jazz Alley
Nitelite, The
Noc Noc
Owl 'n' Thistle Irish Pub and Restaurant

Showbox
Top Pot Donuts
Uptown Espresso and
    Bakery
Vera Project, The
Virginia Inn

EASTLAKE
Cafe Venus and the
    marsBar
Eastlake Zoo

FIRST HILL
Fireside Room
Vito's Madison Grill

FREMONT
Ballroom in Fremont
Buckaroo Tavern, The
Caffe Ladro
Pacific Inn Pub
Red Door Alehouse
Simply Desserts
Star Life on the Oasis
ToST

GEORGETOWN
About the Music
Stella Pizza and Ale

GREENWOOD/
GREEN LAKE
Chocolati
Diva Espresso
Elysian Brewing Company
Latona by Green Lake
Little Red Hen
Luau Polynesian Lounge
Prost!
74th Street Ale House
Urban Bakery, The
Zoka Coffee Roaster and
    Tea Company

KIRKLAND
Kirkland Roaster & Ale-
    house

LESCHI/
MADISON PARK
Attic Alehouse & Eatery,
    The
Leschi Lakecafe and
    G.B.B. Bar

MERCER ISLAND
Roanoke Inn

PIKE PLACE
MARKET
Alibi Room
Kells
Shea's Lounge

PIONEER SQUARE
Catwalk
Club Contour
Comedy Underground
F. X. McRory's Steak,
    Chop, and Oyster
    House
Fenix Underground
Last Supper Club
Marcus' Martini Heaven
Pioneer Square Saloon
Temple Billiards
Zeitgeist Coffee

QUEEN ANNE
Caffe Ladro
Caffé Vita
El Diablo Coffee
McMenamins Queen
    Anne Pub & Brewery
Ozzie's Roadhouse
Paragon Bar and Grill
Sitting Room, The
Uptown Espresso and
    Bakery

RAVENNA/
WEDGWOOD
Duchess Tavern, The
Fiddler's Inn

REDMOND
Old Firehouse, The

ROOSEVELT/
MAPLE LEAF
Cooper's Alehouse
Scarlet Tree

SEATTLE CENTER
Experience Music Project
SkyCity at the Needle

SODO
Studio Seven

UNIVERSITY
DISTRICT/
MONTLAKE
Big Time Brewery and
    Alehouse
Blue Moon Tavern
Cafe Allegro
College Inn Pub
Espresso Express
Giggles
Grady's Grillhouse
Irish Emigrant
Rainbow, The
Star Life on the Oasis

WALLINGFORD
Diva Espresso
Murphy's Pub
Pacific Inn Pub
Teahouse Kuan Yin

WEST SEATTLE
Caffe Ladro
Diva Espresso
Rocksport
Uptown Espresso and
    Bakery

NIGHTLIFE

Music and Clubs

Clubs around Seattle shut down, change format, change names, or get crumbled by earthquakes at an amazing rate. For example, over the past 25 years, the Showbox has been a senior-citizen bingo hall, a flea market, a punk club, closed down, a rock club, a comedy club, closed down again, a private club, a rock club desperately in need of work, and now, in its latest incarnation, a renovated multipurpose music hall. A few of the clubs listed here will no doubt fade into history themselves (or change back into bingo halls). For the latest music listings, check the local daily newspapers (weekend goings-on listings appear on Friday), *Seattle Weekly* or *The Stranger* (the city's alternative weeklies, which come out on Thursday), or the online entertainment guide CitySearch (seattle.citysearch.com).

About the Music

6010 AIRPORT WY S, GEORGETOWN; 206/762-5518 As its name suggests, this south-end lounge is all about the music—the jazz music, that is. Owner Doron Raphaely opened this beautiful, bilevel venue in 2002 to showcase some of the city's fine jazz, soul, and R&B musicians. It's not unusual to find impromptu jam sessions happening at 1am or an occasional hip-hop showcase. *AE, MC, V; no checks; Tues–Sun; beer and wine; aboutthemusic.net; map:JJ7*

Aristocrat's Nightclub

220 4TH AVE S, CHINATOWN/INTERNATIONAL DISTRICT; 206/748-9779 While many of the city's clubs were fretting over format changes, Aristocrat's quietly built itself into the city's premier venue for live DJ music and drum and bass. A former Italian restaurant, the quirky space is full of unexpected twists and turns, every inch of which gets flooded by the energetic crowd. Friday night shows are often 18 and over. *AE, DIS, MC, V; no checks; Thurs–Sat; full bar; aristocratsclub.com; map:Q6*

Ballard Firehouse

5429 RUSSELL AVE NW, BALLARD; 206/784-3516 Because of its predilection toward the nostalgia set (or, as some might call it, the VH1 *Behind the Music* set), this longstanding institution has often evoked more laughter than genuine interest. New management has shifted bookings to focus on reggae and funk, and we'll take that over resurrected Flock of Seagulls any day. *AE, MC, V; no checks; every day; full bar; theballardfirehouse.com; map:FF8* &

Baltic Room

1207 PINE ST, CAPITOL HILL; 206/625-4444 Perhaps as a result of the ever-present candles, everything at this intimate watering hole feels covered in red velvet: the cushy booths and tables, the exquisite drinks, even the appraising glances from other sleek and well-dressed patrons. Though the music is primarily of the DJ variety (theme nights range from dance hall to drum and bass to "I Heart

Shiva," an Indian fusion night), live hip-hop acts flit through occasionally and visiting DJs in town from more cosmopolitan scenes in London, Detroit, and Berlin often stop by for one-night stands. *MC, V; no checks; every day; full bar; thebaltic room.com; map:J2*

Cafe Venus and the marsBar

609 EASTLAKE AVE, EASTLAKE; 206/624-4516 The ruby-red walls and black vinyl booths at Cafe Venus and the marsBar are glossy and stylish, much like most of the bar's clientele. Though a variety of people frequent during the day for the tasty lunch menu, the evenings attract the city's studded-belt punk elite. A diverse array of local bands file across the small stage, and you're practically guaranteed to discover something your friends won't yet have heard of. Come early if you want a booth. *MC, V; no checks; every day; full bar; cafevenus.com; map:F1*

Catwalk

172 S WASHINGTON ST, PIONEER SQUARE; 206/622-1863 This large, high-tech club used to accommodate the small but rabid collection of Goth and industrial bands in Seattle, but lately, it's become an amalgamation of styles and scenes. Lesbian dance promoters Girl4Girl take over on the third Saturday of each month for a blowout party (usually with a costume theme), and cheap live shows that favor no apparent genre happen on Fridays. It's a great room, in any case, and the elaborate fashion statements on any given night are always entertaining. *MC, V; no checks; Fri–Sat; full bar; catwalkclub.net; map:O8*

Century Ballroom

915 E PINE ST, 2ND FLOOR, CAPITOL HILL; 206/324-7263 The Century is a beautiful old theater (formerly an Odd Fellows hall) that started booking music in 1999 in addition to salsa and swing dance nights (with DJs). The light, airy room provides wallflowers and sure-foots alike with one of the best places in Seattle to dance (wood floors!). Swing and salsa dance lessons are available several nights a week, and dancing at all shows is highly encouraged. *MC, V; checks OK; Wed–Sun (hours vary according to bookings); full bar; centuryballroom.com; map:L1* &

Chop Suey

1325 E MADISON ST, CAPITOL HILL; 206/324-8000 When former owner Linda Derschang (also owner of the trendy bar Linda's) jumped ship from Chop Suey in 2003, many thought the club would join its former incarnation, The Breakroom, in dead rock-club heaven. But new management hasn't hurt the stylized Asian-themed club: some might say the shows have improved, as new bookers focus on electronic acts and the diverse local scene. *MC, V; no checks; every day; full bar; chopsuey.com; map:HH6* &

Club Contour

807 1ST AVE, PIONEER SQUARE; 206/447-7704 A polished oasis in the desert of Pioneer Square saloons, Contour is primarily a DJ dance venue, though it does occasionally book live music. It's also a place where beautiful people come to be seen sipping some of the city's best cocktails and noshing premier bar food and where the elegant decor rivals the attractive patrons. It's open until daybreak on Friday and Saturday nights (see the Up All Night sidebar in this chapter). *AE, MC, V; no checks; every day; clubcontour.com; map:N7* &

Comedy Underground

222 S MAIN ST, PIONEER SQUARE; 206/628-0303 For more than 20 years, the Comedy Underground has humbly sent its patrons into fits of giggles, guffaws, and chuckles seven nights a week. Talent can be hit-or-miss—the club considers itself a training ground for new acts—but even a mere titter is worth more when it comes as part of such an enduring tradition. *AE, MC, V; local checks only; every day; full bar; comedyunderground.com; map:O8*

BEST PLACE TO BUY SEDITIOUS LITERATURE?

"Left Bank Books in Pike Place Market if you need immediate inspiration to start a revolution; their selection of titles will be more than enough to help you get your very own FBI file."

Jack Daws, Northwest sculptor

Crocodile Cafe

2200 2ND AVE, BELLTOWN; 206/441-5611 When it first opened its doors in 1991, no one thought the Crocodile Cafe would survive the grunge boom, much less be around 13 years later. But the scene has shifted around the Crocodile; new crops of fine local and national talent are always springing up, ready to step onto its venerable stages. Music ranges from indie rock to pop to singer/songwriters and back again, but all of it (national and local) is consistently excellent. Most nights, the music room charges separate cover from the cafe and bar so you can enjoy the atmosphere, tasty food, and drinks without paying a cover. *MC, V; no checks; every day; full bar; thecrocodile.com; map:G7* &

Dimitriou's Jazz Alley

2033 6TH AVE, DOWNTOWN; 206/441-9729 John Dimitriou's venue isn't just the best jazz club in Seattle, it's one of the best in the nation. His reputation brings international-caliber talent, and the club itself is perfectly designed—you can hear and see from every seat. Dimitriou has added more blues, Latin music, and big bands to the lineup over the past few years, and local artists frequently play during the week. In a counterintuitive move for a jazz club, Dimitriou's has gone smoke-free. Weekends are often packed, so call ahead to reserve tickets. You can guarantee yourself a seat by going early for dinner, although the food isn't quite as good as the jazz. *AE, MC, V; checks OK; Tues–Sun; full bar; jazzalley.com; map:H5* &

Experience Music Project (EMP)

325 5TH AVE N, SEATTLE CENTER; 206/EMP-LIVE OR 877/EMP-LIVE EMP, or as some prefer to call it, the Big Blob, sports a trio of halls where live music is performed regularly. The main attraction is the Sky Church, where bands ranging from They Might Be Giants to Le Tigre take over on weekends. Though there's frequently a full bar attached, all Sky Church shows are all-ages, so feel free to bring the kids (EMP even hosts an afternoon concert series specifically for families). The JBL Theater is a classic-style amphitheater that generally screens films about music. If a live band is playing, go see it; the acoustics here are wonderful. The Liquid Lounge, a surprisingly intimate bar-style venue, hosts live local bands and DJs from EMP's affiliated radio station, 90.3 FM KEXP. *AE, DC, DIS, JCB, MC, V; no checks; every day; full bar; emplive.com; map:C5* &

Fenix Underground

109 S WASHINGTON ST, PIONEER SQUARE; 206/405-4323 The 2001 earthquake put it out of business for nearly three years, but just like its mythological namesake, the Fenix rose again. The new location is glitzier and more mainstream than its former incarnation (no more Goth nights), and the three dance floors are always packed with beautiful people cruising in under the Pioneer Square Joint Cover (see the Pioneer Party sidebar in this chapter). There's an added cafe, too, but, be warned—the food can be a bit dicey. *AE, MC, V; no checks; every day; full bar; fenixunderground.com; map:O8*

Giggles

5220 ROOSEVELT WY NE, UNIVERSITY DISTRICT; 206/526-5653 Name aside, Giggles takes itself seriously as the leading place for edgy, risqué comedy. It draws in touring comedians from TV, film, and radio and almost nothing is sacred on its stage. Like the comedy world in general, bookers seem to prefer the talents of men, though Margaret Cho has dropped in on occasion. *MC, V; no checks; Thurs–Sun; full bar; gigglescomedyclub.com; map:FF6*

Graceland

109 EASTLAKE AVE E, DENNY TRIANGLE; 206/262-0482 Unlike its namesake, Graceland is in no way ostentatious. It's one of the city's true rock clubs, where local and touring alternative rock bands crank their amps up to 11 and attempt to blow out eardrums. The beer is cold, and happy-hour specials are decent, but if you have objections to cigarette smoke, low ceilings, or filthy toilets, this is not the club for you. *MC, V; no checks; every day; full bar; map:H1*

Irish Emigrant

5260 UNIVERSITY WY NE, UNIVERSITY DISTRICT; 206/525-2955 Formerly the University Sports Bar (and, years before that, the Century Tavern), this U District landmark is now strictly Irish in politics, food, and music. They book mostly Irish bands six nights a week (Monday is a trivia contest; see the Mind Games sidebar in this chapter). *AE, MC, V; no checks; every day; full bar; irishemigrant.net; map:FF6*

Last Supper Club

124 S WASHINGTON ST, PIONEER SQUARE; 206/748-9975 The big attractions here are the DJs and the mind-bending digital visual effects that accompany them; the club prides itself on "seamless, flawless sets" and technical prowess. Talent is a mix of homespun DJs and occasional touring mixers, and bookings range from progressive house to trance to dance hall. *AE, DIS, MC, V; no checks; Wed–Sun; full bar; lastsupperclub.com; map:O8* &

Little Red Hen

7115 WOODLAWN AVE NE, GREEN LAKE; 206/522-1168 The Little Red Hen is Seattle's only true honky-tonk. Seated in its brown booths and scuttling 'round its huge dance floor, you'll find the largest collection of cowboy boots north of Wyoming ranch country. The local country bands that grace the stage are consistently excellent. Mondays and Tuesdays offer free country-dance lessons; Wednesday is country karaoke. *AE, DIS, MC, V; no checks; every day; full bar; little redhen.com; map:EE7* &

Neighbours

1509 BROADWAY AVE, CAPITOL HILL; 206/324-5358 Neighbours used to have a monopoly on the gay dance crowd, but in recent years similar venues have popped up like molehills in the surrounding area. Still, none spin quite the same blend of high-energy house, disco, and pop, offer such a flamboyant atmosphere, or have the same array of specialty nights (Sundays are Latin themed, complete with Spanish-language karaoke; Tuesdays are talent-contest nights; and Wednesdays are hosted by drag fixture Mark "Mom" Finley). *MC, V; no checks; every day; full bar; neighbours online.com; map:L1*

Noc Noc

1516 2ND AVE, DOWNTOWN; 206/223-1333 Part chic art bar, part progressive dance party, Noc Noc is an unpretentious, amusing place to pass an evening. DJs spin house during the week, but Sunday night has become one of the most well-trafficked Gothic nights in town. Other special groups who stop by include the city's bike messengers, who gather here en masse to exchange tips on dodging traffic. Well drinks are $1 during happy hour, which runs from 5pm to 9pm daily. *AE, DIS, MC, V; no checks; every day; full bar; clubnocnoc.com; map:J7*

The Old Firehouse

16510 NE 79TH ST, REDMOND; 425/556-2370 Not to be confused with the Ballard Firehouse, this all-ages Redmond venue has helped solidify the alternative rock scene in Seattle's outlying suburbs. For 10 years, it's been one of the only venues that gives teens a chance to see live bands (a recent CD compilation, *All That Was Built Here*, on Missing Records, documented the club's history); and it also provides adults with a window into up-and-coming bands. The friendly atmosphere and cheap sodas more than make up for the lack of beer. Shows are scheduled Fridays and Saturdays, with occasional breaks, so call to confirm lineups. *Cash only; Fri–Sat (hours vary according to bookings); no alcohol; theoldfire house.org; map:EE1*

UP ALL NIGHT

Big-city dwellers will be surprised to find that Seattle is an early-to-bed kind of city. Even on weekends, restaurants generally close up at 10pm and bars at 2am, when it becomes illegal to sell alcohol. Because some of us are true night owls, we've focused here on places where you can find food or fun beyond the midnight hour.

BALLARD'S SUNSET BOWL (1420 NW Market St; 206/782-7310; map:FF8) isn't retro—it simply hasn't been updated since the early 1960s. Which is fine because it's the city's only 24-hour bowling alley, which means a surprisingly large number of people are vying for lanes at 3am. (The city doesn't offer much else in the way of entertainment for its bored teenagers.) If you'd like to sing karaoke in the tiny, aged bar, sign up early—the list fills quickly and the songbook is limited.

Late-night movies are a preferred option for insomniacs. **THE EGYPTIAN THE-ATER** (805 E Pine St, Capitol Hill; 206/323-4978; map:K1) alternates between kitsch classics, cult favorites, and theme-relevant films (Christmas movies during December, horror for Halloween); shows start at midnight on Fridays and Saturdays. Offering similar, if generally more offbeat, late-night fare, the snug, 40-seat **GRAND ILLUSION** (1403 NE 50th St, University District; 206/523-3935; map:FF6) has shows starting at 11pm. Run by local film collective the Northwest Film Forum, the Illusion often screens archival prints and obscure rarities.

In the middle of the night, food is all about the grease factor, and a few 24-hour diners cater to those cravings for buttery hash browns. **BETH'S CAFE** (7311 Aurora Ave N,

Owl 'n' Thistle Irish Pub and Restaurant

808 POST AVE, DOWNTOWN; 206/621-7777 For an old-fashioned evening, hop in one of the horse-drawn carriages that swing around the waterfront and ask the driver to deliver you to this hidden Irish pub on the edge of Pioneer Square. The bookings lean toward Celtic folk bands on weekends, and a variety of other music during the week. There's also a small poolroom and a comfortable dining area up front where you can settle down and peruse an assortment of classic books. *AE, MC, V; no checks; every day; full bar; owlnthistle.com; map:N7*

Paragon Bar and Grill

2125 QUEEN ANNE AVE N, QUEEN ANNE; 206/283-4548 Despite its location on the relatively sedate crown of Queen Anne Hill, the Paragon often bustles just as frantically as any downtown club, particularly on weeknights. Twenty- and thirtysomethings cluster around the long, high bar, jamming to an assortment of live bands that range from pop to singer/songwriter to swing. Call ahead to confirm what you'll be getting that evening. *AE, MC, V; no checks; every day; full bar; map:GG8* &

Green Lake; 206/782-5588; map:EE7) is a longstanding institution, and its 12-egg omelets can bust guts of even the hardiest eaters. The **HURRICANE CAFE** (2230 7th Ave, Denny Triangle; 206/682-5858; map:G5) is generally overflowing with black-clad, angst-filled teens and cigarette smoke during the wee hours, but it does make a mean cup of veggie chili. Those who like their food with a little more class will find sustenance at **13 COINS** (125 Boren Ave N, Denny Triangle; 206/682-2513; map:G3), where pricey Italian and American dishes are the rule. **STELLA'S TRATTORIA** (4500 9th Ave NE, University District; 206/633-1100; map:FF7) and its sister establishment, **TRATTORIA MITCHELLI** (84 Yesler Wy, Pioneer Square; 206/623-3885; N8), offer delicious Italian fare until 4am on Fridays and Saturdays.

Light-footed night owls who groove on laser light shows, fire dancers, and other assorted visual elements will want to check out the after-hours dance party at **CLUB CONTOUR** (807 1st Ave, Downtown; 206/447-7704; map:N7), where a rotating cast of DJs spin house until 9am on weekends. A similarly rave-like environment can be found at **NOC NOC** (1516 2nd Ave, Downtown; 206/223-1333; map:J7), where the DJs spin deep house and hip-hop until the sky goes gray. (See reviews in this chapter.)

For less physical diversion, bookstore **TWICE SOLD TALES** (905 E John St, Capitol Hill; 206/324-2421; map:GG7) stays open until 1am Monday through Thursday, all night every Friday, until 2am Saturday, and until midnight on Sunday. Late-night literature seekers with cat allergies beware, the store's resident bevy of felines has free run of the shelves.

—Tizzy Asher

The Rainbow

722 NE 45TH ST, **UNIVERSITY DISTRICT; 206/634-1761** Catching a show at the Rainbow is like perusing a music snob's CD collection: alongside the standard reggae and jazz, you get oddball experimental music, acoustic singer/songwriters, and high-minded rock bands. No matter what the music selection, the atmosphere is amiable and the cover is usually under $5. *MC, V; no checks; every day; full bar; therainbowlivemusic.com; map:FF7* &

Re-bar

1114 HOWELL ST, **DENNY TRIANGLE; 206/233-9873** The Re-bar has distinguished itself among the city's many hipster-friendly clubs by playing host to theater events, rock musicals, and performance-art events like the monthly Pho Bang, a punk-rock cabaret. Local DJs spin house, old-school, and soul on the off nights and a light-footed crowd turns up to pack the dance floor. Pool tables and pinball provide entertainment for nondancers. *AE, MC, V; no checks; open according to bookings; full bar; rebarseattle.com; map:I2* &

Rocksport

4209 SW ALASKA ST, WEST SEATTLE; 206/935-5838 The Rocksport is the sort of sports bar where everyone roots for the home teams, even when they're losing. It also books live music, but mostly cover bands, so don't go hoping to discover the next big thing. Wednesdays and Thursdays are video game nights, where patrons can play Xbox games on the big screen. *AE, DIS, MC, V; no checks; every day; full bar; rocksport.net; map:JJ8* &

Scarlet Tree

6521 ROOSEVELT WY NE, ROOSEVELT; 206/523-7153 The Scarlet Tree may be best known as a place where you can get a hard drink at 6:30am (and don't think people aren't doing just that), but it also consistently draws crowds for the hard-driving blues bands, as well as the R&B and funk it books. *AE, DIS, MC, V; no checks; every day; full bar; map:EE6*

Showbox

1426 1ST AVE, DOWNTOWN; 206/628-3151 This is the grande dame of Seattle music venues. How many clubs can say they've hosted shows by both Captain Beefheart and Pearl Jam? A recent remodel added a measure of comfort to the cavernous space—more dance floor, more bar space, more air—and the national talent that graces the stage seems to get better and better. The Showbox also occasionally has all-ages shows, so even youngsters can see the inside of an institution. In 2002 the Showbox added the Green Room, a small cocktail lounge in an adjacent space, and this new addition books mainly acoustic acts. *AE, MC, V; no checks; every day; full bar; showboxonline.com; map:J7*

Studio Seven

110 S HORTON ST, SODO; 206/286-1312 For years, the all-ages club scene struggled under a restrictive law that forbade kids from dancing in venues that sold alcohol. Studio Seven (which doubles as a recording studio and practice space complex) is the first attempt at consistently mixing the two since the law was lifted in 2002, and so far, it's been a thriving success. The music here is generally loud and hard-core, so if you're worried about early hearing loss, bring your earplugs. *Cash only; open according to bookings; beer and wine; studioseven.us; map:II7*

Sunset Tavern

5433 BALLARD AVE NW, BALLARD; 206/784-4880 The low ceiling and copious cigarette smoke at this Ballard dive can be off-putting for those not well-versed in rock show etiquette. But if you can survive the body heat and the jostling crowd, you'll be rewarded with a diverse selection of live music from local and touring acts. Bookings lean toward rock 'n' roll and punk, but country and metal have been known to rear up occasionally. A popular weekly event called Rockaraoke gives you the chance to sing karaoke with a live band. *MC, V; no checks; every day; beer and wine; www.sunsettavern.com; map:FF8*

ToST

513 N 36TH ST, FREMONT; 206/547-0240 Unlike other hot spots in Fremont, people flock to ToST (pronounced "toast") for its consistent attempts to provide a diverse selection of musical entertainment. This unassuming space has stepped up its bookings in the past year and has started hosting some of the city's finest hipster troubadours seven nights a week. A generous selection of wines by the glass makes for a mellow, intimate evening. *AE, MC, V; no checks; every day; full bar; tost lounge.com; map:FF8* &

Tractor Tavern

5213 BALLARD AVE NW, BALLARD; 206/789-3599 Almost everyone onstage at the Tractor has that windblown look of alternative country—and so do many members of the audience. It's one of the few clubs in Seattle where you can wear cowboy boots, a plaid shirt, and Levi's and fit in. The booking is consistently excellent (rock, rockabilly, bluegrass, Celtic, and folk are featured in addition to alt country), and the venue itself is intimate without being claustrophobic. *MC, V; no checks; every day (hours vary according to bookings); full bar; tractortavern.citysearch.com; map:FF8*

Tula's

2214 2ND AVE, BELLTOWN; 206/443-4221 Tula's has quietly grown into a noted jazz club. Bookings are mostly local musicians, but the jam sessions attract top-rate talent and it's a great room for music. Advertising is sparse, so make sure to call and check the lineup. *MC, V; no checks; every day; full bar; tulas.com; map:G7*

The Vera Project

1916 4TH AVE, DOWNTOWN; 206/956-VERA As much community organization and teen center as it is rock club, the Vera Project is the only nonalcoholic rock club in town. Kids from all over the area come out as volunteers and run all aspects of the shows—from taking money at the door to providing security to running sound—and the participation provides an uplifting sense of ownership. The bookings vary wildly, so call ahead. *Cash only; open according to bookings; no alcohol; theveraproject.org; map:I6*

The Vogue

1516 11TH AVE, CAPITOL HILL; 206/324-5778 The Vogue, along with the adjacent Bad Juju Lounge, is a frequent haunt for the black-clad, white-faced Goth crowd. The DJs spin mostly darkwave and industrial music, with a heavy emphasis on songs first made popular 10 years ago. The wide dance floor and open booths leave plenty of room to display your best collection of vinyl, velvet, and lace. If you can't see how velvet, vinyl, or lace could combine to make a fashion statement, you have a lot of catching up to do. *MC, V; no checks; Tues–Sun; full bar; vogueseattle.com; map:L1*

Bars, Pubs, and Taverns

Alibi Room

85 PIKE PL, PIKE PLACE MARKET; 206/623-3180 Opened and owned by local Hollywood types (including the ubiquitous Tom Skerritt), the Alibi was conceived as a watering hole for Seattle's burgeoning film set. Unfortunately, that set is fairly few and far between, and the Alibi Room has become a general-purpose bar for a cross-section of Seattleites. It's a great place to celebrity-spot during the Seattle International Film Festival. *AE, DIS, MC, V; no checks; every day; full bar; alibiroom.com; map:J7*

The Attic Alehouse & Eatery

4226 E MADISON ST, MADISON PARK; 206/323-3131 The Attic is a friendly neighborhood bar with all the typical accoutrements—darts, pool, comfy booths, and a sizeable collection of draft beers, of the micro and macro varieties. Like the surrounding Madison Park neighborhood, the bar's constituency seems to straddle the line between rowdy college kids and middle-aged yuppies out for a night away from the kids. *AE, MC, V; checks OK; every day; beer and wine; map:GG6*

Axis

2214 1ST AVE, BELLTOWN; 206/441-9600 Introverts will want to avoid this posh Belltown bar, where much of the polished professional crowd comes to flirt and indulge in thoughtfully chosen wines, specialty cocktails, and gourmet snacks. Even on weeknights, the place is packed, so be prepared to wrestle for a table if you want to sit near the picture windows or in the streetside seating area. *AE, DC, DIS, JCB, MC, V; no checks; every day; full bar; axisrestaurant.com; map:F7* &

Bada Lounge

2230 1ST AVE, BELLTOWN; 206/374-8717 Bada means "ocean" in Korean, and a large screen projects soothing images of tropical fish throughout the evening at this fancy lounge. The decor is Nordic modern (white cubes substitute for chairs) and the patrons are sharply dressed and cell-phone friendly. If you can stand the mobs of people that throng the bar, you'll be rewarded with Bada's signature drink, the Dragon Toe, an incredible concoction made from crushed cucumber and ginger. The Thursday night drink specials come in an assortment of colors that makes Skittles seem drab. *AE, MC, V; no checks; full bar; every day; badalounge.com; map:F7* &

Ballroom in Fremont

456 N 36TH ST, FREMONT; 206/634-2575 This funky but chic club has become one of Fremont's hottest spots. On a good night, entry lines snake out onto the sidewalk and the boisterous crowd can be heard blocks away. There are nine pool tables, but most people seem more interested in dancing and chatting on the wide patio. *MC, V; no checks; every day; full bar; map:FF8* &

Barça

1510 11TH AVE, CAPITOL HILL; 206/325-8263 With its outrageous, carnival-like Saturday nights and tasteful European decor, Barça is the Seattle equivalent to a Barcelona bar during the raging months of summer. A diverse crowd gathers to indulge in tasty bar food, a separate vodka bar, and superb service. It's fascinating to watch the servers maneuver through the tightly packed crowd while bearing enormous platters of fine liquor, never spilling a drop. *MC, V; no checks; full bar; every day; barcaseattle.com; map:L1* &

Belltown Billiards

90 BLANCHARD ST, BELLTOWN; 206/448-6779 Belltown Billiards is a mishmash—part high-tech bar and dance floor, part high-class pool hall, part high-gloss Italian restaurant—but everyone is having too much fun to mind the confusion. The food takes a backseat on weekend nights, when the crowds descend and turn pool into a true spectator sport. *AE, MC, V; no checks; every day; full bar; belltown.city search.com; map:H7* &

Big Time Brewery and Alehouse

4133 UNIVERSITY WY NE, UNIVERSITY DISTRICT; 206/545-4509 Antique beer ads clutter the walls at the U District's most popular alehouse, where the tasty brews are made on the other side of the wall. Students are the prime clientele, though occasional packs of university faculty can be spotted at the hefty wooden tables, discussing literature, math, or politics over a pitcher of hand-crafted beer. Hippies take note: Tuesdays are devoted to the jam band, the String Cheese Incident. *MC, V; no checks; every day; beer and wine; bigtimebrewery.com; map:FF6* &

BLU Video Bar

722 E PIKE ST, CAPITOL HILL; 206/568-4258 BLU is what gay bars look like in the post-MTV generation. Video screens peer down from every available corner of this space-age bar, and the polished silver surfaces reflect spotlights that are, naturally, blue. A flashy gay crowd turns out for regular dance nights and karaoke, and in summer the upstairs patio is packed with beautiful people. *AE, MC, V; no checks; every day; full bar; map:L1* &

Blue Moon Tavern

712 NE 45TH ST, UNIVERSITY DISTRICT; 206/633-6267 It's seedy, it's smoky, and it's beloved: when this lair of legends and gutter dreams appeared to be in the path of the wrecking ball, a cry of protest went up, books on its shady history were quickly printed, and demonstrations were organized. A yearlong battle with developers produced a 40-year lease and a collective sigh of relief from the neighborhood pool players, Beat ghosts, living poets, and survivors of the U District's glory days. Tom Robbins put in his time in this crusty joint, and no wonder—the graffiti-covered booths are filled with strange characters who seem to be in search of a novel. Blue Moon funds the literary journal *Point No Point* and holds an annual poetry and fiction contest. *Cash only; every day; beer and wine; map:FF6*

MIND GAMES

Useless knowledge and beer are natural bedfellows, so holding trivia nights in a bar is a no-brainer. Facts like the number of golf balls on the moon (3) and the largest accordion ensemble (566 accordions!) might seem trivial, but they take on a weighty significance when accompanied by a rich stout and a plate of taters. Trivia night is a longstanding tradition in the British Isles (the *Guinness Book of World Records* was created by a Guinness Brewery manager in 1951), and in the past decade it has spread to Seattle with outcroppings of British- and Irish-themed pubs. Other clubs have caught on and use trivia nights to drum up business on slow days. Any of the following hangouts offer boisterous and brain-teasing environments.

EXPERIENCE MUSIC PROJECT LIQUID LOUNGE (325 5th Ave N, Seattle Center; 206/EMP-LIVE; map:C5), Mondays, 7pm, individual or team play, no entry fee, no cash prizes.

GEORGE AND DRAGON (206 N 36th St, Fremont; 206/545-6864; map:FF8), Tuesdays, 8pm, $5 per team of up to six.

HOPVINE PUB (507 15th Ave E, Capitol Hill; 206/328-3120; map:HH6), second

Brooklyn Seafood, Steak, & Oyster House

1212 2ND AVE, DOWNTOWN; 206/224-7000 If you're looking to meet a lawyer, this is the place: after work, the Brooklyn crawls with suits. On summer weekends, tourists replace lawyers, oohing and aahing at the fresh oyster selection. There's plenty of seating at the wraparound bar and a good choice of beers, although this is more of a single-malt Scotch crowd. *AE, DIS, MC, V; checks OK; every day; full bar; thebrooklyn.com; map:M7* &

The Buckaroo Tavern

4201 FREMONT AVE N, FREMONT; 206/634-3161 The Buckaroo may have cashed in on its reputation as a grizzly biker bar in the movie *Ten Things I Hate About You*, but celebrity stardom hasn't gone to its head. It really is the city's biker bar, and rows of Harleys are perpetually parked out front. If you have a laptop, leave it at home—the Buckaroo doesn't look kindly on nerdy types. *No credit cards; checks OK; every day; beer and wine; map:FF8*

Capitol Club

414 E PINE ST, CAPITOL HILL; 206/325-2149 While the mostly young urban professional crowd yaks away on cell phones or rubs elbows on the outdoor terrace, serious Capitol Club patrons will be wise to sprawl out on the luxurious benches and embroidered pillows that line the walls of this Moroccan-themed bar. Adventurous drinkers should steer toward the lavish house drinks, which come

Tuesday of the month, 8:30pm, $3 per person, up to 6 people per team.

IRISH EMIGRANT (5260 University Wy NE, University District; 206/525-2955; map:FF6), Mondays, 8pm, $5 per team of up to six.

MURPHY'S PUB (1928 N 45th St, Wallingford; 206/634-2110; map:FF7), Tuesdays, 8pm, $4 per round for team of up to four.

THE OLD PEQULIAR (1722 NW Market St, Ballard; 206/782-8886; map:FF8), Tuesdays, 8pm, $5 per team of up to four.

O'SHEA'S EASY STREET PUB (309 NE 45th St, Wallingford; 206/547-6832; map:FF7), Mondays, 8pm, $5 per team.

R PLACE (619 E Pine St, Capitol Hill; 206/322-8828; map:K1), Mondays, 7:30pm, individual or team play, no entry fee, no cash prizes.

READING GAOL PUB AND GRILL (418 NW 65th St, Ballard; 206/783-3002; map:EE8), Mondays, 7pm and 8:30pm, individual play, no entry fee, no cash prizes.

WEDGWOOD ALE HOUSE (8509 35th Ave NE, Wedgwood; 206/527-2676; map:EE6), Sundays, 10pm, no entry fees, no cash prizes.

—Tizzy Asher

laced with extravagances like fresh crushed basil and pomegranate syrup. *AE, MC, V; no checks; every day; full bar; thecapitolclub.net; map:K2*

Cha-Cha Lounge

506 E PINE ST, CAPITOL HILL; 206/329-1101 Under the glowing red lights (which can feel remarkably like heat lamps on a summer night), major players in the Seattle music scene nestle into the circular vinyl booths and high tables at the Cha-Cha for legendary gossip and networking sessions. Food is courtesy of the adjacent Bimbo's Bitchin' Burrito Kitchen (see the Restaurants chapter), and it tends toward the spicy and full of beans. Keep your eyes peeled for local celebrities, but remember, they're as likely to be behind the bar pouring drinks as they are to be sitting next to you. *MC, V; no checks; every day; full bar; map:K1*

College Inn Pub

4006 UNIVERSITY WY NE, UNIVERSITY DISTRICT; 206/634-2307 You won't find stuck-up Whiffenpoofs lingering in the burnished wood booths at the College Inn; this convenient gathering place for university students seems to attract a low-key crowd—the sort of students who don't mind being mistaken for nonstudents. Food is typical pub fare (nachos, sandwiches), and the expansive selection of microbrews on tap and in bottles will help if the conversation turns to postmodernism. *MC, V; no checks; every day; full bar; map:FF6*

Comet Tavern

922 E PIKE ST, CAPITOL HILL; 206/323-9853 One of the last vestiges of the city's flannel-clad grunge element, the Comet Tavern is a huge yet comfortable space with a decent beer selection, occasional live music and DJs, and three fantastic pinball machines in its overhead loft. The heavy wood furniture has been etched and carved by hundreds of hands: careful inspection can occasionally reveal graffiti written by or about one of Seattle's local literary legends. *Cash only; every day; beer and wine; map:L1* &

Conor Byrne's Public House

5140 BALLARD AVE NW, BALLARD; 206/784-3640 Conor Byrne's differentiates itself from the rest of Ballard's pubs by providing an elegant, Old World charm. Giant chandeliers swing lightly above the burnished wood bar and the exposed brick walls feature art from local artists. The stage generally plays host to mellow acoustic folk, traditional Irish music, and various forms of country. Tuesday nights have become a free-for-all variety show led by the divine Miss H, who is said to be Seattle's best hula-hooper. *MC, V; checks OK; every day; beer and wine; conorbyrnepub.com; map:FF8*

Cooper's Alehouse

8065 LAKE CITY WY NE, MAPLE LEAF; 206/522-2923 A mecca for serious brew lovers and home to postgame soccer and rugby bacchanals, this neighborhood pub aims to please in a no-nonsense manner. Patrons can opt for darts or for sports on TV, but beer's the main thing, and Cooper's offers 22 taps, most of them dispensing Northwest microbrews. The Ballard Bitter–battered fish-and-chips (say that fast after a couple of pitchers) are terrific. *MC, V; no checks; every day; full bar; coopersalehouse.com; map:DD6*

DeLuxe Bar & Grill

625 BROADWAY AVE E, CAPITOL HILL; 206/324-9697 The time-honored DeLuxe is where Broadway's most mainstream boulevardiers go for stuffed baked potatoes and electric iced teas. The bar is often crammed, although the retractable wall in front lets you sit on the sidewalk in nice weather and watch the steady stream of passersby. *AE, DIS, MC, V; no checks; every day; full bar; map:GG7* &

The Duchess Tavern

2827 NE 55TH ST, RAVENNA; 206/527-8606 This is the kind of neighborhood tavern that former university students remember fondly decades after graduation. Today's Duchess has cleaned up its act considerably; it's more open and airy than in the past, and there are 20 beers on tap (more than half are microbrews). The darts, the pool table, and the '60s rock make it the perfect place to stop for a pitcher after the game. *AE, DIS, MC, V; no checks; every day; full bar; map:EE6* &

Eastlake Zoo

 2301 EASTLAKE AVE E, EASTLAKE; 206/329-3277 The Eastlake Zoo is the aging hippie of local bars, still holding tightly to its radical ideas nearly 30 years after opening its doors: it's a worker-run collective and the employees have placed an empty water jug on the counter to collect money for the food bank. Along with a solid collection of beer and wine, the bar offers cheap pool, pinball, darts, shuffleboard, and plenty of smoke-stained history on its walls. Sit at the bar and you may get an earful of Marxist commentary. *Cash only; every day; beer and wine; members.aol.com/zootavern.com; map:GG7*

Elysian Brewing Company

1211 E PIKE ST, CAPITOL HILL; 206/860-1920 / 2106 N 55TH ST, GREEN LAKE; 206/547-5929 A low-key combination of brewpub and restaurant, the Elysian often doubles as a meeting place for the jeans and T-shirt Capitol Hill crowd. The grub is delicious (even meat eaters will drool over the barbecue tempeh sandwich, which comes slathered in tangy sauce and cheese) and the freshly brewed beer even better. And with a new location in North Seattle, you'll never want for a glass of Dragon Tooth Oatmeal Stout. *AE, MC, V; no checks; every day; beer and wine; elysian brewing.com; map:HH6, EE7* &

F. X. McRory's Steak, Chop, and Oyster House

419 OCCIDENTAL AVE S, PIONEER SQUARE; 206/623-4800 Visiting F. X. McRory's without having just come from a baseball or football game is like eating kielbasa without sauerkraut: still tasty, but lacking that special punch. This old-school bar offers sports fans a raucous atmosphere where they can toss out sports statistics and banter about who's being traded and for what salary. Fresh oysters and a solid beer selection complete the experience. *AE, DIS, MC, V; no checks; every day; full bar; fxmcrorys.com/fx.html; map:O8*

Fiddler's Inn

9219 35TH AVE NE, WEDGWOOD; 206/525-0752 Now in its 70th year, the Fiddler's Inn feels like a historic space, even though it's officially not. It received a full remodel in 1995, and the decor is rustic and homey, with picnic tables and a large patio. Most nights, acoustic singer/songwriters or mellow bands play live music. *MC, V; checks OK; every day; beer and wine; www.fiddlersinn.org; map:FF6*

Fireside Room

900 MADISON ST (SORRENTO HOTEL), FIRST HILL; 206/622-6400 The clubby lounge in the lobby of the Sorrento evokes a leisurely world of hearthside chats in overstuffed chairs, an unrushed perusal of the daily newspaper, a hand of whist. It's most pleasant for a late-evening drink, particularly when the piano accompanies the music of many and varied conversations. *AE, DIS, MC, V; no checks; every day; full bar; hotelsorrento.com/fireside_room.htm; map:M4*

Five Point Café

415 CEDAR ST, DENNY TRIANGLE; 206/448-9993 Stuffed fish on the wall, nuts in the chairs, rocks in the jukebox—you never know what you'll find here, except extra-strong drinks that have minimal impact on your wallet. With a friendly clientele that ranges from bluehairs and gays to suburban babes and Rastafarians, the place—despite its divey decor and perma-nicotined walls—gives hope that world peace may be achievable after all. *AE, MC, V; no checks; every day; full bar; map:E6*

Fu Kun Wu

5410 BALLARD AVE NW, BALLARD; 206/706-7807 Seattle has always prided itself on being a healthy city; Fu Kun Wu takes that to the extreme (a sign over the entry reads, "The Doctor Is In"). Working from a Chinese herbalist theme, this classy piano bar creates herbal cocktails designed to improve potency and stamina (some contain the African herb yohimbe). If you have no interest in improving your potency, try the Oolong-tini, a blend of tea, vodka, lemon, and sugar. *AE, DIS, MC, V; no checks; every day; full bar; map:FF8* &

Garage

1130 BROADWAY AVE E, CAPITOL HILL; 206/322-2296 The Garage recently leapt from ordinary pool-hall status (if you can call 18 tables ordinary) to uber-club fame by adding a 14-lane bowling alley called Garage Bowl in the adjacent building—Seattle's first new alley in 40 years. Rolling balls around is a surprisingly popular activity: both sides of the club are generally packed with urban hipsters and affluent professionals from the nearby hospitals. DJs spin occasionally, but don't count on live music. (See review in the Restaurants chapter.) *AE, MC, V; no checks; every day; full bar; map:M1*

Grady's Grillhouse

2307 24TH AVE E, MONTLAKE; 206/726-5968 Grady's is a convivial neighborhood pub, comfortable and clean. Come for the good selection of micros on tap and the food, which is a cut above the usual pub fare, but stay away on Husky game days unless you're a die-hard fan. Nonsmokers beware. *MC, V; local checks only; every day; full bar; gradysgrillhouse.com; map:GG6* &

BEST PLACE TO SAMPLE A MICROBREW OR THREE?

"The Blue Moon Tavern, because a couple of Red Hooks in such a genuinely bohemian atmosphere can easily evolve into a metaphysical adventure."

Tom Robbins, author

Hale's Brewery & Pub

4301 LEARY WY NW, BALLARD; 206/782-0737 This gleaming, spacious brewpub, a showcase for locally renowned Hale's ales, also serves as an oasis of sophistication in the Fremont-Ballard industrial neighborhood. Grab a booth, or bring along enough of the gang to fill one of the long tables in the high-ceilinged back room, where live music is performed on weekend nights. At least nine varieties of Hale's pour year-round, as well as a selection of rotating seasonal varieties. *MC, V; checks OK; every day; beer and wine; halesales.com; map:FF8* &

Hattie's Hat

🐷 **5231 BALLARD AVE NW, BALLARD; 206/784-0175** Hattie's Hat is an old-timey place that underwent a major renovation several years ago and now lives on as a hybrid that appeals to both young hipsters and old Ballard fishermen. The food is excellent and the bar is lively even early in the morning. Alt country superstar Neko Case used to work here, and, if you're lucky, you'll find someone who can tell you about those good old days. *MC, V; no checks; every day; full bar; map:FF8*

Hopvine Pub

507 15TH AVE E, CAPITOL HILL; 206/328-3120 Another seedy tavern transformed into a clean pub featuring lots of microbrews. There are hop vines stenciled and sculpted on the walls, wooden booths and tables stained in bright colors, and a smoking area in back. With pizza on the menu and occasional acoustic shows, this is a welcome addition to the Capitol Hill neighborhood. *MC, V; no checks; every day; beer and wine; map:HH6*

Kells

1916 POST ALLEY, PIKE PLACE MARKET; 206/728-1916 Rousing sing-alongs to live Celtic music boom throughout the large pub side of this Irish restaurant every day. Sit near the door in the restaurant and you'll have a breathtaking view of the Olympic Mountains. *AE, MC, V; local checks only; every day; full bar; kellsirish.com; map:I7* &

Kirkland Roaster & Alehouse

111 CENTRAL WY, KIRKLAND; 425/827-4400 Serving microbrews long before the rest of the Eastside caught on, everything seems to shout of beer at the Kirkland Alehouse. Beyond the dispensing of quality beer, beer barrels, taps, and bottles line walls covered with microbrew-label murals. *AE, DC, MC, V; no checks; every day; full bar; map:EE3* &

Latona by Green Lake

6423 LATONA AVE NE, GREEN LAKE; 206/525-2238 The Latona is a light, woody, microbrew-and-cheese-bread lovers kind of place, a favorite with its residential neighbors and lake lizards alike. Things can get cozy in this small but thankfully smoke-free space, which seems more expansive due to high ceilings. Service is extra attentive and accommodating. Most Friday and Saturday evenings, the pub hosts local jazz and folk musicians. *MC, V; local checks only; every day; beer and wine; map:EE7* &

Lava Lounge

2226 2ND AVE, BELLTOWN; 206/441-5660 This long, skinny Belltown bar sports a kitsch tiki-hut theme, from Lava lamps to velvet paintings of bare, busty maidens. Don't expect any froufrou drinks with little umbrellas, however; this is a beer bar (beers are available both bottled and on tap). It's also a great place to meet friends, grab a booth, and get down to serious gabbing and gulping. Pinball and shuffleboard provide added amusement. *MC, V; no checks; every day; beer and wine; map:G7*

Leschi Lakecafe and G.B.B. Bar

102 LAKESIDE AVE, LESCHI; 206/328-2233 It's hard to find the Leschi Lakecafe unless you're looking for it. This large, neighborly bar is tucked on the shore of Lake Washington, in a neighborhood that's much more marina than martini. But on a crisp summer evening, the Leschi provides some of the best beachfront drinking in the city. Take in a view of Mount Rainier and the sound of sailboats gently rocking in the waves, all while sipping one of the many fine beer selections or a smooth cocktail. *AE, DC, DIS, MC, V; no checks; every day; full bar; map:II6*

Linda's Tavern

707 E PINE ST, CAPITOL HILL; 206/325-1220 Linda's is another of the hot spots for local musicians and scenesters: on any given night, a covert business transaction seems to take place just one table over. The crowd here is a multiethnic mix of Gen-Xers and plain folks who come to drink or play pool to the strains of alternative music blaring from the stereo, to watch films on the back porch in summer, or to listen to DJ music (Monday and Tuesday nights). Everyone is made to feel welcome—and that's another nice alternative. *MC, V; no checks; every day; full bar; map:K1*

Luau Polynesian Lounge

2253 N 56TH ST, GREEN LAKE; 206/633-5828 At this tiki-themed hideout smack in the middle of a quiet neighborhood, drinks range from the delicious to the downright bizarre, and if you ask nicely, they'll give you an extra little paper parasol. And yes, you can get a pupu platter (see the Restaurants chapter). *AE, MC, V; local checks only; every day; full bar; luaupolynesianlounge.com; map:EE7*

Manray

514 E PINE ST, CAPITOL HILL; 206/568-0750 White walls, white tables, white bar—the only thing this frosty gay bar lacks is an antiseptic entry chamber that makes sure you don't track in any dirt. Like BLU, Manray is a video bar, which means that TVs flicker from every corner and loud music is de rigueur. If you want a warm, romantic place to chat up a blind date, or if you're prone to spilling glasses of red wine, you should steer clear. *AE, DIS, MC, V; no checks; every day; full bar; manrayvideo.com; map:K1*

Marcus' Martini Heaven

88 YESLER WY, PIONEER SQUARE; 206/624-3323 The folks at Marcus' Martini Heaven know that there are few things in life more pleasing than a well-mixed martini. Like James Bond, the bartenders like 'em shaken, not stirred, and so dry that cacti beg for water. True aficionados may sneer at the array of fruity flavors designed to appease the unconverted, but they shouldn't scoff at the Godiva Chocolate Martini until they've tried it. *AE, MC, V; no checks; Mon–Sat; full bar; map:N8*

McMenamins Queen Anne Pub & Brewery

200 ROY ST, QUEEN ANNE; 206/285-4722 This brewpub—Seattle's first venture for the Portland-based McMenamin brothers—has settled quite nicely into its Lower Queen Anne neighborhood, hosting local residents and Seattle Center visitors alike with characteristic low-key amiability. There's a great selection of McMenamins brews, plus great fries and other reasonably priced pub grub, and the place is smoke-free. *AE, DIS, MC, V; no checks; every day; full bar; mcmenamins.com; map:A5*

Mecca Cafe

526 QUEEN ANNE AVE N, QUEEN ANNE; 206/285-9728 Before its 2003 remodel, the dive bar alongside this greasy spoon was home to many a geriatric drinker. The clientele is now young, cool, and prone to take advantage of the hit-heavy jukebox in the corner. Stop by when you're hungry and order the hand-cut fries. *AE, MC, V; no checks; every day; full bar; map:GG7*

Murphy's Pub

1928 N 45TH ST, WALLINGFORD; 206/634-2110 As Irish pubs go, Murphy's is a pretty classy place (fireplace, antiques, stained glass). Wallingfordians and others pile in to play darts (real, of course, not electronic) or to catch the weekend music (often Celtic). More than a dozen local brews and stouts are poured on draft, and there's a nice collection of single-malt Scotches and single-barrel bourbons, but no well drinks. It's a zoo on St. Paddy's Day. *AE, DIS, MC, V; no checks; every day; full bar; map:FF7*

The Nitelite

1926 2ND AVE, DOWNTOWN; 206/443-0899 A favorite of the hip, young bar-hopping crowd, the Nitelite could well be the queen of retro Seattle lounges. The original decor is from the '40s, with a mind-bending compendium of objects spanning the decades through the '70s. The place was used as a set in the movie *Dogfight* in 1991, and most of the props were kept firmly in place. Check out the train set encased in plastic under the bar. Cheap beer specials, stiff martinis, and syrupy libations for the Cap'n Crunch crowd are what's pouring. *Cash only; every day; full bar; map:I7*

The Old Pequliar

1722 NW MARKET ST, BALLARD; 206/782-8886 Like many of the bars in Ballard, the Old Pequliar appears to have an identity crisis: it's part dive tavern, part classy English pub, and part gourmet eatery. But from one of the comfy booths, all that really matters is the fine selection of liquor and beer and the updated bar menu. Live music of all varieties happens on Fridays, Saturdays, and Mondays, and there is never a surprise cover. *DIS, MC, V; no checks; every day; full bar; map:FF8*

Old Town Alehouse

5233 BALLARD AVE NW, BALLARD; 206/782-8323 The Old Town evokes the look of old Ballard, with an ornate antique bar and icebox, exposed-brick walls, and old black-and-white photos. The Ballard Wedge sandwiches are tasty—and the fries that come alongside are out of this world. *MC, V; no checks; every day; beer and wine; oldtownalehouse.com; map:FF8*

Ozzie's Roadhouse

105 W MERCER ST, QUEEN ANNE; 206/284-4618 The 2003 demise of Sorry Charlie's Piano Bar (rumored to be reimagined as more of a hipster lounge called the

Mirabeau Room) left a void in the karaoke landscape of Lower Queen Anne that Ozzie's Roadhouse is happy to fill. This enormous and labyrinthian bar is one of the city's best singing spots, and karaoke nuts fill every booth, cheering and clapping for their favorites. Not just one but two bars offer microbrews on tap and an array of mixed drinks. *AE, DIS, MC, V; no checks; every day; full bar; map:A7*

Pacific Inn Pub

3501 STONE WY N, FREMONT/WALLINGFORD; 206/547-2967 Should you come for the brew (a dozen on tap, a couple of dozen in bottles and cans) or for the fab cayenne- and herb-spiked fish-and-chips? Most regulars enjoy both at this work-ingman's mainstay where Wallingford and Fremont merge. Old-timers know the PI's owner, Robert Julien, as the wonderful singing bartender at long-gone-but-not-forgotten Jake O'Shaughnessy's. *AE, MC, V; no checks; every day; full bar; map:FF7*

Pioneer Square Saloon

77 YESLER WY, PIONEER SQUARE; 206/628-6444 This is one of the few bars in Pioneer Square that doesn't offer live music—and thus doesn't slap on a cover. The clientele ranges from slackers to corporate types, the taped tunes are good, and there's a dart board in the back. In summer, the patio tables—where you can survey the tourists wandering by—are packed. Between the kindly bartenders, the good (and cheap) wines by the glass, and the unaffected air, this could be the best spot in the city for making new friends. *AE, MC, V; no checks; every day; beer and wine; map:N8*

BEST PLACE TO VIEW ART?
"Howard House and James Harris Gallery have the hottest emerging artists."
Linda Farris, art curator and Contemporary Art Project founder

---

Prost!

7311 GREENWOOD AVE N, GREENWOOD; 206/706-5430 Formerly a funky wine bar, Prost! recently stepped up as the only authentic German beer hall in the city. You'll come out smelling like brats and sauerkraut, but the fine imported beers on tap are worth it. *AE, MC, V; no checks; every day; beer and wine; map:EE7*

Queen City Grill

2201 1ST AVE, BELLTOWN; 206/443-0975 Fluted lights, flowers, and a rosy glow that bathes the room make this one of Belltown's classiest options. On weekends it gets packed with artists, yuppies, and off-duty bartenders pretending they're in New York or San Francisco; we much prefer Queen City on weeknights, when sitting at the curved bar can be quietly lovely (see the Restaurants chapter). *AE, DC, DIS, MC, V; no checks; every day; full bar; queencitygrill.citysearch.com; map:G7*

Red Door Alehouse

3401 EVANSTON AVE N, FREMONT; 206/547-7521 They moved the entire building one block west, but the Red Door remains the same even after its relocation. During the day, suits, salespeople, and salty dogs stop in to down a cold one with a burger and fries. At night it's so crowded with the fraternity/sorority crowd, you could mistake the place for a J.Crew catalog shoot. There's a wide selection of beers, predominantly Northwest microbrews, to complement some terrific (inexpensive) pub grub. Order a bowl of mussels and eat 'em in the beer garden. *AE, MC, V; local checks only; every day; full bar; map:FF7*

Rendezvous (Jewel Box Theater)

2320 2ND AVE, BELLTOWN; 206/441-5823 Up until 2002, the Rendezvous was one of the city's most infamous dives. But after a full renovation and change in owner-ship (by the folks who ran the dearly departed OK Hotel, no less), the Rendezvous transformed into a slick, glamorous establishment, replete with red velvet booths and well-coiffed servers. The bar originally opened in 1926 as a dinner theater, and the new owners have preserved the original screening room, hence the Jewel Box Theater name. Special film events often happen here, as do occasional oddball per-formance art shows and rock shows. *AE, MC, V; no checks; every day; full bar; jewel boxtheater.com; map:F7*

BEST PLACE TO VIEW ART?
"A hot day on Capitol Hill when the tattoo tribe is walking around."
Sherman Alexie, poet, novelist, and screenwriter

Roanoke Inn

1825 72ND AVE SE, MERCER ISLAND; 206/232-0800 The Roanoke Inn isn't the kind of place most people will just happen upon. It resides on secluded Mercer Island, which is usually a destination only for its inhabitants. However, die-hard pub crawlers may want to seek this one out for its history alone. It's known for its some-what checkered past—apparently the upstairs rooms once housed a brothel of sorts, and the main room was the site of many bloody barroom brawls. Today its biggest draw is the outdoor seating on a generous front porch reminiscent of a Southern estate. *AE, MC, V; no checks; every day; full bar; map:II4*

Roanoke Park Place Tavern

2409 10TH AVE E, CAPITOL HILL; 206/324-5882 A relaxed gathering ground where the junior gentry of North Capitol Hill can feel like just folks. Good burgers and beers, and the new Ping-Pong tables are a welcome addition, but loud music often drowns out conversation. The place is packed with drunken frat boys after Husky games. *MC, V; no checks; every day; full bar; map:GG7*

74th Street Ale House

7401 GREENWOOD AVE N, GREENWOOD; 206/784-2955 The 74th Street Ale House and its sister establishments, the Columbia City Ale House (4914 Rainier Ave S, Columbia City; 206/723-5123; map:JJ5) and the Hilltop Ale House (2129 Queen Anne Ave N, Queen Anne; 206/285-3877; map:GG8), are ale houses in the true sense of the word, with regulars lingering at the bar and taps pouring nearly two-dozen brews. The food, however, is more than a cut above pub grub, including a delectable gumbo and several sandwiches and main dishes worthy of a "real" restaurant. All three places are great places for after-work meetings, or for whiling away rainy Sunday afternoons. *MC, V; local checks only; every day; beer and wine; seattle alehouses.com; map:EE7* &

Shea's Lounge

94 PIKE ST, PIKE PLACE MARKET; 206/467-9990 Don't let the near-hidden location (on the top floor of the Corner Market building) keep you from ferreting out this charming little offshoot of Chez Shea. Seven small tables and a minuscule bar are set in a slender, elegant, dimly lit space with enormous casement windows looking out over market rooftops to Elliott Bay beyond. A nice selection of Italian and Spanish wines is complemented by a short but tasteful, mainly Mediterranean menu (see the Restaurants chapter). Utterly romantic. *AE, MC, V; no checks; Tues–Sun; full bar; chezshea.com; map:I7*

The Sitting Room

108 W ROY ST, QUEEN ANNE; 206/285-2830 After taking in a high-minded piece of theater or performance art at On the Boards, a prestigious avant-garde production space, theatergoers can imbibe happily at the Sitting Room. Known for its massive wine list, this glamorous space also features an extensive import and specialty beer menu and an array of delicious snacks and desserts. Expect your server to engage you in a conversation about the show you just saw. *MC, V; no checks; Tues–Sun; beer and wine; map:GG8*

Six Arms Brewery and Pub

300 E PIKE ST, CAPITOL HILL; 206/223-1698 Like its sister establishment, McMenamins on Lower Queen Anne (see review), the Six Arms offers a well-rounded selection of brews, all hand-crafted in the tiny room at the rear of the bar. Tasty pub fare rounds out the menu. It's best not to come with extreme hunger—service can be mellow to a fault. Luckily, an assortment of mini statuary (our favorite is the contented sheep), ornamental light fixtures, and antique books will keep you entertained till the food comes. *AE, DIC, MC, V; no checks; every day; beer and wine; mcmenamins.com; map:K2* &

SkyCity at the Needle

SPACE NEEDLE, SEATTLE CENTER; 206/443-2100 If enjoying a truly sensational view means sipping one of the most expensive drinks you'll ever have in your life, cough up $11 for the hop to the top (only restaurant patrons ride free)—and then drink slowly. Or, if you're feeling particularly daring, ask to see the wine list. A "cheap" bottle will set you back $30 or $40. For a limited vintage, expect to shell out $250, but fine wines taste better in a restaurant that is rotating very, very slowly (see the Restaurants chapter). *AE, DIS, MC, V; checks OK; every day; full bar; spaceneedle.com; map:D6* &

Stella Pizza and Ale

5513 AIRPORT WY S, GEORGETOWN; 206/763-1660 The south-end neighborhood of Georgetown was billed as the next funky artist community, and though this never quite materialized, a few tasty offerings sprang up to offer locals solid neighborhood fare. The pizza at Stella is delicious, as is the fine selection of beer. *MC, V; no checks; every day; beer and wine; map:KK7* &

BEST PLACE TO BE IGNORED?

"The Twilight Exit. Walk in on a weeknight and snuggle into one of their cozy couches with a vodka tonic to be alone with your thoughts and the incredible music on the juke."

Melanie McFarland, Seattle Post-Intelligencer *TV critic*

Temple Billiards

126 S JACKSON ST, PIONEER SQUARE; 206/682-3242 It's not as glossy as Belltown Billiards, but that's just fine with the youngish crowd that shoots pool at the Temple. Word has it the regulars here include certain local band members, so keep your eyes peeled if celebrity-spotting thrills you. There's a decent selection of beer and wine and some tasty sandwiches. *AE, MC, V; no checks; every day; full bar; map:O8* &

Tini Bigs Lounge

100 DENNY WY, DENNY TRIANGLE; 206/284-0931 Located on the jumpin' corner of First and Denny, Tini's adds casual elegance to the KeyArena area. Perch at the bar or grab a more intimate table and dish over a bracingly cold martini (Tini's offers 20 variations). Prices aren't cheap, but the standard's a double; be forewarned—these babies go down smooth. Weeknights are considerably less frantic than Friday, Saturday, and Sonics game nights, when the place packs out in elbow-to-elbow fashion. *AE, MC, V; no checks; every day; full bar; tinibigs.citysearch.com; map:C8* &

The Twilight Exit

2020 MADISON ST, CENTRAL DISTRICT; 206/324-7462 The operating theme of this spacious bar is 1970s kitsch, and the ramshackle decor ranges from absurd (a silver mannequin illuminated by blue light) to adorable (blurry family fishing trip photos). On any given night, you'll find a diverse mix of people chatting and picking tunes from the well-stocked jukebox. Bring quarters: the Exit features one of the city's only table-style Ms. Pac Man games. *AE, MC, V; no checks; every day; full bar; map:HH6* &

PIONEER PARTY

Ever since Seattle was a stopover for prospectors on their way to the Klondike in the 1890s, Pioneer Square has upheld its reputation as the rowdiest part of town. (Sometimes too much so—in 2001, riots on Mardi Gras left one reveler dead and many more injured.) The area has toned down a bit in recent years, but it still sponsors the **PIONEER SQUARE JOINT COVER** on Friday and Saturday nights, where $12 gets you into 10 of the most popular venues (listed below). Before 9pm, cost is $10. Mondays through Thursdays, joint cover is $5. Pay at the door of any one of these clubs and they'll give you a stamp valid for entry at the others. If you can stand the whoops and hollers of the fraternity brothers and the occasional meat-market attitude (best take solitary, introspective drinking elsewhere), you're in for a true Seattle experience.

BOHEMIAN CAFE (111 Yesler Wy; 206/447-1514; map:N7). Officially a reggae club, occasional funk or hip-hop bands can also be seen trouping through on weekends. Bump and grind dancing is the rule, not the exception.

THE CENTRAL SALOON (207 1st Ave S; 206/622-0209; map:O8). A straightforward bar that offers live blues and rock and a classic atmosphere.

DOC MAYNARDS (601 1st Ave S; 206/682-3705; map:N7). A no-frills nightclub that often has live cover bands on the weekends.

FENIX UNDERGROUND (109 S Washington St; 206/405-4323; map:O7). The

Two Bells Tavern

2313 4TH AVE, BELLTOWN; 206/441-3050 Even the most self-conscious hipster lets it all hang out at Two Bells. There is a good selection of local microbrews and imported gems, plus sporadic but creative bookings of solo guitar acts, unusual art exhibits, and poetry readings. Great burgers and sausage plates, and a late-night happy hour complete the experience. *AE, MC, V; no checks; every day; full bar; map:G6*

Virginia Inn

1937 1ST AVE, DOWNTOWN; 206/728-1937 What do you get when you mix arty Belltown dwellers, chic-seeking suburbanites, and babbling pensioners in a historic, brick-tile-and-avant-garde-art tavern on the edge of Pike Place Market? You get the VI, a very enlightened, very appealing, vaguely French-feeling tav with a fine list of libations (including pear cider) and character to burn. You'll have to burn your cigs elsewhere, though. *MC, V; no checks; every day; full bar; map:I7* &

Vito's Madison Grill

927 9TH AVE, FIRST HILL; 206/682-2695 A veritable mishmash of styles (red vinyl booths, shag carpet, etched mirrors, burnished wood), Vito's has been designated as the hip new gathering place for Seattle's electronic and jazz funk elite. Crowds of

Fenix offers DJ dance nights and live shows for those with eclectic taste (see review in this chapter).

J&M CAFE AND CARDROOM (201 1st Ave S; 206/292-0663; map:O8). There's no longer a functioning cardroom in this cafe—just lots of retro dance music and happy dancers.

JUAN O'RILEYS (309 1st Ave S; 206/622-5826; map:O8). Despite its Irish surname, this is a spicy salsa joint where patrons cha-cha to the best in pre-recorded Latin music.

LARRY'S BLUES CAFÉ (209 1st Ave S; 206/624-7665; map:O8). This down-to-earth bar is a good venue for local blues (and for stiff drinks).

NEW ORLEANS RESTAURANT (114 1st Ave S; 206/622-2563; map:O8). The music here is spicy and classy, with zydeco, jazz, and blues being the main focus. Delicious food, too.

OLD TIMER'S CAFÉ (620 1st Ave S; 206/623-9800; map:N7). This former jazz and blues club now features salsa on weekends, as well as blues and karaoke other days.

TIKI BOB'S CANTINA (166 S King St; 206/382-8454; map:P8). Long lines and rowdy crowds are the standard at this franchise Top 40 dance club. Special events and theme nights seem to focus around wearing a wacky piece of clothing (pajamas, wigs, and so on).

—Tizzy Asher

mustachioed men can be seen gathering around giant martinis, sharing stories with hard-core drinkers and obvious long-time imbibers. Local DJs have begun using Vito's as a practice space, and there is occasionally a cover, so bring a little extra cash. *AE, MC, V; no checks; every day; full bar; map:M3*

The Wildrose

1021 E PIKE ST, CAPITOL HILL; 206/324-9210 The center of the universe for the Seattle lesbian scene, the Wildrose has served as community center, coffeehouse, music venue, pool hall, and just plain great bar since 1984. Tables are just as likely to be filled with women reading alone as those dining with friends or drinking in uproarious groups, particularly since the Rose added karaoke to its list of features. *MC, V; no checks; every day; full bar; thewildrosebar.com; map:L1*

Coffee, Tea, and Dessert

Perhaps it's all of our drowsy, gray weather that has caused Seattle to become caffeine addicted. And thanks to the many branches of Starbucks, Tully's, and Seattle's Best Coffee, there's no risk of having to go cold turkey for even a block. But what makes the city really special is its vast array of independent coffee- and

BUBBLE TEA

Cooked up by rival tea stands in Taiwan in the mid-1980s, bubble tea is flavored milk or tea accented by black tapioca pearls, coconut, or fruit jelly. And in Seattle, it's fast becoming the drink of choice with the young college set, the finicky dessert crowd, and Japanese tourists alike. With the wide array of flavors—from plain honey milk tea to tropical fruit like durian—there's something to please every palate.

Tea shops are popping up all over the city, and the ones that stay open late offer an interesting alternative to the bar scene. Animé and karaoke enthusiasts should definitely take note.

EPISODES BUBBLE TEA CAFÉ (13754 Aurora Ave N, #F, North Seattle; 206/365-3281; map:CC7). Episodes uses real fruit instead of a powdered mix, which makes for some of the best bubble tea in the city. The atmosphere is inviting—stay long enough and you'll get incorporated into a card game.

GINGKO TEA (4343 University Wy NE, University District; 206/632-7298; map:FF6). A quiet hangout for university students, Ginko Tea strives for exciting and deli-

teahouses, some of which feature excellent roasterias and bakeries. If you can manage it, stop in at one of the many nonfranchise cafes—it's worth the 10 extra steps to cross the street.

B&O Espresso

204 BELMONT AVE E, CAPITOL HILL; 206/322-5028 Legendary for espresso, extraordinary desserts, and serious conversation, this vigorous Capitol Hill coffeehouse buzzes from morning to 1am (on Friday and Saturday). It's a peaceful place for breakfast and brunch, for a steaming latte and a tart, or for a plate of fried new potatoes with peppers and onions. Lunch and dinner are available, but desserts and coffee are where the B&O really shines; these are some of the best (though they're not the cheapest) homemade desserts in town. *AE, DIS, MC, V; no checks; every day; full bar; map:I1* &

Bauhaus Books and Coffee

301 E PINE ST, CAPITOL HILL; 206/625-1600 At Bauhaus, function follows form. It's a high-ceilinged place with a wall of bookshelves stocked with used art books (Bauhaus doubles as a used-book store—though we suspect the books actually look better than they sell). Big windows afford a view of the Pike/Pine corridor and the Space Needle, which appears oddly inspiring and appropriate in this context. The wrought-iron fixtures and greenish walls lend style, as does the clientele. *Cash only; every day; no alcohol; map:K2*

Cafe Allegro

4002 UNIVERSITY WY NE, UNIVERSITY DISTRICT; 206/633-3030 People who got into the Allegro habit while they were at the University of Washington still find them-

cious flavor combinations: brown rice and barley, fresh pumpkin, young coconut. The less adventurous can choose from the extensive selection of loose-leaf teas.

OASIS TEA ZONE (519 6th Ave S, #120, Chinatown/International District; 206/447-8098; map:FF6). There are many bubble tea stands in the ID, but Oasis is the most active after 8pm. Shaved ice comes drizzled with condensed milk and laden with four types of fresh fruit, and the Thai tea bubble tea is incredible. Board games are provided, as is one pool table with blindingly red felt.

POCHI TEA STATION (5014 University Wy NE, University District; 206/529-1158; map:R7). Pochi is one of the city's oldest stands, and with its lime-green IKEA decor and long list of exotic flavors—including Horlicks, red bean, and durian—it can also be one of the most challenging. The staff is happy to explain anything and everything, however. Come late on Saturday evenings, order Nutella crepes, and watch karaoke in Chinese and Japanese.

—Tizzy Asher

selves gravitating back. It's hard to pin down the cafe's appeal. Perhaps it's the moody, dark-wood decor and often smoke-saturated air; or the cachet of the location (it's not easy to find, set in a U District back alley); or the serious and interesting conversating among its wonderfully international crowd of students. You may feel as if you've been left out of a private joke on your first few visits, but it doesn't take long to become a regular. *No credit cards; local checks only; every day; no alcohol; map:FF6*

Caffe Ladro

2205 QUEEN ANNE AVE N, QUEEN ANNE (AND BRANCHES); 206/282-5313 You won't confuse Caffe Ladro with Starbucks, though the local chain now has multiple locations. It's one of the only cafes in the city to serve organic, fair-trade, shade-grown coffee. The sweets and baked goods are delicious—the carrot cake is worth its weight in gold—as are the soups and sandwiches. There is a second location on Queen Anne (600 Queen Anne Ave N; 206/282-1549; address listed above; map:GG8) as well as franchises downtown (801 Pine St; 206/405-1950; map:J4; and 108 Union St; 206/267-0600; map:J7); in Fremont (452 N 36th St; 206/675-0854; map:FF7); on Capitol Hill (435 15th Ave E; 206/267-0551; map:HH6); and in West Seattle (7011 California Ave SW; 206/938-8021; map:JJ8). *MC, V; checks OK; every day; no alcohol; caffeladro.com; map:A7*

Caffé Vita

813 5TH AVE N, QUEEN ANNE; 206/285-9662 / 1005 E PIKE ST, CAPITOL HILL; 206/709-4440 Locals are rabid about this little cafe tucked in the unlikely neighborhood just north of Tower Records and its larger sister establishment on Capitol Hill. All the beans are roasted to perfection, including the well-rounded Del Sol, the Caffé Luna (French roast), and the organic Papua New Guinea. Beware: All espresso drinks are made with double ristretto shots. *No credit cards; checks OK; every day; no alcohol; caffevita.com; map:B4, L1* &

Chocolati

7810 E GREEN LAKE WY N, GREEN LAKE; 206/527-5467 A new addition to the Green Lake dessert panorama, Chocolati offers delicious, handmade chocolate (what else?) truffles from its nearby production center. The fruit truffles are a refreshing option and the Fish and Chips, chocolate fish with potato chip crumbles inside, are oddly delicious. An array of chilled, blended drinks ranging from the fruity to the decadent will cool off ambitious exercisers who choose to jog the lake path in summer. *MC, V; checks OK; every day; no alcohol; chocolati.com; map:EE7*

Coffee Messiah

1554 E OLIVE WY, CAPITOL HILL; 206/861-8233 This tiny little coffeehouse has the best bathroom in the entire city. We won't reveal the surprise here, but it requires a quarter, so come prepared. After the novelty has worn off, order a frothy caramel latte, enjoy the many religious icons strewn irreverently behind the bar, and have a chat with King Friday, the resident cat. *No credit cards; local checks only; every day; no alcohol; map:I1* &

Dilettante Chocolates Cafe and Patisserie

416 BROADWAY AVE E, CAPITOL HILL; 206/329-6463 / 1603 1ST AVE, DOWNTOWN; 206/728-9144 The name of this Seattle institution is derived from the Italian word *dilettare*, "to delight." And that's exactly what its sinfully rich truffles and butter cream–filled chocolates do. No dieter is safe here—if the truffles don't get you, the rich chocolate tortes, crème brûlée, or Turkish coffee will. The Broadway location inevitably bustles (till 1am on weekends) and the downtown location is a storefront only. Pssst . . . there's a small retail outlet at the candy factory (2300 E Cherry St, Central District; 206/328-1530; map:HH6), with seconds at reduced prices. *AE, MC, V; no checks; every day; beer and wine; dilettante.com; map:GG6, I7* &

Diva Espresso

7916 GREENWOOD AVE N, GREENWOOD (AND BRANCHES); 206/781-1213 This local fave has three locations—it's also in West Seattle (4480 Fauntleroy Ave SW; 206/937-5225; map:JJ8) and Wallingford too (4615 Stone Wy N; 206/632-7019; map:FF7)—and all have excellent coffee and pastries that melt in your mouth. *No credit cards; local checks only; every day; no alcohol; map:EE7*

El Diablo Coffee

1811 QUEEN ANNE AVE N, QUEEN ANNE; 206/285-0693 This colorful Queen Anne shop specializes in coffee of the true Cuban variety: dark, full-bodied, and often mixed with a sinful amount of chocolate. Be sure to check out the Love Grotto, a hidden corner of the cafe where couples can relax on red velvet couches and sip Mexican hot chocolate. Occasional live jazz and Cuban music shows pack the place out. *MC, V; local checks only; every day; beer and wine; eldiablocoffee.com; map:GG8*

Espresso Express

6500 15TH AVE NE, UNIVERSITY DISTRICT; 206/524-6326 Believe it or not, this was one of the very first espresso joints in town, here on the cusp of the U District and Ravenna, and it's consistently remained one of the finest. Though the ambience isn't fancy, Espresso Express has consistently used some of the finest beans around (shipped from Los Angeles, actually), and the quality of their pulls beats Starbucks hands down. If you want nonfat milk, forget it: they don't think it tastes as good, so they offer only low-fat. Like a small piece of Italy in Seattle. *MC, V; local checks only; every day; no alcohol; map:FF6*

BEST PLACE TO SHAKE YOUR BOOTY?

"The Baltic Room on Friday nights, when Jumbalaya mixes up some serious funk to groove the stiffness out of your trunk. And it's blissfully attitude free."

Melanie McFarland, Seattle Post-Intelligencer *TV critic*

Joe Bar

810 E ROY ST, CAPITOL HILL; 206/324-0407 Owner Wylie Bush stocks baked goods from the Hi Spot Cafe in Madrona at this comfortable bilevel space across the street from the Harvard Exit movie theater. The desserts and good espresso drinks add to the we're-all-friends-here atmosphere, fostered by the closely spaced tables and the eager après-film conversation. *Cash only; every day; no alcohol; map:GG6*

Mr. Spot's Chai House

5463 LEARY WY NW, BALLARD; 206/297-2424 Chai has become ubiquitous on the menus of many chain coffee shops, but don't consider yourself an experienced drinker until you've tried the Mr. Spot's homemade house blend, Morning Glory. Made with "good for you" spices such as astragalus, galungal, cardamom, and coriander, it can be a shock for those accustomed to sugary mixes. Don't miss the chai cheesecake if it's available. Live music happens sporadically—call ahead if you're hoping for a quiet night. *AE, MC, V; local checks only; every day; beer and wine; chaihouse.com; map:FF8*

Panama Hotel Tea and Coffee House

607 S MAIN, CHINATOWN/INTERNATIONAL DISTRICT; 206/515-4000 Once a thriving bathhouse and residence, this hotel's beautiful cafe has been refurbished around archival photos of Japantown from pre-Internment Seattle. A glass window set in the floor allows you to peer down into the basement at items left behind by families forced to move inland during World War II. It's a sad and chilling legacy of racism. The Hotel (see review in the Lodgings chapter) has the best tea selection in town and the always-friendly staff is generally willing to explain proper tea-drinking procedures. *No credit cards; local checks only; every day; no alcohol; panamahotelseattle.com/teahouse.htm; map:P6*

Simply Desserts

3421 FREMONT AVE N, FREMONT; 206/633-2671 Simply Desserts cooks up a selection of classic pastries: berry and fruit pies, a white-chocolate strawberry cake that wins raves from everyone, and countless variations on the chocolate cake theme in addition to the lovely chocolate-espresso cake—the most popular being the chocolate Cognac torte and the Bailey's Irish Cream cake. This small spot with an enormous reputation gets plenty busy in the evenings, when chocolate-cake fans from across the city sip espresso and enjoy what may be the best desserts around. *No credit cards; checks OK; Tues–Sun; no alcohol; map:FF8*

611 Supreme Crêperie Café

611 E PINE ST, CAPITOL HILL; 206/328-0292 With its brick walls, extensive wine list, and tasty cocktails, 611 Supreme is Seattle's answer to a dark Parisian creperie, only without the language barrier. The delicate crepes here are decadently stuffed with savory treats like mushrooms and sautéed vegetables or syrupy delights like chocolate sauce and whipped cream. Dessert crepes are big enough for two: amorous couples will enjoy the novelty of nestling together over a giant pancake. (See review in the Restaurants chapter.) *MC, V; no checks; Tues–Sun; full bar; map:K1*

Star Life on the Oasis

1405 NE 50TH ST, UNIVERSITY DISTRICT; 206/729-3542 Delicious baked goods of both vegan and nonvegan varieties are the standard at this cafe, which is housed in a ramshackle space adjacent to the Grand Illusion Cinema (and just recently changed its name from Still Life on the Ave). If you order the black coffee, prepare to stay up way past bedtime—the java at Star Life is famous for its dark, robust roast. Luckily, the new owners were wise enough to extend the hours until midnight. *AE, DIS, MC, V; no checks; every day; beer and wine; map:FF8, FF6*

Teahouse Kuan Yin

1911 N 45TH ST, WALLINGFORD; 206/632-2055 Depictions of Kuan Yin, the Buddhist goddess of mercy, preside over the serene atmosphere at this fine teahouse. Kuan Yin offers a full spectrum of teas, including plenty of blacks and greens, a few oolongs, and some herbals. Complementing these is a multiethnic assortment of panini, piroshkis, and croissants, as well as desserts such as green-tea ice cream, pies, and scones. You're invited to sit in leisurely and lengthy contemplation (quilted tea cozies keep your tea warm for up to two hours). Be sure to chat with the staff: instruction in the ways of tea drinking is dispensed generously and with a philosophical air. *MC, V; local checks only; every day; no alcohol; teahouse choice.com; map:FF7*

Top Pot Donuts

609 E SUMMIT AVE, CAPITOL HILL; 206/323-7841 / 2124 5TH AVE, DOWNTOWN; 206/728-1966 A new venture by the folks at Zeitgeist Coffee, Top Pot offers mouthwatering fresh donuts, delicious coffee, and high-speed Internet in an environment that manages to be both homey and hip. The larger downtown location opened in the fall of 2002 and has quickly acquired the nickname of "donut central." *No credit cards; local checks only; every day; no alcohol; zeitgeistcoffee.com; map:GG6*

Uptown Espresso and Bakery

525½ QUEEN ANNE AVE N, QUEEN ANNE (AND BRANCHES); 206/285-3757 This topnotch coffee hangout turns out a range of superb muffins, scones, and other sweet-and-semihealthy treats. All three locations of the Uptown—it's also in West Seattle (3845 Delridge Wy SW; 206/933-9497; map:JJ8) and has two downtown locations (2504 4th Ave; 206/441-1084; map:F6; and 1933 Westlake Ave; 206/782-8853; map:H4)—are always busy, whether with the quiet post-movie or post-theater crowd at night or with the louder tête-à-têtes throughout the day. Rightfully so, as these are some of the best espresso drinks you'll find in Seattle. *Cash only; every day; no alcohol; map:GG7*

BEST PLACE TO GET A TATTOO OR PIERCING?
"On the ankle."
Greg Nickels, mayor of Seattle

The Urban Bakery

7850 E GREEN LAKE DR N, GREEN LAKE; 206/524-7951 Morning, noon, and night you'll find Green Lake's urban yuppies hanging inside or out of this popular corner spot near the Green Lake shore. Enjoy excellent soups and vegetarian chili, the usual sandwiches and salads, and a world of freshly baked breads, pastries, pies, cakes, and cookies that taste as good as they look. All the requisite coffee drinks, too. *MC, V; no checks; every day; no alcohol; map:EE7*

Victrola Coffee and Art

411 15TH AVE E, CAPITOL HILL; 206/325-6520 Bohemians, erudite snobs, and family-oriented yuppies all happily mingle at this homey neighborhood coffee shop. To find out what's going on in the local literary scene, ask any of the frantic laptop clickers to explain his or her current project and its cultural significance. *V, MC; no checks; every day; no alcohol; victrolacoffee.com; map:GG6* &

Zeitgeist Coffee

171 S JACKSON, PIONEER SQUARE; 206/583-0497 Apart from being one of the finest of Seattle's independent coffee roasters, Zeitgeist is also a mecca for the city's long-laboring but under-recognized arts scene. The Pioneer Square storefront has a monthly featured artist, whose work is showcased on the high brick walls, and the coffeehouse occasionally screens independent films. Zeitgeist closes at 7pm most nights, but stays open until 10pm on the first Thursday of each month for the art walk. *No credit cards; local checks only; every day, no alcohol; zeitgeist coffee.com; map:P8*

Zoka Coffee Roaster and Tea Company

2200 N 56TH ST, GREEN LAKE; 206/545-4277 Owners Tim McCormack and Jeff Babcock bring more than 20 years of experience in the specialty coffee business to this spacious community coffee- and teahouse. Zoka roasts its own signature coffees, with the roaster serving as an appropriate backdrop for live acoustic music on Friday and Saturday nights. A variety of loose teas are available by the cup, by the pot, or in bulk. Complement your drink of choice with a selection from the sandwiches, salads, and baked goods, all made on-site. *MC, V; checks OK; every day; no alcohol; zokacoffee.com; map:FF7*

RECREATION

RECREATION

Outdoor Activities

Part of why people come to Seattle is the access the city offers to "out there." Seattleites—and its visitors—ski, sail, run, row, and in-line skate, sometimes all in one day. You can drive to Snoqualmie Pass and ski the slopes in the morning, then be home in time for an afternoon sail on Puget Sound.

If you're unfamiliar with the region, a good place to start planning your activity is at one of the five local branches of **REI** (Recreational Equipment Inc.), the largest of which is its flagship store downtown (222 Yale Ave N; 206/223-1944 or 888/873-1938; rei.com; map:H2). REI has a generous stock of guidebooks for all outdoor sports, topographic maps, and other equipment (see Outdoor Gear in the Shopping chapter), and hosts numerous clinics, speakers, and other events. The store also rents gear for activities from snowshoeing to camping to paddling. The U.S. Forest Service/National Park Service **OUTDOOR RECREATION INFORMATION CENTER** located in the downtown REI (206/470-4060; nps.gov/ccso/oric.htm; map:H2) provides trail reports, weather information, and referrals.

For some basic information on some of the city's best—or most accessible—outdoor activities, read on. And remember, if you lack skills or experience, get training and guidance before you start.

BASKETBALL

Whether you aspire to pro status or have reconciled yourself to after-work hoops, the city offers 58 public courts upon which to practice your jump shot. Beyond those listed here, you can get more information online from the Seattle Parks Department (www.ci.seattle.wa.us/parks/athletics/basketba.htm).

Denny Playfield

WESTLAKE AVE AND DENNY WY, DENNY TRIANGLE The full court at Denny Playfield is an urban oasis adjacent to a busy street—and a good spot to watch pickup games or play one. No need to bring a ball, really. *Map:F4*

Green Lake Community Center

7201 E GREEN LAKE DR N, GREEN LAKE; 206/684-0780 There is a full lighted outdoor court, as well as a full indoor court, at Green Lake Park, which has a rep as being a hot spot for a pickup game. *Map:EE7*

Nate McMillan Basketball Court

5TH AVE N AND REPUBLICAN ST, SEATTLE CENTER; 206/281-5800, EXT. 1781 Bearing the name of the Sonics's head coach and the team's perky green and yellow colors, this lighted outdoor full court across from Memorial Stadium is open to anyone who wields a ball. Check out the annual Sonics and Storm 4-on-the-Floor Basketball Tournament, for boys and girls ages 10 and up, usually held in August. *Map:C5*

University Heights Community Center

5031 UNIVERSITY WY NE, UNIVERSITY DISTRICT; 206/527-4278 It's a little rough around the edges, but the public outdoor court at this former grade school draws a lot of weeknight and weekend hoopsters. *Map:FF7*

BICYCLING

Despite Seattle's large amount of rainfall and fairly hilly terrain, cycling—from cruising to commuting to racing—is all the rage in and around the city. Many bicycle shops rent bikes for the day or week, from mountain to tandem to kids' bikes. Some even include helmets for free. **AL YOUNG BIKE & SKI** (3615 NE 45th St, Sand Point; 206/524-2642; map:FF6), **BICYCLE CENTER** (4529 Sand Point Way NE, Sand Point; 206/523-8300; map:FF6), and **GREGG'S GREENLAKE CYCLE** (7007 Wood-lawn Ave NE, Green Lake; 206/523-1822; greggscycles.com; and branches on Aurora Ave N and in Bellevue; map:EE7) are all near major bicycle trails. On the Eastside, near the Sammamish River Trail, rentals are available at **REDMOND CYCLE** (16205 Redmond Wy, Redmond; 425/885-6363; redmondcycle.com; map:EE2).

CASCADE BICYCLE CLUB organizes group rides nearly every day, ranging from a social pace to strenuous workouts. Check out the hotline (888/334-BIKE; www.cascade.org) for information about cycling in the Northwest and upcoming events. The legendary **SEATTLE-TO-PORTLAND CLASSIC (STP)** is a weekend odyssey in which 8,000 cyclists pedal from the University of Washington to down-town Portland in late June or early July, rain or shine. Late February's **CHILLY HILLY**, a 33-mile trek on the rolling terrain of Bainbridge Island, marks the beginning of cycling season. Cascade's hotline has information on both rides.

The city's **BICYCLE SATURDAYS/SUNDAYS** (206/684-7583; seattle.gov/trans-portation/bikesatsun.htm) are generally the second Saturday and third Sunday of each month, May through September. Lake Washington Boulevard and Lakeside Avenue, from Mount Baker Beach to Seward Park (map:II5–JJ5) is closed to auto traffic and anyone with a bike is welcome to participate. These pedal-pushing out-ings offer a serene look at the boulevard and are a haven for cycling tykes not yet street savvy.

The city **BICYCLE AND PEDESTRIAN PROGRAM** (206/684-7583; www.seattle.gov/transportation/bikeprogram.htm) provides a biker's map of Seattle that you can order online. (See also the trails listed under Running in this chapter.) Fol-lowing are some of the area's favored rides.

Alki Trail

HARBOR AVE SW AT FAIRMOUNT AVE SW TO FAUNTLEROY WY SW, WEST SEATTLE This 8-mile West Seattle route from Seacrest Marina to Lincoln Park comes with impressive views of downtown and Puget Sound. The first half is on a paved bike/pedestrian path along Alki Beach Park to the Alki Point lighthouse; the remainder is along roads (primarily Beach Dr SW) wide enough for both bikes and cars. On sunny weekend days, the route is often crowded. *Map:II9–KK9*

Bainbridge Island Loop

Start a bike expedition on the island by taking your bicycle on the ferry (wsdot.wa.gov/ferries/)—porting a bike costs only $1 more than the walk-on fee and lets you bypass the long car-ferry lines. The signed, hilly 30-mile route follows low-traffic roads around the island. Start on Ferncliff (heading north) at the Winslow ferry terminal (avoid Highway 305) and follow the signs.

Blue Ridge

NW 105TH ST AT 8TH AVE NW TO 32ND AVE NW NEAR NW 85TH ST, **CROWN HILL** The view of Puget Sound and the Olympic Mountains is spectacular on this less-than-2-mile ride. From NW 105th Street at Eighth Avenue NW (just south of Carkeek Park), head west onto NW Woodbine Way, where the Blue Ridge neighborhood begins. Stay on the ridgetop roads all the way south to Golden Gardens Park at 32nd Avenue NW, near NW 85th Street. *Map:DD8–DD9*

Burke-Gilman Trail–Sammamish River Trail

8TH AVE NW AND LEARY WAY, FREMONT, TO MARYMOOR PARK, REDMOND A popular off-street route for Seattle-area cyclists commuting to downtown, the University District, or Redmond's high-tech campuses, this combined 27-mile path is also a magnet for bicyclists who want great views of the city, waterways, and Lake Washington. Built on an old railway bed, the Burke-Gilman has a trailhead on the Fremont-Ballard border, from which it meanders along the ship canal and Lake Union, through the University of Washington, and along the west shore of Lake Washington. At Bothell's Blyth Park, the trail connects with the Sammamish River Trail, which continues past the Chateau Ste. Michelle Winery, just off the trail at NE 145th Street (a great stop for a picnic lunch), Columbia Winery, and the Redhook Brewery. Plans are afoot to extend the western end of the trail into downtown Ballard. (Also see Top 25 Attractions in the Exploring Chapter.) *Map:FF7–EE1*

BEST PLACE FOR BREAKFAST?

"Mae's in the Phinney district, because they have something for everybody."

Phil Borges, photographer

Elliott Bay Trail

PIER 70 TO ELLIOTT BAY MARINA, WATERFRONT You get a grand view on this brief ride along Puget Sound. The 1.5-mile-long trail skirts the Elliott Bay waterfront, passes between the grain terminal and its loading dock, winds its way through a parking lot of cars just off the ship, and continues to the Elliott Bay Marina. The trail is full of runners and in-line skaters at noontime. *Map:HH8–GG8*

Lake Washington Boulevard

MADRONA DR, MADRONA, TO SEWARD PARK AVE S, RAINIER VALLEY This serene 5-mile stretch between Madrona and Seward Parks is narrow in spots, but bicycles have a posted right-of-way. On Bicycle Saturdays and Sundays, the southern portion (from Mount Baker Beach south) is closed to cars (see introduction above). On other days, riders may feel safer using the asphalt path that follows this portion of the road. Riders can continue south, via S Juneau Street, Seward Park Avenue S, and Rainier Avenue S, to the Renton Municipal Airport and around the south end of Lake Washington, then return via the protected bike lane of Interstate 90. This makes for a 35-mile ride. Take a map with you. *Map:HH6–JJ5*

Mercer Island Loop

MARTIN LUTHER KING JR. WY ON I-90 LID, CENTRAL DISTRICT, TO E AND W MERCER WY, MERCER ISLAND From Seattle, a bicycles-only tunnel (entrance in I-90 lid park at Martin Luther King Jr. Wy) leads to the I-90 bridge on the way to Mercer Island. Using E and W Mercer Way, you'll ride over moderate rolling hills the length of this 14-mile loop. The roads are curving and narrow, so avoid rush hour. The most exhilarating portion of the ride is through the wooded S-curves on the eastern side of the island. *Map:II4–KK4*

Seward Park Loop

S JUNEAU ST AND LAKE WASHINGTON BLVD S, RAINIER VALLEY Take this paved and traffic-free 2.5-mile road around the wooded Bailey Peninsula in Seward Park, which juts out into Lake Washington. The peaceful ride offers a look at what may be the only old-growth forest left on the shores of the lake and at occasional eagles soaring overhead. *Map:JJ5*

GOLFING

Seattle and surrounding area have a number of fine public golf courses, many in wonderfully scenic surroundings.

Bellevue Municipal Golf Course

5500 140TH AVE NE, BELLEVUE; 425/452-7250 This course (5,535 yards), the busiest in the state, is fairly level and easy. Eighteen holes; PNGA rating/slope: 66.3/105. *Map:FF2*

Golf Club at Newcastle

15500 SIX PENNY LANE, BELLEVUE; 425/793-GOLF The rates here are steep, but the view from the two 18-hole courses (5,356 and 6,011 yards) at this hilltop club is impressive; the club also has an 18-hole putting course. PNGA rating/slope: 70/129 and 66/117. *newcastlegolf.com; map:JJ2* &

Interbay Family Golf Center

2501 15TH AVE W, INTERBAY; 206/285-2200 The best par-three course in the city, Interbay is conveniently located and has a driving range and an 18-hole miniature golf course, but it draws a lot of beginners, so the pace can be slow. *Map:GG8*

Jackson Park Municipal Golf Course

1000 NE 135TH ST, LAKE CITY; 206/363-4747 Revamped in 2003, Jackson Park now features new ponds, new greens over its rolling hills, a huge, well-maintained putting green, new chipping green, and a short nine, which is good for teaching kids the basics. Eighteen holes, 5,720 yards; PNGA rating/slope: 66.3/111. *jacksonpark golf.com; map:CC7*

Jefferson Park Golf Course

4101 BEACON AVE S, BEACON HILL; 206/762-4513 Fans of this course boast that it's "the course that Fred Couples grew up on." It's also got a driving range and a nine-hole par-three course. Eighteen holes, 5,857 yards; PNGA rating/slope: 67/110. *jeffersonparkgolf.com; map:JJ6*

Lynnwood Golf Course

20200 68TH AVE W, LYNNWOOD; 425/672-4653 While its woodsy layout and narrow fairways also challenge better players (foursomes of varying abilities can have a good time), this short course (with several par-three holes) is especially suited for inexperienced players. Eighteen holes, 4,741 yards; PNGA rating/slope: 62.0/100.

Riverbend Golf Complex

2019 W MEEKER ST, KENT; 253/854-3673 Riverbend is becoming a better course as its trees grow, and the 18-hole course (6,260 yards) has a nice variety of holes. The complex also includes a nine-hole par-three course and a driving range. PNGA rating/slope: 68.6/112.

West Seattle Municipal Golf Course

4470 35TH AVE SW, WEST SEATTLE; 206/935-5187 A good but forgiving course just west of the Duwamish River, tucked into an undulating valley, which makes for some surprising lies. Tee times are the easiest to come by in the city, views of which are spectacular on the back nine. Eighteen holes, 6,175 yards; PNGA rating/slope: 68.8/116. *westseattlegolf.com; map:JJ8*

Willows Run

10442 WILLOWS RD NE, REDMOND; 425/883-1200 OR 800/833-4787 Willows Run features two 18-hole links-style courses (5,831 and 6,364 yards), both well designed and well maintained, as well as a driving range and a par-three course. PNGA rating/slope: 67.3/114 and 69.8/117. *willowsrun.com; map:EE1*

HIKING

Superlative hiking in Washington is within easy access of Seattle. Day hikers can count on spending just an hour or two in the car before reaching trailheads leading to alpine lakes, rain forests, ocean cliffs, or mountain meadows. For this reason, the national parks, state parks, national forests, and wilderness areas nearby are heavily used, but conservation efforts have managed to stay a small step ahead of the impacts.

Like any outdoor activity, hiking requires a marriage of caution and adventurous spirit. Always carry water and bring extra clothing (wool or synthetics such as polypropylene—not cotton) and rain gear, even if it's 80 degrees and sunny when you set out and you plan only a short hike. Remember, it can rain here almost anytime. Permits may be required for hiking or camping. Check with the local ranger station before setting out, and buy a trailhead parking permit at a ranger station or outdoor equipment store if necessary; a Northwest Forest Pass (www.fs.fed. us/r6/feedemo/) is good at National Forest Service trailheads, picnic areas, and boat launches in Oregon and Washington, and costs $30 per year or $5 per day. In general, national forests require free backcountry permits for hiking, and national parks usually charge fees to enter the park by car but none to hike.

Good hiking guides are published in association with the **MOUNTAINEERS** (300 3rd Ave W, Queen Anne; 206/284-6310 or 800/573-8484 in Western Washington; mountaineers.org; map:A9), a venerable outdoors club whose public bookstore has the largest collection of climbing, hiking, mountain biking, and paddling books in the Pacific Northwest. Another reliable information tap to the outdoors is the Seattle branch of the **SIERRA CLUB** (180 Nickerson St, Ste 202, Queen Anne; 206/523-2147; cascade.sierraclub.org; map:FF8). The **WASHINGTON TRAILS ASSOCIATION** (1305 4th Ave, Ste 512, Downtown; 206/625-1367; wta.org; map:K6), a nonprofit outreach group, welcomes telephone inquiries about hiking, sells maps, and organizes trail-maintenance work parties, group hikes, camping trips, and more. A good source of information in book form is *Inside Out Washington* (Sasquatch, 2001) by Ron C. Judd. Here are some popular nearby hiking areas, described broadly by region.

The most easily accessible hiking area from Seattle (20 miles east of Seattle via I-90), the comely Cascade foothills called the Issaquah Alps have dozens of day trails frequented by both hikers and horseback riders. The **ISSAQUAH ALPS TRAILS CLUB** (PO Box 351, Issaquah, WA 98027; issaquahalps.org) organizes day hikes through the hills, ranging from short (a good way to introduce children to hiking) to strenuous.

The best hiking near Seattle is in the **CENTRAL CASCADES** between Snoqualmie Pass (via I-90 due east) and Stevens Pass (via US Hwy 2 to the north), one to two hours from the city. The Central Cascades are mainly national forest and wilderness areas, including the scenic Alpine Lakes Wilderness. A gorgeous section of the Pacific Crest Trail cuts through the wilderness along the mountain ridges.

Good hiking can also be found farther from the city in the **NORTH CASCADES** (between Stevens Pass and the Canadian border via Hwy 20), with glaciers, summer alpine flowers, and blazing fall colors; part of this area is in remote and rugged **NORTH CASCADES NATIONAL PARK** (360/856-5700 visitor info; nps.gov/noca/). The **OLYMPIC MOUNTAINS** (on the Olympic Peninsula; see the Day Trips chapter) feature **OLYMPIC NATIONAL PARK** (360/565-3130 of 800/833-6388 visitor info; nps.gov/olym/) and striking Hurricane Ridge. In the South Cascades (between Snoqualmie Pass and the Oregon border via US Hwy 12 and others), the highlight is **MOUNT RAINIER NATIONAL PARK** (see the Day Trips chapter).

KAYAKING/CANOEING

In a city that is girdled by water, one of the best ways to explore is by boat. Several locations around Seattle rent canoes and kayaks for day excursions. A good general resource is *Boatless in Seattle: Getting on the Water in Western Washington Without Owning a Boat!* (Sasquatch Books, 1999) by Sue Muller Hacking. For those who want instruction on kayaking, perhaps in preparation for a whitewater trip, one of the oldest kayaking clubs in the nation is the **WASHINGTON KAYAK CLUB** (PO Box

24264, Seattle, WA 98124; 206/433-1983; washingtonkayakclub.org), a safety- and conservation-oriented club that organizes swimming-pool practices, weekend trips, and sea- and whitewater-kayaking lessons. Several companies rent kayaks by the hour year-round, and some will set you up with a car-top rack for longer trips or those farther afield, spring through fall. Here are some favorite places to paddle.

From Tukwila (where the Green River becomes the Duwamish) to Boeing Field (map:QQ5–JJ7), the scenic **DUWAMISH RIVER** waterway makes for a lovely urban paddle. North of Boeing, you pass industrial salvage ships, commercial shipping lanes, and Harbor Island, where the river empties into Elliott Bay. Rent a kayak (and a rooftop carrier) by the day ($48 for a single) or for the weekend ($90 for a single, Friday–Monday) at **PACIFIC WATER SPORTS** (11011 Tukwila International Blvd, Tukwila; 206/246-9385; pwskayaks.com; map:OO6)—and the staff can direct you to one of several spots along the river where you can launch your craft. The current is strong at times, but not a serious hazard for the moderately experienced.

GREEN LAKE's tame waters are a good place to learn the basics. **GREEN LAKE BOAT RENTALS** (7351 E Green Lake Dr N; 206/527-0171; map:EE7), a Seattle Parks and Recreation Department concession on the northeast side of the lake, rents kayaks, rowboats, paddleboats, canoes, sailboards, and sailboats. Rates range from $10 per hour for a rowboat or canoe to $14 per hour for a sailboard or boat. Open daily, except in bad weather, May through September.

Kayaking or canoeing on **LAKE UNION** is a great way to get an up-close look at houseboats or to enjoy great views of the city. If you're ambitious, paddle west from the lake down the Lake Washington Ship Canal, past the clanking of boatyards and the aroma of fish-laden boats to Elliott Bay, or east into Lake Washington. Rent sea kayaks by the hour ($10–$15) or the day ($50–$70) at the **NORTHWEST OUTDOOR CENTER** (2100 Westlake Ave N, Ste 1, Westlake; 206/281-9694 or 800/683-0637; nwoc.com; map:A1) or **MOSS BAY ROWING & KAYAKING CENTER** (1001 Fairview Ave N, South Lake Union; 206/682-2031; map:D1). Both also offer classes; NWOC recommends reservations on good-weather weekends. On **PORTAGE BAY**, closer to the Arboretum, **AGUA VERDE CAFE & PADDLE CLUB** (1303 NE Boat St, University District; 206/545-8570; www.aguaverde.com; map:FF6) rents kayaks hourly for $12 to $16, with discounts for multiple hours.

If you want some summer perspective on the bumper-to-bumper commuter traffic on the Evergreen Point Bridge, rent a canoe or a rowboat at the **UNIVERSITY OF WASHINGTON WATERFRONT ACTIVITIES CENTER** (206/543-9433; depts.washington.edu/ima/IMA.wac.html; map:FF6) behind Husky Stadium. Rates are low ($7.50 per hour for nonstudents) and you can cross the Montlake Cut to mirrorlike waters framed by lily pads and marshlands inside the Washington Park Arboretum (map:GG6).

The trip up the gently flowing **SAMMAMISH SLOUGH** (map:BB5–FF1) is quiet and scenic. Ambitious boaters can follow the slough from the north end of Lake Washington at Bothell all the way to Lake Sammamish, about 15 miles to the southeast, passing golf courses, the town of Woodinville, wineries, and Marymoor Park. In Redmond, you can rent kayaks from **AQUASPORTS PADDLE CENTER** (7907 159th Pl NE; 425/869-7067; map:EE1).

Seattle's proximity to the open waters and scenic island coves of Puget Sound makes for ideal sea kayaking. The nearby **SAN JUAN ISLANDS** to the north provide endless paddling opportunities, though the currents can be strong, and unguided kayaking here is not for novices. Local rental shops or retailers such as REI (rei.com) can help you find information on guided multiday tours, or check out locally published *Canoe & Kayak Magazine* (canoekayak.com).

MOUNTAIN BIKING

Though all of the cycling trails listed above are great jaunts for those with mountain bikes, the advantage of mountain bikes is that they can be taken off-road.

The popularity of mountain biking presents something of a dilemma to environmentalists as well as cyclists. The trails that provide an optimum off-road experience—ones that were once quiet, remote, untouched—are those that often end up closed by the Forest Service because of the damage caused by increasing numbers of mountain bikers. The **OUTDOOR RECREATION INFORMATION CENTER** (206/470-4060) provides information on trail closures. The nonprofit **BACK-COUNTRY BICYCLE TRAILS CLUB** (206/283-2995 hotline; bbtc.org) organizes local rides and is adamant about taking care of regional trails. The best local guidebook is *Kissing the Trail: Greater Seattle Mountain Bike Adventures* (Adventure, 2003) by John Zilly, available at bookstores and biking and outdoor retail outlets. Here are a couple of regional options.

BEST PLACE TO FIND INSPIRATION?

"Victrola coffeehouse on 15th because it's like a family rec room—filled with games and interesting people. The only thing missing is bong smoke."

Frances McCue, artistic director of Richard Hugo House

Deception Pass State Park

SOUTH OF ANACORTES OFF HWY 20 ON WHIDBEY AND FIDALGO ISLANDS; 360/902-8844 An hour and a half northwest by car from Seattle, Deception Pass is without doubt one of the most beautiful wild spots in Washington. And it has more than 16 miles of bike trails that rise and fall up to 1,000 feet of elevation. Trails climb to high rocky bluffs with views of the San Juan Islands, then descend to sandy beaches. The trails are single-track, and not all of the park is open to mountain bikes.

Saint Edwards State Park

OFF JUANITA DR NE, KIRKLAND; 425/823-2992 Up to 12 miles of varied terrain make this park, located in the Juanita neighborhood, great for all skill levels. At 316 acres it is the largest undeveloped area on Lake Washington and has 3,000 feet of shoreline. Be wary as you ride among the tall trees and up and down the 700 feet of elevation: the trails interweave, and it's easy to get lost if you don't pay attention. *Map:CC4*

ROCK CLIMBING

In Seattle and its environs, several indoor climbing walls—or artificial outdoor structures—allow you to get vertical for after-work relaxation or for a good rush on the weekend.

Marymoor Climbing Structure

6046 W LAKE SAMMAMISH PKWY NE, EAST END OF MARYMOOR PARK OFF HWY 520, REDMOND; 206/296-2964 Otherwise known as Big Pointy, this 45-foot concrete brick-and-mortar house of cards just south of the Velodrome was designed by the godfather of rock climbing, Don Robinson. It features climbing angles up to and over 90 degrees. *Map:FF1*

REI Pinnacle

222 YALE AVE N, DENNY TRIANGLE; 206/223-1944 OR 888/873-1938 With more than 1,000 modular climbing holds, this 65-foot freestanding indoor structure (inside the REI flagship store) is very popular. Come early; waits can be as long as an hour and you get only one ascent, but you're loaned a beeper so you can shop while you wait, and the climb is free. *rei.com; map:H2*

Schurman Rock

5200 35TH AVE SW, CAMP LONG, WEST SEATTLE; 206/684-7434 Closed for four years due to damage, 20-foot Schurman Rock reopened in June 2003 thanks to $90,000 in donations. Designed in the 1930s by local scout leader and mountaineer Clark Schurman, the rock incorporates multiple climbing challenges, and a variety of routes and levels of difficulty. It's good for beginners as well as more advanced climbers, and classes are taught on-site. *Map:KK8*

Stone Gardens

2839 NW MARKET ST, BALLARD; 206/781-9828 One section of this indoor climbing gym consists of low overhangs; the rest of the gym offers faces that can be bouldered or top-roped, including a 40-foot outdoor wall with climbs for all levels. There's also equipment you can rent or buy. Staff members offer helpful advice, or you can take classes ranging from one-on-one beginner instruction to several levels of advanced techniques. You can rent the gym for private parties—including instruction—before or after hours. *stonegardens.com; map:FF8*

Vertical World

15036-B NE 95TH ST, REDMOND; 425/881-8826 / 2123 W ELMORE ST, INTERBAY; 206/283-4497 The Redmond location of this rock gym offers 7,000 square feet of textured climbing surface, while the newer, equally striking Seattle club sports 35-foot-high walls and a whopping 14,000 square feet of climbing area. The walls at the Seattle location are also fully textured, making the more than 100 routes varied and interesting. Lessons are offered at both gyms. *verticalworld.com; map:DD2, FF8*

Once you've attained the highest pinnacles indoors and in controlled outdoor settings, take your hardened hands and clenching toes to the great outdoors. But first stop at the **MOUNTAINEERS** (300 3rd Ave W, Queen Anne; 206/284-6310 or 800/573-8484; mountaineers.org; map:A9), the largest outdoor club in the region and a superb resource, offering group climbs, climbing courses, and general information.

ROLLER-SKATING/IN-LINE SKATING/SKATEBOARDING

Roller skaters and in-line skaters compose an ever-widening wedge of the urban athletic pie. In fair weather, they are found anywhere the pavement is smooth, including the downtown waterfront, along Lake Washington Boulevard, and north on the tree-shaded **BURKE-GILMAN TRAIL** that connects with the **SAMMAMISH RIVER TRAIL**, which you can follow all the way to Redmond's **MARYMOOR PARK** (see Bicycling and Running in this chapter). Note: Skate-rental shops won't let you out the door if the pavement is damp.

BEST PLACE FOR A PICKUP GAME?

"Talent-wise it's Green Lake. You spend just
as much time talking as playing."

Sherman Alexie, poet, novelist, and screenwriter

Ballard Skate Park

NW 57TH ST AND 22ND AVE NW, BALLARD; 206/684-4093 This free, skate-at-your-own-risk outdoor park behind the Ballard QFC grocery store opened in spring 2002. Features created by volunteers (with the help of donations) include a half pipe and a bowl. Open daily, 8am to 9pm. *cityofseattle.net/parks/parkspaces/ballardskatepark.htm; map:FF8*

Green Lake

E GREEN LAKE WY N AND W GREEN LAKE WY N This is the skate-and-be-seen-skating spot in town, where hot doggers in bright spandex weave and bob past cyclists, joggers, walkers, and leashed dogs. The 2.8-mile path around the lake is crowded on weekends, but during the week it's a good place to try wheels for the first time. When the wading pool on the north shore of the lake isn't filled for kids or commandeered by roller-skating hockey enthusiasts, it's a good spot to learn to skate backward. Rent ($20 daily or $5–$10 hourly) or buy skates, as well as elbow and knee pads, at nearby Gregg's Greenlake Cycle (7007 Woodlawn Ave NE; 206/523-1822). *Map:EE7*

National Oceanic and Atmospheric Administration

7600 SAND POINT WY NE, SAND POINT Another urban skating site excellent for practicing is the NOAA grounds next to Magnuson Park. This facility can be reached via the Burke-Gilman Trail and offers a quiet workout along a smooth 1-kilometer loop, with one low-grade hill and some exciting turns. *Map:EE5*

Seattle Center Skate Park

5TH AVE AND REPUBLICAN ST, SEATTLE CENTER Situated across from the Space Needle, this 8,900-square-foot facility is authorized for both skateboards and in-line skates. Smooth concrete dips and ridges include a snake run, a bowl, quarter pipes, and a street grind. Open every day, dawn to dusk. *Map:D5*

WE GOT GAMES

With a few notable exceptions—such as the gold rush of the 1890s and the Grunge Rock explosion of the 1980s—Seattle has traditionally maintained a low profile. In recent years, however, as the city has moved into the international spotlight (translation: WTO riots) and absorbed a diverse collection of residents (translation: New Yorkers), a pluckier persona has emerged. About as good an indicator as any of this change of face is the city's reanimated professional sports culture.

Yes, it's true, pro teams haven't exactly choked us in championships. So far that sole honor goes to the Seattle SuperSonics, who way back in the decade of disco (1979 to be precise) gave us cause to splurge on confetti.

However, our reputation as a wimpy, no- or low-achieving sports town is also history— thanks to the **SEATTLE MARINERS**. When the team snagged Seattle its first major-league division title in 1995, giddy doesn't begin to capture the mood of grateful fans. Our boys of summer parlayed pennant fever into the swanky state-of-the-park Safeco Field, inaugurated in 1999 (see Top 25 Attractions in the Exploring Chapter). Meanwhile, Paul Allen, also owner of the Portland Trail Blazers, finagled a new home for his **SEATTLE SEA-HAWKS** (who, have yet to return the favor with a championship season in their new digs). One imploded Kingdome (and nearly $1 billion) later, the two side-by-side stadiums phys-ically—and, more importantly for sports fans, psychologically—dominate our southern waterfront. Today, the confidence permeating the Safe is nearly as inescapable as the

ROWING

In a city graced with two major lakes, many people have discovered an affinity for sleek, lightweight rowing shells and the calm silver-black water of early morning. Seattle has one of the largest populations of adult rowers in the country, and has numerous women-only, men-only, and age-specific clubs. Check out north westrowing.com for a list of local clubs.

The Seattle Parks and Recreation Department runs two rowing facilities: one on Green Lake, out of the **GREEN LAKE SMALL CRAFT CENTER** (5900 W Green Lake Wy N; 206/684-4074; www.greenlakecrew.org; map:EE7), and the other on Lake Washington, through the **MOUNT BAKER ROWING AND SAILING CENTER** (3800 Lake Washington Blvd S, Rainier Valley; 206/386-1913; www.mtbakercrew.org; map:JJ6). Both operate year-round, offer all levels of instruction, and host annual regattas.

A handful of boathouses in the Seattle area field competitive teams and also offer introductory rowing programs. These include the **LAKE WASHINGTON ROWING CLUB** (910 N Northlake Wy, Fremont; 206/547-1583; lakewashington rowing.com; map:FF7), the **POCOCK ROWING CENTER** (3320 Fuhrman Ave E, Eastlake; 206/328-7272; pocockrowing.org; map:FF7), and the **SAMMAMISH ROWING**

swirling aroma of garlic fries. Upper-deck hot shots Ken Griffey Jr. and Alex Rodriguez have been relegated to fading memories (except when Ranger A-Rod comes to town to collect his boos), and M's fans have embraced the team's new imports, Ichiro Suzuki and Shigetoshi Hasegawa (and the subsequent influx of Japanese tourists). By 2001 fans almost seemed to expect that the M's would clinch a history-making tie for most wins in baseball (116). And in the ultimate test of sporting spine, when the team's winningest manager, lovable Lou Piniella, headed to Florida in 2002, M's fans didn't get the shakes. They stepped up to the plate to back new skipper Bob Melvin all the way to what, naturally, they assume will be an impending World Series win.

The city's hoop dreams have been less confidence inspiring. Hopes spiked when Starbucks CEO Howard Schultz spearheaded purchase of the **SUPERSONICS** in 2001, but dipped just two years later when he shocked Seattleites by trading away the face of the Sups, Gary "The Glove" Payton. Still, fans have gamely settled in for a rebuilding season—or two.

On the brighter side, Seattle isn't just a boy's club anymore. In 2000 the WNBA **SEATTLE STORM** started hitting the boards at the KeyArena. They made the playoffs in 2002 and, benefiting from crowd-pleasers such as All-Star guard Sue Bird, are forging a spirited and loyal fan base—who no doubt expect the team to soon don championship jerseys.

—*Shannon O'Leary*

ASSOCIATION (5022 W Lake Sammamish Pkwy, Redmond; 425/653-2583; srarowing.com; map:FF1). Some clubs allow experienced oarspeople to row once or twice without paying fees. Ask individual clubs about guest policies.

RUNNING

Hill climbers love running in Seattle, but the fact of the matter is that you can find a good running course almost anywhere in the city or its surrounding suburbs. Bike paths often do double duty as flat running trails (see Bicycling in this chapter). The mild climate and numerous parks make solo running appealing, yet the city also has a large, well-organized running community that provides company or competition. Pick up a copy of *Northwest Runner* in any running-gear store for information on trails as well as any of a number of annual races for racers, casual or serious. You can find at least one race every spring or summer weekend by checking out the online race calendar (nwrunner.com). One of the finest running outfitters in town, SUPER JOCK 'N JILL (7210 E Green Lake Dr N, Green Lake; 206/522-7711 or 800/343-4411; superjocknjill.com; map:EE7), maintains racing news on its Web site. Some of the biggest are the 3.5-mile ST. PATRICK'S DAY DASH in March, the 6.7-mile Seward Park–to-Leschi SHORE RUN and 5-kilometer RACE FOR THE CURE in June, the 8-kilometer SEAFAIR TORCHLIGHT RUN in July, the SEATTLE MARATHON in

November, and December's 5-kilometer **JINGLE BELL RUN**. Listed below are some popular routes.

The 2.8-mile marked path around **GREEN LAKE** (Latona Ave NE and E Green Lake Way N; map:EE7) has two lanes: one for wheeled traffic, the other for everybody else. On sunny weekends, Green Lake becomes a recreational Grand Central—great for people-watching, but slow going. Early mornings or late evenings, though, it's lovely, with ducks, geese, red-winged blackbirds, mountain views, and rowers and windsurfers on the lake. The path connects with a bikeway along Ravenna Boulevard. A painted line establishes the cycling lane; runners can follow the boulevard's grassy median.

Various paths cut through thickly wooded **LINCOLN PARK** (Fauntleroy Way SW and SW Trenton St, West Seattle; map:KK9), overlooking Vashon Island and Puget Sound. The shoreline is tucked below a bluff, which blocks the sound of auto traffic.

A striking run in clear weather, the **MAGNOLIA BLUFF AND DISCOVERY PARK** route (along Magnolia Blvd W, Magnolia; map:GG9–EE9) offers vistas of the Olympic Mountains across Puget Sound. From the parking lot at Magnolia Boulevard W and W Galer Street, run north along the boulevard on a paved pedestrian trail. Magnolia Park ends at W Barrett Street; continue north for four blocks to Discovery Park, which has numerous paved and unpaved trails.

Formerly part of the Naval Air Station at Sand Point, **MAGNUSON PARK** (Sand Point Way NE and NE 65th St, Sand Point; map:EE5) has many congenial running areas, including wide, paved roads and flat, grassy terrain, all overlooking Lake Washington. On clear days, the view of Mount Rainier is superb.

You can stay on the winding main drive, Lake Washington Boulevard E, or run along any number of paths that wend through the trees and flowers gracing the **WASHINGTON PARK ARBORETUM** (Arboretum Dr E and Lake Washington Blvd E, Madison Valley; map:GG6). Though the charming main unpaved thoroughfare, Azalea Way, is strictly off-limits to joggers, Lake Washington Boulevard connects with scenic E Interlaken Boulevard at the Japanese Garden and then winds down to the lake. The northern lakeside leg, from Madrona Drive south to Leschi, is popular for its wide sidewalks; farther south, from Mount Baker Park to Seward Park, sweeping views make for a pleasing run.

The Eastside's high-visibility running path stretches along the **KIRKLAND WATERFRONT** (along Lake Washington Blvd, Kirkland; map:FF3–EE3) from Houghton Beach Park to Marina Park—a little more than a mile one-way.

MEDINA AND EVERGREEN POINT (along Overlake Dr and Evergreen Point Rd, Bellevue; map:FF4–HH4) offer a scenic run along nicely maintained roads with views of Lake Washington and of some of the area's most stunning homes—two-and-a-half miles each way.

SAILING

Seattle has a great deal of water but, in the summer at least, precious little wind. Thus many sailors hereabouts reckon that sailing season runs from around Labor Day to the beginning of May (although in summer, late-afternoon winds sometimes fill the sheets). Looking toward Seattle from its bodies of water will give you perspectives you can't get from your car, and wannabe sailors can find classes or chartered tours.

SAILING IN SEATTLE (2000 Westlake Ave N, Ste 46, Westlake; 206/298-0094; www.sailing-in-seattle.com; map:GG7) offers three different staffed cruises on a 33-foot sailboat: a 2½-hour sunset cruise on Lake Union; an 8-hour cruise through the Ballard Locks to Puget Sound; or 5 hours on Lake Washington. Rates ($225–$750) are for the entire boat, for up to six passengers. Sit back and enjoy the sights or, even if you've never sailed before, try your hand at sailing with instruction from the on-board crew. Reservations are a must. Sailing in Seattle also offers courses from beginning to advanced.

No more than a mile across in any direction, Green Lake is the perfect place to learn to sail: it's free from motor cruisers, floatplanes, and barge traffic. For beginners who want to learn to sail in a smaller boat and have a few days to pick up the essentials, the **GREEN LAKE SMALL CRAFT CENTER** (5900 W Green Lake Wy N; 206/684-4074; cityofseattle.net/parks/Boats/Grnlake.htm; map:EE7), at the southwest corner of the lake, offers classes. **MOUNT BAKER ROWING AND SAILING CENTER** (3800 Lake Washington Blvd S, Rainier Valley; 206/386-1913; map:II6), on Lake Washington, also offers sailing lessons in small boats. A six- to eight-session sailing class is $120.

Salty dogs who want to be their own skipper should try a classic wooden boat at the nonprofit **CENTER FOR WOODEN BOATS** (1010 Valley St, South Lake Union; 206/382-2628; cwb.org; map:D1). Call and schedule a $5 checkout to show them you know how to tack, jibe, and dock under sail (takes about 30 minutes), and then access to the fleet of 12- to 20-foot rental sailboats is yours. Sailboat rental rates range from $12.50 to $46 per hour; viewing exhibits is free. Visitors are encouraged to touch the center's approximately 100 historic boats and to ask questions of the volunteers. The center also rents rowboats (which require no skills demonstration).

SNOW SPORTS

The rain that falls on Seattle turns to snow at higher elevations in the winter—making for good skiing. And although some call the rain-thickened, heavy snow of the region's skiing areas "Cascade concrete," most mornings a new layer of white has blanketed the slopes. Several ski areas have weekend shuttle buses leaving from Seattle. If you plan to drive, carry tire chains and a shovel, and inquire ahead about road conditions (800/695-7623; wsdot.wa.gov/traveler). All local downhill ski facilities rent skis, snowboards, and other gear. Many rental outlets are available in the city as well.

Though commercial downhill ski areas have ski patrols, skiers in unpatrolled areas or in the mountainous backcountry should heed the constant danger of avalanche. Conditions change daily (sometimes hourly), so always call the Forest Service's **NORTHWEST AVALANCHE INFORMATION HOTLINE** (206/526-6677) before setting out. Finally, if you are heading off into the backwoods, most plowed parking areas near trailheads and along state highways require a Sno-Park permit (360/586-6645; parks.wa.gov/winter/permits.asp), which costs $20 per vehicle for the winter season. A one-day Sno-Park permit is $8 for all areas ($9 from local retail outlets or online).

Below are the ski areas most accessible to Seattleites, with information about downhill and cross-country skiing. For daily updates on conditions in downhill areas, call the Cascade Ski Report (206/634-0200 winter only).

Crystal Mountain Resort

33914 CRYSTAL MOUNTAIN BLVD, CRYSTAL MOUNTAIN, WA 98022; 360/663-2265, 888/754-6199 SNOW CONDITIONS Nine chairlifts lead to more than 50 groomed trails on more than 2,300 skiable acres and a 7,012-foot summit. Two six-person chairlifts make getting up the mountain easy for the beginner or the expert, and there's weekend night skiing all winter long. Nordic skiers will be charmed by Silver Basin's big, broad open area. The ski patrol here monitors your whereabouts if you check in and out. *skicrystal.com; 76 miles southeast of Seattle on Hwy 410*

I-90 Corridor

EXITS 54 TO 71; 800/233-0321 The Forest Service offers a wide variety of marked cross-country trails here, which are free and close to Seattle, but you must have a Sno-Park pass to use the parking lots (see introduction above). At **CRYSTAL SPRINGS/LAKE KEECHELUS** (at the top of Snoqualmie Pass, exit 54), Sno-Parks are at either end of a 11.2-kilometer trail that runs along the shores of Lake Keechelus. Crystal Springs has a concession stand with hot drinks and snacks. **CABIN CREEK** (10 miles east of Snoqualmie Pass, exit 63) has 12 kilometers of trails (some of them groomed); the ones on the south side are easy, and the ones on the north side are intermediate, with plenty of turns. At **IRON HORSE** Sno-Park (exit 71), about 10 miles of easy, flat trails around Lake Easton and Iron Horse State Park are combined with a 12-mile trek from Easton to Cle Elum (not always accessible). For more trails, call the state for a brochure, or contact local outdoor retailers to learn which trails are at their best. *76–91 miles east of Seattle, off I-90*

BEST PLACE TO DINE AL FRESCO?

"In the courtyard at Campagne, because it's less exposed to buses, birds, and bums than a sidewalk cafe, and the menu may be the most exciting in town."

Tom Robbins, author

Methow Valley

NORTH CASCADES SCENIC HWY 20 One of the top Nordic ski areas in the country, the Methow Valley offers the charm of Vermont, the snow conditions of Utah, and the big sky of Montana. Too far from Seattle for a day trip, its 175 kilometers of groomed trails make for a great weekend getaway. The valley towns of Mazama, Winthrop, and Twisp offer an ample number of lodges, guides, lessons, and rental shops. Contact Central Reservations (800/422-3048; www.methow reservations.com) for hut-to-hut skiing or housing/rental reservations. The nonprofit Methow Valley Sport Trails Association (PO Box 147, Winthrop, WA 98862; 800/682-5787; mvsta.com) has more information. *250 miles northeast of Seattle, off Hwy 20*

Mount Baker Ski Area

1019 IOWA ST, BELLINGHAM, WA 98226; 360/734-6771, 360/671-0211 SNOW CONDITIONS The first area to open and the last to close during the ski season, Mount Baker—which has the highest average annual snowfall (595 inches) in North America—is a terrific weekend destination, though most of the lodgings are in Glacier, about 17 miles to the west. The view is remarkable; the runs are varied but mostly intermediate, with one bowl, meadows, trails, and wooded areas. Snowboarders (welcome on all runs) test their mettle in the Legendary Banked Slalom Race, held on the last weekend in January. No night skiing. On the northeastern flank of Mount Baker, Nordic skiers find sporadically groomed trails. Rentals and lessons are available in the main lodge. *mtbakerskiarea.com; 56 miles east of Bellingham, off I-5 on Hwy 542*

Mount Rainier National Park

ASHFORD, WA 98304; 360/569-2211 EXT. 3314 See the Day Trips chapter for details on Mount Rainier.

Stevens Pass

SUMMIT STEVENS PASS, US HWY 2, SKYKOMISH; 206/812-4510, 206/634-1645 WINTER CONDITIONS, 800/695-7623 ROAD CONDITIONS Challenging and interesting terrain makes Stevens Pass a favorite for many skiers, and it's open daily, with seasonal night skiing. Ten chairlifts lead to a variety of runs and breathtaking Cascade views. Snowboarders, welcome on all runs, tend to congregate near the Skyline Express and Brooks lifts, where nearby is a half pipe and a roped-off terrain park. For Nordic skiing, head 5 miles farther east on US Highway 2 to the full-service Stevens Pass Nordic Center, complete with rentals, instruction, hot food and drink, and 25 kilometers of groomed trails over a variety of terrain. The Nordic Center is touted as having the best white stuff within 90 minutes of Seattle, but it's open only Friday through Sunday and holidays. *stevenspass.com; 78 miles northeast of Seattle on US Hwy 2 (Nordic Center, 5 miles east)*

The Summit at Snoqualmie

PO BOX 1068, SNOQUALMIE PASS, WA 98068; 425/434-7669, 206/236-1600 SNOW CONDITIONS Consisting of four neighboring sections along Interstate 90—Alpental, Summit Central (formerly Ski Acres), Summit West (formerly Snoqualmie Summit), and Summit East (formerly Hyak)—this complex offers many options for skiers of all abilities. Linked by a free shuttle-bus service (three are also linked by ski trails), all four honor the same lift ticket, but each has its own appeal. Alpental boasts high-grade challenges, including a nationally recognized run. Summit Central offers intermediate-to-expert runs, and most of the mountain is open for night skiing. Summit West's gentler slopes are ideal for children, beginners, and intermediate skiers. Dozens of ski and snowboard classes operate here. Summit East, the smallest, caters to intermediate skiers. The Summit Nordic Center at Summit East has

50 kilometers of trails—some accessed by two chairlifts—to please skiers of any ability level. The center also offers lessons and ski rentals, a yurt, and a warming hut. *summit-at-snoqualmie.com; 47 miles east of Seattle, off I-90 at exit 52*

TENNIS

Tennis is popular here, but not so much so that it's impossible to get a public court. There's only one indoor public tennis facility in the city: **AMY YEE TENNIS CENTER** (2000 Martin Luther King Jr. Wy S, Rainier Valley; 206/684-4764; map:II6), with 10 indoor courts (there are also 4 unlighted outdoor courts). Most public outdoor courts in the city are run by the Seattle Parks and Recreation Department and are available either on a first-come, first-served basis or by reservation for $6 per hour. Players can make phone reservations up to two weeks in advance (206/684-4077) with a major credit card (AE, MC, V). Otherwise, reservations must be made in person at the scheduling office of **SEATTLE PARKS AND RECREATION** (5201 Green Lake Wy N, Green Lake; map:EE7). If it rains, your money is refunded.

The Eastside has a similar facility, **ROBINSWOOD TENNIS CENTER** (2400 151st Pl SE, Bellevue; 425/452-7690; map:II2), which has four lighted outdoor (two covered) and four indoor courts. Eastside outdoor public courts cannot be reserved in advance. The best time to play is early in the day; in spring and summer, the lines start at about 3pm.

Most private Seattle tennis courts do not sell weekly or daily memberships. Following is a list of the best outdoor public courts in the area.

BRYANT: Two unlighted courts. 4103 NE 65th St, View Ridge; map:EE5

GRASS LAWN PARK: Six lighted courts. 7031 148th Ave NE, Redmond; map:EE2

HILLAIRE PARK: Two unlighted courts. 15803 NE 6th St, Bellevue; map:HH1

HOMESTEAD FIELD: Four unlighted courts. 82nd Ave SE and SE 40th St, Mercer Island; map:II4

KILLARNEY GLEN PARK: Two unlighted courts. 1933 104th Ave SE, Bellevue; map:HH3

LINCOLN PARK: Six lighted courts. 8011 Fauntleroy Ave SW, West Seattle; map:KK9

LOWER WOODLAND PARK: Ten lighted courts. W Green Lake Wy N, Green Lake; map:FF7

LUTHER BURBANK PARK: Three unlighted courts. 2040 84th Ave SE, Mercer Island; map:II4

MAGNOLIA PLAYFIELD: Four courts (two lighted). 34th Ave W and W Smith St, Magnolia; map:GG9

MARYMOOR PARK: Four lighted courts. 6046 W Lake Sammamish Pkwy NE, Redmond; map:FF1

MEADOWBROOK: Six lighted courts. 10533 35th Ave NE, Lake City; map:DD6

MONTLAKE PARK: Two unlighted courts. 1618 E Calhoun St, Montlake; map:GG6

NORWOOD VILLAGE: Two unlighted courts. 12309 SE 23rd Pl, Bellevue; map:II2

RAINIER PLAYFIELD: Four lighted courts. 3700 S Alaska St, Columbia City; map:JJ5

RIVERVIEW: Two unlighted courts. 7226 12th Ave SW, West Seattle; map:KK7

VOLUNTEER PARK: Four courts (two lighted). 1247 15th Ave E, Capitol Hill; map:GG6

WINDSURFING

Definitely not for landlubbers, windsurfing takes athleticism, daring, and a lot of practice. The **COLUMBIA RIVER GORGE** (about 200 miles south of Seattle) is the top windsurfing area in the continental United States (and second only to Maui in the entire country), thanks to the strong winds that always blow in the direction opposite the river's current—ideal conditions for confident windsurfers. Here are some popular locations closer to home.

GREEN LAKE (E Green Lake Dr N and W Green Lake Dr N; map:EE7) is the best place for beginners; the water is warm and the winds are usually gentle, though experts may find it too crowded. You can take lessons and rent equipment at **GREEN LAKE BOAT RENTALS** (7351 E Green Lake Dr N; 206/527-0171; map: EE7) on the northeast side of the lake.

LAKE UNION has fine winds in the summer, but you'll have to dodge sailboats, commercial boats, and seaplanes. To launch, head to **GAS WORKS PARK** (N Northlake Wy and Meridian Ave N, Wallingford; map:FF7). You can rent equipment and catch a lesson from **URBAN SURF** (2100 N Northlake Wy, Wallingford; 206/545-9463; urbansurf.com; map:FF7), which also offers kiteboarding.

Most experienced windsurfers prefer expansive **LAKE WASHINGTON**. Head to any waterfront park—most have plenty of parking and rigging space. **MAGNUSON PARK** (Sand Point Wy NE and 65th Ave NE, Sand Point; 206/684-4946; map:EE5) is favored for its great winds. Choice Eastside beaches include **GENE COULON BEACH PARK** (1201 Lake Washington Blvd N, Renton; map:MM3) and **HOUGHTON BEACH PARK** (NE 59th St and Lake Washington Blvd NE, Kirkland; map:FF4).

On **PUGET SOUND**, windsurfers (and kitesurfers—who can find more information from the Seattle KiteSurfing Association at www.seattlekitesurfing.org) head for **GOLDEN GARDENS PARK** (north end of Seaview Ave NW, Ballard; map:DD9) or **DUWAMISH HEAD** at Alki Beach Park (Alki Ave SW, West Seattle; map:II9).

Spectator Sports

Mere decades ago, Seattle was seen as a nonplayer when it came to big-time professional sports. The city nostalgically clung to the memory of the Seattle SuperSonics's NBA championship in 1979, but it was a long time between celebrations.

Fortunately, as with any good sports story, it was only a matter of time before Seattle's losing streak was reversed. Things began looking up in the late '80s and early '90s, when some all-star athletes brought Seattle national media attention and a much-needed injection of hometown pride. A couple of division-winning seasons and a sports-facility spending spree helped the city regain its sports swagger (see the We Got Games sidebar). Today, a tonsil-ringing enthusiasm makes itself heard in all three houses of the city's pro teams, as well as at the University of Washington and in the lineup of other local sporting sites.

Emerald Downs Racetrack

2300 EMERALD DOWNS DR, AUBURN; 253/288-7000 OR 888/931-8400 Emerald Downs is a sweet little track in Auburn, 25 minutes south of downtown Seattle, where

Western Washington residents can catch the sport of kings. The track has plentiful indoor and outdoor seating, cuisine that goes beyond the usual hot dogs and beer—yakisoba, anyone?—and about 700 color television monitors to ensure that race fans won't miss a thing, plus a sports bar, a gift shop, and an attractive paddock area. Besides the on-site action, Downs visitors can wager on races at tracks around the country. Racing season runs from mid-April to mid-September, Thursday to Sunday (plus Wednesday, mid-July and August). General admission is $4, free for children 17 and under; grandstand seating is $6, clubhouse seating is $6.50 (reservations are available). Free general parking is available (catch a parking shuttle); preferred spaces (a shorter walk) are $4; valet parking (no walk) is $7. *emeralddowns.com; I-5 south to 272nd St exit, east to West Valley Hwy and south to 37th St N*

Everett AquaSox

39TH AND BROADWAY, EVERETT; 425/258-3673 OR 800/GO-FROGS IN WASHINGTON Real grass, real fans, real hot dogs—the AquaSox have it all, including a lime-green frog mascot, Webbly, that is a globally hot collector's item. Watching this Class-A farm team of the Seattle Mariners is always worth the drive to Everett's 4,500-seat Memorial Stadium. The Sox attract a loyal cadre of fans from mid-June through the first week of September. Tickets can usually be bought at the gate and are also available through Ticketmaster outlets. Tickets are $5; reserved seats are $7–$10. *aquasox.com; 30 miles north of Seattle on I-5 at exit 192*

Husky Basketball

BANK OF AMERICA ARENA AT HEC EDMUNDSON PAVILION, UNIVERSITY OF WASHINGTON, UNIVERSITY DISTRICT; 206/543-2200 Around here, real women play hoops—and they play them well. The University of Washington's Husky women's basketball team have long put on a better show (the Husky-Stanford duel is always a hot ticket) than their male counterparts; but the men are gaining ground, and both teams are fun and affordable to watch. The Dawg teams start play in early November and continue through March. General seating costs $6; reserved seats are $8–$14 for women's games, $12.50–$22.50 for men's. *gohuskies.com; map:FF6*

Husky Football

HUSKY STADIUM, UNIVERSITY OF WASHINGTON, UNIVERSITY DISTRICT; 206/543-2200 Beginning in September, the UW's beloved "bad-to-the-bone Dawgs" play top-drawer football in the 73,000-seat Husky Stadium. Tickets are tough to get, so plan ahead, especially for big games; when the Huskies are home, the games are on Saturday. Be sure to pack rain gear, carpool (just follow the cars with the Husky flags), and wear purple. Also, plan to watch game highlights later on TV, as the lovely lake views from the stadium will likely distract even die-hard fans from some of the gridiron action. Tickets are $18–$34. *gohuskies.com; map:FF6*

Seattle Mariners

SAFECO FIELD, BETWEEN ROYAL BROUGHAM WY AND S ATLANTIC ST, SODO; 206/346-4000 Since the team's thrilling foray into the playoffs in 1995, the Mariners have become the undisputed darlings of local sports fans—and the team has even converted a few nonsports types. That stellar '95 season helped catapult attendance through the Kingdome roof and the M's right into an open-air ballpark (see Top 25 Attractions in the Exploring chapter). Besides on-field action, Safeco Field sports a menu offering everything from California rolls to barbecue ribs grilled in an open pit, several Mariners merchandise shops, and a baseball museum. The season lasts from early April through the first week of October. Individual ticket prices range from $6 for center-field bleachers to $50. The $16 upper-deck seats may be the best in the park, with unobstructed vistas of Mount Rainier, Elliott Bay, and downtown Seattle. *mariners.mlb.com; map:R9*

Seattle Seahawks

SEAHAWKS STADIUM, OCCIDENTAL WY S AND S KING ST, PIONEER SQUARE; 888/NFL-HAWK The 67,000-seat Seahawks Stadium opened on the site of the former Kingdome in July 2002. The best bet is to take a free Metro bus from downtown—parking near the stadium is an expensive nightmare. The regular NFL season starts in September (preseason games in August) and runs through December. Ticket prices range from $23 to $79. *www.seahawks.com; map:Q9*

Seattle Sounders

SEAHAWKS STADIUM, OCCIDENTAL WY S AND S KING ST, PIONEER SQUARE; 206/622-3415 OR 800/796-KICK While some American cities are still discovering the world's most popular sport, professional soccer has been kicking around Seattle off and on since 1974, when the Sounders were founded. The 1995–96 A-League champions play at the 67,000-seat Seahawks (football) Stadium, from May through August. Tickets range from $10 to $22. *seattlesounders.net; map:B6*

BEST PLACE TO STAGE A PROTEST?
"Portland perhaps?"
Greg Nickels, mayor of Seattle

Seattle Storm

KEYARENA, SEATTLE CENTER; 206/628-0888 TICKETMASTER Seattle acquired a Women's National Basketball Association (WNBA) franchise in 2000 when this fledgling team blew into town. Games are held during the short NBA off-season (late May through mid-August), but the team has a loyal contingent of fans and some star players. Tickets are comparatively affordable at $8 for binocular level to $60 courtside. *wnba.com/storm/; map:B7*

Seattle SuperSonics

KEYARENA, SEATTLE CENTER; 206/628-0888 TICKETMASTER Since winning it all in the '70s, the Sonics have been an uneven team, especially when it comes to the playoffs. But unpredictability is part of the team's charm, and the Sonics are a consistent winner when it comes to drawing the home crowd. The team tears up the courts from early November to late April, and tickets (ranging from $11 to $129 for near-courtside) often sell out early. *nba.com/sonics/; map:B7*

Seattle Thunderbirds

KEYARENA, SEATTLE CENTER; 206/448-7825 OR 425/869-7825; 206/628-0888 TICKETMASTER Arguably the best buy in local sports, the 1996–97 Western Hockey League champion Seattle Thunderbirds take to the ice in September and play through March—or early May if they make the playoffs. No one could mistake these young icemen for the NHL, but what they lack in finesse (and years) they make up for with sheer energy and some of the most vocal, loyal fans in the region. The T-birds's 36 home games are mostly on weekends; tickets are $8–$18. *seattle-thunderbirds.com; map:B7*

Tacoma Rainiers

CHENEY STADIUM, 2502 S TYLER ST, TACOMA; 253-752-7700 OR 800/281-3834 On clear days at the Mariners Triple-A farm club's Cheney Stadium facility, spectacular views of Mount Rainier play background for these boys of summer. The Rainiers play 72 home games, from early April to September. Tickets range from $5 to $12. *tacomarainiers.com; about 34 miles south of Seattle on I-5, take exit 132 (Hwy 16) west, the 19th street exit east, then turn right on Cheyenne to the parking lot*

DAY TRIPS

DAY TRIPS

South Puget Sound

BAINBRIDGE ISLAND
Take the Washington State Ferry from downtown Seattle's waterfront at Colman Dock (Pier 52), to Bainbridge Island and enjoy approximately 35 minutes of scenery. After docking, it's a short walk northwest along Olympic Avenue to the traffic light; take a left on Winslow Wy E to bustling downtown Bainbridge (locals still call it Winslow).

Lush and green, Bainbridge is bubbling with arts, crafts, and eateries—in July, catch the island's festival of flora, **BAINBRIDGE IN BLOOM** (gardentour.org). For information about visiting the area, contact the Bainbridge Chamber of Commerce (590 Winslow Wy E; 206/842-3700; bainbridgechamber.com). Or just ask the person at the ferry dock when you get there for an island map. Make sure to get the new waterfront trail map as well.

The '70s-era landmark **STREAMLINER DINER** (397 Winslow Wy E; 206/842-8595) is one way to fuel up for a leisurely walk. Or try a tasty orange sweet roll at **BLACKBIRD BAKERY** (210 Winslow Wy E; 206/780-1322).

Don't miss the wide selection of new and used books (and author readings) at **EAGLE HARBOR BOOKS** (157 Winslow Wy E; 206/842-5332) or the whimsical works at the artists' cooperative, **BAINBRIDGE ARTS & CRAFTS** (151 Winslow Wy E; 206/842-3132). If you want to rub elbows with some real live locals, make a pit stop at **WINSLOW HARDWARE & MERCANTILE** (240 Winslow Wy E; 206/842-3101), where you can get island chat and, oh yeah, buy tools.

The Mediterranean food at **BISTRO PLEASANT BEACH** (241 Winslow Wy W; 206/842-4347; see the Restaurants chapter) is a hit, as are **CAFE NOLA**'s (101 Winslow Wy W; 206/842-3822; see the Restaurants chapter) hearty soups and sandwiches, which can be enjoyed on a pleasant outdoor patio. You can also pick up picnic fixings at **TOWN & COUNTRY MARKET** (343 Winslow Wy E; 206/842-3848) or browse the **FARMERS MARKET** in the City Hall Plaza (206/855-1500; see the restaurants chapter) on Saturdays from April to October, 9am to 1pm.

Though walking is the best way to get around downtown, you'll need some wheels to get to the farther reaches of the island; particularly as many of the streets lack sidewalks. What kind of wheels depends on how you want to maneuver the hills that crisscross the island. For a wind-in-your-hair experience, rent a bike right in town at **B.I. CYCLE SHOP** (162 Bjune Dr; 206/842-6413; b-i-cycle.com).

There are many places to park a picnic on Bainbridge. **FORT WARD STATE PARK** (2241 Pleasant Beach Dr NE; 206/842-4041) on the island's south end is good for picnicking, beach walking, or fishing. Or opt for an easier-to-find park: from downtown Bainbridge, take Highway 305 north to the turnoff at Day Road E and follow signs to the small beachfront **FAY-BAINBRIDGE STATE PARK** (15446 Sunrise Dr NE; 206/842-3931 or 800/233-0321), complete with playground, picnic shelters, and Bainbridge's only campground. On the way, visit **BAINBRIDGE ISLAND VINE-YARDS AND WINERY** (682 Hwy 305; 206/842-WINE) for tastings and a self-guided tour of the vineyard. The **BLOEDEL RESERVE** (7571 NE Dolphin Dr; 206/842-7631; bloedelreserve.org) is the island's best stop (see Gardens in the Exploring Chapter). Plan to spend at least two hours perusing the former home of timber magnate Prentice Bloedel. The 150-acre estate features woods, landscaped gardens, and a bird sanctuary. Reservations are required; open Wednesday through Sunday.

Farther north, on the Kitsap Peninsula just north of the island, it's a short drive on the Highway 305 bridge over Agate Passage and up Suquamish Way (the first street on the right after the bridge) to **CHIEF SEATTLE'S GRAVE** and a view of the Seattle skyline. For more information about the chief, head back to Highway 305 and visit the **SUQUAMISH MUSEUM** (15838 Sandy Hook Rd; 360/598-3311; suquamish.nsn.us/museum).

Reward yourself with dinner and a movie off the beaten path in Lynwood Center, on the southwest side of the island. Try fresh-made focaccias and highbrow fare at **RUBY'S ON BAINBRIDGE** (4738 Lynwood Center Rd NE; 206/780-9303), newly at home in historic Olson Manor, then take in the show at the retro **LYNWOOD THE-ATRE** (4569 Lynwood Center Rd NE; 206/842-3080). Appealing tuck-in options for the night are the **BUCHANAN INN** (8494 NE Oddfellows Rd; 206/780-9258, buchananinn.com), a renovated 1912 bed-and-breakfast, or **GAYLE BARD'S OLD MILL GUEST HOUSE** (6159 Old Mill Rd; 206/842-8543), a tiny (three beds!) but charming getaway.

BEST PLACE TO LUNCH DOWNTOWN?

"Salumi, at Third and Main, for home-cured meats and home-made mozzarella cheese. The lamb prosciutto is sent from heaven each day and blessed personally by God."

Greg Kucera, owner of Greg Kucera Gallery

VASHON ISLAND

Take the Washington State Ferry from the Fauntleroy dock in West Seattle to Vashon Island; the crossing is approximately 15 minutes.

Artsy little Vashon Island is only 15 minutes away from West Seattle's southwest shore, but its serene countryside and Baker-to-Rainier views make it seem hundreds of miles away—it even snows regularly in the winter. The island is 12 miles long and 6 miles wide including Maury Island, joined to Vashon by a mudflat. For information on visiting, contact the Vashon–Maury Island Chamber of Commerce (206/463-6217; vashonchamber.com).

The island's long country roads through dense forests and peaceful pastures make it great for biking—once you make it past the killer hill near the ferry dock. Rent bikes at **VASHON BICYCLES** (9925 SW 178th St; 206/463-6225), 4 miles from the ferry dock, accessible by **METRO** bus (206/553-3000; transit.metrokc.gov). Buses stop running around 7pm and don't run at all on Sundays.

Most Vashon beaches are private, but **MAURY ISLAND'S DOCKTON COUNTY PARK** (Stuckey Rd and SW 260th St), facing Vashon's southeast shore across Quartermaster Harbor, is a nice rest stop. A circa 1915 Coast Guard lighthouse stands sentry over the lonely beach and loop walking trail at **POINT ROBINSON** on Maury's easternmost tip, facing Des Moines on the mainland. The point is an ideal spot to watch the sunset over Mount Rainier. Hikers also get access to a bit of beach along the forest trail at **BURTON ACRES PARK** (on a southeast Vashon peninsula east of Burton that extends into Quartermaster Harbor), where reasonably warm inner-harbor waters make for good swimming. You can rent kayaks from **VASHON ISLAND KAYAKS** (206/463-9257) at the Burton Acres boat launch and paddle the inner harbor; staff also lead tours.

You could spend an entire day just visiting island-based companies that market their goods locally and nationally. Unfortunately, corporate fingers have left their prints even in the town of Vashon—the Seattle's Best Coffee plant that grew up on the island is being moved closer to Starbucks headquarters in Seattle (SBC was bought by the coffee giant early in 2003). But Vashon has more homegrown tricks up its sleeve; the **ALL MERCIFUL SAVIOUR MONASTERY** in Dockton on Maury Island (SW 268th St; 206/463-5918; vashonmonks.com) boasts coffee-making (though not roasting) monks. You can get a tour of the grounds and purchase their Monastery Blend Coffee if you call in advance. **WAX ORCHARDS** (22744 Wax Orchards Rd SW; 206/463-9735; waxorchards.com) doesn't do tours, but does sell their trademark preserves, syrups, fudge, and apple cider, made with pure and natural food-preserving techniques. More island goodies can be found at the **COUNTRY STORE AND GARDENS** (20211 Vashon Hwy SW; 206/463-3655), a general store with potted herbs, gardening supplies, outdoor clothing, and 10 acres of fields, flowers, and U-pick filberts, blueberries, and Asian pears. Nearby **MINGLEMENT MARKET** (20316 Vashon Hwy SW; 206/463-9672) offers organic foods, specialty teas, herbs, and local crafts.

BLUE HERON ARTS CENTER (19704 Vashon Hwy SW; 206/463-5131) has an art gallery with rotating exhibits and is home for the live arts events of **VASHON ALLIED ARTS** (206/463-5131; vashonalliedarts.com), including literary readings, dance, folk music, and plays on weekends September through June. It also holds kids' programs, classes, and works in progress. The Blue Heron's crafts gallery and its pottery, woodwork, and textiles are available at the **HERON'S NEST GALLERY** (17600 Vashon Hwy; 206/463-5252), in the center of the town of Vashon.

Early July's **STRAWBERRY FESTIVAL** is the island's biggest event, with a parade, music, and crafts. Don't miss the Thriftway Marching Grocery Cart Drill Team. Maury Island's **FIELD DAY FARM** (23720 Dockton Rd; 206/463-9032) is the area's best U-pick place: strawberries, cherries, pears, vegetables, dahlias, walnuts, chestnuts, filberts, and apples. Call in advance to see what's available at the time of your visit.

For dinner, islanders favor **EXPRESS CUISINE**'s (17629 Vashon Hwy SW; 206/463-6626) superbly prepared pastas, curries, salads, and stews, eaten with gusto by diners who amiably share tables. Vashon's most formal eatery is in the **BACK BAY INN** (24007 Vashon Hwy SW; 206/463-5355; www.thebackbayinn.com), a renovated turn-of-the-century landmark serving Northwest cuisine. Four rooms upstairs are available should you be charmed into spending the night. Island B&Bs range from remote farmhouses to restored Edwardians; for information, call the **LODGING RESERVATION SERVICE** (206/463-5491; vashonislandlodging.com/castlehill.html).

To continue a tour of south Puget Sound, you can leave the island via Vashon's southern ferry terminal at Tahlequah (Tahlequah Rd, on the south end of the island), which drops you off at Tacoma's Point Defiance Park (see Tacoma and Gig Harbor, below).

TACOMA AND GIG HARBOR

Take Interstate 5 south of Seattle 30 miles to exit 133, approximately 45 minutes. Gig Harbor is about 10 miles northwest of Tacoma via Highway 16 (exit 132 off I-5).

Smug Seattleites forget that Tacoma once earned the nickname "City of Destiny" by beating out the Emerald City in the race to win a major rail line. Though Seattle became bigger and glitzier—and Tacoma developed an unfortunate reputation for an aroma drifting out of its paper mills—today Tacoma is trying mightily to reinvent itself. Commuters and visitors alike can enjoy the free rides on its up-and-running electric **LINK LIGHT RAIL** system (while Seattle struggles with its own light rail and monorail development). As downtown cleaned up its act, a branch of the University of Washington moved in and, thanks to years of aggressive historic preservation, history and architecture buffs can still hail Tacoma's classic buildings. Favorites include the Renaissance clock and bell tower of city hall, the Romanesque First Presbyterian Church, and the 92-year-old coppered **UNION STATION** turned **FEDERAL COURTHOUSE** (1717 Pacific Ave; open to the public during business hours). The station's interior is worth a visit just for gawking at its rotunda graced by glass artist (and native son) Dale Chihuly's works.

But it's a couple of newer structures that are garnering attention lately. The most striking is the **MUSEUM OF GLASS** (1801 E Dock St; 866/4-MUSEUM; museumof glass.org; $10 adults). Located along the Tacoma waterfront and designed by Arthur Erickson, the museum's unique profile centers around the Hot Shop Amphitheater, a gigantic silver cone that juts into the Tacoma skyline. In this 9,200-square-foot space, you can watch glass artists in action, as well as try your hand at glassblowing. Linking the Museum of Glass to downtown is the 500-foot-long **CHIHULY BRIDGE OF GLASS**, an enclosed outdoor walkway whose glass walls and ceiling bear hundreds of colorful glass works by Chihuly, who did the work for free. In early 2003, the **TACOMA ART MUSEUM** (1701 Pacific Ave; 253/272-4258; www.tacomaart museum.org; $6.50 adults) moved into new digs nearby, a sleek Antoine Predock–designed stainless-steel building. With the new setting comes a reinvigorated commitment to Northwest art. The third museum in Tacoma's cultural triumvirate is the stately **WASHINGTON STATE HISTORY MUSEUM** (1911 Pacific Ave; 888/238-4373; wshs.org/wshm; $7 adult). Neighbor to Union Station, its building was designed to blend into its surroundings. Inside are intriguing permanent and visiting exhibits on two floors, a museum store, a cafe, and an auditorium. If your goal is to hit all three museums in a day, it's a steal to visit on Tuesdays, when the history museum offers **TRIPLE TUESDAYS**—a joint ticket includes admission to all three for $17 (adults).

BEST PLACE TO BUY A MICROBREW?

"Bottleworks, not only for the great selection of microbrews
and imports, but because they care about beer
and they ask that you do the same."

Jack Daws, Northwest sculptor

Classic old theaters have also become part of downtown Tacoma's renaissance. The lovingly restored **PANTAGES THEATER** (301 Broadway; 253/591-5894; broad waycenter.org), a 1918, 1,186-seat movie house designed by B. Marcus Priteca, now hosts dance, music, and stage presentations; the refurbished 1918, 742-seat **RIALTO THEATER** (310 S 9th St; 253/591-5894; broadwaycenter.org) is the site of smaller performance groups. Both often feature shows mounted by the **BROADWAY CENTER FOR THE PERFORMING ARTS** (901 Broadway; 253/591-5890; broad waycenter.org). The **TACOMA ACTORS GUILD** (Theatre on the Square, 915 Broadway; 253/272-2145; www.tacomaactorsguild.org) draws audiences to performances at Theatre on the Square, next to the Pantages. The **BLUE MOUSE THEATER** (2611 N Proctor St; 253/752-9500; www.bluemousetheatre.com) is the oldest continually operating movie theater in Washington, open since 1923. In addition to other movies, the theater shows the *Rocky Horror Picture Show* every Saturday night. Look up and you'll see little blue glass mice running along the theater's upper portion (mice are courtesy of the omnipresent Chihuly, who is a part owner).

On Tacoma's northwest side is one of the most dramatically sited parks in the country: **POINT DEFIANCE PARK**, with its 500 acres of pristine forest pushing out into Puget Sound. The 5-mile drive and parallel hiking trails provide amazing views of Vashon Island, Gig Harbor, and the Olympic Mountains. This treasure also includes Japanese and Northwest native gardens, a railroad village with a working steam engine, a reconstruction of **FORT NISQUALLY** (originally built in 1833), a swimming beach, the Tahlequah ferry dock for sailings to and from Vashon Island, and the **POINT DEFIANCE ZOO AND AQUARIUM** (5400 N Pearl St; 253/591-5337; pdza.org). This zoo is the official survival and breeding center for the most endangered mammal in North America, the red wolf; the breeding program has grown the population from 14 in 1980 (considered extinct) to approximately 300 today. In the aquarium, don't miss watching seals, sea lions, and the white beluga whale from an underwater vantage point as well as catching the newest exhibit, sea horses. The **RUSTON WAY WATERFRONT**, a 6-mile mix of parks and restaurants filled with people in any weather, connects Point Defiance Park with downtown. **WRIGHT**

PARK (Division Ave and S "I" St) is a serene in-city park with many trees, a duck-filled pond, and a beautifully maintained conservatory, built of glass and steel in 1890.

One of the area's largest estates is **LAKEWOLD GARDENS** (12317 Gravelly Lake Dr SW, off I-5 at exit 124; 253/584-3360; lakewold.org), a beautiful 10-acre site about 10 minutes south of Tacoma that has been recognized as one of the outstanding gardens in America. It has one of the country's largest rhododendron collections, and its design was influenced by park planner Frederick Olmsted and landscape architect Thomas Church. Both men helped Eulalie Wagner design the landscaping.

Nightlife options include **ENGINE HOUSE NO. 9** (611 N Pine St; 253/272-3435) near the University of Puget Sound, a smoke-free beer lover's neighborhood tavern, and the **SPAR** in Old Town (2121 N 30th St; 253/627-8215). If it's food you're after, **ALTEZZO** (1320 Broadway; 253/572-3200) at the top of the Sheraton has a great view of downtown and serves some of Tacoma's best Italian cuisine. The **CLIFF HOUSE** (6300 Marine View Dr; 253/927-0400; cliffhouserestaurant.com) capitalizes on its commanding view of Commencement Bay and its formal airs. Masahiro Endo's stylish downtown Japanese restaurant, **FUJIYA** (1125 Court C, between Broadway and Market St; 253/627-5319), is tucked away but attracts fans with the best sushi and sashimi around, feathery-crisp tempura, and delicious *yosenabe* (seafood stew)—the stair climb to get there will work up your appetite. Worth a look for both food and insider atmosphere, the **SWISS** (1904 S Jefferson Ave; 253/572-2821; theswisspub.com), a former Nordic and Scandinavian lodge turned watering hole, is so popular with the local lawyers and politicians, Tacoma mayor Bill Baarsma and state congressman Norm Dicks literally have barstools with their names on them. The pub also carries a variety of art by local artists, as well as a permanent collection of—what else—Chihuly glass.

Other top Tacoma eateries include **STANLEY & SEAFORT'S STEAK, CHOP, AND FISH HOUSE** (115 E 34th St; 253/473-7300), with a panoramic view of the city, harbor, and the Olympic Mountains; **BIMBO'S** (1516 Pacific Ave; 253/383-5800), an Italian restaurant serving hearty pasta dishes; **EAST & WEST CAFE** (5319 Tacoma Mall Blvd; 253/475-7755), a charming Asian restaurant; and the **DASH POINT LOBSTER SHOP** (6912 Soundview Dr NE; 253/927-1513) and the **LOBSTER SHOP SOUTH** (4015 Ruston Wy; 253/759-2165). The city's downtown revitalization has also seen the opening of an **EL GAUCHO**. Local brewery **HARMON'S** (1938 Pacific Ave; 253/383-BREW) offers the range of pub fare—fish-and-chips, burgers, soups and salads, and homemade microbrews.

Among Tacoma's appealing bed-and-breakfast options are **CHINABERRY HILL** (302 Tacoma Ave N; 253/272-1282; chinaberry@wa.net; chinaberryhill.com), an 1889 Victorian mansion in the city's historic Stadium District restored as a garden retreat with bay views and fireplaces, and **THE VILLA BED & BREAKFAST** (705 N 5th St; 253/572-1157; villabb@aol.com; villabb.com), an Italian Renaissance mansion exuding Mediterranean style and the opulence of the roaring '20s in the heart of the historic north end. The **SHERATON TACOMA HOTEL** (1320 Broadway Plaza; 253/572-3200) is considered the best hotel in town. Adjacent to the Tacoma

Convention Center, most rooms look out over Commencement Bay or have Mount Rainier views.

Of course, one of the most notable sights of the city is the **TACOMA DOME** (253/272-6817; tacomadome.org), the country's largest wooden dome, hosting trade shows, concerts, and sporting events, including Tacoma Sabercats hockey games. But when it comes to sporting events, nothing beats going to **CHENEY STADIUM** in west Tacoma (2502 S Tyler St, from Seattle take I-5 south to exit 132/Hwy 16 west) to watch the **TACOMA RAINIERS** (253/752-7707; tacomarainiers.com), the Seattle Mariners Triple-A affiliate.

To visit nearby **GIG HARBOR** (253/851-6865 Chamber of Commerce), drive about 60 minutes on Highway 16, west across the Tacoma Narrows Bridge. Once a fishing village and still home port for an active commercial fleet, Gig Harbor is part suburbia, part weekend getaway. Boating remains important, with the town's good anchorage and various moorages attracting gunwale-to-gunwale pleasure craft. When the clouds break, Mount Rainier dominates. It's also a picturesque spot for browsing the numerous interesting shops and galleries lining Harborview Drive. Traffic is congested and parking limited because the city was built for boats, not cars, but it's still a good place for festivals, including an arts festival in mid-July and the Maritime Gig in mid-June. A **FARMERS MARKET** features local produce and plants on Saturday, May through October.

Seafood served with a French accent and outdoor dining on a deck overlooking Gig Harbor make the **GREEN TURTLE** (2905 Harborview Dr; 253/851-3167) the best restaurant in town. **MARCO'S RISTORANTE ITALIANO** (7707 Pioneer Wy; 253/858-2899) is a favorite, with fare ranging from traditional Italian to more original specials. Both are owned by members of the same family. The **TIDES TAVERN** (2925 Harborview Dr; 253/858-3982) is a popular watering hole perched over the harbor—boaters like to tie up at its dock—that is often packed to capacity, especially on the deck on sunny days. Originally a general store, it's a full-service tavern with pool table and live music on weekends.

Gig Harbor's **PARADISE THEATER** (9916 Peacock Hill Ave NW; 253/851-7529) has a full season of dinner shows from mid-September to June and offers outdoor shows during the summer. Bring a picnic and a blanket for this summer tradition. There's also an improv group on Friday nights. At the **MARITIME INN** (3212 Harborview Dr; 253/858-1818), downtown and across from the waterfront, each of the 15 rooms has a theme, such as the Canterwood Room's golf motif.

KOPACHUCK STATE PARK west of Gig Harbor is a popular destination (follow signs from Hwy 16), as are **PENROSE POINT** and **ROBERT F. KENNEDY STATE PARKS** on the Key Peninsula farther west (Hwys 16 and 302 to Longbranch Rd). All have beaches for clam digging (call 800/562-5632 for red-tide warnings). At **MINTER CREEK STATE FISH HATCHERY** (12710 124th Ave; 253/857-5077), also on the Key Peninsula, you can watch the developmental stages of millions of salmon, daily.

OLYMPIA

Take Interstate 5 south of Seattle 60 miles, approximately 1¾ to 2 hours.

Though the Nisqually Earthquake shook things up in 2001, Olympia has been taking steps to get back on its feet. Reconstruction of the state capitol is in full swing, and though legislators are in temporary quarters, the main draw of this capital town still happens in late winter, when both the legislature and the city's three college campuses are in session.

The **LEGISLATIVE BUILDING** (14th Ave SW and Capital Wy; 360/586-8687) will be closed for its $100-million renovation until late 2004. In the meantime you can take free tours of the well-manicured lawns of the **CAPITOL CAMPUS** (360/586-8687; tours@leg.wa.gov) seven days a week, featuring a plant conservatory, Tivoli fountain, Temple of Justice (which you can tour as well), and views out over the Capitol Lake and memorials. Tours of the **GOVERNOR'S MANSION** are also available. Call for reservations and information. The government buildings are a study in classical architectural style as seen through the lenses of passing decades (it took about 40 years to complete the campus plan), from Beaux-Arts to art deco to the modernist **WASHINGTON STATE LIBRARY**, which is definitely worth a look—particularly to see the Kenneth Callahan mural (most of the other art has been temporarily removed while office space is shifting all around). Take the stairwell down at the mosaic on your right, and you will see the mural wrapping around the upper band of the room below. Each section depicts a different stage of Washington state's history. The **WASHINGTON STATE VISITOR INFORMATION CENTER** (14th Ave SW and Capitol Wy; 360/586-3460) has plenty of additional information about the campus.

Just south of campus, the **WASHINGTON STATE CAPITOL MUSEUM** (211 W 21st Ave; 360/753-2580; wshs.org/wscm) has an outstanding collection of Native American baskets and memorabilia from the territorial government's early days and from the state's founding in 1889. The capital isn't just for adults, though. Kids will love the **HANDS-ON CHILDREN MUSEUM** (106 11th Ave SW; 360/956-0818), filled with interactive exhibits that will entertain (and educate) the tykes for hours.

Olympia's downtown has a variety of galleries, offbeat shops, cafes, and entertainment venues. **BATDORF AND BRONSON COFFEE ROASTERS** (200 Market St NE; 800/955-5282; batdorf.com) boasts a large following of folks who would never even consider going to Starbucks. A large blackboard lists an ample variety of coffees, teas, and espresso drink offerings. On Capitol Way, historic **SYLVESTER PARK** hosts summer concerts, holiday lights, and year-round demonstrations, with the stately old stone Capitol Building—originally built as the Thurston County Courthouse—overlooking the park. A nearby boulder at the corner of Capitol and Legion Ways marks the end of the Oregon Trail. Grab a sandwich or a slice of cake at **WAGNER'S EUROPEAN BAKERY AND CAFÉ** (1013 Capitol Wy S; 360/357-7268). Olympia's best-known restaurant, **THE URBAN ONION**, is right across the street in the **OLYMPIAN HOTEL** (116 Legion Wy; 360/943-9242). The Onion's signature sandwich, the Haystack—sprouts, tomatoes, guacamole, olives, and melted cheese piled high on whole-grain bread—draws crowds for lunch; breakfast and dinner are also served. There's also the venerable **SPAR** (114 4th Ave NE; 360/357-6444), which features Saturday night jazz, a cigar-smoking room in back of the lounge, historic photos, and lots of character.

Downtown doesn't fold up its sidewalks after business hours. The **WASHINGTON CENTER FOR THE PERFORMING ARTS** (512 Washington St SE; 360/753-8586; washingtoncenter.org) offers a range of performances, including dance, symphony, and theater. The **CAPITOL THEATRE** (206 E 5th Ave; 360/754-5378) is a showcase for locally produced plays, musicals, and Olympia Film Society–sponsored screenings, including an October film festival. The activity continues into the weekend with the **OLYMPIA FARMERS MARKET** (700 Capitol Wy N; 360/352-9096), selling produce, flowers, and south Sound crafts Thursday through Sunday during the growing season. Not far away is **PERCIVAL LANDING** (at the foot of State St), a waterfront park with a tower providing views from Budd Inlet and the capitol dome to the snowcapped Olympic Mountains. One of the country's top liberal arts colleges, the **EVERGREEN STATE COLLEGE** (Evergreen Pkwy; 360/866-6000), to the west of town on Cooper Point, has a woodsy campus with an organic farm and 3,100 feet of beachfront property. The college also hosts a range of cultural events throughout the year.

There are a number of nature-appreciation side-trip options in the area, such as Tumwater Falls and Capital Lake, southwest of downtown. Five miles farther south off Pacific Highway SE is **WOLF HAVEN** (3111 Offut Lake Rd, Tenino; 360/264-HOWL), a nationally renowned conservation organization that teaches wolf appreciation, invites the public to join its wolves in a "howl-in" (Saturday nights, June through September, reservation required), and gives hourly tours Wednesday through Monday year-round except February. And the **NISQUALLY WILDLIFE REFUGE** (100 Brown Farm Rd; 360/753-9467; nisqually.fws.gov), 10 miles north of Olympia just off I-5, offers a 5.5-mile bird-watching hike through its wetlands sanctuary.

Snoqualmie Valley

Take Interstate 90 east of Seattle approximately 30 miles to exit 27, Snoqualmie–Fall City, about 40 minutes.

Seattle's eastward-oozing suburbs have caused the loss of many sleepy farm hamlets of yesteryear, but Snoqualmie Valley's relatively bucolic stretch of cow country just west of the Cascades is still great for weekend biking or driving, especially if you like U-pick berry farms, roadside stands, and local cafes.

From the town of Snoqualmie off I-90, Highway 202 heads south to North Bend and north to Fall City, then Highway 203 takes over heading north through Carnation and Duvall—both highways are crisscrossed by a web of backroads leading to dairy farms, quiet lakes, and beaches along the Snoqualmie River. Cyclists should stick to backroads to avoid weekend traffic. Mountain bikers, hikers, and horseback riders can hit the Snoqualmie Valley Trail, an old railroad right-of-way connecting Stillwater (between Carnation and Duvall) and Tokul (south of Fall City); the trail continues north to the Snohomish County line just north of Duvall, and south to Snoqualmie.

Head into downtown **SNOQUALMIE** and climb aboard the **SNOQUALMIE VALLEY RAILROAD** (38625 SE King St; 425/888-3030 fares and schedules; trainmuseum.org) for a scenic upper-valley tour. That's just one part of the "living" Northwest Railway Museum; there's also a Santa Train during early December weekends (reservations required) and numerous railroad artifacts. If you're hungry, head to **ISADORA'S** (8062 Railroad Ave SE; 425/888-1345), a cozy cafe and a funky shop full of country collectibles. Not far to the south, North Bend's main attraction is the **FACTORY STORES OF NORTH BEND** (exit 31 off I-90; 425/888-4505) outlet mall.

Continue north on Highway 202 to the region's 268-foot-high natural wonder, **SNOQUALMIE FALLS**. The **SALISH LODGE** (6501 Railroad Ave SE; 425/888-2556 or 800/826-6124; salishlodge.com) is adjacent to the falls and is a high-end stay-over spot. You can look out at the nearby gorge from the restaurant—where you can gorge yourself on its famed four-course breakfast—but you can't see the falls. You can see them from a cliffside gazebo, or hike down to the gorge bottom for a closer look.

BEST PLACE TO FIND INSPIRATION?

"At a beach burn at Golden Gardens Park. Someone's usually staging one on any given weekend over the summer, but the best are thrown by Burning Man tribes—dementia set to a glorious inferno. Leave the kids at home."

Melanie McFarland, Seattle Post-Intelligencer *TV critic*

Continue northwest to **FALL CITY**. For lunch, the perfect place to stoke up for an active day on the Snoqualmie is **SMALL FRYES** (4225 Preston–Fall City Rd; 425/222-7688), a burger stand with seasoned french fries and tasty milk shakes (try banana or mocha malt). From Fall City, take Highway 203 north (Hwy 202 heads west to Redmond).

South of Carnation, **TOLT RIVER–JOHN MACDONALD PARK** (31020 NE 40th St; 206/296-2964), at the confluence of the Tolt and Snoqualmie Rivers, is a fine place for a barbecue in a reservable picnic shelter. Throw a Frisbee on the grass, ride an inner tube where the Tolt empties into the Snoqualmie, camp, or watch teenagers dive from the Tolt Hill Road Bridge. Mountain bikers can hit the 7.4-mile Snoqualmie Valley Trail here, meander over the Snoqualmie River into the Tolt River Campground and through part of the Snoqualmie Valley, and see eye-popping views of the Cascades and Mount Si along the way.

CARNATION is home to **REMLINGER FARMS** (32610 NE 32nd St; 425/333-4135 or 425/451-8740; remlingerfarms.com), one of the biggest and best produce markets around. You can buy their farm-grown fruits and veggies (U-pick or not), baked goods, gift items, and canned foods. Its restaurant out back serves lunch, desserts, and candy. Kids love it in summer because the farm has a petting zoo, pony rides, puppet shows, and a small theme park with rides. Open May through October.

From Carnation, Highway 203 follows the Snoqualmie River west, then north, to **DUVALL**, which has preserved its small-town storefronts despite commercial growth. **GARDENS AND SUNSPACES MAIN STREET GALLERY** (15611 Main St NE; 425/788-9844) is an indoor sanctuary of fountains, sundials, garden statuary, and fine art. End your day on the Snoqualmie at the **DUVALL CAFE** (15505 Main St NE; 425/788-9058), which offers surprisingly upscale dinners (as well as enormous breakfasts and fresh lunches). Don't pass up dessert, especially the pie.

FERRY RIDES

No activity better captures the spirit of Seattle than a ferry ride—both for commuters who use them for transportation and for sightseers who want to simply enjoy the sunset or the city skyline from an unobstructed vantage point.

Most of the ferries on Puget Sound are run by **WASHINGTON STATE FERRIES** (206/464-6400 or 888-808-7977; wsdot.wa.gov/ferries). The largest ferry system in the country, it operates 10 routes serving 20 terminal locations and transporting some 27 million passengers a year. On weekend and evening runs, ferries often don't have room for all the cars, so be prepared to wait unless you walk on or ride your bike (fare is much cheaper for pedestrians and cyclists). Wi-Fi service is even being tested on the Seattle–Bremerton, Seattle–Bainbrige, and Edmonds–Kingston routes. Rates range from $3.50 one way for foot passengers traveling from West Seattle to Vashon to $44.25 each way for a car (under 20 feet long) and driver going from Anacortes to Sidney, British Columbia (RV and trailer drivers, take note: beyond 20 feet, the fee goes up and is determined by vehicle length and height; check the Web site for pricing detail). The bike surcharge is $1 from Seattle to Bainbridge, Vashon, or Bremerton. Passengers pay both ways to Canada, but stateside pay only on westbound ferries (so if you're island hopping, head to the westernmost destination first and work your way back).

Three ferry routes leave downtown from the main Seattle terminal at Colman Dock (Pier 52, Alaskan Wy and Marion St; map:M9). The small, speedy walk-on ferry takes mostly commuters to **VASHON ISLAND** (Monday through Friday only; 25 minutes). Tight budgets mean that it is the sole remaining passenger-only ferry, having avoided the axe thanks to the pier protests of some diehard riders. The car-ferry trip to **BREMERTON** takes an hour. The **SEATTLE–BAINBRIDGE ISLAND** run takes 35 minutes. If sightseeing is your objective, take the Bremerton trip. It's a bit longer, but the scenic ride crosses the Sound skirts the south end of Bainbridge Island and passes through narrow Rich Passage into the Kitsap Peninsula's land-enclosed Sinclair Inlet.

In recent years, the population of Bainbridge and Vashon Islands has increased and more folks are commuting by ferry. As a result, drive-on passengers should arrive early, especially when traveling during peak hours (mornings eastbound, evenings westbound; summer weekends: Friday and Saturday westbound, Sunday eastbound). Schedules and fees vary from summer to winter (with longer lines in summer). Americans traveling to Canada should bring a passport or other proof of U.S. citizenship, such as a birth certificate. Other major Puget Sound routes are listed below.

EDMONDS–KINGSTON (30 minutes)

Kingston, close to the northern tip of the Kitsap Peninsula, is reached from Edmonds, about 15 miles north of Seattle (take the Edmonds/Kingston Ferry exit, exit 177, from I-5 and head northwest on Hwy 104).

FAUNTLEROY–VASHON ISLAND–SOUTHWORTH (15 minutes to Vashon plus 10 minutes to Southworth; 35 minutes from Seattle to Southworth)

Vashon, an idyllic retreat west of Seattle, can be reached via passenger ferry from downtown Seattle, Monday through Friday, or every day via car ferry from the Fauntleroy Ferry Dock in West Seattle (exit 163 off I-5; map:LL9). Vashon is the first stop on a trip from the Fauntleroy terminal to Southworth on the Kitsap Peninsula (see Vashon Island in this chapter).

VASHON–TACOMA (15 minutes)

At the southern end of Vashon Island is the Tahlequah Ferry Dock, from which the ferry departs for Point Defiance Park, on the northwest edge of Tacoma.

MUKILTEO–CLINTON (20 minutes)

From Mukilteo, 26 miles north of Seattle (exit 189 off I-5), a ferry goes to Clinton on pretty Whidbey Island (see Whidbey Island in this chapter).

KEYSTONE–PORT TOWNSEND (30 minutes)

From Keystone, 25 miles up Whidbey Island from Clinton, a ferry reaches Port Townsend on the Olympic Peninsula, one of the most enchanting towns in the state (see Port Townsend in this chapter). This route is subject to cancellation due to extreme tidal conditions.

ANACORTES–SAN JUAN ISLANDS–SIDNEY, BC (crossing times vary)

The remote San Juan Islands are reached by ferry from Anacortes (82 miles northwest of Seattle, exit 230 off I-5). There are 743 islands at low tide, but only 172 have names. Gene Hackman owns one, and only four have major ferry service: the boat stops on Lopez, Shaw, Orcas, and San Juan Islands. Once a day (twice a day in summer), the ferry continues on to Sidney on British Columbia's Vancouver Island, just 15 minutes north of Victoria by car. It returns in the early afternoon. During the summer, you can reserve space for your car on this crowded run.

SEATTLE–VICTORIA, BC (2 hours)

The *Victoria Clipper* fleet (206/448-5000 Seattle, 250/382-8100 Victoria, or 800/888-2535 outside Seattle or BC; victoriaclipper.com) offers the only year-round ferry service to Victoria from Seattle. The waterjet-propelled catamarans carry foot passengers only between Seattle and Victoria four times a day from mid-May to mid-September, and once or twice a day the rest of the year. Reservations are necessary. (See Victoria in this chapter).

PORT ANGELES–VICTORIA, BC (1½ hours)

The privately run Black Ball Transport's (360/457-4491; cohoferry.com) *MV Coho* makes four daily runs in summer, and two runs daily in spring and winter (with an extra run for a few days in October for the Canadian Thanksgiving Day and U.S. Columbus Day) from Port Angeles, on the Olympic Peninsula, to Victoria, on Vancouver Island.

An option for returning to Seattle is to continue north on Highway 203 to US Highway 2 at Monroe, from which you can head west toward Everett on US 2 or southwest to Seattle on Highway 522 for a loop tour.

North Puget Sound

WHIDBEY ISLAND

Take Interstate 5 north about 25 miles, past Lynnwood, then take Highways 526 east and 525 north about 5 miles to Mukilteo; driving time is about 45 minutes. Take the Washington State Ferry from Mukilteo to Clinton; the crossing is approximately 20 minutes.

You don't have to go to the San Juans to get away from it all when the pretty villages, viewpoints, sandy beaches, and rolling farmland of Whidbey Island are so close. The island is ideal for a family outing of sightseeing, beachcombing, and clam digging (call 800/562-5632 for red-tide warnings). And the long island's roads are good for biking.

BEST PLACE FOR SEAFOOD?

"Chinook's at Fisherman's Teminal. Consistently the best seafood in a friendly, down-home, nonchic atmosphere."

Charles R. Cross, *author of* Heavier Than Heaven:
The Biography of Kurt Cobain

The ferry lands at **CLINTON** on Whidbey's south end. Drive north on Highway 525 and Langley Road to **LANGLEY**, about 10 minutes north. First Street is a browser's dream filled with shops and galleries. Swap stories with Josh Hauser of **MOONRAKER BOOKS** (360/221-6962). **THE COTTAGE** (360/221-4747) sells adornments and elegant clothing; **VIRGINIA'S ANTIQUES** (360/221-7797) features Asian and American wares; and **WHIDBEY ISLAND ANTIQUES** (360/221-2393) is a two-in-one shop with both restored and unrestored pieces. The **STAR STORE** (360/221-5222) is a genuine mercantile outpost with a grocery and deli, gifts, and gadgets galore; upstairs, the **STAR BISTRO** (360/221-2627) specializes in seafood, Northwest cuisine, and martinis.

Langley is also home to a number of fine galleries. More than 40 island artists and craftspeople sell their wares at the **ARTISTS' GALLERY COOPERATIVE** (314 1st St; 360/221-7675). **MUSEO** (215 1st St; 360/221-7737; www.museo.cc) offers work by local and regional glass artists as well as rotating exhibits from artists nationwide; **HELLEBORE** (308 1st St; 360/221-2067) features glass art made in the studio. Many of the galleries in the area are open late on the first Saturday of the month. **GAL-LERIO** (111 Anthes St; 360/221-1274) is hard to miss—just look for a turquoise stucco building with a giraffe on the side of it to see Kathleen Miller's hand-painted silk and wool clothing and enamel jewelry, as well as husband Donald Miller's art photography. **GASKILL/OLSON** (302 1st St; 360/221-2978) specializes in original Northwest art and fine crafts. And don't miss the **CLYDE THEATRE** (213 1st St; 360/221-5525), host to live theater productions and regularly scheduled films.

If you want to stay in downtown Langley, try Linda Lundgren's retreat, the **GARDEN PATH INN** (111 1st St; 360/221-5121; www.whidbey.com/gp), with two handsomely furnished suites. The interior designs are also on display at her adjoining shop, Islandesign. Excellent B&Bs abound. **HOME BY THE SEA** (2388 E Sunlight Beach Rd; 360/321-2964; homebytheseacottages.com) is right on the water, ideal for beach walking and bird-watching because the tide goes out three-quarters of a mile every day. You can sleep on a (moored) stern-wheeler houseboat at **LONE LAKE COTTAGES AND BREAKFAST** (5206 S Bayview Rd; 360/321-5325; lonelake.com). Or you can try for a room at the idyllic **INN AT LANGLEY** (400 1st St; 360/221-3033; innatlangley.com).

CAFÉ LANGLEY (113 1st St; 360/221-3090) is a busy eatery specializing in Mediterranean dishes. Join native islanders for a microbrew, along with a burger and fries, at the classically dumpy **DOG HOUSE BACKDOOR RESTAURANT AND TAVERN** (230 1st St; 360/221-9825). Or take a picnic to **DOUBLE BLUFF BEACH** northwest of Langley—the perfect place to fly kites, spot bald eagles, watch a sunset, or stroll an unspoiled beach. When the tides are right, this is also one of the Sound's best clam-digging beaches. **WHIDBEY ISLAND VINEYARDS AND WINERY** (5237 S Langley Rd; 360/221-2040), a mile south of town, specializes in small bottlings of rhubarb wine, estate-grown grapes, and a full line of Eastern Washington–grown varietals.

Continuing west and north on Highway 525, you'll pass Freeland at Holmes Harbor and, just beyond, the road west to South Whidbey State Park. Halfway up the island on its narrowest section is Whidbey's **GREENBANK FARM** (corner of State Hwy 525 and Wonn Rd; 360/678-7700; greenbankfarm.com), famed for its loganberry products such as jams, jellies, and liqueurs (all available for sampling). You can also sample and buy 36 regionally produced wines in the store. The farm is a fun picnic spot, especially during the two-day Loganberry Festival in July.

Continue north to Keystone, where Highway 525 ends and Highway 20 begins; follow it north into **COUPEVILLE**, the state's second-oldest incorporated town. It started as a farming community in 1852, and a fort was added after Indian scares. Part of the fort, the **ALEXANDER BLOCKHOUSE**, remains on Alexander Street and is open for tours. The **ISLAND COUNTY HISTORICAL MUSEUM** (908 NW Alexander St; 360/678-3310; www.islandhistory.org) recalls Whidbey Island's past.

Downtown is made up of souvenir and antique shops and a few restaurants. Stop by the **JAN MCGREGOR STUDIO** (19 Front St; 360/678-5015), which specializes in Japanese antique furniture, hand-woven silks, and the pottery McGregor makes using rare porcelain techniques (Thursday through Sunday in winter, every day in summer). Drop by **TOBY'S 1890 TAVERN** (8 NW Front St; 360/678-4222) for Penn Cove mussels, burgers, beer, and pool. The **KNEAD & FEED** (4 Front St; 360/678-5431) offers homemade breads, pies, and soups, or you can join the locals for coffee and a slice at **GREAT TIMES ESPRESSO** (12 Front St; 360/678-5358). Annual community events include the **PENN COVE MUSSEL FESTIVAL** the first weekend in March and the **COUPEVILLE ARTS & CRAFTS FESTIVAL** the second weekend in August (Whidbey Island Visitor Center; 360/678-5434).

You can ride the bike lane on Engle Road 3 miles south to **FORT CASEY STATE PARK**, a decommissioned fort with beaches and commanding bluffs. The Washington State Ferry (206/464-6400 or 888/808-7977; wsdot.wa.gov/ferries) to Port Townsend leaves from Admiralty Head in Keystone, just south of Fort Casey (see Port Townsend below).

Other good places to explore include the bluff and beach at 17,000-acre **EBEY'S LANDING** and **FORT EBEY STATE PARK** northwest of Coupeville. Highway 20 winds north around Penn Cove to Oak Harbor. The Whidbey Island Naval Air Station, an air base for tactical electronic warfare squadrons, dominates **OAK HARBOR**, making it a home for active and retired military folk. Check out **LAVENDER HEART** (4233 N DeGraff Rd; 360/675-3987), which makes topiaries at a working studio in a remodeled barn on what the owner says is one of the Northwest's oldest holly farms. Old and young alike will enjoy **BLUE FOX DRIVE-IN THEATRE** and **BRATT-LAND GO-KARTS** (1403 Monroe Landing Rd; 360/675-5667; bluefoxdrivein.com). You can get good Mexican food at **LUCY'S MI CASITA** (31359 Hwy 20; 360/675-4800), then have a 27-ounce Turbo Godzilla margarita in the lounge upstairs.

At the north end of the island is pretty **DECEPTION PASS STATE PARK**, with 2,300 acres of prime camping land, forests, and beach. Here the beautiful, treacherous gorge of Deception Pass has highly hazardous currents—don't go in the water. You can cross the bridge over Deception Pass that links Whidbey to Fidalgo Island and the mainland via Highway 20 to I-5; or take the Whitney–La Conner Road south to La Conner in the Skagit Valley.

SKAGIT VALLEY

Take Interstate 5 north of Seattle 60 miles, then take exits 221, 226, or 230 west to La Conner; approximately 1 hour.

The Skagit Valley may be little more than a blur to northbound tourists most of the year, but during early spring the area blossoms into color worth slowing down for. In fact, if you pull off the highway during the annual **TULIP FESTIVAL**, you'll have to slow down because the roads are gridlocked most weekends in early April. Many of the country roads are level, making biking an ideal way to get around the traffic. There's also plenty of parking at several I-5 exit ramps, where travelers can hop shuttles. You can also avoid traffic hassles by taking a *Victoria Clipper* boat/bus tour (206/448-5000 or 800/888-2535 outside Seattle; victoriaclipper.com); tours leave Seattle's waterfront every morning during the festival, boats dock in La Conner, and buses take visitors throughout the countryside. There's still plenty to see after the tulips are cut. Tourists swarm U-pick farms during the June strawberry season, continuing with raspberries, blueberries, and sweet corn, and ending in October with pumpkins. A wide range of vegetables, fruits, and honey are also available at fresh-fruit stands throughout the area.

Right off I-5 at exit 226, **MOUNT VERNON** is the "big city" to folks in Skagit and Island Counties. It's a rural town where good restaurants outnumber taverns and video stores; it's a college town (even if Skagit Valley College is only a small community college); and it's a major shopping center thanks to the **OUTLET MALLS** between Mount Vernon and Burlington that feature such stores as J.Crew, Liz Claiborne, and Tommy Hilfiger.

If you take I-5 exit 230 to **LA CONNER** instead, you'll cruise through Conway, where locals meet to eat panfried oysters, charbroiled burgers, and onion rings at the classic **CONWAY PUB** (18611 Main St; 360/445-4733). Five miles west of town, don't miss **SNOW GOOSE PRODUCE** (15170 Fir Island Rd; 360/445-6908), a huge roadside stand open late February to mid-October and worth its own day trip. Get a waffle cone, a wide range of local produce, fresh-caught Hood Canal shrimp, and specialty foods including cheese and pasta.

Although La Conner was founded by trading post operator John Conner in 1867, much of the town remains unchanged today. In those days, the area's fishing and farming communities traded by water—the Skagit River, the Swinomish Channel, and many small streams and sloughs. The arrival of trains and interstate highways made the town a backwater and haven for different drummers and artists, including Guy Anderson, Morris Graves, Mark Tobey, and writer Tom Robbins. The result is a culturally rich town—made more so by the contributions of the nearby Swinomish Indians. Adding to the town's atmosphere is an American bazaar on First Street with **SHOPS** such as Cottons, Nasty Jack's Antiques, and Ginger Grater. Try **HUNGRY MOON DELI** (110 N 1st St; 360/466-1602) for soup and a sandwich.

TILLINGHAST SEED COMPANY (623 Morris St; 360/466-3329), at the southern entrance to town, is the oldest retail and mail-order seed store in the Northwest (since 1885), complete with seeds bred specifically for the Northwest, plus a nursery, florist shop, and general store. **GO OUTSIDE** (111 Morris St; 360/466-4836) is a small garden and garden-accessories store. **GACHES MANSION** (703 S 2nd St; 360/466-4288) is an example of American Victorian architecture, with a widow's walk that looks out on the Skagit Valley. The old mansion is filled with period furnishings and houses the Northwest's only quilt museum (open Wednesday through Sunday). Don't miss the **MUSEUM OF NORTHWEST ART** (121 S 1st St; 360/466-4446; museumofnwart.org), featuring the work of Northwest artists. At the town's edge, the **HERON** in La Conner (117 Maple St; 360/466-4626; theheroninn.com) has pretty-as-a-picture rooms and a tempting hot tub out back.

Kitsap and Olympic Peninsulas

BREMERTON

Take the Washington State Ferry from Colman Dock (Pier 52) in downtown Seattle to Bremerton; the crossing is approximately 1 hour.

It's not easy to make an industrial area look pretty, especially if that industrial center is in the heart of a city's downtown, as Bremerton's U.S. Naval Shipyard is. Though some say it's a good place to pass through—headed somewhere else—a few attractions in the area near the ferry terminal make downtown Bremerton worth a stop, and an art scene is emerging.

Start at the promenade along the shore from First to Fourth Streets with picnic tables, benches, a shipworker statue, and views south to Sinclair Inlet. The walkway ends near the U.S.S. Turner Joy, a destroyer that played a pivotal role in U.S. involvement in Vietnam. The ship, open for self-guided tours (daily in summer, Thursday through Sunday in winter), has a POW memorial featuring a reproduction of a cell from Vietnam's infamous "Hanoi Hilton." Get tickets at the Ship's Store Gift Shop. The shop also sells tickets for **KITSAP HARBOR TOURS**'s (360/377-8924; visitkitsap.com/harbortours) narrated 45-minute trip around the harbor (daily in summer), providing close-up views of battleships, nuclear subs, the carrier U.S.S. Carl Vinson (when it's not at sea), and the eerie mothball fleet. The company also offers a cruise to **TILLICUM VILLAGE**'s salmon dinner and stage show on **BLAKE ISLAND** (also accessible from Seattle; see Boat Tours under Organized Tours in the Exploring chapter). The naval theme continues at the free **BREMERTON NAVAL MUSEUM** (130 Washington St; 360/479-7447), open daily in summer, Tuesday through Sunday in winter; 10am to 5pm. Two doors south, the comfortable **FRAICHE CUP COFFEEHOUSE** (120 Washington Ave; 360/377-1180) offers pastries and espresso drinks.

The **AMY BURNETT FINE ART GALLERY** (412 Pacific Ave; 360/373-3187) started the growth spurt, but the arts district on Fourth Street now includes **COLLECTIVE VISIONS** (360/377-8327), **VIEWPOINTS GALLERY** (360/4400-3843), **METROPOLIS GALLERY** (360/373-4709), and a **GALLERY TOUR** the first Friday of the month. (The corner of Fourth Street and Pacific Avenue also boasts a plaque commemorating the origin of Harry S. Truman's campaign slogan, "Give 'Em Hell, Harry," which was shouted by a bystander in the crowd.) Plays at the art deco **ADMIRAL THEATRE** (515 Pacific Ave; 360/373-6743) are also adding life to downtown.

Just a five-minute drive north of downtown on Washington Avenue, across Port Washington Narrows on the Manette Bridge, the Manette district boasts a few antique stores, a used-book shop, and three good restaurants: the popular **BOAT SHED** (101 Shore Dr; 360/377-2600) is much loved for its seafood, clam chowder, and deck view; the intimate Northern Italian restaurant **FISCHIARE LA FERMATA** (2204 E 11th St; 360/373-5927); and **PETE'S JERSEY SUBS** (2100 E 11th St; 360/377-5118) for subs and an excellent vegetarian cheesesteak sandwich.

At the Bremerton Ferry Dock you can hop a **HORLUCK TRANSPORTATION COMPANY** (360/876-2300) foot ferry for the 10-minute crossing of Sinclair Inlet to **PORT ORCHARD**. The ride ends at the Sidney Dock, a block from Bay Street's antique stores, taverns, and cafes. (The ferry runs until 8:15pm weekdays, 6:45 pm Saturdays–Sundays; $1 for adults.) Must-sees include the **OLDE CENTRAL ANTIQUE MALL** (801 Bay St; 360/895-1902) and the **WATERFRONT FARMERS MARKET** on Saturdays, April to October.

From Bremerton you can skip the ferry and drive 7 miles around the west end of Sinclair Inlet via Highways 3, 16, and 166 and make a few additional stops at places including **SPRINGHOUSE DOLLS AND GIFTS** (1130 Bethel Ave; 360/876-0529), with its huge collection of modern dolls and teddy bears as well as the flouncy **VICTORIAN ROSE TEAROOM**. Attend a monthly Victorian High Tea and keep your floral china teacup as a souvenir (reservations required). On Highway 16 just beyond milepost 28, don't miss **ELANDAN GARDENS** (3050 W Hwy 16; 360/373-8260), an open-air art gallery/nursery/gift shop along the shore specializing in priceless bonsai (closed Monday and in January).

Head the other direction from Bremerton, north on Highways 3 and 308 to Keyport at the north end of Dyes Inlet, and you'll see the free **NAVAL UNDERSEA MUSEUM** (610 Dowell St; 360/396-4148; num.kpt.nuwc.navy.mil), with exhibits on naval history, undersea technology, and the submersible that helped explore the *Titanic*. For a post-museum snack, stop at the sandwich shop in **KEYPORT MER-CANTILE** (15499 Washington Ave; 360/779-7270).

You can return via Poulsbo and continue south on Highway 305 to the Bainbridge ferry. Or you can return to Bremerton on Highway 3, continuing south to explore Hood Canal.

BEST PLACE TO SEE AND BE SEEN?

"Pike Place Market, because shopping for fruit and vegetables is both a sensual and a reasonable thing to do."

Frances McCue, artistic director of Richard Hugo House

HOOD CANAL

Take the Washington State Ferry from Colman Dock (Pier 52) in downtown Seattle to Bainbridge Island; crossing is approximately 35 minutes. From the Bainbridge Ferry Dock, take Highway 305 north across Agate Passage and through Poulsbo to Highway 3; driving time approximately 45 minutes. South leads to the east shore of Hood Canal; north leads to the Hood Canal Bridge at the mouth of the canal, with its crossing to Highway 104 and US Highway 101, which in turn meanders south along the west shore of the canal—your return route.

Hood Canal, a 65-mile-long, fishhook-shaped inland waterway, lies west of Puget Sound, between Kitsap Peninsula and the Olympic Peninsula to the west. The eastern arm of Hood Canal extends from Belfair southwesterly along Highway 106 to Union. The area is filled with mansions and homes built by urbanites seeking summer getaways with Olympic Mountain views. From Union, the canal turns north at the Great Bend; US 101 follows the west shore of the less domesticated western arm, which has long stretches of forested slopes and accessible beaches. Three rivers that plunge down from the Olympics to Hood Canal's western arm offer trail access to the mountains: the **DUCKABUSH**, the **HAMMA HAMMA**, and the **DOSEWALLIPS**. US 101 and Highway 104 lead north and west to the mouth of Hood Canal, closing the loop tour described below.

From Highway 3 just outside Poulsbo, head south toward Silverdale and follow signs west to Seabeck. On the Kitsap Peninsula's west shoulder is **SCENIC BEACH STATE PARK**, with picnicking, campsites, and a view of the Olympics. On the way to Seabeck (via Seabeck Highway), stop to watch a play at the **MOUNTAINEERS'**

FOREST THEATER (3000 Seabeck Hwy; 206/284-6310; foresttheater.com). To reach the southern tip of the peninsula, follow back roads south through Holly and Dewatto to reach the Belfair-Tahuya Road, or return to Highway 3 and drive south to Belfair to Highway 300 southwest, which follows the north shore of the canal's east arm. At the tip of the peninsula, overlooking the canal's Great Bend, sprawling **TAHUYA STATE PARK** embraces beach and forest and is sought out by mountain and motor bikers, hikers, and horseback riders.

BEST PLACE TO VIEW ART?
"The new James Turrell SkySpace at the Henry Art Gallery because it's amazingly simple. And no one can say, 'I could do this.' "
Greg Kucera, owner of Greg Kucera Gallery

Returning north on Highway 300, **BELFAIR STATE PARK**, 3 miles south of Belfair, is one of the peninsula's busiest parks. Campers must reserve in summer (800/452-5683). You can swim, fish, or dig clams. Just north of the state park, South Belfair's **HOOD CANAL–THELER WETLANDS** (E 22871 Hwy 3; 360/275-4898) features 3.8 miles of wheelchair-accessible trails through marshes, woods, and the Union River estuary. A wooden causeway over a tidal marsh provides a view of the head of the canal's expanse. The interpretive center gives insight into the value of wetlands.

From Belfair, continue south on Highway 3 a short way to Highway 106 and follow it southwest. The big, safe, shallow pool and fast-food concession makes **TWANOH STATE PARK**, on the south shore of Hood Canal's eastern arm, popular with families. Farther southwest, the **UNION COUNTRY STORE** (E 5130 Hwy 106; 360/898-2641) offers exotic groceries, produce, wines, and wonderful fresh-daily dips (free tastings) plus calzone, lasagnas, and fettuccines. Barbecued pork ribs smoked in peach wood is the weekend special. Continue west to cross the Skokomish River and meet US 101, where you turn north to follow the canal's west shore.

Stop at **POTLATCH STATE PARK**, 3 miles south of Hoodsport, for a picnic or a refreshing dip. At low tide, you can gather oysters on the beach. **HOODSPORT WINERY** (23501 Hwy 101; 360/877-9894; www.hoodsport.com), a mile south of Hoodsport, will match its wine to your oysters. Sample one of the four fruit wines, white varietals, or such reds as the legendary Island Belle, made from grapes grown on nearby Stretch Island (to the east in Case Inlet), as you look out on the canal.

Hoodsport serves as the gateway to the Lake Cushman area. Just west of the lake's development, the Olympic National Park boundary is marked by a ranger station, campground, picnicking, and trailheads. The short **STAIRCASE RAPIDS TRAIL** along the upper Skokomish River is a pleasure. From Hoodsport to Quilcene, Hood Canal's west arm boasts many recreational areas in the **OLYMPIC NATIONAL**

FOREST and **OLYMPIC NATIONAL PARK;** the many ranger stations along US 101 provide all the information you need to visit. **HOODSPORT RANGER STATION** (just off US 101 on Lake Cushman Dr; 360/877-5254) has single-sheet maps for a range of hikes along the canal's southern sector.

Public beaches where oystering is permitted along the canal's west reach include Cushman Beach, Lilliwaup Recreational Tidelands, Pleasant Harbor State Park (near the mouth of the Duckabush River), Dosewallips State Park (a choice stop, with 425 acres of meadows, woodlands, and beach), and Seal Rock Campground. Most have clam beds. North of Seal Rock, Bee Mill Road heads eastward from US 101 to the Point Whitney State Shellfish Laboratory, with an interpretive display and a good oyster and swimming beach. Check the state hotline (800/562-5632) for red-tide warnings. North of Hoodsport, and just south of the Hamma Hamma River, shucked **OYSTERS** may be purchased at **HAMMA HAMMA OYSTER COMPANY SEAFOOD STORE** (35846 N US 101; 360/877-5811). Call ahead to check hours.

Gardeners will find a paradise of their own at **WHITNEY GARDENS** (306264 US 101; 360/796-4411 or 800/952-2404; whitneygardens.com) in Brinnon, which is between Dosewallips State Park and Seal Rock. You can see the rainbow of colors from blooming rhododendrons, azaleas, and camellias in early spring or stroll the 7-acre retreat's leafy corridors of weeping spruces, colorful maples, and magnolias. The gardens are open every day (small fee). There's a nursery and small picnic area. You can also eat at the folksy, unassuming **HALFWAY HOUSE** (US 101 at Brinnon Ln; 360/796-4715), where tourists and locals mingle.

Just 5 miles south of Quilcene off US 101, 2,750-foot **MOUNT WALKER** is one of the canal's most spectacular viewpoints, providing views of Seattle, Mount Rainier, and the Cascades. You can reach it by driving up a 5-mile dirt road that snakes around the mountain (summer only) or hiking the 2-mile trail up. Bring a picnic. Also worth a stop is the **WALKER MOUNTAIN TRADING POST** (near the Mount Walker turnoff from US 101; 360/796-3200), which crams a variety of antiques and collectibles into a pioneer home. On the highway's west side, north of the Mount Walker turnoff, **FALLS VIEW CAMPGROUND** is a short hike from a lovely waterfall on the Quilcene River.

The Quilcene Ranger Station (360/765-2200 or 360/765-3368), just south of Quilcene, has information about outdoor recreation at the canal's north end, including advice on shellfishing. **QUILCENE** has the world's largest oyster hatchery and possibly the purest salt water in the West. The mellow **WHISTLING OYSTER** (360/765-9508) is where knowing locals go for food, darts, and shuffleboard. In the heart of town, the **TWANA ROADHOUSE** (360/765-6485) features fresh soups, sandwiches, homemade pies, hand-dipped ice cream, and quick, cheery service.

North of Quilcene, just before the junction of US 101 with Highway 104, the **OLYMPIC MUSIC FESTIVAL** (206/527-8839; olympicmusicfestival.org) holds forth at 2pm on Saturdays and Sundays, June through mid-September, in a turn-of-the-19th-century barn/concert hall. Listeners sit inside on hay bales or church pews, or outside on the grass. Bring a picnic, or buy dinner at the well-stocked deli on site. The site is a real farm, and youngsters are encouraged to pet the animals. The music is sublime, performed by the Philadelphia String Quartet with guest artists from around the world. Reservations advised.

Head east on Highway 104 and cross the Hood Canal Bridge to close the loop at Highway 3 south of Port Gamble. Or continue north on US 101 to Discovery Bay and Highway 20 north to Port Townsend.

PORT TOWNSEND

Take the Washington State Ferry from Colman Dock (Pier 52) in downtown Seattle to Bainbridge Island; crossing is approximately 35 minutes. From the Bainbridge Ferry Dock, head northwest on Highway 305 to Highway 3. Follow Highway 3 north to the Hood Canal Bridge and cross it to continue west on Highway 104, turn off north onto Highway 19, which merges into Highway 20. Follow Highway 20 north into Port Townsend, 50 miles northwest of Seattle (approximately 2 hours).

In the mid-1800s Port Townsend was quite the rollicking town, where whiskey flowed free, brothels flourished, and sailors were often shanghaied. The seaport still draws throngs, but today it's the Victorian architecture and beautiful waterfront that attract. Avoid the hassle of parking—especially during festivals—by stopping at the Park and Ride (at Haines Place near Safeway, as you enter town) and riding the shuttle, which runs every half hour to uptown (Lawrence Street) and downtown (Water Street).

BEST PLACE FOR A ROMANTIC STROLL?

"Alki Beach on a sunny weekend day, or at sunset. You get the shimmering water and the skyline in one gleaming swath—a great setting to marvel at what a stunning city we live in."

Melanie McFarland, Seattle Post-Intelligencer *TV critic*

Hidden away near the Park and Ride, **KAH TAI LAGOON PARK** is favored by birders, walkers, bikers, and waterfowl. Downtown parks are **JACKSON BEQUEST TIDAL PARK**, behind Elevated Ice Cream (see below) on Water Street; compact **POPE MARINE PARK** is at the end of Adams Street and has picnic tables, logs, and playground equipment; and the 130-year-old **UNION WHARF** has a pavilion with views of Mount Baker and Mount Rainier.

Downtown, stroll along Water Street and soak up the town's mix of 19th-century charm and modern-day shops, galleries, and restaurants. **EARTHENWORKS** (702 Water St; 360/385-0328) houses crafts and fine art. The **ANTIQUE MALL** (802 Washington St; 360/379-8069) houses 35 little shops offering the standard mix of old stuff plus Port Townsend's answer to Underground Seattle: a display of artifacts from the area's old Chinatown. The Chinese Colony was destroyed by fire at the turn of the 19th century, and the items were discovered when the mall basement was excavated. **PACIFIC TRADITIONS**, in the Water Street Hotel lobby (637 Water St; 360/385-4770), sells masks, Salish blankets, and jewelry created by artists from the Olympic Peninsula. A superior bookshop, **IMPRINT BOOKSTORE** (820 Water St;

360/385-3643), is stocked with classics, contemporary works, and a fine selection of regional guidebooks. **WILLIAM JAMES BOOKSELLER** (829 Water St; 360/385-7313) across the street sells used and rare books. **APRIL FOOL & PENNY TWO** (725 Water St; 360/385-3438) specializes in collectibles, dollhouses, and whimsical greeting cards. **THE WINE SELLER** (940 Water St; 360/385-7673) offers a large selection of wines, beers, and coffees.

ELEVATED ICE CREAM COMPANY (627 Water St; 360/385-1156) has the best ice cream in town, plus a sundeck overlooking the bay. Have soda in a nostalgic setting at **NIFTY FIFTYS** (817 Water St; 360/385-1931). **FIN'S COASTAL KITCHEN** (1019 Water St; 360/379-3474) at Flagship Landing has a fresh daily menu prepared by European-trained chefs, plus a balcony view. **BREAD & ROSES BAKERY** (230 Quincy St; 360/385-1044) is known for great breads, pastries, light lunches, and open-air seating. **SALAL CAFÉ** (634 Water St; 360/385-6532) has breakfast and innovative meals, served in the dining room or the atrium overlooking Franklin Court, where concerts are held. The classic **ROSE THEATRE** (235 Taylor St; 360/385-1089) has daily showings of contemporary American and foreign films.

You can go uptown by ascending the stairway at Taylor and Washington Streets or by driving past the old Episcopal church and rusty-red **OLD BELL TOWER**. From here you can see venerable mansions a few blocks away from Lawrence Street's pizzerias, cafes, and galleries. Sadly, **ALDRICH'S**, the old general store in the heart of uptown, burned down in 2003. The owners plan to rebuild, but until then stock up for a picnic at other area grocery stores and delis—including **PROVISIONS** (939 Kearney St; provisionspt.com), a Euro deli stocked with specialty meats, cheeses, and ready-made takeout—or browse the **FARMERS MARKET** (Madison and Washington Sts, Saturdays May–Oct, or Lawrence and Polk Sts, Wednesdays June–Sept; ptfarrmersmarket.org; 206/379-6957 ext. 119). Then head for the emerald lawns, rose arbors, playground, and beach access of **CHETZEMOKA PARK** at Jackson and Blaine Streets. You can dig clams if the tide's right (call 800/562-5632 for red-tide warnings).

Or visit **FORT WORDEN STATE PARK**, once an army base and now inexpensive lodgings (great for families) and the headquarters of the Centrum Foundation, which puts on summertime concerts, plays, festivals, and workshops. The **COMMANDING OFFICER'S QUARTERS** (360/344-4452; commandingofficersquarters.com) at the end of Fort Worden's Officers' Row faithfully reproduces the life of a turn-of-the-19th-century officer and family. **BLACKBERRIES** (in the heart of Fort Worden; 360/385-9950) serves appetizing meals in a rustic dining room. The beach's **PORT TOWNSEND MARINE SCIENCE CENTER** (360/385-5582; ptmsc.org) has touch tanks and aquariums that allow children to tickle a seastar (closed in winter; call for hours). Up on Artillery Hill, visit the bunkers and gun emplacements from the fort's heyday.

You can gain insight into Port Townsend's tawdry past at the **JEFFERSON COUNTY HISTORICAL SOCIETY MUSEUM** in city hall (540 Water St; 360/385-1003; jchs museum.org), which includes the city's original courtroom, jail, and a replica of a Victorian bedroom. The 130-year-old **ROTHSCHILD HOUSE** (360/379-8076 group tour reservations) at Jefferson and Taylor Streets features original furnishings and beautiful herb and rose gardens. Every September, Port Townsend holds a **HISTORIC HOMES TOUR** (Port Townsend Visitors Information Center, 360/385-2722; ptchamber.org). To experience Port Townsend's quaint history more fully, stay at the exquisitely turreted, Victorian **F. W. HASTINGS HOUSE / OLD CONSULATE INN** (313 Walker St; 360/385-6753 or 800/300-6753; oldconsulateinn.com).

The city has two marinas downtown and a Washington State Ferry dock. From here, you can take a short ferry ride across Admiralty Inlet to the Keystone ferry dock on Whidbey Island. Port Townsend's annual **WOODEN BOAT FESTIVAL** (360/385-3628; woodenboat.org/festival), on the first weekend after Labor Day, is centered at Point Hudson at the end of Water Street. Attractions include concerts, entertainers, and, of course, boats. And don't miss the annual Kinetic Sculpture Race in early October, when locals race anything they can get to move.

Mount Rainier and Mount St. Helens

MOUNT RAINIER

Take Interstate 5 south from Seattle to exit 142; then take Highway 161 south through Puyallup, Graham, and Eatonville; head east on Highway 7 to Elbe. Take Highway 706 east through Ashford to the park's southwestern (Nisqually) entrance; 100 miles southeast of Seattle, approximately 2¼ hours.

Before there was the Space Needle, there is and always was Mount Rainier, the dominant element of the skyline on a sunny day in Seattle. Seattleites measure the quality of a summer day by the mountain's presence: if it's sunny and the mountain is "out," it is a great day indeed. Originally called Tahoma, this volcano defies simple description. It isn't just a majestic geological landmark that has become associated with Washington, it's a moody Native American god and a magnetic force of nature that creates its own weather and draws admirers from all over the world.

On your way to Mount Rainier, you can visit **NORTHWEST TREK WILDLIFE PARK** (11610 Trek Dr E, Eatonville; 360/832-6117; nwtrek.org), a natural habitat 55 miles south of Seattle off Highway 161 and 60 miles from the Nisqually entrance to the national park. Bison, caribou, moose, elk, and deer roam in pastures, peat bogs, ponds, and forests, while visitors watch from trams. Naturalists narrate the hour-long, 5.5-mile trip. Admission is $8.75 for adults, less for children and seniors, free for kids under 3. The steam-powered trains of the **MOUNT RAINIER SCENIC RAILROAD** (schedule varies seasonally; 360/569-2351 or 888/STEAM-11), based in Elbe on Highway 7, provide mountain views but don't get close enough.

The closest accommodations near the park's Nisqually entrance are around Ashford. **WELLSPRING** (54922 Kernahan Rd, Ashford; 360/569-2514;) has two spas surrounded by evergreens. If your massage or sauna (or hour-long hot tub soak for $10) has you too relaxed to travel, consider spending the night. **ALEXANDER'S COUNTRY INN** (37515 Hwy 706 E, Ashford; 360/569-2300 or 800/654-7615; alexanderscountryinn.com) offers B&B-style rooms (with free, full-course breakfasts) with modern-day comforts in a turn-of-the-19th-century inn. Make reservations for a fine meal, including panfried trout—caught out back in the holding pond.

Six large guest rooms and a private outdoor 23-jet Jacuzzi spa are available at **MOUNTAIN MEADOWS INN B&B** closer to Mount Rainier (28912 Hwy 706 E, Ashford; 360/569-2788; mt-rainier.net). The 24-room **NISQUALLY LODGE** (31609 Hwy 706 E, Ashford; 360/569-8804; escapetothemountains.com) offers reasonably priced respite to those willing to trade charm for a phone, TV, and air-conditioning.

A mile past the Nisqually entrance to **MOUNT RAINIER NATIONAL PARK** (entry fee $10 per car; 360/569-2211; nps.gov/mora) is Sunshine Point Campground (open year-round), and 6 miles farther is the village of Longmire, home to the simple **NATIONAL PARK INN** (360/569-2411; guestservices.com/rainier), a wildlife museum, a hiking information center, and a cross-country skiing rental outlet. The 235,625-acre park is a lushly forested reserve with the 14,410-foot-high volcano as its centerpiece. Tour the mountain by car, hike or snowshoe it, ski nearby, or climb to its summit. The most popular summertime option is to drive a loop around the mountain: follow the road from Longmire to Paradise (you can use it during daylight hours in winter, but it's best to carry tire chains and a shovel and check conditions beforehand on the 24-hour information line, 360/569-2211) to Highway 123 over Cayuse Pass to Highway 410 just west of Chinook Pass (both passes are closed in winter), then take the road west to Sunrise (open only when it's snow-free, usually July 1 through Labor Day).

BEST PLACE TO BE IGNORED?

"Bad Alberts is great—you could be a celebrity and everyone would leave you alone, not including the servers!"

Kathy Casey, chef and culinary diva

The park road winds past Cougar Rock Campground (reservations required, 800/365-2267), many scenic viewpoints, and waterfalls as it climbs to **PARADISE**. At 5,400 feet on the mountain's south side, it is the park's most popular destination because it offers the most complete services in the park, including rustic accommodations at **PARADISE INN** (mid-May to October; 360/569-2413; guest services.com/rainier), the **JACKSON MEMORIAL VISITORS CENTER**'s 360-degree view, and a network of spectacular hiking trails that are ideal for cross-country skiing, snowshoeing, or inner-tubing in the winter; Paradise has a guided snowshoe walk in winter.

The park road continues east to Highway 123 at the Stevens Canyon entrance; head north over Cayuse Pass to Highway 410, then continue north to the Sunrise Road at the White River entrance; White River Campground is on the way up to Sunrise. About 1,000 feet farther up, the **SUNRISE** visitor area offers a view of the peak from the northeast. It's the highest point open to cars and is open only in summer. A number of naturalist talks will enhance your experience. They range from a half-hour slide show (at Paradise) or a 2-mile geologic walk (at Sunrise) to a 6-mile alpine ecology hike (at Paradise).

STALKING SHELLFISH

A geoduck (pronounced "gooey-duck") is an ungainly creature, a huge, 2-pound clam with a foot-long siphon that it can't completely retract into its shell. Doesn't matter, though; geoducks inhabit deep sands in Puget Sound tideflats, from which only the tip of the siphon protrudes. The creatures are rarely discerned, except by habitués of beaches at low tide—and by visitors to Pike Place Market, who stare in disbelief at the bizarre appearance of the limp, harvested specimens displayed on ice. Geoducks are profoundly difficult to dig from their lairs, 3 feet deep in the sand.

Luckily for anyone interested in a genuine Puget Sound experience, many shellfish species are much easier to obtain than geoducks. Native butterclams and littlenecks, and introduced species such as Manila clams, are found in shallower habitats; mussels and oysters live on subtidal rocks. If you're willing to make a day trip of it, hike a bit, and dig a little, you're sure to come back with a bucket full.

State regulations establish seasons and harvest limits for all shellfish, and you'll need a modestly priced license, available at sporting goods and hardware outlets where fishing licenses are sold. Make sure your destination is one that's open to public digging. Beginners need a tide table (you'll need at least a modest minus tide, the lower the better) and a good guide (the Audubon Society's *Pacific Coast* [Knopf, 1985] nature guide is excellent). Be sure to call the state's red-tide hotline (800/562-5632 in state only), which

There are also 305 miles of trails within the park, including the 93-mile Wonderland Trail, which circles the mountain. Backcountry permits are required for camping and are available at ranger stations and visitors centers. The campgrounds at Ohanapecosh (just south of the Stevens Canyon entrance) and Cougar Rock require reservations (800/365-2267), while sites at White River, Ipsut Creek (on the park's northwest corner), and Sunshine Point are first-come, first-served.

It's also possible to ski the area in winter and spend the night at a hut-to-hut ski trail system south and west of the park. **MOUNT TAHOMA SKI HUTS**, run by the Tahoma Trails Association (PO Box 206, Ashford, WA 98304; 360/569-2451; skimtta.com), has more than 75 miles of trails, three huts, and one yurt. Rooms at **WHITTAKER'S BUNKHOUSE** (30205 Hwy 706; 360/569-2439; welcometo ashford.com) are basic and cheap. Near the Sunrise Road on Highway 410 is **CRYSTAL MOUNTAIN** (360/663-2265; crystalmt.com), said to have the state's best skiing (see Snow Sports in the Recreation chapter).

Or you can climb the mountain, either with a concessioned guide service such as **RAINIER MOUNTAINEERING** (30027 Hwy 706 E, Ashford; 888/89-CLIMB; rmiguides.com) or in your own party. For the latter, you must register at one of the park's ranger stations and pay $30 for a pass, which will last you a year. The guide service offers a one-day training session that teaches all you'll need to know to make

lists any areas in which mollusks are contaminated by paralytic shellfish poison (PSP) or other marine biotoxins; in some years, much of Puget Sound is off-limits by late August.

Unfortunately, when the legendary Seattle songwriter/entrepreneur Ivar Haglund rejoiced in his "happy condition / Surrounded by acres of clams," it was a more bucolic time. Today, because of urban pollution, no beaches in the immediate Seattle area are advisable for clam digging. The nearest spots are Dash Point and Saltwater State Parks in Federal Way, south of Seattle; the best places are a ferry ride away, such as the beach at Double Bluff Park, a 3-mile-long walk-in park on Whidbey Island. Hood Canal is the place to hunt oysters: two of the best areas are Shine Tidelands and Hood Spit, both just on the west side of the Hood Canal Bridge, requiring a ride on the Bainbridge Island or Edmonds–Kingston ferry. (See Hood Canal in this chapter.)

What to do with your loot? Steam clams or mussels in a pot, or use them to make clam chowder or mussel stew (don't overcook them or they'll get tough). Real enthusiasts like to take along an oyster knife and shuck a couple of their finds right on the beach. Add a dash of lemon juice and you can have lunch on the spot. And if you somehow manage to extract a geoduck from the sand, it's excellent diced up in a stir-fry—yes, siphon and all (dip the siphon briefly into boiling water and remove the skin first). With geoducks, you need only one for a meal.

—*Eric Lucas*

the two-day climb. The climb can be done year-round, but late May to mid-September is the best time to go. It's best to climb with a guide service unless you're qualified to do it solo. Rainier can be as dangerous as it is enchanting.

To complete your loop around Mount Rainier, continue north and west on Highway 410 through Enumclaw back to Highway 161. Or return to Elbe on Highway 7 and turn south to Morton on US Highway 12 to reach Mount St. Helens from the north.

MOUNT ST. HELENS
Take Interstate 5 south from Seattle to exit 49, then follow signs east via Highway 504; approximately 150 miles south of Seattle, a two- to three-hour drive.

Temperamental Mount St. Helens last blew its top on May 18, 1980. The 8,365-foot simmering remains are worth the trip. It's best to go on a clear day when you can see the regrowth on the mountain.

Just off I-5 at exit 49/Castle Rock, where Highway 504 begins, start your visit at the Mount St. Helens **CINEDOME THEATER** (360/274-9844; thecinedome.com), where you can see *The Eruption of Mount St. Helens* on a three-story-tall, 55-foot-wide screen. The seat-rattling rumble alone is worth the $6 (adult) admission.

As you travel east along Highway 504 (the Spirit Lake Memorial Hwy), there are five interpretive centers, each of which complements the others. The Washington

State Park and Recreation Commission's **MOUNT ST. HELENS VISITORS CENTER** (milepost 5; 360/274-2100; www.fs.fed.us/gpnf/mshnvm/) commemorates the blast with exhibits, a walk-through volcano, hundreds of historical photos, geological/anthropological surveys, and a film documenting the destruction and rebirth. Cowlitz County's **HOFFSTADT BLUFFS VISITORS CENTER** (milepost 27; 360/274-7750; mt-st-helens.com) features a restaurant, a gift store, and a memorial to those who died in the blast. Helicopter tours are available here. Weyerhaeuser-operated **FOREST LEARNING CENTER** at North Fork Ridge (milepost 33; 360/414-3439; weyerhaeuser.com/sthelens) covers the eruption's impact on tree farms. The Forest Service's **COLDWATER RIDGE VISITOR CENTER** (milepost 43; 360/274-2131), with priceless views of the black dome resting in the middle of the 2-mile-wide steaming crater and of Coldwater and Castle Lakes (both formed by massive mud flows), focuses on the landscape's amazing biological recovery. The final stop is the Forest Service–run **JOHNSTON RIDGE OBSERVATORY** (milepost 52; 360/274-2140; www.fs.fed.us/gpnf/mshnvm/) that provides a view directly *into* the crater and concentrates on the eruption itself, how geologists monitor volcanoes, and what we have learned since the eruption.

BEST URBAN WATERFALL?

"Waterfall Park, Pioneer Square. The gushing cascades over the wall of assembled rocks are loud enough to drown out the noise and the distractions of the city."

Michael Medved, film critic and host of syndicated radio talk show originating at KNWX AM 770

It costs $3 per adult to visit one of the Forest Service visitors centers ($6 for more than one center, free for children under 4). There are other viewpoints lining roads approaching the mountain (from the south, Hwy 503 via Woodland and Cougar; from the north, US Hwy 12 east to Randle, then Forest Roads 25 and 99), but all the visitors centers are on Highway 504. Those who enter from Randle via Forest Road 99 will get a dramatic view of the blowdown destruction. Although there is no camping in the Mount St. Helens National Monument, there is in the 1.3 million-acre **GIFFORD PINCHOT NATIONAL FOREST** (360/891-5000; www.fs.fed.us/gpnf/) surrounding the monument, with its more than 50 campgrounds and excellent fishing. Call ahead for road and campground conditions.

To climb the mountain, budget at least six or seven hours. Registration can add another day, however, because you must get a permit ($15 per person) well in advance—call monument headquarters (360/247-3900) for the procedure—and you must register at **JACK'S STORE AND RESTAURANT** (23 miles east of Woodland on Hwy 503 just west of Cougar; 360/231-4276). It's best to climb in May and June (when there's still enough snow to tame the ash). Bring good hiking boots, drinking water, sunscreen, sunglasses, crampons, and an ice ax. There are still glaciers on the crater's rim, so only the experienced should make the climb. Extend your mountain sojourn by staying at the moderately priced, 49-room **SEASONS MOTEL** (200 Westlake Ave, Morton; 360/496-6835 or 877/496-6835; whitepasstravel.com/seasons. htm), located about halfway between Mount St. Helens and Mount Rainier on US 12.

British Columbia

VICTORIA

While Vancouver is a very popular BC stop for residents of Washington, it's more of a weekend getaway. (For details, pick up Northwest Best Places *14th Edition [Sasquatch, 2003; 15th Edition available as of Fall 2004].) Victoria, however, is easily doable in a day. Just take the passenger-only Victoria Clipper from Pier 69 in downtown Seattle; the crossing is 2½ hours.*

Justifiably famous as a city of British charms and romance, many people are beginning to see Victoria as a soft adventure destination as well. Ever since the Cousteau Society rated it as having the second-best winter diving in the world, it's become a big diving destination. Biking and whale-watching are also popular.

First, you have to get there. The waterjet-propelled catamaran called the *Victoria Clipper* (206/448-5000 Seattle, 250/382-8100 Victoria, or 800/888-2535 outside Seattle and BC; victoriaclipper.com) takes foot passengers—Victoria is very walkable—from Seattle, with four trips a day between May and September, once or twice a day off-season. (See the Ferry Rides sidebar in this chapter for other waterborne options.) You can also fly **KENMORE AIR** (425/486-1257; kenmoreair.com) from Lake Union to the Inner Harbor for $177 round-trip; **HELIJET AIRWAYS** (800/665-4354; www.helijet.com) from Boeing Field south of Georgetown; or **HORIZON AIR** (800/547-9308; horizonair.com) from Sea-Tac Airport.

Visit **TOURISM VICTORIA** (812 Wharf St; 800/663-3883; tourismvictoria.com) for useful information on where to go biking, diving, hiking, and whale-watching, and for information on dozens of other activities. Victoria has an extensive system of biking trails, and **CYCLE BC RENTALS** (950 Wharf St; 250/385-2453 or 866/380-2453; cyclebc.ca) is just a block away. The 78-mile (125-km) **GALLOPING GOOSE TRAIL** is just across the Johnson Street Bridge. If diving is your thing, it's a quick **KABUKI CAB** (bicycle cab) ride or 10-minute walk to the **OGDEN POINT DIVE CENTER** (199 Dallas Rd; 888/701-1177; www.divevictoria.com), where the experts can outfit you and have you out diving in the breakwater in no time flat.

For more traditional touring, hop on one of **TALLY HO'S** (250/383-5067) horse-drawn carriages for a fun city history lesson. The one-hour narrated tour, with humorous historical asides, starts at the **PARLIAMENT BUILDINGS** (Belleville and Menzies Sts) and winds through Beacon Hill Park to the waterfront and James Bay. The company also offers private tours. The **ROYAL BRITISH COLUMBIA MUSEUM** (Belleville and Government Sts; 250/387-3701; www.rbcm.gov.bc.ca) has dramatic dioramas of natural landscapes and reconstructions of Victorian storefronts, as well as a Northwest Coast Indian exhibit of spiritual and cultural artifacts (open daily).

The **ART GALLERY OF GREATER VICTORIA** (1040 Moss St; 250/384-4101; www.aggv.bc.ca) features a world-class Asian art collection, including North America's only Shinto shrine, and engaging contemporary exhibits throughout the year (open daily). It's in the Rockland neighborhood, a five-minute walk from downtown. Also nearby is **CRAIGDARROCH CASTLE** (1050 Joan Crescent, off Fort St; 250/592-5323; craigdarrochcastle.com), built by coal tycoon Robert Dunsmuir in the 1890s to compensate his wife for having to live in the then wild hinterlands. Open daily.

Want to see more homes? There are five **VICTORIA HERITAGE HOMES** (admission varies; seasonal closures; sidneybc.com/heritagetours) downtown, including Helmcken House (behind Thunderbird Park, east of the Columbia Museum), Point Ellice House (Bay and Pleasant Sts), Craigflower Manor (110 Island Hwy), Craigflower Schoolhouse (Admirals Rd and Gorge Rd W), and painter Emily Carr's childhood home, the Carr House (Government and Simcoe Sts).

Another grand old building worth a visit is the **FAIRMONT EMPRESS** (721 Government St; 250/384-8111 or 250/389-2727 tea reservations; fairmont.com). The turn-of-the-19th-century Edwardian edifice isn't just a landmark, it's still an operating hotel. Afternoon tea at 12:30pm (summer only), 2pm, 3:30pm, and 5pm is a Victoria tradition. The hotel's Bengal Lounge is known for its curry buffet and martinis. Also still in use is the **MCPHERSON PLAYHOUSE** (3 Centennial Square; 250/386-6121 or 888/717-6121), another classic building. The former Pantages vaudeville house offers evening entertainment throughout the year. The free *Monday Magazine* contains the city's best weekly calendar of events.

BEST PUBLIC ART?
"The Fremont Troll. Should be the worst, but is easily the best."

Amanda Wilde, afternoon host on 90.3FM KEXP

Victoria has more than just old buildings. Just south of downtown, the 177-acre **BEACON HILL PARK** provides spectacular water views and beautiful landscaping (some of it wild). Within the park, the **BEACON HILL CHILDREN'S PETTING ZOO** is a kid-friendly minizoo that includes a turtle house, aviary, and petting corral (admission fee; closed in winter). **CRYSTAL GARDEN** (713 Douglas St; 250/381-1213; bcpcc.com/crystal) is a turn-of-the-19th-century swimming-pool-building-turned-glass conservatory with a tropical theme, a fine place to spend a rainy day (admission fee; open daily). Just across the street is the **VICTORIA CONFERENCE CENTRE**, linked to the Empress Hotel by a beautifully restored conservatory. Also within walking distance of the park is **ABIGAIL'S HOTEL** (906 McClure St; 250/388-5363 or 800/561-6565; abigailshotel.com), a four-story, 22-room Tudor manor.

What would a trip be without shopping? The area around the Empress Hotel is a great place to browse. **W & J WILSON CLOTHIERS** (1221 Government St; 250/383-7177) sells European-style clothing and Scottish cashmere sweaters; **SASQUATCH TRADING COMPANY** (1233 Government St; 250/386-9033) offers

Cowichan sweaters and Native art; **OLD MORRIS TOBACCONIST** (1116 Government St; 250/382-4811 or 888/845-6111) carries fine pipes, tobaccos, and Cuban cigars; and **MUNRO'S BOOKS** (1108 Government St; 250/382-2464 or 888/243-2464), an early-20th-century bank-building-turned-bookstore, is one of Canada's largest independent bookstores. Don't forget the Victoria creams at **ROGERS' CHOCOLATES** (913 Government St; 250/384-7021 or 877/663-2220); the **ENGLISH SWEET SHOP** (738 Yates St; 250/382-3325) for chocolates, black-currant pastilles, and Pontefract cakes; or **BERNARD CALLEBAUT CHOCOLATERIE** (621 Broughton St; 250/380-1515) for beautiful Belgian chocolates.

MARKET SQUARE (between Wharf and Store Sts on Johnson St) is a restored 19th-century courtyard surrounded by three floors of shops and restaurants. A few blocks farther north at Fisgard Street is **CHINATOWN**, marked by the Gate of Harmonious Interest. A growing number of upscale boutiques, non-Chinese bistros, and lofts are now encroaching on the area's original mix of Chinese restaurants and green grocers, however. Walk through **FAN TAN ALLEY**, the country's narrowest thoroughfare, which originally was a discreet passageway into the area's opium dens and gambling parlors. Visit **PANACEA, THE FURNITURE ART COMPANY** (532 Fisgard St; 250/391-8960) and have a bubble tea—a concoction of green or red tea and fruit flavorings poured over tapioca pearls. On Fisgard Street, enjoy an unpretentious Chinese dinner at **WAH LAI YUEN** (560 Fisgard St; 250/381-5355). A block north of Chinatown you can stop in at the Victoria institution **HERALD STREET CAFFE** (546 Herald St; 250/381-1441) for tasty West Coast cuisine, a great wine cellar, and walls festooned with funky art.

Antique hunters should head east of downtown, up Fort Street, to **ANTIQUE ROW**—the 800 to 1100 block—which boasts block after block of shops, ending with **FAITH GRANT THE CONNOISSEUR SHOP** (1156 Fort St; 250/383-0121). Visit **BASTION SQUARE** (bounded by View and Fort Sts and Wharf and Government Sts) for sidewalk restaurants, galleries, and the **MARITIME MUSEUM OF BRITISH COLUMBIA** (250/385-4222; mmbc.bc.ca), the location of Victoria's old gallows. The museum has apparently become a hot spot for ghost sightings. If you want to learn about others, take the **GHOSTLY WALKS** (250/384-6698; www.discover thepast.com/discvr/gwalks.htm) tour. Held nightly in July and August and weekends during October's Ghosts of Victoria Festival, the tours start at the Visitor Info Centre and visit alleys, squares, and many of Olde Town's happy haunting grounds. Admission is $12 for adults. Back among the living, don't miss Bastion Square's great gardeners' shop, called **DIG THIS** (250/385-3212).

Located 13 miles (21 km) north of town is one of Victoria's most impressive landmarks, the **BUTCHART GARDENS** (250/652-5256; www.butchart gardens.com). The result of Jenny Butchart's mission to relandscape her husband's limestone quarry is now a mecca for gardening enthusiasts, with 50 acres of beautifully manicured gardens. It's best to go early in the morning, when the dew is still on the grass, or late afternoon in summer, after the busloads of tourists have departed. Afternoon tea and light meals are served in the garden's teahouse. Entertainment and fireworks are featured on Saturday night in July and August (admission fee; open daily).

VIA RAIL CANADA (450 Pandora Ave; 888/842-7245; viarail.ca) has a morning run from a mock-Victorian station near the Johnson Street Bridge to Courtenay, with stops in between. The $54 advance purchase fare allows you to get on and off the train as many times as you like, but the train only makes one departure per day from each end. It's a slow, scenic trip and there's no food served aboard.